STUDIES IN THE EARLY HISTORY O

Series Editors: Stuart Airlie and Paul Kershaw

Mercia

Studies in the Early History of Europe

Series Editors:
  Stuart Airlie, University of Glasgow
  Paul Kershaw, University College London

Established in the tradition of Leicester University Press's highly regarded *Studies in the Early History of Britain*, this major new series offers scholars and students definitive analyses of some of the key subjects in European history between the disintegration of Roman imperial hegemony in the west in the fifth century and the twelfth-century cultural renaissance.

Interdisciplinarity is central to the project. *Studies in the Early History of Europe* aims to address all aspects of early medieval political, cultural and social history, and the insights of archaeology, anthropology, art history and literary and cultural studies all fall within its scope.

Recent scholarship has radically altered our picture of the 'barbarian world' of early medieval Europe. *Studies in the Early History of Europe* reflects this new understanding, while at the same time maintaining a commitment to original historical research. Work by outstanding younger scholars will sit alongside that of established figures in the field. In keeping with its European vision, the series also endeavours to bring the work of leading continental historians to the attention of an Anglophone audience.

An important objective of the series is to place Anglo-Saxon and Celtic Insular history in its European context: hence the publication of this first volume. Other subjects the series intends to cover include: historical writing, the reception of patristic thought, ethnicity and identity, the lives of key individuals in early medieval society, tenth-century Europe, the 'feudal transformation' and Christian Spain.

Mercia
An Anglo-Saxon kingdom in Europe

Edited by Michelle P. Brown and Carol A. Farr

continuum

Continuum

The Tower Building, 11 York Road, London, SE1 7NX
15 East 26th Street, New York, NY 10010

First published in 2001 by Leicester University Press

British Library Cataloguing-in-Publication Data

A catalogue record for this book is available from the British Library.

ISBN 0-7185-0231-0 (hardback)
     0-8264-7765-8 (paperback)

Library of Congress Cataloging-in-Publication Data

Mercia, an Anglo-Saxon kingdom in Europe/edited by Michelle P. Brown
    and Carol A. Farr.
        p. cm. — (Studies in the early history of Europe)
    Includes bibliographical references and index.
    ISBN 0–7185–0231–0 (hb) — 0-8264-7765-8 (pb)
        1. Mercia (Kingdom) 2. Anglo-Saxons—Mercia (Kingdom)
        3. England—Civilization—To 1066. I. Title: Mercia. II. Brown, Michelle
    (Michelle P.) III. Farr, Carol Ann, 1949– IV. Series.

DA670.M52 M43 2001
936.201′5—dc21
    00-069642

Typeset by BookEns Ltd, Royston, Herts.
Printed and bound in Great Britain by MPG Books Ltd, Bodmin, Cornwall

Contents

Part III   The Material Culture of Mercia

Part IV   The Visual Culture of Mercia

Part V   Mercia in Retreat

Illustrations

Maps

Figures

Contributors

Edel Bhreathnach is a Post-Doctoral Fellow at the National University of Ireland, Galway

Michelle P. Brown is Curator of Manuscripts, The British Library

T. M. Charles-Edwards is Jesus Professor of Celtic at Jesus College, Oxford University

Robert Cowie is Senior Archaeologist, Museum of London Archaeology Service

Carol A. Farr is Lecturer at the Mary Ward Centre in London

Peter Featherstone is an independent scholar

Jane Hawkes is Lecturer in History of Art, University of York

David Hill is Senior Research Fellow, Manchester Centre for Anglo-Saxon Studies, University of Manchester

Della Hooke is Honorary Fellow, Institute for Advanced Research in Arts and Social Sciences, University of Birmingham

Simon Keynes is Elrington and Bosworth Professor of Anglo-Saxon, University of Cambridge, and a fellow of Trinity College, Cambridge

Richard H. I. Jewell is an independent scholar

Janet L. Nelson is Professor of Medieval History, King's College London

David Parsons is University Fellow and Emeritus Reader in Church Archaeology at the University of Leicester

Jane Roberts is Professor of English Language and Medieval Literature at King's College London

Pauline Stafford is Professor of Medieval History, University of Liverpool

Alan Vince is Archaeological Consultant, Alan Vince Archaeological Consultancy, Lincoln

Leslie Webster is Deputy Keeper, Department of Medieval and Modern Europe, The British Museum

Martin Welch is Senior Lecturer, Institute of Archaeology, University College London

Gareth Williams is Curator of Early Medieval Coins, The British Museum

Alex Woolf is Lecturer in Celtic and Early Scottish History and Culture, University of Edinburgh

Barbara Yorke is Professor of Early Medieval History, King Alfred's College, Winchester

Acknowledgements

We dedicate this volume to our partners, Cecil and Richard, and extend our particular thanks to Richard for assistance with the bibliography.

Permission to reproduce photographs and drawings (other than those of the individual authors) is gratefully acknowledged.

Chapter 4, Figures 4.1 and 4.2 C. A. Farr; Figure 4.3 Richard Gem in Wilkinson and McWhirr (1998)

Chapter 15, Figures 15.1 and 15.2 by kind permission of the Trustees of the British Museum

Chapter 16, Figure 16.1 (a) English Heritage

Chapter 17, Figures 17.1–17.4, The Courtauld Institute of Art, Conway Library; Figure 17.5 The Board of Trustees of the Victoria and Albert Museum

Chapter 18, Figures 18.1, 18.4a, 18.6, 18.7, 18.8 by kind permission of the Trustees of the British Museum; Figure 18.4c Dr M. O. Budny

Chapter 19, Figures 19.1, 19.3a and 19.4b by courtesy of the British Library Board; Figure 19.2 Bibliothèque Nationale de France, Paris; Figures 19.3b and 19.4a the Syndics of Cambridge University Library; Figure 19.5a, b Biblioteca Apostolica Vaticana

Chapter 21, Figures 21.1 and 21.3 courtesy of the British Library Board; Figure 21.2 by kind permission of the Dean and Chapter of Canterbury

The Vespasian Psalter, London, B.L., Cotton MS Vesp. A.i, ff. 30v–31. The British Library.
Courtesy of the British Library Board.

Abbreviations

A	The Winchester manuscript (Cambridge, Corpus Christi College, MS 173)
AC	*Annales Cambriae* in Morris (1980)
Alcuin, *Epist.*	'Alcvini sive Albini epistolae', *Epistolae Karolini Aevi* II, in Dümmler (ed.), (1895) (reprinted Munich, 1978): 1–481, with number of letter
ASC	*Anglo-Saxon Chronicle*, in Plummer (1892–9), trans. in Whitelock (1979), no. 1, or in M. Swanton (1996)
AU	Annals of Ulster
BMFacs.	E.A. Bond, *Facsimiles of Ancient Charters in the British Museum*, 4 vols. (London, 1873–8)
C	The Abingdon manuscript (London, British Library, Cotton MS Tiberius B.i)
CCSL	*Corpus Christianorum, Series Latina*, Turnhout, Brepols (1953-)
E	The Peterborough manuscript (Oxford, Bodleian Library, MS Laud 636)
EHD (1955)	Whitelock (1955)
EHD (1979)	Whitelock (1979)
HE	Bede, *Historia Ecclesiastica*
HH, *HA*	*Henry, Archdeacon of Huntingdon: Historia Anglorum/ The History of the English People*, ed. D. Greenway, Oxford Medieval Texts (Oxford, 1996)
JW, *Chron.*	Darlington, McGurk, and Bray (1995); and McGurk (1998)
MGH	*Monumenta Germaniae Historica*
OSFacs.	W.B. Sanders, *Facsimiles of Anglo-Saxon Manuscripts*, 3 vols., Ordnance Survey (Southampton, 1878–84)
PL	*Patrologia Latina*, 221 volumes, J.P. Migne (ed.), Paris, J.P. Migne and Garnier Frères (1841–80) (with volumes reissued by Garnier to 1905)
S	Sawyer, 1968 (revised edition [S 1–1602], ed. S.E. Kelly, available online at <www.trin.cam.ac.uk/chartwww/>), with number of document
WM, *DAntG*	Scott (1981)

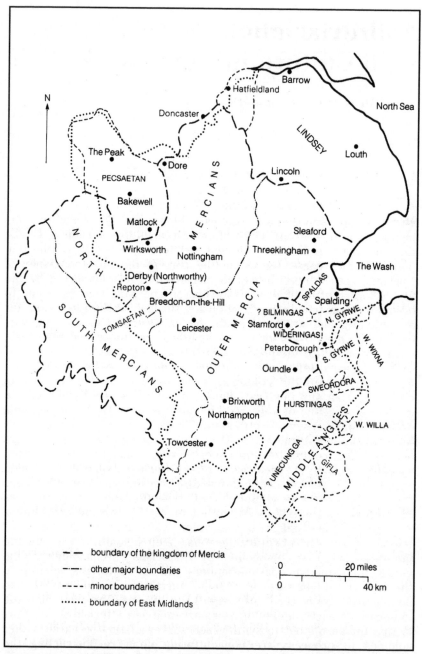

Map 1 Mercia. A suggested reconstruction of the political geography of the Tribal Hidage (after C. R. Hart, 'The Kingdom of Mercia', in *Mercian Studies*, ed. A. Dornier, 1977).

Introduction: Mercia, a Culture in Context

Michelle P. Brown and Carol A. Farr

There is a mystique associated with Mercia which is almost semi-mythical and of the sort which often surrounds lost kingdoms. Unlike the other major Anglo-Saxon successor states, there is little recollection of this former contender within the current regional topography of England. The Mercian heartland has been largely overtaken by the visible legacy of the Industrial Revolution and King Offa has come to occupy a role in popular imagination as a shadowy warlord, notorious for his brutality and attributed with the construction of an enigmatic earthwork, Offa's Dyke, which, like its Roman precursor, Hadrian's Wall, is chiefly famed for the popular footpath which follows it.

The focuses for more informed studies of early Anglo-Saxon England have been the 'golden ages' of Northumbria, promoted by its chief historian and publicist, Bede, and of Alfred's Wessex and the gradual emergence of a unified kingdom, along with the phenomena of Viking onslaught and settlement. The absence of a contemporary Mercian apologist and the patchy nature of such evidence as has survived the course of subsequent events, and the West Saxon ascendancy, have ensured that, until recently, scholars have tended to err on the side of caution, afraid of over-interpreting what does remain. In 1977 a collection of papers, edited by Ann Dornier as *Mercian Studies* (1977a), attempted to rectify this by providing a valuable overview of some of the evidence available at that time. Over the past quarter of a century there has been a wealth of exciting and innovative work accomplished by historians, archaeologists, linguists, numismatists, palaeographers and art historians relating to the history and culture of England during the period of Mercian domination, from the early eighth to ninth centuries, and the implications and contexts of its emergence and aftermath. The time is ripe for an up-to-date synthesized survey of this research. Other volumes in progress are concentrating upon reconstructing the history of the Mercian supremacy, or hegemony, as it is often termed, and upon the achievements and failures of its rulers. The present volume takes as its focus the detailed study of the material evidence – literary, documentary, art historical and archaeological – and a consideration of other contemporary, parallel cultures which help to provide an historical and cultural context.

The origins of Mercia, like those of the other early Anglo-Saxon kingdoms, are shrouded in the mists of time and in the myths of origin promoted by the ruling dynasties that were successful in their bids for power. Those fostered in the circles of King Æthelbald and his successors, which equated the royal house of the Iclingas with the stock whence sprang the Mercian *gens*, are explored by Barbara Yorke in Chapter 1. Such constructs may be contrasted with the archaeological evidence for the mixed origins of the varied groups of Germanic and acculturated British backgrounds who, from around 500 onwards, adopted an Anglian identity in material culture and were brought under Mercian rule, as discussed by Martin Welch. From the mid-seventh to early ninth centuries, Mercian authority expanded from its origins in the Trent Valley to embrace nearly all the territories from the Thames to the Humber and was also felt throughout East Anglia and the South East. One of the principal sources for reconstructing the processes of alliance and subjugation by which this was achieved, and of identifying the lost tribes thereby absorbed, is the Tribal Hidage. Peter Featherstone examines its provenance, date and purpose in Chapter 2 and proposes that many of these minor tribal groupings were retained within the larger kingdom as provinces run by ealdormen, creating power bases which in turn impacted upon the court hierarchy and provided a measure of stability and continuity, despite succession crises in respect of the royal dignity. Here, as in other chapters, a scenario emerges of the construction of a 'Greater Mercia' in which the core territories were supplemented by the acquisition of tributary regions (an inner zone of the hegemony) and the overlordship of other Southumbrian kingdoms (an outer zone), the latter often vigorously contended as in the case of Kent. A cultural reflection of such zones and their interaction is perceived in Michelle Brown's discussion of the Mercian '*Schriftprovinz*' and is similarly signalled in other aspects of visual and material culture – church archaeology and architecture, sculpture and metalwork and carving (in the discussion of which Leslie Webster, in Chapter 18, examines the complex relationships and diffusion of such Mercian masterworks as the Gandersheim Casket, the Pentney brooches, the Witham pins, the Ormside bowl and the St Ninians Isle chapes and sword pommel). In Chapter 7, Alex Woolf points to the possible occurrence of a similar phenomenon in the construction of a Pictish 'Verturian hegemony' around the core of Fortriu. The preconditioning factor in the rise of both is presented as their struggles with Bernicia in the 670s and the failure of Ecgfrith of Bernicia to maintain the dominant position inherited from his father, King Oswiu of Northumbria. Edel Bhreathnach's study of contemporary Ireland in Chapter 8 also reveals a number of intriguing similarities to developments in Mercia: the creation of a number of core dynasties, of amorphous origins, which expanded through the accretion of other groups claiming a common ancestry; a corresponding growth of royal and ecclesiastical authority, of clerical alliances with emergent dynasties and competing claims and absorption of lesser secular and ecclesiastical units; the creation and promotion of cults, especially those with dynastic overtones; the role of women; the entry of royal personages into religious life, voluntarily or otherwise, and its use as a dynastic mechanism – perhaps of the sort employed in the case of the 'pretender' to the throne of Kent, Eadberht Praen, on whose behalf Charlemagne and the Pope intervened but whose opposition to King Coenwulf led to his mutilation and imprisonment. The historical record may retain little evidence of direct links between Ireland and Mercia, but similarities in general political and social trends, coupled with the discovery of links, however discrete, in the art historical and archaeological material, raise some intriguing possibilities.

The role of aristocratic women in the politics of family and succession is explored by Pauline Stafford in Chapter 3. Mercia displays an unusually high level of representation of politically significant women, even in the depleted historical record. Offa's wife, Cynethryth, not only witnessed his crucial documents but had coinage struck in her name. His daughters made influential marriages; one of them, Eadburh, wife of Beorhtric of Wessex, thereby achieved notoriety. Abbess Cwoenthryth, daughter of King Coenwulf, was politically active in the affairs of Church and State and was acknowledged as his heir. The ending of an independent kingdom of Mercia culminates with two unique early medieval instances of female rule – Æthelflæd, Lady of the Mercians, and her daughter, Ælfwyn, who was removed by her uncle, King Edward of Wessex.

In addition to military campaigns and alliances and the politics of the marriage bed, the Church played a fundamental role in the cohesion of this extended hegemony. The traditional date for Peada's conversion, 653, is taken to mark the commencement of the conversion of Mercia, with the foundation of *Medeshamstede* (Peterborough), with Northumbrian support, and St Chad's mission to Lichfield and the Mercian heartland around 670. In Chapter 4 David Parsons discusses the artefactual evidence for the early stages of the Christianization of Mercia, the topography and landholding of its early Church, the possibility of interaction with the post-Romano-British Church in western Mercia and the possible pre-Anglo-Saxon origins of the foundation of Worcester, the focus of an independent Hwiccan bishopric. Sites and fabric, such as Brixworth, Flixborough, Repton and Wing, are discussed, as is the evidence of hagiography and dedications with its dynastic implications. The development of a hagiographic and literary tradition surrounding the most significant such cult, that of St Guthlac of Crowland, is assessed in Chapter 5 by Jane Roberts, who considers not only the material produced during the eighth century, such as Felix's *Life* with its promotion of the future King Æthelbald of Mercia and of Guthlac's links with Repton, site of the royal mausoleum, but the Mercian literary output during the Alfredian revival, including Bishop Werferth of Worcester's translation of Gregory's *Dialogues*, the Old English Bede and the Old English Martyrology.

The *Mierce* or 'Marcher People' were to some extent defined, as their name suggests, by their relationships with their neighbours – hence Mercia's unique ability to serve as a mirror of the whole Anglo-Saxon microcosm. In Chapter 6, Thomas Charles-Edwards discusses their complex dealings with the Welsh: from Penda's alliances with them against the Northumbrians, leading to the deaths of King Edwin at the battle of Hatfield (633) and of King Oswald at *Maserfelth* (Oswestry, 642), which set Mercia on the path towards overlordship; through the obscure period of Welsh history from the 670s to 820s during which Wales may have formed part of the outer zone of Mercian hegemony, much as did East Anglia, Kent, Sussex and Wessex. An initial military clientship of mutual convenience may have gradually been transformed into something far more onerous, accompanied by a sharper definition of a frontier in the face of a hardening of attitudes between the two Churches after an initial period of more positive interaction of Britons and 'English'. Subsequently, forceful campaigns to extend Mercian overlordship in Wales were conducted by Coenwulf and, later, Æthelflaed while Alfred pursued a policy of 'protection' of the southern Welsh kingdoms against Mercia, the sons of Rhodri Mawr and the Vikings. Finally, the removal of the Mercian 'third party' in West Saxon/Welsh relations with Edward the Elder's forcible removal of Aelfwyn, the last independent ruler of Mercia, paved the way for the absorption of Wales into a new *imperium*. The role of Offa's Dyke in this complex web of relationships is examined by David Hill, in Chapter 12, who discusses the 'frontier', the principal 'March' from which Mercia derived its identity, as a dynamic and topographically fluctuating source of turbulence, in both directions, connected with English attempts to control Wales through overlordship. Although the precise role of the two major earthworks in these processes remains elusive, the picture that emerges is one not of a trade frontier, but of a political border which was an essential feature of the state.

In Chapter 9, 'Carolingian Contacts', Janet Nelson considers the substance of the evidence for direct relations between Offa and Charlemagne, as well as the broader context of trade and ecclesiastical contacts between their realms. The picture which emerges is one in which Offa may have aspired, and on occasion have been encouraged, to think of himself as 'a contender' upon the bigger stage; well illustrated by Charlemagne's proposal of a marriage between Offa's daughter and his son Charles (which was rapidly withdrawn when Offa countered with an over-ambitious request that his son should receive the hand of Charlemagne's daughter, Bertha). However, she highlights the differences in scale and the nature of their internal achievements and international relations, placing the Mercian 'hegemony' in a more realistic context. Offa could be useful to Charlemagne, on occasion, and was accorded due diplomatic regard when being addressed, but this was in no sense a relationship of equals. Nonetheless, this study, along with others in the volume, indicates that the growth of the Mercian supremacy was part of a broader trend of consolidation and extension of regimes and larger territorial areas of overlordship. Pictland, Ireland and Wales were experiencing similar phenomena; the Bernician house had attempted something similar in the North and had, in so doing, occasioned its own eclipse; Mercia was soon to do the same. What its rulers perhaps failed to realize, and what helped to facilitate and to render tangible the success of their West Saxon successors and their Carolingian 'big brothers', was the fundamental need for strong ideological foundations to underpin political and administrative constructs and to compensate for the animosity and competition that such expansionism aroused. The trappings of a perceived need for such cultural ideology may, nonetheless, be perceived in the quality and the self-conscious exoticism of the visual imagery of Mercia, with its cross-referential amalgam of cultural components as seen in its manuscripts, metalwork, sculptural and architectural monuments. This was not 'borrowed' from the Carolingian orbit, but seems to have prepared and simultaneously explored the ground in which the aesthetically and ideologically fertile seeds of East Christian art and classicism (as explored by Richard Jewell in Chapter 17) were sown. The value of the spiritual basis for intellectual and cultural constructs, so prized by the circles of Charlemagne and Alfred, may also have been well recognized by Mercian religious, as the continued provision of liturgical books, the growth of a vibrant devotional genre (expressed in the Tiberius group prayerbooks, with their emphasis upon spiritual health and the solidarity of purpose of the communion of saints, as discussed by Michelle Brown in Chapter 19) and the construction of cults may indicate. In Chapter 16 Jane Hawkes similarly relates the ambitious iconographic programme of the Sandbach crosses, in the diocese of Lichfield, to the debate concerning ecclesiastical authority, the divine source of which they affirm, stimulated by the visits of the papal envoys in 787 and 803. Yet these remained, in many ways, 'add-ons' rather than tangible manifestations of an underlying conceptual motivation.

The Carolingian Empire may have been of a very different order of scale and complexity to that of Mercia: its dynastic longevity was not that much greater – but its ideological image was imperishable. That Offa was only too well aware of the crucial importance of ensuring dynastic continuity is demonstrated by his ruthless removal of any potential counter-claimants to the rule of his son, Ecgfrith, and his determination to have him consecrated as king of the Mercians during Offa's own lifetime. This unorthodox event occurred in 787, but in the process Offa had found it necessary to reorganize the southern English Church, obtaining hard-won papal permission to establish a new archbishopric at Lichfield. This proved as short-lived as the hapless Ecgfrith, who died some four and a half months after his sire, on 17th December 796, but it served to harden the attitude of churchmen such

Map 2 Mercia in Europe. The 'Carolingian Empire' in the period of its greatest
Under the Carolingians)

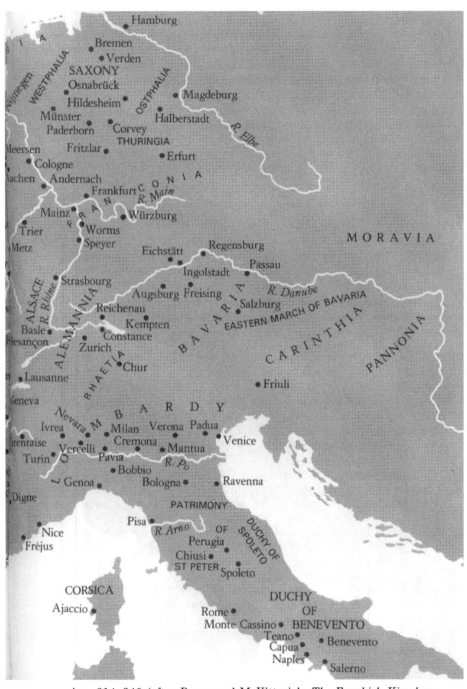

expansion, 814–840 (after Rosamond McKitterick, *The Frankish Kingdoms*

as archbishops Jænberht and Wulfred and to further their promotion of solidarity among the episcopal ranks in the face of attempts to extend royal and lay control (this assertion of episcopal rights eventually finding its most powerful expression in the canons of the Council of Chelsea in 816). Offa may have absorbed the lessons of Æthelbald's reign concerning the subjugation of men, but neither fully grasped the longer term need to touch their hearts and minds. From his vantage point in Charlemagne's kingdom, Alcuin lamented such dangerous times in his homeland, concurring with the psalmist (Ps. 127): 'Except the Lord build the house, they labour in vain that build it; except the Lord keep the city, the watchmen waketh but in vain.'

In Chapter 11, Della Hooke's discussion of landscape and environment gives an impression of the tremendous regional diversity of Greater Mercia, from the Peaks and the Welsh Marches to the coastal and riverine trading centres – access to which was a compelling factor in Mercian expansion, especially towards London and the Thames. Supplementation of the Roman road system suggests that this was still at least partially in use, although probably primarily for military use as the term 'highway' ('army-way') implies. Saltways also served to disseminate the products of the brine extraction industry at centres such as Droitwich and other industries, such as lead mining at Wirksworth, would similarly have benefited from a communications network. The watermill at Tamworth and the fish weirs at Chelsea and Colwick on the Trent also indicate advances in food provision. Settlement and economy were essentially rural in character, with 'central places', such as the estate centres of royal vills and minsters nonetheless serving as foci for economic redistribution. Multiple estate units focused upon such *caputs* were gradually subject to fragmentation into smaller estates and parishes, with tribute simultaneously commuting into services and money renders. Hooke, Welch and Vince (Chapters 11, 10 and 13) portray a hierarchy of settlement, from single farms to larger settlements with some indications of continuous occupation from the Roman to the medieval periods. An element of post-Roman continuity may be indicated by burial practices at sites such as Wasperton and Blacklow Hill, while the transfer of a Roman farm unit to an Anglo-Saxon one may be preserved at Orton Hall Farm (west of Peterborough) and the Roman town of Wroxeter may have continued as a settlement until replaced as a focus by the nearby Atcham Hall. Regional centres feature, some polyfocal and with royal connections (such as Tamworth and Northampton, where a possible royal hall may have functioned in a monastic context, as at the Carolingian centre of Paderborn, and at Flixborough). Some, such as Newark, subsequently became market towns. Mid-Saxon urbanization is easier to demonstrate in eastern Mercia, at centres such as Northampton, Bedford and Nottingham, than in the more rural interior. Major urban development would have to wait for the Anglo-Saxon *burhs* and Danish boroughs of the late ninth and tenth centuries. However, as Vince's discussion in Chapter 13 shows, the archaeological record may be misleading; potential sites have been located and there is significant evidence in the form of traded goods to indicate commercial development. It is instructive that the commercial heart of London – *Lundenwic* – remained undiscovered until the mid-1980s. Robert Cowie's summary of exciting recent archaeological work in Chapter 14, especially in the vicinity of Aldwych and Covent Garden, indicates the complexity of this industrial and international trading centre, close to the ecclesiastical focus which remained within the old Roman town. Above all there is the eloquent witness of the coinage which, as Gareth Williams shows in Chapter 15, provides evidence not only of trade and of a monetary economy, but of the aspirations and the governmental capacities and constraints of Mercia's rulers at different points in its history.

The overlordship so energetically forged and wielded by a series of powerful Mercian rulers – notably Æthelbald (716–757), Offa (757–796) and Coenwulf (796–821) – was not supported by dynastic continuity, despite Offa's labours and the promotion of a perception of ultimate common ancestry. Different kin groups vied for prominence, not unlike their Irish contemporaries the Uí Neill, and matters relating to their possible backgrounds are discussed in the contributions by Yorke, Featherstone, Williams and Keynes. The 'collapse' of the Mercian supremacy may be viewed from a number of perspectives. For some scholars it occurs in the 820s as an almost inevitable result of the overbearing methods employed in its construction – the Mercian iron gauntlet giving way to the West Saxon velvet glove – and of a dynastic crisis provoked by the absence of an individual strong enough to seize and retain personal rule. Coenwulf stepped forcefully into the breach in 796, but there was apparently no such leader to hold things together following his death during a military campaign in Wales. This, coupled with ongoing disputes in Kent, undoubtedly assisted Ecgberht of Wessex in his defeat of one of the hapless and rapidly ousted successors to the throne, Beornwulf, at Ellendun in 825 and his subsequent conquest of Mercia in 829. But other scholars have been quick to point out that by 830 the kingdom had been regained by Wiglaf, whether in his own right or as a client of Wessex. Pressure from Viking attack brought Mercia into even closer contact with Wessex, King Burgred's immediate response to the invasion of Mercia in 867–868 being to appeal to the West Saxons for help, before finally departing for Rome with his wife and intimates in 874. Hostile West Saxon sources, and many modern historians, might write off Mercia at this point and refer disparagingly to the Viking's puppet-ruler, Ceolwulf II (874–*c*. 879), as a 'foolish king's thegn', yet even at this stage the charter and coinage evidence presents a picture of some continuity of rule and identity within the kingdom. Then, as earlier, the ealdormen of its component regions may have served to ensure some stability and the system of mutual dependence and extension of royal control inherent in the Mercian promotion of bookland may also have stood the kingdom in good stead. As Gareth Williams shows in Chapter

20, the early basis for Mercian military success, based on the personal bond between lord and follower, was retained, and indeed consolidated through documented property tenure, and although aggressive warfare was probably limited to an elite, defensive warfare probably involved a wider section of society, which also undertook increasing responsi-bility for the construction and maintenance of roads, bridges and fortresses under Mercian rule. Wessex may have built on these foundations and extended such obligations to the construction of an effective network of *burhs*, but their use as part of a campaign of reconquest of the Danelaw was significantly furthered by Alfred's daughter, Æthelflæd, as 'Lady of the Mercians'. The 'kingdom of the Mercians' retained its identity and played an often crucial role in the balance of power that sustained the 'kingdom of the English' forged by Alfred and his successors.

Part I

The Mercian Polity: Church and State

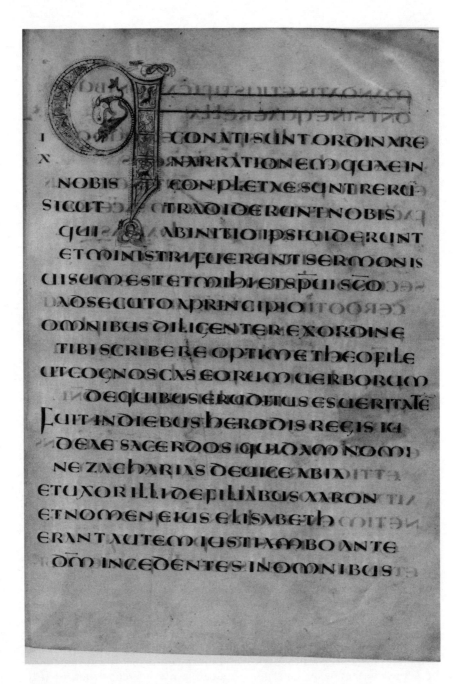

1 The Origins of Mercia

Barbara Yorke

The question of the origins of Mercia is a microcosm of the larger question of the origins of Anglo-Saxon kingdoms. Some kingdoms were apparently securely established by the seventh century when the attention their rulers received from missionaries of various nationalities provided the raw materials for Bede's celebrated account of the 'Ecclesiastical History of the English People', but their origins unfortunately occurred at a time outside the reach of his historical narrative. Questions of origins could be answered relatively easily in the nineteenth century, when Bede's edited version of the account of the Anglo-Saxon *adventus* provided by Gildas and entries in the *Anglo-Saxon Chronicle* were taken at face value to suggest that the invaders arrived already led by the men who would establish themselves as the founders of dynasties as soon as they had completed their conquest of the hapless natives (Sims-Williams, 1983b). The earliest attempts at archaeological analysis could be fitted into this format with brooches and pots seen as the spoor of parties from the earliest settlements penetrating via the river systems into the heart of darkest post-Roman Britain (Collingwood and Myres, 1936; Leeds, 1936).

Those days of innocence are, of course, long over. But in the place of the earlier consensus there is currently discord and confusion in which rival, often mutually contradictory, narratives jostle for attention, and the results of the theoretical constructs of different disciplines have yet to be reconciled (e.g. Higham, 1992b; Gelling, 1993; Scull, 1993; Lucy, 1999). Exploration and reconciliation of the evidence from different regimes of academic study for the origins of Mercia would take more space than can be allowed for in one short chapter, and in view of the range of current debate such syntheses might be considered premature. Rather, as a contribution to the cross-disciplinary consensus that may one day emerge, this historian will stick to her last and concentrate on how the origins of the province were presented in written records produced by the Mercians and their neighbours in the seventh, eighth and ninth centuries. It will remain to be seen whether what emerges is purely a literary construct, or if it has a potential contribution to make to the vexed question of the origins of Mercia and of other kingdoms.

Anglian descent

In his oft-cited addition to Gildas's account of the Anglo-Saxon *adventus*, Bede identified the *Merci* as one of the peoples (*gentes*) who had come to Britain from *Angulus*, the Continental German land which lay between that of the Jutes and the Saxons, and which, he says, was largely depopulated in his day because of the scale of the migration to Britain (*HE* I, 15). In a later chapter Bede reveals that he knew that the situation was in fact more complex and that there were many peoples (*nationes*) in Germany from whom the *Angli* and *Saxones* derived their stock and origin (*genus et originem*) (*HE* V, 9). Bede's limited observations seem broadly in accord with archaeological evidence. Fifth-century finds from the Anglian areas of England do suggest the presence of peoples from several different areas of Germany and Scandinavia, but those of the sixth century, especially the more elaborate forms of female dress, imply the evolution of an Anglian identity which drew upon the traditions of several different Germanic provinces (Hines, 1995). 'Anglian dress' is found over a wider area than that covered by fifth-century finds, including the area of historic Mercia, giving rise to current interpretations of such forms of dress as an indicator of ethnic identity assumed by a diverse population, including many of the indigenous inhabitants of Roman Britain (Bassett, 2000). The exact context that gave rise to the formation of Anglian identity is harder to pin down in the absence of written sources for much of the politics of the fifth and sixth centuries. But the archaeological evidence suggests that the desire to stress Germanic origins, and the distinction between Anglian and Saxon found in province names and apparently in dialect, as well as in Bede's narrative, was a real phenomenon and not just one imposed on the evidence by the early written sources or by later commentators who made use of them (Hines, 1994).

Also present in the country from an early date was an Anglo-Saxon version of an archetypal migration myth that explained the formation of new peoples through the arrival of the founders of new dynasties (Moisl, 1981; Yorke, 2000). It was Gildas who recorded how the leaders of the *Saxones* had come across the sea in three *cyulis* (keels), a word of Germanic origin, which, together with a reference to a Germanic prophecy that they would remain 300 years in the island, suggests that Gildas had information that came ultimately from the Anglo-Saxon settlements (Winterbottom, 1978: 26; Sims-Williams, 1983a; Higham, 1994a: 35–66). So although it was in the *Historia Ecclesiastica* that these leaders were identified as Hengest and Horsa, which may have been an invention of Bede or of churchmen in Kent, and considerably developed versions of Kentish and West Saxon foundation legends are known, the basic format was apparently in circulation as early as the late fifth or early sixth centuries (depending on when Gildas is thought to have lived and written). It would therefore seem to be the case that, well before conversion to

Christianity, Anglo-Saxons of eastern England were actively promoting through the symbolism of jewellery and clothing the importance of links with northern Germanic areas and were utilizing myths in which the formation of a new people was embodied in accounts of the migration and victories of their leaders. These accounts may have been embellished after conversion, and interest in them may have been stimulated by knowledge that other post-Roman people such as the Goths and Burgundians believed (perhaps because of a convenient tie-up with classical ethnography) that they had migrated from Scandinavia (Reynolds, 1983; Heather, 1996: 9–50), but it is not necessary to conclude that they were purely the invention of literate commentators of the seventh century or later (Yorke, 2000).

Mercian foundation legends

Brief references suggest that Mercia may have possessed a foundation account of how the kingdom and its ruling dynasty came into existence, comparable to the more detailed versions that have survived for Kent and Wessex, albeit in forms adapted to suit later needs and contexts. The key evidence is that of the early eighth-century *Vita S. Guthlaci* where it is recorded that Guthlac's father Penwalh was *de egregia stirpe Merciorum* and could trace his descent *digesto ordine* ('in set order' presumably in a genealogy) 'through the most noble names of famous kings, back to Icel in whom it began in days of old' (Colgrave, 1956: 72–5). Icel, who appears five generations above Penda in the genealogies of the Anglian collection (Table 1.1; Dumville, 1976), would appear to have been regarded as the founder of the dynasty and of the Mercian people. The traditional reckoning of 30 years per generation would reach back to the middle of the fifth century, perhaps revealing the influence of Bede's calculation of a date of *c.* 450 for the Saxon *adventus* on the development of Mercian traditions. As Mercia was not a maritime province, presumably the founders of the dynasty would have to be represented as moving inland from a more easterly base. Henry of Huntingdon recorded under the year 527 that 'there came at frequent intervals from Germany large numbers of men who settled East Anglia and Mercia, but as yet these kingdoms had not been brought under one king' (Greenway, 1996: 98–9). Some support for seeing the Mercian royal house as originating in East Anglia has been seen in the incidence of place-names incorporating the name 'Icel' in eastern England (Myres, 1986: 185), but the evidence is really too slight to postulate the former existence of an extended tradition of how the Iclingas came from East Anglia to Mercia (Davies, 1977).

In common with several other kingdoms, by the end of the eighth century the Mercians were claiming that their ancestors included traditional Germanic heroes. The upper reaches of the genealogies of King Æthelred of Mercia (675–704) in the Anglian collection and of Penda in the *Anglo-Saxon Chronicle* s. A. 626 contain the names of

Table 1.1 The descent of Pybba from Woden

Anglian Collection	Anglo-Saxon Chronicle, 626	Beowulf
Pybba	Pybba	
Crioda	Creoda	
Cynewald	Cynewald	
Cnebba	Cnebba	
Icil	Icel	
Eamer	Eomær	Eomer
Angengeot	Angelþeow	
Offa	Offa	Offa
Wærmund	Wærmund	Garmund
Wihtlæg	Wihtlæg	
Weoðulgeot		
Woden	Woden	

Wihtlæg, his son Wærmund and grandson Offa, all, apparently independently, attested in the works of the Danish historians, Saxo Grammaticus and Sweyn Aageson, writing in the latter part of the twelfth century (Chadwick, 1924: 114–20; Chambers, 1967: 32–4). Wærmund (in the form Garmund) and Offa also feature in *Beowulf*, together with a grandson of Offa called Eomer (ll. 1949–1963). The latter also appears in this position in the genealogy of Æthelred, where he is given as the father of Icel. The elaborate upper reaches of the genealogies in the Anglian collection have been contrasted with the simple descent from Woden given by Bede for Hengest and Horsa (Sisam, 1953a). Genealogies clearly evolved over time, often in response to political alliances or propagandic needs (Dumville, 1977). King Offa of Mercia (757–796) may have deliberately developed parallels between himself and his heroic namesake. Matthew Paris's *Vitae Duorum Offarum* (Chambers, 1967: 217–43) seems to have drawn on material with origins in the reign of Offa that was preserved in his community at St Albans, one of the religious houses favoured by the king (Vaughan, 1958: 189–94). Complimentary references to the heroic Offa in *Beowulf* and *Widsith* (ll. 35–44), including allusions to the establishment of a boundary in the latter that may have been intended to bring to mind the historical Offa's eponymous dyke, may also reflect a deliberate parallelism of the two Offas at the Mercian court in the later eighth century (Whitelock, 1951: 58–64). However, the less than complimentary references in *Beowulf* (ll. 1931–1950) to the heroic Offa's wife Thryth (who could be seen as a parallel for the historic Offa's queen Cynethryth) suggest that the convention could be subverted satirically by enemies of Offa or of Mercian royal women (Earle, 1892: lxxv–lxxxvii). The unflattering portrayal of Cwoenthryth (daughter of Offa's successor Coenwulf) in the *Lives* of her brother St Kenelm may also owe something to the bad reputation attributed to Thryth (Wright, 1939: 93–106).

But although Offa may have encouraged citations of the heroic Offa and his relatives, he may not have been the first to link them with the Mercian royal house. The matter cannot be proved one way or the other, but King Æthelred may himself have celebrated his descent from the heroic ancestors who were included in his genealogy that was written down in the late eighth century. Tales of Wærmund and Offa may have been among the accounts of 'the valiant deeds of heroes of old' which inspired the young Guthlac (in the late seventh century) to an early career of what seems to have been unheroic pillaging (Colgrave, 1956: 80–1). The fact that the name was given in the seventh century to a prince of the East Saxons (who abdicated by 709) (Yorke, 1985: 22–3) may also suggest knowledge of the heroic Offa in England before the eighth century. Offa of Mercia may therefore have been so christened to deliberately recall a well-known hero by a royal branch line who saw a chance of coming to power. Offa, Wærmund and their associates were denizens of that shadowy heroic Germanic world that Mercians and other Anglians sought to evoke through the imagery of their metalwork in the sixth century (Magnus, 1997; Webster, 1997: 237).

Offa and Wærmund provided the Mercian royal lines with a noble descent which aspirant kings may have been as eager to claim in the sixth century as in the eighth. Did they also help to provide not only a noble, but a divine descent – if indeed these things can be distinguished? Many of the heroes claimed by Germanic dynasties in western Europe have a hazy identity which hovers between the heroic and the divine, their original status often fudged by later euhemeriza-tion (Moisl, 1981). However, Mercian claims to divine origins, like those of other Anglo-Saxon dynasties, are less equivocally made through claimed descent from Woden. Whether Woden was actually ever seen as a divine ancestor has been questioned (John, 1992). Certainly Bede's blithe comment that it was from Woden's stock that 'the royal families of so many kingdoms claimed their descent' (*HE* I. 15) suggests that he followed the line suggested by Bishop Daniel to Boniface that gods who behaved like men and begat descendants were men not gods (Tangl, 1916: no. 23; Talbot, 1954: no. 11). Bede and other churchmen could allow Woden to stay in the royal genealogies as a founding hero, but it is unlikely that they would have voluntarily included him had he not been there already, especially as, through contacts with missionaries and traders, English churchmen must have been aware of Woden/Odin's status as a god among other Germanic peoples. That the cultivation of Woden was part of the process by which royal houses hoped to enhance their status in the pre-conversion period has emerged as even more likely after the strong arguments produced in recent years for a Woden cult underpinning emergent kingship in Scandinavia in the sixth and seventh centuries following much work on the imagery of bracteates (Axboe, 1982; Gaimster, 1998). Not only are bracteates found in eastern England that were either imported from Scandinavia or embrace the forms of some of the Scandinavian series (though not the most explicit A and B types), but so are other representations that seem to be linked with Woden cults, notably the figures with spears and bird-headed helmets on the Sutton Hoo helmet (Bruce-Mitford, 1978: 186–220).

The earliest Mercian kings

Gods and heroes may help us to understand how the earliest Mercian kings sought to underpin their power and why the subject of the origins of Mercia was of enduring interest at later Mercian royal courts, but they do not help us pinpoint the actual origins of Mercian kingship. Regnal lists included in the Anglian collection (Dumville, 1976), in BL, Cotton Tiberius A. xiii ('Hemming's Cartulary'), in the preliminary tables of the *Chronicle of John of Worcester* (Thorpe, 1848: 264–7), and the one which presumably lay behind the Mercian entries in the *Anglo-Saxon Chronicle* (Whitelock *et al.*, 1961), all begin with the reign of Penda. Bede could only provide regnal years from the reign of Penda onwards, but he knew that there had been an earlier king called Cearl whose daughter had married Edwin of Deira and that their children had been born during Edwin's period of exile (*c.* 604–616) (*HE* II. 14). The only narrative sources that attempt to go back further are post-Conquest in date. The *Historia Anglorum* of Henry of Huntingdon claims that Crida (Creoda) began to rule in 585, when the kingdom of Mercia began, that he was succeded by Wibba (Pybba) who ruled three years, and that he was followed by Ceorl (Cearl) who ruled for ten years (Davies, 1977). The information was subsequently copied by the St Albans historians Roger of Wendover and Matthew Paris (Greenway, 1996: cii–iii). One would have more confidence with this tradition if it showed any independence of other known sources. As it is, the name of Cearl/Ceorl could have been taken from the *Historia Ecclesiastica* and the names of Crida/Creoda and his son Wibba/Pybba from the version of Penda's genealogy given in the annal for 626 in the *Anglo-Saxon Chronicle*. In trying to fit the regnal years into his annalistic format it appears that Henry of Huntingdon assumed that Crida/Creoda was the individual of that name recorded in the *Anglo-Saxon Chronicle* as dying in 593, though the context of that annal implies that its Crida was a West Saxon.

The four Mercian genealogies in the Anglian collection have Pybba as their common gateway ancestor. Æthelred was the grandson of Pybba; Æthelbald and Ecgfrith, the son of Offa, claimed descent from Eowa, son of Pybba, and Coenwulf from Coenwalh, son of Pybba. Coenwalh is otherwise unknown, but the ninth-century *Historia Brittonum* implies that Eowa had ruled and had been subject to King Oswald of Northumbria, for it says that Penda 'first freed the kingdom of the Mercians from the kingdom of the northerners', following the battle of Cocboy/*Maserfelth* of 642 in which both Eowa and Oswald were slain (Brooks, 1989a: 165–8). With the Northumbrian tradition of the enigmatic Cearl, with whom no later ruler claimed a connection, we can trace Mercian rule back to *c.* 600. If the implication of Edwin's marriage to Cearl's daughter is that Cearl sheltered Edwin in exile, in the face of Æthelfrith of Bernicia's determination to stamp out his Deiran rivals, one could argue that Mercia was already relatively strongly established by the early years of the seventh century (Higham, 1992a). On the other hand, the early documentary evidence has also been interpreted as evidence for the relatively late emergence of Mercia as a consolidated kingdom of any size in the second half of the seventh century (Dumville, 1989a). There has been greater agreement between modern commentators that the reigns of Penda (d. 655) and his son Wulfhere (658–675) were of crucial importance in laying the foundations for the great overlordships of Æthelbald (716–757) and Offa (757–796) in the following century (Stenton, 1971: 202–38).

If we could trust the tradition that Crida ruled before Cearl, it would push the known existence of the kingdom back to the last quarter of the sixth century. This is the period from which a reliable historical horizon of dated reigns begins for most of the kingdoms with early written traditions. Are we seeing the origins of kingdoms here, or only the limits of living memory projected back from the time when record keeping began in earnest in the seventh century (Dumville, 1977: 92–3)? It appears that the best the surviving written sources will allow us to say is that there were probably men calling themselves 'kings of the Mercians' by *c.* 600; what they meant by that title is another question again.

The Mercians

The name *Mierce/Merci* means 'the borderers', but it is not immediately clear who or what they were most significantly considered as bordering, though the western British is the explanation that has been generally preferred (Stenton, 1971: 40; Brooks, 1989a: 160–2). The simplex name-form recalls those of the Hwicce and Gewisse (Coates, 1990; Sims-Williams, 1990: 16–18). Such names may be of older formation than the kingdom names incorporating a geographical location, and could have originated as the names of mobile *comitatus* groupings rather than of settled peoples. Kings do not have to be seen necessarily as emerging through some natural evolutionary process of competition between the most significant families of a district (Scull, 1993, 1999). Some may have begun life as the leaders of Viking-type solidarities who imposed themselves by force on settled peoples, as some Scandinavian leaders did in western Europe in the ninth century.

By the seventh century there was a clear geographical area which was associated with the Mercians. Bede, writing of arrangements after the battle of the Winwaed of 655 in which Penda had been killed, described a division into North and South Mercians of 7,000 and 5,000 hides respectively, with the River Trent forming the boundary between them (*HE* III. 24). In the vicinity of the Trent are some of the key places for Mercian rulers in the late seventh and eighth centuries: the royal nunnery of Repton, the royal vill of Tamworth and the site of the Mercian bishopric at Lichfield (which had formerly been a British centre, perhaps acquired by King Wulfhere) (Bassett, 2000). This is surely the core area of the historic kingdom defined as 'original Mercia' in the Tribal Hidage, from which the other peoples of the list appear to radiate (Brooks, 1989a: 160–2; Featherstone, this volume).

But the Mercia of the Tribal Hidage is given an area of 30,000 hides not the 12,000 recorded by Bede, and if that were taken literally (as opposed, say, to being seen as a penal assessment), the 'original Mercians' would have to incorporate the territories of some of the neighbouring peoples of the list (Hart, 1977). This is just one of the many problems that make the Tribal Hidage something of a poisoned chalice for historians of Mercia. A consensus has yet to be reached on many of the key issues concerning it. A range of dates from the early seventh century to the late eighth century has been assigned (Rumble, 1996a), and opinion is divided over whether it was produced in Mercia (Stenton, 1971: 296–7; Hart, 1977; Keynes, 1995: 21–5) or Northumbria (Brooks, 1989a: 159; Higham, 1995: 74–111). As it only survives in manuscripts of the late eleventh century or later, and in collections of material assembled for legal and antiquarian interest rather than practical use, we cannot hope to recover its original form and provenance (Wormald, 1996a). Errors have evidently crept in during copying, leading to some hopelessly distorted names, but its contents may have been subject to other additions and emendations over the years which are not so easily recognizable. It may be a composite document rather than one that can be assigned to a particular regime or administrative dictat. The 'peoples' in it have been interpreted either as representing early settlement groupings (Davies and Vierck, 1974), or as originating as units of administration (Campbell, 1979a: 47–50; Foard, 1985: 201–8). The Tribal Hidage has been viewed both as an example of the strength of Mercian overlordship (Hart, 1977), and as evidence for the failure of Mercia to become a fully integrated kingdom (Keynes, 1995). In short, if we had the correct key, the Tribal Hidage could be the gateway to understanding the origins of Mercia, but without it there are too many uncertainties for it to support secure hypotheses.

What defined a people as being Mercian? The two main alternatives are that people were either Mercian because they lived in a certain geographical area or because they accepted the authority of Mercian kings. The geographical identity came to dominate, but in the seventh and eighth centuries being Mercian seems to have been a more flexible commodity. People under the authority of the Mercian kings might always be referred to as the Mercians, but they might not always be exactly the same people – the extent of their authority might fluctuate depending on the military success of kings at different points in their reigns. The Mercians could have moved from being a 12,000 hide to a 30,000 hide people in a relatively short space of time. Someone living in the Peak District may have been both one of the Pecsaete, answerable to a local lord or administrator, and at various points in the seventh century also a Mercian or a Northumbrian depending on the destination of his tribute payments. A family in the vicinity of Lichfield that had begun the reign of Wulfhere considering themselves to be British by allegiance, language and custom, might after conquest by Wulfhere have preferred to adopt the English language and some of the customs such as dress that would signify they were not challenging the Mercian identity imposed upon them (Bassett, 2000). King Æthelbald of Mercia experimented with different titles to express his overlord-ship of other southern peoples, but King Offa preferred to remain *rex Merciorum* and saw himself as expanding the boundaries of what constituted Mercia (Stenton, 1918). As Bede defined it in his *Ecclesiastical History*, a *gens* like that of the Mercians was ruled by a king, and everyone who recognized his authority was a member of his *provincia* (Yorke, 2000). The origin of the concept of a Mercian people is inextricably bound up with the origins of their ruling house.

Conclusion

Isidore of Seville defined a people, that is a *gens*, 'as a multitude sprung from one principle' (*Etymologiae* 1X. ii. 1), by which he meant that in early medieval Europe there was a belief that the whole of the people descended from a common founder (Loud, 1981; Reynolds, 1983). That is what was embodied in the Anglo-Saxon foundation myths in which the whole of the Kentish or West Saxon peoples apparently arrive with their leaders in three or five boats. It would appear to be what Felix is alluding to when he describes Æthelbald of Mercia as being *de egregia stirpe Merciorum*, 'of the distinguished stock of the Mercians', and *de inclita Merciorum prole*, 'of the famous stock of the Mercians' (Colgrave, 1956: 72–3, 124–5); the royal house was interpreted as the stock from which the Mercian people had sprung. Such beliefs about the origins of kingdoms are good examples of an 'imagined community' or an artificially created, collective remem-brance of the past which takes the place of genuine memories (Anderson, 1991). It explains why the origins of kingdoms are so hard to trace because the type of records modern historians would like to possess have been replaced by the accounts which Anglo-Saxons felt were needed. Gildas and archaeological evidence may help trace the beginnings of these created remembrances, and so perhaps of the royal houses which generated them, back into the sixth century, but any genuine traditions that had come down from an early period would have been honed and redefined in subsequent centuries as kingdoms themselves grew and reformed themselves, so that there are further problems in identifying the antiquity of different layers. The origins of the Mercian kingdom cannot be recovered in detail, and the creation of the kingdom must have been only part of the history of the people who lived in what was to become Mercian territory. We have instead glimpses of the official account of Mercian origins, presumably sponsored by the ruling house, but the fact that the creation of a shared history was deemed important and that it might obliterate any memories of a disunited past, bears witness to the impact that kings had within the territories that became their kingdoms, however, and whenever, they may have been created.

2 The Tribal Hidage and the Ealdormen of Mercia

Peter Featherstone

Between the mid-seventh century and the turn of the ninth, the influence of Mercia expanded from its origins in the Trent valley to encompass virtually all of the territory between the Thames and the Humber, as well as enjoying considerable influence over East Anglia and the South East. During the years of expansion, many minor kingdoms and principalities were absorbed into the Mercian kingdom, either through subjugation or voluntary alliance and the only record we now have of these 'lost' peoples is in the assessment list known as the Tribal Hidage (Table 2.1). There are good reasons for believing that many of the minor tribes that were absorbed by Mercia were retained within the political infrastructure of the larger kingdom as provinces run by ealdormen, and it is this possibility that forms the focus of this chapter. In some ways it covers similar ground to Cyril Hart's 'The Kingdom of Mercia' in *Mercian Studies* (Dornier, 1977a); however, whereas Hart discussed the topography of the Tribal Hidage through a study of parish and shire boundaries, I shall be looking in more detail at the document itself, discussing its provenance and purpose and its relationship to the ealdormen of Mercia.

The Tribal Hidage survives in seven medieval manuscripts. It comprises a list of 35 peoples or 'tribes', each given in the genitive plural and accompanied by an assessment in hides. Although often referred to as a tribute list (Hart, 1971: 133; 1977: 44; Davies and Vierck, 1974: 225; Sawyer, 1998: 110), there is nothing in the text itself to confirm this theory. Certainly, assessment for tribute or taxation remains the most probable purpose of the list; nevertheless, there are indications that the text may have been tampered with or updated, which opens the possibility that the list meant different things at different times in its history. The Tribal Hidage as we have it may bear little resemblance to the lost original and this must be borne in mind when analysing the text.

Any investigation of the Tribal Hidage should proceed from the manuscripts. David Dumville (1989) has identified three separate recensions of the text. Recension A, the earliest and most complete text, survives as an Old English version in B.L., Harley MS 3271, an

Table 2.1 The Tribal Hidage (derived from the text in Harley 3271)

Tribe	Hidage	Suggested locations (Hart, 1971; Davies and Vierck, 1974)
Myrcna landes	30,000	'the area first called Mercia'
Wocen saetna	7,000	Wreocensaetan
Westerna	7,000	Magonsaetan
Pecsaetna	1,200	Peak dwellers
Elmedsaetna	600	Elmet dwellers
Lindes farona mid haethfeld land	7,000	Lindsey with Hatfield Chase
Suth gyrwa	600	Located around Peterborough 'in the
North gyrwa	600	region of the Gyrui' (*HE*, III. 20)
East wixna	300	Possibly located around Wisbech in
West wixna	600	Cambridgeshire
Spalda	600	Spalding, Lincolnshire
Wigesta	900	?Wiggenhall in Norfolk marshlands
Herefinna	1,200	?*Hyrstingas* of Hurstingbourne, Huntingdonshire
Sweordora	300	Associated with Sword Point, Huntingdonshire
Gifla	300	R. Ivel, Buckinghamshire
Hicca	300	Hitchin, Hertfordshire
Wihtgara	600	Isle of Wight
Noxgaga	5,000	?Wokingham, Berkshire and Woking, Surrey
Ohtgaga	2,000	?Surrey
Total	**66,100**	
Hwinca	7,000	Hwicce
Ciltern saetna	4,000	Chiltern dwellers
Hendrica	3,500	?North Oxfordshire vs Buckinghamshire
Unecung-ga	1,200	?Buckinghamshire
Arosaetna	600	River Arrow, Warwickshire
Faerpinga	300	Charlbury, Oxfordshire
Bilmiga	600	Northamptonshire vs Rutland
Widerigga	600	Wittering and Werrington, Northamptonshire
East willa	600	?Willeybrook, Northamptonshire vs the Old Well
West willa	600	Stream of the Fen area
East engle	30,000	East Angles
East sexena	7,000	East Saxons
Cantwarena	15,000	Men of Kent
Suth sexena	7,000	South Saxons
West sexena	100,000	West Saxons
Total	**242,700**	(*recte* 244,100)

eleventh-century manuscript of unknown provenance (Ker, 1957: 309–12). Harley 3271 is a curious document written in many different hands that all date to roughly the same period. It also contains a six-line Latin piece on the characteristics of nations, which is appended to the end of the Tribal Hidage, as well as a miscellaneous collection of texts on various subjects. These include an incomplete copy of a treatise on Latin Grammar by abbot Aelfric of Eynsham (*c.* 955–*c.* 1020); a letter from Aelfric to Sigeweard in which he discusses various points in the Old and New Testaments; calculations on the date of Easter and other feast days; the number of months, days, mealtimes and hours in the year; and a table of lucky and unlucky days of the moon. It would appear that great care was taken to update the information in the manuscript and in the Tribal Hidage in particular. A marginal note written in a different hand to that which penned the Tribal Hidage adds information that the Faerpingas *is in Middelenglum*, a comment probably derived from Bede (*HE* III. 21), while the word *hund* was appended to the assessment of the Herefinna and the final total. The haphazard arrangement of the texts and the multiplicity of hands that produced the manuscript make it difficult to discern a single underlying purpose. However, it may have acted as a reference work, chiefly for ecclesiastical matters, or possibly even as a school book (cf. Barnwell, 1991). The Tribal Hidage, coupled as it is with a piece that describes the characteristics of nations, may have served as a sort of verbal atlas, describing the relative sizes or resources of the peoples listed.

Recension B exists only in a seventeenth-century copy made by Henry Spelman in his *Archaeologus in modum Glossarii ad rem antiquam posterium* (Dumville, 1989: 225–30). In form and content Spelman's list greatly resembles Harley 3271, except that it assigns 3,000 hides to the Hendrica rather than 3,500, and it varies slightly in aspects of spelling, for instance, Eyfla for Gifla, or Fearfinga for Faerpinga; most significantly, there are several instances where an 'i' in Harley 3271 has been replaced by a 'y' in Spelman's copy, e.g. Hwynca versus Hwinca. These differences indicate that Spelman's copy was not taken from Harley 3271 and that his version of the Tribal Hidage represents a separate mode of transmission. His exemplar may have been a Latin text, for although the tribal names retain their Old English forms, the word *hidas* is used throughout as though it were a first declension, Latin accusative plural and the entry for Mercia reads: *Myrcna continet 30,000 Hidas*. However, Spelman copied the text as part of a Latin treatise on the subject of the hide and it is clear from the concise, tabulated way in which he presented the Tribal Hidage that the version he has preserved for us has been highly edited; hence, we must consider the possibility that the Latin embellishments were Spelman's own.

Recension C comprises six Latin manuscripts of the thirteenth and fourteenth centuries which represent a separate mode of transmission from Harley 3271 or the copy of the Tribal Hidage recorded by

Spelman (see Davies and Vierck, 1974: 288–92; Rumble, 1996b: 36–53). Four of the manuscripts belonged to the Guildhall of the City of London (John Rylands Library, Latin 155 (1204 x 1215); B.L., Cotton MS Claudius D.ii (*c.* 1310); Cambridge, Corpus Christi College, MS 70 (by 1313 x 1314); Oxford, Oriel College, MS 46 (*c.* 1330)) while the other two hail from the Royal Exchequer at Westminster (Red Book of the Exchequer (*c.*1225); B.L., Hargreave MS 313 (*c.* 1250). The Tribal Hidage is presented in all six manuscripts grouped together with the Burghal Hidage under the heading *De numero hydarum Anglie in Britannia* making it likely that the compilers of these manuscripts were unaware that they were dealing with two documents that hailed from very different origins.

The four Guildhall versions of the Tribal Hidage belonged to a collection of legal texts compiled by the citizens of London in the early thirteenth century, which Felix Liebermann named the *Leges Anglorum Londoniis collectae* (Liebermann, 1894). Within the *Leges Anglorum*, the combined document of the Tribal Hidage and Burghal Hidage is preceded by a text that describes the internal divisions of the *regnum Britanniae ... quod modo uocatur regnum Anglorum* and is followed by Latin texts of the laws of the West Saxons kings, Ine and Alfred. The *Leges Anglorum* was compiled in the early thirteenth century at a time when the citizens of London, who had become a commune in 1191, were becoming involved in the opposition to King John. The citizens' chief concern was to see the enforcement of law through reference to legal custom rather than through the exercise of royal will (Holt, 1965: 48–9, 79–80); hence the *Leges Anglorum* was presumably intended to act as a record of native English legal custom (Rumble, 1996b: 45).

The thirteenth-century copy of the Tribal Hidage in the Red Book of the Exchequer may have served a similar function. It is preceded by the legal text *Blodwite* and is followed by a list of those shires governed by West Saxon, Danish and Mercian law, the latter including some material similar to that concerning the *regnum Britanniae* in the Guildhall manuscripts. The other Exchequer version of the Tribal Hidage, found in Hargreave 313, is a highly flawed text and may have been produced as part of a training exercise for a new scribe (Rumble, 1996b: 53).

Despite the division of its manuscripts between the Guildhall and Westminster, there was probably a single archetype for all six manuscripts. All six manuscripts add an 'r' to W(r)ocensaetna; a 'c' to O(c)htgaga; an extra syllable to Bilmiga; they render the Wideriga as Wyderinga; and like Recension B they frequently use 'y' where an 'i' was used in Recension A. One further feature that distinguishes this group is that all the manuscripts omit Wessex from the list, while ascribing its 100,000 hides to the South Saxons. The irony of this omission is that the archetype for Recension C probably belonged to the Exchequer which in the pre-Conquest period is thought to have resided at Winchester, the capital of Wessex (Rumble, 1996b: 47).

The collection of legal texts in which Recension C was preserved was probably used as evidence of legal precedent; however, the purpose of the Tribal Hidage within the collection is ultimately defined by its association with the Burghal Hidage. The Burghal Hidage was a document that was primarily concerned with defence of fortified *burhs* in the South of England. Version A of the Burghal Hidage contained a calculation that made a direct association between hides and men: 'If each hide is represented by one man, then each pole (of wall) can be furnished with four men' (Rumble, 1996a: 30, 34). Unfortunately, version B of the Burghal Hidage, that which is associated with Recension C of the Tribal Hidage, does not include the calculation; however, it remains possible that the composite document was viewed as an ancient population census rather than a tribute list.

All three recensions of the Tribal Hidage are descended from a lost original that pre-dates the earliest manuscript; the provenance and purpose of that lost original have been the source of considerable debate among modern scholars. To some extent the purpose of the Tribal Hidage can be determined by examining the text itself. Looking at the entries in the list it becomes immediately clear that Mercia was at the forefront of the compiler's mind. The list begins with an assessment of the Mercian heartlands around the Trent valley at 30,000 hides and then proceeds in a topographical progression to describe those peoples who were located in adjacent regions (Hart, 1971: 133–57; 1977: 47–54; Davies and Vierck, 1974: 230–6). The Wocen saetan have been identified with the Wreocensaetan of the area between Wroxeter and the Mersey to the West of the Trent valley, while the Westerna have been associated with the Magonsaetan, who occupied lands around Leominster and Hereford. Next on the list are those peoples to the North of the Mercian heartlands: the Pecsaetan of the Peak district and the people of Elmet, near Leeds. To the East are the people of Lindsey and Hatfield Chase of Lincolnshire and the North and South Gyrwe who may have been located around Peterborough. Many of the smaller units that follow have also been located in the East Midlands. Place-name evidence suggests that the Spalda were active around Spalding, Lincolnshire, whilst the Sweodora have traditionally been associated with Sword Point in Whittlesea Mere, Huntingdonshire. The clockwise progression is broken by the inclusion of the Wihtgara of the Isle of Wight, but then it picks up again to list the tribes to the South of the Mercian heartlands. The Hwinca, or Hwicce of Worcestershire and Gloucestershire, the Ciltern saetan of the Chilterns and the Faerpingas who have usually been associated with the Feppingas of North Oxfordshire. With the exception of Northumbria, the other kingdoms of the so-called heptarchy, that is, Kent, the East Angles, and the East, South and West Saxons, are appended to the end of the survey. The tribes that I have mentioned here are those which can be positively located. Nevertheless, attempts to locate the other peoples listed have tended to confirm the general picture that Mercia was at the centre of the world mapped out by the Tribal Hidage.

The hidage assessments also reveal something of the criteria under which the assessment was made. The round figures quoted for each tribe belie any notion that the Tribal Hidage is the result of an accurate survey of land-holdings; nor does there seem to have been a single, discernible pattern of assessment that applies to the list as a whole. The smaller tribal units were apparently assessed using a duodecimal system based upon multiples of 300 (Hart, 1977: 46); for instance, the Faerpinga were assessed at 300 hides, the Spalda at 600, the Wigesta at 900 and the Pecsaetan at 1,200 (see Table 2.1). This formula may be associated with the system of accounting used for Mercian coinage, where there were 240 pennies to the pound (Chadwick, 1905a: 31; Hart, 1977: 46); however, it should not be taken as an indication that the Tribal Hidage was directly associated with payments made in coin. There is little numismatic evidence to indicate that coin use was sufficiently widespread during the period of the Mercian hegemony for all payments of tax or tribute to have been made in coin.

It is harder to divine a simple formula of assessment in the hidages of the larger tribes such as the Hwicce (7,000), Kent (15,000), East Anglia (30,000) or Wessex (100,000). There is clearly no mathematical formula at work here and it may be that some of these figures bore a symbolic significance. The assessments of 7,000 hides are reminiscent of the 'seven thousand, hall and throne' that were bestowed upon Beowulf by King Hygelac of the Geats as a reward for defeating the monster Grendel (*Beowulf*: lines 2195–6), while the 100,000 hides assigned to Wessex recall Hygelac's gift of 'a hundred thousand of land and treasure rings' to the Princes Wulf and Eofor elsewhere in the same poem (line 2994). Such endowments are also recorded in the historical sources; hence, the *Anglo-Saxon Chronicle* recounts that in 648 King Cenwalh of Wessex granted 'three thousand of land' to his kinsman Cuthred, whilst Bede tells us that after the death of Penda in 655, Oswy of Northumbria divided the kingdom of Mercia, taking for himself the land of the North Mercians, assessed at 7,000 hides, while leaving the South Mercians, assessed at 5,000 hides, in the hands of Penda's son, Peada (*HE* III. 24). Although in most of these cases it is not specifically stated, in all of these references hides were probably meant or understood. These apparently abitrary figures may have been symbolic of the relative status of the recipient. From Beowulf's reward it would appear that 7,000 hides was considered 'an appropriate endowment for a prince who had proved himself' (Sawyer, 1998: 111); 30,000 hides would perhaps distinguish Mercia and East Anglia as powerful kingdoms; while 100,000 hides marked Wessex as an early medieval superpower. Significantly, royal lines can be identified for most of the larger units. Mercia, Wessex, Kent, the East Angles and the East and South Saxons maintained their royal lines into the eighth century and beyond. Furthermore, a genealogical table survives for the kingdom of Lindsey (7,000 hides) and charter evidence demonstrates that the royal line of the Hwicce lasted until at least the 780s. Significantly, royal lines can also be demonstrated for some of the smaller units. Bede mentions a *princeps* of the South Grywe who married into the East Anglian royal house (*HE* IV. 19) as well as the kings of Wight whose royal line was extinguished by Cadwalla of Wessex in 686 (*HE* IV. 16).

The Tribal Hidage would therefore seem to be a catalogue of kingdoms and principalities, some of whom boasted their own royal lines, assessed in figures that were symbolic of relative status. The topographical progression of the list indicates that Mercia was at the forefront of the compiler's mind and the fact that the list was used in some form of bookkeeping is suggested by the totals that are offered in the text. Whoever compiled the list was interested in the total hidation of Southumbria; however, it must be stressed that this information might be of use whether the compiler were levying taxes or merely taking a rough count of heads.

We now come to the slightly more contentious issue of date and provenance. Due to its concentration on Mercia, the Tribal Hidage has usually been assigned a Mercian origin. Cyril Hart (1971 and 1977) declared it to be a product of the reign of Offa (657–696); drawing attention to the discrepancy between Bede's Mercia at 12,000 hides (*HE* III. 24) and the Tribal Hidage at 30,000 he argued that Mercia must have expanded their territorial claims since the 730s when Bede was writing his history (Hart, 1971: 157; 1977: 44). Conversely, Wendy Davies assigns the Tribal Hidage to the reign of another Mercian king, Wulfhere (658–675), since in Wulfhere's reign Mercia's expansionist interests took them north towards Elmet and south towards Wight (Davies and Vierck, 1974: 226–7). An alternative to the Mercian origins of the list has been offered by Nicholas Brooks who suggests that the Tribal Hidage was not Mercian at all, but the work of the Northumbrian overlord Oswy (642–670) who annexed Mercia in 655–658 (Brooks, 1989: 159). Brooks rejected a Mercian provenance for the Tribal Hidage on the grounds that 'An early medieval king did not impose tribute on his own kingdom' (Brooks, 1989a: 159; see Higham, 1995: 75–99). While I welcome the broader perspective that Brooks has offered for the authorship of the Tribal Hidage, I cannot accept his reason for rejecting a Mercian provenance. On the one hand, it has not been proven that the Tribal Hidage was a tribute list, while on the other the idea that a king would not levy taxes or 'tribute' from his own people seems untenable, for it presumes that one must acquire an empire before one can gather revenue. On the whole, it seems more likely that the Tribal Hidage originated in Mercia since the perspective of the document is decidedly Mercian.

There remains the question of date. It is appropriate that current opinion should be divided between a date in the late seventh century and a period that post-dates Bede since the document appears to belong to both eras. Indeed, the Tribal Hidage has the air of a document that is looking toward the past. It opens with an assessment of 'the area first called Mercia', a statement which has been interpreted as indicating that, at the time of writing, the name Mercia applied to a wider area (Davies and Vierck, 1974: 225). This creates problems with assigning the Tribal Hidage as it now stands to Wulfhere. Although Wulfhere certainly dominated much of southern England during his reign, he does not appear to have considered his dominion to be an extension of his regnal authority. For instance, in 665 the East Saxon kings, Sigehere and Sebbi accepted the overlordship of Wulfhere (*HE* III. 29); however, although Wulfhere was empowered to dispose of the London bishopric (*HE* III. 7), the royal dynasty of the East Saxon kingdom continued until at least 823 (S.187). Similarly, the royal houses of the Hwicce, Lindsey, the South Saxons and Kent all bowed to Wulfhere's authority, but retained their royal status well into the eighth century. As such, it does not seem likely that someone living in Wulfhere's day could look back to a time when the name Mercia was applied to a smaller area.

Conversely, Mercian foreign policy in the late eighth century seems to have switched from domination to absorption of surrounding kingdoms. In the 780s the sub-kings of the Hwicce were replaced by ealdormen whose direct allegiance was to the king of Mercia (S.55, 57, 58, 63 and 113; see *ASC* 800 [802]). Similarly, the kings of the South Saxons were demoted to ealdormen of Mercia in the 770s (S.108 and 1183) and the native dynasty of Kent disappeared from the historical records in the 780s (S.35–38). Although the kingship of Kent was revived in the reign of Coenwulf (796–821), who placed his brother Cuthred (798–807) on the Kentish throne, autonomy in Kent was a thing of the past. The policies pursued by Offa in the late eighth century ensured that in the ninth century the name Mercia covered virtually all of the area between the Thames and the Humber. Hence, when the Danes conquered most of Mercia in the late ninth century, ealdorman Æthelred (*c.* 879–911) was able to govern what remained of Mercia from Gloucestershire and the western provinces. I suggest that it is into this late ninth-century context that the Tribal Hidage fits in its extant form. Under this thesis 'the area first called Mercia' does not simply refer to a time when the name Mercia applied to a smaller area; rather, it makes a written claim to rights over the ancient homeland of the Mercians, which at the time of writing lay in the hands of the Danes.

The 100,000 hides assessment of Wessex also points to a late ninth-century date. I cannot accept Davies' assertion that 100,000 hides were 'a fair comparative estimate of West Saxon influence' in Wulfhere's reign, since at that time Wessex had yet to conquer Cornwall, Wight or the Jutish kingdom of Hampshire (Davies and Vierck, 1974: 236; see Yorke, 1995: 57–60). It is possible that the large assessment may have been a punitive fine imposed upon Wessex by an overlord (Hart, 1971: 156–7); but this assumes that the Tribal Hidage was a tribute list, a fact of which I am not wholly convinced. On the whole, I tend to side with Peter Sawyer's insistence that the 100,000 hide assessment of Wessex was intended to symbolize the West Saxons' role as a leading superpower, a situation that best describes Wessex at the end of the ninth century (Sawyer, 1998: 111). The West Saxon entry may even have been added in Wessex itself. The very survival of the Tribal Hidage when so many other Mercian documents perished at the hands of the Danes suggests that it was preserved outside the Danelaw, possibly in western Mercia or in Wessex. Furthermore, the fact that it became associated with the Burghal Hidage in the thirteenth century also implies that it fell into West Saxon hands at some point in its transmission (Rumble, 1996b: 47). We cannot escape the fact that the details of the survey, such as the inclusion of Elmet and the assessment of Wight separately from Wessex, point to an earlier date, but nor can we ignore the reflective nature of the document as a whole. Under the circumstances I would suggest that, as it stands, the Tribal Hidage is a document of the late ninth century that was compiled using material that probably dates back to the late seventh (Sawyer, 1998: 111).

Of course, if this theory is correct, then we must assume that the Tribal Hidage was preserved for a reason. The most probable reason is that the divisions of the Tribal Hidage continued to have some form of political significance from the seventh century to the ninth. This is certainly the case for Kent, East Anglia and the East, South and West Saxons and so may be true of the more obscure tribal units, which could have survived as political divisions of the extended kingdom of Mercia. As we have seen, the sub-kings of the Hwicce were replaced by an ealdorman in the 770s; however, the name of the principality was preserved, not least of which by the bishops of Worcester, who were alternatively known as the bishops of the Hwicce until at least the late tenth century (S.1324, 1352). The Wreocensetan and Westerna also survived as divisions of Mercia. A Worcester charter of 855 was said to have been drawn up at that time 'when the pagans were in the land of the *Wreocensetun*' (S.206), while a charter of 872 makes mention of one Nothheard, *praefectus et comes regis* of the Magonsaetan (S.1782; c.f. S.677, 1264), another name for the Tribal Hidage's Westerna. The role of the Westerna or Magonsaetan as a division of Mercia continued at least until 1016 when, at the battle of Ashington, the ealdorman Eadric led the Magonsaetan in a disgraceful flight from the forces of Cnut (*ASC*).

A continuing political function for the smaller units of the Tribal Hidage is harder to prove. Bede makes reference to the Feppingas (*HE* III. 21) and the Gyrwe (*HE* III. 20; IV. 6, 19), and the latter even warrant a mention in the twelfth-century *Liber Eliensis*, though this may have been using Bede (Blake, 1962: 14, 21). There are no direct references to the Spalda outside the Tribal Hidage, but we do have the names of two Mercian ealdormen who were active in the region around Spalding which may have been associated with the Spalda (Hart, 1971: 144–5; Davies and Vierck, 1974: 232). The first was one Cuthbert *princeps* who was granted land at Swineshead, near Spalding, by Abbot Beonna of Medeshamstede, in the late eighth century (S.1412), and the other was Aelfgar, son of Aelfgar, a *comes* of Coenwulf, who made a generous endowment of lands in the Spalding region to Siward, abbot of Croyland, in 810 (S.1189). However, although Cuthbert and Aelfgar clearly held land in the region, it does not necessarily indicate that they were in any way associated with the Spalda.

Nevertheless, there is good circumstantial evidence to suggest that the smaller units of the Tribal Hidage survived as regional divisions of the Mercian kingdom throughout the eighth and ninth centuries. The evidence concerns the structure of the Mercian court as revealed through the witness lists of charters. Charters for the late seventh century and the opening years of the eighth are extremely rare and unreliable; however, the extant charters of Æthelbald (716–757) and more particularly Offa and his ninth-century successors contain clear patterns within their witness lists that reveal a great deal about the nature of the Mercian court during this period and more particularly the number of ealdormen who served under the king. There is no rule as to the number of ealdormen who appear as witnesses in any one charter; the lowest number found in a charter is one (e.g. S.129, 135, 141) while the largest is 19 (S.173); most charters from the period feature between six and twelve. However, if we look at the pattern formed by the careers of individual ealdormen, a different story comes to light. If one follows the careers of all the major attestors in the charter record over the period 716–850[1] it soon becomes clear that, regardless of individual names, the charters from any one moment feature some or all of the top ten regular attestors of their specific period. Take the ealdormen of Offa's reign: the most consistent witnesses of Offa's reign were Brorda (757–799: 18 appearances), Berhtwald (757–796: 20 appearances), Eadbald (757–789: 11 appearances), Esne (764–802: 16 appearances) and Eadbald (777–781: 7 appearances). To these names we might add a couple of ealdormen who appear late in Offa's reign such as Heaberht, who appears in at least fourteen charters from between 762 and 809, and Wicga (789–805) who appears in ten. To these we might add a number of ealdormen who appear to have enjoyed long careers, but who feature in a relatively small number of charters; one such possibility is Lulling who features in only three extant charters falling in the years 772–799 (S.108, 139 and 155). There are also a considerable number of noblemen whose careers shone brightly but very briefly. One of the two ealdormen named Eadbald makes seven appearances in the extant charter record, but only in the years 777–781, whilst Æthelmund, the

---

1. The absence of surnames makes positive identification of individuals difficult; however, the recurrence of names in the charters makes identification easier. Nevertheless, it must be stated that there are cases where caution must be exercised. For instance, Brorda, whose career I have assigned to the years 757–799, was not the only Brorda to appear in Offa's charters. A second Brorda appears in the period 774–779 (S.110, 111, 114, 147) and then disappears, raising the possibility that instead of two careers spanning 757–799 and 774–779, we have two careers spanning 757–779 and 774–799.

ealdorman of the Hwicce whose career can be traced over a nine-year period between 793 and 802, appeared in about five charters. In other words, there appears to have been a solid core of around five regular attestors to Offa's charters, whose numbers were regularly swelled by five or six others of almost equal significance.

The same phenomenon can be observed in the courts of Offa's successors. Heardberht, whose career began under Offa, signed at least 16 charters under Coenwulf before 816; Beornnoth appears as a witness 14 times in charters from the period 801–825; Eadberht (809–825) appears in 17; Cynehelm and Heafrith, both signing in the period 801–811, witnessed eight and five charters, respectively; and Eahlheard who signed 814–825 made nine appearances. In the second quarter of the ninth century the recurring names included Sigered (814–848: 7), Mucel (814–857: 12), Ealdred (823–852: 10), Aelfstan (825–852; 10) and Humberht (835–857: 10). In other words, the witness lists of the extant charters of each Mercian king in the late eighth and early ninth centuries are dominated by a limited group of around ten recurring names.

Perhaps more importantly, there were, in addition to this core group of the most powerful of the king's subjects, a large number of men who made only one or a handful of appearances, usually in the same charters as the favoured few. This feature of Mercian charters implies that there may have been a graded hierarchy at the royal court. In any one charter of the eighth and ninth centuries one might expect to find between five and ten regular witnesses plus a selection of other witnesses who never appear anywhere else. In charter S.173 (814) there are no fewer than 19 lay witnesses, all of whom are ascribed the Latin title *dux*, a word that by the early ninth century was synonymous with ealdorman (Thacker, 1981: 203–7). This implies that, in addition to the top ten ealdormen of Mercia, there were at least as many again holding office, but only very rarely being acknowledged by the historical records.

The reason for this graded hierarchy at court might have been based on something as mundane as royal favour; however, the continuity of the hierarchical structure argues against such a simple answer. The witness lists of Coenwulf's early charters are crammed with names from the reign of Offa: Brorda, Eadgar, Æthelmund, Esne, Wicga, Heaberht all feature in the charters of Coenwulf. Similarly, a great many of Coenwulf's chief men, Beornnoth, Eadfrith, Eadberht, Wulfred and so forth, witnessed the charters of at least two of Coenwulf's successors. If the position an ealdorman held at court were a simple reflection of the favour in which he was held by the reigning monarch, then one would expect a greater reshuffling of the 'core' group of witnesses in the charter record when the crown changed hands. The obvious solution to the longevity and resilience of the careers of the men at the top is that their personal power bases were too great for them to be easily shifted.

Thus, we have a court structure that appears to consist of 10 or 11 powerful magnates and a similar number of lesser lords. Where else can such a pattern be found if not in the Tribal Hidage? If one omits Wessex, Kent, the East and South Saxons, the East Angles and Wight from the reckoning, there are still 11 units of the Tribal Hidage whose assessment is greater than 1,000 hides: Mercia, the Wreocensaetan, the Westerna, the Pecsaetan, Lindsey, the Herefinna, the Noxgaga, the Ohtgaga, the Hwicce, the Ciltern saetan, the Hendrica and the Unecung-ga. A direct relationship cannot be proven between the 11 regular attestors at court and the 11 larger units of the Tribal Hidage; however, it seems unlikely that an ealdorman who led a province of 7,000 hides, such as the Hwicce, would enjoy equal standing at court as one who governed a land of 300, such as the Hicca.

3 Political Women in Mercia, Eighth to Early Tenth Centuries

Pauline Stafford

The politics of family and succession, and with them the significance of women in politics, is a feature common to all the early English kingdoms. Mercia is no exception. Rather, it is remarkable for the series of women, from the reign of Offa until the end of the independent Mercian kingdom, who played roles significant enough to have left traces in the surviving evidence. Offa's wife and widow, Cynethryth, for example, not only appeared in the witness lists of his charters, and in disputes concerning his inheritance but had the rare honour of having coins struck in her name. From at least the middle of the ninth century, her successors as queens in Mercia witnessed charters with a regularity far from common in early medieval Europe, and never again matched in England until the quasi-regency of Emma alongside Cnut after 1017. The daughters of Offa married kings of Northumbria, Wessex and possibly East Anglia – and in the case of Eadburh, wife of Beorhtric of Wessex, achieved notoriety in later West Saxon history if not power in her own lifetime. No less notorious in later legend was the daughter of Coenwulf, Abbess Cwenthryth. Her contemporary importance was signalled by her position as her father's heir, and her consequent involvement in disputes over monastic lands with Archbishop Wulfred. Against such a background it comes as less of a surprise that the history of independent Mercia ended with women, and with two unique instances of early medieval female rule. Æthelflaed, Lady of the Mercians, stood almost alone in early medieval Europe as a ruler in her own right, not in the name of an underaged son or brother. On her death in 918 some in Mercia seem to have contemplated transferring her power and authority to her daughter Aelfwyn. And when the long shadow of Mercian power reached into the history of the tenth century, it was embodied in Aelfgifu, a female descendant of Æthelflaed's Mercian grandmother. King Eadwig married Aelfgifu, and his brother and supplanter, Eadgar, felt it necessary to come to terms with her. If the political women of the early Middle Ages demand our attention everywhere, they should certainly receive it in the history of the Mercian kingdom.

Cynethryth, Offa's queen, was the first Mercian political woman who can be studied in any detail. Her significance derived first from her marriage to Offa, a union rooted in the Mercian past. Her name encourages speculation that she represented a surviving branch of Penda's successful late seventh-century ruling family. Penda's own queen was *Cyne*wise (*HE* III. 24, in Colgrave and Mynors, 1969: 150); his [probably their] daughters included *Cyne*burh and her sister *Cyne*swith (*HE* III. 21, in Colgrave and Mynors, 1969: 144; Hugh Candidus, in Mellows, 1949: 50–1). It would have made sense for Offa, who claimed remote descent from Penda's line, to underpin that claim with a marriage into the same prestigious family, though this must remain speculation. What is more certain is that the marriage he made was full and legitimate, including in whatever senses eighth-century churchmen recognized these terms. In this respect Offa had taken the opportunity to define himself against his predecessor, Æthelbald, and to connect again with earlier Mercian traditions.

The arrival of Christianity in the seventh century had had a complex impact on the emerging English kingdoms and their family politics. Monastic foundations, as well as expressing the enthusiasm of recent conversion, opened up new possibilities for political control, including through women and family members. Christian ideas and ideals in the area of marriage became a new factor in succession and legitimacy, and in the related position of king's wife and queen. Bede and later sources hinted at the significance of these new ideals. This is clearest in the evidence for Mercian royal women featuring alongside their male relatives as heads of monasteries: Werburg at Ely, Threckingham (Lincs) and perhaps Hanbury (Staffs), Cyneburh and Cyneswith as joint founders of Castor near their brother Wulfhere's Medeshamstede/ Peterborough (John of Worcester s.a. 675, in Darlington *et al.*, 1995; Hugh Candidus, in Mellows, 1949: 50–1). Here the impact of Christianity is clear. As far as the position of queen was concerned, however, Christianity encountered established roles. Cynewise, wife of the pagan Penda, was important enough to hold a Northumbrian hostage such as King Oswiu's son (*HE* III. 24, in Colgrave and Mynors, 1969: 150). But Christianity may have underlined such importance. Two Christian Northumbrian women, daughters of Oswiu, married Mercian kings in the seventh century. Both fell victim to accusation: Alchflaed was accused of plotting in the royal household and Osthryth was eventually murdered by a group of Mercian nobles (*HE* III. 11; IV. 21; V. 24 s.a. 697, in Colgrave and Mynors, 1969: 126–8, 207, 292). Alchflaed and Osthryth attracted the sort of suspicion common to in-marrying women, especially those representing rival and aggressive powers. Northumbrian women were not necessarily safe in seventh-century Mercia. But it may have been Christian queens as much as Northumbrian daughters who were attacked – and not merely in the context of pagan–Mercian reaction. Christianity offered new opportunities for female power. Osthryth had certainly manipulated the novel Christian technologies of power – relics and monastic foundation (*HE* III. 11, in Colgrave and Mynors, 1969: 126–8; S 76). New bases for queenship may have been emerging *c.* 700.

If so, Æthelbald set his face against them. His reign suggests a reaction, and his actions are susceptible to new interpretations in the light of possible changes in marriage, family politics and the power of queens in the wake of conversion. Boniface accused him of failing to take a legitimate wife and of consorting with nuns (Whitelock, 1979: 816–22). Æthelbald's sexual mores came under scrutiny in large part because he was asserting lay claims over monastic lands. Æthelbald had not had a Christian wife but only unions which in Christian eyes appeared as fornication. Fornication, like concubinage, is a slippery term in the story of early medieval marriage, not least because of its use in succession dispute to label and undermine rivals. It is of only limited use in assessing the nature of Æthelbald's marital practice. That was defined in the critical eyes of Boniface and pointedly contrasting actions of Offa. Both, however, must suggest that Æthelbald's unions lacked some of the critical elements which might be held to define Christian marriage. In a world where religious houses were controlled and inhabited by royal women, his propensity for nuns appears more than an acting out of sexual fantasy. Æthelbald, no less than Offa, may have sought out politically important sexual partners. But he did not, apparently, make them queens. There are no queens recorded during the reign of the fornicating, nun-snatching Æthelbald – and, as Cynewise, Alchflaed and Osthryth indicate, this is not because there had been none in pagan or early Christian Mercia. This absence confirms some of Boniface's allegations. As in sixth- and early seventh-century Francia, marriage probably made queens. It was marriage not the sexual partnerships of her son and grandsons which the Frankish queen Brunhild saw as a threat to her situation at court (Nelson, 1986: 29). Æthelbald may have seen it as a similar threat to his strategies of succession. But as Brunhild also discovered, Christian intervention in marriage definition was already complicating arguments about legitimacy, and restricting room for manoeuvre.

Whether or not Æthelbald realized the implications of this, Offa did. His union with Cynethryth was marriage, full and legitimate – and as such a deliberate rejection of the choices of his predecessor. It confirmed the legitimacy of his future heirs, while complicating if not undermining the claims of a previous clutch. Whether by accident or design it also laid a basis on which the power of Cynethryth and that of subsequent Mercian queens would be built, though that construction was not to be a simple linear development.

Offa's marriage was, like Æthelbald's 'fornications' a strategy of succession, and one with markedly different implications for his wife and queen. The emphasis on the birth of heirs from full and legitimate marriage in the papal legates' decrees issued in 786 recognized in retrospect a strategy Offa had already adopted (Whitelock, 1979: 836–

40; Wormald, 1999: 106-7). This emphasis is inconceivable had Offa not been certain that his son fulfilled those criteria. The decrees were no simple statement about Christian marriage but aimed at other possible claimants to the Mercian throne. Offa was ruthlessly concerned to prune collateral lines in favour of his own direct heirs. After Ecgfrith's untimely death Alcuin remarked on the results of this for royal succession. But murder of relatives was only one mechanism for effecting such a strategy. Offa had deliberately eschewed the practices of Æthelbald. His marriage to Cynethryth was full and legitimate, and was so in the interests of her children. Its consequences expanded to develop her interconnected roles of mother, wife and queen.

At the heart of these lay maternity. It was not the marriage but the birth, or at least the first charter appearance, of her son Ecgfrith in 770 which marked Cynethryth's public recognition. The date of Cynethryth's marriage to Offa is unknown. Her first charter witnessing, the first witness of a Mercian queen since Osthryth (S 59 and 70; Osthryth, see the much debated S 76), was implicitly as the mother of an heir to the throne, and one whose legitimacy was to be stressed through his mother's status. From 770 until his consecration as his father's successor in 787, she was a regular witness, though more often without than with her son. Yet her public presence was arguably tied in with him, underscoring if not publicly representing his claims until he came of age – if 770 was the year of his birth, he would have been 15 in 785.[1] His majority and consecration initiated his own regular witnessing, and her eclipse.

Her later appearances confirm a significance integral to the familial strategies of Offa's politics. She witnessed in 786-788 on three occasions, in the consecration year 787 with the whole royal family, Ecgfrith and Offa's four daughters (S 125, 127, 129). The late 780s saw the marriage of Eadburh, Offa's daughter and probably hers, to Beorhtric of Wessex. Negotiations for the marriage of the eldest daughter, Aelfflaed, to Æthelred I of Northumbria, which took place in 792, may have begun at that time (*ASC* MSS D and E s.a. 792, in Whitelock, 1979). Aelfflaed was already of full marriageable age in the late 780s, if her witness of a debatable charter of 770 can be taken as evidence (S 59). Royal daughters feature even more rarely in eighth-century English charters than royal wives and mothers. The late 780s were a time of family arrangements which were also political. After this, Cynethryth witnessed no further charters until the brief reign of her son (S 150, 151). Dickins (1936-8) interpreted her re-emergence as a sinister seizure of power, but it rather confirms the familial, specifically maternal aspects of her power. Alcuin, in his letters to

---

1. Fifteen was a significant male age in the tenth century and possibly before. Eadgar was chosen as king of Mercia when he reached 15; his own son Æthelred seems to have assumed personal power in 984, when evidence suggests he would have been 15.

Offa's court, underlined that maternal, parental authority. He called on Ecgfrith to obey and respect it (Alcuin, in Dümmler, 1895, 4, no. 61).

Alcuin, however, referred to Cynethryth not only as Ecgfrith's mother but also as the mistress of the royal household, so busy about the king's business that she had little time to read his letters. His loyalty and counsel were thus directed through others at the palace (Alcuin, in Dümmler, 1895, nos 61, 62 and 102). Cynethryth's maternity was of a peculiarly legitimate and legitimizing nature, thanks to the nature of her marriage itself, and the implications of that marriage spilled out beyond motherhood. Alcuin recognized the position of wife as household mistress, created by marriage. This was what Brunhild had feared in a daughter- or granddaughter-in-law. Offa could not easily raise a mother for legitimate sons without creating a consort in the royal court. Alcuin's is the voice of the practised courtier, but there are more neutral, if more problematic, witnesses to the elevation of the queen.

The titles given to Cynethryth in the charters call her 'queen', often 'queen of the Mercians', and in 780 'queen of the Mercians by the grace of God'.[2] Not even in Ecgfrith's reign was she *mater regis*. Coins were struck in her name. She counts alongside Angelberga, mid-ninth-century wife of Louis of Italy, and Emma, wife of the tenth-century penultimate Carolingian ruler Lothar, as the only non-Byzantine woman to be so honoured after the end of the Constantinian house in the West (Grierson and Blackburn, 1986: 69, 195, 248, 279–80, 576–7, 580). Accidents of survival have no doubt affected our picture of the volume, and perhaps of the uniqueness of these three – but their coinage nonetheless remains remarkable. Cynethryth's is the most numerous and the earliest. Offa associated his wife in the ideological messages he conveyed through his coinage. Like his, some of her coins carry a profile bust of the queen. In only one, a coin which seems to have re-used an obverse designed for a coin of Offa, was she depicted wearing a diadem, but her title was given: 'regina M', 'queen of the Mercians', paralleling that of Offa (Blunt, 1961; Lyon, 1968; Grierson and Blackburn, 1986). The coins, like Offa's, are difficult to date, but they appear to pre-date the late heavy pennies of the reign. They may be linked to the birth of Ecgfrith, though his consecration is another possible date; so too, perhaps on the basis of the *dei gratia* title, is 780. Although the coins of the Byzantine Empress Irene, struck in the 780s, may have been an inspiration (Grierson and Blackburn, 1986: 279–80), they could not have been the direct model because they depict frontal busts. The inspiration seems rather to be directly from late antique

---

2. See e.g. S 59 and 60 – both with Ecgfrith, and where she is queen of the Mercians. This title is not, however, confined to her appearances with him, see also e.g. S 120 and 121, and, in 780, S 116, 117 and 118.

coins themselves, and especially from the Empress Helena's coinage of the fourth century.[3]

The references back to late Antiquity and its imperial models indicate the developing Mercian concept of hegemony, which was imperial and dynastic, inclusive of Offa's family and his wife. Its complex nature was expressed not only through tribute and battles, and through charters and their relegation of subject kings but also through a series of marriages of his daughters. It was to be handed on to his son. The mother of that son, if not of those daughters, was given unprecedented standing, and by reference to one of the most iconic female royal figures, the mother of the Emperor Constantine and the finder of the True Cross. It is tempting to see Offa's inspiration in this, as in much else, arising from his Carolingian contemporaries, in particular Charles the Great. Certainly the concern with succession and the acknowledgement that this had to include the mothers of future kings as well as their fathers had been stressed in Francia in the 750s; if there is a parallel to Cynethryth, Charles's mother, Bertrada, is a better candidate than any of his wives. Charlemagne never elevated a queen as Offa raised Cynethryth. It is no accident that queenship went on to develop so strongly in ninth-century Mercia.

The association of Cynethryth in Offa's kingship extended to his – and her – control over monasteries and their lands, where she was not only his partner but his heir. The extent to which eighth-century Mercian royal power had involved the exploitation of this control is well known (Levison, 1946: Appendix IV; Brooks, 1984: cap 7; Cubitt, 1995: cap 8). Already in the first generations of conversion Mercian women had been involved in the monastic foundations which expressed power and piety. The women of Offa's family continued the tradition. His daughter Æthelburh appears to have held Fladbury (S 62), and, along with her sister, may have had some claims on Glastonbury (S 152). Cynethryth and Offa together erected, acquired and granted a series of monasteries dedicated to St Peter; a series which may have included Bedford, Bath, Westminster, Northampton, *Medeshamstede*/Peterborough and Bredon (Levison, 1946: 29–31; Cubitt, 1995: 226 n 93). After Offa's death she held Cookham, about which dispute arose with the Archbishop of Canterbury. In the resolution of this she received another unidentified monastery 'aet Pectanege' in 798 (S 1258). At Cookham and at Fladbury Offa's wife and daughter took over houses which earlier Mercian rulers had held: Cookham had been Æthelbald's house, Fladbury a foundation of Æthelred and Osthryth (S 1258 and 76). The women of Offa's family shared in the extension and consolidation of its power, and when a new family took over, new female members stepped into those same roles.

---

3. Blunt (1961: 46–7) supports the idea of a direct borrowing from classical Rome. Ann Gannon's forthcoming PhD thesis (Cambridge) notes the copying in seventh-century England of Helena coins, and possibly here as well. I am very grateful to Ms Gannon for allowing me to see sections of her forthcoming thesis.

Coenwulf, Offa's successor in Mercia and in Kent, held Kentish royal monasteries (S 1434) as well as Offa's own house at Winchcombe (Levison, 1946: 249 citing BL Cotton Vitellius C VIII, Winchcombe Annals). By the 820s, if not before, they were in the hands of his daughter, Cwoenthryth – who inherited both her father's control and his long-running struggle over it with Archbishop Wulfred.

At the Synod of Clofesho in 798 Cynethryth was named as the heir of her husband. Coenwulf's daughter, Cwoenthryth, was named as her father's heir in a similar dispute over monastic property (S 1258 and 1434). These statements must be read carefully. The naming of an heir in a dispute may be no neutral statement of inheritance right. It may be a strategic way of gathering disparate claims in the hands of a single person, with whom they can then be negotiated or even extinguished. But such a strategy cannot be entirely unrelated to inheritance practice and norms. Claims on behalf of women as heirs in early ninth-century Mercia were thinkable and arguable; for widows on the property of their husbands but also for daughters, on the inheritance of their fathers. Cynethryth was a widow, Cwoenthryth a king's daughter, but both were also abbesses at the time they were named as heirs. Female monasticism was central to the early English Church. It was built on the enthusiasm of conversion and on female claims to share family inheritance, which it in turn strengthened. The foundation of a monastic house could be a way of endowing women, providing for them and protecting their vulnerable claims with religious sanctions (Leyser, 1989: Section II). Those claims were familial, stemming from women's position as family members, but they were also religious, undergirded by their status as abbesses. The disputes which Mercian royal attitudes to monasteries provoked defined these claims maximally, with women as full heirs. A century before Æthelflaed and Aelfwyn made the ultimate claims to a husband and father's inheritance, one basis for their actions seems already to have been laid.

Like the daughters of Offa, Cwoenthryth is remarkable for her appearance as a charter witness in 811 (S 165). Thus 811 was a significant year. At what looks like a meeting of royal heirs, or at least of his surviving family, Coenwulf was accompanied not only by his daughter but also by his brother's son, Coenwald, and by another 'king's kinsman' (*propinquus regis*), Cyneberht. Coenwulf's son, Cynehelm/Kenelm, appears to have predeceased his father. The royal meeting in 811 may have been the one at which the consequences of that death were dealt with. Male heirs were gathered, and a female. Cwoenthryth's inheritance-worthiness may have been recognized now. But not as far as the throne was concerned. No woman apparently made any claim to succeed either Offa or Coenwulf. In this sense the later actions of Æthelflaed and Aelfwyn would be unique.[4] But in

---

4. Note, however, that in the later legend Cwoenthryth was alleged to have aspired precisely to this. It is difficult to know whether to attach any credibility to this legend; see Rollason (1983).

another respect the meeting in 811 signalled the future. With Coenwulf in that year were not only his blood heirs but also his [perhaps second] wife Aelfthryth.[5] Although the marriage had taken place some years earlier, it was only from that year that she became a regular witness of Coenwulf's charters, foreshadowing later Mercian queens of unusual prominence. To some extent Aelfthryth and her successors look back to Cynethryth, whose career created a tradition of female power, albeit a broken one. Like her they flourished in the context of Mercian kings' needs for heirs of undoubted legitimacy, born of a true queen. In the ninth century even more than in the case of Cynethryth, however, queenship would crown wife and partner as well as mother.

Perhaps driven by his search for an heir, perhaps in deliberate contrast to the ruthless purging of collaterals which had left Offa's male line extinct, perhaps stimulated by the conflict with Archbishop Wulfred over the claims of lay families and kin *vis-à-vis* bishops, Coenwulf brought members of his family to the fore, including the wife by whom he may still have hoped to produce a son. Neither of his two successors, Ceolwulf I or Beornwulf, followed his example as far as their wives were concerned. But strategy, and with it the place of queens, changed permanently in the reign of Wiglaf. His wife, Queen Cynethryth, witnessed the two genuine charters of his reign, in the first along with her son, Wigmund (S 188 and 190). In the reign of his successor, Beorhtwulf, Queen Saethryth witnessed every charter of her husband from 840 to 849. Burgred's queen, Æthelswith, followed suit, witnessing all his charters until she followed him into exile in the 870s. The public prominence of these ninth-century Mercian queens is unusual. It is testified to in charters and their witness lists. These documents, like the meetings which they record, were normally in England male preserves (Stafford, forthcoming). This was the tradition to which Æthelflaed would be heir. Unfortunately the obscurity of ninth-century Mercian history makes it difficult to interpret.

It is linked in some way to the shifting dynastic situation. In ninth-century Mercia kings' sons rarely if ever succeeded fathers, and even the kinship of successive kings is difficult to establish.[6] In these circumstances kings may have chosen important royal women as their brides in order to consolidate their own position as well as to influence that of their heirs. In two cases the choice of high status wives can be

---

5. S 165; Aelfthryth had appeared earlier in 808, S 163 – at an Easter meeting at Tamworth, and perhaps in 804, S 159, though the witness list has here been tampered with if not conflated with a later one (see Kelly, 1995, no. 16). S 156 may preserve the name of an earlier wife, Cynegyth, though since this was modelled on a charter of Wihtred, S 15, the name may have been lifted from the original. Note, however, that Coenwulf's son was named *Cyne*helm and he had a kinsman, perhaps affinal, called *Cyne*berht.

6. If Wigmund ruled briefly after his father, he would be the only example of a father–son transmission. The only suggestion that this might have been the case comes in the much later *Life* of Wigmund's son, Wigstan, who came to be venerated as a murdered prince at Repton. See Rollason (1981 and 1983).

demonstrated. Burgred's wife, Æthelswith, was daughter of Æthel-wulf, king of Wessex, and Æthelred married Æthelflaed, daughter of Alfred of Wessex (*ASC*, MS A, s.a. 853, in Whitelock, 1979; Asser, cap 75, in Stevenson, 1959). West Saxon evidence has ensured our knowledge of the identity of these West Saxon brides. The Viking context of these two marriages made them alliances between kingdoms and thus sets them apart. But their difference should not be overstressed. Æthelflaed, as we shall see, played to internal Mercian insecurity as well as external anti-Viking alliances. She helped establish a husband whose claims to the Mercian throne were as debatable as those of most of his ninth-century predecessors. Had they, like him, sought high status brides? Were Aelfthryth, Cynethryth and Saethryth women of royal Mercian birth whose own blood and claims strengthened those of their equally shadowy husbands? The name of Wiglaf's wife, Cynethryth, seems to hark back to kin of Coenwulf if not earlier royal lines. The later *Life* of his grandson Wigstan gives the name of Wigstan's mother, wife of Wiglaf's son Wigmund, as Aelfflaed – a name borne by a ninth-century abbess of Winchcombe, a house on which descendants of Offa and of Ceolwulf I had claims.[7] As for so much in the history of ninth-century Mercia, tantalising hints take the place of solid evidence.

Late ninth- and tenth-century West Francia provides an illuminating parallel. Here queenly anointing, and queenly power and activity more generally, developed rapidly in a similar context of a contest between rival families for the throne. The queen as heir-bearing consort became crucially important (Lot, 1891; Lauer, 1900 and 1910; Erkens, 1993; Nelson, 1997; Stafford, 1998). But so too did her high birth, and her wider political roles. By 987 it could be dangerous for a West Frankish king to take a wife whose origins did not enhance or rather match his own status, as Charles of Lorraine, the last of the Carolingians, found to his cost. As her husband's and son's securest ally, a tenth-century West Frankish queen held strongholds, organized defence, negotiated with others and received allegiances. Ninth-century Mercian queens were not important solely as the mothers of sons. Only one, Cynethryth, appears, as her namesake Offa's wife had done, with her son. It is unclear which of these women had sons; the presence of unidentified Mercian princes/aethelings in the later ninth and early tenth centuries suggests that some of them did (S 539; *ASC* MS A s.a. 904, recte 903, in Whitelock, 1979). But dynastic change enhanced their status as more than bearers of royal heirs. The absence of evidence other than the charters deprives us of the narratives and letters in which their other activities could be traced. Æthelflaed, as a queen, fortified *burhs* and organized defence in the early tenth century.

---

7. S 1442, though as a widowed queen/princess she might have had claim on such a royal house whatever her origin.

It may be only the silence which shrouds ninth-century Mercia which has deprived us of knowledge of the precedents she followed.[8]

In tenth-century Francia, queenly anointing developed as an intrinsic part of the growth of queens' importance. The first certain anointing of a western queen was that of Judith, daughter of the Carolingian Charles the Bald and wife of Æthelwulf of Wessex, in 856 (Nelson, 1997). This should arguably be understood as much in English – and Mercian – context as in Frankish. Æthelwulf made Judith his queen, the initiative did not come entirely from Charles the Bald. The *ordo* on which Archbishop Hincmar based that of Judith was the First English *Ordo* for the consecration of a king, which Æthelwulf surely supplied. What inspired Æthelwulf in 856? Certainly not recent West Saxon practice, from which he departed radically in raising Judith as queen. The most recent royal marriage he had witnessed was that of his daughter Æthelswith to the Mercian king Burgred, three years before. Was Æthelswith anointed? Was Hincmar the first to adopt an English king's *ordo* to consecrate a queen? Where does Mercia, with its significance in the history of royal anointing established by the events of 787, stand in the subsequent development of those rites? At the very least, Æthelwulf took with him to West Francia the memory of Æthelswith's elevation as a Mercian queen. It does not strain credulity to see it as an inspiration for his young bride's new position.

In ninth-century Mercia as in tenth-century West Francia, queenship may have developed its own momentum. As queens became a significant part of the political landscape, no king could afford to be without one. Obscure as it is, ninth-century Mercian history may be a crucial chapter in the history of English, if not European, queenship.

Æthelflaed was its heir. Although there were Mercian princes at the end of the ninth century, none of them established his claim to follow his father on the throne. In the 870s and 880s it passed first to Ceolwulf II, perhaps a member of the earlier Ceolwulf's family, and then to Æthelred – who ruled debatably under the lordship of the West Saxon king, Alfred, and even more debatably under that of Alfred's son, King Edward the Elder. Æthelred married Æthelflaed, Alfred's eldest daughter, Edward's sister, probably in 887/8.[9] Æthelflaed thus followed her aunt, Æthelswith, as a Mercian queen. Marriages which knit alliances between rulers of Wessex and Mercia against Viking attack doubtless confirmed the status of both women. Æthelflaed was also important to her husband within Mercia. Her mother, Ealhswith, was a Mercian royal woman (Asser, cap 2, in Stevenson, 1959),

---

8. The association of queens, strongholds and defence certainly had its parallels in other English kingdoms – see Bebba who gave her name to Bamburgh (*HE*, III. 6, in Colgrave and Mynors, 1969: 119) and for Queen Æthelburh demolishing a stronghold which Ine had built at Taunton (*ASC* MS A *s.a.* 722, in Whitelock, 1979).

9. She does not appear in S 218 and 219, his charters of 883/4, but is there by 888, S 220, and in S 217, whose correct date may be 887.

probably a descendant of King Coenwulf on whose inheritance Ealhswith's brother, Athulf, seems to have had claim (S 1442). Æthelred sought not merely a West Saxon alliance but also a strengthening of his Mercian claims through female Mercian royal blood. Through her mother, Æthelflaed – and her brother Edward – boasted Mercian royal descent. Ealhswith was as important to her children and her son-in-law as their father Alfred. The Chronicles which were produced close to the courts of Æthelflaed and Edward both drew attention to this woman whom the documents of Alfred's own reign had studiously ignored.[10] It is with Ealhswith's daughter and grand-daughter that the history of Mercian royal women, and the history of an independent Mercia itself, came to an end.

Æthelflaed was the last Mercian queen, first alongside her husband Æthelred, then ruling alone after his death in 911. In the Celtic kingdoms to the West, she was recognized unambiguously as a queen and ruler.[11] Yet descriptions of her in West Saxon and Mercian sources raise questions about her status, as about that of an independent Mercia itself. Neither she nor Æthelred were ever called *rex/regina* in the surviving English documents. In contrast to his royal predecessors, Ceolwulf and Burgred, no coins were struck in Æthelred's name, nor in that of Æthelflaed when she succeeded him. Charters were granted by them but with the permission, witness or presence of King Alfred or Edward the Elder. All this points to a non-royal, subordinate status in an alliance which was rapidly becoming a domination of Mercia by Wessex. But in the shifting political situation of early medieval hegemonic rule the language of alliance and domination can be strategic and aspirational, part of the technology of power not a simple measure or description of it. It must be read carefully and contextually.

The coinage evidence is most straightforward but no general guide. London was the critical mint. It had passed into Alfred's control and struck no coins in the names of Æthelred or Æthelflaed. But the situation in London was not necessarily that in Mercia as a whole, nor one recognized by all. The charters tell a more ambiguous story. First Æthelred, then Æthelred and Æthelflaed together, and finally Æthelflaed alone, granted charters in their own names, transferring

---

10. See *ASC* (Whitelock, 1979) MS A (the West Saxon version) *s.a.* 902 and 904, and MS B (which contains the so-called Mercian Register) after 901 – the only entry in the latter before it turns its attention to its theme, the military victories of Æthelflaed.

11. Annales Cambriae (Williams ab Ithel, 1860), *s.a.* 917 – *regina*; Brut y Tywysogion, *s.a.* 918 (Jones, 1955) – *vrenhines* (cf. Alfred - *vrenhin, s.a.* 898); Annals of Ulster (MacAirt and Mac Niocaill, 1983), *s.a.* 918 – *famosissima regina saxonum*. These Chronicles are late, and not all independent, but they seem to represent at least two separate traditions. 'Regina' may not mean the same in the Celtic kingdoms as in tenth-century England, but the author of the Brut equated her and her father Alfred with the masculine and feminine versions of the Welsh title. Wainwright (1975a) is still essential reading on all this, though he interprets the ambiguity and contradictions of the sources within a rather modern gender framework.

the rights and claims which would normally denote the regal status of the grantor (S 221, 225 and 224). In some, but not all, the permission or witness of King Alfred was recorded. The critical factor here seems to have been the beneficiary of the charter. In all cases where this was the church of Worcester, Alfred's lordship was acknowledged (S 217, 218, 223, 346, 1282); in the couple for other beneficiaries, it was not (S 220, St Albans; S 219, Worcestershire, but for a lay beneficiary). This may be because Worcester was in 'free Mercia', i.e. Mercia under West Saxon 'protection', while others were in more disputed territory. It may also have been because Werferth, Bishop of Worcester, was Alfred's close ally, and thus chose to stress, or overstress, the subordination of Æthelred and Æthelflaed. Control in the early Middle Ages is the sum total of allegiances like those of London and Werferth. The problem in late ninth-century Mercia is that most of the other components of the sum are unknown.

The evidence for West Saxon overlordship becomes even more attenuated in the reign of Æthelflaed's brother, Edward the Elder. Æthelred and Æthelflaed, and Æthelflaed alone, now acted without any reference to Edward (S 221, Much Wenlock; S 225, Abingdon; S 224, Burton), except in four cases, all of which should probably be dated to 903. In the charters of this year Edward *rex*/king and Æthelred and Æthelflaed 'who then held the *principatus* and *potestas* of the Mercian people under the aforesaid king' were petitioned together. All three charters concerned the land of ealdorman Æthelfrith, who was the son-in-law of Æthelflaed and Edward's uncle Athulf, brother of Ealhswith, who had just died. One is explicitly concerned with the dowry of Edward's and Æthelflaed's cousin, Æthelgyth – the woman whose Mercian descendant, Aelfgifu, Edward's grandson, King Eadwig, would later marry. All three charters are family business, and one if not all involved the claims of Æthelflaed and Edward as Ealhswith's heirs and not just as the rulers of Wessex and Mercia (S 367, Christ Church; S 367a, St Pauls; S 371, Glastonbury; cf. S 361, Worcester 900/904 with all three acting together). The language used to describe their respective rule was carefully chosen; it did not claim royal authority for Æthelflaed and Æthelred but maximized their power under Edward's kingship. The context of 903 was familial. Inheritance claims were settled, against a background of rebellion and threat from their paternal cousin, Æthelwold. He was at large and threatening Edward if not Æthelred and Æthelflaed with his Viking allies; he was not killed until the battle of the Holme in December 903. This was no time to stoke up other family tensions. In this context and in these Kentish, West Saxon and London charters, Edward's kingship was recognized, and Æthelred and Æthelflaed were relegated – just.

After 903, there is evidence of alliance but no further explicit subordination. Although the titles continued to deny Æthelred and Æthelflaed regal status, charters spoke of them 'holding the monarchy of the Mercians by the grace of God' (S 221) and of

Æthelflaed alone 'by the gift of Christ's mercy ruling the government of the Mercians'(S 225 *largiente clementia Christi gubernacula regens Merceorum*) or as 'Lady of the Mercians [*domina Merceorum*] by the virtue of divine grace' (S 224). Unlike her aunt Æthelswith, Æthelflaed was never 'regina', whether here or in the Mercian chronicle, the Mercian Register. Rather she was 'Lady', like her own mother, Ealhswith. The use of that title for her mother, and the significance of Ealhswith and her claims for her daughter, complicate still further the reading of it for Æthelflaed. For Ealhswith, in the peculiar circumstances of late ninth-century Wessex, it denoted not a 'queen' but certainly a 'king's wife', and one whose status had transformed the simple 'lady' into 'Lady' (Stafford, 1997: 56–8, and Stafford, forthcoming). For the rest of the tenth and eleventh centuries it was a title of English queens. Its use for Æthelflaed seems yet another instance of studied ambiguity.

Æthelflaed's situation is difficult to interpret. It was complex and changing, like the relationship of Wessex and Mercia, of which she was an embodiment but in which she was also a dynamic factor. Depending on date, circumstance and geographical position, contemporaries variously chose to stress or ignore elements of subordination in this relationship. Issues presumably changed in significance. Had Æthelred, for example, undergone formal inauguration or anointing as king when he took over effective power in Mercia in the 880s? Absence of this, for whatever reason, could have proved critical later. Even though Æthelred and Æthelflaed exercised most if not all the powers of king and queen, and increasingly so in the equal alliance of brother, brother-in-law and sister after 899, formal recognition of that through a retrospective king-making would have been a provocative act, especially after Æthelwold's rebellion. Ironically, the co-operative sibling partnership after 899, knit more tightly by the fostering of Edward's eldest son Athelstan at Æthelflaed's court, could have precluded, could even have been felt to render unnecessary, any clarification of the situation.

After Æthelred's death, Æthelflaed, a West Saxon royal daughter and sister *and* a Mercian royal woman and queen, was uniquely placed to satisfy all sides in this delicate balance between two old kingdoms. There were those in Mercia who felt that another woman, her daughter Aelfwyn, could continue to embody this balance after Æthelflaed's death in 918. Edward thought otherwise, removed her and took over rule in Mercia. Æthelflaed's multiple female identities, which had made her so acceptable, were, as in the case of all women, her own. They were not transmitted to her daughter, who was more emphatically Mercian. The early tenth century is an example of how family rule, with its complex ties of blood and marriage, can express notions of unity and separation, and most fully and successfully in the composite identity of women. In early tenth-century Mercia the context for this expression was a specific recent history of powerful queenship. Æthelflaed's independent female rule, and Aelfwyn's summary disposal by her uncle, indicate both the possibilities, and the limitations, this could produce.

Æthelflaed was, from 887/8, increasingly from 899, and alone from 911, Lady, quasi-queen of the Mercians. Her rule was a product of familial politics, but it was characterized by that most traditionally unfeminine and most traditionally royal activity – warfare. She was responsible for attacks on Viking strongholds and for defence through the construction of her own, and was one of the architects of a Northern British alliance against further Viking activity. In a rule which paralleled that of her brother in this as in many ways, she and Æthelred undertook the remodelling of the New Minster, Gloucester, and the transfer thither and to Chester of the key royal relics of St Oswald and St Werburg. And either during, or just after, her reign, the first surviving Mercian Chronicle was produced to give an account of this daughter of Alfred who was a Mercian queen.[12]

It is an interesting account. It focuses almost exclusively on Æthelflaed's campaigns and fortress building, on her quintessentially regal activity. But more so than in the West Saxon chronicles of Edward and Alfred, with which it surely belongs in general inspiration, this chronicle of Æthelflaed's Mercia stresses divine aid at her side. It was with God's aid that she took control of Derby in 917 and Leicester in 918. After Æthelred's death, when she went to Tamworth 'with all the Mercians' to build a *burh* but also perhaps to take power, she acted 'with God's help'. An independent female ruler was unusual to say the least. Its presenters might well choose to strike a special note of divine legitimation. The creation of this appropriate female royal image was not retrospective but a contemporary manipulation of symbols. Æthelflaed's first action after the death of Æthelred was the building of the *burh* of Shergeat. It was begun on the Eve of the Invention of the Cross, a feast associated with St Helena, that same iconic figure of female rule with whom Cynethryth had been linked on her coinage. Elizabeth I was not the first woman to rule an English kingdom. Nor, apparently, was she the first to realize the power of imagery in negotiating that novel situation.

Cynethryth, and her ninth-century successors, give every impression of having been significant women. But for the most part their lives must be pieced together from recalcitrant evidence. In the case of Cynethryth and Cwoenthryth, their traditional roles in relation to monastic houses, combined with the complications of family politics, have combined to produce black legends surviving in much later sources which distort our pictures of both women, even as they indicate some of the sources of their power. Æthelflaed has been more fortunate. Ironically, as a warrior queen, she moved fundamentally

---

12. It is difficult to date this Chronicle, which now survives in MSS B and C of the *Anglo-Saxon Chronicle*, where it breaks off abruptly in mid-sentence in 924. MS D continues the entry and adds others for 925 and 926, though it is possible that D was here using Northern annals (see Cubbin, 1996: xxxi).

outside the gender expectations of later historians and chroniclers. In doing so she escaped the obloquy which so readily attaches to female roles in family politics and which is heaped especially on those in the early Middle Ages whose views of property and inheritance did not chime with those of ecclesiastical reformers (Stafford, 1997: 148–56). While Cynethryth and Cwoenthryth stood exposed to both denigrations, Æthelflaed became a potential heroine to be associated later with the emergence of an English nation against Viking attack. Her activity in the traditionally masculine, and the traditionally chronicled, royal sphere of warfare separated her from the world of family and inheritance around which the curtains of feminine secrecy and the bedroom were so easily hung. Like a latter-day Elizabeth I she became a wonder to later ages. In her own day, she, or those close and sympathetic to her, moulded her own image. In this crucial respect she was a West Saxon: in her sensitivity to self-presentation she was her father's daughter.

It is thus doubly important to remember that Æthelflaed was heir to the traditions of Mercian political women. These were rooted in family, household and inheritance and in control of monastic lands as well as perhaps in warfare and defence. Imagery linked her to Cynethryth and the elevation of a Mercian queen and mother. The claims of a wife, widow and daughter arose from family roles but in Mercia had been particularly sharply defined in dispute with churchmen. The dynastically shifting, Viking-threatened ninth century had witnessed a steadily developing queenship. Æthelflaed was the beneficiary of a century and a half which had made queens a familiar, acceptable and necessary part of Mercian political life. Her undoubted importance is a fitting end to their story.

Figure 4.1 Castor, Cambridgeshire: 'Apostles panel' sculptural fragment. Photo: Carol A. Farr

4 The Mercian Church: Archaeology and Topography

David Parsons

Introduction

By the mid-seventh century Mercia was entirely surrounded by Christian neighbours. Kent had been the first English kingdom to receive Christianity following the landing of Augustine in AD 597, and despite apostasy the faith had spread to London (not yet a Mercian city) and Essex, and to East Anglia. After a start in the 620s, which was overtaken by military and political events, Northumbria had been the subject of a vigorous missionary campaign by Irish monks, whose influence rapidly spread south from their Holy Island base. To the south, Wessex had also received foreign clergy and established a church, while to the west, Wales had inherited the Christianity and perhaps some of the Church organization of late Roman Britain. The Mercians can hardly have been unaware of these developments as they formed their military alliances with the Welsh and sought to intermarry with the already Christian dynasties round about. The traditional date of Peada's conversion, 653, is held to mark their introduction to Christianity, which was swiftly followed by the founding of the monastery at *Medeshamstede*, the later Peterborough, with Northumbrian support. These early developments have recently been the subject of a thesis by Avril Morris, who is now pursuing her research at doctoral level (Morris, 1999). The influence of this monastery, located as it was on the Fenland edge, spread well into the west Midland heartland of Mercia proper, which surprisingly had to wait until *c.* 670 for its own missionary bishop in the person of Chad.

Unlike Kent and Northumbria, Mercia cannot boast surviving fabric from the churches of the first phase of Christianity. The archaeological remains of the pre-Norman church at Peterborough appear to belong to the later Anglo-Saxon period, while the historically attested royal nunnery of Castor nearby is represented by a single fragment of stone carving at least a century later than the date of its foundation some time in the seventh century (Figure 4.1). The tangible remains of the first phase of Christianity in Mercia have to be sought in other forms of evidence.

Artefactual evidence

The material comes from so-called 'pagan' burials conventionally dated to the seventh to eighth centuries, or is typologically comparable with it. These burials represent the 'Final Phase' of traditional inhumation with grave goods, to use the description coined by E. T. Leeds in the 1930s; more recently they have been referred to overtly as 'conversion-period' graves, especially since the publication of Helen Geake's doctoral thesis (1997). This is not the place to debate this interpretation of the Final Phase; both the concept and the methodology are being subjected to criticism in reviews, such as that of Hines (1999), and discussed in a highly theoretical manner by Schülke (1999 and forthcoming) and others. It is sufficient to acknowledge the dangers inherent in interpreting Final Phase material, in particular the imprecisions of dating, the likelihood of circular argument and the dubious nature of inferences about lifestyle based on grave goods. It is nevertheless clear that there is a body of material, some of which certainly was, and some of which may have been, affected by Christian ideology and Christian symbolism.

Two aspects of Final Phase cemetery archaeology have been much discussed in the past. The first is the possibility that the shift of burial grounds from one site to another in the same locality may be related to the coming of Christianity: the classic case in Mercia is Leighton Buzzard, Bedfordshire (Hyslop, 1963). The second is the resurgence of barrow burial, a phenomenon represented dramatically at both extremes of greater Mercia. At the southern end is the famous Taplow site in Buckinghamshire, where the barrow stands close to the site of the old church and within the precinct of the graveyard (Meaney, 1964: 59). This juxtaposition has been frequently discussed, though the chronological relationship between the church and the mound is unknown. Richard Morris considers Taplow in the context of high-status sites and a possible continuity from 'pagan' barrow burial, as at Sutton Hoo (where the Christian overtones of some of the grave goods are undeniable, if ambiguous), and the patently Christian royal mausoleum complex at Repton, Derbyshire (Morris, 1989: 256, 460–1) (Figure 4.2). The discovery in 1995 of parchmarks almost due east of the Taplow barrow and its subsequent recording have served to highlight the importance of the site (Stocker and Went, 1995). The parchmarks are interpreted as an apse-ended single-cell church, for which the authors suggest an eighth- or ninth-century date, secondary to the 'burial monument of the immediate pagan past' (ibid.: 449).

At the northern end of Mercian territory is the equally well-known cluster of barrows in the Peak District of Derbyshire and Staffordshire (Ozanne, 1963). Several of the barrows have yielded material of a Christian or semi-Christian nature. Most famously the male grave at Benty Grange produced the boar-crested helmet with a silver Latin cross inlaid in the nasal and a leather cup similarly decorated with silver crosses (ibid.: 20; Webster and Backhouse, 1991: no. 46). The

Figure 4.2 Repton, Derbyshire: St Wystan's Church, crypt. Photo: Carol A. Farr

helmet is a significant 'transitional' piece: there is no attempt to conceal the symbol of the new religion, but the traditional boar, with its background of pagan animal rites, is equally if not more prominent. Whether this combination of motifs should be interpreted as the owner of the helmet 'hedging his religious bets' or merely as an example of the currency of two cultures in the seventh century is not clear. Similarly overt is the pendant cross from White Low, near Winster. It is an unmistakably Christian piece, which Ozanne compares with examples from outside Mercia: Wilton (Norfolk), Stanton (Suffolk), and several examples from Kent (Ozanne, 1963: 26), and there are other pendants found with a composite brooch, all but one of which are decorated with cruciform motifs, from Boss Hall near Ipswich (Webster and Backhouse, 1991: nos. 33a and 33b). In Mercia itself there are further examples of pendant crosses, though none of them is similar in form to the White Low cross. Most striking is the equal-armed cross which formed the centrepiece of an elaborate necklace belonging to a high-status woman buried at Desborough, North-amptonshire (ibid.: no. 13). Since this chapter was originally written, a further example from Holderness has been published (MacGregor, 2000).

A few of the latest furnished graves in west Oxfordshire also contained some clearly Christian objects (Blair, 1994: 70–2, with Fig. 49). These include two pendant crosses, one of sheet bronze and silver foil from Standlake, the other of silver from a necklace found at Lechlade. Both of these crosses are of the expanded-arm variety and more closely comparable in shape with the East Anglian examples than with those in more northern parts of Mercia. The finds from west Oxfordshire also include a gold bracteate from Ducklington, which bears an applied filigree cross. Blair's illustration also shows a so-called 'thread box' from North Leigh, made of bronze and with a cruciform design. Such boxes may perhaps be interpreted as reliquaries.

Returning to the north of Mercia, another object from the White Low barrow is worthy of attention. This is a silver gilt disc (perhaps intended as a brooch, but lacking any fastening) with concentric bands of garnet *cloisonné* and filigree (Ozanne, 1963: 26–8). The outer bands of filigree decoration are divided by four symmetrically-placed bosses, which are joined to the rim and to the central area by radial filigree 'arms'. Like many of the developed Kentish circular brooches, the basis of the design is cruciform, though whether this is merely a geometrical device or whether it has Christian significance is uncertain. In addition to this, however, the design of the missing central boss and the surrounding garnet settings of the inner zone can be read in two ways as representing a cross with expanded arms. Both the ambiguity of the reading and the fact that the cross arms are not distinguished from the background by the use of material of a different colour (e.g. blue glass) suggest that if a Christian message was intended, it was deliberately semi-concealed. This may not mean so much a tentative adherence to Christianity as a lack of certainty about what was going to be the dominant force in the mixed religious culture suggested by the Benty Grange helmet. Alternatively, such objects may be interpreted as being closely related to the mainstream of Christian art as it developed in the late seventh and early eighth centuries. Michelle Brown has drawn attention to the mystic significance in the design of carpet pages in such manuscripts as the Book of Durrow and the Lindisfarne Gospels, where the cross motif is similarly half concealed (Brown, M., 2000).

Not far from the Peak District, an equally intriguing find was made in 1860 at Womersley, near Pontefract, in an isolated inhumation burial (Meaney, 1964: 303). The site is on the edge of the 'grey area' described as 'the no-man's land in North Derbyshire and South Yorkshire' (Brooks in Bassett, 1989: 162) between the Mercians and Northumbria. The object concerned, which would not have been out of place in a Derbyshire barrow, is a gold bracteate-like pendant with applied filigree and an area of garnet *cloisonné*. The circular field is divided by filigree strips into four areas shaped like the expanded arms of a cross, such as those from Wilton and Stanton, alternating with four areas of background. The lower, left and right arms are filled with tight filigree scrolls; the upper arm is set with *cloisonné* garnets, which seem to offer a frontal view of an animal's head flanked by down-curving narrow bands of filigree, perhaps representing horns. The interpretation of this head is very subjective, but it may be that of a ram. This pendant may once again represent the fusion of the two cultures and the uncertainties of the seventh century, which may derive from the belief system of the owner or manufacturer of the pendant, but which could also be explained as a resurgence of the inherent ambiguity of Iron Age art.

Topography and land-holding

When the practice of Christianity became more fully visible, Mercia conformed to patterns already established in Kent, Northumbria and elsewhere: the foundation of monasteries and minsters was pioneered by the kings and their magnates, while nunneries and double houses were set up by queens and royal princesses, usually on estates directly under their control. These estates included public buildings of different sorts surviving from previous periods, principally the Romano-British and late prehistoric. The ownership of redundant forum complexes and forts seem to have devolved onto the local rulers of Anglo-Saxon England, whether or not of royal status. The reuse of such sites may indeed have begun before the end of the Roman period, depending on the resolution of the dating problems associated with the early phase of the church of St Paul in the Bail, Lincoln (Jones, 1994: 331–3). Here a church was built across the courtyard of the forum in the late Roman or post-Roman period and was accompanied by east–west burials; it developed through several medieval and post-medieval phases until the nineteenth century, but became redundant and was demolished in 1971.

Similarly positioned was St Nicholas in Leicester, though in this case the church was built in the open *palaestra* or exercise yard, a building probably surrounded internally by a verandah and located in the *insula* to the immediate west of the forum. The still surviving stretch of Roman wall to the west of the church appears to have been incorporated in the church structure, though the extent of the survival of the baths complex west of the wall at any given date is unclear. Warwick Rodwell's ingenious suggestion that the Roman cold bath may have served as a baptismal tank is thought-provoking, but depends on two assumptions – that the church was the cathedral of the short-lived Leicester diocese and that there is masonry of a sufficiently early date incorporated in the otherwise late Anglo-Saxon structure (Rodwell, 1984: 6; Blair, 1992: 245). Neither proposal is capable of proof, and the cathedral hypothesis is at variance with the (unpublished) opinion of local historians that the church of St Mary de Castro is a more likely candidate for cathedral status (C. V. Phythian-Adams, personal communication; Parsons, 1996: 11–13). Nevertheless, the significance of the St Nicholas site should not be underestimated, since it conforms to a pattern of reuse of Roman enclosures, which outside Mercia notably includes a number of Saxon Shore forts. The conversion of forum complexes to Christian use is attested elsewhere in Mercia, for example, at St Albans and Gloucester (Rodwell, 1984: 5–6, 7). Without excavation these developments are undatable, so that it is unclear whether the examples in London belong to the period of Mercian control or to an earlier phase of the city.

Leicestershire also provides the classic example of the reuse of prehistoric hillforts as sites for monasteries and minsters: Breedon on the Hill (most recent discussion Parsons, 1996: 15–16, 24–5; see also Jewell, Chapter 17 in this volume). The interpretation of hillforts as central places which may have had an administrative role in their respective regions leads to a recognition of them as the 'public buildings' of the prehistoric period, and thus the potential equivalents of Roman forts and fora. Their perceived status, as well as practical advantage, may lie behind their reuse for secular purposes in post-Roman Britain and for ecclesiastical purposes in Anglo-Saxon England. They were evidently, like the Saxon Shore forts, the rulers' property to dispose of, as is clear from the Breedon memoranda (Stenton 1933: 182). The second and third memoranda name Friduric as the donor of real estate on which the monks of Medeshamstede were to found their *monasterium*. He is described as *princeps*, and there is a good chance that he was or subsequently became sub-king of the Middle Angles, a major if artificial part of 'greater Mercia'. The status of Friduric and coincidentally of Breedon is emphasized by the third memorandum, which records the addition to the original grant of property now accepted as belonging to Repton (Dornier, 1977b: 158; Rumble, 1977). Repton was the monastery in which St Guthlac received the tonsure (see Roberts in this volume) and which later became the burial place of the Mercian kings. Its chronology is vague, and it is unclear whether the monastery was already in existence when Repton was granted to Breedon, 675 × 691 (Stenton, 1933: 183, n. 4), or whether the third Breedon memorandum is effectively an abstract of its foundation charter.

The two grants of land together totalled 51 *manentes*, a substantial endowment if *manentes* are thought to be the equivalent of hides, though the 31 *manentes* of the third memorandum have been explained as the same number of Domesday vills belonging to the Derbyshire minsters of Repton, Melbourne and Derby itself (David Roffe, personal comm.). The number is an odd one, but is not inconsistent with the frequent grants of 50-hide estates elsewhere for the founding of early monasteries. A Mercian example of this is Hanbury in Worcestershire (Dyer, 1991: 199–20), whose charter purports to date from 657 × 674, and whose church, like Breedon's, is situated in a prehistoric hillfort.

Perhaps the most dramatic discovery of the recent past has been the hillfort identified in the centre of Aylesbury, with archaeological evidence for Christian burial outside the present precinct of St Mary's church, but within the presumed enceinte of the fort (Farley, 1979). Unlike both Breedon and Hanbury, where villages were established at the bottom of the hill, the settlement of Aylesbury grew up around the hillfort and eventually encroached both upon it and upon the originally more extensive graveyard around the church. In view of Aylesbury's *-byrig* place-name suffix and of its place in the history of dynastic monasticism in the Midlands (see below), this insight into its early development is particularly significant.

Earlier enclosures of a rather different type formed the basis of some of the first Christian sites in the former independent kingdom of Lindsey. Using a combination of documentary and topographical evidence, David Stocker explores a number of religious houses where physical remains are non-existent, in some cases despite archaeological excavation (Stocker, 1993). His prime example, Crowland, is known mainly from the *Life of St Guthlac*, which is discussed in detail elsewhere in this volume. Located in the south of Lincolnshire not far from Peterborough, the site is effectively an island in the fens and 'had been of ritual significance at some time in its past' on account of several barrows and other mounds, possibly funerary, that have been identified there (ibid.: 101–6, esp. 106). The monastery at Bardney, a Mercian royal foundation of the late seventh century (see below for its dynastic connections), occupied an island site between the River Witham and two of its tributaries, where as at Crowland there is some evidence for earlier ritual use. There was a 'family' at least three churches, which may have been linked liturgically (ibid.: 107–10). A similar situation existed, albeit on a smaller scale, at Partney, which Stocker argues developed as a daughter house of Bardney, with South and North Kyme as a possible addition to a postulated monastic group (ibid.: 110–13). More general discussion of the early church in Lincolnshire inevitably includes the position of Lincoln and the location of the bishop's see, and this debate is carried forward in more detail in the same volume by Richard Gem (Gem, 1993b).

An insight into the rather different situation along Mercia's western frontier is provided by a fresh interpretation of the conversion of the Hwicce, an identifiable sub-group in the south-west of greater Mercia, who were given their own bishop in 680, based on Worcester. Steven Bassett has argued persuasively that the late Romano-British church survived in western Mercia and was responsible for the conversion of the incoming Anglo-Saxon settlers (Bassett, 1992: 18–20) and that the Anglo-Saxon bishopric was imposed on an existing organization in the Worcester area. From both topographical and documentary evidence he concludes that the church of St Helen pre-dated the Anglo-Saxon cathedral and may have been the see of an earlier Romano-British bishop (Bassett, 1989 and 1992: 20–6). It has also been suggested that the St Helen dedication may indicate pre-Anglo-Saxon origins. Bassett, basing himself on earlier work by Carolyn Heighway, uses a range of archaeological, topographical and documentary evidence to propose a similar British origin for the church of St Mary de Lode in Gloucester (Bassett, 1992: 20–4), and argues a comparable case, though on more tenuous evidence, for St Michael's, Lichfield (ibid.: 29–35). While there is no early fabric in any of the churches discussed, the topographical evidence plays a large part in the argument for their early establishment. Bassett concludes that Christianity in the Severn valley and its Anglo-Saxon hinterland is likely to have had a British origin.

Hagiography and family connections

One of the developments in scholarship over the past ten or twenty years has been the new awareness that saints' lives and genealogies generally contain useful nuggets of historical information, however fanciful their content appears to be. In some cases this provides supporting evidence for sites already known from documentary or topographical data; in others it enables us to add further sites to the list of those likely to have sheltered Christian communities, even though no early church fabric has survived. In the latter category there are two intriguing examples situated on either side of the Oxfordshire–Northamptonshire border to the south of Banbury, which follows the River Cherwell. On the Oxfordshire side is the village of Adderbury, whose large and magnificent parish church dates from the thirteenth to the fifteenth century. There is no trace of Anglo-Saxon masonry, or of reused carved stonework, one of the classic indicators of an earlier church, and often of one of some status. At Domesday most of Adderbury was in royal or episcopal hands, and an earlier 50-hide royal landholding can be reconstructed from the Domesday and earlier documentary evidence. The place-name is significant, consisting of the Old English personal name Eadburh and the suffix *-burh*. Stenton (1942) argued that women's names in combination with this suffix almost certainly indicate a religious rather than a military site (though it is clear from the foregoing discussion that pre-Anglo-Saxon fortifications were frequently reused as sites for religious houses). It is therefore no surprise to find that Eadburh is recognized as one of a number of saintly royal princesses, many of whom claimed descent from Penda, the last pagan king of Mercia. She is associated with Aylesbury and with Bicester, to which her remains were translated in the twelfth century, and she is credited with the training of St Osyth, herself abbess of Aylesbury. Osyth is supposed to be the daughter of another of Penda's daughters, Wilburh, who married 'King' Frithuwold, the founder of a monastery at Chertsey; Osyth's birth is said to have taken place at her father's palace at Quarrendon, near Aylesbury (Blair, 1989: 106–7). The Eadburh legend therefore suggests an otherwise unknown early Mercian religious house at Adderbury as well as confirming the minster at Aylesbury implied by the archaeological evidence discussed above.

On the east (Northamptonshire) side of the Cherwell lies King's Sutton. Like Adderbury, the church is outstanding for its late medieval features, notably the west tower and spire, but with earlier work in the chancel interior in the shape of Romanesque blind arcading, heavily restored. The west tower is clasped by the broad side aisles, a feature regarded as indicative of a possible pre-Conquest core and perhaps of high status (Richmond, 1986: 183–6). The status of the church in the later Middle Ages is confirmed by its becoming a prebend of Lincoln Cathedral, and other documentary evidence, discussed by Franklin (1984: 81–3), strongly suggests that it was an ancient Anglo-Saxon minster. There is, however, no evidence of any pre-Conquest fabric or residual carved stonework. Nevertheless, a legendary passion of an extraordinary saint provides the link to the formative period of Anglo-Saxon Christianity. According to this account, a child called Rumwald was born on the royal estate of Sutton to a daughter of Penda and her Northumbrian husband. The legend is pervaded by the symbolism of the number three: the child survives three days, preaches on the Trinity and predicts his burial successively at three locations – King's Sutton itself, Brackley and Buckingham. At all these places there is evidence for a St Rumwald cult later in the Middle Ages, in the case of King's Sutton in the form of a bequest as late as 1525 to an altar of St Rumwald (Serjeantson and Longden, 1913: 354). The legend is interesting on two accounts. The first is the implication of a substantial royal estate in the seventh century, embracing much of south-west Northamptonshire and part of Buckinghamshire, an early landholding apparently pre-dating the shire boundary which later divided it. An echo of this primitive land unit can be found in the name of the later prebend: Sutton-cum-Buckingham. The second point of interest is the possibly fictional reference to another of Penda's supposed daughters, which puts Sutton, along with Adderbury, into the category of houses founded by royal princesses in the late seventh or early eighth century. Whatever the truth of the legend, the involvement of early royalty in minster foundation was clearly appreciated.

Unless Rumwald's mother was Cyneburh, as some have suggested, a further daughter of the royal family, along with her sister Cyneswith (and in some accounts her cousin Tibba) were responsible for the foundation of a double monastery at Castor, only a few miles west of Peterborough (Morris, 1999: 44–5). Again, there is no Anglo-Saxon fabric surviving in the church, though its twelfth-century successor takes one of the forms regarded as typical of former pre-Conquest minsters: an aisleless cruciform layout with central space or tower. There is, however, a precious survival in the shape of a fragment of Anglo-Saxon stone carving showing a saintly figure (? apostle) under an arch (Figure 4.1). Several limited campaigns of excavation have established settlement of Middle Saxon date around the site of the church, but no masonry buildings have been identified and the small finds have included nothing of specifically ecclesiastical significance. The excavation report nevertheless optimistically reports 'the conspicuous number of feminine ornaments' and a high proportion of finds from one of the sites denoting 'a strong female presence' (Green *et al.*, 1986-7: 144–5). Archaeologically, however, the early nunnery is virtually invisible. To carry the dynastic story a step farther, Cyneburh was closely related both through her own marriage and that of her brother Æthelred (king of Mercia at the time of the Breedon foundation) to the Northumbrian Osthryth, who was responsible for the translation of the remains of her uncle St Oswald to Bardney in Lindsey, of which Bede gives such a dramatic account (*HE* III. 11). He further indicates that the royal pair were substantial benefactors of the Lincolnshire monastery. These cults are discussed in more detail by Alan Thacker (1985: 2–8).

Turning now from Mercians with northern dynastic alliances to others with southern connections, three saints claim our attention. The memoranda discussed above named as founder and benefactor of the Breedon/Repton monasteries the *princeps* Friduric. He is surely the same as 'S. Fretheric' recorded in the twelfth-century Peterborough Chronicle of Hugo Candidus, in an amplified version of the Old English list of saints' resting places as one of three saintly monks who were interred at Breedon (Mellows and Mellows, 1980: 32). It was not of course unusual for high-status founders to enter their own monasteries as inmates or even as abbots/abbesses, as witness the withdrawal of King Æthelred of Mercia to Bardney in the early eighth century. The first abbot of Breedon, however, was Hædda, who later appears in documents as abbot of Woking and Bermondsey in Surrey. This apparently long-range territorial connection is also referred to by Hugo Candidus in his list of monasteries founded from *Medeshamstede* (Mellows and Mellows, 1980: 8), and the order of the list suggests that the Surrey houses were offshoots of Breedon (Dornier, 1977b: 159–60). This point has been taken up by Blair, who also argues that the Surrey monastery at Chertsey was endowed with an estate 'carved out of the Woking *regio*' in the charter of 672 × 674 (Blair, 1991: 104; 20–1; and 1989, 105–7). The charter was granted by Frithuwold, described as sub-king, and the first witness was Frithuric, the later saint of Breedon. The identical first elements of these men's names makes it likely that they were closely related, if not brothers, and this implies a significant link between a Mercian, perhaps Middle Anglian, noble family and early monastic development in the Thames Valley area. The connection between Frithuwold and the family of Penda of Mercia has been referred to above. The Mercia–Thames Valley link is enhanced by the third member of the trio of saints, Frideswide (Frithuswith), again likely to be a close relation of the founders of Chertsey and Breedon. She was and is associated with a nunnery at Oxford, supposedly founded for her by her father (Blair, 1994: 52–4).

Sites and buildings

Possible monastery sites

From the topographical, documentary and hagiographical evidence discussed above it is clear that Mercia was well endowed with monasteries from the late seventh century onward. The extent to which these early houses would stand scrutiny from the standpoint of later definitions of monasticism and whether their primary purpose was the pastoral care of the laity has been debated elsewhere (Blair, 1995b; Cambridge and Rollason, 1995). It is likely that there were many mixed communities of monks and clergy performing both functions, as seems to have been the case, for instance, at Breedon (Parsons, 1996: 24–5). For the purposes of the present chapter the minster/monastery question does not need to be resolved, and the term 'monastery' is used to indicate houses of religious communities of whatever kind. In the case of most examples referred to above, there is a dearth of material remains from the Anglo-Saxon period generally, the principal exception being the friezes and associated sculptural material at Breedon, which are discussed in detail elsewhere in this volume (pp. 248–54). Sites where there is either upstanding pre-Conquest fabric or archaeological evidence include Brixworth, whose church is discussed below. The slight documentary evidence consists of the twelfth-century Peterborough list of houses supposedly founded from *Medeshamstede*, where Brixworth takes precedence over Breedon and the Surrey monasteries mentioned above. Archaeological evidence for this monastery was uncovered by excavation in 1972, when a ditch – possibly part of the *vallum monasterii* – and burials of eighth- to ninth-century date were recorded (Everson, 1977). This and subsequent excavations have not been extensive enough to reveal any substantial evidence of the monastic layout, and the same is true at Deerhurst, Gloucestershire, where there is also a significant church of Anglo-Saxon date still surviving (Rahtz and Watts, 1997).

The monastery at Much Wenlock, Shropshire, which was in existence by the last quarter of the seventh century, has been subjected to archaeological investigation on several occasions. Excavations in the crossing of the medieval priory church by D. H. S. (later Dean) Cranage in 1901 and by Jackson and Fletcher in 1962–63 revealed a small building thought to be of seventh-century date. New investigations by Humphrey Woods in 1981–86 led to a claim that this was a surviving Roman building brought back into use after the foundation of the monastery (Woods, 1987: 58–63), but this view was immediately contested by Lord Fletcher and more sharply by the Biddles (Fletcher *et al.*, 1988). Without first-hand knowledge of the site it is difficult to be certain about the interpretation of the excavated evidence, and there are several walls of early medieval date or earlier whose relationships and purpose are not entirely clear. Of the rectangular building first excavated by Cranage, one can say at least that its form is not inconsistent with an early medieval date. The eastern apse claimed by previous excavators was not found by Woods, but there was evidence for a segmental niche in the East wall of the building. An interior apse in a square-ended building is a fairly common occurrence in the pre-Romanesque archaeology on the continent of Europe, and parallels for Wenlock would not be difficult to find.

Excavation has also taken place at sites where there is no Anglo-Saxon church fabric or documentary evidence to suggest the former existence of a monastic house. The range of finds from these sites has suggested high status, and writing materials in particular have led to the inference of a literate society most likely to be found in a monastic context. The point of reference is the material from the site of a known monastery at Barking, Essex (Webster and Backhouse, 1991: nos 67 a–w), although with the foundation date possibly as early as *c.* 675 this can hardly count as a Mercian house. Notable among the finds were copper alloy and iron styluses. Copper alloy styluses were also a feature of the site excavated at Brandon, Suffolk (Webster and Backhouse, 1991: no. 67 r–t), where the mainly eighth- to ninth-century dates of the finds can be held to justify including this example in a survey of Mercian rather than independent East Anglian monasticism. The material recovered also includes an inscribed gold plaque bearing the symbol of St John the Evangelist, but many of the finds were secular, if not actually domestic, and the interpretation of the site as monastic is not secure. The largely informal layout did, however, 'place emphasis on the location and accessibility of the church', which was accompanied by a group of high-quality buildings (Webster and Backhouse, 1991: no. 66). Materials of comparable type and date have also been uncovered at another site in 'outer Mercia', Flixborough, Lincolnshire (formerly Humberside) (Webster and Backhouse, 1991: no. 69). The settlement seems to have begun around 700 and to have been abandoned in the 870s; some of the buildings had glazed windows and a literate society is indicated once again by an inscribed plaque, made of lead on this occasion, and by no fewer than sixteen styluses, one of which uniquely is of silver. The high living standards implied by the food debris do not immediately suggest monastic self-discipline, and arguments have been put forward in favour of a secular site of very high status, where the keeping of records and the writing of documents were part of an aristocratic life-style. It may not, however, be appropriate to seek to distinguish between high-status domestic sites and monasteries in this way, in view of Bede's strictures on the 'irregular' family monasteries of the early eighth century in his letter to Archbishop Ecgbert (Whitelock, 1979: no. 170). The picture Bede paints of houses which were scarcely monastic in the strict sense of the word leads one to wonder whether there was any noticeable difference in the material culture of a 'lax' monastery and that of a totally secular aristocratic family home. The graphic description by Gregory of Tours some 150 years earlier of the nuns' revolt in Poitiers makes it clear that some religious at least expected to find their normal high-status creature comforts in the confines of a monastic house.

Early church fabrics

The dearth of early church remains in Mercia is not total. At Wroxeter, Shropshire, a church ascribed by the Taylors to period A (1965: 694–95) was built in the south-west corner of the Roman town. Frequently rebuilt and extended, the first phase of this church is represented only by part of the present north wall of the nave, whose masonry unsurprisingly contains large quantities of Roman *spolia*. Its diocesan setting and its possible British origin are discussed by Bassett (1992: 35–9). At nearby Atcham the side walls of the nave survive, likewise dated by the Taylors to period A, which they defined as approximately 600–800 (1965: 31–2, 17).

It is probable that parts of the present church of St Wystan at Repton, Derbyshire, also date from the late seventh century, when the monastery is mentioned specifically in the *Life of St Guthlac* and by implication in the third of the Breedon memoranda (see above, pp. 56 and 60). Intensive archaeological investigation in the 1970s and 1980s, both above and below ground, has greatly increased our knowledge of the development of the church fabric, though the phasing remains relative rather than absolute. The earliest masonry identified is the lower walling of the crypt (much of it below the Anglo-Saxon ground level), which is now thought to have been a free-standing burial chamber, on to which the body of a conventional church was later built (Taylor, 1971, 1977). This is assumed to have been the burial place of the kings of Mercia on the basis of documentary references in the ninth century and later to St Wistan (a royal prince murdered in 849) being buried in the 'mausoleum of his grandfather Wiglaf' (king of Mercia 827–40), and it is known that Æthelbald, king in the first half of the eighth century, had previously been buried in Repton. The original structure of the crypt did not yet have the four twisted stone columns, the wall pilasters flanking the primary recesses in the outer walls, the stone vaulting or the stairways leading down from the body of the church (Figure 4.2). It was a plain square underground space, to which the listed features were successively added. The connecting passages from the church are interpreted as a development necessitated by the need to make access possible for pilgrims as the cult of St Wistan grew in importance, and thus by definition later than 849. The precise dates of the insertion of the vaulting and its supports and of the original exterior walls are not known, but presumed to be before the mid-ninth century. The body of the church must have existed before the cutting of the passages to the crypt. The upper walling of the chancel above the crypt and of the surviving portions of the north *porticus* contains features of later pre-Conquest type, which may date from the last century of Anglo-Saxon England.

Churches of the Carolingian period

The second half of the Taylors' sub-period A3 and their B1, i.e. *c.* 750–850, sees the appearance of more substantial church buildings in Mercia. At Brixworth, Northamptonshire, the earliest church attested by surviving fabric had a rectangular nave and a square 'central space' totalling over 30 metres in length (Figure 4.3). Excavations in 1981–82 showed that the construction of the present church is likely to have taken place during the century under discussion (Audouy, 1984), despite the oft-repeated statement of A. W. Clapham which assigned a seventh-century date to it. The excavations also showed conclusively that the ranges of *porticus* along the north and south sides of the nave were intended from the beginning, since their foundations were identical in technique to those of the nave. The arches which led into these *porticus*, with their mainly two orders of Roman brick pseudo-voussoirs are supported on rectangular piers rather than on the columns of a regular basilica. Comparative examples elsewhere in Europe, such as Steinbach and Seligenstadt in Germany and several in northern Italy date from the early ninth century or later, so on several grounds the 'Carolingian' date for Brixworth seems certain. Stone-by-stone drawing has been carried out on all elevations with exposed masonry, and the individual stones coded according to their petrological origin. This has enabled a detailed analysis to be undertaken, and the published results for the west wall of the nave have made possible a clearer understanding of the development of the west end of the church (Sutherland and Parsons, 1984). The existence of a primary opening in the west wall of the nave at first-floor level has long been recognized, and it now appears that it may have led to – or been approached from – a long first-floor gallery in the west forebuilding one or two steps higher than the sill of the opening. On the Continent such western complexes are a feature of Carolingian architecture.

Another western complex has been recognized from the excavations at Cirencester Abbey, Gloucestershire (Wilkinson and McWhirr, 1998: 23–39) (Figure 4.4). In his contribution to the excavation report, Richard Gem describes the rectangular element west of the nave subdivided by a north–south wall or arcade as 'certainly not ... a "westwork"' (in Wilkinson and McWhirr, 1998: 37), but as displaying features which would develop on the Continent into a full westwork. Other characteristics of this church, the archaeological evidence for which was very tenuous, include a ring crypt, another Carolingian feature (which it shares with Brixworth), and aisles flanking the nave subdivided into long compartments by north–south walls. It is unclear from the excavated evidence whether these were solid walls or simply the sleeper foundations for arches spanning the aisles. The same uncertainty obtains at Brixworth, where the compartments surrounding the nave were much smaller in scale. Nevertheless, the overall dimensions of the two churches were not dissimilar: Gem proposes 35m for the length of the Cirencester nave, while the nave and central space together at Brixworth measure approximately 31m; the Cirencester church was rather narrower, with the nave measuring internally about 6.4m against Brixworth's 10m and total internal width 13.7m against *c.* 18m. As reconstructed, however, the Cirencester building appears to have been more sophisticated with important parallels in Carolingian Europe. A date in the first half of the ninth century has been proposed, and the church can been seen as the natural product of the contacts with the Carolingian Empire developed by Offa of Mercia in the second half of the eighth.

At Wing, Buckinghamshire, the Anglo-Saxon fabric consists of a nave with north and south arcades of three bays, substantial parts of a north aisle and a polygonal apse with crypt beneath (Taylor and Taylor, 1965: 665–72). The nave walls are plastered, and few details of construction can be seen, but the arches of the arcades are of one plain order, supported on rectangular piers and rising from stepped imposts. In these three respects there is great similarity between Wing and Brixworth. The arches are roughly similar in height; at Wing they are somewhat wider, but the supporting piers are somewhat narrower than those at Brixworth. The length of the Wing nave is much the same as that at Brixworth, but there is no separate 'choir' space to the east of it; instead, there is a further short bay to the east of the arcades, where continuous walling has been pierced by openings of later date, which may represent a 'central space' comparable with that at Repton (see above). At the west end of the nave, round-headed doorways high in the side walls indicate a probable west gallery across the church. Here the comparisons are not with Brixworth, but with Tredington, Warwickshire, and Jarrow. The north aisle has the appearance of an undivided space, but could be the residue of a series of chambers separated by cross-walls of the Brixworth type, though no archaeological investigation has taken place which might have proved or disproved this hypothesis. It is worth noting, however, that the blocked doorway at the sound end of the east wall now has a parallel in the eastern chamber of the north range at Brixworth, where remains of a jamb lining were discovered during the 1981 excavations (Audouy, 1984: 11, with figs 4 and 5). Much of the apse and crypt belong to a later date, though there is sufficient evidence to indicate an earlier crypt structure, which might be contemporary with the nave. Taylor and Taylor (1965: 671) considered the nave to be of similar date to Brixworth, which on the basis of the excavations carried out twenty years ago is likely to be late eighth or early ninth century, as noted above.

A combination of excavation and survey of the standing fabric was carried out at Deerhurst, Gloucestershire, from 1971 to 1984, and research still continues (Rahtz, 1976; Rahtz and Watts, 1997; Taylor, 1977). Understanding of the fabric and its development has increased enormously as a result compared with the relatively simple phase diagrams published by Jackson and Fletcher in the early 1960s. In particular, the sequence for the progressive construction of the *porticus* around the nave has been refined, and the development of the structure is now seen as considerably more complex. In the present context what seems important is that, unlike Cirencester and Brixworth, Deerhurst church was not planned from the start with ranges of side chambers. In this respect the layout of the early phases of the church appears to be less well developed than either Brixworth or Cirencester and may thus be earlier in date. Absolute dates are difficult to determine, but the summary of stratigraphic and structural sequences at Deerhurst (Rahtz and Watts, 1997: Table IX) suggests an origin in the seventh or eighth century, with the *porticus* being added progressively through the ninth and into the tenth. The complexities of this church and its development cannot, however, be addressed in a general synthesis such as this.

Postscript: Bampton, Oxfordshire

The progress of John Blair's research at Bampton is being watched with great interest. Here is a church complex which has developed from a minster first mentioned in the 950s and with standing fabric no earlier than the Romanesque period. There are, however, indications of an earlier origin for the Christian use of what appears to have been a pagan ritual site. The axial alignment of church and chapel sites is consistent with the linear groups of churches found in both England and Europe from the seventh to the ninth century (Blair, 1994: 64). The most recent publication by Blair makes clearer the relationship between the churches and the prehistoric barrows on the site and reports the earliest evidence so far for the Christian use of the site in the form of east–west inhumations, one of which yielded a calibrated radiocarbon date of 680–870 (Blair, 1999). On the basis of what has so far been established at Bampton it is clear that much remains to be discovered about the early church in Mercia by means of archae-ological and topographical research on sites which architecturally seem devoid of any Anglo-Saxon significance.

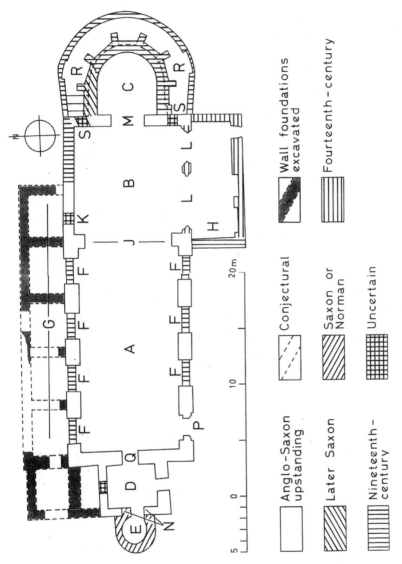

Figure 4.3 Brixworth, Northamptonshire: All Saints Church

Anglo-Saxon upstanding

Later Saxon

Nineteenth-century

Conjectural

Saxon or Norman

Uncertain

Wall foundations excavated

Fourteenth-century

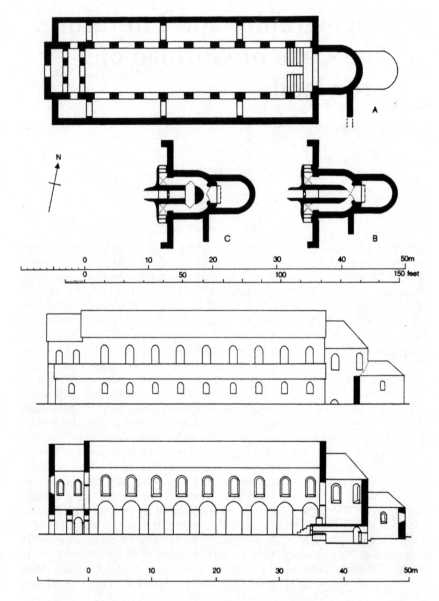

Figure 4.4 Cirencester, Gloucestershire: ninth-century minster church, reconstructed plan, south elevation and longitudinal section (after Wilkinson and McWhirr, 1998)

5 Hagiography and Literature: The Case of Guthlac of Crowland

Jane Roberts

Two main phases of hagiographical writing are confidently assigned to the Mercian area. First and foremost, there is the *Vita sancti Guthlaci*. Described by Stenton as 'the one historical work which has come down from the ancient Mercian kingdom' (Stenton, 1971: 178), it was written towards the middle of the eighth century (Colgrave, 1956: 19; Lapidge, 1996: 10). Second, because of the disruptions caused by Vikings, when King Alfred looked for helpers in his programme of making available in English those books most necessary for all men to know,[1] works with a distinct hagiographic thrust, for example the Dialogues of Gregory, were among translations made by Mercians. Some scholars argue that Mercia already had a tradition of English prose, but there is no evidence to support dating any of the extant texts that remain, apart from a group of charters, as early as the middle of the ninth century. Notoriously, there is no agreement as to the date or provenance of most Old English poetry, but because Guthlac of Crowland is the one English saint commemorated in the four codices, it is often assumed that the Guthlac poems and therefore, by extension, the other poetic saints' lives of the Vercelli and Exeter Books, were Mercian compositions, 'probably from East Mercia like Felix's Life' (Sisam, 1953b: 134). Despite the disappearance of a separate kingdom of Mercia, perhaps even in Alfred's reign, interest in the saints of Mercia continued as part and parcel of the elaboration of saints' lives in general throughout the later Middle Ages.[2] New legends grew up, attaching themselves to names of benefactors and

---

1. Sweet (1871: I. 7) 'sumæ bec, ða ðe niedbeðearfosta sien eallum monnum to wiotonne'.
2. Among recent historians who have paid scrupulous attention to these lives are Thacker (1985) and Rollason (1978, 1983, 1989). Good brief accounts of many lives, together with bibliography, are to be found in Farmer (1978), whose spellings, where different from those I have chosen, are added in brackets, with F. following.

forgotten men and women from long before. There is much to marvel at in the adventures and miracles of a surprising number of saintly children and grandchildren of Penda. Their post-Conquest lives come from an England with little sense of the vanished Mercian kingdom, but with a willingness to listen to stories that gave a seeming individuality to names from the past. With Guthlac, were it not for the considerable body of Anglo-Saxon writings, some of the post-Conquest legends might equally amaze us into disbelief. The conventions of hagiography change, and even Guthlac, for whom there are written records from little more than a generation after his death, was not immune to improvement and amplification. Felix's *Vita sancti Guthlaci* exercised a brake on over-elaboration, whereas other Mercian royal saints gave great scope for invention. It is interesting therefore to begin with an overview of some of the major changes the Guthlac cult underwent after the Anglo-Saxon period (Birch, 1881; Bolton, 1954; Roberts, 1970; Iamartino, 1992), before considering what other hagiographical writings have come down to us from the historic kingdom of Mercia.

Sometime towards the middle of the eighth century a man named Felix drew together materials about Guthlac of Crowland (*V. Guth.*, Prologue: 60). We assume that Felix, who shows knowledge of Bede's life of Cuthbert, wrote his life of Guthlac after Bede completed his *Historia Ecclesiastica*, for Bede makes no mention of Guthlac. Who this Felix was, we do not know. Because Felix says in his Prologue that he wrote the life in obedience to the commands of his lord King Ælfwald, it is often asserted that he was an East Anglian, and some have pointed to the likelihood of his having been named in memory of the first bishop of the East Anglians. Ælfwald, who ruled East Anglia from possibly as early as *c.* 713 up to 749, was probably closely related to Ecgburh (Edburga, F.), daughter of King Aldwulf, his predecessor as king of East Anglia. Ecgburh was abbess of the Mercian monastic foundation at Repton during the years of Guthlac's life in Crowland (*V. Guth.*, c. 48: 146–9), and is indeed given more attention in the life than Ælfthryth, foundress of the abbey and abbess during the two years of Guthlac's religious training there (*V. Guth.* c. 20: 84–5). Thus, despite the dedication of the *vita* to an East Anglian king, the impetus for the writing of the life of Guthlac probably came from Repton, a Mercian religious foundation and for a time the burial place of Mercian kings (Rollason 1989: 118 and n.59). Felix's *vita* first consolidated the legend of Guthlac.

Although Felix is often described as a monk of Crowland, there is no convincing documentary or archaeological evidence for any large monastic settlement at Crowland before the Benedictine revival of the latter part of the tenth century. Felix makes no reference to any such monastery, but presents a Guthlac who, like other western followers of the desert fathers, imposed austerities upon himself and chose the life of a separate cell rather than the membership of a larger brotherhood. When Felix was writing, the anchorite of Crowland was a man named

Cissa (*V. Guth.*, c. 48: 148–9), and there is nothing in his chapter about King Æthelbald's vision at the saint's burial place to indicate that the king of Mercia had founded a monastery at Crowland (*V. Guth.*, c. 52: 164–7). There was the oratory, enriched by containing the saint's body, and around it as like as not a few scattered cells that prefigured the later monastery. There is, added to a ninth-century copy of the *vita*, a twelve-line acrostic, reading 'BEATUS GUDLAC' down the left-hand side and 'BARTHOLOMEUS' up the right-hand side (Birch, 1881: xix–xxi; James, 1909: 105–6), perhaps made for an early shrine (Colgrave, 1956: 27; Henderson, 1985: 83). The first abbot of the monastery founded in *c.* 971 was Thurkytel, and his Crowland was to become one of the great Benedictine foundations associated with the reformers of monastic life in England.

The absence of identifiable Crowland materials about Guthlac from before the twelfth century can be put down to the sudden fire of 1091 in Abbot Ingulf's time (Chibnall, 1969: 346–7). By then Crowland had the tombs of two major saints, having acquired the body of Waltheof (Waldef (1), F.), earl of Northumbria and of Huntingdon and Northampton. Earl Waltheof was beheaded in 1076, after years of uneasy dealings with and rebellion against William the Conqueror, and soon became an English martyr, with miracles reported from his tomb at Crowland Abbey. Compilations newly made in the late twelfth and early thirteenth centuries provide the first important evidence of the growth and elaboration of Guthlac's cult at Crowland itself. Much of the entertaining history of early Crowland attributed to Ingulf lacks credibility (Riley, 1893: ix–xv): little of it can have been written before the late twelfth century, and it is likely that even the eleventh-century materials of the *Historia Croylandensis* were put together at a much later date, perhaps as late as the fifteenth century. Therefore we cannot trust the story of duplicate charters saved from the 1091 fire because they had luckily been removed from the muniments room to serve as copying-texts for young scribes. When Orderic stayed at Crowland for five weeks some time between 1114 and 1123, he was told of a charter given by Æthelbald to Guthlac and of a monastery founded by the king, and the forged charter he used might later have been used in the Pseudo-Ingulf (Chibnall, 1969: 338–9 and n. 2). Otherwise, except for the pseudo-Ingulf writings, charters are not mentioned between the years 1091 and 1415, that is not until they apparently proved useful in disputes about property ownership. Another fire occurred in the mid-twelfth century, in which further historical materials could have been lost. One of the best-loved legends of Crowland Abbey is attributed to Ingulf (Riley, 1893: 59, 64ff., 102–3, 223), that five old men survived from the old monastery, emerging after Viking times to welcome Thurkytel's reinforcements. These sempects – old monks maybe, but Swiftian struldbrugs I have always thought them – are an imaginative elaboration of Orderic's simple statement that 'from the day of its first foundation by the king to the present the island of Crowland has never been without holy monks'.[3] More reliable is the information to be found in a book still extant, Douai, Public Library MS 852, a record from the twelfth and thirteenth centuries of Crowland's historical materials, which was at Crowland when seen there by John Leland shortly after the dissolution of the monasteries. This manuscript gives an account of the translation of the bones of St Guthlac on 23 August 1136, together with further Guthlac miracles. An *Abbreviatio* of Felix's *vita* commissioned by Prior Wulfwine of Crowland from Ordericus Vitalis was written into the Douai manuscript (Chibnall, 1969: 322–33).

The ambition of thirteenth-century abbots leaves its marks among the Douai materials: there are celebrations of the acquisition of the relics of St Neot by Crowland in 1213 and of the translation of Earl Waltheof to a marble tomb in 1219, both in Henry Longchamp's abbacy. The thrust of the Guthlac biographies commissioned by Henry Longchamp was very different. Peter of Blois adds no new incident within the materials derived from Felix, instead rewriting, simplifying, commenting, incorporating more scriptural references and more direct speech.[4] He used the Douai manuscript for miracles additional to those in Felix's *vita*. Henry of Avranches used as the main source for his hexameters the new life by Peter of Blois, introducing rather more changes, extending some descriptive passages and adding lengthy digressions, for example on ambition.[5] A third, rather different document, the Harley Roll, may also come from the abbacy of Henry Longchamp. Roundel XVIII includes among Crowland's properties Frieston Priory, which was not granted until 1141; and its depiction of the saint's shrine provides evidence for the even later date of after 1196, when Guthlac's tomb was moved to a raised position above the high altar (Warner, 1928: 18; Henderson, 1985: 84).

Felix was well versed in hagiographic convention, as is clear from the ways in which he fleshed out the details of Guthlac's life with phrasing, motifs and scene-types familiar from well-known legends. Among the greatest influences on him as a writer were the Evagrian life of Anthony and Bede's life of Cuthbert.[6] His borrowings are, however, the literary trappings of a well-made legend, and behind them lie clear indications of the nature of Felix's working materials, from which it is possible to gain an impression of the nuggets of hard information the life contains. The prologue, a fine piece of learnedly modest writing, names as witnesses to the life 'a certain most reverend Abbot Wilfrid' and a 'certain priest Cissa' (*V. Guth.*, Prologue: 64–5 and c. 28: 92–3), Guthlac's successor at Crowland (*V. Guth.*, c. 48:

---

3. Chibnall (1969: 340–1) 'nec unquam post primam instaurationem quam idem rex fecit; sedes Crulandiæ religiosorum habitatione monachorum usque in hodiernum diem caruit.'
4. The life is printed in Horstmann (1901: II. 698–727).
5. The poem is edited by Bolton (1954). See also Bolton (1959: 47–52).
6. See Kurtz (1926); also the discussion and notes that accompany Jones's translation (1947) and Colgrave's edition (1956).

148–9).[7] The life proper begins with the identification of Guthlac's father, Penwalh, a leading man among the Middle Angles, descended from famous kings stretching back to Icel, the founding king of the Mercian dynasty (*V. Guth.*, cc. 1, 2: 72–5). How far the Middle Angles had self-government is hazy. Stenton (1971: 120) regards them as having fallen under Mercian control by the middle of the seventh century when Penda sent his son Peada to rule there. So was Penwalh, alliterating pleasingly with Penda and Peada, ealdorman of the Middle Angles? In due course Penwalh married a noblewoman named Tette (*V. Guth.* c.3: 74–5). The house in which their child was to be born was marked out by a miraculous hand (*V. Guth.*, cc. 5–8: 74–7). For Henderson, this portent, new to hagiography and possibly the earliest appearance of the *manus dei* motif in insular traditions, resonates with memories of the ordination of God's son as king on Mount Sion in Psalm 2 (1985: 76–7). The boy was baptised Guthlac and had a dutiful and even-tempered childhood (*V. Guth.*, cc. 10–15: 76–81). However, says Felix, remembering 'the valiant deeds of heroes of old ... he changed his disposition and gathering bands of followers took up arms'.[8] Apparently he fought in the Welsh borders, for later (*V. Guth.*, c.34: 108–11), in Crowland days, when Guthlac was praying one evening, he was suddenly overtaken by a 'dream-filled sleep'[9] in which he thought he heard the shouting of a large crowd. Quickly awake, he went out of his cell, and he recognized the words and speech of Britons. Felix adds the explanation that in other days Guthlac had lived among the Britons and therefore understood their 'sibilant speech'.[10] For nine years he was a successful war-lord, before his decision to leave the 'fleeting riches and the contemptible glory of this present life' and to become a monk at Repton.[11] During his two years there 'he was initiated in canticles, psalms, hymns, prayers, and church routine'.[12] He was plainly eager for a life of even greater austerity, and indeed was not over-popular with his brother monks for refusing 'any draught of intoxicating drink ... except at the time of holy communion'.[13] Inevitably, the life of the desert called and he set out in search of a solitary place, arriving there on the feast of St Bartholomew, in whom he therefore placed his trust (*V. Guth.*, cc. 24–27: 86–93).

---

7. Sims-Williams (1990: 172–3, fn. 135), points out that Patrick Wormald's identification of Abbot Wilfrid with Bishop Wilfrith of Worcester (718–43 × 45) confirms an early dating for the *vita*.
8. *V. Guth.*, c. 16: 80–1 'valida pristinorum heroum facta ... adgregatis satellitum turmis, sese in arma convertit.'
9. *V. Guth.*, c. 34: 108–11 'imaginato sopore'.
10. *V. Guth.*, c. 34: 110–11 'strimulentas loquelas'.
11. *V. Guth.*, c. 18: 82–3 'caducas mundi divitias contemtibilemque temporalis vitae gloriam'.
12. *V. Guth.*, c. 23: 86–7 'canticis, psalmis, hymnis, orationibus moribusque inbutus'.
13. *V. Guth.*, c. 20: 84–5 'non ullius inebriantis liquoris ... excepto communicationis tempore'.

This is where the account of the solitary life begins, and Felix now presents the most striking sequence of chapters in his life of Guthlac, those stretching from the beginning of Guthlac's solitary life at Crowland to his victory over his demonic tormentors at the gates of hell. They deal with the temptations of a 'desert' saint – a desert of fenland marshes and waterways. Yet, this is a solitary life in the Antonian tradition, except that Guthlac's vision of the gates of hell, unparalleled in the Evagrian life of Anthony, is more akin to accounts of the visions of Fursey. This temptation sequence was treated as of a piece in the Guthlac homily that ends the Vercelli Book collection of English poetry and prose (Scragg, 1992: 383–92). What comes before the temptation sequence in the *vita* is preliminary fleshing out of the early life, chapters that end with a double statement of the arrival at Crowland on St Bartholomew's day (Roberts, 1977). Hitched to its other end is a series of tales and miracles filled with circumstantial references to validating figures, some named and obviously important in their time and therefore in Felix's eyes. The life is well stocked with incident: Guthlac puts devils to flight, feeds ravens and swallows, and heals the sick. He often displays a remarkable foreknowledge of varied events; and from his second year in Crowland he was visited daily by an angel of consolation.[14]

It has been said that the prophets of the desert have always drawn crowds. So it was with Guthlac. Quite apart from the two attendants who travel into the fenlands with Guthlac, once Guthlac was at Crowland others found their way there. In the saint's miracles that follow the temptation sequence witnesses are named. Some are closely connected with the Crowland hermitage. There is Tatwine, the old man who first ferried Guthlac to Crowland (*V. Guth.* c. 25: 88–9). And Beccel (Bettelin (1), F.), the companion who, jealous of Guthlac's position, once thought to kill him but remained faithfully with him and was trusted with Guthlac's dying confidences (*V. Guth.* cc. 35, 50: 110–13, 150–61). A strange legend was to grow up about Beccel (Bettelin (2), F.), that before his Crowland days he abducted the daughter of an Irish king, took her to England, pregnant, and while he was off seeking help for the birth of their child the unfortunate princess died with the child at the teeth of a wolf.[15] (A credible saint works wonders for a thin legend: compare, for example, the incursion of Chad into the legend of Wulfhad and Ruffin.) Beccel was to tell two people of Guthlac's dying confidences: Pege, the saint's sister who lived as a hermit nearby; and an anchorite named Ecgberht (*V. Guth.*, cc. 50, 53: 150–61, 166–71). Some others play a central part in a typical hagiographical episode. Among named companions of the future King Æthelbald are Ecga and Oba (*V. Guth.*, cc. 42, 45: 130–3, 138–41), but essentially we are told

---

14. *V. Guth.*, c. 50: 156–7 'angelum consolationis meae'.
15. Horstmann (1901: I. 162) 'lupinibus dentibus'. For discussion of this saint see Oswald (1954), Crawford (1968) and Thacker (1985: 18–19).

as little about them as about the 'paterfamilias' from the people of the Wissa, cured of blindness after Guthlac's death (*V. Guth.*, c. 53: 166–71). Abbot Wilfrid witnessed swallows settling on Guthlac's arms, knees and chest, and he turns up also with King Æthelbald (*V. Guth.*, cc. 39, 40: 120–7). A young East Anglian nobleman named Hwætred was freed from madness (*V. Guth.*, c. 41: 126–31). Headda, bishop of Lichfield (not Hedda of Winchester, F., as mistakenly identified in later tradition), when he visited Crowland, had in his entourage a certain Wigfrith, who declared that he could judge Guthlac because 'he had lived among the Irish, and there had seen false hermits and pretenders of various religions'.[16] Poor Brother Wigfrith. Bishop Headda was so impressed by Guthlac that he consecrated his oratory and Guthlac as a priest. And Guthlac, displaying not just his knowledge of things unknown but a very human pride in the recognition shown him, looked over to Wigfrith who was sitting some distance away and said to him: 'Brother Wigfrith, what do you now think of the cleric whom yesterday you promised to judge?'[17] The first bishops of the Middle Angles and the Mercians were Irish, or like Chad of Lichfield, trained in Ireland, and it would seem that Wigfrith's training had followed in that tradition.

Guthlac, Felix tells us, himself recognized, one day while praying, the signs of his approaching death. He was seized with shooting internal pain:[18]

> Now for seven days he was wasted by dire sickness and on the eighth day he reached his end. For he was taken ill on the Wednesday before Easter, and again on a Wednesday, on the eighth day, being the fourth day of the Easter festival, his illness came to an end and he went to be with the Lord.[19]

The length of Guthlac's illness and even the days of the week follow the summary of events set out by Bede for the last week of Cuthbert's life suspiciously closely, but, working from the evidence of the *Old English Martyrology* and of the later Latin calendars that Guthlac's feast was celebrated on 11 April, his death can be dated to 714, the year noted in the Anglo-Saxon Chronicle (Plummer, 1892: 42). In that year Easter day fell upon Sunday, 8 April. So 714 can be supported from Felix's narrative when checked against the Easter tables. Oddly,

16. *V. Guth.*, c. 46: 142–5 'inter Scottorum se populos habitasse et illic pseudo-anachoritas diversarum religionum simulatores vidisse'.
17. *V. Guth.*, c. 47: 144–7 'O frater Wigfrith, quomodo tibi nunc videtur ille clericus, de quo hesterno die iudicare promisisti?'
18. *V. Guth.*, c. 50: 152 'intimorum stimulatio'.
19. *V. Guth.*, c. 50: 152–3 'Septem enim diebus dira egritudine decoctus, octavo die ad extrema pervenit. Siquidem quarta feria ante Pascha egrotare coepit, et iterum octavo die, quarta feria, quarto etiam lumine paschalis festi, finita egritudine ad Dominum migravit.'

the Douai manuscript is a year out, specifying the date 715 in words added to Felix's account,[20] a date found widely from Ordericus Vitalis onwards, who after all worked up his *Abbreviatio* at Crowland. In his presentation of Guthlac's death Felix draws on techniques and wording used in the Evagrian life of Anthony as well as on Bede's Cuthbert, itself indebted to the Evagrian life. Charles W. Jones points out that 'Felix is no fumbling amateur': arguing that the *vita* 'follows a plot structure more clearly than any other saint's life of the period', he sees Felix as standing 'clear as a man of purpose and intelligence' (1947: 85–6). Harsher critics term Felix's style hisperic or hermeneutic, complaining about the excesses of Aldhelm or of the Irish.[21] Felix's life of Guthlac was widely read, for he constructed an instructive biography which remained popular even after simplified revisions came into circulation from the twelfth century. The thirteen manuscripts known to modern scholarship date from a late eighth-century or possibly early ninth-century fragment (flyleaves in British Library, Royal MS 4 A. xiv) to the early fourteenth-century Gotha collection of English, Welsh and Cornish saints (Colgrave 1956: 26–44).

Apart from Guthlac himself, the figure that stands out most of all in the life is another Mercian princeling, the future King Æthelbald, also a descendant of Icel. According to Felix he visited Guthlac often at Crowland. After Guthlac's death, Æthelbald, then an 'exile dwelling in distant parts', hastened to the tomb, to seek in prayer the intercession of his dead friend and counsellor.[22] That evening he saw a vision of 'the blessed Guthlac standing before him robed in angelic splendour' and prophesying that he would be king within a year (*V. Guth.*, 52: 164–5).[23] This penultimate chapter of the life ends: 'For from that time until the present day, his happiness as king over his realm has grown in succeeding years from day to day'.[24] Felix may have dedicated the life to an East Anglian king, but it is the Mercian king on whom he heaps praise. Had Abbess Ecgburh, daughter of King Aldwulf, a hidden agenda other than her wish to have commemorated a Repton alumnus? If we are to believe Boniface, Æthelbald was not generally known for the saintliness of his behaviour once he had gained the throne. Did Æthelbald, grandson of Penda's brother Eowa rather than, as his predecessors, a descendant of Penda, feel a need for his own royal saint?

Late in the ninth century, probably in response to Alfred's educational reforms in neighbouring Wessex, two major hagiographical

---

20. Colgrave notes the Douai insertion in his collations (1956: 58, note 19); see also his discussion (1956: 158, note 19).
21. Colgrave (1956: 17–18 and note 1) identifies borrowings from the *Hisperica Famina* which he notes as probably having come through Aldhelm.
22. *V. Guth.*, c. 52: 164–5 'exul ... in longinquis regionibus habitans'.
23. *V. Guth.*, c. 52: 164–5 'beatum Guthlacum coram adstantem angelico splendore amictum'.
24. *V. Guth.*, c. 52: 166–7 'Ex illo enim tempore usque in hodiernum diem infulata regni ipsius felicitas per tempora consequentia de die in diem crescebat.'

works were produced in Mercia, in English. Wærferth, bishop of Worcester, translated Gregory's Dialogues, according to Asser at the king's command. An anonymous translator, also Mercian, made a version of Bede's history, thereby giving accounts in English of the few Mercian saints Bede included. Foremost among them is Chad of Lichfield, first bishop of Mercia and Lindsey. Bede's is the only Latin life of the saint from Anglo-Saxon England. The twelfth-century English life (Vleeskruyer, 1953), derived from Bede, may have looked also to the Alfredian translation (Roberts, 2000). Bede apparently gained most of his Mercian information from Lastingham, the northern monastery founded by Chad's brother Cedd. He names other early Mercian bishops: Ceollach, Diuma, Jaruman, Seaxwulf, Trumhere and Winfrith; and Higebald (Hybald, F.), an abbot of Lindsey, territory sometimes under Northumbrian domination, sometimes Mercian. Higebald was probably from Bardney in Lindsey, notoriously the monastery that at first refused to house Oswald's bones, until, as Bede relates, miracles softened the hearts of the monks, and it has been persuasively argued that 'it may have been Mercian resentment that excluded Oswald' (Wallace-Hadrill, 1988: 104). Wherever Maserfelth was, it was, by the time Queen Osthryth of Mercia had Oswald's remains translated to Bardney Abbey, very likely under Mercian control (Stancliffe, 1995b: 85), and the cult was to become as important in Mercia as in Northumbria (Thacker, 1985: 4; Thacker, 1995: 127). It is noteworthy that pre-reformation church dedications to St Oswald cluster predominantly in the north and midlands (Binns, 1995: 268–71). Certainly with the ninth-century translation of Bede's history, Oswald can be said to have entered Mercian literature.

The *Old English Martyrology*, another Mercian production that goes back to this time (Whitelock, 1966: 96; Bately, 1988: 95, 103), frequently acknowledges Bede as its source for the saints of Britain. The midlands area is represented by notices for Chad and Higebald and for two saints of Britain unknown to Bede: Guthlac and his sister Pege. The Guthlac entry runs:

> On ðone ændleftan dæg þæs monðes bið Sancte Guthlaces geleornes ðæs anceran on Brytone, þæs lichoma resteð on þære stowe ðe is cweden Cruwland. His nama is on Læden belli munus, ond his halignes wæs sona getacnad æt his acennisse mid heofonlicum tacnum. Men gesegon cuman fægre hand of heofonum ond gesegnian þæs huses duru ðe he wæs on acenned, ond eft to heofonum gewat. Ond ymb an geár ðæs þe he on ancorsetle wunade, he geearnadede ðæt him spræc án Godes engel to æghwelce æfenne, ond eft on ærnemergen, ond him sæde heofonlico geryno.[25]

---

25. Kotzor (1981: II. 52–3) 'The death of the hermit St Guthlac in Britain, whose body lies in the place that is called Crowland, is on the 11th day of the month. His name is *belli munus* in Latin and his holiness was symbolised immediately at his

Just why were these details selected for so brief a digest of the life, given that the most striking event in Guthlac's legend was his being lifted into the air by evil spirits who carried him 'to the accursed jaws of hell'?[26]

We are given a few details only in the passage. First, there is the saint's day: his death (departure or 'geleornes') is 11 April. The word *geleornes* is one of the clues for the origins of this piece of English, perhaps pointing further north than the West Saxon kingdom, into Mercia, and corroborating composition in the age of Alfred. It is the sort of form that got tidied out in later copies of early texts, and it is replaced by 'gewytennys' in the other extant version of this entry in the *Old English Martyrology*. Brief straightforward notes of date, place and name are followed by two miracles: the miraculous hand presaging the saint's birth; and his morning and evening angelic visitor. The miraculous signs accompanying Guthlac's birth look to *V. Guth.*, cc. 4–7: 74–7, the sentence about the angel of consolation to Chapter 50. Both these miracles are found linked together, marked by neumes for singing, in part of a Guthlac office in a late eleventh-century Worcester manuscript:

> From the second year, said blessed Guthlac, in which I lived in this hermitage, I have always had, morning and evening, colloquy with an angel of the Lord who lightened my hardships, who gave me messages of eternal joy. Therefore my soul magnifies the Lord.
>   Magnificat
> Through the intervention of our saint Guthlac let us worship the Lord.
>   Psalm 1
> In that same birth of blessed Guthlac there was manifested his future through a heavenly miracle.
>   Psalm 2
> A radiant human hand, reaching with a cross to before the door of the house in which he was to be born, was seen plainly by all.
>   Psalm 3
> As all the onlookers marvelled, the hand marked the door with the sign of the cross and so was received into the heavens.[27]

---

cont.
   birth through heavenly signs. A lovely hand was seen to come from the heavens and mark the door of the house in which he was born, and it returned to the heavens. And one year after he was living in his hermitage he received the reward that an angel of God spoke to him each evening and again in the early morning and told him heavenly mysteries.'
26. *V. Guth.*, 31: 104–5 'ad nefandas tartari fauces'.
27. James (1909: 480) 'Secundo anno inquit beatus GUTHLACUS quo hanc heremum inhabitaui, mane ad (et) uespere, semper angelum domini colloquutorem habui, qui meos labores leuigabat qui michi aeterna gaudia nuntiabat hinc anima mea dominum magnificat. Magnificat. Per sanctum interuentorem nostrum Guthlacum

The great gift of the angel of consolation miracle leads into the Magnificat and is followed by a sentence in which the saint is invoked. This evening service begins the week's singing of the psalter. After the Venite the singing of the hand of God miracle begins. Psalm 2 follows very appropriately, its image of the son of God evoking the birth of Christ. In the *vita* a woman cries out: 'Stand still, for a man child who is destined to future glory has been born into this world.'[28] Is it mere coincidence that these two incidents from the *vita* form the neumed part of this late eleventh-century Guthlac office from Worcester? The *Old English Martyrology* refers over and over again to sacramentaries or massbooks (Roberts, 1997: 156–7), and it is possible therefore that its compiler saw as part of his task the explanation of events and festivals celebrated in the course of the year. Coincidentally, a collect found at the end of the 'John of Tynemouth' life of the Guthlac also draws on the angel of consolation theme (Horstmann, 1901: 2. 10–11, note 14). The context of worship and prayer may explain the selection of miracles in the *Old English Martyrology*, rather than direct consultation of Felix's life.[29] Neumes are not given for the Magnificat or for the first three psalms, where notes would not have been needed, and they cease with Psalm 4:

> Psalm 4.
> News of the strange miracle immediately spread through the country and made evident how great a boy had been born.
> Psalm 5.
> His varied life: a gentle boyhood, a military adolescence, the rest divine sanctity. He used the noble strength of his youth in war so that he might know what the practice of sacred warfare might entail. Blessed Guthlac's customary abstinence in his diet was a scrap of bread with water after sunset.[30]

---

cont.

adoremus dominum deum nostrum. Venite exult. [I]n ipso ortu beati guthlaci quis esset futurus aparuit miraculo celesti. Beatus uir. Visa est palam cunctis humana manus de celo fulgida cum cruce ante hostium domus puerperi porrecta. Quare f. Cunctis uidentibus admirabilis manus signo crucis signauit hostium et sic recepta est in celum.' The text in Birch (1881: 70–1) is more fully edited.

28. *V. Guth.*, c. 8: 76–7 'Stabilitote, quia futurae gloriae huic mundo natus est homo.'
29. The Hereford Breviary celebrates the 11th April with a prayer of intercession at Vespers, and at Matins the first six of nine brief readings draw on the content of *V. Guth.*, cc. 1–27; the opening two report on the miraculous hand (Frere and Brown, 1903–15: II. 140–2).
30. James (1909: 480) 'Domine quid mult. Mox inauditum miraculum patriam impleuit & quantus puer natus esset in mundo claruit. Cum inuocarem. Vita eius diuersa benigna pueritia bellicosa adholescentia cetera sanctitas theorica.
'Ingenuas uires adholescentie bellis exercuit et cetibus ut sciret quid diuine militie deberet conuersus.
'Ordinata erat beati Guthlaci abstinentiam uictus eius post solis occasum panis ordeaceus cum aqua.'

The three Guthlac sentences without neumes refer respectively to *V. Guth.*, cc. 9, 12–19 and 28: 76–7, 78–83 and 94–5.

A translator of the *Vita sancti Guthlaci* seems also to have been at work in Mercia during the age of Alfred, contributing to the revival of learning sparked off by the king's call for English versions of 'those books most needful for all men to know'. A recasting of this early translation, dated to the second half of the eleventh century, followed after a copy of the late West Saxon translation of the first books of the Bible.[31] This English life is neatly parcelled into prologue and 22 chapters. Its redactor edited it carefully, seeking to eliminate out-of-date or unfamiliar words and probably at the same time cutting out passages from the copy-text. Part of this English translation of Felix is paralleled in the last homily of the tenth-century Vercelli Book, which gives a better idea of the nature of the vocabulary of the original. This Guthlac homily, essentially an abstracted portion of the original translation excerpted for use as a reminder of the temptations of the hermit saint, focuses on the most striking elements of the legend (Roberts, 1986). The hermit saint undergoes three temptations, and each is defused, as in Felix's life, with a scriptural verse, given in full in the English version whereas readers of the Latin were expected to fill out etc.[32] First, Guthlac is tempted to despair, and cries out: 'In my distress I called upon the Lord' (Psalm 17:7):

In tribulatione invocavi Dominum, et reliqua. (*V. Guth.*, 29: 96)	'Min drihten, [in] minre geswencednesse ic [ðe] clypige 7 cige. Ac gehyr ðu me 7 me gefultuma in minum earfeðum.'[33] (Vercelli, lines 31–3)	'*In tribulatione mea invocavi Dominum, et reliqua.*' Þæt ys on englisc: 'Min drihten on minre geswincnysse ic þe to clypige, ac gehyr þu me and gefultuma me on minum earfeðum.' (Vespasian, p. 121: 81–7)

Next he is tempted to excessive fasting, and he draws strength from 'Let my enemies be turned back' (Psalm 55.10):

---

31. Gonser (1909). See Ker (1938: 18–40) for separation of Cotton Vespasian D. xxi, ff. 19–40, from Bodley, Laud Misc. 544.
32. The Vercelli text is cited from Scragg (1992), the Vespasian from Gonsor (1909) and the Latin from Colgrave (1956).
33. The manuscript has 'mid' for Scragg's 'in' and lacks Scragg's 'ðe'. He also amends the manuscript 'geswencendnesse'.

Convertantur inimici mei retrorsum, et reliqua. (*V. Guth.*, 30: 100)	'Min dryhten god, syn mine fynd a onhinder gecyrred, for ðan ic þe ongite 7 geþence, for ðan þu eart min scyppend!' (Vercelli, lines 76–8)	'Syn mine fynd, min drihten god, á on hinder gecyrde, forþon ic þe ongite and oncnawe, forþon þe þu eart min scyppend.' (Vespasian, p. 126: 74–8)

Then he is dragged through rough places, and he declares: 'The Lord is at my right hand, lest I should be moved' (Psalm 15:8):

Dominus a dextris est mihi, ne commovear. (*V. Guth.*, pp. 102, 104)	'Dryhten me is on ða swiðran healfe; for ðam ic ne beo oncyrred.' (Vercelli, lines 112–13)	'Drihten me ys on þa swyþran healfe, forþon ic ne beo oncyrred [fram þe].'[34] (Vespasian, p. 130: 162–4)

The articulation of narrative leads in each episode to familiar words of thought and prayer.[35] Together *Elene* and the Guthlac homily form a 'booklet' or distinct block of material within the Vercelli Book, probably brought together as complementary texts (Ó Carragáin, 1981: 75–8). *Elene*, one of the four Old English poems containing the name Cynewulf spelled out in runes, is acknowledged to be among the most shapely of Anglo-Saxon poems (Sisam, 1953b: 14).[36] By contrast, the Guthlac homily opens abruptly: 'Wæs þær in þam [fore]sprecenan iglande ...'. The 'aforesaid' island is, so far as this homily is concerned, previously unmentioned, but anyone who knew of Guthlac would have known that Crowland was his island. The ending of the Guthlac homily is more surprising. In the Vespasian life as in Felix, Bartholomew instructs Guthlac's demon persecutors to take him safely back to the place that they had taken him from, and a throng of blessed spirits celebrates his victory (*V. Guth.*, c. 33: 106–9), singing 'The saints shall go from strength to strength'.[37] The homily ends very differently:

---

34. Gonsor (1909: 130) emends 'for þe' out of his text.
35. For the identification of three episodes in the Vercelli homily see Pilch (1990: 315–6).
36. The *Fates of the Apostles* is also in the Vercelli Book; *Christ II* and *Juliana* are in the Exeter Book.
37. *V. Guth.*, c. 33: 106–9 'Ibunt sancti de virtute in virtutem.'

7 þa æfter þam fleah se haliga Guðlac mid þam apostole, s*ancte*
Bartholomei, to heofona rices wuldre, 7 hine se hælend þær
onfeng, 7 he þær leofað 7 rixað in heofona rices wuldre, a butan
ende on ecnesse. Amen, *fiat*.[38]

With the focal events of the Guthlac legend complete, and the demon
attackers defeated, the Vercelli compiler ends by stating that Guthlac
ascended to heaven in his patron saint's company and that Christ received
him there. The assumption that Bartholomew should ferry Guthlac to
heaven suits the material excerpted from the life, perhaps reflecting some
alternative traditional telling of the saint's death. Or maybe the Vercelli
homilist could not, any more than the *Guthlac A* poet, 'see the point of
Guthlac's return to the wilderness' (Jones, 1995: 286 n 77).

There is a surprising amount written about Guthlac in Old English,
far more than about Cuthbert. Both are important in calendars and
litanies, but only Guthlac of Crowland, with two poems in the Exeter
Book miscellany, is the subject of poetry in English from the Anglo-
Saxon period.[39] Neither of the Guthlac poems is a straightforward
narrative life, in the way that Cynewulf's *Juliana* is or his *Elene*. These
both relate closely to Latin sources: the divisions of *Elene* indeed
'correspond fairly closely' with the lections of the two nearest Latin
texts (Gradon, 1958: 19). The *Guthlac B* poet presents, so far as we
can see from what is extant of his poem, his version of Felix's account
of the saint's death as a struggle between Death and a soldier of Christ
(Rosier, 1970). It is an assured piece of writing, drawing effortlessly on
verbal reminiscences of a familiar canticle in leading into the stealthy
figure of Death (Roberts, 1979: 38–9) and building for Guthlac's
companion a growth towards understanding (Brown, 1996). Here are
the most elaborated tricks of Anglo-Saxon poetic diction: successive
and crossed alliteration, compounds piled high, sporadic decorative
rhyme, lengthy simile. This writer wished to manage in English as fine
a death-bed scene as the Evagrian Anthony and Bedan Cuthbert which
lay behind Felix's account. Clearly, he knew the genre very well, he
admired it, and he had therefore every reason to strike out anew with
his own interpretation of Guthlac's death.

Guthlac A is very different. A reflective poem, like the so-called
elegies it tends more to debate than narrative. It is the only saint's life of
the poetic corpus that does not follow an identified source text (Roberts,
1988). The poem opens with a short picture of a righteous soul at death.
An angel comes to meet the soul, to carry it forward to heaven over
broad ways, joyfully, amidst great light, an itinerary that draws on a well-

---

38. Scragg (1992: 392), lines 149–52 'And then, afterwards, the blessed Guthlac flew
    with St Bartholomew the apostle to the glory of the heavenly kingdom, and the
    saviour received him there. And He lives and reigns there in the glory of the
    heavenly kingdom, always, without end, in eternity. Amen. Fiat.'
39. The Guthlac poems are cited from Roberts (1979). Muir (1994) should be
    consulted for more recent work on these poems.

known homiletic exemplum, the three utterances at the going out of the soul. What way, asks the poet rhetorically, must a man behave on earth to merit such an end (lines 26–9)? The answer, that is the greater part of the poem, looks to the 'desert' temptation of Guthlac as one pattern by which heaven can be attained. A lot of ink has been wasted trying to prove that this poet did or did not use Felix in his creation of Guthlac's temptation, pointlessly. Where Felix created a narrative, this poet is intent on exploring Guthlac's opposition to temptations that beset a solitary, a chosen soldier of Christ.[40] There is little circumstantial detail, and human companions play no part. There is not even Tatwine to ferry Guthlac through water-logged fens: there are no fens or waterways; and the unnamed place of temptation is revealed by God. Devils cluster terrifyingly about in nearby hills. The one constant is the teaching of Guthlac's angel of consolation, here his 'sawelcund hyrde' (spiritual guardian, lines 317–18), with whom he often talked. What man, we are asked, was greater than Guthlac?

> Hwylc wæs mara þonne se?
> An oretta   ussum tidum,
> cempa, gecyðeð   þæt him Crist fore
> worldlicra má   wundra gecyðde.[41]

This Guthlac erects a cross to mark his chosen place in his desert (lines 179–80). He opposes demons with forceful words: 'Her sceal min wesan| eorðlic eþel, nales eower leng';[42] and he taunts them with the horrors of hell (lines 623–36, 666–83a). It would be easy to visualize him using a whip on them, as in the Harley Roll (Roundel XII). Bartholomew adjudicates command of 'þy wonge' (that field, line 702) to him, whereupon it transmutes into a 'sigewong' (victory field, line 743) and is described as a green field ('se grena wong', line 746), a metaphor for paradise attained. With this image of how one man merited heaven in the age of our times ('in ussera| tida timan', lines 753–4), the poet circles back to his framing materials. It is an interesting coincidence that the last homily in the Vercelli Book relates to the desert temptation of Guthlac, but the *Guthlac A* poet need have known some sentences only of the parallel chapters of Felix's *vita*, whether in readings, prayer or song. He seems not to have known the bleak flatness of the fens, and it is unlikely that he had before him Felix's text. Or at least, it is not possible to match sentences from Felix's Latin with sections of his poem as it is for

---

40. The 'miles christi' theme is noted in particular by Kurtz (1926: 144–6); Roberts (1981); Hill (1981); Iamartino (1992). The eremitic background is sensitively explored by Clayton (1996).
41. *Guthlac A*, lines 401b–4 'One hero, a soldier, in our times testifies that Christ manifested in his sight more miracles on earth.'
42. *Guthlac A*, lines 260b–1 '(This) earthly dwelling-place here is to be mine, not yours any longer.'

Guthlac B. The *Guthlac A* poet's Crowland is visualized afresh with properties from lives of other hermits, let us say the hills of the Evagrian life of Anthony rather than fenland waterways about Crowland, and some other place of composition that the East Midlands might therefore be sought. There is, after all, evidence to support the foundation of St Guthlac's collegiate church in Hereford in King Æthelbald's reign (Sims-Williams, 1990: 60 and note 25; 146 and note 16). Some recent critics, arguing from content, have proposed that *Guthlac A*, in its monastic interests, reflects the context of the Benedictine revival (Conner, 1993a: 163; 1993b; Jones, 1995), but an earlier dating cannot be ruled out (Fulk, 1992: 399–400).

By contrast with the amount of documentation for Guthlac of Crowland, two lists in English, of 'þa halgan þe on Angelcynne restað' (Liebermann, 1889: 1 'the holy men and women who lie among the English') and of 'Godes sa*nctum* þe on Engla lánde ærost reston' (Liebermann, 1889: 9 'God's saints who first lay in England'), found together in early eleventh-century manuscripts, furnish the earliest written evidence for many of the saints of Mercia. Their openings are complementary. Augustine, who brought Christianity to the English, is named first in the 'halgan' list, whereas the 'sanctum' list, noting saints and their burial places, opens with Alban, Britain's protomartyr. The 'halgan' list, organized by the reception of Christianity which fans out from Augustine's mission, more or less people by people through the marriage of Christian princesses to royal pagan husbands, provides a summary of notable royal converts and benefactors. It is perhaps tendentious to differentiate the lists as historical and hagiographical, but that they are different in kind is signalled not just by the choice of 'halgan' and 'Godes sanctum' in their respective openings. Strikingly, not all the people named in the first list are granted a preceding 'sancte', but 'sancte' is general in the second. The 'halgan' list is essentially a who's who for the royal families of the Anglo-Saxons. Mercian saints, and some legendary material, appear in the list because of the marriage of Eormenburg of Kent (or 'Domne Eue' (Ermenburga, F.)) to Merewalh, a son of Penda of Mercia. Their children were Mildburh (Milburga, F.), abbess of Wenlock, Mildred, abbess of Minster-in-Thanet after her mother's death, and, less credibly, Mildgyth and Merefin.[43] A letter Boniface wrote to a monk at Wenlock makes it clear that Mildburh was then abbess of Wenlock (Sims-Williams, 1990: 98–9), and the 'sanctum' list records that she was buried there. There are no other literary records of any substance from before the Conquest. Another grandchild of Penda, Werburgh (Werburga, F.), daughter of Wulfhere of Mercia and a Kentish princess named Eormenhild (Ermengild, F.), also occurs in the 'sanctum' list as buried first at Hanbury in Staffordshire and later at Chester. The

---

43. See Rollason (1978, 1983); Sims-Williams (1990: 50) doubts the existence of Merefin and Mildgyth.

earliest evidences of a Werburgh legend again come from post-Conquest sources (Horstmann, 1887: xvi–xxvi; Thacker, 1982).

Alban, who is described as a 'martir on Breotone' and given top billing in the 'sanctum' list, is followed by Columba of Iona. Thereafter the organizing principle of the 'sanctum' list is roughly geographical, moving southwards according to the places where God's saints lie. Immediately after Columba come saints buried in Northumbria, Cuthbert first, followed by three further Northumbrian entries: Oswald; John of Beverley; and three saints buried at Ripon, Ecgbyrht (Egbert, F.), Wilfred and Wihtburh. None of the Monkwearmouth–Jarrow saints of the *Martyrology* is included: no Benedict Biscop, Ceolfrith, Eastorwine. There is no entry for Abbess Hilda of Whitby. Eadberht (Edbert, F.) and Ethelwald (Ethilwald, F.) of Lindisfarne are not included, and Aidan appears much later in the list, because his body lies with Patrick and many other saints in Glastonbury. The Mercian entries begin with Chad and Cedd, named together with the otherwise unknown Ceatta for Lichfield. The ratio of Northumbrian to Mercian saints has shifted strikingly from that of the *Old English Martyrology*, with a proportionately far greater representation of saints from the Mercian area.[44] The brief statement about Guthlac, which notes that his body lies in Crowland and that the 'mynster' (monastery or, later, abbey) is in the middle of the 'Girwan fænne' (the fens of the Gyrwe people), is fairly typical of a longish entry in this list. Some of these Mercian entries supply the first evidence for the cults of midland saints whose legends were to blossom in the later Middle Ages. There are, for example, more descendants of Penda: his daughters Cyneburg (Cyniburg, F.) and Cyneswith at Castor near Peterborough, and Edburga of Bicester; his grandsons Wulfhad and Ruffin at Stone, Rumwold at Buckingham. Later Mercian princes are also named: Wigstan at Repton (Wistan, F.), Kenelm at Winchcombe. It may well be, as Thacker argues, that the cults are obscure because of 'the extinction of the Mercian royal house and the traditions associated with it after the Viking invasions and the West Saxon reconquest which followed them' (1985: 18). He points to the evidence for the celebration of ancient cults and the translation of relics to new homes from the early tenth century. Mercian saints are, as we have seen, well represented in the 'sanctum' list, a recognized part of the heritage of early eleventh-century England. Their legends continued to grow and multiply, in Latin, in English and in French, but they are not part of the literary tradition extant from the historical kingdom of Mercia. As Eckenstein (1896: 108) observed long ago, 'the historical information we have about them is meagre'.[45]

---

44. The greater representation of entries for the middle of the country by comparison with the north is plotted on a map in Rollason (1978: 88).
45. There lurk in the shadows numbers of less well attested figures. Listed by Farmer are: hermits (Adulf, Adnoth, Arnulf, Barloc, Etheldrith of Crowland, Hardulph of Bredan, Huna, Modwenna, Tibba); abbots (Aldwyn of Peartney,

With Guthlac of Crowland, it is different. There is a body of
literature, both from the period when Mercia dominated much of
England and from the waning years of the much diminished Mercian
kingdom of later Anglo-Saxon England. Across time Guthlac's legend
too altered and was made anew. Odd stories crept into the records.
Quite what was tradition, what invention, is hard to tell, and perhaps,
from the literary point of view, irrelevant. Henry of Avranches makes
much of a lost psalter, and he explains the separate hermitage of Pega
as enforced by her brother after a demon took on her form to tempt
him to break fast before sunset: Guthlac required her to move further
away, and they did not see each other for the rest of their lives. A less
stylish English poem has the devil in 'Forme of Godes aungel' attempt
to 'him brynge . into glotenye'.[46] According to the pseudo-Ingulf
tradition Pege's holiness was such that the church bells in Rome rang
out for an hour when she arrived there as a pilgrim; she left a scourge
and psalter belonging to her brother in Abbot Kenulph's hands when
she went to Crowland for the elevation of Guthlac's relics (Riley, 1893:
9). Whether or not you can believe in Kenulph as the second abbot and
successor of Guthlac,[47] there does seem to be something behind the
psalter, and perhaps the trigger for it lies in the tale (*V. Guth.*, c. 37:
115–19) in which Guthlac writes on parchment stolen by a jackdaw.
Henry Longchamp's seal shows Bartholomew giving a scourge to
Guthlac, who is holding a book, and early in the sixteenth century the
abbey still had a great book called 'St Guthlac's Psalter' as a relic on
the altar.[48] Whereas for many of the saints of Mercia there is little
evidence, the legend of Guthlac of Crowland undoubtedly engaged the
attention of many audiences throughout the Anglo-Saxon age and
beyond. In the words of the *Guthlac A* poet, Guthlac became 'mongum
... bysen on Brytene' (an example for many in Britain, lines 174–5)
once he took possession of his hermitage. Guthlac's influence is
visible, the evidence remains, a trail of prose and poetry from the
eighth century forwards.

---

cont.

    Botulf of Icanhoe, Credan 2, Elstan); abbesses (Cyniburg 3, Ethelburg 1,
    Hildelith, Osith) and patrons (Cyniburg 2, Eudelm, Frideswide, Wendreda);
    bishops (Egwyn, Erkenwald); monks (Herefrith, Owin from Chad's story);
    possible Britons (Aldate, Wannard); kings venerated in Mercia (Ethelbert 2, the
    East Anglian king venerated at Hereford, Sebbi of the East Saxons); mere names
    (Cett from the 'sanctum' list); and martyrs who died at the hands of the Vikings
    (the hermits Fremund, Tancred, Torthred and Tova of Thorney, Abbot Hedda of
    Peterborough).

46. Bolton (1954: 227, lines 147–70 of the Cambridge, Corpus Christi College 145
    version of the *South English Legendary*).
47. Chibnall (1969: xxviii) suggests that his name was probably abstracted from a
    boundary marker at Crowland and rationalized as a forgotten abbot.
48. See Roberts (1970) and Henderson (1985) for fuller information on such
    traditions.

Part II

Parallel Cultures

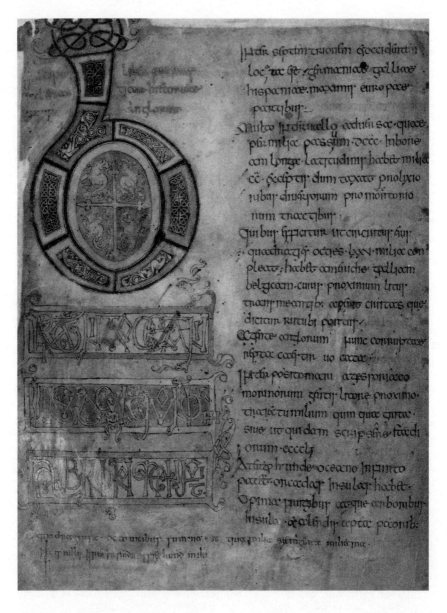

The Tiberius Bede, London, B.L., Cotton MS Tib. c.ii, f. 5v © The British Library, courtesy of the British Library Board

6 Wales and Mercia, 613–918

T. M. Charles-Edwards

The history of Wales between the rise of Mercia under Penda (d. 655) and Mercia's incorporation into a united England is like crossing a river in a dense fog, jumping from one insecure stepping-stone to another.[1] It is possible to have a broad conception of the political culture and situation of Wales in the seventh century and again in the ninth; these are the banks of the river, not always secure, but in-between all is guesswork. Mainly because of Bede, there are pockets of narrative material for the seventh century; for the end of the period Asser's Life of King Alfred is brief but invaluable on his native country;[2] by then, also, the *Annales Cambriae* were becoming a slightly less exiguous record.[3] Alongside such standard sources we have some sculpture, though the richest period in Welsh epigraphy was over by 650;[4] poetry, of which most, at least, offered a retrospective view of the seventh century from the vantage-point of the ninth and tenth;[5] a tenth-century collection of royal genealogies;[6] the *Historia Brittonum* of 829–830 (and also later versions), which displayed more interest in Northumbria than in Mercia;[7] and some charters, of varying

---

1. W. Davies, *Wales in the Early Middle Ages* (1982: 90–114); J. E. Lloyd, *A History of Wales* (1939: 178–202).
2. Asser, *Life of King Alfred*, ed. W. H. Stevenson (1904), esp. cc. 79–80, transl. S. Keynes and M. Lapidge, *Alfred the Great: Asser's Life of King Alfred and Other Contemporary Sources* (1983: 93–6).
3. *Annales Cambriae*, ed. E. Phillimore, 'The Annales Cambriae and the Old Welsh genealogies from Harleian MS. 3859', *Y Cymmrodor*, 9 (1888: 141–83). This text is reprinted with a few additions from later MSS in *Nennius, British History, and The Welsh Annals*, ed. and transl. J. Morris (1980). The principal account is K. Hughes, 'The Welsh-Latin Chronicles: Annales Cambriae and Related Texts', *Proc. Brit. Acad.*, 59 (1973: 233–58), reprinted in her *Celtic Britain in the Early Middle Ages* (1980: 67–85). For other discussion, see M. Lapidge and R. Sharpe, *A Bibliography of Celtic-Latin Literature* (1985: no. 135).
4. V. E. Nash-Williams, *The Early Christian Monuments of Wales* (1950); this corpus is currently being revised.
5. J. Rowland, *Early Welsh Saga Poetry* (1990), provides texts, translations and an extensive discussion.
6. *Early Welsh Genealogical Tracts*, ed. P. C. Bartrum (1966: 9–13).
7. 'Historia Brittonum', ed. E. Faral, *La Légende arthurienne*, 3 (1929: 4–62) (Chartres, as far as it goes, in parallel with Harleian). Faral's Harleian text is reprinted with a translation in *Nennius, British History, and the Welsh Annals*, ed.

reputation.[8] In addition to such sources, there is the single best-known monument of the period, Offa's Dyke; yet this is better appreciated for what it tells us of the governmental capacities deployed by a Mercian king than for any light it sheds on conditions in Wales (see Hill, Chapter 12 in this volume).[9]

Wales and the Britons

Bede was interested in seventh-century Britons for only three reasons: because they failed to preach Christianity to the English; because they were at odds with Rome over Easter; and because they were involved in the struggles between Mercia and Northumbria for dominance in Britain. There was no reason, therefore, why he should drop more than the odd hint about the political shape of Wales. Furthermore, we should be quite clear at the outset that Bede had no concept of Wales or of the Welsh in the modern sense; neither, more importantly, did the Welsh themselves. For both, the Britons as a whole were the ancient enemies of the English; they included the Britons of Armorica, Dumnonia and Cornwall, and also of what is now northern England and southern Scotland.[10] The modern Welsh term for themselves, Cymry, may be first attested in a poem in praise of Penda's ally Cadwallon of Gwynedd;[11] yet, as the name Cumberland attests, it was to be many centuries before *Cymry* came to mean only the Welsh rather than the

---

cont.

    and transl. J. Morris (1980); a later recension is *The Historia Brittonum, 3, The 'Vatican Recension'*, ed. D. N. Dumville (1985).

8. The Book of Llandaf, ed. J. Gwenogvryn Evans and J. Rhys, *The Text of the Book of Llan Dâv* (1893), of which pp. xliii–xlviii contain an edition of the marginalia from the Lichfield Gospels; on the Llandaff charters, see W. Davies, *The Llandaff Charters* (1979); 'Vitae Sanctorum Britanniae et Genealogiae', ed. A. W. Wade-Evans, *History and Law Series*, ix (1944): 124–36 = Vita S. Cadoci, §§ 55–68, contain the Llancarfan charters. D. Jenkins and M. E. Owen, 'The Welsh Marginalia in the Lichfield Gospels. Part I', *Cambridge Medieval Celtic Studies*, 5 (1983: 37–66), and 'The Welsh Marginalia in the Lichfield Gospels. Part II: The "Surexit" Memorandum', *Cambridge Medieval Celtic Studies*, 7 (1984: 91–120).

9. C. Fox, *Offa's Dyke* (1955); D. Hill (1974a), 'Offa's and Wat's Dykes – some exploratory work on the frontier between Celt and Saxon', in *Anglo-Saxon Settlement and Landscape*, ed. T. Rowley, British Archaeological Reports 6 (1974: 102–7); Hill (1974b), 'The interrelation of Offa's and Wat's Dyke', *Antiquity*, 48 (1974: 309–12); Hill (1977), 'Offa's and Wat's Dykes: some aspects of recent work, 1972–1976', *Transactions of the Lancashire and Cheshire Antiquarian Society*, 79 (1977: 21–33); F. Noble, *Offa's Dyke Reviewed*, ed. M. Gelling, British Archaeological Reports, Brit. Ser. 114 (1983); M. Gelling, *The West Midlands in the Early Middle Ages* (1992: 101–19); W. Davies, *Patterns of Power in Early Wales* (1990: 62–7).

10. T. M. Charles-Edwards, 'Language and society among the insular Celts, AD 400–1000', in M. J. Green (ed.), *The Celtic World* (1995: 711–13).

11. Moliant Cadwallon, ed. R. G. Gruffydd, 'Canu Cadwallon ap Cadfan', in R. Bromwich and R. Brinley Jones (eds), *Astudiaethau ar yr Hengerdd* (1978: 27–34), at 29, ll. 12, 28.

Britons. Throughout the entire period dealt with in this book, the Britons of Wales conceived of themselves as forming one people with other Britons to the North and to the South: all might be called, indifferently, *Brittones* in Latin, *Brython* or *Cymry* in Welsh. For this chapter, therefore, 'Welsh' will mean 'Britons who lived in the area later defined as Wales'.

There is only one qualification to this inclusive sense of Britishness, embracing people who lived from Stirling to Nantes, namely that by the end of our period there was also another sense of *Brittones*, co-existing with the first, according to which it applied especially to the Welsh. In this new sense an annal for 722 could talk both of the Cornishmen and of the South Britons, *Dexterales Brittones*, meaning the southern Welsh.[12] Asser has the same double sense of Britain and the Brittones.[13] By his time, therefore, in the late ninth century, and that of the earliest extant version of the *Annales Cambriae* in the tenth, the subject of this chapter had a recognized identity.

The Welsh and the rise of Mercia

By the end of the seventh century the Mercians were no longer strictly the 'Marcher People', *Mierce*.[14] They now had western satellites from the Cheshire Plain over into the Severn Valley and down as far as the mouth of the Wye: Westerne, Wreocensæte, Magonsæte, and Hwicce.[15] The Welsh frontier in the late seventh century was a place where ambitious princes of the *Iclingas*, the Mercian royal lineage, might hope to make a reputation as war-leaders: Guthlac's acquaintance with the Welsh was acquired during his period as a young dynastic hopeful, and hence an exile among the Britons, rather than from the situation of his parental residence among the Middle Angles.[16]

The borderlands between the Welsh and the English were, for more than a generation, *c.* 610–658 and perhaps as late as 679, the target of

---

12. *Annales Cambriae*, ed. Phillimore, s.a. 722.
13. *Asser's Life of King Alfred*, ed. Stevenson, has both Britain = the island of Britain – p. 1 (dedication), cc. 21, 49 – and Britain = Wales, cc. 7, 79, 80.
14. N. P. Brooks, 'The formation of the Mercian Kingdom', in S. Bassett (ed.), *The Origins of Anglo-Saxon Kingdoms* (1989b: 162).
15. Texts: D. N. Dumville, 'The Tribal Hidage: an introduction to its texts and their history', in Bassett (ed.), *The Origins of Anglo-Saxon Kingdoms* (1989b: 225–30). Discussion: W. Davies and H. Vierck, 'The contexts of the Tribal Hidage: social aggregates and settlement patterns', *Frühmittelalterliche Studien*, **8** (1974: 223–93); C. R. Hart, 'The Tribal Hidage', *TRHS* **21** (1971: 133–57); Brooks, 'The formation of the Mercian kingdom', (1989a: 159, 160–1, 167).
16. *Felix, Life of St Guthlac*, ed. and transl. B. Colgrave (1956), cc. 16–18, 34 (to be driven into exile was a common fate of members of a dynasty contending for the kingship; two other examples are Æthelbald, Felix, Life, c. 40, Cædwalla of Wessex, Bede, *HE* IV. 15; for the tensions arising from the presence of exiles in another country, see the letter of Waldhere, bishop of London, to Berhtwald of Canterbury, *EHD* i, no. 164, and Bede, *HE* II. 12).

Northumbrian military intervention. The principal events are recorded by Bede; what makes a proper interpretation difficult is not just Bede's own Northumbrian standpoint and particular concerns, but problems over the dating and interpretation of Welsh sources. The first attested intervention led to the battle of Chester, the final victory of Æthelfrith, 'the most rapacious wolf', 'most desirous of glory, who ravaged the people of the Britons more than all the leaders of the English.'[17] Æthelfrith's opponents, for Bede, were simply Britons;[18] the *Chronicle of Ireland*, here probably derived from Iona annals, dates the battle to 613 and states that Selyf ap Cynan was killed.[19] The Welsh genealogies attribute Selyf to a dynasty associated with Powys, a kingdom not named in a contemporary source until the ninth century. This is consistent with the notion that the kingdom of Powys was the successor to the Romano-British *civitas* of the Cornovii, within whose territory Chester was placed.[20] Æthelfrith's victory thus threatened to establish Northumbrian rather than Mercian power at the northern end of the Welsh borderlands.

Although Æthelfrith died in battle only three years later, and his successor was of the Deiran rather than the Bernician dynasty, this made no apparent change to Northumbrian interest in the Britons. Indeed, Edwin, king of Northumbria 616–633, remained until the end of the Middle Ages the emblem of English hostility to the Welsh. His power appears to have exceeded anything achieved by his predecessor; according to Bede he subjugated Anglesey, the heart of Gwynedd, as well as the Isle of Man, and so established Northumbrian power in the Irish Sea.[21] When Edwin was killed at the battle of Hatfield in 633, his defeat came about through an alliance of the king of Gwynedd, Cadwallon, and a young Mercian prince, Penda.[22] It led to a year during which Northumbria was increasingly dominated by Cadwallon until he unexpectedly fell in battle against Oswald, Æthelfrith's son.[23]

Oswald was described by Bede as enjoying a power similar to that of Edwin.[24] That this entailed intervention in the Welsh borderlands emerges from the location of his last battle, fought in 642, in which he

---

17. Bede, *HE* I. 34. For the nature and background to this story see C. Stancliffe, 'The British Church and the mission of Augustine', in R. Gameson (ed.), *Saint Augustine of Canterbury and the Conversion of England* (1999: 124–30).
18. Bede, *HE* II. 2.
19. *The Annals of Ulster*, ed. S. Mac Airt and G. Mac Niocaill (1983), s.a. 613.3 (the Annals of Ulster are usually the best representative of the Chronicle of Ireland which ran up to 911).
20. M. Gelling, *The West Midlands in the Early Middle Ages* (1992: 27–8), outlines the issues.
21. Bede, *HE* II. 5, 9. For the possible significance of this achievement, see J. R. Maddicott, 'Two frontier states: Northumbria and Wessex, c. 650–750', in J. R. Maddicott and D. M. Palliser (eds), *The Medieval State: Essays Presented to James Campbell* (2000: 39–40).
22. Bede, *HE* II. 20.
23. Bede, *HE* III. 1.
24. Bede, *HE* II. 5; III. 6.

was killed by an army led by Penda. This battle was called Maserfelth by Bede, but the battle of Cogwy in the *Annales Cambriae* and the *Historia Brittonum*.[25] Clare Stancliffe has recently reconsidered the evidence for the location of Maserfelth and has confirmed the traditional site of Oswestry.[26] The situation of the battle, close to what became the western boundary of one of the Mercian satellites, either of the Westerne or of the Wreocensæte, has reasonably been explained in the context of an alliance between Penda and the Welsh, probably of Powys.[27] Bede does not allude to any such alliance in 642: its existence is inferred from the site of the battle, much later Welsh sources, which on their own would not merit any confidence, and the analogy of the alliance between Penda and Cadwallon in 633. The suggestion is, therefore, that the alliance of 633 against one Northumbrian king was repeated, though perhaps with different Welsh participation, in 642 against another Northumbrian king. Both in 633 and in 642 the force behind the alliance was the desire to resist or even to destroy a military hegemony established by the Northumbrians. The contexts of the two battles, of Hatfield in 633 and of Maserfelth in 642, were different. In 633 Cadwallon and Penda were challenging Edwin, whose ancestral kingdom was Deira, and they were making this challenge close to the Deiran frontier. In 642 Oswald, like Edwin, king of the Northumbrians, but a Bernician, had led an army to a site lying in-between the Mercian territories and those of the Welsh. By 642, the leadership of the alliance may well have passed to the Mercian ruler Penda. According to the *Historia Brittonum*, in 655 the king of Gwynedd, Cadafael, was one of Penda's many allies in his last expedition, which issued in Penda's defeat and death at the hands of Oswald's younger brother Oswiu, at the battle of the Winwaed, close to Leeds. Both Mercia and the Welsh were, therefore, involved in the struggle for military overlordship in Britain in the period *c.* 625–679.

The Mercians came to secure their overlordship over 'the Southern English' by opposing the Northumbrian ambition to dominate the English frontier zone with the Britons from Lothian to Shropshire. As the career of Cadwallon demonstrated, the rule of the English in Northumbria remained fragile. Until Edwin conquered Elmet and Oswald (so it seems) subjugated the last remaining territory of the Gododdin, English Northumbria was nearly surrounded by British

25. Bede, *HE* III. 9; *Annales Cambriae*, s.a. 644; *Historia Brittonum*, ed. Faral, c. 65.
26. C. Stancliffe, 'Where was Oswald killed?', in C. Stancliffe and E. Cambridge (eds), *Oswald: From Northumbrian King to European Saint* (1995b: 84–96). A different view, but after much less thorough discussion, is taken by M. Gelling, 'The Early History of Western Mercia', in S. Bassett (ed.), *The Origins of Anglo-Saxon Kingdoms* (1989b: 188–9).
27. J. Rowland, *Early Welsh Saga Poetry* (1990: 124–5); Stancliffe, 'Oswald, "Most holy and most victorious king"' (1995a: 56).

kingdoms.[28] The rapidity of Northumbrian advance between the beginning of the reign of Æthelfrith and the death of Oswald suggests that power must have been built around regular plunder and huge land grants available to the king's military followers. Its expansion was so fast that it cannot have been sustained by a war of English peasants seeking to drive British peasants off the land. To a somewhat lesser extent the same must be true of Wessex.[29] There was no reason why extensive conquests of British territory in northern Britain should not lead to conquest of British territory in what became Wales: one has to remember that there was no such thing as Wales in the later sense, and no reason to think that while, say, Elmet was a reasonable target for attack, Powys and Gwynedd were not. Nor was it inevitable that Mercia would ally with the Welsh against northern kings from Æthelfrith to Oswald: Eowa, a Mercian king (and ancestor of the eighth-century kings Æthelbald and Offa), may well have supported the Northumbrians.[30] The fact remains that Penda did ally with the Welsh and that his alliance set him on the road to overlordship over England south of the Humber.

The Welsh and the Mercian supremacy

After the battle of the Trent in 679, and still more after the death of Ecgfrith in battle against the Picts at Nechtansmere in 685, Northumbria ceased to be a threat to the Southumbrian hegemony of the Mercian kings. No longer did the Welsh and the Mercians make common cause in order to withstand Northumbrian invasion. This period of about 150 years, from 679 to 825, is the least well understood in the whole of Welsh history. Hardly any interest was shown by external observers and we are reduced for the most part to making deductions from the exiguous entries in the *Annales Cambriae*.

   The Mercian hegemony had three zones. In the centre was Mercia proper, including such places as Repton, Lichfield and Tamworth, the land that was Mercia before Penda and his sons made their kingdom the dominant force in southern England. Wrapped around this core were satellite peoples, probably mostly with their own rulers, but often colonized by Mercian nobles. Beyond this zone lay another, more loosely dependent, indeed sometimes entirely independent, consisting of kingdoms with their own dynasties, quite separate from that of the Mercians. Around the core, therefore, there was an inner and an outer

---

28. For Elmet, see Bede, *HE* IV. 23/21; *Historia Brittonum*, c. 63; for Lothian, K. H. Jackson, 'Edinburgh and the Anglian occupation of Lothian', in P. Clemoes (ed.), *The Anglo-Saxons: Studies Presented to Bruce Dickins* (1959: 35–47).
29. Ine's Laws, 23.3; 24.2; 32; 33; 54.2; 74, ed. F. Liebermann, *Die Gesetze der Angelsachsen* (vol. i, 1903; ii, part i, 1906; ii, part ii, 1912; iii, 1916), i. 100–2, 114, 120.
30. Brooks, 'The Formation of the Mercian Kingdom' (1989a: 166).

zone. The inner zone consisted of such peoples as those who inhabited the various Middle Anglian regions, of Surrey and Essex, and also of the Westerne, the Wreocensæte and Magonsæte along the Welsh border. In the outer zone lay the kingdoms of Kent, Sussex, the East Angles and Wessex. The rulers in the inner zone, even if they started as kings, were reduced to sub-royal status; and some may never have had kings but only *principes* or *duces*; the rulers in the outer zone were kings, and when the Mercians imposed their own candidates, this was violently resented.

What is difficult if not impossible to determine is whether the Welsh were part of this structure. If they were, they evidently belonged to the outer zone; if they were not, they belonged to a different political sphere, as did the Northumbrians. Not all kingdoms in the outer zone were in precisely the same degree of subservience to the king of the Mercians. Kent was a special case because of the desire of Mercian kings to impose their own candidates as archbishops of Canterbury. The evidence is simply not sufficient to sustain definite conclusions, but a reasonable case can be made for seeing the Welsh kingdoms as part of the outer zone of the Mercian hegemony, just as their northern brethren were sometimes subject to the Northumbrians, sometimes to the Picts, and occasionally resisted both their powerful neighbours.

In the second quarter of the seventh century, as we have seen, leadership in the alliance between the Welsh of Gwynedd and Powys and the Mercians shifted from Gwynedd to Mercia. The effect was that the north Welsh kings, those principally concerned with Northumbrian aggression, were normally, though perhaps not invariably, clients of the king of the Mercians. Their clientship may not have extended beyond the military sphere: when Penda summoned kings and 'royal leaders' to withstand Northumbrian attack or to invade Northumbria, Welsh kings received the summons along with English rulers, both of the outer and the inner zones.[31] At the end of the period, in the late ninth century, we can trace the outlines of a process by which Mercian authority in Wales was undermined. By this stage, it seems that Welsh subjection to Mercian kings had been more widespread geographically and more extensive in terms of the obligations imposed than it had been in the mid-seventh century. The clientship that Welsh kings sought to escape in the ninth century was not the same as the clientship of the age of Penda. Unfortunately, we have only the odd hint to guide us to an understanding of what had happened between 679 and 850, between the end of Northumbrian overlordship in southern England and the years immediately preceding the arrival of the Viking Great Army.

---

31. *Historia Brittonum*, cc. 64–5. There is nothing to prove that any Welsh were included in 'all the southern peoples' summoned by Wulfhere to fight against Northumbria (Stephen, *Life of Wilfrid*, c. 20), but it is quite likely that some were.

Two views of relations between Mercia and Wales

Two stories may be told on the basis of the extant evidence. They are entirely incompatible, but neither is demonstrably wrong. They may be set out briefly so that a judgement can be made as to which is the most likely to be correct.

The first story denies the existence of any settled Mercian overlordship over Wales in the period 679–796, from the battle of the Trent to the death of Offa, succeeded after a few months by Coenwulf.[32] In order to sustain its view of what happened, the first story draws a sharp contrast between the Welsh as military clients of Mercia in the mid-seventh century and the much more extensive subjection of the ninth. The military clientship of the seventh century was a voluntary arrangement dictated by Northumbrian aggression. Its voluntary character is underlined by changes in leadership: Penda had been a client of Cadwallon; he became the overlord of Cadafael. The context was of a landscape in which there was not yet a sharp divide between land settled by Britons and English. There were still many pockets of British speakers, illustrated by place-names such as Walton as well as many Britons mixed with, and often the tenants of, English neighbours.[33] This was especially so in Northumbria: in terms of population, Bernicia, the most successfully aggressive English king-dom of the seventh century, was the least English. In the mid-seventh century, also, English Christianity was assisted, though not usually initiated, by Welsh neighbours and subjects.[34]

In the period 670–768 Christianity came to divide Britons from English, no longer as pagan versus Christian, as in the sixth century, but as two Churches that refused communion one with the other on the grounds of heresy.[35] Archbishop Theodore, as well as Wilfrid, bishop of York, regarded those Britons and Irish that adhered to the 'Celtic' Easter as heretical and schismatical, not just misguided.[36] Churches

---

32. See F. M. Stenton in C. Fox, *Offa's Dyke* (1955: xx–xxi); P. Wormald, 'The Age of Offa and Alcuin', in J. Campbell (ed.), *The Anglo-Saxons* (1982b: 119); W. Davies, *Patterns of Power* (1990: 62–71).
33. Gelling, *The West Midlands* (1992: 106–11).
34. P. Sims-Williams, *Religion and Literature in Western England, 600–800* (1990: 54–86). In Northumbria, the use of the British name of Lindisfarne in the Irish annals (here very probably derived from Iona annals), is perhaps symptomatic of contact between Aidan and the Britons.
35. The initial date, 670, is chosen because it was with the arrival of Theodore in 669 and the installation of Wilfrid in the see of York in 670 that a hard line began to be adopted; 768 derives from an entry in the *Annales Cambriae* recording the adoption of the Roman Easter in Gwynedd.
36. Penitential of Theodore (the version of the Discipulus Umbrensium), ii. 9, ed. P. W. Finsterwalder, *Die Canones Theodori Cantuariensis und ihrer Überlieferungsfor-men* (1929: 322–4); transl. J. T. McNeill and H. M. Gamer, *Medieval Handbooks of Penance* (1938: 206–7); Stephen, *Vita S. Wilfridi*, cc. 12, 14–15, ed. and tr. B. Colgrave, *The Life of Bishop Wilfrid by Eddius Stephanus* (1927: 24–5, 303); contrast Bede, *HE* III. 17.

that in the middle of the seventh century are likely to have had close and cooperative relations with their British neighbours now cut off those relations.[37] In the same period, the landscape on the English side of the frontier was systematically anglicized, yielding a situation in which British place-names were rarer in Shropshire than they were in Staffordshire further east and much rarer than in Herefordshire to the south. Quite contrary to England as a whole, and quite contrary also to the Mercian dependencies of the Hwicce and Magonsæte to the south-west, British place-names in central and western Mercia get rarer as one goes west towards Wales until one reaches the frontier zone itself.[38] In linguistic and cultural terms the frontier became much more sharply defined and much more impervious in the eighth century. At the very same period, since the Northumbrian threat was removed, so also was any military necessity for an alliance. The warfare that is attested between Coenred (704–709), Æthelbald (716–757), Offa (757–796) and the Welsh was just conflict between independent kingdoms, not an attempt to restore an overlordship against the threat of rebellion.[39] One episode in that warfare was the recovery by its native dynasty from the English of control over Powys, a recovery recorded in a ninth-century inscription but which should itself be dated to the reign of Æthelbald or to the years immediately after his death, when first Beornred and then Offa became king.[40] Offa's Dyke was a defensive structure and did not merely delimit the boundary, as Fox believed; it was designed to keep an habitually hostile power at bay, above all from the central area of the frontier, the very area that was undergoing a thorough anglicization.[41]

This story switches direction, however, in the ninth century. It has to explain why, by *c.* 850, there was a traditional Mercian overlordship over most of Wales.[42] This overlordship it attributes not to the Mercian hegemony as a whole, stretching back to the seventh century, but to the campaigns of Coenwulf, the last great Mercian king. The final part of his reign saw successive campaigns in Gwynedd (816,

---

37. Sims-Williams, *Religion and Literature* (1990: 114). 'Only the influence of the neighbouring Welsh church is conspicuous by its absence'.
38. Gelling, *The West Midlands* (1992: 66–9).
39. *Felix, Life of Saint Guthlac*, ed. Colgrave, c. 34 (that Guthlac was an exile among the Britons is evidence that the Britons in question were independent of Coenred); Annales Cambriae, s.aa. 722, 760, 778, 784, 797 = 796.
40. *The Pillar of Eliseg: Early Welsh Genealogical Tracts*, ed. Bartrum, 1–3 (mainly on the basis of a reading by Edward Lhuyd). The dating depends exclusively on the number of generations between Cyngen, who had it set up, and who may be identified with the king of Powys who died in 854, and his great-grandfather, Elise, who recovered Powys from the English; Continuation of Bede, s.a. 757, ed. Colgrave and Mynors (1969: 574), suggests a possibly favourable moment for the recovery of Powys.
41. D. Hill (three citations in n. 9).
42. *ASC* 853 with 830.

822), Dyfed (818) and in Powys (822).[43] These are not to be compared with his campaign of 798 to re-establish Mercian control over Kent.[44] That occurred two years after his accession in 796, when Mercian overlordship over the outer zone of its hegemony was in peril. His Welsh campaigns took place at the zenith of his power, and they should therefore be interpreted as new conquests rather than as attempts to hold onto old lordship. On this view, the Mercian hegemony reached its greatest territorial extent in the years immediately before it lost almost all authority south of the Thames.

The other story, however, sees the ninth-century Mercian hegemony in Wales as the lineal descendant of the authority acquired by Penda over southern England. In the first place, there is no mention in the sources, exiguous though they are, of any great rebellion, during which the Welsh threw off the overlordship of the Mercians. The Welsh recovery of Powys, apparently after a period of direct English rule, recorded on the Pillar of Eliseg, may be compared with other periods when Mercian kings displaced local English dynasties;[45] and, in any case, it refers solely to Powys. Similar incidents were to occur in the ninth century, when the Mercian overlordship over much of Wales can hardly be denied.[46] On the other side, the famous list of so-called 'Bretwaldas', that notoriously ends with Oswiu of Northumbria, cannot be argued to indicate an end to English overlordship over the Britons after Oswiu's death: that list was probably taken by Bede from a Kentish document of c. 670, and Ecgfrith of Northumbria was to enjoy an overlordship over the southern English between 675 and 679 very similar to that held by his father 655–658.[47] Second, it appears that

---

43. This information derives mainly from the B recension of the Annales Cambriae, mostly supported by the C recension; these were, however, independent versions and there is no textual reason to think that the extra information they contain was a later addition; the earliest version (A) has been thoroughly abbreviated. The further material in the other versions is to be found in the old and unsatisfactory edition by J. Williams ab Ithel, *Annales Cambriae*, Rolls Series (1860).

44. *ASC*, s.a. 798; S. Keynes, 'The control of Kent in the ninth century', *Early Medieval Europe*, 2 (1992: 113).

45. For example, Kent from 785–796 (Stenton, *Anglo-Saxon England* (1971: 206)), East Anglia after 794, when the king was beheaded by command of Offa (*ASC*).

46. *Annals of Ulster*, ed. S. Mac Airt and G. Mac Niocaill (1983, s.a. 865.4), if this refers to Wales rather than to the northern Britons.

47. Stephen, *Life of Wilfrid*, c. 20, where Ecgfrith is said (a) to have made Mercia tributary after defeating Wulfhere's attack on Northumbria, and (b) after Wulfhere's death (675) to have 'ruled in peace for some time more widely'; Bede, *HE* II. 5; as is well known, this list occurs in Bede's text associated with the death of a Kentish king (the only one to appear in the list); it shows a notable sensitivity to Kentish interests (Kent was the only part of Britain not subject to Edwin); and it ignores not just Æthelbald, mentioned later by Bede as having a similar authority (*HE* V. 23), but also Ecgfrith, the principal benefactor of Wearmouth-Jarrow. The nine years assigned to Ecgfrith in HB c. 65 may perhaps be explained not as a scribal error but as a statement from a North Welsh perspective, according to which the battle of the Trent put an end to Northumbrian overlordship.

Æthelbald claimed an overlordship over southern Britain and not merely the southern English.[48] Bede's description of the territorial scope of his authority first details all the dioceses of the southern English (specified in terms of kingdoms, *prouinciae*), and then adds 'and the other southern provinces up to the boundary of the River Humber'; the latter ought to be British.[49]

Offa's warfare in Wales is likely to have had a similar background to his warfare in southern England: Kent threw off his overlordship for a time after defeating Offa in 776; under Cynewulf the West Saxons appear to have remained independent, in spite of defeat at Bensington in 779.[50] Even in the twelfth century, when English overlordship over Wales was not seriously questioned, campaigning was often necessary to support one ruler against another. Offa's Dyke, even if it be admitted to be defensive, did not mark the limit of English settlement: numerous such settlements survived on the western side of the dyke. On the other hand, it may be associated with Welsh rebellion and with the desire to protect those lands in Shropshire that had been systematically anglicized under royal authority.

After 768, when paschal differences probably no longer divided the Welsh and English,[51] but the Welsh still kept their independence of Canterbury, Offa is shown as having influence in Wales at the very least. The papal legates who came to Britain in 786 divided their efforts between the province of Canterbury, where Offa and Cynewulf collaborated to receive them in a special council, and Northumbria, the kingdom of Ælfwold. After attending the council with Offa and Cynewulf:

> when counsel had been taken with the aforesaid kings, bishops and elders of the land, we, considering that that corner of the world extends far and wide, allowed Theophylact, the venerable bishop, to visit the king of the Mercians and the parts of Britain.[52]

---

48. The Ismere charter, Sawyer, *Anglo-Saxon Charters*: no. 89, *EHD* i, no. 67; T. M. Charles-Edwards, 'The continuation of Bede', in A. P. Smyth (ed.), *Seanchas: Studies … in Honour of Francis J. Byrne* (2000: 137–39); F. M. Stenton, 'The Supremacy of the Mercian Kings', *EHR*, **33** (1918: 438–44) = Stenton, *Preparatory to Anglo-Saxon England* (1970: 538).
49. Bede, *HE* V. 23: 'Et hae omnes prouinciae [the English dioceses/kingdoms] ceteraeque australes ad confinium usque Hymbrae fluminis cum suis quaeque regibus Merciorum regi Aedilbaldo subiectae sunt.' The list even includes kingdoms currently without a bishop (Sussex, the Isle of Wight); the only frontier mentioned is to the north, the Humber.
50. Stenton, *Anglo-Saxon England* (1971: 208).
51. Assuming that the adhesion of Gwynedd to the Roman Easter, recorded in *Annales Cambriae*, s.a. 768, was the final episode: the northern Britons had conformed much earlier under the influence of Adomnán of Iona, if they were the 'nonnulla [pars] etiam de Brettonibus in Brittania' of Bede, *HE* V. 15.
52. *Epistolae Karolini Aevi*, ed. E. Dümmler, MGH, Epp. 4 (1895, **4**: 20) (Alcuini Epistolae, no. 3), 'permisimus Theophylactum, venerabilem episcopum, regem Merchiorum et Britanniae partes adire'; *EHD* i, no. 191.

Having already conducted the formal business in council, Theophylact went first to Offa and then to 'the parts of Britain'. It may reasonably be inferred that these 'parts of Britain' were other than the English dominions already dealt with in the council and that they were in fact the non-English parts of Britain subject to Offa, namely Wales. They were treated independently from the areas covered by the council because they were not part of the province of Canterbury, and perhaps also because they were solely the business of Offa and not of Cynewulf.

Coenwulf's aggression against the Welsh did not begin, as the first story would suggest, in 816, but immediately after his accession. Just as he attacked Kent, deposed the Kentish king Eadberht Præn, and brought him back in chains into Mercia, so also he or his subordinates slew the king of Gwynedd, Caradog.[53] Coenwulf's campaigning later in his reign may thus be seen as an attempt to maintain by violence a hegemony that was under severe threat.[54]

Both stories have their good points. In favour of the first is the strong possibility that the Mercians lost their authority over Wales in the reign of Coenred. Yet the arguments for the second account of events seem more convincing. In particular, the second story allows for periods when Mercian power collapsed in Wales as it did elsewhere in the outer zone; it does not assert that Mercian hegemony was uninterrupted, only that it was the settled ambition of Mercian rulers to dominate Wales and that, for most of the time, they had the power to attain that ambition.

Wales and the end of the Mercian supremacy

When the West Saxon Ecgberht ended Mercian power over almost all England south of the Thames, he went on to assert a supremacy over England south of the Humber and even sought the subjection of the Northumbrians. This further expansion of West Saxon power did not endure and was not revived until the conquests of the Viking Great Army changed the shape of Britain. Yet immediately before Ecgberht lost control of Mercia, he campaigned against the Welsh and secured their submission.[55] The following years saw, on the whole, a peaceful arrangement by which the Thames remained, though only approximately, the boundary as far east as London.[56] The West Saxon

---

53. *Annales Cambriae*, s.a. 798.
54. For Coenwulf's dispute with Wulfred, archbishop of Canterbury, whose loyalty was crucial, see N. Brooks, *The Early History of the Church of Canterbury* (1984: 175–80); Keynes, 'The Control of Kent' (1993b: 117–18).
55. ASC 830. While the annal puts Wiglaf's recovery of Mercia first and the Welsh campaign second, the two events may have been in reverse order or contemporaneous. By expressing it as he did, the annalist ended with a West Saxon triumph instead of a reversal.
56. Essex may have remained for a time subject to Wessex: D. N. Dumville, *Wessex and England from Alfred to Edgar* (1992), Chap. 1; on the other hand, S. Keynes,

assistance given in 853 to Burgred, king of the Mercians, so as to secure the submission of the Welsh was granted in the same year that Burgred married Æthelwulf's daughter; it was also consistent with a division of authority by which the West Saxons had their 'Welsh' sphere, namely Cornwall, and the Mercians had theirs – Wales.

West Saxon interest in assuming authority over Wales revived under Alfred after he had won the battle of Edington in 878. Alfred's triumph over the Great Army and the baptism of Guthrum coincided with the death of Rhodri Mawr, king of Gwynedd, in battle against the English. Those involved in the latter battle are not defined any further than as English, but given Alfred's commitments elsewhere they can hardly have been other than the Mercians, probably led by Ceolwulf.[57] As is notorious, Ceolwulf is described by the West Saxon chronicler as 'a foolish king's thegn', but against the Welsh he was a formidable leader.[58] Ceolwulf's reign, however, came to an end during the next year, 879.[59] His successor, Æthelred, was not recognized as king by the West Saxons, although he was married to Alfred's daughter, Æthelflæd. He was also defeated by the Welsh of Gwynedd in the battle of the Conwy in 881, a battle which precipitated the collapse of Mercian authority in Wales.[60]

What is striking, given Alfred's close associations with Mercia, is that the West Saxon king took an active part in undermining Mercian power over the Welsh. This is apparent from the contemporary and well-informed account by Asser in chapter 80 of his *Life of Alfred*. According to Alfred, the southern Welsh kings felt exposed to attack either, in the case of Dyfed and Brycheiniog, from Gwynedd, or, in the case of Gwent and Glywysing, from 'the force and tyranny' of Ealdorman Æthelred and the Mercians. As a result all of them sought the lordship of Alfred. Eventually, Anarawd son of Rhodri abandoned his alliance with the Viking rulers of York and subjected himself to Alfred on the same conditions as Æthelred. These events are best seen as occurring between Æthelred's defeat at the Conwy in 881 and the renewed Viking onslaught on England in the autumn of 892. Although Alfred may have done much to reconcile the Mercians to West Saxon supremacy, he was quite prepared to play his part in ending Mercian power in Wales. By 892 he had two leading Christian subordinates, the ealdorman of the Mercians and the king of Gwynedd:

---

cont.

    'King Alfred and the Mercians', in M. A. S. Blackburn and D. N. Dumville (eds), *Kings, Currency and Alliances: History and Coinage of Southern England in the Ninth Century* (1998: 33), does not accept this argument for the 880s; for Mercian possessions south of the Thames, see S no. 1271 = *EHD* i, no. 87.

57. The subsequent Mercian defeat in 881 was seen by the *Annales Cambriae* as 'God's revenge for Rhodri'.
58. *ASC* s.a. 874.
59. Keynes, 'King Alfred and the Mercians' (1998: 12 n. 48).
60. *Early Welsh Genealogical Tracts*, ed. Bartrum: 101 (ABT § 7 [q]).

in terms of the treaty arrangements between Alfred and these two, they were in exactly the same position.

One danger for Alfred was that these two rulers might combine together. Although there was no rebellion on the scale of that mounted by Cadwallon and Penda against Edwin, there is one annal which suggests that Alfred's settlement of Wales could be undermined by his principal client rulers. The *Annales Cambriae* have an entry for 894 according to which 'Anarawd with the *Angli* came to ravage Ceredigion and Ystrad Tywi'. Asser's account shows that in the 880s south-west Wales felt itself vulnerable to attack from Gwynedd, and that Hyfaidd, king of Dyfed, sought Alfred's protection as a result. The likelihood is that *Angli* was used instead of the annalist's usual *Saxones* so as to make it quite clear that Alfred and the West Saxons were not implicated.[61] Alfred was in any case heavily involved with the Viking threat; his commitments elsewhere are presumably the reason why Gwynedd and Mercia could combine against his Welsh clients.

There is no evidence that Alfred's hegemony over Wales recovered from this reversal of his policy. Three characteristics mark the final phase of Welsh–Mercian relations in the quarter of a century between 893, when Asser stopped writing his *Life of King Alfred*, and the winter of 918 when, not long before Christmas, a rapid *coup d'etat* saw the last native ruler of Mercia being led off into confinement in Wessex.[62] This short period saw the revival of Mercian power in Wales, the triumph of the descendants of Merfyn Frych in all regions outside the South-East, and renewed Viking pressure on Gwynedd.

The evidence for Mercian power in Wales is twofold, but to appreciate its significance we need to remember the Wales described by Asser, the Wales of the 880s. Asser distinguished the far south-east, Gwent and Glywysing, threatened by 'the power and tyranny of Æthelred and the Mercians', from the south-west, Dyfed, and the central south-east, Brycheiniog, both threatened by the power of the sons of Rhodri Mawr. Two aggressive powers drove the southern Welsh kingdoms into the welcoming embrace of King Alfred; after their defeat at the battle of the Conwy in 881, the Mercians only hoped to retain lordship over the lands to the south of the Brecon Beacons and to the east of Swansea; the sons of Rhodri threatened the rest. Three annal entries, one in the 'Mercian Register' and the others in the

---

61. D. P. Kirby, 'The political development of Ceredigion, c. 400–1081', in J. L. Davies and D. P. Kirby (eds), *Ceredigion County History*, gen. ed. I. G. Jones, i, 'From the earliest times to the coming of the Normans' (1994: 318–42), at 331, describes Anarawd as having received 'Anglo-Saxon assistance' whereas Hyfaidd was previously enabled to resist because of 'West Saxon aid'. For Kirby, Llywarch ap Hyfaidd was dispossessed of Ceredigion and Ystrad Tywi after 894. This may well be right.

62. *ASC* C 919 = the beginning of December 918, if the annal usually assigned to 919 was just a continuation of that for 918: see F. T. Wainwright, 'The chronology of the Mercian Register', *EHR*, 60 (1945: 388–9); Wainwright, *Scandinavian England: Collected Papers*, ed. H. P. R. Finberg (1975b: 127–9).

Parker Chronicle (a West Saxon text), show how the political balance had changed since the renewed Viking attack in the autumn of 892. These entries may be taken in reverse chronological order. When Edward the Elder carried out his coup against Ælfwyn in 918, he secured not just Mercia itself but also supremacy over three Welsh kings: Hywel, Clydog and Idwal. Hywel (later known as Hywel Dda) and Clydog were sons of Cadell ap Rhodri, who had died in 909.[63] Their father, Cadell, appears to have acquired the kingdom of Dyfed within the last six years of his life; and it was to this new acquisition that Hywel had succeeded. Previously Cadell may have been king of Powys;[64] and Clydog probably succeeded him in this older possession, perhaps acquired in 881–882, after the battle of the Conwy. In place, therefore, of Hyfaidd, a ruler of Dyfed who had made himself objectionable to St David's, but who had eventually submitted to King Alfred, we now have Hywel ap Cadell, king of Dyfed, and Clydog ap Cadell, king of Powys, from a dynasty earlier based in the north, in Gwynedd. Indeed, it was less than a hundred years since, in 825, Merfyn Frych, the eponymous ancestor of the Merfynion, as they came to be called, had said farewell to his native Isle of Man and had established himself as king of Gwynedd.[65] The last of the three kings, Idwal, was the ruler of Gwynedd in succession to his father Anarawd, who had died in 916.[66] The annal entry suggests, therefore, two things: first, three kings, all from the Merfynion, ruled the three major kingdoms of Gwynedd, Powys and Dyfed (to the last of these three were probably also attached Ceredigion and Ystrad Tywi). In less than a century from 825, the Merfynion had gained power over most of Wales. Second, Edward gained the allegiance of these three kings when, and only when, he became the ruler of Mercia. The implication is that Æthelflæd, described in both the Irish and the Welsh annals as queen, had secured, at least by the last years of her reign, the submission of the Merfynion, and with it an hegemony over all Wales outside the far south-east.[67] It is conceivable that this hegemony only dated from the death of Anarawd in 916, but it is more likely that its roots lay in the alliance made in 893 or 894, revealed in the joint campaign by Anarawd and the *Angli* in 894.

Three important kingdoms lay outside the sphere of the Merfynion: Brycheiniog, Glywysing, and Gwent. Once one admits that the Merfynion were subject to Mercia in the years running up to 918, it becomes very likely that the weaker kingdoms in the south-east also

---

63. *Early Welsh Genealogical Tracts*, ed. Bartrum: 11 (HG § 1), 101 (ABT § 7 [h]).
64. His name, Cadell, echoed that of the founder of the Cadelling dynasty of Powys.
65. For the Man origins of Merfyn Frych, see P. Sims-Willams, 'Historical need and literary narrative: a caveat from ninth-century Wales', *Welsh History Review*, 17 (1994–5: 11–20). I am assuming that the move to Gwynedd was, at least partly, induced by Viking pressure.
66. *Annales Cambriae* 915 = 916; *Chronicum Scotorum*, ed. Hennessy, 915 = 916.
67. *Annales Cambriae*, s.a. 917 = 918; *Annals of Ulster*, 918. 5.

had an English overlord. Two entries, one in the Parker Chronicle and the other in the Mercian Register, suggest that Brycheiniog lay within the Mercian sphere while Glywysing and Gwent were subject to King Edward. In 914 Cyfeilliog, bishop of Ergyng (Archenfield), was captured by Vikings and then ransomed by Edward the Elder.[68] Although he is described as bishop *on Ircingafelda*, he appears to have had property mainly in Gwent.[69] The dynasties of Gwent and Glywysing were branches of a single lineage, and the two kingdoms, originally one, were sometimes recombined.[70] It is unlikely that Gwent and Ergyng would have been subject to one English overlord, while Glywysing was subject to another. From this one piece of evidence, therefore, we may conjecture, with all due caution, that Glywysing, Gwent and Ergyng were all subject to the overlordship of Edward. In 916, however, Æthelflæd sent an army to Brycheiniog which succeeded in taking the island fort on Llangorse Lake and capturing the queen.[71] The fort or, to give this type of structure its usual Irish name, *crannóg*, was known to the English by the name of the lake itself, 'Brychan's Lake', *Brecenan Mere*, called after the half-mythical founder of Brycheiniog, Brychan.[72] Whether this was a punishment for the killing of Abbot Ecgbryht, recorded in the same annal entry, is uncertain, but it was probably a reprisal for something. Æthelflæd, the acknowledged superior of three kings of the Merfynion, including the ruler of Dyfed in the far south-west and Gwynedd in the north-west, is unlikely to have allowed Brycheiniog, far closer than Dyfed to Mercia, to remain independent. Hence this is more likely to have been a punitive expedition against an errant client than an attack on an independent kingdom.

A plausible account of these isolated items of evidence takes its start from the crisis of 892–895, brought about by the renewed Viking invasions in the autumn of 892. The Merfynion, led by Anarawd ap Rhodri, made an alliance with Æthelred of Mercia, the husband of Æthelflæd. This alliance overturned, so far as Wales was concerned, the system of alliances constructed during the 880s, in which Alfred had made himself successively the patron of more and more Welsh kings, gradually extending his influence from the south-east to Gwynedd in the north-west. Now the Merfynion submitted to Æthelred instead of Alfred, but, in return, were given a free hand to extend their

---

68. *ASC* A 918 = 914.
69. W. Davies, *The Llandaff Charters* (1979: 122–4).
70. W. Davies, *An Early Welsh Microcosm* (1978: 94–5).
71. *ASC* B and C (in 'the Mercian Register'), s.a. 916. A powerful case has been made for associating the Llywarch Hen cycle of saga englynion with Brycheiniog, and, somewhat more speculatively but plausibly, with the Mercian attack of 916: P. Sims-Williams, 'The provenance of the Llywarch Hen poems: a case for Llangors, Brycheiniog', *Cambrian Medieval Celtic Studies*, **26** (1993: 27–63).
72. E. Campbell and A. Lane, 'Llangorse: a tenth-century royal crannog in Wales', *Antiquity*, **63** (1989: 675–81); M. Redknap, *The Christian Celts: Treasures of Late Celtic Wales* (1991: 16–25).

power into south-west Wales, and even received Mercian military support in the joint campaign of 894. This challenge to Alfred's support for the independence of Hyfaidd of Dyfed was to lead eventually, probably between 903 and 909, to the conquest of Dyfed.[73] This might have come sooner if Gwynedd itself had not come under severe Viking pressure after Anarawd abandoned his alliance with Viking Northumbria in order to submit to Alfred.[74] The West Saxon overlordship in Wales was reduced to the far south-east, exactly the area to which the Mercian hegemony in Wales had been reduced immediately after Æthelred's defeat at the battle of the Conwy in 881.

After 918, when Mercia was incorporated into the English kingdom of Edward, the prospects for the Welsh kingdoms became much less promising. The alliances of Alfred with the Welsh in the 880s had been directed both against Mercia and against the Vikings; similarly, the alliance between Mercia and the Merfynion of the 890s was directed partly at loosening Alfred's grip on Wales. Now there was no English third party and no corresponding reason to shelter the Welsh from the full burden of fiscal exploitation. That such exploitation now followed is implied by the Welsh poem *Armes Prydein*:[75] even if William of Malmesbury's story about Æthelstan's meeting with the Welsh at Hereford and his imposition of an unheard-of tribute is suspect, some such event very probably occurred.[76] The Welsh were now among the principal victims of a new imperium.[77]

---

73. That is, between the death of Hyfaidd's son, Llywarch, in 903 and the death of Cadell ap Rhodri in 909 (dates from *Annales Cambriae*). There is no need to identify the moment of collapse with the beheading of Rhodri son of Hyfaidd in 904, although it may have occurred then.
74. W. Davies, *Patterns of Power in Early Wales* (1990: 52–5).
75. *Armes Prydein*, ed. I. Williams (1955); English version by R. Bromwich (1972); on the date see D. N. Dumville, 'Brittany and "Armes Prydein Vawr"', *Etudes Celtiques*, **20** (1983: 145–59).
76. *William of Malmesbury, Gesta Regum Anglorum*, ii. 134. 5, ed. and tr. R. A. B. Mynors, R. M. Thomson and M. Winterbottom, Oxford Medieval Texts (1998, I: 214–16). On William's willingness to prefer a later source to an earlier one on the grounds of style, see M. Lapidge, 'Some Latin poems as evidence for the reign of Athelstan', *Anglo-Saxon England*, **9** (1981: 62–71).
77. I hope to consider the issues raised in this chapter more fully in a forthcoming book, *The Origins of Wales*.

7 The Verturian Hegemony: A Mirror in the North

Alex Woolf

Despite their reputation as the mystery people of early medieval Britain the Picts have a history which shares remarkable similarities with that of the Mercians. Both peoples were later than most of their neighbours in adopting Christianity and no indigenous narrative accounts survive from either kingdom. In addition to these general parallels, both kingdoms established regional hegemonies for themselves following the failure of Ecgfrith of Bernicia to maintain the dominant position in Britain which he had inherited from his father Oswiu. In the ninth century both kingdoms were effectively destroyed in the chaos of the first Viking Age and supplanted by erstwhile client-kingdoms.

The Picts differed from the Mercians in as much as they were a native people, descended from those Britons who had remained beyond effective Roman control and who had retained their Celtic language and culture with far less of the Latin veneer which characterizes medieval Welsh language and society (Forsyth, 1997: 16–30). The exact chronology of the conversion of the Picts to Christianity is unclear. Adomnán, the ninth abbot of Iona (679–704), clearly believed that a significant portion of the Picts had still been pagan a century before his time, during the *floruit* of his predecessor St Columba (Adomnán, *Vita Columbae*, e.g. 2: 33–4, in Anderson and Anderson, 1991). The Pictish king whom he claims Columba encountered, Bridei son of Meilocon, is presented as pagan yet not overtly hostile to the Church, much as Bede presents Penda (*HE* III. 21, in Colgrave and Mynors, 1969). It is equally unclear to what extent the Picts represented a unified kingdom in Columba's day. Bede, in his account of Columba's missionary activity (*HE* III. 4, in Colgrave and Mynors, 1969), describes Bridei son of Meilocon as a *rex potentissimus*, a phrase which might imply that he was not the only king amongst the Picts. The location of Bridei's fortress by the mouth of the River Ness (Adomnán, *Vita Columbae* 2: 33, in Anderson and Anderson, 1991) may also suggest that he was a local king in the Moray Firth region rather than ruler of a unified Pictish kingdom.

The creation of something approaching a unified Pictish polity appears, in fact, to have been an achievement of the seventh rather than the sixth century or earlier. Just as the Iclingian dominions – so-called after Icel, the apical figure in the Mercian royal pedigree – in the English Midlands consisted of that land 'which was first called Mercia' and a number of other Middle Anglian and West Anglian satellite *regna*, so the historical Pictish kingdom seems also to have comprised a core territory and outer provinces. The core territory was that province known to the Gaelic-speaking chroniclers as Fortriu, a name related to the Roman-period tribal name Verturiones (Watson, 1993: 68–9), and probably representing a Pictish form something like *Uerteru. Fortriu appears to have been centred upon the middle Tay but its exact extent is uncertain. Some versions of the Pictish king-list name seven sons of 'Cruithne' (the eponymous ancestor of the Picts) who appear to be eponyms of provinces. These are Fib, Fidach, Fotla, Fortrenn, Cait, Ce and Circinn (Anderson, 1980: 245, with discussion at 139–45). The rather fanciful tract *De situ Albaniae* (Howlett, 2000), from the late twelfth century, describes the extent of seven Pictish provinces without naming them and scholars have frequently attempted to match these districts against the eponymous sons of the king list. A consensus has emerged that the province described as comprising the earldoms of Strathearn and Menteith is likely to be Fortriu. This identification is, however, questionable. First, the section of the king-list which preserves the names of the eponymous sons of Cruithne is written in Gaelic orthography, rather than Pictish, and is unlikely to date to a period before the late ninth century at the very earliest. Second, examination of *De Situ Albaniae* suggests that it is entirely a composition of the twelfth century and is unlikely to have anything genuine to contribute about the Pictish provinces save that they were deemed to be seven in number at some earlier stage. This earlier stage of the tradition need not, itself, go back to Pictish times (Broun, 2000). This text is of no value for students of the Picts and tells us far more about twelfth-century Scotia.

The pre-eminence of Fortriu among the provinces of the Picts is emphasized by the fact that it is the territory most frequently mentioned by name. The name first occurs in the *Annals of Ulster* under the year 664.3, in an entry which reads *Bell[um] Lutho Feirnn, .i. i Fortrinn* – 'The battle of Lutho Feirnn (site unknown), i.e. in Fortriu'. We are not told who the combatants were but in the previous year the same chronicle notes the death of Gartnait son of Domnall, who appears as a king of the Picts in the king-lists. It is most likely that this battle in Fortriu is connected in some way with the accession of his successor Drust son of Domnall – either as part of a succession dispute or as part of a conflict with Oswiu of Bernicia who was certainly claiming dominion over 'the greater part of the Pictish gens' by the end of his reign (*HE* III. 24, in Colgrave and Mynors, 1969).

The next mention of Fortriu comes in the *Annals of Ulster*'s obituary of Bridei son of Beli (*AU* 693.1, in Mac Airt and Mac Niocaill, 1983) who is described as *rex Fortrend*. This king is most famous as the

leader of the Pictish force which killed Ecgfrith of Bernicia and wiped
out his army in 686 (*AU* 686.1, in Mac Airt and Mac Niocaill, 1983; *HE*
IV. 24, in Colgrave and Mynors, 1969; Nennius, *Historia Brittonum* 57
and 65, in Morris, 1980) and is thus popularly viewed as an anti-
Anglian hero whose deeds pre-figure those of Wallace and Bruce (e.g.
Cruickshank, 2000: 74). There are certain facts about his career,
however, which may lead us to suppose otherwise. From the king-lists
it can be deduced that his reign began in 671 or 672 (Anderson, 1980),
and indeed the expulsion of his predecessor Drust is noted at *AU*
672.6. Taken together with the information supplied by Stephan of
Ripon (*Vita Wilfridi* 19, in Colgrave, 1927) that following the death of
Oswiu, in 671, the Picts threw off Bernician over-lordship and were
only subjugated after an invasion of their territory by King Ecgfrith and
the *audaci subregulo* Beornhaeth, it is hard to escape the supposition
that Bridei began his reign as a Northumbrian *sub-regulus*. There is
certainly no obvious point at which he might have re-asserted himself
subsequently for, from that time forth, Stephen claims, until the killing
of Ecgfrith, the Picts remained loyal. The *Historia Brittonum* (57, in
Morris, 1980) also supplies the information that Bridei and Ecgfrith
were *fratrueles* – parallel cousins. Since it is extremely unlikely that
Oswiu and Beli king of Dumbarton, Bridei's father (MacQuarrie, 1993:
9), were brothers, one can only assume that Bridei's mother, like
Eanfled, Ecgfrith's mother, was a daughter of Edwin of Deira (Woolf,
1998: 161–2). Such a relationship would certainly make sense of the
verse ascribed to Riagail of Bangor in which the battle between
Ecgfrith and Bridei is presented as a squabble over grand-paternal
inheritance:

> Today Bridei fights a battle
> over the inheritance of his grandfather,
> unless it is the wish of the Son of God
> that restitution be made.

> Today the son of Oswiu was slain
> in battle against grey swords,
> even though he did penance
> it was a penance too late.
>   (text Radner, 1978: 54, translation adapted from
>   Radner, 1978: 55, and Clancy, 1998: 115)

It might even be argued that the rise of Fortriu and the creation of a
Verturian hegemony amongst the Picts can be ascribed to this period
of Bernician domination. The early 680s see conflict within the Pictish
regions with a siege of Dunottar (*AU* 681.5, Mac Airt and Mac Niocaill,
1983), a great promontory fort 20 kilometres south of Aberdeen, and
an expedition by Bridei to Orkney (*AU* 682.4, Mac Airt and Mac
Niocaill, 1983), as well as a siege of Dundurn in upper Strathearn (*AU*
683.3, Mac Airt and Mac Niocaill, 1983). The most likely extent of

Fortriu, if we take it to be a Bernician protectorate, would be the southern marches of Pictavia comprising the later medieval provinces of Fife, Strathearn and perhaps also the centre of royal power in the central Middle Ages, Gowrie. Fortriu would thus comprise a swathe of territory bordered on the south by the Forth with its northern frontier running from the hills behind Dunkeld and Rattray down to the Tay at Invergowrie (see map). The strength of Fortriu in relation to the other provinces may have lain not just in its superior agricultural potential but in its ability to maintain tributary structures set in place during the 20 years or so of the Bernician *imperium*.

That Fortriu remained the dominant province within Pictavia seems to be borne out by the ninth-century annals which describe Constantín son of Uurguist (789–820) and his brother Onuist (829–834) as kings of Fortriu at their deaths (*AU* 820.3 and *AU* 834.1, in Mac Airt and Mac Niocaill, 1983). Fortriu is mentioned again shortly after Onuist's death (*AU* 839.9, in Mac Airt and Mac Niocaill, 1983) when the men of Fortriu are heavily defeated in battle by the heathens. John Bannerman (1999) has suggested that the reappearance of Fortriu in this era may reflect the breakdown of its hegemony in the chaos of the early Viking Age. Most Pictish kings in the intervening century or so had been noticed by Irish chroniclers simply as 'kings of the Picts'. Bannerman's hypothesis is plausible, but alternative explanations, such as different sources lying behind these annals, one more familiar than the other with Pictish terminology, are also possible. In either case, it seems to reflect the fact that the core region of what historians, medieval and modern, have tended to call the Pictish kingdom, was the province of Fortriu and that control beyond this region reflects a regional hegemony, very similar to that exercised by Mercia in the English Midlands.

The sub-kingdoms within this hegemony appear from time to time but very rarely. Adomnán, writing in the late seventh century, describes Columba's encounter with a sub-king of Orkney (Adomnán, *Vita Columbae* 2: 42, in Anderson and Anderson, 1991). Such a sub-king may have existed in Columba's time (the late sixth century) but the political relationship described might as easily reflect conditions in Adomnán's own time, *c.* 690, following Bridei son of Beli's expedition to Orkney (*AU* 682.4, in Mac Airt and Mac Niocaill, 1983). During the reign of the first Onuist son of Uurguist (729–761) we hear of his drowning of a king of Atholl (*AU* 739.7, in Mac Airt and Mac Niocaill, 1983), a region usually presumed to be Pictish. In the late eighth century a list of obits includes Dub Talorc, 'king of the Picts this side of the Mounth' (*AU* 782.1, Mac Airt and Mac Niocaill, 1983), presumably reflecting a Gaelic perspective and indicating someone ruling either on the north-west coast or more likely on the Moray plain, some way north of Fortriu. Moreover, it is likely that Gaelic Dál Riata and perhaps the British kingdom of Dumbarton were also under Verturian domination from the middle of the eighth century (Charles-Edwards, 2000; Woolf, forthcoming).

One interesting feature of the relationship between Fortriu and the region immediately to its north can be identified in the sculptural tradition. While settlement archaeology for the eighth and early ninth centuries is as unforthcoming in Scotland as it is in England, the Pictish sculpture of this period is famous. The two main classes of stone monument produced by the Picts have been known to scholars as Class I and Class II stones. While the Class I stones are undressed monoliths incised with the enigmatic Pictish symbols, those traditionally known as Class II monuments are dressed cross slabs decorated with sculpture in relief which includes, as well as the symbols, decorative motifs such as interlace and figurative representations of both religious and secular themes (Foster, 1996: 71–9). Current scholarship is moving away from such a rigid classification and favours a more descriptive approach referring to 'incised symbols' or 'relief cross slabs', etc. The two hundred or so monuments with incised symbols are distributed throughout the mainland north of the Forth, with the significant exception of Gaelic Argyll, and in the Northern Isles, with one or two outliers in the Hebrides and south of the Forth. Cross slabs carved in relief, which can be dated on art historical grounds to the eighth and ninth century, have a more circumscribed distribution. There are only some sixty or so of these monuments known, complete or in fragments, but of these only about half a dozen come from the area we have tentatively identified as Fortriu.

The greatest concentration of cross slabs is to be found in what would become the later medieval province of Angus, with particular concentrations at St Vigeans (Allen and Anderson, 1903: 234–42, 267–81) and Meigle (Allen and Anderson, 1903: 265–305, 328–40). While both Meigle and St Vigeans were churches in the later Middle Ages, neither was a major ecclesiastical centre, and the collections of monuments at these sites serve to demonstrate how completely the ecclesiastical order of Scotland was transformed during the Viking Age. The province of Angus, which contains these concentrations of ecclesiastical sculpture lies immediately to the east of Gowrie and thus, in all probability, of Fortriu. In the context of the present volume it is perhaps of interest to compare the relative poverty, in sculptural terms, of Fortriu when compared to Angus with the similar contrast between the diocese of Lichfield and that of Leicester within the Mercian heartland. The absence of surviving Pictish charter material, if indeed it ever existed, makes it impossible to trace the patterns of royal endowment of monastic sites in detail. It may be, however, that as within the Mercian hegemony, major endowments to the Church took place largely within 'subject' provinces rather than in the 'tribal homeland' of the dominant group. The great ecclesiastical establishments of Angus may have fulfilled a spiritual and political role analogous to that played by monasteries such as Medeshamstede and Breedon to the east of the Mercian homeland (Plunkett, 1998a). South of the Tay, in Fortriu proper, the greatest monument to late Pictish sculpture is not a cross slab but the so-called St Andrew's Sarcophagus

(Foster, 1998), a box shrine constructed to hold the remains of a king. As at Repton (Biddle and Kjølbye-Biddle, 1985) we see a monastic centre within the imperial province functioning as a royal mausoleum.

To conclude this brief attempt to draw out some parallels between the Mercian hegemony in southern Britain and the 'Verturian' hegemony at the north end of the island, we can see that both *imperia* grew out of the struggle with the Bernicians in the 670s. The kings of Fortriu do not seem to have achieved a unified Pictish state but they did go some way towards the production of an increasingly centralized over-kingship. It would be interesting to know if events such as the drowning of the king of Atholl (*AU* 739.7, Mac Airt and Mac Niocaill, 1983) were part of a process of suppressing sub-kingdoms and replacing the *reguli* with royal officers, the precursors of the later mormaers ('great-stewards'), analogous to those that we can observe in Mercia. Unfortunately the documentary records of the Picts are even less well preserved than those of Mercia. In terms of chronicle narratives both peoples are poorly served but the existence of a relatively extensive, if geographically uneven, diplomatic record of the acts of Mercian kings is completely unparalleled for the Picts. Whether such records existed or not, they have not come down to us and we are left with no idea as to how the court of the kings of Fortriu operated and are entirely dependent upon sculptural remains to estimate their interest in ecclesiastical endowment. The Verturian *imperium* was destroyed by the Danes in the last quarter of the ninth century and when a new power arose in its place, although it adopted many of its trappings, it claimed as its progenitor one of the erstwhile subject kingdoms, Dál Riata, rather than Fortriu. The name of Fortriu was preserved for a while as a poetic name for the dominions of the kings of Alba, as the new territory was called, but was all but forgotten by the twelfth century.

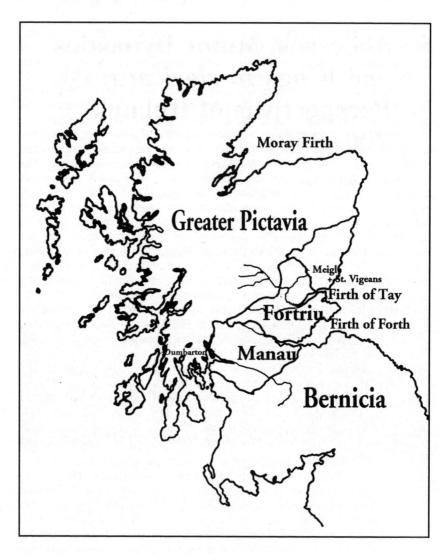

Map 3 Pictland and Bernicia

8 Abbesses, Minor Dynasties and Kings *in clericatu*: Perspectives of Ireland, 700–850

Edel Bhreathnach

Introduction

Seventh-century Ireland witnessed the creation of a number of powerful dynasties that were to remain part of the Irish political landscape in various guises into the late medieval period. These dynasties sprang from amorphous origins, frequently following the model whereby a core dynasty expanded through the accretion of other ambitious dynasties which claimed a common ancestry. The eponymous ancestors belonged to a sufficiently distant past to allow for easy expansion of their descendants (for an example of this construct, see Charles-Edwards, 1993: 120 (Table 2.6)). The Irish model was not unlike that of the early Anglo-Saxon use of *-ingas* names 'derived from shadowy figures of indeterminate status and date' (Bailey, 1989: 114–15). Thus in Ireland, for example, Uí Néill dynasties of the North and Midlands claimed common ancestry from Níall Noígiallach, Éoganachta of Munster from Éogan Már and in Leinster, Uí Dúnlainge and Uí Chennselaig from Cathaír Már and their more immediate ancestors, Dúnlaing and Énna Cennselach. The merging of smaller groupings into larger, more consolidated dynasties in the seventh century had been a difficult process, involving intense internecine strife and often bloody subjugation of less successful or ailing dynastic contenders. The Church in seventh-century Ireland also underwent similarly profound changes, and in many instances these changes were related to events in secular society. It is evident that the structure of the Church in Ireland was complex, sophisticated and not as peripheral or peculiar as often portrayed (Etchingham, 1999). Seventh-century hagiographical sources such as the lives of the three primary Irish saints, Patrick, Brigit and Columba reflect the main concerns of the Church at the time – the promotion of their respective cults (and the ensuing authority such success might guarantee), alliances with the emerging dynasties and competing claims for smaller churches whose fortunes had declined for various reasons, one of which was the devastation caused by a series of plagues (Doherty, 1991).

Ireland emerged from the vicissitudes of the seventh century with ecclesiastical and royal institutions that were to be the foundations of authority in Ireland until the twelfth century (for a survey, see Ó Corráin, 1995). They were not immutable and were constantly subject to changing alliances, to declining fortunes and to the intervention of extraordinary individuals. The prominent Uí Néill dynasties of the seventh century, Cenél Conaill and Síl nAedo Sláine, for example, gave way to their rivals for the kingship of Tara, Cenél nEogain and Clann Cholmáin, by the mid-eighth century. The eighth and ninth centuries in Ireland were marked particularly by the regulation of centralized royal and ecclesiastical authority. Ecclesiastical law, the *cáin*-law or *lex*, which was first clearly attested in 697 with the promulgation of *Cáin Adomnáin* to deal with the protection of non-combatants (Ní Dhonnchadha, 1993), gained popularity and was imposed by leading ecclesiastics with the approval of secular authorities (Charles-Edwards, 1999: 43–59). Royal assemblies (*rígdála*) are mentioned in the annals, some of them related to the promulgation of *cána*, others to the resolution of particular political problems. Armagh, as the primary church in Ireland, was assiduous in the eighth and ninth centuries in enforcing its authority throughout Ireland, evident through the promulgation of the *Lex Patricii* and in written sources, including the compilation of the Patrician dossier in the Book of Armagh. Other churches, such as Clonmacnoise, Kildare and Emly, maintained close connections with important dynasties and could be regarded as royal protectorates. Materially, the ecclesiastical and secular power of this period finds expression in the luxury items produced at the time, including the Ardagh and Derrynaflan Chalices, the Tara Brooch and the Moylough Belt-shrine. Culturally, there was a conscious effort to codify and to recast, often with political intent, chronicles, genealogies, laws and saga literature.

The overall impression of consolidation of power and stability in eighth- and ninth-century Ireland masks, however, a much more complex society. In the past, it led scholars to coin such phrases as 'Ireland of Saints and Scholars', 'The Golden Age' and to regard the Viking incursions from 795 as instituting the passing of the old order (Binchy, 1962). While revision of views regarding the contribution and impact of the Vikings in Ireland has been forthcoming in recent years (Clarke *et al.*, 1998), the diverse strands affecting Ireland from *c.* 700 to 850 have yet to be fully evaluated. This chapter does not offer a general survey of the period, therefore, but rather attempts to deal with this diversity by concentrating on three specific topics, namely, the church of Kildare, disturbances among minor population groups and the retirement and deaths of kings *in clericatu*.

Kildare: a royal protectorate and church of powerful women

The church of Kildare was recognized from the seventh century at least as one of the primary churches in Ireland. Located at the head of a fertile plain known in the sources as *Cuirrech Liphe* 'the Curragh of the [river] Liffey', it was placed in a strategically crucial area in the province of Leinster. Any population group, dynasty or king who wished to claim superiority in Leinster could not sustain their claim without exerting authority over this plain. Brigit, foundress of Kildare, whose historicity has been bedevilled by her obvious links with her homonymous pagan predecessor (Ó Riain, 1995: 150–6), was guardian of Leinster, a role eloquently expressed in a poem attributed to a certain Orthanach úa Cáellama Cuirrich,[1] probably a bishop of Kildare who died in 840 (Meyer, 1912: 12 with modified translation):

> Slán seiss, a Brigit co mbúaid,
> for grúaid Lifi lir co tráig,
> is tú banfhlaith buidnib slúaig
> fil for clannaib Catháir Máir.

> Sit safely enthroned, o victorious Brigit/on the bank of the abundant Liffey to the seashore/you are the sovereign lady with companies of a host/who presides over the families of Catháir Már.

The reference to the descendant of Catháir Már alludes to the rival dynasties of Leinster, the most prominent of which by the mid-eighth century were Uí Dúnlainge and Uí Chennselaig. Whereas royal patronage of Kildare is usually regarded as primarily associated with the Uí Dúnlainge dynasty (Ó Corráin, 1981: 328–9), which was the emergent power in Leinster when sources become abundant in the seventh century, they were not the first dynasty to identify its importance. At an earlier remove, the kingship of Leinster was dominated by Dál Messin Corbb and Uí Fhailgi, both of which were associated with Kildare. For example, Conláed, represented as the first bishop of Kildare in the seventh-century *Life of Brigit* by Cogitosus (Connolly and Picard, 1987: 23 paragraph 28), reputedly belonged to Dál Messin Corbb (Mac Shamhráin, 1996: 45–7). Kildare developed rapidly as a centre producing hagiography as part of its attempt to use the cult of Brigit to rival the interests of other churches (Armagh, Clonmacnoise, Durrow and Iona) in the Irish Midlands. By 850 it is suggested that a number of lives of Brigit either in Latin or in Old Irish had been compiled, although not necessarily all in Kildare (McCone, 1982; Sharpe, 1982).

---

1. His name may be translated as 'Prayerful one of the Slender Hand of the Curragh'.

In the period 700–850, the annals record with regular frequency the obits or other activities of the abbots, abbesses and bishops of Kildare. The obits of eight abbesses are recorded, many of them in their office for a lengthy duration. For example, Condal, daughter of Murchad, seems to have held office from the death of her predecessor in 773 to her death in 797, while Muirenn, daughter of Cellach, ruled from 805 to 831. Provided that the annalistic record is accurate and has not overlooked other abbesses, such lengthy incumbencies are indicative of a stable institution and probably of a privileged lifestyle. The role of the abbess of Kildare, as part of the ruling triumvirate in the church (abbot, abbess, bishop), has so far been measured by comments made in the lives of Brigit, which, for example, range from claims according her episcopal status to joint governance with a bishop (Ó Riain, 1995: 151–2). This approach is primarily dictated by the absence of information in other sources as to her actions, apart from her death. However, some hints about her role become evident when familial affiliations, slightly later references, Anglo-Saxon and Ottonian parallels, and other topoi in Brigitine hagiography are explored. Abbesses of Kildare to the twelfth century generally belonged to provincially dominant families (Uí Chennselaig, Uí Dúnlainge or Uí Fhailgi) or to the geographically extensive Fothairt,[2] who claimed Brigit as their own from the earliest sources. Sebdann, daughter of Corc, (d.732) was of the Fothairt (Ó Corráin, 1981: 329), while Muirenn, daughter of Cellach, (d. 831) belonged to Uí Dúnlainge. She was the daughter of a king of Leinster and also the sister of a king of Leinster, while her three brothers were abbots who ruled Kildare in the first three decades of the ninth century (Moody *et al.*, 1984: 259–61). The abbess, depending on her origins, either represented the interests of a dominant dynasty in the primatial church of Leinster or maintained the cult of Brigit and her foremost associate, Conláed. An idea of how this position was expressed in a real sense is gained from the description in the Fragmentary Annals of Ireland of the return of the co-ruler of Munster and abbot of Inis Cathaig (Scattery Island, County Clare), Flaithbertach mac Inmainéin, to Munster in 909 after his defeat at the battle of Belach Mugna (near Castledermot, County Kildare):

> Flaithbertach was brought to Cell Dara [Kildare] then, and the clergy of Leinster reproached him severely, for they knew that it had been he alone who had urged the hosting and the battle, and that Cormac [Cormac mac Cuilennáin, co-ruler of Munster, bishop, killed at the Battle of Belach Mugna in 908] had come against his will. However, after the death of Cerball, king of the

---

2. If the Fothairt, who were scattered throughout Leinster (and elsewhere), were favoured clients of Uí Dúnlainge, and as such, then the latter gained adherents across the province and probably could not object strenuously to an occasional abbess of Fothairt origin being an incumbent of the office at Kildare.

Laigin [Leinster], Flaithbertach was released, which was at the end of that year, according to some. Muirenn, successor of Brigit [Muirenn daughter of Suairt of the Fothairt d. 916], along with a large group of clergy and many relics, escorted him to Mag nAirb [on the borders of Leinster, Osraige and Munster], and when he arrived in Munster he made peace there. (Radner, 1978: 158–9)

In this instance, the abbess of Kildare led the clergy of Leinster and enforced her authority through the medium of relics. The use of relics to impose authority was a normal practice in Ireland from the late eighth century onwards (Doherty, 1984), although the role of the abbess of Kildare is almost unique. Cogitosus, in his seventh-century *Life of Brigit*, speaks of the bodies of Brigit and Conláed laid on the right and left of the ornate altar at Kildare 'in tombs adorned with a refined profusion of gold, silver, gems and stones' (Connolly and Picard, 1987: 25, paragraph 32.1). Conláed's remains were placed in a shrine of gold and silver in 800 (*AU*, in Mac Airt and Mac Niocaill, 1983), although significantly no reference is made to Brigit's remains. Such elaborate dedications could be endowed by women, as also witnessed in the Fragmentary Annals of Ireland, which claims that in 868 Flann, wife of the northern king, Áed Finnliath, 'was building a church to St. Brigit at Cell Dara, and she had many carpenters in the wood chopping down and shaping trees' (Radner, 1978: 133). The situation at Kildare, in which royal women, powerful abbesses, endowments and relics merged, finds many parallels elsewhere. Likely parallels might include the 'holy cousinhood' of seventh-century Anglo-Saxon princesses, Osgyth of Aylesbury, Eadburh of Bicester and Cyneburh of Castor (Campbell, 1986a: 218; Blair, 1989: 106). Leyser's observation that a notable number of Saxon and Lower Rhenish illuminated manuscripts and processional crosses of the Ottonian period and the eleventh century were created for and commissioned by women abbesses (Leyser, 1989, reprint of 1979: 50) appears to offer a parallel to the role of women at Kildare. The great Ottonian tenth- and eleventh-century abbesses of Essen, Mathilda, Sophia and Theophano, probably characterize the zenith with regard to the power of royal women in the Church (Backes and Dölling, 1969: 197–201; McKitterick, 1990, 91–100), of which the situation at Kildare was a relatively pale echo.

Kildare's part in the complex political fabric of Leinster is epitomized by a series of events dating from 804 to 833. In that period the obits of four sons of Cellach son of Dúnchad, king of Leinster (d. 776) are recorded: Fáelán, abbot of Kildare (804), Fínshnechta Cetharderc, king of Leinster (808), Muiredach (823) and Áed (828), abbots of Kildare. In addition, the obits of Flann son of Cellach, abbot of Finnglas (Finglas, County Dublin) and of Eterscél son of Cellach, bishop of Glendalough are recorded in 812 and 814, respectively. It is possible that both were also brothers of Fínshnechta

Cetharderc, king of Leinster, which if correct, illustrates the considerable influence of one generation of royal kinsmen on the prominent churches of North Leinster and Brega. The annals recount that Fínshnechta died of an illness in Kildare suggesting that, apart from naturally retreating to the church – and likely royal vill – of his brother and dynasty, a king might expect superior care in Kildare than in any of his 'secular' residences.

Kings of Leinster did not always behave benignly towards Kildare. Two protagonists for the kingship of Leinster, Rúaidrí son of Fáelán and Bran son of Muiredach, fought each other in 782 at *bellum Cuirrich in confinio Cille Daro* (*AU*, in Mac Airt and Mac Niocaill, 1983). In 834, Cellach son of the aforementioned Bran attacked Kildare itself and killed many on St John's Day in the autumn. Violence at Kildare was not confined to secular intruders. Clerics occasionally indulged in violent deeds, as witnessed by the killing of bishop Echthigern by a priest in 762 and by a fracas which took place in 836 between Feidlimid mac Crimthann, king of Munster and Forannán, abbot of Armagh at the oak church (*dairthech*) of Kildare. While it is difficult to gain any impression of the physical nature of Kildare from many references, some offer an insight into components of its structures. For example, bishop Echthigern was reputedly slain at St Brigit's altar in the *dairthech* (Annals of Clonmacnoise). The seventeenth-century Annals of the Four Masters (s.a. 755, in O'Donovan, 1848–51) claim that Echthigern was killed *etir an cróchaingel 7 an altóir* 'between the chancel-screen and altar'. Despite being a late source, it is never-theless useful to speculate as to what might be meant, since it makes sense in relation to archaeological evidence elsewhere and to Cogitosus's description of the church at Kildare. Cogitosus describes the elaborate partitions in the church of Kildare that divided men from women and clergy from laity.

> The first of these walls, which is painted with pictures and covered with wall-hangings, stretches widthwise in the east part of the church from one wall to the other. In it there are two doors, one at either end, and through the door situated on the right, one enters the sanctuary to the altar where the archbishop offers the Lord's sacrifice together with his monastic chapter and those appointed to the sacred mysteries. (Connolly and Picard, 1987: 26, paragraph 32.2)

The compound *cróchaingel* appears to consist of *cró* 'enclosure, fold, pen' and *caingel* 'chancel-screen, lattice' (borrowed from Latin *cancella*). The additional notes in the ninth-century Book of Armagh refer to a testament made by Fith Fio *iter cróchaingel 7 altóir Dromma Lías* 'between the chancel-screen and altar of Druimm Lías' (Bieler, 1979: 172, paragraph 9(1)). A possible parallel to Kildare's *cróchaingel* 'chancel-screen', albeit in stone rather than in wood, may be the fragmentary baluster-shafts uncovered at Monkwearmouth, interpreted by Cramp as likely to be 'part of a low balustrade either at the base or top of an enclosure, for example surrounding the sanctuary or choir' (1984: 24–5).

Minor dynasties and population groups in the formation of the kingdoms of the eighth and ninth centuries

Commentaries relating to Ireland during this period have tended to concentrate on the deeds of the major or nascent dynasties, and where ailing or minor population groups were concerned, these were studied only if they impinged on the greater powers (for papers dealing with the origins and activities of some minor population groups see Byrne, 1966; Ó Corráin, 1986; Ó Muraíle, 2000). However, as with Mercia, both in its 'original' and 'extended' definitions, large Irish kingdoms consisted of the dominant dynasties and their competing segments, and also of many other population groups, who – depending on their local power and extent – were subject in various forms to the greater powers. The impact of these minor population groups on the polity of the period under review may be divided into four broad categories: (i) when defeated and subjected to a stronger or emerging dynasty; (ii) when they cause disruption to major dynasties; (iii) when involved in internecine warfare among themselves; and (iv) when fighting other minor dynasties.

Cooperation from lesser people within a kingdom or on the borders of a kingdom was essential if a dynasty was to extend and maintain its authority. In many instances, therefore, the implementation of a policy of subjection of minor kingdoms signalled the emergence of a new and dominant dynasty. Dealing severely with miscreants was necessary, a requirement amply demonstrated in the annalistic vocabulary. The use of phrases, including *foirdbe, prostrati sunt, strages* suggest that the defeated party was shown little mercy and, in some cases, that they were deprived of their local kingship and lands or even slaughtered. This would appear to have happened in 744 when the Déis (later to emerge as Dál Cais) severely defeated Corcu Modruad (a kingdom roughly co-extensive with the Burren, County Clare), and when in 754 the Osraige destroyed the Fothairt Fea, a border people in Leinster. Difficult people within an extended kingdom found no favour as the hapless Luigni (located on the borders of counties Mayo–Sligo) experienced in the late eighth century. They were defeated in 762 by the over-kings of Cenél Coirpri, whose kingdom extended from North Mayo to Donegal Bay and eastwards into the Midlands, and were again slaughtered in 789 by their immediate –and more powerful – neighbours, Uí Ailello. In 752, Cenél Coirpri also routed the Brecraige, a Midlands population group whose territory lay west of Lough Iron, County Westmeath. The earlier dynasties of the eastern and north-eastern Midlands fell foul of the designs of greater dynasties from the beginning of the historic period. Recent studies have shown that the rise of elements of Síl nÁedo Sláine (of the southern Uí Néill) was at the expense of the Cíannacht Breg, whose territory extended south of the River Boyne in the seventh century (Byrne, 2000; Byrnes, 2000). Their title was usurped in the eighth century by Síl nÁedo Sláine kings north of the Boyne, which led Cíannacht Breg kings to assume the more restrictive title 'king of Árd Cíannachtae' (roughly co-extensive with the barony of Ferrard, County Louth) instead of 'king of Cíannachta'. However, Cíannacht Breg continued to be active in the eighth and ninth centuries even in the area south of the Boyne to the Liffey that they had effectively ceded in the seventh century. In 770 they defeated Uí Théig of North Leinster at Áth Cliath (later Dublin), although it seems to have been a hollow victory insofar as many of them were drowned at full tide, presumably while crossing the River Liffey. The men of south Brega (the territory between the rivers Boyne and Liffey) roundly defeated them in 817. Similarly in Connacht, the once powerful and extensive Cíarraige were squeezed by the rising Uí Briúin, particularly in Mag nAí, the great central plain of Roscommon (Ó Muraíle, 2000: 166–7).

Relatively minor dynasties could re-emerge on occasion and cause disturbance not to the liking of greater powers. The North Midlands Gailenga created disorder at *Oenach Tailten* 'The Fair of Tailtiu' in 827 while it was being celebrated by the king of Tara, Conchobar, son of Donnchad (d. 833). It is clear from the pre-Norman genealogies that the Gailenga were extensive landholders in the East and North Midlands, and as such their support was probably vital to an over-king's authority and to the stability of the region (Byrne, 1966: 394). That the Gailenga continued to irk Uí Néill over-kings and cause disturbance in and around their core territory is apparent from their killing of the abbot-bishop of the church of Kildalkey, Co. Meath, in 837 (s.a. Annals of the Four Masters, in O'Donovan, 1848–51). This type of activity undoubtedly prompted Máelsechnaill I (d. 865) – Conchobar's nephew – to deal harshly with the Gailenga and their allies the Luigni. The annals record that in 847 Máelsechnaill destroyed (*togail*) Inis Locha Muinremair (understood to be a crannóg on Lake Ramor, County Cavan) 'overcoming there a large band of wicked men of Luigni and Gailenga, who had been plundering the territories in the manner of the heathens' (*AU*, in Mac Airt and Mac Niocaill, 1983). Despite this type of subjugation by a greater power, however, the Gailenga and their allies were resilient and continued to irritate their over-kings until the twelfth century.

Internecine warfare and war among minor dynasties merited a specific term, *belliolum* 'skirmish', in the sources. This type of outbreak often involved warfare between immediate neighbours, as with Cenél nArdgail and Cenél Lóegairi in the East Midlands in 800, the Sogain and Aicme Móenmaige in the kingdom of Uí Maini in Connacht in 803 (Kelleher, 1971: 74) or the Midland population groups Corcu Roíde and Uí Moccu Uais in 812. Literary sources suggest that some form of common bond may have existed among these minor dynasties or population groups, reflected in the use of collective terms such as *aithechthúatha*, *déisi* 'vassal or subject people' and *echtarthúatha*, 'outside people'. Indeed, it might be argued that the events of the eighth century offer a possible context for the redaction of texts dated to the period, most notably *Indarba* or *Toirche na nDéisi* 'The Expulsion or Migration of the Déisi' (Meyer, 1901 and 1907), which tells of the migration and subjection of the vassal people of Ireland.

Dia rogba(i) ind fhlaith bachaill: further reflections on kings who opted out[3]

Clare Stancliffe, in her consideration of the custom of Anglo-Saxon and Irish kings entering religious life from the seventh century onwards, noted that in the case of Irish kings, the movement increased dramatically after *c.* 700, becoming a veritable flood in the last quarter of the eighth century (1983: 165). Noting that this apparent increase might be due to a greater coverage of that period by the sources, Stancliffe also postulated that the habit might have stemmed from Irish – or possibly British – churches (ibid.: 161), and questioned whether 'such conversions are explained solely in terms of concepts of a king's role, leaving nothing to individual choice' (ibid.: 176). The following comments reflect further on Stancliffe's observations in the context of cases of 'opting out' by eighth- and ninth-century Irish kings.

Taking the staff, or in Etchingham's recently coined terminology, becoming a paramonastic adherent of a church (on the concept, see Etchingham, 1999: 290–318), was a relatively common phenomenon among kings from the seventh century. One term associated with this in the annals is *bachall* 'staff(-bearing)', which symbolizes the requirement that a convert from worldly evil must abandon arms-bearing. A gloss on the law-tract *Bretha im Fuillema Gell* explains that *gabullorga* 'forked staves' were appropriate to such persons – perhaps a reference to tau-shaped pilgrim staffs – while according to the law-tract on status *Críth Gablach*, the lord who took the pilgrim staff had no need of a defensive fort (*dún*), but only a house, constructed for him by ecclesiastics (Etchingham, 1999: 296, 388). It is instructive to examine the circumstances in which kings 'opted out' in Ireland and to identify the churches to which they retired, either permanently or intermittently. The following is a list of the incidents of such opting out between 700 and 850, including any possible context and location:

1. 705: Cellach, son of Rogellach, king of Connacht, died after entering religion (*post clericatum*). He is credited with the defeat

---

3. I owe inspiration for the title of this section to Colmán Etchingham's discussion of the phenomenon in Etchingham (1999: 388–9) and to Clare Stancliffe's parallel discussion in an Anglo-Saxon and Continental context (Stancliffe, 1983).

of Loingsech, son of Óengus, king of Tara, at the battle of Corann in 703.

2. 707: Bécc Bairrche, son of Blathmac, king of Ulaid, took the pilgrim's staff (*bachall*) and died in 718. He may have been involved in the battle of Mag Cuilinn in 703 between the Ulaid and British in which Radgann's son 'an enemy of God's churches' was slain. His sons defeated rivals in 714.

3. 723: Selbach, son of Ferchar Fota, king of Dál Riata entered religion. In 717, he had defeated the Britons of Dumbarton at Minuirc, but was defeated by Cenél nGabráin at the naval battle of Ard Nesbi in 719. He re-emerged in 727 and fought at the battle of Irrus Foichnae. He died in 730.

4. 723: Indrechtach, son of Muiredach, king of Connacht, died in Clonmacnoise *i n-ailithri* 'on pilgrimage, in ecclesiastical retirement'.

5. 740 and 744: Domnall Midi, son of Murchad, king of Tara, entered religion in 740 and again in 744. He may have originally entered religion following a defeat of his followers (*muintir*) in 739, but returned to arms in 743 when he defeated the northern Uí Néill. He continued an active life to his death in 763 and was reputedly buried at Durrow. In 764 the churches of Clonmacnoise and Durrow fought each other, the community of Durrow led by Domnall's son, while Clonmacnoise was led by Domnall's brother.

6. 756: Fergus, son of Cellach, king of Connacht, died on pilgrimage.

7. 765: Flaithbertach, son of Loingsech, king of Tara, died in religion in Armagh in 765. He appears to have abdicated when defeated by Áed Allán at the battle of Mag nÍtha in 734.

8. 778: Niall Frossach, son of Fergal, king of Cenél nÉogain, died on pilgrimage in Iona.

9. 782: Artgal, son of Cathal, king of Connacht, took the pilgrim's staff and made a pilgrimage to Iona in 782–783. He had been victorious in 778 when he defeated his rivals in Connacht, Uí Maini, at the battle of Mag nDairben. He died in Iona in 791.

10. 783: Domnall, son of Cethernach, king of Uí Garrchon, died in religion.

11. 784: Donnchad, son of Dub dá Túath, king of Uí Maini, took the pilgrim's staff.

12. 789: Gormgal, son of Éladach of the Gailenga (Byrne, 1966: 392–3), king of Knowth, died in religion.

13. 797: Cummascach son of Fogartach, king of South Brega, died in religion.

14. 808: Fínshnechta Cetharderc, king of Leinster, died of an illness in Kildare (see p. 118).

15. 826: Máel Dúin, son of Gormgal, king of Uí Méith, died in religion.

16. 849: Máel Bresail, son of Cernach, king of Mugdorna, was killed by Vikings after he had converted to religion (*post conuersionem suam ad clericos*) (see Etchingham, 1999: 296–7).

Certain conclusions may be drawn from this information. While kings retreated from dynastic politics into religion following a defeat (nos. 4, 5 and 7), this context does not explain all cases. In the case of Cellach, son of Rogellach (no. 1), Bécc Bairrche (no. 2) and Artgal, son of Cathal (no. 9), they were victors of decisive battles in years immediately prior to their retreat into religion. It may be significant that the term *bachall* as opposed to *in clericatu* is used to describe Bécc Bairrche and Artgal's deed, suggesting that they may not have retired fully, but literally became pilgrims. Domnall Midi, son of Murchad (no. 5), was so closely linked to the church of Durrow and the Columban church – he promulgated the Law of Columba in 753 – that Durrow may have counted among his royal vills. His association with Durrow was probably similar to that of the king of Leinster, Fínsnechta Cetharderc (no. 14), who retreated to Kildare at the end of his life. Abdication could lead to a king fully embracing clerical life or spending a lengthy period in a church, which explains the period between Flaithbertach, son of Loingsech's apparent abdication in 734 and his death in Armagh in 765 (no. 7). A royal family's propensity to enter religion or become pilgrims is evident in relation to the Uí Briúin kings of Connacht, four of whom, Cellach (no. 1), Indrechtach (no. 4), Fergus (no. 6) and Artgal (no. 9), appear to have 'opted out'. The obvious prevalence of the custom in the 780s could have been prompted by an outbreak of disease during that decade. The annals record that smallpox and influenza appeared in Ireland in 779, 783 and 786. The *Annals of Ulster* proclaim in 786 'A great windstorm in January. An inundation in Dairinis. A horrible vision in Clonmacnoise, and great penance done throughout Ireland' (Mac Airt and Mac Niocaill, 1983). That such circumstances caused kings to enter religion is clear from the context of the near contemporary text *Cáin Éimíne Báin* 'The Law of Éimíne Bán'. The text explains that, during an epidemic, the nobles of Leinster came to their king to find out what they should do in the face of tribulation, whether each should go to his local church to take the staff (*dia eclais dúthaig do gabáil bachla*) or whether they should go to one place together (*i n-oentaid na ríg*). They decided to band together and to seek the advice of the saint, Éimíne Bán, with whom they discussed what had impelled them to do penance towards God and to take the staff (Poppe, 1986: 40–1).

The death of Máel Bresail, son of Cernach, king of Mugdorna (no. 16), at the hands of the Vikings, *post conuersionem suam ad clericos* in 849 has been interpreted as possibly resulting from a raid on a church (Etchingham, 1996: 64). The phrase used in the annals suggests that Máel Bresail underwent the process of a layman's conversion to that of an *athláech* 'ex-layman', the stages of which are laid out in an appendix to the tract *Míadslechtae* (Etchingham, 1999: 296–7). The Viking aversion to his conversion may not have been accidental in that Máel Bresail was merely an unfortunate victim of a raid, since the Vikings and Mugdorna were not on good terms. In 837 the Vikings were defeated by the men of Brega at Deoninne in the territory of Mugdorna Breg, while two years following Máel Bresail's murder (851), his brother, Eochu, son of Cernach, styled king of Fir Rois, was killed by them. As to the churches which attracted royal pilgrims, we can only surmise from the scant references to specific churches (Armagh, Clonmacnoise, Iona, Kildare) that the larger churches attracted them not least because they were their patrons and could accommodate them to a suitably high standard. However, *Cáin Éimíne Báin* indicates that lesser kings could seek solace and do penance in their local church in times of crisis.

Conclusion

Direct links between Ireland and Mercia are not as well attested as links between Ireland and other Anglo-Saxon and British kingdoms. Kathleen Hughes (1970) identified Irish influence on early English prayer and made particular reference to the *lorica* of Laidcenn, copies of which are included in the ninth-century Books of Cerne and of Nunnaminster. On the basis that the Book of Cerne was copied in part from a Hymnal of Aedilwald, whom she identified with Æthelwald, bishop of Lichfield from 818 to 830, and therefore Mercian in origin, Hughes considered Irish links with Mercia. Though less extensive than Irish associations with Northumbria, recorded contacts are sufficient to suggest an Irish presence in the kingdom from at least the seventh century. Hughes noted two significant references to the Irish in Mercia during the period under consideration. Charlemagne corresponded with Offa between 793 and 796 requesting him to recall an Irish priest to his home diocese – presumably somewhere in Offa's kingdom – for judgement. The Council of Celchyth, held in 816 and attended by Southumbrian bishops and the king and aristocracy of Mercia, attacked the bishops of the Scotti because the validity of their orders was suspect to the English church (Hughes, 1970: 60–1; 1971: 56–7). Stylistic similarities between the Book of Cerne and the *Tiberius* group of prayer-books and late eight- or early ninth-century Irish manuscripts, including the Books of Armagh and Mulling and the Stowe Missal also suggest contemporary links with Mercia, possibly through Wales (Brown, 1996: 117–18; see Charles-Edwards, Chapter 6 in this volume). With regard to material goods, Susan Youngs has attributed two enamelled buckles from Melton Mowbray, Leicestershire, dated to the seventh or eighth century, to Ireland (Youngs, 1997: 194). An eighth-century Irish-style annular brooch was found at Bonsall, Derbyshire, on the Mercian–Northumbrian border (Smith, 1914: 230, fig. 5). Further evidence of exchange in works of art or at least of the transmission of ideas between Ireland and Mercia in the late seventh or eighth centuries may be deduced from the occurrence of an Irish enamelled mount at the church of St Mary and St Hardulph, Breedon-on-the-Hill, Leicestershire (Youngs, 1989: 60–1 no. 50). The paucity of well-attested connections between Ireland and Mercia in the period *c.* 700 to 850, however, belies the many attributes common at the time to the kings and kingdom of Mercia and kings and kingdoms of Ireland: strong and expanding dynasties, the consolidation of royal and ecclesiastical authority at the expense of earlier, ailing and border churches and dynasties.

Acknowledgements

I wish to thank Michelle Brown, Thomas Charles-Edwards and Raghnall Ó Floinn for their comments on early drafts of this chapter.

9 Carolingian Contacts

Janet L. Nelson

Contacts and contexts

As now in the modern European Union, there was a great deal of subsidiarity in early medieval Europe. Power operated at different levels including the local and the regional. Many historians have drawn attention to the microcosmic nature of early medieval social and political structures, and rightly stressed the workings of power in localities and regions (Davies, 1988; Wickham, 1995a; Brown, P., 1996: 7, 11–13, 216–32). In some places, very small-scale polities persisted over centuries, whether more or less independent, as in the districts of Saxony or the kingdoms of Ireland, or as sub-structures overlain by wider authorities, as in Brittany or the Rhineland (Hässler, 1999; Davies, 1993; Innes, 2000; see also in this volume Charles-Edwards, Woolf, Bhreathnach, Featherstone). At the same time, there were countervailing pressures that tended to produce large political units. Some were ideological: Roman traditions continued to be put into the heads of elite and land-owning persons, by parents and teachers, long after the preconditions for Roman government had gone (Riché, 1976; McKitterick, 1989b); and the Latin Church operated, after a fashion, Christendom-wide, since for some religious purposes, many roads still led to Rome (Levison, 1946; Angenendt, 1990: 252, 341). Also, operative across the boundaries between successor-states to the Roman Empire and other areas, and between Christian and non-Christian states, were strong economic pressures: the basic poverty of early medieval Europe drove elites to cream off wealth across very large geographical areas, producing what can look like two-class societies of powerful and non-powerful, warriors and peasants (Duby, 1974; Fouracre, 1992; Depeyrot, 1994: 37–62).

The conjuncture of the ideological and the economic did not determine outcomes. In Italy, a powerful Roman successor-state was succeeded, after further variations on that theme, by political parcelization. Power was split between regional aristocracies who, by the tenth century, had cornered the peninsula's military and commercial resources (Wickham, 1981; Tabacco, 1989). Eighth-century Saxony consisted of perhaps a hundred districts, ruled by what Bede, characteristically interested in this unfamiliar set-up, and drawing on biblical terminology, called 'satraps', who sometimes joined together to make war under a common leader chosen by lot (*HE*, V. 10, in Plummer, 1896; McClure and Collins, 1994). In Scotland, conquest seems to have contributed more than ideology to the creation, by *c.*900, of a large kingdom covering over 20,000 square kilometres (Davies, 1993; Broun, 1994; Henderson, 1994; Wormald, 1996b). Variety notwithstanding, the dominant trend was towards the formation of larger states. Where historians used to claim sharp, catastrophic disjunctures, caused by internal collapse or external force wielded by assorted barbarians, Arabs, or Vikings, recent historiography, at least as far as the Continent is concerned, tends to see continuities, or cyclical higher-level change overlaid on lower-level stability (Nelson, 1995; Fouracre and Gerberding, 1996).

Can these more general European models be mapped onto Anglo-Saxon England in the eighth and ninth centuries? In some ways, very easily. Bede differentiated between regions (*regiones*) and provinces (*provinciae*) and kingdoms (*regna*); he distinguished princes (*principes*) from kings (*reges*) and kings who had authority (*imperium*) over many provinces (Campbell, 1979a; Campbell, 1979b). Bede wrote when Æthelbald, king of Mercia, was putting together just such a composite kingdom, though Æthelbald was famously absent from Bede's list of kings with *imperium*; and both Æthelbald and Offa were equally absent from a ninth-century West Saxon extension of Bede's list. These absences are attributable to the bias of non-Mercian authors. What Bede described already in the seventh century, and what the availability of charter evidence shows clearly for the eighth, was a process of early state-building (Brooks, 1989a). Warrior-kings, like Machiavelli's manly prince, bent fortune to their will. But Aristotle's dictum that kingship was brought into being by aristocrats to protect their own position against the common people, was probably borne out in Mercia as in other Anglo-Saxon regions. By the 670s, a group of Mercians were the first Englishmen to be recorded (by Bede, *HE* IV. 22) as able to articulate class consciousness: responsible for guarding a Northumbrian prisoner-of-war who claimed to be 'a peasant and a poor man' (he was in fact one of the enemy king's warband, and feared the Mercians' vengeance), the Mercians spotted from 'the way he looks, behaves and speaks' (*vultus et habitus et sermones*) that he was 'not of common stock but of noble family'. The pattern of social evolution towards greater stratification, and of political evolution towards larger concentrations of power, reproduced the transformations that occurred, first among the barbarians in their various Continental kingdoms from the fifth century onwards, then in the empire of Charlemagne on a truly Continental scale.

Yet there were important structural differences between Mercia and, for instance, the kingdom of the Franks. The Mercian kings of the Middle Angles, recorded only from the seventh century onwards, inherited little (if anything) in the way of functioning Roman imperial institutions. They, unlike the Franks, had to re-create a state more or less from scratch. Mercian kings had military followings (Æthelbald was killed by one of his followers), and used regular envoys on diplomatic business abroad (Bullough, 1993: 121), but the evidence for royal administrative officers, active in the realm at large, is very slim. They summoned assemblies to royal estate-centres, but those places were quite small, and the lists of attestations of these kings' charters are brief. A state of sorts, supported by Anglian noble landowners and capable of making war on neighbours regularly and effectively, was a going concern in Mercia before the Church entered the picture. But it was only in the eighth century, with documentary forms and institutional models transmitted in the laws of Christian Roman emperors via the Theodosian Code, that Mercian kings found a convenient way of claiming to impose public military services on all their people (Brooks, 1971). On the Continent, by contrast, barbarian incomers had, as early as the fifth century, established regimes in provinces where the Roman state and the local Roman aristocracy had already endowed the Church; and if it was only the Carolingians who systematically exploited the Theodosian legacy, there had been no break in the legal traditions and practices of the formerly Roman provinces of Aquitaine and Provence (Nelson, 1989: 89–98).

In Mercia, even after conversion that came relatively late compared with other Anglo-Saxon kingdoms, the Church remained relatively poor, dependent on the aristocracy as much as on kings. Mercian kings could not base their state on the Church. They could require a royal monastery to provide board and lodging for royal messengers, but when St Boniface complained bitterly of King Æthelbald's extracting support services for his army from peasants and even monks on lands that churches had been given, the king gave way, at the Council of Clofesho, in 746/7 (Cubitt, 1995: 110–13). Just three years before, the Carolingian mayor of the palace Karloman had informed his bishops that:

> because of the wars which threaten, and the hostility of the rest of the peoples that surround us, we have decided, with the advice of the servants of God, and of the Christian people, to keep for a while longer a portion of church property. (Fouracre 2000: 139)

The contrast with the Franks became starker from the mid-eighth century, for the Carolingians, now kings, harnessed the Frankish Church firmly to their state. Particular churches would grant lands (*precaria*) to laymen with the king's approval, and the king would feel quite justified in claiming some say in the selection of tenants, and then demanding military service from them for the *res publica* (Nelson, 1983; Nelson, 1987). As Charlemagne extended his empire, the churches in annexed provinces like Lombardy were brought into its institutional ambit, and military services were exacted from church tenants (Nelson, 1995: 390). Ecclesiastical geography favoured Frankish royal control. The key archiepiscopal sees – Rheims, Rouen,

Sens, Cologne, Mainz – lay in the heartlands of Francia, hence under the king's thumb. Mercia lacked an archiepiscopal see, and so its bishops owed obedience to a metropolitan in another kingdom, Kent.

Christian rituals were built into the very fabric of the Carolingians' state. Oaths of fidelity had to be sworn by 'all', effectively all adult men from small-scale landowners to magnates (excluding dependent peasants and the unfree), who came to local public courts to swear their oaths to royal commissioners (Nelson, 1995: 425; Nelson, 1990: 10, 20). Oaths were sworn to Charlemagne in conquered Bavaria, as well as in Francia (Bitterauf, 1967 Freising no. 186). Rebel Thuringians were made to confess their offence to the king at Worms, then sent away with royal officers:

> some into Italy, some into Neustria and into Aquitaine, ... to the tombs of the saints so that they might swear fidelity to the king and his children ... Some were arrested on their return journey and had their eyes torn out, some reached Worms and were arrested there and sent into exile, and had their eyes torn out there. (*Annales Nazariani* 786, ed. Pertz, 1826b: 42–3, trans. King, 1987: 155)

Charlemagne was determined that oaths should be used only to sustain the vertical authority of kingship and lordship:

> those presuming to engage in a conspiracy of any sort and sealing it with an oath are to have judgement passed on them ...: whenever some evil has been perpetrated as a consequence, the authors of the deed are to be put to death while their helpers are to be flogged, one by the other, and to cut off each other's noses. (Capitulary of Thionville (806), no. 44, *c*.10, ed. Boretius, 1883: 124, trans. King, 1987: 249)

Christian rituals did not exclude, indeed were complemented by, the savage rites of lordly vengeance. With some justification, Charlemagne's empire has been called 'a village chiefdom extended to the limits of the universe' (Duby, 1971: 23).

In the end, the most important difference between Mercia and the Frankish Empire was one of scale. Mercia itself covered some 25,000 square kilometres, and in Offa's reign, including satellite kingdoms, perhaps four times that. The Frankish kingdom under the Merovingian dynasty in the seventh century had extended its sprawling, loose hegemony east of the Rhine to cover perhaps 600,000 square kilometres: the Carolingians' realm from the mid-eighth century, through a process of conquering and absorbing other regions and *regna*, became very large indeed, until by *c*.800, the empire of Charlemagne covered 1,200,000 square kilometres. But it was not just a matter of scale. Charlemagne ruled more intensively too, imposing burdens of military and governmental service on both high and low, summoning provincials bearing gifts to assemblies in Francia, sending out commissioners to check and cajole local office-holders, requiring reports in writing on local court proceedings, and lists of those who failed their obligations (Nelson, 1990: 1–36). As part of the process of conquest, Saxon hostages, listed as 'x son of y', suggesting both nobility and youth, were distributed among loyal provincial elites, who then had to present them for inspection at royal centres (Capit. no. 115, and cf. Capit. 32, c.12, ed. Boretius, 1883: 233–4, 84). Within its own limits, this was a bureaucratic state. A village-chiefdom 'extended to the limits of the universe', if it is to survive, necessarily becomes something other than a village-chiefdom. Not only did the empire of Charlemagne survive for some sixty years as a large composite state, but thereafter, when split into plural states, each one continued for at least a generation more as a microcosm of its universal original – still composite, still relatively bureaucratic (though less so in East Francia), still large compared with Anglo-Saxon kingdoms, even Mercia (Reuter, 1991: 84–94; Nelson, 1992: 19–74; Delogu, 1995: 303–13).

The differences between Mercia and the Carolingian Empire, though they result, up to a point, from scarcity of evidence in the one case, plentiful sources in the other, are nevertheless real. If annalistic evidence for contemporary contacts, and awareness of their significance, were all there was, it would be near impossible to write a chapter on any kind of Anglo-Saxon contacts, least of all Mercian ones, with the Carolingians. The *Anglo-Saxon Chronicle* barely notices events in the Frankish realm, unless these impinge on the Continental Saxons, as in 782: 'in this year the Old Saxons and the Franks fought' (Whitelock, 1979: 179). The death of 'King Charles' is noted under 814. Nor do the Royal Frankish Annals notice Offa at all. Apart from a single episode involving the Northumbrian king Eardwulf, his exile and restoration by papal and Frankish *legati* in 808,[1] and the ransom of one of those envoys in 809 (he had been captured by 'pirates', presumably Scandinavians, and the ransom was paid by 'a man of King Coenwulf'), there is no mention of any Anglo-Saxon kingdom in the near-century, 741–829, these annals cover (*Annales regni Francorum* 808–9, in Kurze, 1895: 126–8, trans. King, 1987: 100–1). Such mutual neglect is instructive, and not wholly to be explained away by annalists' myopia. Different early medieval worlds were, for many people and for much of the time, self-enclosed, and only certain individuals were involved in

---

1. Was any Frankish force made available to Eardwulf? It is worth comparing the activities of Bishop Jesse of Amiens, sent as Charlemagne's envoy (*missus*) to Italy in 808, which aroused a fierce protest from Pope Leo III: 'in our view this *missus* is not suitable (*non idoneus*) ... We do not know if it is by your orders that your *missi*, who have come to do acts of justice, have brought large numbers of men with them and installed them in the cities and caused them to levy large taxes' (Leo III, Ep. 2, ed. Hampe, 1898: 89, 91). An envoy sent to Italy with a large military retinue could turn into a viceroy.

regular contacts between them. Entrée to that parallel world of communications is supplied above all by letters, notably those of Alcuin, a Northumbrian resident in Francia, who kept in touch with a wide range of correspondents in various Anglo-Saxon kingdoms, especially Northumbria. The value of the letter-collection whose compilation he himself supervised is enhanced by his two fairly lengthy returns to England, in 786 and 790–793, and by his absence from court for almost all of the last eight years of his life. Thanks to those returns, and those absences, the range of Alcuin's correspondents was significantly widened during substantial periods between 786 and 804 (Godman, 1982; Wormald, 1982; Bullough, 1983; Garrison, 1995: esp. ch. 3).

Largely because the two major eighth-century Anglo-Saxon letter-collections are those associated with the West Saxon Boniface and the Northumbrian Alcuin, and because Alcuin seems to have fed information to the compilers, probably based at York, of Northumbrian annals (Wallace-Hadrill, 1965: 155; Whitelock, 1979: 127, 263–76), Mercia is under-represented in the evidence for contacts between Anglo-Saxon kingdoms and the Continent. Northumbrians do seem in any case to have taken a larger interest in the Continental Saxons than the Mercians did. It was the king and queen of Northumbria, not Mercia, who wrote to Bishop Lul of Mainz to ask him to help ensure a hearing for their envoys at the court of Charlemagne in 772/3, in the aftermath of Charlemagne's first Saxon campaign (Ep. 121, ed. Tangl, 1916: 257–8, trans. Whitelock, 1979: 833–4). It is also true that Mercia, until quite late in the eighth century, seems to have engaged in relatively fewer Continental contacts than did Northumbria, East Anglia, Kent and Wessex. Mercia was in origin, if not a landlocked kingdom, then one less coastally orientated than its neighbours. Yet the Trent gave access to the sea and beyond that the Continent. Archaeological and architectural evidence shows when Mercian rulers and elites became interested in that access. The monastery of Breedon-on-the-Hill, just 5 kilometres from the Trent though well upriver from its confluence with the Humber, and only a day's journey from Tamworth, favourite residence of the eighth-century kings, was adorned at just this period with stonework influenced by the art of Francia and the Mediterranean world (Cramp, 1977; Jewell, Chapter 17 in this volume), while the high-status site at Flixborough, Lincs., also of eighth-century date, has revealed the effects on material culture once Mercian power stretched itself towards places linked with Continental trade (Loveluck, 1998; cf. Stafford, 1985: 102). The imposition on Breedon of hospitality service for 'envoys from across the sea', and the importance of the London mint in Offa's reign, were symptomatic of these widened horizons and resources (Stewart, 1986; Bullough, 1993: 121–2; Blackburn, 1995: 550). But did all this put Mercia on a par with the kingdom of the Franks?

Imitation and flattery

It has been claimed that Charlemagne imitated Offa, as well as vice versa, in the fields of coinage and legislation (Blunt, 1961; see also Williams, Chaper 15 in this volume).[2] True, it seems highly likely that Offa undertook a major revaluation of coinage in 792, before Charlemagne's revaluation in 793/4. But since the revalued penny was of significantly different weight in each case (1.7 gr. for the Frankish, and 1.45 gr. for the Mercian), the two decisions need to be prised firmly apart. Offa increased the weight of the Mercian penny to something above that of the Frankish one (1.3 gr.) as it had been since the 760s. Charlemagne fairly promptly altered, and substantially increased, the weight of the Frankish penny, throughout the empire (Grierson, 1965: 506–11; Day, 1997: 29). It seems fairly clear that the intent, in both kingdoms, was to ensure that foreign coin had to be exchanged at entry, thus implying that both kings were intent on exploiting the income from this exercise (Blackburn, 1995: 548–50). Further, in comparing the volume of these coinages, hence the profits rulers stood to make in Mercia and Francia, it is worth contrasting Offa's three mints (London, Canterbury and an East Anglian site) with Charlemagne's 40 (Blackburn, 1995: 549).

As for Offa's 'Laws', these are almost certainly to be identified as the decrees of the Legatine Mission that summoned a council in Mercia in 786 (Wormald, 1991; Wormald, 1999: 106–7), and those decrees influenced Charlemagne's *Admonitio Generalis* of 789 (Cubitt, 1995: 153–90). Yet the men behind 786 were less Pope Hadrian's than Charlemagne's, since one of the two legates, the Italian Bishop George of Amiens, had long since become a Frank by adoption (Levison, 1946: 127–9; Bullough, 1991: 130), while their clerical support team included the Frankish abbot Wigbod sent by Charlemagne for the express purpose of 'helping' the legates, and Alcuin, who very probably had a hand in both the 786 decrees and Charlemagne's *Admonitio* three years later (Kasten, 1997: 146–7). Offa's 'Laws' can thus be seen as Carolingian-inspired.

The marriage alliance mooted between Charlemagne's son Charles and Offa's daughter in 790 was clearly a Frankish initiative, and linked with the Young Charles' promotion in that or the previous year (Classen, 1972: 110–11). The man chosen to negotiate the match was Gervold, recently appointed abbot of St-Wandrille, and before that bishop of Evreux in the province of Rouen. According to *The Deeds of the Abbots of St-Wandrille*, written up *c.*840 but on the basis of documents preserved at the abbey (Wood, 1991), Gervold had already

---

2. On eighth- and ninth-century Mercia, the work of Simon Keynes, Patrick Wormald and Anton Scharer is especially thought-provoking. See Keynes (1990); Keynes (1998); Wormald (1982); Wormald (1991); Scharer (1982) and Scharer (1988).

for many years served as superintendent of the kingdom's trade, collecting the taxes and tolls in various ports and cities but especially in Quentovic. It is known that very strong bonds of friendship existed between him and Offa, most mighty king of the Angles or Mercians. Letters sent from Offa in which he declares that he will be Gervold's dearest friend and intimate are still extant. On the orders of the most invincible king Charles, Gervold on many occasions served in person as an ambassador to the aforementioned king Offa. His final mission was concerned with the daughter of the said king, whom the younger Charles was seeking in marriage. Offa would not agree to this unless Bertha, daughter of the great Charles, was given in marriage to his son, and the most mighty king [Charles], somewhat angered (*aliquantulum commotus*), gave the command that no-one from the island of Britain or the people of the Angles was to set foot on the shores of Gaul for the purposes of trade. (*Gesta sanctorum patrum Fontanellensis coenobii*, in Lohier and Laporte, 1936: 84–7, trans. King, 1987: 334).[3]

While the author of *The Deeds* goes on to say that Gervold dissuaded Charlemagne from this retaliatory action, two letters of Alcuin (Epp. 7 and 9, in Dümmler, 1895, 2) written late in 790 show that contacts between Mercia and Francia had indeed been disrupted: 'sailings have been forbidden to traders on both sides, and have come to a stop'. Alcuin was then staying in Northumbria, and begged the influential Abbot Adalard of Corbie (Charlemagne's cousin) for information about the cause of the dispute, suggesting that he himself might be sent back to Francia to help resolve it. He may have overestimated his own influence, for he remained in Northumbria. The bits of information do not entirely coincide, and given Alcuin's evident lack of knowledge (he was after all in Northumbria, not Mercia), his claim that measures were taken on both sides may not be correct. On the other hand, he was in a position to know that cross-Channel communication had become difficult, and his contemporary testimony is to be preferred to the St-Wandrille author's denial that Charlemagne carried out his threat. *The Deeds'* intent is to present Gervold as a man with the power to sway not just one but two kings. Yet the phrase 'somewhat angered' strikes me as rather precisely calibrated: there was all the difference in the world between seeking a foreign king's daughter as bride for your son, and sending your own daughter abroad. Charlemagne, in the 780s, had contemplated giving his eldest daughter in marriage to the Emperor in Constantinople; but that alliance was plainly in a different league. No such gift could be considered in the case of his second

---

3. Given the nature of this source, Whitelock (1979: 21) may have been unwise to infer from it that 'Englishmen in general' were 'apparently regarded [by Charlemagne] as Offa's subjects'. Whitelock (1979: 341) translates *Angli* as 'Englishmen', whereas King, as quoted above, translated 'Angles'.

daughter Bertha, now aged perhaps 11, and Offa's son. Offa's counter-request was a serious affront. Yet the appropriate response was a measured blend of anger and contempt: to be 'just a bit incensed' was the perfect put-down. The proof of the pudding is the fact that no marriage took place – which perhaps suited Charlemagne quite well at the time. The Young Charles could wait.

Offa's imitation of Charlemagne is clearest in his sustained and ultimately successful efforts to have his son and heir anointed king, in 787. This act of pre-mortem succession was a demonstration of paternal power, intended to assure the continuance of a single royal descent line: something new in Mercian history (cf. Goody, 1968: 1–56, esp. 8–12; Lewis, 1978). There can be little doubt that the use of the ritual of anointing in such a context was inspired by a pair of Carolingian royal inaugurations just six years before (Wallace-Hadrill, 1965: 157–8; Wallace-Hadrill, 1971: 113–15; Nelson, 1986b: 285). But there were important differences. First, the anointings of the Carolingian infant-kings in 781 were performed by Pope Hadrian, in Rome, and so were intended to supply a similar legitimacy to that conferred by Pope Stephen II on Charlemagne and his brother in 754. Second, these rituals were associated with post-baptismal anointings performed by Hadrian on Charlemagne's sons, so that a bond of spiritual co-fatherhood was forged between pope and king, and subsequently emphasized in papal correspondence (Classen, 1965; Angenendt, 1984: 75–91; Nelson, 1996: 102, 110). Third, however, the anointings of 781 were linked with the establishment of two kingdoms, one, Italy, under new Carolingian management (Delogu, 1995: 304), the other, Aquitaine, plain new (Collins, 1990). In other words, the Carolingian rituals pertained to inheritance that was designed to be not just partible but potentially permanently so, and, according to the *Divisio regni* of 806, without further subdivision, assuming that each son had at least one male heir (Classen, 1972: 125).

The main explanations for these differences were, first, that Charlemagne's position was intimately linked with papal authority in a way that Offa's was not, and, second, that Charlemagne's multiple acquired kingdoms were destined for redistribution whereas Offa planned to leave a single son as sole heir to his expanded realm. Was this latter difference the result of accident, in that Offa had only one son? No, for the reverse of the coin of bloody usurpations was that Mercia had not been partitioned for generations before 786. Was Mercia too small, or its royal lands too poor, to partition? That seems unlikely, though tenth-century Saxony would provide a parallel (Gillingham, 1971; Reuter, 1991: 148–50; see Yorke, 1983). In a thought-provoking structural comparison of Mercia with Wessex, Patrick Wormald argued that the West Saxon kings were richer in land than the Mercian kings and also did better in holding on to that land. Wormald admitted there was little real evidence for these contrasts (Wormald, 1982: 141–2). The agrarian richness of the Midlands is likely to have been well exploited by the eighth century, and it was in the midst of that richness that the Mercian kings' heartlands were situated (Stafford, 1985: 6, 78, 102). I am unconvinced that the West Saxon kings 'could afford not to pressurise the Church' as the Mercian kings had. Earlier medieval kings everywhere found it convenient, and affordable, to do so from time to time. Ine did so already in the early eighth century, if he is indeed the butt of the complaints of Abbess Eangyth and her daughter Bugga (*Epistolae selectae* III, in Tangl, 1916: no. 14). Alfred certainly pressurized several churches, including those of Canterbury and Winchester (Nelson, 1986c). Charlemagne, despite his enormous landed resources, was a patron discriminating to the point of stinginess, and he imposed military obligations on all the churches he could (Nelson, 1983: 117–32). Nor is it easy to be sure that the West Saxon kings 'could afford to be less generous [than the Mercians] in the immunities they gave laymen'. In the ninth century, charter evidence indicates that Æthelwulf was indeed generous to his thegns (Keynes, 1994b), as on occasion were his Carolingian contemporaries. Wormald is certainly right, though, to bring kings, Church, and lay aristocracy into the same frame. Alfred used something like the Carolingian system of precarial grants, that is, arrangements whereby churches agreed to the temporary use of their lands by men nominated by the king. It was possible for everyone to have their cake and eat it.

The royal anointings of Charlemagne's sons did not mean that their sub-kingdoms escaped Charlemagne's supervision. In Aquitaine, after the aristocracy tried to take advantage of the boy-king Louis by filching royal estates, Charlemagne promptly sent his own overseer of estates (*provisor villarum*) to ensure the restoration to the public service (*obsequium publicum*) of the misappropriated lands – 'and these orders were carried out' (Astronomer, *Vita Hludowici* c.6, in Tremp, 1995: 302–3). In Italy too, Charlemagne continued to supervise his son Pippin's regime (Bougard, 1995: 27–9, 32, 51; Kasten, 1997: 138–60). He sent *missi* to tackle local grievances, but the locals had no doubt who ultimately received their appeals for justice (Nelson, 1996: xxvi). Charlemagne devolved power, but retained ultimate responsibility for ruling his vast empire. No rebellion against either sub-king followed the setting-up of those two sub-kingdoms. In Mercia, there is no evidence as to how, or whether, Offa divided his power with Ecgfrith between 787 and 796, but Alcuin referred to the bloodshed Offa had perpetrated to secure Ecfrith's succession (Ep. 122, in Dümmler, 1895, **2**: 179). The anointing of Ecgfrith was a response to the extreme discontinuity that had characterized Mercian successions in the past and continued to plague other Anglo-Saxon kingdoms. Fortunately for Offa, partition was not an option he had to consider; nor would he know that the bloodshed had been in vain, since Ecgfrith outlived him only by months, and the succession then passed to a man who did not even claim more than a distant kinship with Æthelbald or Offa.

Offa among 'the big men of Europe'?

In a letter conventionally dated 784 × 91, Pope Hadrian wrote to tell Charlemagne that he had received from him a letter

> relating that Offa, king of the people of the Angles, had sent your royal excellence a document to show that some enemies (*aliqui emuli*) of yours and his would be informing our Apostolic Person that that same King Offa was suggesting to you ... that you ought to evict us from the Holy See ... and that you should establish another rector there from among your own people. What was written appeared most abominable and mischievous to your eyes ... and in every respect false, since Offa has not ... urged you to any such thing ... I myself had heard nothing of these allegations, which are incredible in our eyes. (*Codex Carolinus*, ed. Gundlach no. 92, trans. King, 1987: 305)

Charlemagne had spiked the rumour; and in any case the pope claimed to find it 'incredible'. But Hadrian was happy, nevertheless, to have Charlemagne's assurances, and to welcome envoys from both Charlemagne and Offa.

A likely date for Offa's sending of envoys, and for his being well aware of what enemies might say, has been argued to be the year 784 or 785, when Offa was putting heavy pressure on Archbishop Jaenberht of Canterbury to consecrate Ecgfrith as king (Stenton, 1971: 213; Wallace-Hadrill, 1975 (1965): 157; Brooks, 1984: 117–18). On the evidence of this letter, Nicholas Brooks has presented Offa as 'a king who exercised unparalleled influence at the courts of Charlemagne and of the pope' (Brooks, 1984: 111). According to Michael Wallace-Hadrill, the letter shows Offa 'in touch with the big men of Europe' (Wallace-Hadrill, 1975 (1965): 157). But 'influence' and contacts are not the same thing, and Anglo-Saxon concerns cannot supply the only context for this letter. As Brooks acknowledged, Offa's activities could just as well have aroused 'enemies', and caused intrigue in Francia and Rome, rather later in the 780s. Something similar can be said from the Continental side too: if Pope Hadrian felt insecure, even 'frightened' (Wallace-Hadrill, 1975 (1965): 157), he had plenty of reasons for doing so. Charlemagne had not fulfilled what papal sources regarded as a firm promise to hand over to the papacy a very large tranche of central Italy (Noble, 1984: 85–6, 160–1). Concessions made by Charlemagne in 781 had proved impossible for the pope to secure on the ground, both in the Sabina and in Campania (Wickham, 1995b; Costambeys, 1998). Hadrian's relations with Charlemagne had been severely jolted at the turn of 786–787, when, in the aftermath of a revolt that posed the most serious political problems he had yet faced in Francia, the king had appeared in Italy, marching south from Florence, where he spent Christmas, 'with all possible speed' to Rome, en route for a campaign against Benevento

(*Annales regni Francorum*, revised, 786, in Kurze, 1895: 73; King, 1987: 120). Disturbing that frontier had two dangerous consequences elsewhere, in Bavaria and Byzantium. Charlemagne wanted Pope Hadrian involved in all three areas, yet the options the king took were at odds with Hadrian's perceptions of papal interests. Charlemagne's stalling over his daughter's marriage with the Byzantine emperor wrong-footed the pope, whose sights were set on a peaceful resolution to the long-running iconoclast dispute (*Annales regni Francorum*, revised, 786, in Kurze, 1895: 75; King, 1987: 120). The pope was dragooned into underwriting Charlemagne's new hard line with Bavaria (*Annales regni Francorum*, original version, 787, in Kurze, 1895: 74–6). In Benevento, Charlemagne huffed and puffed, failed to prevent his envoys' entrapment, and, in early 788, flouted Hadrian's advice and reverted to a policy of using the local dynasty as client-rulers – a policy that soon proved as unworkable as before (*Codex Carolinus*, ed. Gundlach, no. 80; cf. Nelson, 1998).

It was not as if the papal position had been secure previously. The papal *Lives* throw lurid light on Roman politics in the 760s and early 770s. It was in a situation of endemic factional violence that the existence of the permanently manned *scholae*, that is, hostels, of Anglo-Saxons, Franks, Lombards and Frisians, right next door to St Peter's, could assume a significance that was other than symbolic. The potential military importance of these establishments, hinted at in the context of 799 (*Life of Leo IV* c. 19, in Davis, 1992: 189), and realized in the mid-ninth century (*Life of Sergius II* c. 46, in Davis, 1995: 95), was surely there already in the late 780s. Perhaps Offa exerted enough leverage to harass Hadrian into approving the creation of a new archbishopric at Lichfield in 787 (*ASC* 787, letter of Coenwulf to Leo III (798), in Whitelock, 1979: 180, 860). But Charlemagne's leverage at Rome was clearly far greater: hence the rumour that Offa had 'suggested to him that he evict' the pope, and replace him by a Frank. If there is any truth in this tale, it may be that Offa suggested what Charlemagne was already half-inclined to consider, at one particularly difficult moment.

Exiles and enemies

In another letter, this time addressed by Charlemagne to Archbishop Æthelheard of Canterbury and Bishop Ceolwulf of Lindsey (Alcuin, Ep. 85, in Dümmler, 1895, **2**: 127–8; Whitelock, 1979: 847; Bullough, 1993: 116, n. 78), the conventional theme of friendship stressed in the opening sentences supplies the occasion for Charlemagne to remind his addressees that they had met and spoken with one another – whether when Æthelheard was en route to Rome for his pallium (though no such visit in recorded in the *Anglo-Saxon Chronicle*) or on some other mission (for he was evidently one of Offa's trusted men; Brooks, 1984: 120).[4] Charlemagne sent back, along with this letter,

some Mercian exiles, the men of a lord named Hringstan, who had also
evidently been living under Charlemagne's protection. Hringstan had
died, and his men were no longer guaranteed houseroom at the
Frankish palace. While Hringstan had repeatedly said that he had fled
Mercia in fear of his life, Charlemagne now voiced his own belief that
Hringstan 'would have been faithful to his lord [i.e. Offa] had he been
allowed to stay in his own land' and hoped that the two churchmen
could obtain 'peace' for his followers from Offa. The most revealing
line in the letter is Charlemagne's assertion that though he had kept
Hringstan with him (*apud nos*) for 'quite some while', he had done so
'on account of reconciliation, not hostility'. Presumably the two terms
of that last phrase were to be understood as having two different
referents: that is, Charlemagne had hoped that Hringstan would be
reconciled with Offa, and he had not hoped to exploit the exile's
presence out of any hostile intent of his own towards Offa. Wallace-
Hadrill remarks that Charlemagne's 'excuses for sheltering [Hringstan
and his men] in the first place sound rather thin' (Wallace-Hadrill,
1965: 163). Granted that, it is noteworthy that in this letter, Offa is
termed not just Charlemagne's 'brother', but his 'dearest brother'.

The excuses sound the thinner when it is recalled that Hringstan
and his men were not the only Mercian exiles harboured in Francia. In
789, Ecgberht, a son of the Kentish king Ealhmund and a claimant to
the West Saxon kingdom, was exiled by Offa and King Beorhtric of
Wessex to 'the land of the Franks' where he stayed for three years
(*ASC* 839, Whitelock, 1979: 187). Though there is no direct evidence,
it seems very likely that Charlemagne was his host, and even that
Ecgberht's eventual return was sponsored by Charlemagne. The
Northumbrian exiled king Eardwulf, helped by Charlemagne and
restored by his *missi*, has already been mentioned; and another
probable Kentish royal exile will be considered presently. Thrice is
surely beyond coincidence. What this evidence strongly suggests is
that Charlemagne's powerful proximity posed a permanent threat for
Offa. 'If you have the Frank as your friend, you don't have him as your
neighbour' (Einhard, *Vita Karoli* c.16, Holder-Egger, 1911: 20). By
contrast, Offa is never mentioned as posing an equivalent threat to
Charlemagne. No Frankish rebel is recorded as finding refuge with a
neighbouring ruler. Though Charlemagne's Saxon opponent, Widukind, was briefly harboured by the Danish king in 777, and the
Lombard prince Adelchis, son of the deposed King Desiderius, found
long-term shelter in Constantinople, whence he attacked via Bene-

---

4. The forthcoming book of Donald Bullough will clarify much about the letters in
    the Alcuin letter-collection, and about Alcuin's role as Charlemagne's advisor.
    Meanwhile I have relied on Bullough (1991; 1983), and Bullough (1993), for the
    attributions of 'Charlemagne's' letters. Another eagerly awaited book is the
    revised Cambridge (1995) PhD thesis of Mary Garrison. I am very grateful to
    both these scholars for help and advice on the key author for the subject of this
    chapter.

vento, Charlemagne eventually neutralized both threats by his own diplomatic and military efforts. The king of the Danes who received Widukind in 777 sent envoys to Charlemagne in 782, and in 793, Alcuin was obliquely promising the bishop-abbot of Lindisfarne that he would seek Charlemagne's intervention to secure the return of 'boys carried off by the pagans and held in captivity' (Ep. 20, Dümmler, 1895, **2**: 58, trans. Whitelock, 1979: 846).

Aachen, small beer by comparison with Constantinople, or Córdoba, or Baghdad (Barraclough and Parker, 1993: 108–9), was impressive by comparison with any other central place in the Christian West (Nelson, 2000). The range of Charlemagne's foreign contacts was extraordinarily wide: his allies included 'the king of the Persians' in Baghdad and his 'beloved and honourable brother, Michael, glorious emperor and Augustus' in Constantinople (*MGH*, Epistolae IV, Epistolae variorum no. 37, ed. Dümmler 1895, **2**: 556), the amir of Fustat in north Africa, the governors of Barcelona and Huesca in Muslim Spain, the king of the Asturias, and 'kings of the Irish'. These multiple bonds of *amicitia* (friendship), Einhard thought (*Vita Karoli* c. 16, Holder-Egger, 1911: 19), 'augmented the glory of his realm'. Thus Charlemagne bestowed rich gifts on the Irish kings, and, variously, to submissive Avars, Slavs and Danes. If the Franks' neighbours feared them, those neighbours' neighbours found the Franks their allies. Beyond the hostile Sorbs and Wilzes were the Abodrites, 'our Slavs' (*Annales Laureshamenses* 798, ed. Pertz, 1826a: 34, trans. King, 1987: 143). But Einhard and the author(s) of the Frankish annals were more anxious to report the lavish gifts Charlemagne received from exotic quarters: the beautiful pavilion tent from the Asturias, more fine tents, and also robes and spices, candelabra and a wonderful water-clock from Baghdad, and last but not least, the gift that Charlemagne asked for, an elephant (*Annales regni Francorum* 798, 807, in Kurze, 1895: 102, 123–4, King, 1987: 90, 98; Einhard, *Vita Karoli* c. 16, Holder-Egger, 1911: 19; *Annales regni Francorum* 802, in Kurze, 1895: 117, King, 1987: 95).

Kings as brothers

Some, exclusively English, historians have suggested that the relationship between Charlemagne and Offa was one between equals (Stenton, 1970: 215; Whitelock, 1979: 22; Wormald, 1982: 101; cf. Kirby, 1991: 175). The evidence consists essentially of two letters. One is a mere note, probably composed by Alcuin on Charlemagne's behalf, datable no more precisely than to 793–796, in which Charlemagne asks Offa to cooperate in returning a miscreant Irish priest from Francia to Ireland via Mercia. 'We request you ... to give orders for him to be conveyed, according to opportunity of time and transport, to his homeland' (Ep. 87, Dümmler, 1895, **2**: 131; Bullough, 1993: 116 and n. 78). The priest had been accused of eating meat during Lent, and though adequate evidence was lacking, there were worries about discrediting the priesthood in the eyes of the 'ignorant people'. The priest had been residing in the diocese of Cologne, whose bishop was Hildebold, one of Charlemagne's closest confidants. It was perhaps because Hildebold was about to be, or had just been made, Charlemagne's special ecclesiastical adviser permanently resident in the palace (Capitulary of Frankfurt (July 794), *c.*55, Boretius, 1883: 78) that both king and bishop were especially concerned about the situation. The likelihood of a date of summer 794 for this letter might be strengthened further by Alcuin's availability in Charlemagne's palace to act as draftsman (Frankfurt, *c.*56, Boretius, 1883: 78).

The letter's subtext is Charlemagne's responsibility for the religious well-being of Christian people wherever they are. He is concerned about correct priestly conduct *ibique* – there in Ireland too – as well as in the lands regulated by 'our bishops'. In the letter's address formula, he has the title 'by the grace of God king of the Franks and defender of the Holy Church of God'. The request is polite, but authoritative: that Church included the Irishman's *patria*, and Offa's, as well as the Frankish realm. This, again, is the spirit of Frankfurt, where Charlemagne summoned bishops from every province to condemn heresies, for which Paulinus of Aquileia wrote a lengthy theological statement on behalf of the bishops of Italy, and from which Alcuin drafted two letters: one from the Frankish bishops to their Spanish confrères, and another for Charlemagne to send to Archbishop Elipand of Toledo and the bishops of Spain (Bullough, 1991: 187, though cf. Cavadini, 1993: 77). When Charlemagne, in the salutation of his more or less contemporary letter to Offa, greets his *frater et amicus* (brother and friend), he names himself first, and with a title that makes universal claims, Offa second, and with the simple title *rex*. It is a standard feature of medieval epistolography that the salutation clause always names the superior first, the inferior second. This little letter needs to be read alongside the big letter sent in Charlemagne's name to the Spanish bishops:

> We claim, according to the share of our strength, to serve and preach ... the orthodox faith handed down by apostolic teachers and kept by the Church universal ... Correcting you is what makes us glad, for we desire to have you as our associates in the Catholic Faith so that the joy Christ promised his disciples may dwell in us and our joy be fulfilled in you. To fulfil that joy, and on the compulsion of fraternal love, we have ordered a synodal council of holy fathers to be assembled from all the churches under our rule ... Furthermore, we have summoned some men of ecclesiastical discipline from regions of Britannia so that the Catholic Faith may be investigated by the diligent consideration of many ... We have ordered that three statements be drawn up, first, presenting the view of the Pope and the Holy Roman Church and the bishops in those parts, second, saying what the ecclesiastical teachers and bishops of the churches of Christ in

the nearer parts of Italy wish to be believed ..., and third, containing the orthodox faith of those holy fathers the bishops and venerable men who fill worthy offices for God in Germania, Gaul, Aquitaine and Britannia. (*MGH*, Concilia II (i), ed. Werminghoff, 1906: 158–60)

Fraternity did not imply equality for this Big Brother writing in 794 to his (little) brother in Britannia.

No more did it in Charlemagne's second letter to Offa (probably composed not by Alcuin but by some other adviser, though preserved in an English manuscript; Ep. 100, Dümmler, 1895, **2**: 144–6, trans. Whitelock, 1979: 848–9; Bullough, 1993: 116, n. 78), this time as a 'man to be respected, and dearest brother'. Again, Charlemagne's name and multiple titles are elaborated first ('king of the Franks and Lombards and patrician of the Romans'), and in the nominative case, Offa's second, in the dative, and with a singular title ('king of the Mercians'). The preliminaries focus, as ever, on friendship, this time between 'more elevated personages of this world'. Charlemagne has received letters 'at various times' from Offa, and 'endeavours to reply adequately'. The king by the grace of God rejoices in Offa's sincerity of Catholic faith. Next, Charlemagne complains about 'people who have fraudulently joined up with pilgrims', people evidently from Mercia, whose goal is profit, not religion: if they are really traders, they must pay tolls. Moving on to merchants (*negotiatores*), relations are admitted to cut both ways: Mercian merchants may not always have been properly treated in Francia, and in future must have justice, but Frankish merchants in Mercia must have the same, 'according to the ancient custom of trading' (with an echo of the Theodosian Code that some in Offa's entourage might have relished). So much by way of niceties, and the diplomatic everyday.

The heart of the letter deals with serious stuff. First, Charlemagne mentions 'the priest Odberht', to be identified with the Kentish prince Eadberht, who, 'along with other exiles, sought the wings of our protection, being in fear of death'. On his return from Rome, Eadberht wished, 'as he keeps repeating, not to accuse you, but to go on pilgrimage (*peregrinare*)', presumably to the shrines of various Frankish saints (as had the former Frankish rebels of 785–786, mentioned above). Charlemagne tells 'Your Belovedness' that he has sent Eadberht and his companions on to Rome where the pope and Archbishop Æthelheard, 'your archbishop', would judge their case, because, 'so your letters have informed us, they had bound themselves by a [religious] vow' – hence Eadberht's description as 'the priest'. But there Charlemagne is clearly quoting Offa: he thinks it 'more safe' that the pope should decide on the status of the exiles, that is, whether they are indeed religious in the technical sense, since 'the opinion of some people is different'. The allusion here seems to be to the forced tonsuring of someone, perhaps more than one person, of royal blood in order to disqualify them for secular rulership. Charlemagne makes no

promise to return Eadberht to Mercia once he is back from Rome: on
the contrary, Eadberht's wish for pilgrimage is to be taken seriously. Is
there an ironic contrast with the false pilgrims from across the
Channel whom Charlemagne has just denounced? Once this letter is
set alongside the one to Archbishop Æthelheard about Hringstan's
companions, a thematic link is clear – and the 'thin' excuses of the
Hringstan letter sound thinner still in the Eadberht one!

But before drawing further conclusions, let us briefly consider the
two other serious points in Ep. 100. The much-discussed 'black stones'
that Offa had asked for are authoritatively dealt with elsewhere in this
volume (see Parsons, Chapter 4 in this volume): sufficient here, then,
to endorse the hypothesis that stones whose length is in question
sound more like columns than mill-stones. Charlemagne stalls over
that request, on the grounds that Offa has left him uncertain as to what
he wants. Charlemagne's riposte leaves Offa in no doubt at all about
what is wanted on the Frankish side: 'our men demand' (*nostri
deposcunt*) that the cloaks sent from Offa's realm should revert to being
the size in which 'they were accustomed to reach us in the old times'.
The temptation is irresistible to link this 'demand' with Charlemagne's
personal complaint in a story told by Notker the Stammerer, though
here the blame for palming off unwontedly short cloaks on the Franks
(and selling them at the same price as the large ones) is blamed on
Frisians. (Perhaps Mercian cloaks were exported through Frisian
middlemen?[5]) Charlemagne's objections were inimitably blunt:

> What's the use of these little bits of cloth? I can't cover myself up
> with them when I'm in bed. When I'm riding, I can't protect
> myself against wind and rain. When I have to go and answer a call
> of nature, I suffer because my legs are frozen! (Notker, *Gesta
> Karoli* I, 34, in Haefele, 1959: 47–8)

In short, the request about the stones was not equivalent to the
complaint about the cloaks. In the one case, Charlemagne hinted at an
unheard-of, even excessive, request, in the other, he frankly protested
about shoddy goods – consignments that any connoisseur of
contemporary masculinity should have blushed to condone.

The last section of the letter is about gifts and *quid pro quos*. The
gifts go in just one direction, from Charlemagne to select Anglo-
Saxons. The bishoprics of Northumbria and Mercia receive dalmatics
and fine cloths in return for prayers on Charlemagne's behalf ('to show
our faith and love') for the soul of the recently deceased Pope Hadrian.
Charlemagne correctly quotes Augustine: 'to intercede for a good man
profits him who does it'. Gifts go, too, to the metropolitan sees,

---

5. King Alhred and Queen Osgifu of Northumbria sent Lul twelve cloaks in 773
   (Tangl, Ep. 121, Whitelock, 1979: 834). Presumably these cloaks were full
   length?

tactfully (given the contentions surrounding Lichfield's elevation) unspecified; and to Offa, 'a belt and a Hunnish sword and two lengths of silk' – an exquisitely balanced choice. Charlemagne did not need to add that such gifts honoured the giver; but he did tell Offa to have intercessions made 'for us and for our faithful men, and indeed for the whole Christian people', so that God might deign 'to protect and exalt the realm of the Holy Church'. The rhetoric recalls Frankfurt.

Re-reading each piece of evidence for Offa's Continental contacts in the context of the rest is also to put Offa's regime in context. Looked at from Francia, Offa was certainly a king with whom it was worth keeping in touch. He could be addressed as an exalted personage, and mutual trade between his kingdom and Charlemagne's was of value to both (Ep. 100). He could be appreciated as a potential helper in ridding the Frankish Church of an unworthy priest (Ep. 87). But if Offa's charters have allowed historians, since Stenton, to infer Offa's 'supremacy', the letters reveal his Achilles' heel. The fraternal love invoked in diplomatic correspondence should be set against the hard evidence, in these same texts, for exiles and enemies. Charlemagne may sometimes have encouraged Offa to punch above his weight. But, despite Alcuin's classically derived notion that friendship meant 'equality of friends' (Alcuin, *Disputatio Pippini cum Albino*, *PL* 101: col. 978), the idea of an equal relationship between these two rulers, or between their realms, is a mirage that would have deceived no eighth- or ninth-century viewer. Historians (could they be any but English historians?) who think otherwise should look at a map, ponder the subsequent histories, and legacies, of Mercia and Francia, and reflect on what shaped the historiography of England in the later nineteenth and twentieth centuries. The twenty-first century will assuredly be another story.

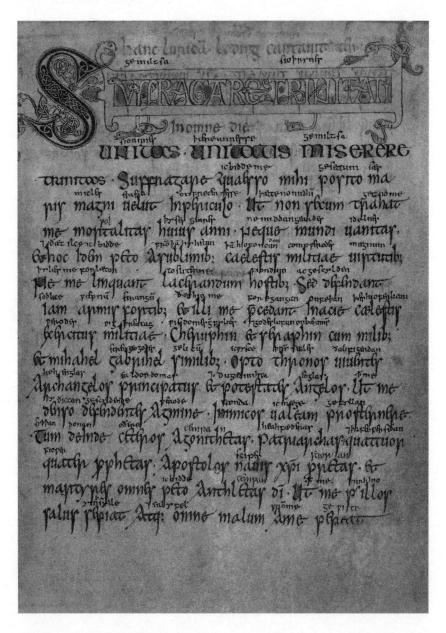

The Book of Cerne, Cambridge University Library, MS Ll.1.10, f. 43
© Cambridge University Library, courtesy of the Syndics of Cambridge
University Library

Part III

The Material Culture of Mercia

The Book of Cerne, Cambridge University Library, MS Ll.1.10, f. 21v, © Cambridge University Library, courtesy of the Syndics of Cambridge University Library

10 The Archaeology of Mercia

Martin Welch

This survey of the current archaeological evidence in the Midlands, with special reference to the North Midlands, covers the period from *c.*425 to *c.*875, that is from after the end of Roman Britain to the Danish conquest of northern and eastern England. Its approach is thematic, looking in turn at burial practices and sites, including elite burials; then rural settlements; pagan and Christian religious monuments; specialized production and trade centres; and finally fortification and frontiers. As each of these topics could be developed into individual papers, a selective approach is taken here.

Its geographical range is a compromise between concentrating on the original Mercian kingdom and the concept of Southumbria. The Mercians, as first described, occupy lands to the north and south of the middle Trent valley. Southumbria is the reality of Mercian overlordship over the kingdoms and provinces south of the Humber, as exercised for much of the period between the reign of Wulfhere (657–674) and Beornwulf's decisive defeat in 825. We know the names and territories of some of the Mercian sub-units, notably the *Tomsætan* in the tributary valley of the Tame to the south of the Trent, together with their western neighbours, the *Pencersætan* of the Penk valley (Hooke, 1996: Fig. 1) and their northern neighbours, the *Hrepingas*, who have been identified with Repton on the Trent in Derbyshire (Rumble, 1977) (see Yorke Chapter 1 and Featherstone Chapter 2 in this volume).

As the Mercian kingdom evolved from the seventh into the eighth century, it absorbed previously independent kingdoms, both British and Anglo-Saxon. Lindsey in North Lincolnshire and the *Hwicce* of Worcestershire and Gloucestershire are examples. In the process the Midlands became Mercian from Cheshire, the Peak District and the Humber estuary in the north to as far south as Berkshire, a territory disputed with the West Saxon kings (Yorke, 1995: 62–4). During the last quarter of the ninth century the North and East Midlands became Danish and are often referred to as the territories of the Five Boroughs: Derby, Leicester, Lincoln, Nottingham and Stamford. Our view of the Mercian landscape in the West Midlands has been illuminated by both land diplomas (commonly referred to as charters) and the place-name record (Hooke, 1996; and Hooke, Chapter 11 in this volume). For the

North and East Midlands, however, the equivalent evidence has been obscured by the renaming of estates allocated to new Danish owners between the ninth and eleventh centuries.

Cemeteries and burial practices

An Anglo-Saxon migration from north-west Germany and southern Scandinavia is demonstrable in archaeological terms for the fifth to early sixth centuries. It is much more than a transfer of artefacts. We see the introduction of new dress fashions, different burial practices and structures, new rural settlements, featuring *Grubenhäuser* (also known as sunken-featured buildings), not to mention a different ship-building technology. German archaeologists have demonstrated a contemporary depopulation within North Germany, most relevantly with the abandonment of settlements and cemeteries in the Weser-Elbe coastlands occupied by the Saxons (Böhme, 1986: cf. Abb.54 with Abb.69) and the Angeln region within Schleswig-Holstein for the Angles (Müller-Wille *et al.*, 1988) (see Yorke, Chapter 1 in this volume).

At the time of the migration, these peoples either cremated or inhumed their dead (Welch, 1992: 54–70). Selected calcined bone, often both human and animal, was buried in an urn, and typically was accompanied by objects, which might be burnt or unburnt (McKinley, 1994; Bond, 1996). Some of the latter might have possessed a ritual significance, e.g. combs and toilet implements. Normally the urn was a pot, but it could be an organic container (wood, leather or textile), and for the cremated social elite of the late sixth or early seventh century, as at Sutton Hoo (Suffolk) mound 5, it was a bronze bowl (Carver, 1998: 81).

Pottery was handmade and could be plain, but when decorated had linear, plastic or stamped designs. Most archaeologists have assumed that ceramic urns were primarily made for burial use (e.g. Richards, 1987: 51–91), but it seems equally plausible to this writer that the burial function was secondary to use as a domestic container. It could have been selected from household stock for re-cycling as an urn. Modern ethnography reveals that handmade pottery is usually made by women producing on a household scale (Freestone and Gaimster, 1997: 11–12, 14, 18, 30, 36–7, 146–7). If Anglo-Saxon handmade pots were created by women rather than men, then both their form and ornament should provide a particularly reliable guide to ethnic identity. Designs would be passed from mother to daughter and thence by marriage from settlement to settlement (Welch, 1992: 109–10).

On the other hand, pottery fabric studies reveal that a small proportion of pottery from cremation cemeteries was not made locally. There is also the recent identification of handmade pottery in the East Midlands containing granodiorite as a temper to strengthen the clay. The geological origin of the temper was the Mountsorrel granite outcrop in the Charnwood Forest of Leicestershire (Williams and Vince, 1997: Fig. 7). This suggests centralized production and trade, but perhaps the trade was in the granite temper, rather than in the finished pots.

Inhumation normally involved an individual grave with the fully-dressed corpse laid on its back (supine). It could also contain items associated with social status, such as weapons with up to 50 per cent of adult men and keys with some women. Furnished inhumation in North Germany in the Migration Period may well represent a modification of Late Roman burial practice, introduced by Germanic warriors who had retired from Roman military service. Roman practice had moved from cremation to inhumation during the third century AD, but normally Roman inhumation involved neither weapons nor elaborate dress fittings. Instead the emphasis was on a variety of accompanying vessels, whether to sustain the deceased in the grave or to accompany the journey to another world. It is very rare to find an Early Anglo-Saxon cemetery which consists entirely of cremations or inhumations. Usually at least a few of the alternative practice are present, though there are also cemeteries in which both are equally popular. Cremation went out of fashion during the seventh century, probably as a result of Christian hostility, with the belief that the body should be kept intact for the Resurrection.

For the majority of cemeteries in the Midlands, however, we are reliant on old records of partial discovery of burials revealed by development activity, particularly quarrying (Meaney, 1964). Excavations by archaeologists in the second half of the twentieth century are the exception and several important sites remain unpublished, such as the sixth-century inhumations of 1971–1972 investigated just outside Little Chester Roman fort (*Derventio*), near Derby (Dool et al., 1985). Elsewhere in the North Midlands, however, we are dependent on finds recorded between the eighteenth and early twentieth centuries.

Fortunately, the situation is rather better in the East Midlands with final reports available for cemeteries at Wakerley, Northamptonshire (Adams and Jackson, 1992), Empingham II, Rutland (Timby, 1996), Thurmaston, Leicestershire (Williams, 1983), and both Broughton Lodge, Willoughby-on-the-Wolds (Kinsley, 1993) and Millgate, Newark (Kinsley, 1989) in Nottinghamshire. Further north in Lindsey there is the relatively large cemetery at Castledyke South, Barton-on-Humber (Drinkall and Foreman, 1998), but other key reports are awaited. Examples are the cremation cemeteries at Elsham and Cleatham (Manton) and the inhumation cemetery at Welbeck Hill (Irby) in Lindsey (Leahy, 1993) and another urnfield at Loveden Hill (Hough-on-the-Hill) in south-west Lincolnshire, near Newark (Sawyer, 1998a: 217). There are also the 35 cremations and 15 inhumations inserted into the counterscarp of the Roman ditch at Great Casterton in Rutland, near Stamford (Sawyer, 1998a: 216) and a recently excavated cemetery with fifth-century cremations and sixth-century inhumations at Alwalton, Cambridgeshire, just west of Peterborough (Howe, 1984).

A series of relatively large Anglo-Saxon urnfields are found spaced across the landscape. These represent a key feature of the 'Anglian' regions of eastern England, i.e. East Anglia, the East Midlands, Lincolnshire and eastern Yorkshire, as far north as Sancton in the Wolds (Timby, 1993). Such cremation cemeteries were used over a much shorter timespan than their continental counterparts, however, involving no more than a couple of centuries. They are, therefore, correspondingly smaller with no more than a few thousand urns each. Nevertheless, they have been interpreted as communal burial grounds, serving the needs of a whole district rather than a single settlement community. This is a working assumption, however, and has yet to be confirmed by archaeological fieldwork.

Thus, while a contemporary settlement has been partially excavated adjacent to the urnfield at Spong Hill (North Elmham) in Norfolk (Rickett, 1995), we do not yet know its full extent, nor the locations of any associated settlements. It is plausible that the Spong Hill settlement was associated solely with the adjacent sixth-century inhumation burial area located on the north edge of the cremations. The earliest cremations at Spong Hill probably pre-date the middle of the fifth century and certainly continued for some time after the last inhumation took place here. Alternatively, there may have been a very extensive settlement complex on Spong Hill from the fifth to the seventh centuries.

It seems reasonable to interpret the communities represented by the urnfields as immigrants from North Germany or South Scandinavia. Typically the earliest pottery containers and burnt dress fittings indicate that from Suffolk to Yorkshire, cremators belonged to two different Germanic tribal groups. For example, pots with incised 'standing arch' designs or with elaborate bosses (known as *Buckelurnen*) are typical of the Saxon region west of the Elbe estuary and can contain Saxon brooches as well. There are usually many more pots with simple linear decoration and sometimes with small shoulder bosses, which are typical of the Anglian region in Schleswig-Holstein. Once again, these can be found with Anglian brooches, including early cruciform brooches. Revealingly, this same admixture can be found in the cemeteries of the eastern half of the Weser-Elbe coastal region, as at Issendorf (Janssen, 1972; Hässler, 1994). So the founders of the English urnfields might well have been ethnically-mixed migrants from the lower Elbe basin.

The character of Anglo-Saxon pottery urns changes *c*.500, when new English 'Anglian' regional pottery fashions begin to be developed. Typically these feature stamped designs and the new pots are matched by items from a new repertoire of female dress fittings, giving rise to a new 'folk' costume. We seem to be witnessing the active creation of an Anglian regional ethnic identity for these communities, whose geographical distribution broadly matches the eighth-century list of Anglian peoples given in a famous passage by Bede (Plummer, 1896: 31). They include the Middle Angles and the Mercians in the Midlands.

If we are right to exclude the Newark cemetery as too far downstream for the 'original' Mercians, then there are only two cremation cemeteries in the middle Trent valley which might convincingly represent founding Germanic settlements. One was discovered during railway construction in 1866 at King's Newton (Melbourne), Derbyshire, for which we have illustrations of a dozen urns (Meaney, 1964: 76). The other at Barton-under-Needwood, Staffordshire produced a great number of urns containing bone dug out of a ballast pit in 1851. Unfortunately none of these pots were described or illustrated (Meaney, 1964: 220).

Inhumation cemeteries are much smaller in scale and generally conform to a population size appropriate to a hamlet of three to six households or farm units. A maximum of ten farms has been estimated for the extensive settlement complex at Mucking in Essex (Hamerow, 1993), but most excavated settlements were considerably smaller. Generally, these cemeteries seem to be founded in the late fifth or the early sixth century in the Midlands, but very few of them were still in use as late as the middle or the second half of the seventh century. Castledyke South, Barton-on-Humber (Drinkall and Foreman, 1998) is one of the rare exceptions.

As already mentioned, around 500 Anglian women begin to be buried wearing a distinctive costume with new, specifically Scandinavian elements (Hines, 1984). In particular, there is now an undergarment with long tailored sleeves fastened at the wrists with metal clasps (Hines, 1993), as well as a pair of brooches to fix a tubular overdress at the shoulders. With richer graves we find an additional large brooch to fasten a cloak, perhaps with a hood (Owen-Crocker, 1986: 33, Fig. 30; Hines, 1997). By contrast, in the South Midlands a 'Saxon' dress fashion is more common. This uses brooch types also found in the Thames valley, particularly pairs of saucer and disc brooches (Owen-Crocker, 1986: 30, Fig. 22). The cemeteries of the Avon valley (Ford, 1996: 92–5) as far south-west as Beckford (Conderton), Worcestershire (Evison and Hill, 1996) contain fastenings from both dress 'provinces', but the 'Anglian' costume has been replaced by the 'Saxon' here well before the middle of the sixth century.

In their turn, these regional fashions disappear by a date no later than the beginning of the seventh century. Thereafter fewer individuals are accompanied by metal dress fittings. Indeed, the whole burial repertoire changes with weapons becoming much rarer during the seventh century and fully-dressed burials were replaced by shroud-wrapped corpses during the eighth century (Geake, 1997).

The sixth-century inhumation cemeteries occupy the gaps between the large urnfields of the East Midlands (e.g. Leahy, 1993: Fig. 4.2). At present there is no widely accepted methodology for determining whether inhuming communities represent or include Germanic immigrants. They could be acculturated British communities, which have adopted an 'Anglian', or in the South Midlands a 'Saxon', cultural identity. In many cases they might be mixed communities of natives and immigrants, though there are strong grounds for seeing all cremations as the descendants of Germanic immigrants.

The Wasperton cemetery located by the Avon between Warwick and Stratford is particularly relevant here, with its 25 cremations and 182 inhumations (Geake, 1997: 186). While the cremation minority implies some Anglo-Saxon presence, one group of inhumations share a common orientation (north to south) together with Late Roman burial characteristics. These involve hobnailed footgear, nailed coffins and decapitated burials, and there are some others which mix Roman and Anglo-Saxon practices. We still await the full report and the available published record is insufficient to tell us whether we are looking at a British farming community, which became Anglo-Saxon in the late fifth century, or a new Anglo-Saxon community, which chose to bury in a recently abandoned sub-Romano-British cemetery. It is theoretically possible that DNA analysis from the organic content of human bone or teeth might throw new light on this issue. In the meantime, we can use genetically diagnostic features in the teeth, wormian bones and other aspects of the skeletal record, but we need good bone preservation and this is rare in practice.

Continuity from the Roman period has also been argued for some cemeteries on the basis of a location close to a major Roman road and Roman roadside settlements and small towns (Kinsley, 1989: 5, Fig. 2; Kinsley, 1993: 175, Fig. 104). This may simply reflect the continuing value of Roman roads throughout the early medieval period. There are other cemeteries which seem more closely related to the major waterways, such as the Trent and Avon. Characteristically though, both cemeteries and contemporary settlements in the valleys were located on gravel terraces well above the floodplain.

Warrior elite burials

The warriors who forged the Mercians into a military force capable of challenging all-comers are archaeologically invisible in the North Midlands at present. A recent cemetery excavation in the Lakenheath US airbase (Suffolk) revealed two inhumed warriors, each buried with a horse, within a ring ditch implying a barrow mound (Caruth and Anderson, 1999; Anon., 1999). Their equivalents can be found in several East Midlands cemeteries, as at Broughton Lodge (Vierck, 1970–1971: 190–2, 218–20; Kinsley, 1993: 58–61, Figs 16, 28, 45, 90). The Salin's Style I animal ornament on the mounts in one of the Lakenheath graves was from a harness still attached to the horse and can be attributed to the first half of the sixth century. By the end of that century, equivalent warriors were normally buried apart from the farming communities which supported them. They might be placed under an isolated barrow adjacent to and commanding a routeway, as at the Caenby crossroads in Lindsey (Everson, 1993: Fig. 8.1).

Alternatively, they can be found in a separate elite barrow cemetery, as at Sutton Hoo (Suffolk) overlooking the River Deben (Carver, 1998).

A plough-damaged, isolated grave containing a pattern-welded sword, a hanging bowl and an iron helmet was found unexpectedly beside a Roman road at Wollaston, near Wellingborough, Northamptonshire (Meadows, 1996–1997; Meadows, 1997). The iron helmet plates resemble those of the well-preserved eighth-century helmet from Coppergate in York (Tweddle, 1992), while the boar figurine on the crest matches another famous helmet excavated in 1848 from the Benty Grange barrow in the Derbyshire White Peak (Bateman, 1861: 28–33; Bruce-Mitford, 1974: 223–42). This too had an associated hanging bowl and it seems that a date bracket covering the first half of the seventh century would be equally appropriate for the Wollaston 'prince'.

The 'princely' warrior buried at Benty Grange may have been a Mercian Angle, ruling the British of the Peak District on behalf of his king, the people listed as the *Pecsætan* in the *Tribal Hidage* document (Hill, 1981: 76–7, map 136). Alternatively, he could have been a British ruler who had agreed terms with his Mercian neighbours and adopted an Anglian identity. Whichever was the case, it is conceivable that he derived revenue from lead mining, with silver extraction as its valuable by-product, in addition to food rents from his lands. Certainly lead was being mined at Wirksworth by the ninth century (Campbell, 1982: 226–7). Indeed, men such as those buried at Benty Grange, Caenby and Wollaston would have been the patrons of metalsmiths and other specialist craft workers. The 1981 excavation of a smith's hoard near Tattershall Thorpe (Lincolnshire), attributable to the later seventh century (Hinton, 1993, 2000), is a find which demonstrates the range of craft skills needed to produce fine decorative metal fittings.

From the mid-seventh century onwards, kings and leading nobles began to be buried within side chapels or crypts of churches. The Repton double monastery in Derbyshire was a burial place favoured by eighth-century Mercian kings, including the canonized Wystan (Biddle and Kjølbye-Biddle, 1985: 235). The royal burials themselves have not survived in the Repton church, but a fragment of a sandstone cross discarded in a pit adjacent to the east opening of the crypt perhaps depicts such a king (ibid.: 237ff.). It shows a mounted warrior with a moustache, who holds his small round shield in his left hand and wields a sword over his head with his right hand. The reins of his stallion rest over his forearm, while his seax is in its scabbard at his waist. This is a powerful image of secular authority in a Christian context and is perhaps a portrait of King Æthelbald, who died in 757.

Settlements

The Midlands contains numerous finds of Anglo-Saxon buildings, frequently represented by the distinctive pit of the *Grubenhaus*, also known as the sunken-featured building (or SFB). These are relatively easy to recognize and can be detected also as cropmarks on air photographs. Thus there are three *Grubenhäuser* widely spaced within a Romano-British farmstead at Willington in Derbyshire (Wheeler, 1979). Continuity, implying the intact transfer of a Roman farm unit to an Anglo-Saxon farm, has been proposed for the Orton Hall Farm site, just west of Peterborough by the River Nene. There is a *Grubenhaus* and also rectangular buildings based on earthfast posts revealed by excavation amidst the ruins of a Roman villa (Mackreth, 1996). The rectangular halls functioned principally as farmhouses and have a fairly standard plan across Early Anglo-Saxon England from Hampshire to Northumberland (James *et al.*, 1984; Welch, 1992: 14–28). While this site did produce an antler comb of fifth-century type, the metalwork finds and most of the decorated pottery certainly belong to the sixth century. Continuity is by no means certain at this site, and Anglo-Saxon settlers may have moved into an abandoned farm. Also in the East Midlands, the Raunds project in Northamptonshire has demonstrated an interesting sequence of settlement on one site from the Early Saxon period through to the Middle Saxon and into the Late Saxon period (Dix, 1986–1987: 18–25, Figs 12–14).

The only settlement in the North Midlands which has been investigated on a large scale is Catholme in the parish of Barton-under-Needwood (Staffordshire), occupying a gravel terrace of the Trent. It may well be associated with the Wychnor inhumation cemetery found in 1899 (Meaney, 1964: 223). Gavin Kinsley is currently preparing the final report on Catholme, but a summary of its six phases appeared in 1984 (Losco-Bradley and Wheeler, 1984). The few handmade potsherds and a plain strapend do not provide an adequate basis for establishing a chronology, but radiocarbon dates provide a probable range between the sixth and ninth centuries. Farm and household units are clearly defined by ditches and fence lines and there were 15 buildings in the first phase, three of which were *Grubenhäuser*.

Parallels have been noted between some of the Catholme rectangular halls and buildings excavated at a Romano-British rural settlement of the second and third centuries at Dunston's Clump (Ranby parish) Nottinghamshire (Garton, 1987). Even now though, relatively few Romano-British settlements below the status of villas have been excavated, and the issue of a British contribution to the Anglo-Saxon small hall is still not settled. Perhaps Catholme and its associated cemetery belonged to an acculturated British community which had adopted an Anglian identity by the sixth century. The near invisibility in archaeological terms of both native British settlements and cemeteries in the post-Roman period means that we cannot establish convincingly the British contribution to Anglo-Saxon material culture in the Midlands. We have to look as far west as Wroxeter (Shropshire) before we can trace a sequence of Late Roman and post-Roman occupation in a former Roman town (White and Barker, 1998).

A new type of rural settlement emerges in the late sixth and the seventh century with massive, imposing timber halls matching descriptions of royal feasting in *Beowulf*. The type site is the Bernician royal *villa* of *Ad Gefrin*, identified with the excavated settlement at Yeavering in Northumberland (Hope-Taylor, 1977). Air photography has identified similar halls at Atcham near Shrewsbury in Shropshire, perhaps an Anglo-Saxon replacement for the post-Roman centre at Wroxeter (Welch, 1992: Fig. 26). In Warwickshire such halls occur at Hatton Rock (Welch, 1992: Fig. 27) and Long Itchington within what is later a royal estate (Hooke, 1996: 111–12, Fig. 7; Hooke, Chapter 11 in this volume) and in Oxfordshire at Drayton and Long Wittenham (Welch, 1992: pls 28 and 29). Limited excavation took place across Hatton Rock and more extensively at Yarnton just north of Oxford (Nenk *et al.*, 1992: 258).

These so-called 'palaces' are probably better described as estate centres for the collection and consumption of food and drink renders by a lord, often a king, and his entourage. The timber hall to the east of St Peter's church in Northampton is particularly interesting, as it was replaced in the ninth century by a masonry hall (Gem, 1993a: 39, Fig. 3). The stone hall is comparable in scale to the first phase of the Carolingian royal hall constructed *c.*776 and excavated in 1963 at Paderborn in Germany (Williams *et al.*, 1985; Gai, 1999: Abb.1 and 5). At Northampton, the masonry of the church, the second hall and contemporary mortar mixers suggest that the hall belonged to a monastery, providing entertainment for royal and noble travellers by its abbot (Welch, 1992: 47–50; Blair, 1996: 98–108). If it was a royal residence within a monastic enclosure, as was the case at Paderborn, it would have belonged to the Mercian kings. Presumably a similar hall and associated buildings would have stood within the inner enclosure at Tamworth (Rahtz and Meeson, 1992: 1–5, Fig. 2).

Religious centres

The identification of a pair of enclosures, one circular, the other rectangular, at Blacklow Hill in Warwickshire as a pagan religious site (Wilson, 1992: 64, Fig. 20) can be added to a growing corpus of such enclosures datable to the pre-Roman Iron Age and the Roman period assembled and discussed by John Blair (1995a). The rectangular enclosure contained a large number of empty pits, but also two centrally located inhumation graves, one of which contained an iron narrow seax, implying a late sixth- to early seventh-century date (Ford, 1996: 69). Its full publication is awaited, but it can be compared to the western burial complex in Area D at Yeavering (Hope-Taylor, 1977: 108–16) and to a structure on Slonk Hill in Sussex (Blair, 1995a: 16–19, Figs 11 and 12).

The eighth-century church at Repton with its famous crypt has been the subject of detailed structural survey complemented by selective research excavation of its exterior. The most remarkable find here was the human charnel of at least 249 individuals deposited in a separate two-cell stone sunken structure well to the west of the church (Biddle and Kjølbye-Biddle, 1992). This collection of bones is coin-dated by five silver pennies to 873–874, precisely when a great Danish army stayed in a winter camp at Repton. The interpretation has been influenced by the allegedly robust and non-local character of the adult males aged between 15 and 45 or more years, who formed 80 per cent of the charnel deposit. They are interpreted as Scandinavians, even though there was little evidence of battle trauma on their bones. By contrast, the female bones have been identified as a different population group, possibly Mercian.

A great ditch incorporated Repton church into the Viking camp defences and cut through the monastic cemetery. This writer can offer an alternative thesis, however, which assumes that monastic Christian burials were removed by local forced labourers in constructing this ditch. The workmen and their local lords might well have insisted on reinterring consecrated burials as charnel in a former mausoleum. The fact that the condition of the bone from the cemetery is now different from that of the charnel is not surprising, as its local environment had been significantly changed. On the other hand, if the 'robust' male charnel is unmatched within the pre-Viking Repton cemetery, my suggestion would be ruled out.

Excavation and detailed surveys have also been made at the fine basilican church of Brixworth in Northamptonshire (Audouy, 1984; Sutherland and Parsons, 1984), now attributed to the mid to late eighth century (Gem, 1993a: 34), while the crypt and the ninth-century polygonal apse above it at the church of Wing in Buckinghamshire have been compared to their equivalents at Repton (Gem, 1993a: 34, 51, 53, Figs 8A, 9B, pls IXA and B; see Parsons, Chapter 4 in this volume). The eighth- to ninth-century sculptured panels preserved in the church at Breedon-on-the-Hill in Leicestershire can be taken to be representative of the artistic achievements of Mercian stonemasons (Cramp, 1977; Tweddle, 1991; see Jewell, Chapter 17 in this volume). As yet though, very few Anglo-Saxon monasteries have been extensively excavated in England, apart from Jarrow and Monkwearmouth in Northumbria. So the identification of a settlement made up of rectangular timber buildings at Flixborough (Lindsey) as a nunnery on the basis of finds of inscriptions and styli for writing on wax tablets is very significant (Whitwell, 1991; Reynolds, 1999: 119–22), the publication of which is eagerly awaited.

Production and trading centres

Salt extraction exploiting the brine springs at Droitwich, Worcestershire can be traced back to at least the Iron Age and Roman periods at Upwich (see Hooke, Vince and Cowie, Chapters 11, 13 and 14 in this volume). Excavation there also revealed compelling evidence for salt extraction in the Early and Middle Anglo-Saxon periods. During phase 4, ten stone-built boiling hearths were associated with stakes for wattle screens to shelter the hearths. Dating evidence was provided by handmade pottery, including stamp-decorated sherds, one of which is paralleled by a sixth-century pot from the Anglo-Saxon cemetery at Bidford-on-Avon (Hurst, 1997: 17–27, 75–8, Fig. 68). A period of flooding intervened depositing thick alluvium, followed by construction of a wicker revetment, aligned stakes and a brushwood trackway along the river bank in phase 5. This was accompanied by extensive dumping of charcoal and ash, but only a small amount of pottery. Radiocarbon dates suggest the alluviation belongs in the seventh to mid-eighth centuries (Hurst, 1997: 27–32, 78–9, 106–10). From the seventh century onwards we have documentary and place-name evidence for the Droitwich salt industry and its distribution network (Hooke, 1998b: 2–6, Figs 2 and 4; see Hooke, Chapter 11 in this volume). Nantwich, together with Northwich and Middlewich in Cheshire possessed comparable brine wells both in the Roman period and later in the Middle Ages, and so might also have been exploited by the Mercians (McNeil, 1983).

The well-known waterlogged timber structure of the Tamworth watermill with its horizontal wheel is associated with one of the most important Mercian royal vills, but need not have been in royal ownership. There is no dating evidence for the first mill here, but dendrochronology and radiocarbon dates imply a felling date for the timbers used in a replacement second mill erected in the middle of the ninth century. It is possible then that the first mill was constructed within the later eighth century. The broken millstones were mostly of sandstone, but also of imported Rhineland lava. The temptation to link the lava millstones to Charlemagne's letter agreeing to Offa's request for *petra nigra* (Whitelock, 1979: 849) should be resisted, as this might well refer to Tournai marble (Rahtz and Meeson, 1992: 73). Other waterlogged timber structures in a former channel of the Trent at Colwick have been radiocarbon dated to 810–880 and interpreted as fish weirs, principally for trapping eels (Salisbury, 1981 and 1991). The recent find of related structures on the Thames foreshore at Chelsea are likely to have had the same function, rather than support landing stages for those attending the Chelsea synods (Cubitt, 1995). Fish weirs are an increasingly recognized find from estuaries and rivers in this period.

An international trading and manufacturing centre which developed on the north bank of the Thames in London along the Strand between the Fleet and Trafalgar Square is the *Lundenwic* of contemporary sources (Vince, 1990). Its existence has been demonstrated archaeologically with the preservation of gravelled streets and side alleys and their frontage buildings revealed in advance of the redevelopment of the Royal Opera House, Covent Garden (Nenk *et al.*, 1997: 268–9, see Cowie, Chapter 14 in this volume). To the east, an episcopal church probably existed from the mid-seventh century within the Roman walled area of *Lundenburh*, quite possibly under the present St Paul's Cathedral. The tradition that an Anglo-Saxon royal palace existed in Cripplegate is not borne out by the archaeology there (Milne, forthcoming), however, so we cannot locate a Mercian royal palace in London between the late seventh and early ninth centuries (cf. Cowie, Chapter 14 in this volume).

Defences

The final theme is the issue of fortification in the later eighth and ninth centuries in response to the growing Viking menace. An absence of impressive defences is a characteristic feature of the trading *emporia*, such as *Lundenwic* and *Hamwic* (Southampton). A boundary ditch around *Hamwic* marks its limits but provided no real barrier, though the ditch at Covent Garden in London would have been rather more effective for defence. There is charter evidence for the duties of building fortifications, roads and bridges during Offa's reign, however, and in 792 a Kentish charter refers to defence against pagan seamen (Campbell, 1982: 132). It has been suggested that the early tenth-century system of West Saxon defensive strongholds or *burhs* listed in the *Burghal Hidage* (Campbell, 1982: 152–3) may have been imitating measures taken a century or more earlier by Offa and his successors. There is evidence for bank rampart defences at Hereford (Shoesmith, 1982) and at Tamworth with its 'palace' enclosure (Rahtz and Meeson, 1992: Fig. 2) of the pre-Viking period.

Finally no survey of Mercian archaeology can fail to refer to the achievement in mobilizing labour services involved in the construction of Offa's Dyke (see Hill, Chapter 12 in this volume). A long-term programme of field survey and small-scale excavation initiated by David Hill (Campbell, 1982: 120–1) has contributed to our understanding of the construction and maintenance of this frontier work, designed to prohibit access by the Welsh to the Midlands. Both marker trenches and individual sections built by work teams have been identified, but artefacts to provide dating evidence are notable for their absence.

A radiocarbon date from an excavation on Wat's Dyke to the east of the northern section of Offa's Dyke suggests that this is one of the linear earthworks constructed in the immediate post-Roman period, such as the Wansdyke, and not a precursor to Offa's Dyke ordered by his predecessor Æthelbald (Gaimster *et al.*, 1998: 150–1). Whatever the chronological relationship between these earthworks, the sheer scale of Offa's Dyke itself, covering nearly 150 miles, cannot fail to impress. If it is an attempt to match the achievement of Roman frontiers, then perhaps it reflects the contemporary creation of the Carolingian Empire on the Continent. Although a case has been made for place-names such as Burton representing defensible locations within a pre-Danish defence system (Gelling, 1989b), it is clear that

the *burhs* of Mercia proved inadequate against the Danish 'great army'.
Reality failed to match Mercian royal aspirations.

Conclusion

It is not possible to define a distinct archaeology for the early Mercians
in the North Midlands. They are related to the peoples who settled
East Anglia and the East Midlands in the fifth to sixth centuries and
who adopted in *c.*500 an Anglian identity reflected in both dress
fittings and pottery. As yet, we cannot define the contribution of the
native population, but can suspect that many British adopted an
Anglian ethnicity. Mercian rural settlements are poorly known at
present, but there is the emergence of a social elite in elaborate
burials marked by mounds and by great halls, usually of timber and
later in stone. We are learning more about their economy, with
industries such as salt extraction and their trading networks, though
true towns do not exist in the Midlands prior to the Danish conquest.
The dominance of architectural and art historical studies for the
archaeology of the Christian period is being reduced by the results of
fieldwork and excavation in the past 30 years.

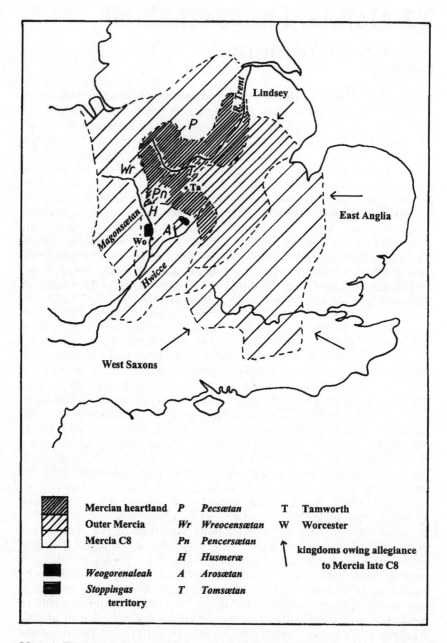

Map 4 The expansion of Mercia in the eighth century from its heartland in the Trent basin, showing places referred to in the text

11 Mercia: Landscape and Environment

Della Hooke

Territorial organization in early Mercia

From its heartland in the valley of the Trent, Mercia at the beginning of the eighth century extended northwards to a frontier with Northumbria which extended from the Mersey estuary to that of the Humber; to the east only the kingdoms of Lindsey and East Anglia lay beyond its grasp and to the south it was already making inroads into the territory of Wessex (see map 4). The early kingdom of the Hwicce had been subsumed, its kings demoted to the status first of princes or under-kings and then, after AD 800, of ealdormen. To the west, its frontier marched with that of the Welsh kingdoms and especially with that of Powys, against which Offa may have constructed the linear dyke which still bears his name (Hill, 2000). It was during the later eighth century that Mercia was to exert its maximum supremacy – eastwards across Lindsey and East Anglia to the North Sea, southwards over the lands of the South Saxons as far as the south coast and south-westwards over the remainder of Wessex as far as the Tamar estuary – beyond, Cornwall, all that was left of the former British kingdom of Dumnonia, continued to maintain a measure of autonomy into the tenth century.

There is still much to be understood about early Anglo-Saxon administrative units. As the Anglo-Saxon kingdom developed, it had incorporated not only lesser kingdoms like that of the Hwicce but numerous smaller sub-groups. Some may have been of early origin, with British antecedents, others are likely to have been more recently created land units. The Hwicce, for instance, included a folk group known as the *Husmeræ* who were based in the Stour valley in what is now north Worcestershire, their lands extending north-eastwards to the uplands of the Clents. The *Weogoran* were a tribe based around Worcester, *Uuigorna civitate*, in the Severn valley, and the *Arosætna* probably occupied the Arrow valley in what is now Warwickshire (Hooke, 1985a). On its northern frontier the *Pecsætna* occupied the Peak district while the *Pencersætan* and *Tomsætan* were based in the valleys of the Penk and Teme of southern Staffordshire, respectively.

In what was to become Shropshire, the *Wreocensætan* occupied the land around the Wrekin. It is not easy to reconstruct the boundaries of these peoples for many changes to the boundaries of administrative units had already been made by the end of the early medieval period but in many cases the extent of their territories can be suggested (Hooke, 1983, 1985a). The focal regions of early territories are often the easiest to recognize: these were usually located in areas that were geographically favourable, such as river valleys which were relatively fertile and provided ease of access, and even if early centres did not survive as administrative or political foci, their sites were often considered to convey a symbolical status to later foundations such as early minsters.

The recognition of *caput* centres or royal vills helps to identify some early land units. These were often provided with minsters, with the ecclesiastical function often outliving the secular. The sites of the early minsters can most easily be recognized within the kingdoms of the Hwicce and the Magonsæte, the two south-western kingdoms subsumed into Mercia by the eighth century. One of the reasons for this is that many of them were noted in the documents of the church of Worcester. Many royal vills and early minsters appear to have been the focus of 50-hide units and it is clear that administrative units were clearly organized on a fiscal basis by the seventh century. In Herefordshire, most of which fell into the southern part of the Magonsætan kingdom, Coplestone-Crow (1989: 6–9) notes the 50-hide unit centred upon the minster endowed at Leominster by King Merewalh but claiming a foundation *c.* 660, apparently to serve the former British kingdom of Leen (Rennel of Rodd, 1963). This may represent the notional 50-*trefi* unit of a Welsh commote. Similar 50-hide units can be reconstructed around some of the early Hwiccan minsters. Within the Hwiccan kingdom, the central core of estates belonging to the minster at Evesham is represented by the 50-hide unit of central *Fisseberg* on both sides of the River Avon (Cox, 1975). Cropthorne, on the south bank of the Avon, was a royal vill at the focus of another 50-hide unit. What is less clear is how such units relate to both earlier or wider territorial divisions.

Royal centres can be identified from a number of sources but charters are one of the most important. Unfortunately, these thin out northwards towards the core of the Mercian kingdom. Tamworth, located in the valley of the Tame in what is now Staffordshire, lay at the heart of the territory of the South Mercians and in probable *Tomsætan* territory and seems to have been Offa's 'capital'. Penkridge lay at the focus of the *Pencersætan* land beside the River Penk. In the eighth and ninth century, Mercian kings favoured Winchcombe in the north Cotswolds. King Coenwulf referred to the region around as 'his inheritance' and restricted the leasing out of estates to a period of only one lifetime (Finberg, 1972: 51, 229). It became a royal burial place and in 825 was the recognized place of custody for the archives of the Mercian royal house. Other royal vills were scattered across the kingdom and many were presumably the centres at which the king and his court would have stayed in the days that kings regularly made circuits of their lands; they survived as vills at which renders and payments were collected from their appendant estates. Sometimes charters were signed at them, showing that the king or his leading nobles did indeed continue to visit from time to time (e.g. Wellesbourne, Warks.) but with charter evidence lacking for most of northern Mercia one is forced to examine the Domesday Book for a knowledge of royal ownership there and by 1086 the king had acquired sundry additional estates.

The eastern section of the Hwiccan kingdom is an area which reveals early territorial divisions particularly well. Alcester, Roman *Alauna*, early medieval *Alencestre*, standing at the confluence of the rivers Alne and Arrow (tributaries of the Warwickshire Avon), was the hub of this region in Roman times. Although the process by which the *Arosætan* territory, like the rest of the west midland region, became 'Anglo-Saxon' is not understood, pagan burials have been found in both the Arrow and Alne valleys and an expanse of territory across the headwaters of the Alne was apparently given to a group (possibly of Anglo-Saxon origin) known as the *Stoppingas*. The extent of their territory is suggested by that of the medieval *parochia* of the minster established at Wootton Wawen in the early eighth century to serve them (Bassett, 1983) (Map 5). While the lands appendant to Alcester seem to have been close to 100 hides at the time of Domesday Book, that of the *parochia* was assessed at just short of 50 hides (49 hides and 12 acres in 1086, the 12 acres part of the manor of Oldberrow in Arden (Hooke, forthcoming), as if this was a secondary land unit of early Anglo-Saxon origin). Alcester failed to survive as an urban centre although it appears to have retained its ecclesiastical status, being referred to as 'the celebrated place called Alne' where an ecclesiastical council was held in 709 (Haddan and Stubbs, 1871: 281, 283). No early minster is recorded but this may be due to the predatory land claims of the Worcestershire minster of Evesham which successfully acquired most of the potential Arrow valley estates by the eleventh century (there are traditions of the townspeople and smiths of Alcester refusing to listen to the preachings of Ecgwine, the bishop of Worcester who founded the abbey at Evesham in the eighth century). At an early stage, Bidford on Avon, a few kilometres to the south, seems to have replaced Alcester as the favoured centre of the royal estate which dominated this region.

Where early multiple estate units can be recognized, focused upon a *caput* such as a royal vill or a minster parochia, they often included both richer regions of more intensive cultivation and more marginal zones, as in most Welsh commotes. But more distant estate linkages also become apparent. The *Arosætan* and *Stoppingas* territories clearly overlay a pattern of linkages which ran from the more intensively cultivated Feldon to the more heavily wooded Arden and a pattern of drove ways can be suggested, fossilized in present-day roads, bridle

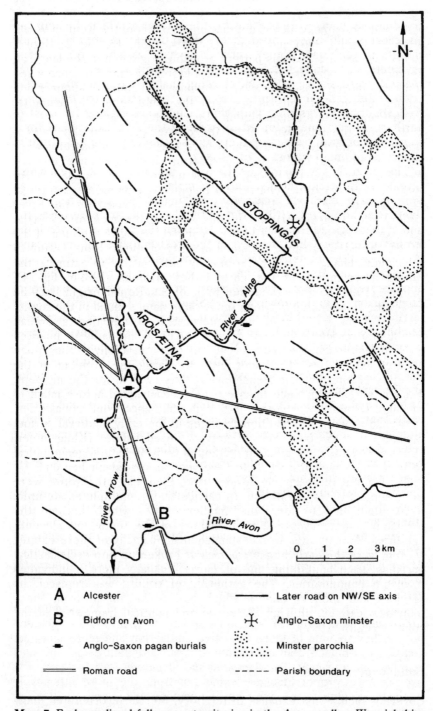

Map 5 Early medieval folk group territories in the Arrow valley, Warwickshire

paths and footpaths, which is not dissimilar to that of the Kentish Weald (Map 5). Ford (1976) and others (Bassett, 1986, 15, Fig. 7; Hooke, 1996) have argued that this pattern probably originated in the late Iron Age or Roman periods, arising out of a system of transhumance when stock was moved seasonally away from cultivated zones to summer and autumn pastures. If this is so, then the multiple estate/'commote' pattern represents a fragmentation of earlier territories.

In Kent, the links were from the coastal plain and the Vale of Holmesdale into the central Weald where seasonal wood-pastures were known as 'dens'. It can be seen, again from charter evidence, that the Wealden dens originally belonged to the men of the various lathes. An authentic eighth-century charter, for instance, grants swine-pastures in 'the wood of the men of the Lympne district [based on the River Limen] (the *Limenwara*) and in the wood of the men of Wye (the *Weowara*)' (Sawyer, 1968: S 1180), clearly referring to the men of the lathes, the administrative divisions of early medieval Kent. Owing to subsequent changes, it is unfortunately not possible to estimate the *sulung* assessments of the early lathes (Brooks, 1989b: 69–74). Balkwill (1993) believes the lathes to be of post-Roman origin since he finds little relationship between the *wīchām* names found in the county (derived from Latin *vicus* and interpreted as denoting a Roman administrative centre within a defined territory) and lathe or hundred divisions, although the term occurs in four out of five cases upon hundred boundaries. This does little to clarify the problem of the antiquity of long-distance transhumance links which, for the moment, remains unresolved. Such links can be reconstructed across much of England. Obviously, estate owners, especially successful monasteries, were also to gather in additional estates in the early medieval period, causing some to doubt the antiquity of linked estates (Klingelhöfer, 1992), but as the most efficient method of utilizing natural geographical resources the system is likely to have been an old-established one.

Throughout the early medieval period, then, early territories were to be subject to fragmentation. In particular, the multiple estate units were subdivided to form the smaller estates which became the township communities and proto-manors of the tenth and eleventh centuries. As churches were established upon many of these estates so, too, were the early minster *parochiae* broken up into ecclesiastical parishes, each containing one or more – usually more – individual township communities. The gathering of tribute was replaced by services and money renders which had to be raised from these individual estates, altering the social and political framework of the country (Faith, 1997).

Landscape regions

Covering such a vast expanse of territory, Mercia incorporated many different landscape types. Its northern frontier crossed the southern

Pennines and incorporated most of the Peak District, a region divided into the millstone grit landscape of the Dark Peak to the north and the limestone area of the White Peak to the south. The spine of upland diminishes in height southwards to rise again in the South Staffordshire and Birmingham Plateau; lower-lying claylands lie to the west forming the Shropshire, Cheshire and Staffordshire Plain. Beyond, to the west, outlying uplands continue the higher land of the Welsh Border across southern Shropshire and parts of Herefordshire before giving way to the central clay plain of Worcestershire. To the east the land falls slowly into Lincolnshire and the Trent basin. The Jurassic limestone and the chalk escarpments form a continuous arc to the south-east, the chalk outcrop standing out above the clays of the Thames and Hampshire basins but almost encircling the sandstone outcrop of the Weald in Kent.

The northern hills were lightly settled areas of largely seasonal pasture. A tenth-century charter, only discovered in 1983 (Brooks *et al.*, 1984), provides the only detailed charter evidence for the Peak region, referring to an estate on the Derbyshire Peak fringe to the north-east of Ashbourne. It grants five hides of land at Ballidon, but casts little light upon the nature of the countryside – it is likely that the area was largely sheep pasture, grazed by flocks driven up the old Roman track from Ballidon itself (Hodges, 1991: 97–8, Fig. 66) incorporating land that was to become the site of a Cistercian grange (reign of Henry II or Richard I), a common occurrence in this part of the country.

Knowledge of the landscape in the early medieval period is still incomplete. While environmental evidence from archaeological excavation is yielding essential information, at present sites are few and wide apart. The location of early medieval woodland, for instance, has to be estimated from incomplete and often later sources. Past estimates often disagree: the Ordnance Survey in 1935 suggested extensive patches of dense woodland on the Cheshire Plain while Stenton suggested more woodland in the Peak District (mapped in Hill, 1981: Fig. 23). While woodland regeneration soon after the end of the Roman period has been suggested by pollen diagrams produced for sites on Exmoor, Durham and other sites in northern England (Higham, 1992b), and from soil profiles in the weald, elsewhere palaeoenvironmental studies have failed to identify a significant increase in woodland at this time. There appears to have been more woodland regeneration towards the end of the early medieval period and it has been argued (Hooke, 1998a) that this arises due to an increased interest in hunting by the later Anglo-Saxon kings, following similar trends on the Continent. In well-wooded regions the *haga* term appears to refer to enclosures or linear features associated with the retention and capture of game, often on royal estates, and it is often in those areas in which a concentration of the incidence of this term occurs that the Norman forests were eventually to be formally and legally recognized.

A belt of woodland probably extended in early medieval times from the Humber estuary into Gloucestershire, roughly following the scarp slope of the Jurassic escarpment. The incidence of the *lēah* place-name element certainly suggests this for the scarp face of the Cotswolds in Gloucestershire where woodland is still present today. Bruneswald and its outliers occupied the Bedfordshire and Cambridgeshire claylands and extensive woodlands extended across the clay-with-flints covered chalk of the Chilterns and into East Anglia, especially on the claylands of Norfolk, Suffolk and Essex. Extensive woodland tracts ringed the Hwiccan kingdom, from Morfe and Kinver through Wyre and Malvern to Dean on the west and from Kingswood through Kemble to Wychwood (the latter beyond its seventh-century boundary). The frontier of this kingdom was only open along its eastern boundary with Greater Mercia, where it ran through an area cleared and intensively settled by Roman times, for its north-eastern boundary continued through the woodlands of Arden in the north-east (Hooke, 1985a: 79, Fig. 20). In the south of England, the most extensive tracts probably included Selwood, the later forested areas of Wiltshire, Somerset, Dorset and Hampshire, and of course, the Weald, an area of woodland said in 892 to be 'a hundred-and-twenty miles long or longer from east to west, and 30 miles broad' (Swanton, 1996: 85). In most of these areas the *lēah* term in place-names confirms the landscape character of these regions as that of wooded countryside.

The *lēah* term appears to mean variously both 'wood' and 'woodland clearing' (Johansson, 1975) and it is obvious from the Worcestershire place-name and charter evidence that land use could change in connection with the *lēah* term from specifically meaning 'wood' to places associated with crops and animal sheds or to places of young saplings where wood was apparently regenerating (Hooke, 1978–79). Wager (1998: 154–5) is probably right to consider the term as being indicative of secondary woodland. Certainly the *lēah* place-names tend to cluster along the edge of more heavily wooded tracts, whether applied to early or later settlements. Map 6 shows the area known as *Weogorenaleah*, 'the woodland of the Weogoran', within which the church of Worcester was granted an extensive estate entitled *Wican* in the eighth century (Sawyer 1968: S 142, S 180). It has to be remembered that most early place-names were only recorded in documents because they had become estate or settlement centres and it is only later charter boundary clauses that refer to the features disassociated from settlement: here the term almost always means 'wood' (Hooke, 1990: 399). However, it would not be far wrong to envisage a landscape made up of mostly open, rather than dense, woodland and the term may convey an economic usage as wood-pasture.

The charter boundaries are most detailed in the later Anglo-Saxon period, by which time Mercia had been decimated by Danish attack and settlement and had lost its supremacy to Wessex. However, in a swathe of England that extends from Dorset in the south-west into Yorkshire in the north-east changes were taking place that were to alter the

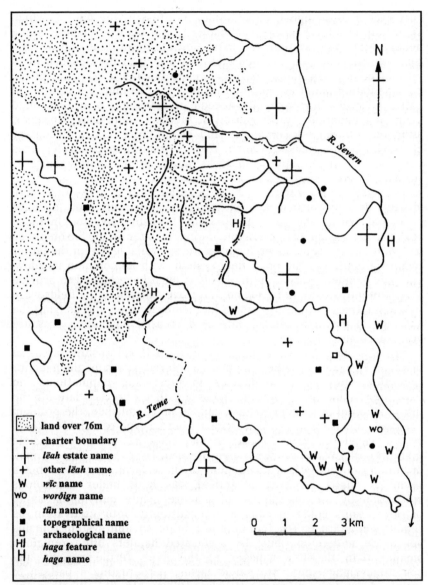

Map 6 *Weogorena lēah*, to the west of Worcester in the kingdom of the Hwicce, showing place-name and charter evidence of woodland and woodland features

character of the English countryside. At present, the date at which open field farming became established is still open to dispute: some believe that the system of open field farming that led to the reorganization of common fields around a central nucleus had been introduced into England by the eighth century (Hall, 1981) but reliable documentation is not available until the tenth. Timing is crucial for, if early, the system had been introduced early enough to provide a sound agrarian foundation for the period of Mercian supremacy. However, although reference to common land occurs in a mid-ninth-century charter of Cofton Hacket in north Worcestershire, specific references to subdivided fields only occur from the mid-tenth century onwards (Hooke, 1988a, 1990).

The system only seems to have been adopted in areas that were already densely settled and cleared for agriculture and to have developed within the later Anglo-Saxon township division. In these regions, increasing estate fragmentation in later Anglo-Saxon times had deprived many such estates of pastures available within the larger territorial unit, and the open field system, with its common meadow-land and compensatory system of fallow, must have helped to provide this continuing need. In regions of intensive cultivation the fields were to extend across whole townships by medieval times, intensifying the shortage of pasture relieved only by decreased population pressure after the Black Death.

In more marginal zones, such as much of Herefordshire, areas of open field remained smaller and more scattered – perhaps the need for reorganization of the fields due to increasing populations and extending arable never became necessary. If no precise date for the introduction of open field farming can yet be established, the problem is equally apparent in western Britain where a type of infield–outfield system developed. Such a system may underlie some of the field systems of the Welsh Border region (Rowley, 1972: 137). The common ownership of land was a component of these farming systems but a relatively restricted area of infield was kept under continuous cultivation by the liberal use of manure, while outlying areas of marginal land could be taken intermittently into cultivation as requirements arose. Whether this is a more ancient system remains yet to be understood but the associated hamlets often remained smaller than the new villages of the more fertile regions and sometimes languished into single farms, perpetuating a pattern of mainly dispersed settlement (Hooke, 1998a: 115–36). Whether the more organized open field system was an introduction from elsewhere – for it appears in Scandinavia (Berglund, 1994) and western Europe at about the same time – or whether it represents the development of a native system remains, as yet, unclear but archaeology seems to present evidence of earlier enclosed fields on the relatively rare occasions that such evidence has been found.

Hand in hand with the development of the open field system was the increasing nucleation of settlement, apparently based upon the new estate/manorial divisions of the later Anglo-Saxon period. Many of these bore *tūn* settlement names and the more successful ones became the villages of later times, especially as churches and chapels were founded to serve these new communities. *Tūn* settlements begin to proliferate in the mid-eighth century and to increase in late Anglo-Saxon times, often associated with the personal names of apparent estate holders, although in part this may reflect increasing documentation (Gelling, 1978: 180–5; Hooke, 1997a: 72–6). It is now clear that nucleation was a slow process that was still proceeding in medieval times, and even in heavily nucleated regions outlying settlements which have left no further trace in the documentary record were still present in the eleventh century (Hooke, 1985b). In more sparsely populated regions nucleation was seldom a dominant characteristic. The different settlement patterns are well exemplified throughout central and southern England with clear contrasts between the Arden and Feldon regions of Warwickshire, for instance, or the Vale of the White Horse and the Chieveley region of Berkshire (the Vale has now been taken into Oxfordshire) (Hooke, 1988b). It is clear that they reflect natural resources and farming systems. Herefordshire again offers examples of this: while most of the county shows evidence of an irregular field system made up of tiny but numerous patches of open field within a township, often related to scattered hamlets, in the more heavily settled area of the Wye valley to the north of Hereford villages developed and the open fields extended to cover much of the individual township area by the late medieval period, by then organized in this region into the more typical midland three or four field system.

Communications and trade

The estate centres of royal vills were by no means necessarily urban centres. Indeed, most lay in rural countryside where they could draw upon a wide range of agricultural resources. The minsters, too, were often established in similarly rural locations and the early minster was a simple monastic cell, probably surrounded by an earthen bank or *vallum* which enclosed the ecclesiastical buildings including the church and ranges of outbuildings. But recent excavations at West Heslerton and other 'central places' have shown how even a rurally placed central place could draw in commodities from a world-wide trading network: cowrie shells from the Red Sea, hone-stones from Scandinavia, ivory purse rings (Powlesland, 1997). In return, Britain was exporting such goods as textiles which included woollen cloaks from the Cotswolds, and rich embroideries, leather, minerals such as lead, hunting-dogs, salt and possibly honey; slave trading 'was possibly the most important trade in early medieval Europe although it began to decline after the seventh century when the church reacted strongly against it' (Hodges, 1982: 125–9). Coastal and riverine trading centres were established, often bearing *wic* place-names, and the need to guarantee access to such outlets must have been a powerful factor impelling Mercia's expansion, particularly towards London and the Thames. The Bishop of Worcester was granted freedom of toll in the port of London, *Lundentunes hyðe*, in the eighth century (743 × 745) (Sawyer, 1977; 1968: S 98) and much of the trade here is likely to have been in salt.

Droitwich was the great inland brine-producing centre of Anglo-Saxon England and it lay within the kingdom of the Hwicce. Here brine flowed freely from underground springs and had supported a valuable salt trade since at least Iron Age times. In Anglo-Saxon times the brine was evaporated in leaden vats over 'ovens' fired with wood and the salt was transported across the Hwiccan kingdom and beyond via a series of long-established saltways which can be accurately traced from the early medieval documentary evidence. These radiated outwards from Droitwich but not necessarily directly – often following well-established routes along main valleys (Hooke, 1981b, 1985b). South-eastwards, they appear to have led to the Thames at Lechlade and from here the salt would no doubt have been carried by barge to London. Droitwich itself was probably not an urban centre – rather, a collection of separate industrial settlements clustered around the salt springs and the evaporation 'ovens' which included Middelwich, *Upewic* and Netherwich, reflecting the application of the Latin *vicus* to 'a street or quarter where particular trades concentrated' (Smith, 1956: 257–64).

In addition to the saltways, other highways can also be recognized, providing communications throughout the kingdom and across the rest of the country (Hooke, 1981a). Many of the Roman roads remained in use (often referred to by the *strǣet* term used for a made-up road); other major highways were named as *herepæð* routes. Although the term originally meant 'army way' it became generally applied to highways in southern England in later Anglo-Saxon times. Although rivers were normally forded or crossed by ferries (Forsberg, 1950: 20–3), some major bridges were being constructed in the Anglo-Saxon period, recorded, for instance, at Rochester in Kent when those responsible for the restoration of the bridge were listed in 974 (Birch, 1885–99: B 1321, B 1322; Robertson, 1986: no. 52, 106–9).

True urban centres were slow to develop. This growth was driven by several factors – economic and defensive, neither a new concept but developing in response to the events and circumstances taking place in Anglo-Saxon England. The establishment of *burhs* as centres from which to organize defence against the Danes was a major factor in southern England, initiated by Alfred during the resurgence of Wessex (but imitating earlier fortifications as at Hereford against the Welsh). The fortification of midland centres such as Warwick and Worcester followed. The complete redrawing of administrative boundaries within Mercia may have been in part a political measure as Wessex took advantage of the break-up of its former adversary (the eastern sector of the kingdom had fallen to Danish rule) to establish its dominance. The new urban *burhs* were able to fulfil a greater administrative function as county towns and to facilitate the regularization of trade and marketing. Thus Worcester was fortified in the late ninth century by Æthelred and Æthelflæd, the ealdorman of Mercia and his wife (the daughter of Alfred), who *hehtan bewyrcean þa burh æt Weorgerna Ceastre eallum folc to gebeorge*, 'ordered the burh (Whitelock gives 'borough') at Worcester to be built for the protection of all the people' (Sawyer, 1968: S 223; Whitelock, 1979: 540–1). An important part of the revenue from the new town was to be drawn from market tolls and it was ordered that the church should take half the profits while the ealdorman was to retain the rest.

Although this period marked the end of Mercian supremacy, the region was to continue to play an important economic and political role within the new 'England'. The church of Worcester, its bishop serving the diocese which had been established to serve the Hwiccan kingdom, continued to produce and preserve documents within its scriptorium at Worcester which remain an important source of evidence for the late Anglo-Saxon landscape. The way that it managed its estates, leasing out for limited periods the new 'proto-manors' which were to become the forerunners of the Domesday vills, continued to exhibit contemporary trends in late Anglo-Saxon estate management and administrative organization (Dyer, 1980: 30–6, 39–50; Hooke, 1997b). Other churches, such as Winchester and Canterbury, were equally prolific in producing documentation relating to their estates (Hill, 1981: 22, Fig. 31). Monasteries such as Glastonbury and Ely were becoming immensely wealthy. Increasingly, the Church was to enjoy guaranteed revenues of jurisdiction and to become increasingly involved in the organization of military service. Cash began to replace payment in kind in a growing monetary economy.

Secular landholders also, however, held great estates extending across the country: King Athelstan was to amass the royal holdings of Wessex, Mercia and Northumbria, although royal estates were to be dissipated by mid-tenth-century reforms. The ealdormen of Mercia, successors to the early princes, gained new powers as they built up their own estates and power bases: under Danish patronage, Leofric, the younger son of an ealdorman of western Mercia, became earl of Mercia and his family became dominant in the former Mercian homeland, hostile to the Godwine family established in Wessex – old rivalries re-emerging on the eve of the Norman conquest. By the end of the Anglo-Saxon period the setting for feudal England was in place. Farming, however, exploiting the natural but managed resources of woodland, heath, pasture and arable, remained the mainstay of the economy. The landscape itself was continuing to develop the regional characteristics which were to prevail thoughout the Middle Ages and which were to contribute towards the appearance of the rural countryside as we see it today.

12 Mercians: The Dwellers on the Boundary

David Hill

Mercia was the land of the boundary and, in particular, of the March in the sense that we still use it, the Welsh Marches. From the slender materials available it can be shown how important Welsh warfare on the troubled frontier was to Mercia and how frequent was that warfare. The sources also indicate that the frontier was one on which the Saxon was as frequently the victim as the Celt.

The sources for the relations between the Welsh and Mercians in the early medieval period are primarily documentary. Foremost is the *Anglo-Saxon Chronicle*, which deals almost exclusively with West Saxon matters, so that the Welsh do not figure largely in the annals between the initial settlements and 830. There are some other English sources which relate to the question of the relations between the Saxons and the Welsh, in particular Asser's *Life of King Alfred*, the account of Athelstan preserved by William of Malmesbury and an agreement usually called 'The ordinance concerning the Dunsætæ'. The Welsh sources, while not abundant, are by no means negligible. The main narrative comes from the *Annales Cambriae*.

The archaeological evidence is limited. There are the great earthworks standing as landmarks in our study, Wat's and Offa's Dykes and the remains of the Anglo-Saxon town of Cledemutha, just to the south of Rhuddlan. These represent contemporary limits set by the kings of Mercia and of England. Among the material remains there are the sculpted stones, in particular the Pillar of Eliseg. The coin hoards are mainly late and a penny of Hywel stands in isolation. There may, apparently, be information to be gleaned from the poetry.

From these various sources a picture can be constructed of warfare and disturbance on the frontier for lengthy periods of time in the eighth, ninth and tenth centuries:

> From an incidental reference in Felix's *Life of Guthlac* we learn that in 704–709 'the Britons, the dangerous enemies of the Saxon race, were oppressing the nation of the English with war, pillage and devastation of the people'. (Whitelock, 1955: 711)

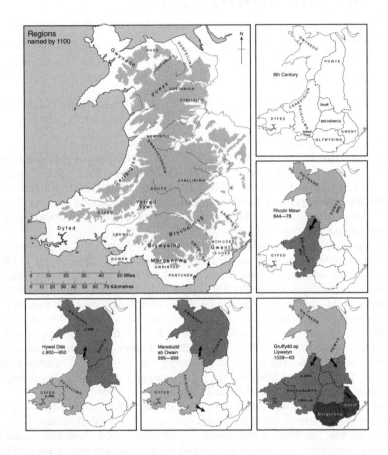

Map 7 Regions named by 1100

In 722 the Welsh won three battles (AC).
In 743 'Æthelbald, king of Mercia, and Cuthred, king of Wessex, fought against the Welsh' (E).
In 753 'Cuthred, king of Wessex, fought against the Welsh' (E).
In 760 there was 'a battle between the Britons and the Saxons, that is the battle of Hereford' (AC).
The Pillar of Eliseg, so called from the name of the king it commemorates, is a free-standing cross shaft at Llantysilio-yn-ial just north of the Abbey of Valle Crucis. The inscription is now worn away, but was recorded by Edward Lhuyd in 1696. The

translation reads in part: 'It was Eliseg who annexed the inheritance of Powys ... throughout nine (years) from the power of the English, which he made into a sword-land by fire' (Rhys, 1908). The reign of Eliseg is usually dated to the mid-eighth century.

For 778 is recorded 'the devastation of the South Britons by Offa' (AC).

And for 784 'the devastation of Britain by Offa in the summer' (AC).

In 797 the battle of Rhuddlan took place (AC).

In 798 'Caradog king of Gwynedd [was] killed by the Saxons' (AC).

In 816 'Saxons invaded the mountains of Eyri and the kingdom of Rhufoniog' (AC).

In 818 'Coenwulf devastated the Dyfed region' (AC).

In 822 'The fortress of Degannwy [was] destroyed by the Saxons and they took the kingdom of Powys into their own control' (AC), Coenwulf having died in 821 (A,E) at Basingwerk in Flintshire (Hardy and Martin, 1888: 90; Stenton, 1971: 230).

In 830 'King Egbert led the army among the Welsh, and he reduced them to humble submission' (A).

In 849 'Meurig was killed by Saxons' (AC).

In 853 'Burhred, king of Mercia, and his councilors asked King Ethelwulf that he would help them to subject the Welsh. He then did so, and with the army went through Mercia into Wales, and they made them all subject to them' (A; see also Keynes and Lapidge, 1983: 69).

There is a puzzling reference in a charter of Burgred, king of the Mercians, which is dated 855, from an unknown Oswaldesdun (Sawyer, 1968: 206), *quando fuerunt pagani in Wreocensetun* ('when the pagans were in the province of the Wrekin-dwellers'). There is no other record of these pagans, presumably Vikings; neither English nor Welsh sources mention any incursion, which obviously would have been major to reach so deep inland. The most likely would be a Dublin- or Ireland-based expedition, but there is a chance that there was collaboration between Viking and Welsh to bring them so deep into the country, and the slight chance that they were Welsh.

When one of the more notable forgers of the Middle Ages was putting together the so-called 'pseudo-Ingulf', the writer did not invent everything from the start. To add verisimilitude, and to save himself effort, he used genuine sources for the framework; some of those sources may be lost to us. Dealing with the events of 871, he writes: 'In the meantime, Bürgred, king of the Mercians, was busily engaged with the Britons, who, by their frequent irruptions, disquieted the western borders of his kingdom of Mercia' (Riley, 1854: 49). If genuine tradition stood behind this account it would indicate a raid or expedition in that year.

In 877 'Rhodri and his son Gwriad [were] killed by Saxons' (AC).

In 880 the battle of Conway was recorded, with a comment that it was 'vengeance for Rhodri at God's hand' (AC).

Asser wrote that at the time that he was called to Alfred's court, apparently in the opening months of 885, 'and for a considerable time before then, all the districts of right-hand [southern] Wales belonged to King Alfred, and still do. That is to say, Hyfaidd, with all the inhabitants of the kingdom of Dyfed, driven by the might of the six sons of Rhodri [Mawr], had submitted himself to King Alfred's royal overlordship. Likewise, Hywel ap Rhys (the king of Glywysing) and Brochfael and Ffyrnfael (sons of Meurig and kings of Gwent), driven by the might and tyrannical behaviour of Ealdorman Ethelred and the Mercians, petitioned King Alfred of their own accord, in order to obtain lordship and protection from him in the face of their enemies. Similarly, Elise ap Tewdwr, king of Brycheiniog, being driven by the might of the same sons of Rhodri [Mawr], sought of his own accord the lordship of King Alfred. And Anarawd ap Rhodri, together with his brothers, eventually abandoned his alliance with the Northumbrians (from which he got no benefit, only a good deal of misfortune) and, eagerly seeking alliance with King Alfred, came to him in person; when he had been received with honour by the king and accepted as a son in confirmation at the hand of a bishop, and showered with extravagant gifts, he subjected himself with all his people to King Alfred's lordship on the same condition as Æthelred and the Mercians, namely that in every respect he would be obedient to the royal will' (Keynes and Lapidge, 1983: 96).

In 894 'Anarawd came with the Angles and laid waste Ceredigion and Ystrad Tywi' (AC).

In 915 was built 'that stronghold at Chirbury, and then that at Weardbyrig' (C).

In 915 (D) or 917 (A) 'a great raiding ship-army ... raided in Wales ... where it suited them, and took Cameleac, bishop in Archenfield, ... and then King Edward ransomed him back for 40 pounds'.

In 916 'Abbot Ecgberht, guiltless, was killed with his companions ... And three days later Æthelflæd sent an army into Wales and broke down Brecenanmere and there took the wife of the king as one of thirty-four' (C).

In 921 'King Edward ... rode and took the stronghold at Tamworth, and all the nation of the land of Mercia which was earlier subject to Athelflaed turned to him, and the kings of Wales: Hywel and Clydog and Idwal, and all the race of the Welsh, sought him as their lord' (A).

Also in 921 'King Edward built the stronghold at the mouth of the Clwyd' [Cledemutha] (C).

Three incidents which would have occurred in 923–925 are recounted in William of Malmesbury's *De Gesti Regorum Anglorum* ('Concerning the Acts of the Kings of the English'). While this account is obviously flawed, and its authenticity has recently been questioned (Lapidge, 1981: 71, but see Wood, 1981), it may be based on fact. The incidents are:

1. After taking over Northumbria 'And since a noble spirit, once roused, attempts greater things, [Edward] forced Idwal, king of all the Welsh, and Constantine, king of the Scots, to yield their kingdoms. Yet not long afterwards, moved by pity, he restored them to their former position to rule under himself, declaring that it was more glorious to make a king than to be a king' (Whitelock, 1955: 277).

2. '§133. King Edward, after many noble achievements both in war and in peace, a few days before his death repressed the contumacy of the city of Chester, which was in revolt in alliance with the Britons; and then having placed there a garrison of soldiers, he was seized by sickness, and ended the present life at the residence of Farndon' (Whitelock, 1955: 279).

3. '§134. [Athelstan] was much beloved of his subjects out of admiration of his courage and humility, but like a thunderbolt to rebels by his invincible steadfastness. He forced the rulers of the North Welsh i.e. the Northern Britons, to meet him at the city of Hereford and to submit after they had resisted for some time; thus he carried into effect what no king before him had even dared to think of, that they were to pay to him annually in the name of tribute 20 pounds of gold, 300 of silver, to add 25,000 oxen, besides as many dogs as he chose, which could discover with their keen scent the dens and lurking-places of wild beasts, and birds which were trained to make a prey of other birds in the air. When he had departed from there, he turned himself to the ... Corn-Welsh; ... fixing their boundary of their province beyond the river Tamar, just as he had established the river Wye as the frontier for the North Britons' (Whitelock, 1955: 280–1).

In 943 'Idwal son of Rhodrii and his son Elisedd [were] killed by the Saxons' (AC).

In 951 'Cadwgan son of Owain [was] killed by the Saxons' (AC).

We have little to show in the way of trade or commerce across the frontier, in fact the paucity of finds of any kind for the period from Wales is such that we are not entitled to argue anything from the lack of goods and materials originating from Anglo-Saxon England and found within the confines of modern Wales. The only straw that we have is that it has proved so far impossible to find original gateways in the line of Offa's and Wat's Dykes, leaving us with the impression that there was little or no traffic across those lines.

There is often little from our sources in the way of scale, for we are going to be dealing with a range of events which include raids, rule or settlement. Certainly, there is an indication of occupation as well as of raiding. There are periods of dependence on the Mercian and English crown but that is really an innovation of the 830s and beyond; it may be that it only worked formally after the end of the tenth century. A state can survive a raid or a lost battle, but the implications of recognizing overlordship, the acceptance of hegemony, is a different matter. The effects of it are as nothing compared with the situation where the actual ruler is a Mercian with Mercian officials and the village (or whatever unit the community was divided into) has a 'lord' or 'thegn' who was Saxon. The ultimate stage comes when the whole folk are Saxon, in other words when there is a complete settlement of ethnic Saxons. These events are not simply incidents, unconnected and essentially meaningless. For Mercia, with its satellites facing usually separate and disunited Welsh kingdoms and principalities, the border was an essential feature of the state. Mercia's organization, even its very name, depended on its military response to its borders, particularly its Celtic border, while to the Welsh the extinction of their state was always a threat. The elimination of Celtic independence and the settlement by Saxons were a distinct possibility throughout this period.

There was therefore a dynamic frontier reflecting the range of relationships between the parties on either side. Even ignoring the impact of the Vikings, the fluctuation of frontiers is complex. The first half of the eighth century appears to be a time of Welsh local supremacy in the border warfare, perhaps enough to bring onto themselves the attentions of Æthelbald, king of Mercia, with his vassal Cuthred, king of the West Saxons, in 743, followed by a devastation of the Archenfield. Æthelbald's reign must mark the attempt of the Mercians to make permanent settlements within the lands of the Welsh, otherwise there would not have been the fairly recent oppression of the Mercians for Eliseg to react to, moving the frontier permanently back in favour of Powys in the decade up to 773. It is in this period that a context for Offa's Dyke may be sought. The devastations that followed when Offa regained the hegemony of Southumbrian England continued up until the death of the king of Gwynedd in 798. Although the sources do not enable us to be categoric about the state of the frontier from the death of Offa until, after a period of great activity in the North Wales marches from 816 in 822, Deganwy was destroyed and Powys occupied, there does seem to have been a genuine attempt to hold North Wales, otherwise the battle of Conway in 880 lacks a context. There may in fact have been a see-sawing of the frontier, for in 830 what part of Wales was reduced by a triumphant Egbert? Certainly, the period of the late 840s, leading to the necessity of both West Saxons and Mercians coming together in 853 to reduce the Welsh again, would appear to mark one of the periods of Welsh dominance on the border, and a possible context for Wat's Dyke. There are difficulties in that case in moving the border in the north back to the Conway for the battle of 880, followed by the possible settlement of the Strathclyde immigrants, but we do seem to be faced with an attempt to move the border permanently to include

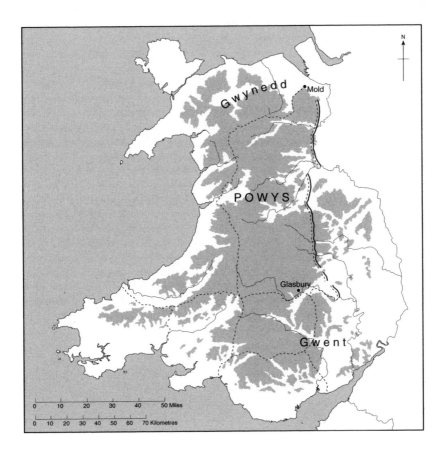

Map 8 Powys and Offa's Dyke

into England the richest agricultural area in Wales (the Vale of Clwyd currently has the largest concentration of Grade One agricultural land in Wales).

That Wales remained a serious threat for a generation would appear to be borne out by the construction of fortresses along the border such as Chirbury, built in 915, although they may simply have been to do with the Danish Wars. The events of 921 when Cledemutha was built could be interpreted as an attempt by Edward the Elder to re-establish his North Wales provinces and form a 'Clwydshire', the rising of ?923 by Idwal, the North Welsh and Chester putting paid to that, although it brought Edward to the north-west to stabilize the situation. There is no particular reason to disbelieve the claim that Athelstan dispossessed

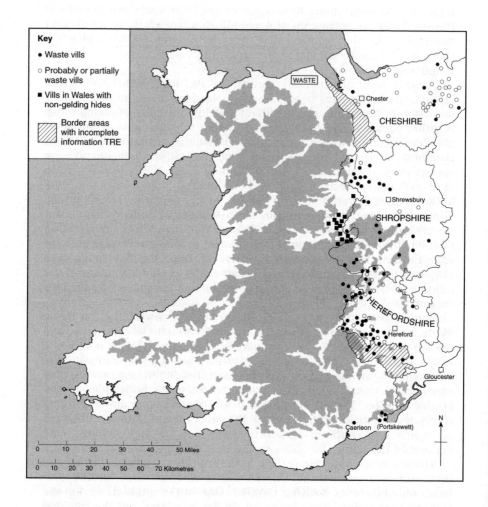

Map 9 Domesday waste in 1066 as an indicator of previous Welsh raids. *Note*: High ground stippled (after David Hill, *An Atlas of Anglo-Saxon England*, University of Toronto Press, 1981)

Idwal after the revolt at the close of Edward's reign, and it is in this period of the submission at Hereford, whatever the precise details, that a long period of English supremacy was ushered in with the taxes and stewards of the Armes Prydein ('The Prophecy of Britain') (Bromwich and Williams, 1972) and the series of meetings recorded in the charters. It would also seem to be the context for the expansion of

English settlement along both sides of the Wye south and west from Hereford and the setting up of Archenfield, although these permanent movements of the frontier may well have been earlier (Map 7). However, for all the activity at Hereford, the Vale of Clwyd was forever abandoned to the Welsh.

Turning from the overall picture to the local situation on the ground, there may have been a no man's land between the two peoples for much of the time, the result of the impossibility of living close together because of skirmishing and raiding, with one side or the other withdrawing in periods of weakness. The nature of that no man's land is difficult to assess, but there is enough indication to suggest that in certain areas it was a land given up only to hunting. There is a certain tendency for West Saxon kings to have hunting lodges on the borders between themselves and the Cornish, or Corn-welsh. Lodges in the Tamar valley and Alfred's hunting on the fringes of Bodmin Moor point to this form of land use, and examples may be found in the destruction in 1065 of the hunting lodge at Portskewett in Monmouthshire built for King Edward the Confessor by Earl Harold. And one of the suggested purposes for the royal palace at Basingwerk is to take advantage of the hunting on the Clwydian mountains and the sea marshes along the Dee estuary.

Domesday records for some Herefordshire settlements: 'on these waste lands there have grown up woods in which Osbern hunts, and thence he has whatever he can take. Nothing else.' There is also the whole of the Vale of Montgomery given over only to hunting. The Shropshire entries record similar patterns of waste as well as reminding us that devastation could be found on both sides of the border in 1066. Yale, described as 5 leagues long and one and a half broad, was waste in 1066. If we see the exact frontier as often a band of no man's land with no agriculture, we may be approaching some version of the truth.

Elsewhere we have the setting of the frontier on a river, the Wye in the ordinance concerning the Dunsætæ and the Dee in the pre-Domesday reference to King Gruffyd. One of the suggestions for the Dykes has therefore been for some similar boundary, but the fact that the Dyke is not a frontier, crossing fields and settlements, stands against this. What Domesday must show us is that it was possible for a series of raids and incessant warfare on the part of the Welsh to devastate completely a belt of land 10 miles broad down the frontier and effectively throw that frontier back from Holywell/Basingwerk to the River Dee, incorporating an area of prime agricultural land 18 miles wide: moreover, an English king accepted the situation. That these periods could be extensive and 'won' by the Welsh can be demonstrated from Domesday and from the Pillar of Eliseg. The Armes Prydein, probably from a South Welsh background, and the Colloquy *De Raris Fabilis*, perhaps from Cornwall but with Welsh connections (Davies, 1982: 213), indicate that, whatever the princes were doing, there was a deep pool of resentment among some sections of the Celtic population against the Saxons. This resentment may well lie behind some of the minor outbreaks along the border and would certainly allow a Welsh king to act against the English if opportunity allowed.

When struggling with the reality of all this action on the border we have to people the Marches and therefore search to man the frontier. Professor Earle (1857) dealt with great clarity and insight into Offa's Dyke and its setting. He made serious suggestions about conservation, discussed the 'agreed frontier' and reviewed the evidence for the supporting administration for the Mercian and English relations with the Welsh kingdoms. He started with the Chronicle entry for 896: 'That same year Wulfric, the king's horse-thegn, passed away: he was also the Welsh reeve' (A). Dorothy Whitelock remarks that 'it is uncertain what this term implies' (Whitelock, 1965: 58), but Earle felt that the conclusion was justified that the *wealh gerefa* could be rendered as 'patroller-general of the Welsh Marches'. However this conclusion rests on whether or not the scribe intended *gefera*, which then leads to the 'patroller', or left out a letter and Whitelock is right in reading *gerefa*, leading to 'reeve'. Earle linked this functionary with the charter (Sawyer, 1968, no. 207) dated 855 where Burgred, King of Mercia, freed land of various dues for the monastery of Blockley, Worcestershire, from: 'the feeding and refection of those men we call in Saxon, Walhfæreld'. Earle rendered this word as 'the military company on Welsh duty', a body which he equated with those mentioned in the Chronicle entry for 1053: 'Also the Welsh men killed a great part of the English people of the guard near Westbury' (C).

These *weardmanna* recall the place-name given to the fort founded in 915, *weardbyrig*. The identification of Westbury is usually taken as being that in Gloucestershire, though there is no reason to ignore Westbury in Shropshire, only 5 miles from the Welsh boundary on the Severn, while Westbury on Severn is nearly twice as far and the wrong side of the Forest of Dean. Apart from these military men the mechanism for the control may be seen through the hostages mentioned in the 'Ordinance concerning the Dunsæte', and there clearly is some recognized person who will meet *bona fide* travellers at the frontiers. The messengers and guides are mentioned by Asser, Domesday and in charters. There are other tiers, however, as indicated by the local arrangements referred to in the ordinance and the mention of 'stewards' in the Armes Prydein. What is clear is that there were established in Wales the collection of taxes and tribute and the authority of stewards, probably Saxon. The relationship of these mechanisms with the Welsh princes and kings is unclear.

In summary, the frontier was dynamic, both in the turbulence it apparently constantly generated and in the serious attempts to move the frontier one way or the other, connected also with English attempts to control Wales through overlordship, though the role in these developments of the two major earthworks is not clear.

13 The Growth of Market Centres and Towns in the Area of the Mercian Hegemony

Alan Vince

Introduction

It is possible to overstate the case for the sophistication of the economy of Mercia in the seventh to ninth centuries. In the Roman period, the Midlands and East Anglia were integrated into the Roman empire. Imported goods, represented mainly by pottery in the archaeological record, occur on sites of all kinds and the quantity and range of artefacts found on these sites indicates that dress accessories, tools, household fittings and ornaments were being moved over long distances, no doubt alongside other goods which we have no direct knowledge of. In the later twelfth century and later the same is true. Sufficient surplus was being generated in the countryside to not only support the Church and the landholding class but also to leave the peasant some disposable income. In the centuries in-between, however, archaeological sites are often almost barren of artefacts. Parts of western Mercia were aceramic – there is no locally made pottery of fifth- to tenth-century date from any site west of the Severn – and in many cases elsewhere the entire artefact assemblage amounts to less than a dozen objects. Spread across the centuries of occupation, these finds might reflect the occasional, once-in-a-lifetime, passing of a trader. Alternatively, they may simply indicate that few middle Saxon settlements have been excavated and that what we have is simply the debris from settlements which lay outside the excavated area. The example of *Lundenwic*, which was, apparently, unknown archaeologically before the mid-1980s should warn us about making any categorical statements on the basis of negative evidence.

The subject of this chapter, therefore, is difficult to address. It is at present possible to make a very minimal case for the growth of market centres and towns in Mercia in the seventh to ninth centuries, to the extent of denying their existence. On the other hand, almost the same evidence can be interpreted optimistically. The crucial point, for the development of the subject, is to find alternate models which are capable of testing using either existing archaeological data or at least where archaeological data if acquired might discriminate between them.

A case in point is the mechanism of transfer of goods. Documentary sources suggest that food renders were an important redistributive mechanism and even the derivation of the word 'lord' shows the importance of redistribution in the seventh to ninth centuries. Redistribution in certain societies seems to have been capable of achieving the entire circulation of goods whereas in others it was one of a number of mechanisms. In our own times it survives mainly as a means of cementing relationships through the ritualized giving of gifts, as at Christmases and birthdays, and in a fuller form within the family. Undoubtedly, economic life in the seventh to ninth centuries included the collecting of renders and the subsequent redistribution of those goods through the giving of gifts and formal meals. But how can we recognize redistribution in the archaeological record? Naturally enough, archaeologists have turned to the faunal remains record and O'Connor, for example, has suggested that the animal bones found at Fishergate, York, are consistent with that site being a centre for the consumption of animals supplied as part of a food render (1991: 282–3). And yet, Northumberland at that time, like Mercia, was a coin-using society. What might the archaeological differences be between food debris acquired through render and that acquired through a monetary exchange?

Even the use of coin itself is not a clear-cut case for the existence of a monetary economy. Grierson (1959) has made the case that coins, especially those of high face value, were often used in gift exchange or for the payment of tribute or fines rather than trade and exchange. It may be that the re-introduction of coinage to Anglo-Saxon England was achieved as much through this means as through commercial contacts with Merovingian France or the Eastern Empire. Nevertheless, there is a point during the development of Anglo-Saxon coinage where it becomes clear that the quantities being produced and the range of contexts in which they occur is incontrovertible evidence for their widespread use in commerce. For much of Mercia that point is probably close to 700, which implies that for maybe two generations coins were being produced in Essex and Kent but not used in the majority of the Mercian economy.

For trade to flourish roads and river communication would also have been crucial. In the Roman period the road network throughout Mercia was well developed. Much of this network emanated from London and by and large the system survives today. However, in almost every case the surviving routes link Roman towns which later re-emerged as medieval towns. It was therefore almost inevitable that the road system would be revived too and is no evidence that the roads survived throughout the fifth to ninth centuries. Contemporary evidence comes mainly from documentary sources rather than archaeology. In those parts of Mercia outside of the Danelaw the bounds of estates often survive and when plotted on the ground quite often use roads as part of their boundaries. Sometimes roads are actually mentioned in the charters. Not all of these are of obvious Roman date. Some may in fact be even earlier routeways but others may have been constructed during the seventh to ninth centuries. A case can certainly be made for this being the case in Middlesex where some routes headed toward the middle Saxon settlement of *Lundenwic* rather than the Roman and medieval walled city. In general, however, there is little that can be done to prove that a Roman road was being used in the seventh to ninth centuries. The very fact that additions were made to the Roman system does, however, suggest that they were being used.

Roads, however, were used for other purposes than trade. Their original function was to a great extent as part of the military occupation of Britain, both to allow the Roman army to rapidly move about the country overland and to allow the provisioning of their forts. Again, there is some evidence that this military function continued into the seventh to ninth centuries, for example the use of the term 'army street' (*herepaþ*) and similar terms for roads later known as the King's Highway on which special protection for travellers and merchants was in force.

Ports and landing stages are even less in evidence during the seventh to ninth centuries. Hodges (in Nielsen *et al.*, 1993) has speculated that the earliest post-Roman ports would have been seasonally occupied beach markets, of the sort which seems to have existed in Funen, Denmark, at Gudme during the fifth and sixth centuries. Structural evidence would be unlikely to survive on such sites, if it ever existed, and the most that might be hoped for would be evidence for the loading and unloading of goods, in the form perhaps of cargo broken in transit and discarded. By the mid-seventh century we have evidence for such an *emporium* at Ipswich (Wade, 1988). The site in question produced evidence for a revetted waterfront and local and imported artefacts, principally pottery. However, it if were not for the fact that the site later developed into a major port it is unlikely that the evidence found would itself have suggested the existence of an emporium. The revetment, for example, is little more than might be expected to protect any section of river bank from erosion rather than a major engineering feat (Wade, 1988: Fig. 52). Remains of Hodges Type A emporia will therefore always be difficult to find, even assuming that they existed at a locality. Therefore, the origins of international trade must be sought by looking at some of the consequences of this trade rather than directly.

Towns, markets and trade in the fifth, sixth and early seventh centuries

Settlements of the early Anglo-Saxon period, dating roughly from the early to mid-fifth century to the mid-seventh century are now known throughout the Midlands. In most cases, however, the evidence for their size, internal layout, organization and economic basis is slight or non-existent. Difficulties in dating archaeological features within this period severely limit interpretation, even when, as at West Stow in Suffolk, what appears to be the entire settlement has been excavated and published (West, 1985). At Mucking a site interpreted during excavation as being a large contemporary settlement has been re-interpreted during post-excavation analysis as the remains of a much smaller settlement whose focus shifted during its life (Hamerow, 1993). Intensive field surveys, such as those carried out in North-amptonshire and Leicestershire, indicate intensive small-scale settle-ment in those counties and a survey of Anglo-Saxon pottery findspots in the East Midlands suggests that a similar density of occupation existed in Lincolnshire and the Trent Valley. Evidence from Nottinghamshire and Derbyshire away from the River Trent either suggests a culturally different settlement pattern or much less intensive occupation. Faunal remains studies of some of these settlements indicate a mixed economy and for the Orton Hall Farm site, on the fen edge near Peterborough, the evidence suggests a change from specialized cattle-rearing in the Roman period to a broader, less specialized economy in the early Anglo-Saxon period (Mackreth, 1996). Both the walled Roman towns of the Midlands and the large 'villages' or unwalled towns which grew up at nodal points along the road network seem in some cases to have been abandoned and in others to have been succeeded by early Anglo-Saxon settlements. However, there are no finds from these successor sites to suggest that their inhabitants were leading an urban life.

Despite this negative evidence, there is reason to believe that there was some cross-Channel trade during this period, although whether it was continuous from the end of the Roman period or re-established after a break is unclear. For example, at sites such as Newark on Trent and West Halton, both riverine settlements along the Trent, as well as at Barton upon Humber, sherds of probable Merovingian imported pottery have been found. At Mucking too there is evidence for the increasing use of imported pottery during the lifetime of the settlement. In each case the number of sherds is minute in comparison with the total number of pottery vessels found and exactly how these finds should be interpreted is unclear. A better indication that the rural economy of the Midlands was not entirely based on self-sufficient mixed agriculture is given by the distribution of pottery tempered with fragments of acid igneous rock. Such vessels have a wide currency in the area later to become Mercia.

The urban role of religious communities

A strong argument can be made for the Church having a major influence on the development of the economy of Mercia. Our archaeological evidence is poor but there are grounds for thinking that several religious communities in Mercia in the seventh to ninth centuries were associated with large secular settlements. Amongst these are Barking Abbey and Ely, which has also recently been proposed as a mint for Series Q *sceattas* (Newman, 1999: 43–4).

There are several ways in which religious communities might have stimulated urban development:

1. Some early Christian communities seem to have been sizeable. A large community would have been a market for food, clothing and luxury goods over and above those that could be provided by the community itself. It is easy to imagine a sequence of development starting with the periodic supply of goods by traders but leading to the foundation of a permanent secular settlement, as may have happened in the eleventh century at Bury St Edmunds.

2. Attendance at religious ceremonies might have provided a convenient opportunity to meet and exchange goods within the territory of the church. Again, there is evidence that this happened later in the medieval period and no reason to doubt that it might have happened during the seventh to ninth centuries. There were clearly fewer churches at that time than later, and consequently their congregations would have been drawn from wider regions than the medieval parishes. The effort involved in attending a church would therefore have been greater and the desire to make use of that opportunity for trade or exchange therefore greater.

3. Some seventh- to ninth-century religious communities seem to have sold on surplus produce. Continental sources, for example, show that the nuns of Fulder in Frisia produced more cloth than they could use and sold on the surplus and Penelope Rogers, in an as-yet unpublished paper, has proposed that the same may be true at Flixborough during its brief monastic phase. Even if monastic communities did produce a surplus, the extent to which this was simply a non-commercial exchange of luxury goods, such as textiles, metalwork and books, rather than extending to higher volume, lower status, goods is uncertain. Demonstrating that any craft was operating at a commercial level is difficult using archaeological evidence alone and, as noted above, the churches would have provided a large market for luxury goods. Later in the medieval period religious communities were clearly involved in large-scale production of wool and other goods but it is likely that this was a development of the eleventh century or later.

4. The location of some early religious communities suggests that they were sited partly to take advantage of good water connections. However, it is also clear that the same locations could be interpreted as being sited to avoid secular involvement, by being surrounded by water or fen (as at Crowland Abbey; see Roberts and Parsons, Chapters 5 and 4 in this volume).

5. The church structure itself provided potential sanctuary for

traders and security for valuable goods and cash. Again, there is documentary evidence for the use of the parish chest by secular merchants in the later medieval period and no reason to doubt that the Church could have had a similar role earlier on.

All of these arguments are strong but they do not take the place of actual proof that the Church did have any role in urban development or trade. Excavations on early monastic sites need to examine not only the church buildings and ancillary buildings but also test the existence of contemporary secular settlements. At Beverley, in Northumbria, for example, it seems clear that the medieval town was laid out in the eleventh or twelfth century, although this does not prove that there was not an earlier secular settlement near the mid-Saxon monastery.

Palaces and elite residences as urban nuclei

Following the discovery of extensive settlement at Northampton of seventh- to ninth-century date there has been considerable interest in the possibility that high status secular residences, usually termed palaces by present-day archaeologists, might exist at various places in Mercia (Williams *et al.*, 1985). The Northampton remains include mortared stone structures and were clearly part of an important site. They were discovered during rescue excavations in the core of the medieval town and the earliest defences of the late Saxon town probably enclosed them. The excavator has interpreted the site with palatial complexes on the continent, such as that at Aachen, but John Blair remains to be convinced that the site was, in fact, secular. In his view, secular palaces were impermanent affairs, given to shifting location every generation or so. He sees them as the upper end of the rural settlement hierarchy and as being essentially similar to those sites in character (Blair, 1996).

Despite this, the orthodox view is still that royal and aristocratic sites may well have formed the nuclei around which early towns grew. Eleventh-century and later documentation hints at a class of settlements, held directly by the king or one of his officials (in Domesday Book usually the Earl), which seem to have been centres for the collection of tax. Often these places are referred to in documents as the King's *tun* or *vill*. The theory goes that such centres were occupied periodically by the royal entourage and by a residual staff in his absence and that, among other functions, they were collecting points for food renders in the seventh to ninth centuries. Excavations at Flixborough, situated close to the junction of the Trent and the Humber, have revealed a large, rich settlement with many signs of high status (see also Parsons and Webster, Chapters 4 and 18 in this volume). These include the presence of the bones of large sea mammals – such as whales, dolphins – which contemporary laws suggest were the prerogative of the king, and many examples of high quality metalwork. Several interpretations of the site have been made since its discovery in the late 1980s, including an identification of the site as *Donnamuth*, a monastic site known from documentary sources and its place-name to lie on the Trent, close to its junction with the River Don. Current thinking would suggest that for most of its life the settlement was a royal vill, although the possibility of a short-lived monastic phase is conceded. In the medieval period the settlement seems to have shifted up the hill before finally being deserted in the late medieval period. At no stage did the medieval village have urban status or show any signs of being anything but an agricultural settlement. Likewise, the mid-Saxon settlement, despite its obvious wealth, shows little sign of being engaged in trade. Imported pottery and Ipswich ware have been found, but in very low quantities. One example, of course, cannot disprove that other royal settlements did not develop into urban centres and there may well be good reasons for Flixborough's failure to develop. For example, in the Roman period the site lay close to the northern end of Ermine Street, from where a ferry crossing led to Brough-on-Humber, whereas by the twelfth century the routeway had been diverted eastwards, crossing the Ancholme at Brigg to reach Barton, thus sidelining Flixborough.

Fieldwork in the East Midlands, notably in Northamptonshire, has shown that a hierarchy of settlement can be recognized on the ground. Three levels of settlement have been proposed (four if one counts Northampton itself). At the base is the small rural settlement, probably no larger than a single farm. Next come larger settlements which often have longer lifetimes (in some cases starting in the Roman period and continuing into the medieval) and above those were regional centres (sometimes polyfocal) which may have documentary or place-name evidence for a direct royal involvement. Where these centres have been examined archaeologically, they often produce sherds of Ipswich ware (Blinkhorn, forthcoming). In some cases such sites emerge in the medieval period as market towns, founded in the eleventh or twelfth centuries. At Newark, for example, excavations have shown that extensive early Anglo-Saxon settlement underlies the medieval town and castle (Dixon *et al.*, 1994). To date, however, mid-Saxon Newark has eluded discovery, probably because, like so many of these settlements, its focus has shifted. Direct or indirect involvement by the king or the secular elite in urban development during the seventh to ninth centuries is therefore quite possible in Mercia but, as yet, unproven.

Coastal and riverine trading settlements

Until comparatively recently it could also be said that the major trading settlement at London, *Lundenwic*, was not known from archaeology but only through documentary sources which were capable of several interpretations. In the space of 15 years, however, the archaeology of

Lundenwic has become well known (see Cowie, Chapter 14 in this volume). From the late seventh century onwards, there was a large, permanently occupied town lying immediately to the west of the Roman walled city. A case for a similar settlement existing at York was made in the late 1980s on the basis of the Fishergate excavation, although the interpretation of that site is disputed (Kemp, 1991; O'Connor, 1991). Together with evidence from Wessex (*Hamwic* situated on the opposite side of the Itchen from the Roman walled settlement at Bitterne) and Kent (the undefended Fordwich situated downriver of the Roman walled town of Canterbury), it began to look as though a pattern had been established and that to find the urban centres of Mercia we should look close to, but not on the same site as Roman towns located on navigable rivers. Only East Anglia provided a different model, where the remains of the mid-Saxon trading settlement of Ipswich lay underneath the medieval and modern town (Wade, 1988). However, despite archaeologists now being sensitized to the possibility of large trading settlements existing in Mercia, no such settlement to rival that of London has yet been found. The River Trent, for example, provided access to the Continent and the east coast of the British Isles to sea-going ships, perhaps even as far inland as Nottingham. Certainly, the ninth-century Viking army seems to have sailed up the Trent to Torksey and thence to Repton while in the early eleventh century Swein Forkbeard and his army landed at Gainsborough. Treasure hunters using metal detectors have reportedly found the Viking age site at Torksey and amongst the reputed finds from the site are Northumbrian *stycas* and Arabic *dirhems*. Torksey lies just to the south of a Roman ferry crossing which linked Ermine Street to Doncaster and York via Tillbridge Lane. It is also extremely close to the Roman capital at Lincoln. In theory, the site could hardly be bettered in terms of its location. There is even a Roman walled settlement on the opposite side of the Trent, Littleborough. This is sometimes identified as *Tiowulfingcastre*, mentioned in Bede's *Ecclesiastical History* (II. 16, in Colgrave and Mynors, 1969: 100) as the location of the mass baptism of the people of Lindsey by Paulinus, Bishop of York in the mid-seventh century. Nevertheless, without archaeological study of the site and its local context, anything that might be said about Torksey in the seventh to ninth centuries is pure speculation. However, a word of caution is required. One of the characteristics of *Hamwic,* Ipswich, and *Lundenwic* is the high frequency of imported and non-local pottery found in the settlements and in sites in the surrounding catchment zones. No pottery finds from the mid-Saxon Torksey site have been reported but pottery collections from sites in the lower Trent valley and central Lincolnshire have been surveyed as part of the East Midlands Anglo-Saxon Pottery Project. This survey shows very few finds of imported pottery – certainly not a concentration – and Ipswich ware is actually absent from the mid-Saxon settlements closest to Torksey. We have too few examples to start laying down strict rules on what to expect at an *emporium* site but this negative evidence does emphasize how important it is to obtain proper archaeological evidence of mid-Saxon Torksey.

Recently, a case has been put forward for the existence of an *emporium* at Ely, in the Cambridgeshire fens, based on the discovery of traces of extensive mid-Saxon settlement (as yet unpublished). The location of this site in the seventh to ninth centuries would have been rather different to its current situation, since much of the surrounding fenland was probably freshwater fen (in contrast with the Lincolnshire fens, where fieldwork has indicated intensive, and unexpected, mid-Saxon settlement, Hayes and Lane, 1992: 127). On the Mercian–East Anglian border, finds made during the construction of a bypass at Thetford suggest that the late Saxon planned town may have been preceded by a mid-Saxon settlement lying immediately to the northwest, lining the southwest bank of the river (Andrews, 1995; Andrews and Penn, 1999). Unfortunately there has been little opportunity as yet to investigate this site archaeologically and much of what was recovered came from the use of metal detectors.

The lack of archaeological investigation at the most likely candidates for Mercian *emporia* sites is a serious problem, especially where those sites are undergoing predation. It is likely that at least one of the candidates will turn out to have been a mid-Saxon trading settlement but until details of their size, foundation dates, histories, layout, activities carried out within them and trading contacts become available, there is little that can be written.

Inland towns

In the last three decades of the twentieth century campaigns of investigation took place in many of the towns of Mercia. In every case documentary records could demonstrate that the place was urban in the tenth or eleventh centuries and in many cases these records have now been amplified by archaeological evidence demonstrating the size and layout of the towns and, less convincingly, their growth or decline. Evidence for seventh- to ninth-century occupation is a lot scarcer and it seemed until recently that most of these sites were at most sparsely occupied during this period. This applies not only to those medieval towns lying in and over Roman walled predecessors (as at Leicester, Cirencester and Gloucester, for example) but also to industrial towns such as Stafford and Stamford, both places where pottery was produced in quantity in the late Saxon period. There are exceptions, however. Excavations on several sites in Bedford showed that there was extensive mid-Saxon settlement on the north side of the river, whereas that part lying south of the river has been demonstrated to be a late Saxon development. Among the pottery from the Bedford sites are several Ipswich ware sherds and at least one continental import. Mid-Saxon pottery, including Ipswich ware, has also been found on sites in Nottingham, where a defensive circuit pre-dating the late

Saxon period has also been discovered (although its exact date is uncertain). Investigation of several of these sites in the western part of Mercia has been hampered by the lack of recognizable finds. Excavations at the centre of Gloucester, for example, revealed timber buildings of ninth-century or earlier date together with rush matting and wooden artefacts. If it were not for the exceptional preservation on the site, there would have been little sign at all of occupation preceding the late Saxon period (Heighway *et al.*, 1979). Furthermore, since the main indication of the non-agricultural nature of mid-Saxon urban sites is the presence of non-local artefacts, such as pottery, metalwork and coins, and these are all much less common in the west of Mercia than the east, it will always be easier to study possible seventh- to ninth-century inland urbanization in the east of the kingdom.

At present, it seems that most of the inland towns of Mercia came into existence in or after the late ninth century. Even where mid-Saxon occupation has been found on the site of a later town, there is at present little evidence to demonstrate the nature of the early settlement. The three sites which at present stand apart from this general rule are Northampton, Bedford and Nottingham. Each of these sites has been shown to be occupied in the mid-Saxon period and the finds include Ipswich ware, differentiating the sites from contemporary rural settlements. We are still, however, a long way from being able to show that any of the major features of the later towns originated in the mid-Saxon period. This is in contrast with Ipswich, where the street pattern of the core of the medieval town has been demonstrated to originate in the mid-Saxon period. Jeremy Haslam (1987) has made a case for several of these midland towns being planned foundations of King Offa. To date, this can be disproved in some cases and remains unproven in others.

Rural fairs and markets

In the 1980s, as a result of the increased use of metal detectors by treasure hunters, a number of sites were recognized as producing more than usual quantities of mid-Saxon metalwork. In some cases the sites were investigated in conjunction with archaeologists while in others knowledge of the sites is partial. In some cases the location has been kept obscure so as to stop rival treasure hunters plundering the site and in others there is suspicion that provenances have been deliberately confused so as to hide the fact that the sites are scheduled ancient monuments.

Discussion of those sites which have not been studied by archaeologists is futile, since even the list of artefacts recovered may well be biased in favour of those with monetary value on the antiquities market. Nevertheless, the discovery of these sites has at least made archaeologists realize that the recovery of metalwork from ploughsoil can provide invaluable knowledge and, where a partnership has been established, it has proved to be very informative. At present, the best examples of such partnerships lie outside of Mercia. Julian Richards' work at Cottam, in the Yorkshire Wolds, for example, has shown that metalwork was in common use on small rural settlements connected by trackways to presumed larger centres in the valleys (Richards, 1999). Detailed plotting of metal finds and features revealed in air photos together with selective excavation has shown that the metal finds were discarded within agricultural settlements. Excavations in Suffolk, at Barham and Coddenham, have failed to find contemporary occupation on either site, although that at Barham is adjacent to a medieval village, suspected to have existed in the mid-Saxon period. Finally, fieldwork in Norfolk has shown that one such scatter of mid-Saxon metalwork originated in a monastic settlement (A. Rogerson, pers. comm.).

At present, therefore, the concept of 'productive site' as a class of mid-Saxon archaeological site appears to be under serious attack by those who would instead see the sites as being examples of sites known through traditional archaeological methods but which for unexplained reasons have produced unusually large numbers of finds when metal-detected. There is, nevertheless, a need to consider whether any of these sites was the site of a mid-Saxon fairground. Barham, for example, could be interpreted as a fairground lying on the outskirts of a permanent settlement. Fairgrounds are unlikely to produce much evidence if tackled using traditional archaeological methods, such as air photography and fieldwalking. Unlike markets, there is unlikely to have been any attempt to maintain a hard surface so metalling is unlikely.

Conclusion

Several decades of urban archaeology have failed to provide conclusive answers to even basic questions, such as were there towns in Mercia in the seventh to ninth centuries? Much of the evidence for trading comes from the recognition of traded goods and if the distribution system is effective, these will in the main end up in the households of those with the wealth or status to acquire them, rather than the ports, towns or fairs through which they may have been transported. One of the difficulties, therefore, is to distinguish high status sites not directly involved in trading from low- or medium- status sites through which the same goods passed and where they may occur through accidental breakage. Nevertheless, despite the lack of answers, we are now in a good position to take the study further. Sites worthy of investigation have been identified and the questions to be posed of those investigations have been formulated.

14 Mercian London

Robert Cowie

During the Middle Saxon period London served as an important, perhaps the only, seaport for the landlocked kingdom of Mercia. It was part of a network of maritime trading settlements located in the coastal areas of north-west Europe. Typically these *emporia* were large undefended settlements situated on navigable rivers where, in addition to trading, a range of specialist crafts and industries were undertaken (Hodges, 1982; Clarke and Ambrosiani, 1991; Hill and Cowie, forthcoming). London's counterparts in England included *Hamwic* (Southampton) in Wessex, *Gipeswic* (Ipswich) in East Anglia, and *Eorforwic* (York) in Northumbria, while on the Continent they included Dorestad and *Quentovic*. Such settlements are commonly referred to as *wics*, which has become the accepted generic term in archaeological literature for a range of pre-Viking trading centres, as their names often included the *wic* suffix, which meant (in this context) trading settlement or harbour. London, for example, appears in various guises in Middle Saxon documents, including *Lundenwic* and *Lundenuuic* (John Clark, pers. comm.; Vince, 1990: 86, Fig. 43). It is suspected, but by no means proven, that *Lundenwic* and other English *wics* were royal creations (see below).

Like many *wics*, London was located near natural and political boundaries, for it lay on the southern border of the kingdom of Essex, which was marked by the Thames. The kingdom of Surrey lay on the opposite bank, and Kent, Mercia and Wessex were within easy reach. It was, therefore, ideally located to act as a port of trade between these Anglo-Saxon kingdoms. It was also well placed for cross-Channel connections; by sailing vessel it would have been less than two days journey to *Quentovic*, while it would have taken only about three days to reach Dorestad.[1]

The site of *Lundenwic* was first identified in 1984 by Martin Biddle and Alan Vince, who suggested that it lay around Aldwych (or

---

1. The journey times from *Lundenwic* to *Quentovic* and Dorestad are based on a rate of travel by sail of 82 miles per day (see Carver, 1990).

Old *wic*[2]) and the Strand, about a kilometre to the west of the site of Roman London (Biddle, 1984; Vince, 1984). Their theory was confirmed the following year, when excavations at Jubilee Hall in Covent Garden uncovered evidence for dense Middle Saxon occupation (Whytehead, 1985; 1988). Since then, excavations have revealed evidence for the Middle Saxon settlement at more than 40 sites in the area around the Strand and Covent Garden.[3]

Prior to these discoveries, evidence for Middle Saxon London had mainly come from documents and seventh- and eighth-century coins issued in London. It was known from these sources that London became an episcopal see in 604, when the cathedral church of St Paul's was built for Mellitus, bishop of the East Saxons (*HE* II. 3; *Anglo-Saxon Chronicle* (E)).[4] They also indicated that the port, established in London by the early 670s, had developed into a major international trading centre by the early eighth century. London was described by Bede in about 730 as an 'emporium for many nations who come to it by land and sea' (*HE* II. 3; Colgrave and Mynors, 1969: 142–3).

Documentary sources also indicated that London, although an East Saxon settlement, was for much of the time dominated by neighbouring kingdoms. During the seventh century London was intermittently under Kentish control. It briefly came within the Mercian sphere of influence when Wulfhere became overlord of Essex in the mid-660s, but apparently reverted to Kentish control during the reigns of Hlothhere and Eadric (673–685?). Towards the end of the seventh century, or early in the eighth century, Ine of Wessex (688–726) may have assumed control of London, since he refers to Eorcenwold, the East Saxon bishop, as 'my bishop' in his law-code (Whitelock, 1955: 364). Mercian ascendancy was re-established by or during the reign of Æthelbald, and continued until the mid-ninth century, apart from a brief period of West Saxon control in 829–830.

The walled area of the former Roman city

Whereas the Strand settlement developed into a bustling port in the Middle Saxon period, it seems that the walled area of the former

---

2. The place-name derives from *vetus vicus*, mentioned in 1199, and occurs variously as *Aldewich*, *Aldewic* and *Aldewyk* in thirteenth-century documents (Gover *et al.*, 1942: 166). Until recently the place-name was thought to mean 'the old dairy farm', but the identification of the site of *Lundenwic* makes it clear that it alludes to the old *wic* (Biddle, 1984: 25–6; 1989: 27).

3. The results of excavations undertaken in *Lundenwic* up to October 1991 are summarized in a gazetteer (Cowie, 1988a), and all finds of Middle Saxon date recorded up to December 1998 are listed and mapped in a new survey of Saxon London (Cowie with Harding, 2000: 199–206, Map 10).

4. The episcopal succession was interrupted by the apostasy of the East Saxons between 617–618 and about 653 (see *HE*, III. 7; Colgrave and Mynors, 1969: 153).

Roman city remained largely uninhabited. It has been suggested that occupation of the intramural area had continued uninterrupted since the end of Roman provincial rule, albeit on a diminished scale (Wheeler, 1934: 290; Biddle, 1989: 22), but in the face of considerable negative evidence this view is no longer tenable.

The destruction of the Saxon ground surface by later activity across a large part of the excavated area of the City may partly explain the scarcity of Early and Middle Saxon finds there, but one might, nevertheless, expect some deep features of fifth- to ninth-century date to survive if urban occupation had continued, or at the very least the presence of residual artefacts dating to this period. This is not the case. Finds of known or probable Middle Saxon date from the walled area include a small quantity of residual pottery from four sites to the south of St Paul's,[5] a single potsherd from New Fresh Wharf, a double inhumation burial at Rangoon Street[6] and two foreshore burials at Bull Wharf.[7] To this short list might be added a bone comb from Lombard Street, although this possibly dates to the early part of the Late Saxon period (Riddler, 1990: 13–14). Middle Saxon dates have also been suggested for the remains of a church at St Alban, Wood Street (Grimes, 1968: 206), and for an arched doorway in the south-west corner of the church of All Hallows Barking (Kendrick and Ralegh Radford, 1943: 17–18). However, these structures are now considered to be later, and are most probably eleventh-century in date (Vince, 1990: 71; Schofield, 1994: 81–82).

Nevertheless, the abandoned city appears to have retained considerable symbolic importance, possibly because it had once been a Roman administrative and ecclesiastical centre.[8] This may explain why, in 601, Pope Gregory had intended Augustine to establish his seat at London rather than at Canterbury,[9] and why it was chosen as the site of the cathedral church of St Paul's. It is thought that this church was built on or near the site of Wren's cathedral, although no

---

5. The group comprises sherds of chaff-tempered pottery from the riverside wall in Upper Thames Street (Rhodes, 1980), St Peters Hill/223–225 Upper Thames Street and Horn Tavern, 29–33 Knight Rider Street (Vince, 1983: 33, 36–7), and a sherd of Ipswich ware from Pilgrim Street (Cowie, 1988a: 45).

6. The two bodies were found one on top of the other in the dark earth. They were aligned with their heads to the north (Bowler, 1983). They produced radiocarbon dates calibrated to 660–870 [BM 2214R] and 680–945 [BM 2215R] at 68 per cent confidence level (Bowman *et al.*, 1990: 70).

7. The burials were of women, probably in their thirties, and faced east. One had been interred in a grave, while the other had been laid on a bed of reeds on the foreshore (Ayre *et al.*, 1996: 20). The latter appears to have been placed between sheets of bark, which produced a calibrated radiocarbon date of 775 +/- 105 years (Wroe-Brown, 1998: 75).

8. Historical sources indicate that London had a bishop, Restitutus, who attended the Council of Arles in 314.

9. Pope Gregory expressed his wish that London should become the primary see in a letter written in 601, and quoted by Bede (*HE*, I. 29; translation in Colgrave and Mynors, 1969: 105, 107).

physical remains of the Saxon building have ever been recorded. Churches dedicated to St Augustine and St Gregory, respectively to the east and west of St Paul's, are also considered to be possible Middle Saxon foundations. In addition, a royal hall may have been sited in the intramural area. A possible location for the hall was the site of the Roman Cripplegate Fort, an area which later became known as Aldermanbury, 'the fortified enclosure of the alderman' (Dyson and Schofield, 1984: 307–8; Biddle, 1989: 23), although this now seems less likely in view of recent research by Gustav Milne.

The picture that emerges is of at least one church, and possibly a royal hall, surrounded by a small number of buildings belonging to the ecclesiastical and, possibly, royal communities, situated on the western hill of the City. The ruins of some Roman buildings would still have been visible, but most traces of the Roman town would have been hidden beneath a thick layer of naturally formed soil, the so-called dark earth. Large parts of the intramural area would have become uninhabitable marsh following the breakdown of the Roman drainage system. Archaeological evidence indicates boggy areas along the Walbrook and its tributaries (Maloney with de Moulins, 1990: 79–81), on the site of the former amphitheatre (Porter, 1997: 148) and behind the Roman riverside wall (Millett, 1980: 14).[10]

The Strand settlement

Current knowledge of the Strand settlement's development is mainly based upon the distribution of datable artefacts in stratigraphic sequences, especially that of the pottery (Blackmore, 1988a; 1989; 1999; forthcoming). The two most common categories of pottery in *Lundenwic* are chaff-tempered wares, which were mainly used in the period from about 650 to 750, and Ipswich ware, which dominated the market from about 750 to 850. Shell-tempered wares occur much less frequently but have been particularly useful in the identification of later phases of occupation, since their use is thought to have begun in the last quarter of the eighth century. Imported wares from the Continent have also proved invaluable for dating purposes. They include Walberberg buff wares, which were imported during the late seventh and earlier eighth centuries, Badorf and Tating wares from the mid-eighth century, and red-painted wares from the early ninth century. Coins can usually be dated more closely, but unfortunately they are found infrequently, and most date from 700–750. Radiocarbon dating has been used to establish the date of several burials, and timbers from two waterfront sites have been dated by dendrochronological analysis (see below). Archaeomagnetic dating has occasionally

---

10. Some of these boggy areas were reclaimed in the Late Saxon period, but others were not drained until the twelfth or thirteenth centuries.

been used, but has so far contributed little to our understanding of the settlement's development. This is partly because of the scarcity of features suitable for archaeomagnetic dating, and because the calibration curve for the thermo-remanent magnetism of the Middle Saxon period is tightly looped.

The origins of the Strand settlement are still unclear, although it is thought that a modest settlement may have been established in the area by the late sixth or early seventh centuries. Evidence for the putative early settlement is limited and mainly depends on small assemblages of artefacts from excavated sites, a few stray finds and a small number of inhumation burials (Vince, 1988: 83–4; Blackmore, 1997: 124–5). The burials were in two groups. One was located at St Martin-in-the-Fields, near the West end of the Strand, where sarcophagi containing two glass palm cups and a spearhead were discovered during the construction of the church in 1722–1726. The other group comprises at least fourteen inhumation burials widely scattered to the west of Drury Lane. Most were undated, but radiocarbon dating suggests that a burial at Jubilee Hall and two others at the Royal Opera House were interred during the seventh century.[11] A fourth burial in the group, excavated at 67–68 Long Acre, was that of a man, possibly a foreign visitor of some status, who was wearing a belt buckle of Frankish-Alamannic type dated to 640–670 (Blackmore, 1997: 124). A fifth burial, at 45–7 Floral Street, produced an elaborate composite disk brooch dated to the second half of the seventh century (R. Humphrey, pers. comm.).

The nature of the early settlement is uncertain. It may have comprised scattered farmsteads akin to the settlement pattern at Norwich (see Atkin, 1993: 129–31) or, as at Ipswich (see Wade, forthcoming), it may have been a small, nucleated settlement. It is also possible that it began as an impermanent market place or fair, of the type first classified by Richard Hodges as a type A *emporium* (Hodges, 1982: 50–2), where occupation may have been seasonal. Such activity would probably leave relatively little physical trace, and would explain the paucity of the archaeological evidence.

Excavated remains indicate that during the second half of the seventh century the Strand settlement rapidly grew. The burial ground to the west of Drury Lane was built over (Blackmore *et al.*, 1998: 62), and next to the river an embankment was built which incorporated a revetment dated by dendrochronology to 679 or soon after (Cowie, 1992: 164; Tyers *et al.*, 1994: 16–17). The settlement's expansion appears to have begun at about the time when Wulfhere was overlord of Essex and Surrey, when Mercia first gained control of London. This

---

11. The inhumation at Jubilee Hall gave a radiocarbon date of 1370+/–60 b.p. [HAR–8936], calibrated to 630–675. The two at the Royal Opera House produced radiocarbon dates of 1408+/–46 b.p. [UB-4456] and 1367+/–46 [UB-4457] calibrated respectively to 607–660 and 640–673. These calibrations are to one standard deviation, using the calibration curve in Stuiver and Pearson (1986).

would fit with the documentary evidence, since the earliest surviving reference to the Saxon 'port of London' (*portum Lundoniae*) occurs in 672–674 in a charter of Wulfhere's sub-king Frithuwold (Sawyer, 1968: No. 1165). Wulfhere would have had much to gain from developing London as a seaport, since hitherto Mercia had had no direct access to the sea and the Continent. Kent, on the other hand, possessed a number of ports, including Fordwich, Sandwich and Sarre (Tatton-Brown 1984: 16–22). Significantly, the first known use of the *Lundenwuuic* (*Lundenwic*) name form[12] occurs only a few years later in the laws of Hlothhere and Eadric. The *wic* suffix (and its variants *wich* and *uuic*) appears to have been used specifically in connection with the extramural port, and its usage occurs only during the period that the Strand settlement was occupied.

Excavations at the Royal Opera House suggest that the settlement became more densely occupied during the late seventh and early eighth centuries. As more streets and buildings were added, space in the settlement became increasingly restricted and the layout of properties became more clearly and permanently defined (Blackmore *et al.*, 1998: 62). By the early to mid-eighth century *Lundenwic* had probably grown to its full extent, when it may have covered an area of between 55 and 60 hectares (Cowie and Whytehead, 1989: 708–9; Cowie with Harding, 2000: 182–3). The limit of the site appears to extend from Aldwych north along Kingsway as far as Great Queen Street, which with Shorts Gardens roughly marks the northern edge of *Lundenwic* at its maximum extent. It then turns south, running between Leicester Square and Charing Cross Road, through the National Gallery and into Trafalgar Square (Cowie and Whytehead, 1989: 708; Cowie, 1989: 68). The south side of the settlement was bounded by the River Thames, which in the Middle Saxon period lay about 100m south of the Strand. The exact line of the waterfront has yet to be plotted, but its approximate position may be conjectured from the embankment at York Buildings, and from the remains of possible Middle Saxon embankments at 12 Buckingham Street and beneath Charing Cross Station (Cowie, 1992: Fig. 2b; see below). A site in Temple Place, 150m south of the Strand, was clearly in the river in the Middle Saxon period, since foreshore deposits were found there; these produced two sherds of Ipswich ware, a fragment of an annular loomweight and a copper-alloy strap-end finely decorated with a Trewiddle-style beast (Bowsher, 1999).

---

12. The name *Lundenwic* appears in the *Anglo-Saxon Chronicle* (E) in the entry for 604 but, since this document was compiled at a much later date, this does not necessarily indicate the use of the *wic* suffix in the early seventh century.

Infrastructure

Lundenwic lay near the hub of a network of extant Roman roads radiating from the site of *Londinium* (*Augusta*). These roads were probably the principal land routes linking *Lundenwic* to its hinterland. Watling Street, for example, would almost certainly have been a major highway between London and Mercia. The Roman road leading to Watling Street passed within 200m of the northern edge of *Lundenwic*, along what is now New Oxford Street and High Holborn. It is referred to as 'the wide army street' (*wide here straet*) in Edgar's charter of 959 (Gelling, 1953: 102–3; Sawyer, 1968: no. 670), and may have been 'the public way' (*viam publicam*) mentioned in Frithuwald's charter. The Strand and Fleet Street are also thought to have been on the line of a Roman road leading from Ludgate in the city (see Merrifield, 1983: 121). The road is first mentioned in a charter of 1002 (Sawyer, 1968: no. 903), which refers to it as *Akemannestraete*, meaning Bath Road. Its name suggests that in the Saxon period it was considered an important route to the west. The road would also have been the most direct route between *Lundenwic* and the walled area, and would have overlooked the entire length of *Lundenwic*'s waterfront. The two Roman roads may have been joined in the Middle Saxon period by the road referred to as *Oldewich Lane* in 1393 and as a *street called Aldewyche* in 1398, part of which is now Drury Lane (see Gover *et al.*, 1942: 185).

The best physical evidence for the roads of *Lundenwic* was found at the Royal Opera House, where a large-scale open area excavation revealed a network of narrow gravel streets (Blackmore, 1997: 125; Blackmore *et al.*, 1998: 60–1). The earliest road on this site was laid out in the late seventh century. It was 3m wide and flanked by narrow drains. The road was well maintained; during its use, which continued until the settlement was abandoned in the mid-ninth century, it was resurfaced at least ten times. Side streets leading off from the road were also maintained, but not to such a high standard. Patches of gravel metalling at several other sites in *Lundenwic* may also represent roads.

A massive amount of gravel would have been used in the construction and repair of *Lundenwic*'s streets. It would almost certainly have been quarried locally at gravel pits such as those found on the site of the National Gallery's Sainsbury Wing, which lay just beyond the western edge of the settlement (Cowie, 1989: 60–65). The scale of the gravel extraction at this site has prompted the suggestion that it was a communal effort controlled by a central, probably royal, authority (Cowie and Whytehead, 1989: 710).

Much of the traffic passing to and from *Lundenwic* would, however, have been waterborne. It is not certain how rivercraft and seafaring ships using the port were berthed, although it is generally assumed that vessels were beached on the gently shelving foreshore (Cowie and Whytehead, 1989: 710). It is also possible that embankments, such as the one at York Buildings, provided dry, level areas against which ships could be drawn, and possibly on which smaller vessels could be placed.

They would also have been convenient places to load and unload cargoes, and possibly to undertake trading, for it is suggested that most transactions of riverborne trade were undertaken on the waterfront during the Saxon period (Milne and Goodburn, 1990: 629). The embankment at York Buildings was at least 17m wide, and between 0.20 and 0.80m high. It may have continued along the waterfront for a considerable distance, since traces of embankment were possibly recorded at Buckingham Street and Charing Cross Station, which were respectively about 60 and 150m upstream from the excavated section. It was constructed of brushwood, including alder branches, weighed down with rubble. Within the embankment was a row of stakes aligned roughly parallel to the Thames, and a crude revetment of stakes with wattle and vertically set oak planks orientated at right angles to the river. The evidence suggests that the embankment had been built in stages. Initially a block of foreshore was enclosed and infilled. The embankment was then extended, along the riverside and out into the channel, by reclaiming adjacent blocks of foreshore.

The river level during the Middle Saxon period must have been lower than in Late Saxon times, since the top of the embankment lay between 0.80m and 1.30m OD (Ordnance Datum). Late eighth- to ninth-century buildings next to the river at the Treasury, Whitehall, were even lower; one had a sunken floor at Ordnance Datum, which was replaced by a surface-laid building at 0.61m OD.[13] This suggests that the tidal level, which had fallen in the Late Roman period, had not yet recovered to the first-century level, when the Mean High Water Spring tides may have reached about 1.5m OD (Milne, 1985: 84–5; Brigham, 1990: 143–9; Milne, 1992: 78–9). Nevertheless, river levels may have begun to rise during the eighth or ninth centuries as part of the York Buildings embankment was covered by alluvial clay, and the lower of the two buildings at the Treasury had probably been abandoned because of increasingly wet conditions.

Buildings

Buildings in the settlement were located either next to streets and/or around yards. Their remains are mainly represented by alignments of slots and postholes in the ground, which mainly marked the position of external walls, and internal features including earthen floors, hearths and oven bases. Fragments of burnt wall daub from buildings damaged or destroyed by fire are commonplace across the settlement, and often have timber and wattle impressions. The remains of timber buildings have been identified at several sites, notably the Royal Opera House where more than 60 were recorded. Typically, they were surface-laid

---

13. Information from a draft report by Michael Green.

and rectangular in plan. Those at the Royal Opera House had an average length of 12m and a width of a little over 5.5m. Their walls were usually made of wattle (possibly in panels) supported by posts either set in the ground or in sill-beams, although a few comprised vertical staves. Wattle walls were plastered with daub made from the local brickearth, to which plant matter (possibly in dung) had sometimes been added (Goffin, 1988: 114–9). Some daub walls were crudely coated with limewash. External doors were usually in the long walls, although a few were in the gable ends, and some had porches and gravelled thresholds. Roofs were presumably made of organic materials, probably timber and thatch, but no evidence survives to confirm this. Hearths were often made of fragments of Roman tile and stone set in brickearth. The buildings served as both living quarters and as workshops. Domestic rubbish and waste from crafts and industries were disposed of in pits, disused wells and middens. These were located in open areas and yards adjacent to the buildings. Water was obtained from wells dug into the underlying river terrace gravel, and lined with timber frames, wattle or barrels.

Trade and commerce

Documentary evidence suggests that Kentish and Mercian kings played an important part in the regulation of trade in *Lundenwic*. For example, the laws of the Kentish kings Hlothhere and Eadric decreed that the transactions of their countrymen buying property in London should be overseen by the king's town-reeve (*wic-gerefa*) (Whitelock, 1955: 360–1). A number of eighth-century documents indicate that maritime trade in the port was under royal control. These comprise charters issued by Æthelbald of Mercia, to the Abbess of Minster-in-Thanet, and to the bishops of Rochester, Worcester and London exempting them from tolls on their ships landing there (Sawyer, 1968: nos. 86, 88, 91, 98, 1788; see Kelly, 1992).

The archaeological evidence strongly supports the view that *Lundenwic*'s primary function was as a trading centre. Indeed, the settlement's links with the Continent and other parts of England are clearly indicated by imports, such as lava quernstones from the Mayen-Niedermendig area of the Rhineland, and whetstones and burnishers possibly from Norway. Much of the Continental pottery in *Lundenwic* comprises grey and blackwares from northern France (Blackmore, 1988a; 1989; 1997: 126; 1999). Pottery from Normandy and the Seine valley and from Rhenish production centres at Walberberg and Badorf in the Vorgebirge has also been recovered.

Trading links with the Low Countries were apparently in existence by the late seventh century, since Bede (*HE*, IV. 22; Colgrave and Mynors, 1969: 405) records that a Northumbrian prisoner captured by the Mercians in 687 was sold in London to a Frisian. Further evidence of contact with the Continent is given by Willibald, who tells us that

Boniface sailed from London to Dorestad in 716, and from London to *Quentovic* in 718 (Robinson, 1916: 43, 48–9).

Lundenwic relied on local and regional trade for food, hones, querns and pottery, as well as raw materials (such as wool, antlers and metals) for its artisans. For example, large numbers of cooking pots, storage jars and pitchers were imported from Ipswich, suggesting a considerable volume of coastal trade with East Anglia. By sailing ship the journey to Ipswich would probably have taken less than two days. Other English wares are thought to have come from Surrey, the East Midlands and probably the North Downs or the Chilterns (Blackmore, 1988a: 87–9; 1989: 80–5; 1999; Vince, 1990: 100–1).

Industry

There are no clearly discernible specialized zones of industrial activity in *Lundenwic*, and tools and waste from various crafts and industries are intermingled across the entire excavated area of the settlement. Scattered waste from bone and antler working, iron-working and the production of copper-alloy objects suggests small-scale production by artisans working in dwellings and workshops (Cowie and Whytehead, 1989: 712–3). Two buildings at the Royal Opera House have been tentatively identified from concentrations of slag as smithies. Limited evidence for the production of silver objects was also found at this site. It is thought that rows of rectangular pits at the site may have been used by tanners to process hides or skins (Bowsher and Malcolm, forthcoming). The pits were about 3.00m long, 1.50m wide and at least 0.70m deep.

Other artefacts from *Lundenwic* represent different stages of textile production. Fibre preparation is indicated by the remains of carding combs from Maiden Lane (Blackmore 1988b: 128, 130) and the Royal Opera House, suggesting that wool may have been imported as a raw material. Purple staining and deposits on a number of sherds suggests that pots may have been used to make and store vegetable dyes such as madder (Blackmore, 1988a: 85, 87; 1989: 76, 80). Spindlewhorls are often found, and loomweights are especially common. It would seem from their widespread distribution that spinning and weaving were undertaken in most households. The dating of these objects suggests that cloth production increased from a modest level in the seventh century to become a major industry by the mid-eighth century (Blackmore, 1997: 127). Some woven garments may have been produced specifically for export. It is even possible that the cloaks mentioned by Charlemagne in a letter to Offa (see Whitelock, 1955: 782) were manufactured in *Lundenwic*; at the very least it is likely that they were shipped from the Mercian seaport to the Continent.

From the seventh century London was an important centre for coin production in South-East England. Indeed, some of the earliest Anglo-Saxon coins to be issued include gold coins bearing the legends

LONDINIV and LONDENVS, which are thought to have been minted in London during the 630s (Grierson and Blackburn, 1986: 161–2). In the late seventh century a considerable proportion of the new silver coinage was apparently minted in London. Indeed, it is possible that coins from London account for over a third of all known *sceattas* of this period (Vince, 1990: 112). In the 710s coins with the (D)E LVNDONIM mint-mark were produced (Grierson and Blackburn, 1986: 181, 188). It is possible that Æthelbald of Mercia issued these, and a subsequent issue, bearing the legend DE LVNDONIA, dated to the 730s is almost certainly associated with this Mercian king (Grierson and Blackburn, 1986: 186). It is not known exactly where in London these coins were struck; they may have been minted in the walled area, but the possibility that moneyers were operating in the *wic* cannot be ruled out.

Food supply

As *Lundenwic* grew it would have become increasingly reliant on farming communities in its hinterland for food and other materials necessary to support its artisans and visiting merchants and sailors. Large assemblages of plant remains and animal bones from the settlement bear witness to the diet of its inhabitants, and provide valuable information about the agricultural economy of the surrounding region. Cereals, mainly barley and wheat, were brought to the settlement as cleaned or semi-cleaned grain from which chaff and large weed seeds had already been removed (Davis and de Moulins, 1988; de Moulins and Davis, 1989).

Quernstone fragments are ubiquitous in *Lundenwic* suggesting that most households ground their own flour. The barley was probably used for brewing and in soups and stews, and the wheat for making bread and possibly brewing. Peas and horse beans, which may have been either fresh or dried, were also eaten, as were hazelnuts, apples/pears, blackberries/raspberries, strawberries, elderberries, and sloes/plums. Most fruit was probably wild, although some may have been cultivated. It is thought that more exotic foods found in *Lundenwic*, such as grapes, figs and lentils, may have come from the Continent, possibly as dried fruits and pulses. The grapes, however, may have been grown locally for eating or for making wine, since vines grew in some parts of England during the eighth century (see Hagen, 1995: 221), and in the late eleventh century the Domesday Book records that some were cultivated at Westminster (Morris, 1975: 4.2). Indirect evidence for the consumption of wine in the settlement is provided by Continental tablewares including pitchers and beakers (Blackmore and Redknap, 1988: 225). Rhenish wine may have been imported in amphorae, which are represented by a small number sherds of Badorf ware, and in barrels, some of which were re-used to line wells.

Faunal assemblages from *Lundenwic* are dominated by cattle, which were bred mainly for beef, and were often slaughtered at a young age to provide good quality cuts of tender meat. Pork and mutton were consumed in smaller quantities (West with Rackham, 1988; West, 1989; Reilly, in progress). There is evidence to suggest that livestock were killed and/or butchered at specific places in or close to *Lundenwic*, including a 'butchery site' at Exeter Street (Farid and Brown, 1997), and the sites of possible farms at the National Gallery (Rackham *et al.*, 1989: 167–70) and the Treasury (Chaplin, 1971: 136). Chickens and geese were occasionally eaten, as were their eggs. Fragments of hatched eggs indicate that geese were bred in the settlement (Sidell, in progress), and it is possible that larger animals were also kept. Unlike the monastic sites at Jarrow and Barking, *Lundenwic* and its counterparts at *Eorforwic* and *Hamwic* have produced very little evidence for wild birds. The somewhat restricted range of animals at these *wics* suggests that they may have been provisioned from royal food-rents (O'Connor, 1991: 276–82; forthcoming).

Fish, eels, oysters and mussels were consumed in considerable quantity (Locker, 1988; 1989). The eels and freshwater fish, including cyprinids, salmonids, roach, rudd and pike, probably came from the Thames and its tributaries, and may have been caught in traps such as those recently discovered on the Thames foreshore at Barn Elms, Chelsea and Isleworth, and in the Blackwater Estuary in Essex.[14] The eels were probably mainly caught during their seaward migration in mid-winter (Locker, 1988: 149). Shells from the Royal Opera House suggest that the oysters were not farmed, but were gathered from uncultivated beds along the coast of Essex and Suffolk (Winder and Gerber-Parfitt, in progress). Of the sea fish eaten in the settlement, herring was particularly well represented, but other marine species included cod, whiting, haddock, hake, gurnard, red sea bream, brill and ling, all of which could have come from the North Sea (Locker, 1988; 1989). Ling, which is found in northern waters, was probably dried or salted for the long journey down to London. Flatfish, such as plaice and flounder, were fairly common, and may have been caught in the Thames estuary.

The hinterland of Mercian London

Little is known of *Lundenwic*'s relationship with its immediate hinterland, for as yet only a handful of rural and monastic settlement

---

14. The three fishtraps on the Thames foreshore were found during the Thames Archaeological Survey. Each comprised two converging rows of posts, marking the position of wattle barriers. Their calibrated radiocarbon dates suggested that they were built between the mid-seventh century and the end of the ninth century (Mike Webber, pers. comm.). Seven similar fishtraps have been found in the Blackwater estuary, three of which have been dated by radiocarbon to between 600 and 950 (note in *British Archaeology* 41 (1999): 5).

sites have been found in the surrounding region (Cowie and Whytehead, 1989: 714). In archaeological terms the most productive of these was at Barking, about 12km to the east of *Lundenwic*, where Eorcenwald founded the abbey of St Mary for his sister Æthelburh in about 666.[15] Excavations on this site apparently revealed part of the monastic complex, including the remains of timber buildings, timber-lined wells and a leat which presumably channelled water from the nearby River Roding to a mill (MacGowan, 1987; 1996). The site produced a number of items which may reflect the ecclesiastical nature of the settlement, notably fragments of gold thread, possibly from religious vestments or nuns' apparel, and styli (Webster and Backhouse, 1991: 88–90). Otherwise the range of artefacts recovered from Barking was similar to that found in *Lundenwic* (Blackmore and Redknap, 1988: 231–4), although Continental pottery does not appear to have been as common (Redknap, 1992: 378). It seems likely that at least some of the Gallic and Rhenish items found there were imported directly from the Continent, since the abbey's position on the Roding would have given easy access to the Thames estuary and the North Sea, although foreign goods may possibly have come via *Lundenwic*.

Evidence for Middle Saxon settlement has been found closer to *Lundenwic* at four Thameside sites. The nearest was about 0.5km upstream from the *wic*, at the Treasury, Whitehall, where the site of a farm is dated to the late eighth to ninth century (Green, 1963). Animal bones from the site were identified as a mixture of domestic food and commercial debris (Chaplin, 1971: 124–38), and it seems likely that some of the farm's produce would have been intended for *Lundenwic*. A short distance to the south, at Westminster Abbey, Middle Saxon activity is indicated by a small assemblage of residual pottery dated to between *c.*730 and 850 (Blackmore, 1995) and a coin of Ecgberht of Wessex (Stott, 1991: 309, no. 62). These finds lend credence to the tradition that the abbey had Middle Saxon antecedents (see Rosser, 1989: 12). Limited evidence for Middle Saxon settlement has also been found a little further up the Thames at Chelsea (Farid, 1997) and Battersea (Blackmore and Cowie, forthcoming). The Surrey bank opposite *Lundenwic* was virtually uninhabited, and mainly consisted of low islands surrounded by marsh and mudflats. Nevertheless, there is documentary evidence that a minster had been founded at *Vermundesei* (identified as Bermondsey) by the eighth century (Blair, 1991: 95, 102). This fits well with the discovery on the site of the medieval abbey at Bermondsey of residual Middle Saxon pottery and three *sceattas*, suggesting the presence of a settlement near the edge of habitable land, about 3km south-east of *Lundenwic*.

---

15. The exact date for the foundation of Barking Abbey is uncertain, but 666, the year given in the Chertsey register, is generally accepted (Clapham, 1913: 70–1; Knowles and Hadcock, 1971: 256).

The end of *Lundenwic*

Evidence from the Royal Opera House suggests that *Lundenwic* may have been in decline by the late eighth century, for at this site the construction of buildings and other activity apparently decreased from about this time. By about the mid-ninth century occupation throughout the Strand settlement had evidently ceased altogether. There is evidence for increased activity in the intramural area during the mid- to late ninth century, suggesting that the focus of settlement had shifted back to the City at this time.[16] It may be significant that during the last few decades of the Strand settlement's existence no direct reference is made in documents to the port or to ships landing there. Overall, the evidence suggests that the trading centre had been failing for some time before its final abandonment.

Various factors may have played a part in the waning fortunes of the Strand settlement. It is possible, for example, that *Lundenwic* suffered a series of major fires during the period in question, since according to the *Historia Regum* London was devastated by fire in 764, 798 and 801 (Whitelock, 1955: 239). Although the accuracy of this record is uncertain, it is clear from archaeological evidence that many of the buildings in *Lundenwic* had burnt down. This is not surprising considering the nature of the settlement, where open fires were used for cooking, heating and other purposes, and buildings were chiefly made of highly combustible materials. Moreover, because the buildings were closely spaced there would have been a considerable risk that accidental fires would quickly spread. Conflagrations such as those recorded in the *Historia Regum* would have been a major economic setback from which the settlement may never have fully recovered.

It is possible that changes in the tidal regime may also have played a part in the shift in settlement location (see Vince, 1991a: 419). If river levels rose during the eighth and ninth centuries *Lundenwic*'s embanked waterfront would have become increasingly prone to flooding, and the resulting accumulation of alluvial clay may have impeded activities.

It would seem, however, that the most important factor leading to the eventual abandonment of the Strand settlement was warfare. By the 830s *Lundenwic*'s decline may have reflected the faltering economies of its Carolingian counterparts, which had been hit hard by a series of civil wars beginning in 829 (see Hodges and Whitehouse, 1983: 163, 164). Even greater was the impact of Viking raids on the towns and monasteries of north-west Europe, particularly during the mid-ninth century. The *Anglo-Saxon Chronicle* records that Vikings

---

16. Evidence for activity at waterfront sites around Queenhithe (originally Æthelred's Hythe) in the City during the second half of the ninth century. At one site, Bull Wharf, the presence on the Saxon foreshore of two Northumbrian *stycas* dated to the 840s (Wroe-Brown, 1998: 75) suggests that activity may have commenced shortly after the first Viking attack on London.

attacked London in 842 and 851, and that in 871–872 a Viking army over-wintered there. Two ditches, located well inside the site of *Lundenwic* at Maiden Lane (Cowie, 1988b: 71–3) and the Royal Opera House (Blackmore *et al.*, 1998: 63), are dated to the ninth century, and were probably dug during the period of Viking activity. Both were 2m deep and are thought to have been defensive; they might represent an attempt to defend a limited area of *Lundenwic*, or the fortifications of a Viking camp.

Four coin hoards from central London were probably concealed or lost during the Viking raids (see Dolley, 1960; Blackburn and Pagan, 1986: 294; Pirie, in progress). One at the Middle Temple may have been deposited at the time of the first Viking attack. Two others, at Westminster Bridge and Waterloo Bridge, are dated to about 872 when Halfdan's Danish army took up winter quarters in London. The hoard at Waterloo Bridge was found on the west side of the second pier from the Surrey bank (Andrew, 1911: 102), suggesting that the hoard had been lost or thrown from a vessel (Vince, 1991a: 418). This may also be the case with the Westminster Bridge hoard. Only one coin hoard has been found on the site of the Strand settlement. It was discovered during excavations at the Royal Opera House, and consisted of Northumbrian *stycas*, which may have been hidden in 851 (Pirie, in progress). Interestingly, the hoard lay in dark earth above the latest Saxon occupation levels, suggesting that by about the time of the second Viking attack all or part of the extramural settlement had been deserted long enough for soil to form on the site. It is possible, therefore, that the Strand settlement may not have survived the first Viking onslaught. Villages and monasteries in the countryside around London would also have been extremely vulnerable to attack by raiders, and Viking activity might account for the apparent abandonment in the mid- to late ninth century of settlements at Barking (Redknap, 1991a: 359), Battersea (Blackmore and Cowie, forthcoming), Bermondsey (Blair, 1991: 103) and the Treasury.

Conclusion

The identification of the site of the Mercian seaport and its subsequent investigation have greatly increased our knowledge of Middle Saxon London, and have provided much information not covered by documentary sources. The evidence suggests that for well over a century London was of immense economic and political importance to the kingdom of Mercia, both as a major trading link to eastern England and the Continent, and as a royal and ecclesiastical centre. Whether or not the Strand settlement was fully urban remains a moot subject. It would be fair to say, however, that the development of *Lundenwic* and similar Anglo-Saxon trading centres in the seventh and eighth centuries represents the first major step in the evolution of medieval towns in England.

Acknowledgements

The author is indebted to all those involved in the investigation of Mercian London, but particular thanks must go to Lyn Blackmore (who commented on the text), John Clark and Alan Vince for their unstinting help, encouragement and advice.

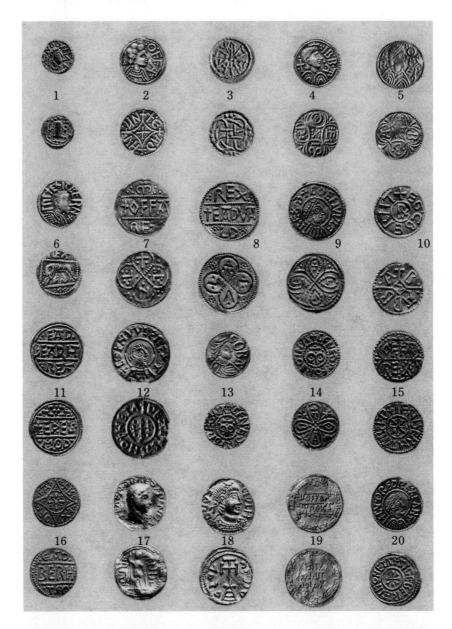

Figure 15.1 Mercian coins © The Trustees of the British Museum. Reproduced by kind permission of the Trustees of the British Museum. 1. Silver penny of Æthelbald, king of Mercia, minted in London; 2. Silver penny of Offa, king of Mercia, moneyer Eadhun; 3. Silver penny of Beonna, king of East Anglia; 4. Silver penny of Offa, moneyer Ibba, minted in Canterbury; 5. Silver penny of Offa, moneyer Ibba, minted in London; 6. Silver penny of Æthelberht, king of East Anglia, moneyer Lul, minted in East Anglia; 7. Silver

15 Mercian Coinage and Authority

Gareth Williams

The origins of Mercian coinage are obscure, since before the middle of the eighth century few Anglo-Saxon coins carried inscriptions, and the vast majority of those that did are either debased versions of Roman inscriptions or seem more likely to represent the names of the moneyers who produced them than of recognizable rulers or places. An early gold coinage, mostly concentrated in the south-east, gave way *c.* 670 to a coinage of small, thick, silver pennies, often misleadingly known as *sceattas*. A large variety of these are known, and the different series are attributed to different areas largely on the basis of distribution of individual finds, while a relative chronology is established on the basis of developments in weight, metal purity and style. Interpretation of this nature is necessarily speculative. The combination of different coin types in hoards provides better evidence for the chronology, but hoards are comparatively rare for this period, and it is difficult to assign coins to any individual ruler with great certainty. The attribution of a transitional pale-gold coinage inscribed *Pada* to Peada, a sub-king of both Penda of Mercia and Oswiu of Northumbria, is no longer accepted, while the attribution of pennies of the Frisian-derived 'porcupine' type, with

cont.

penny of Offa, king of Mercia, moneyer Lul, minted in East Anglia; 8. Silver penny of Eadwald, king of East Anglia, moneyer Lul, minted in East Anglia; 9. Silver penny of Coenwulf, king of Mercia, moneyer Lul, minted in East Anglia; 10. Silver penny of Ecgberht, king of Kent, moneyer Udd, minted in Canterbury; 11. Silver penny of Eadberht Praen, king of Kent, moneyer Ethelmod; 12. Silver penny of Coenwulf, king of Mercia, moneyer Dealla, minted in Canterbury; 13. Silver penny of Cynethryth, portrait type, moneyer Eoba, minted in Canterbury; 14. Silver penny of Cynethryth, non-portrait, moneyer Eoba, minted in Canterbury; 15. Silver penny of Offa, king of Mercia, and Archbishop Jaenberht, minted in Canterbury; 16. Silver penny of Offa, king of Mercia and Bishop Eadberht, probably minted in London; 17. Gold mancus of the moneyer Pendraed; 18. Gold mancus of the moneyer Ciolheard; 19. Gold dinar of Offa, king of Mercia, imitating dinar of Caliph al-Mansur; 20. Silver penny of Cuthred, king of Kent, moneyer Sigeberht, minted in Canterbury.

the runic inscription *Æthiliræd,* to Æthelred of Mercia (674–704) is at best uncertain.[1]

What does seem clear is that coinage must have become established in Mercia no later than the reign of Æthelbald, although none survives which bears his name. The first half of the eighth century saw the spread of coinage across much of southern England, and since this spread coincided with the establishment of a broad hegemony over the area by Æthelbald, it would be implausible to suggest that none of this widespread coinage was his, although much of it was probably issued by sub-rulers in East Anglia, Kent and Wessex. Michael Metcalf (1966, 1977) has suggested that from the early 730s Æthelbald himself had at least two centres of production, one at London, issuing mint-signed coins (see Figure 15.1, no. 1), and one further west, possibly in Oxford.

Developments in the early Anglo-Saxon coinage tended to be closely linked to developments on the Continent. The decline in the seventh-century gold coinage and the shift to silver are mirrored in the Frankish coinage, and throughout the early eighth century there were close monetary ties between southern England and Frisia, although the paucity of documentary evidence makes the respective political and economic importance of these links unclear. The mid- to late eighth century saw a revolution in the form of the Anglo-Saxon penny, and it is clear that this was also inspired by Frankish examples. Following Pepin the Short's seizure of the Frankish kingdom in 751, he reformed the coinage in 754–755, introducing a slightly higher weight standard, better silver, and a somewhat broader, flatter penny. His coins also gave some indication of his name and title. Pepin's son Charlemagne (768–814) also customarily placed his name on the coins, and his pennies were also broader and flatter than the earlier Merovingian pennies, with a considerable degree of uniformity in their design. A further reform in 793–794 led to a substantial increase in both diameter and weight (Grierson and Blackburn, 1986: 204–10).

The Carolingian reforms had a major impact in England, and especially in the kingdom of Mercia under the powerful king Offa (757–796). Offa's coinage is one of the most varied of all the Anglo-Saxon rulers, as well as being both interesting and attractive (see Figure 15.1, no. 2). It is also particularly complex to interpret. Offa's overlordship in southern England at times gave him direct authority in both East Anglia and Kent, and coins bearing his name were issued in both of those kingdoms as well as in Mercia, but coins in the names of both East Anglian and Kentish kings are also known, and matching the sequence of the coinage with the chronology suggested by manuscript evidence is problematic.[2]

---

1. The basic classification of the different series used by modern numismatists was established in Rigold (1961 and 1966). For a more recent and comprehensive discussion of early Anglo-Saxon coinage, see Metcalf (1993–4).
2. The standard text on Offa's coinage remains C. E. Blunt (1961). A more recent interpretation is provided by D. Chick (1997), together with the more detailed references supplied there.

The practice of placing rulers' names on coins was adopted throughout England, including Northumbria, and the kingdoms south of the Humber also adopted first a somewhat broader and heavier penny inspired by Pepin's reform, and in the final years of Offa's reign an even heavier penny following Charlemagne's reform of 793–794, although they did not reach the same standards as Charlemagne's reformed coinage, nor were the designs controlled with such uniformity. Offa's diplomatic and economic contacts with Charlemagne are well known and have been much discussed (see Nelson, Chapter 9 in this volume), and it is not surprising that he should follow Carolingian examples, but clearly both East Anglian and Kentish rulers were also influenced by the Carolingian reforms. What is less clear is whether they did so as a result of direct Frankish influence, or whether they were influenced by Offa.

Christopher Blunt (1961), in his study of the coinage of Offa, suggested that broader pennies were first introduced in Kent, the kingdom with closest trading links with the Franks, and therefore most susceptible to Frankish monetary influence, with Offa only introducing his own coinage after he established his own direct authority in Kent in the late 770s and took control of the Kentish mint at Canterbury. This view was based on the similarity of style between some of Offa's coins and those of the Kentish kings, and the fact that a number of moneyers' names appear both on Kentish coins and on those of Offa, and even of his Mercian successor Coenwulf. According to Blunt's theory, all of Offa's coinage was struck in Canterbury, with the exception of a further stylistically distinct group attributed to an unknown mint in East Anglia. This attribution was based on the fact that moneyers of this group also struck coins in the names of East Anglian kings, and it is implied that it was only under Offa that the broad penny was introduced in East Anglia.

Comparatively little of this would now be accepted without qualification, largely because the growing hobby of metal detecting has brought to light a number of relevant finds, which between them present an important body of evidence which was unavailable to Blunt. Most significantly, the adoption of the broad penny in England may have taken place considerably earlier than Blunt suggested, with Kent the last, not the first, of the three southern English kingdoms in which this took place. Transitional pennies, larger than the earlier anonymous types but smaller than those of the later eighth century, were issued in East Anglia in the name of Beonna, probably around 760 (see Figure 15.1, no. 3), before the subjection of East Anglia by Offa, and only a few years after Pepin's reform of the Frankish coinage (Pagan, 1968; Archibald, 1985; Archibald and Fenwick, 1995). Among the moneyers who struck coins for Beonna was one called Wilred, who is also known to have struck coins for Offa. Although these share some features with other coins of Offa, Derek Chick has suggested that stylistically they appear to be earlier than any of the coins classified by Blunt, and that Offa's coinage in East Anglia may have begun as early as *c.* 765. He has also suggested that it is politically unlikely that Offa would have initiated his Mercian coinage in East Anglia (or indeed Kent) before issuing coins in Mercia himself. Chick therefore postulated the existence of an earlier Mercian issue, as yet undiscovered, which provided a model for the Wilred coins, which represent Offa as 'OFRM' *(Offa rex Merciorum)* (Chick, 1997: 48–9, 57).

While not providing an exact stylistic model for the Wilred coin, three coins have been discovered, struck for Offa by the moneyer Mang, which also give Offa the title 'OFRM', and like the Wilred coins give the moneyer's name in two lines divided by a horizontal cross (see Figure 15.1, no. 4). Like the coins of Beonna, these are comparatively small and appear to represent a transitional phase between the earlier small flan coins and the broad pennies of the late eighth century. Chick (1997: 55–7) plausibly interprets these as an early coinage struck in Mercia before any of the coins of Blunt's primary phase, and suggests that Offa's coinage may have begun in Mercia itself as early as *c.* 760. Offa's coinage may even extend further back into the small-flan coinage. A single coin of this type, now in Paris, apparently carries Offa's name, although the lettering goes off the edge of the flan (Metcalf, 1993–4, **3**: 608). Furthermore, one cannot exclude the possibility that Offa may have struck anonymous coins in the earliest years of his reign.

This introduces a further problem with Blunt's classification, which rested partly on the assumption that Offa's coins were solely produced in mints in the subject kingdoms of Kent and East Anglia. As mentioned above, the distribution of the earlier small flan pennies suggests that before Offa's reign coins were already being struck in London, and it would be remarkable had a king as powerful as Offa been able to extend his authority into the neighbouring kingdoms of East Anglia and Kent without also having the power to maintain established rights in the most important trading centre in his own kingdom (Metcalf, 1963). Blunt himself, together with Stewart Lyon and Ian Stewart, later argued that a London coinage could be discerned in the reign of Offa's eventual successor Coenwulf, and that this could be traced back into Offa's own reign (Blunt *et al.*, 1963). This idea was developed further by Stewart (1986), who suggested that the distinctions between Blunt's Groups 1 and 2 are as much to do with regional differences between a Kentish mint at Canterbury and a Mercian mint at London, with the notable feature that coins with a royal bust tend, with notable exceptions, to be products of the London mint (see Figure 15.1, nos 4 and 5). His argument that London may actually have been the leading mint during the reign of Offa is now generally accepted, although the stylistic distinction between some coins of Canterbury and London remains problematic (Chick, 1997).

The existence of a London mint challenges the assumption that Offa only issued coinage after he took control in Kent, and allows for separate patterns of development in each of the three kingdoms in which Offa exercised authority. In Mercia, as discussed above, recent evidence suggests that Offa introduced a transitional broad penny along Carolingian lines as early as *c.* 760, struck in London, where minting was already established.[3] Broad pennies continued to be struck in London throughout the reign, with the number of moneyers increasing substantially later in the reign. The importance of the London mint reflects the fact that Offa remained in control in Mercia throughout his reign.

In East Anglia, a similar transitional coinage was begun around the same time under Beonna, and when Offa took control of East Anglia he also took over at least one of the East Anglian moneyers and the coinage, although it may now have changed to reflect Mercian designs. Offa's control of East Anglia was less secure than in Mercia, however, and the coinage reflects a brief resurgence of East Anglian independence under Æthelberht, whom we know from other sources was executed on Offa's orders in 794 (Blunt, 1961: 49–50). Following Æthelberht's death, Offa resumed control of both the kingdom and coinage of East Anglia. Following Offa's own death in 796, the coinage indicates another brief attempt at independence, this time under a king Eadwald, who is known only from his coins, and seems to have ruled there *c.* 796–798. There is little doubt of his East Anglian origins, since coins almost identical in size and design to the heavy coinage of Offa were struck in his name by the moneyer Lul (like many moneyers, a man of flexible loyalties) who had earlier struck coins for Æthelberht, and who went on to strike coins for Coenwulf after he re-established Mercian supremacy *c.* 798 (Blunt, 1961: 50). The coinage thus acts as an index of the fortunes of Mercian political authority in East Anglia in the late eighth century (see Figure 15.1, nos 6–9).

The same is true to some extent in Kent, although the evidence there is less clear-cut. Although there is no doubt that anonymous small flan pennies were struck in Canterbury in the first half of the century, it is less clear whether the broad penny was introduced in Kent by Offa or by the Kentish kings Heaberht and Ecgberht. Both Heaberht and Ecgberht are known to have ruled in Kent *c.* 765, and Ecgberht appears again in the 770s. Sir Frank Stenton (1971: 206–7) pointed out that Offa's authority in Kent may have been severely diminished after the battle of Otford in 776. It seems clear that Offa established authority in Kent, lost it and then regained it, but the precise sequence of both authority and coinage is problematic. The most recent sequence, proposed by Chick (1997), seems plausible, but by no means certain. This would see a brief coinage by Heaberht, *c.* 765, immediately followed by coinage in the name of Offa. Following the battle of Otford, Kentish control was reasserted by Ecgberht (Figure 15.1, no. 10), with the reappearance of coins in the name of

---

3. Pagan (1986) points out that it may be misleading to talk of mints as such in this period, as there is no evidence to suggest a common workshop shared by the various moneyers.

Offa after he re-established Mercian overlordship in Kent around the end of the decade. Thereafter, coins continued to be struck in the name of Offa in large quantities for the rest of his reign. Following Offa's death, Eadbert Praen re-established both an independent kingdom and coinage, but by 798 Coenwulf had re-established Offa's Mercian empire (Figure 15.1, nos 11–12).

In addition to the light which coinage sheds on Offa's political authority, there are three aspects of Offa's coinage which have a more than purely numismatic interest. First, there are the silver pennies in the name of his wife Cynethryth, apparently issued at Canterbury by the moneyer Eoba (Figure 15.1, nos 13–14). The coins give Cynethryth the title *Regina M[erciorum]*, and are unique in western Europe in this period as a coinage in the name of a queen consort. Asser's *Life of King Alfred* describes Offa's daughter Eadburh in terms that suggest that Mercian queens may have been accustomed to more authority than those in other Anglo-Saxon kingdoms, a possibility further supported by charter evidence (Keynes and Lapidge, 1983: 71–2, 235), but there is nothing in the historical sources to suggest that Cynethryth exercised real political authority either in Mercia or in Kent (cf. Stafford, Chapter 3 in this volume). Alternatively, it has been suggested that the coins were issued for donations by Cynethryth to the Church (Archibald, 1991: 247). However, the similarity between these and other coins of Offa points to them having been part of the general currency rather than purely religious issues.

The coins can also be interpreted as part of Offa's strategy of self-promotion, acting as he believed a great ruler should be seen to act. There is no Frankish parallel for such a coinage, but Stewart (1986: 41) has pointed out that a near-contemporary parallel can be observed in the coins of the Empress Irene in Byzantium, although Irene's sole coinage probably postdates that of Cynethryth by some years (Zipperer, 1999). A more likely explanation is that Offa was consciously imitating Roman practice. A number of late Roman emperors issued coins in the names of their wives, and Offa may well have been familiar with such coins (Blunt, 1961: 46–7). It is certainly consistent with the attitude that caused Offa to address Charlemagne as 'brother' that he should affect behaviour which he regarded as appropriate for a Roman emperor.

It is also possible that Cynethryth's coins may reflect an unusual grant of income by Offa to his wife. Grants of estates to royal women were common in the early Middle Ages, and it is not inconceivable that Offa might have granted Cynethryth the right to the income derived from a single moneyer. Cynethryth's coinage was struck by a single moneyer, Eoba, and a large proportion of Eoba's portrait coinage during the reign of Offa was struck for Cynethryth rather than Offa himself. Such a grant would be unique, but so is Cynethryth's coinage itself (see Stafford, Chapter 3 in this volume).

Such a grant would also fit with another important development in the reign of Offa, the appearance of coins in the name of the archbishop of Canterbury. It is likely, given Frankish influence on the early Anglo-Saxon coinage, and that episcopal coinage was common in the kingdom of the Franks, that the archbishops had minting rights from the beginning of the Anglo-Saxon coinage but, if so, their coins were as anonymous as most others before the mid-eighth century. A precedent was set for Offa in the coinage of Eadberht of Northumbria (737–757/8), since Eadberht's reign saw the appearance of coins in the name of his brother Ecgberht, archbishop of York, and archiepiscopal issues remained a feature of the Northumbrian coinage until its collapse in the mid-ninth century.[4]

Until recently, the earliest known coins in the name of an archbishop of Canterbury were those which carried Offa's name on one side, and that of Archbishop Jaenberht on the other (Figure 15.1, no. 15). Such a joint coinage seems odd, given the recorded hostility between Offa and Jaenberht, and Chick plausibly suggests that this joint coinage only existed because the archbishop's right to issue coins already existed. Support for this idea may be found in the recent discovery in Yorkshire of a coin in the name of Jaenberht alone. This may be linked stylistically with the coins of Ecgberht II of Kent, and Chick suggests that this issue pre-dates the joint coinage with Offa, probably with a gap in between, from the late 770s to *c*. 783–784, when Offa first reasserted his authority in Kent. It is within that period that Chick also assigns the earliest coins of Cynethryth (Chick, 1997: 54–9), and it is possible that Offa was usurping the archiepiscopal minting rights and granting them to his wife. The same period perhaps also saw a coinage which has been attributed to Bishop Eadberht of London (see Figure 15.1, no. 16). It has been suggested that the coinage in the name of Eadberht may date from *c*. 786, as an attempt to buy Eadberht's support for Offa's plans to divide the province of Canterbury, and to establish a Mercian archbishopric at Lichfield (Metcalf, 1963: 39). However, Chick (1997: 53) has suggested that the Eadberht coinage appears to be earlier than this stylistically, and is more likely to date from the late 770s. This would also represent a temporary usurpation of Canterbury's minting rights, and may indicate an earlier stage in Offa's attempts to diminish the authority of Canterbury, and that at this early stage Offa's ambitions focused on London rather than Lichfield. It is also possible that the bishops of London may have had earlier minting rights in the anonymous coinage, and that this was now recognized on the coins, as with the kings and archbishops, but this would not explain why no later coins in the name of any bishop of London are known, nor is there documentary evidence for later bishops of London trying to claim this as an ancient right. Whatever the precise reason for the issue of Eadberht's coinage, it was apparently short-lived, and coinage in the name of Jaenberht revived,

---

4. For the Northumbrian coinage, see Pagan (1970); Metcalf (1987); and Pirie (1996).

now in a joint issue with Offa. A joint royal and archiepiscopal coinage continued under Offa with Jaenberht's successor Æthelheard.

Another feature of Offa's coinage is the survival of gold coins. Although the Carolingians issued gold *solidi*, few Anglo-Saxon gold coins have survived other than the early coinage of the seventh century. Offa is unique among later Anglo-Saxon rulers in having two surviving examples. A third Mercian coin is attributed to Coenwulf, rather than Offa, on the basis of style, although it only carries the name of the moneyer, Ciolheard, who struck pennies in the names of both rulers, as well as for Ceolwulf I (Pagan, 1965; Stewart, 1978). The function of these gold coins is debatable, and the rarity of later Anglo-Saxon gold coins may indicate that they were occasional issues intended only for presentation, and not as any part of the circulating currency.

There are, however, a number of references to a unit of gold called a *mancus*. While this would appear originally to have represented a weight of gold, some references appear to coins, and there are grounds for supposing that the *mancus* may have had the equivalent value of 30 silver pennies (Lyon, 1969; Nightingale, 1983). While it might seem rash to postulate the existence of a regular gold coinage on the basis of a handful of coins spread across the period between the reigns of Offa and Edward the Confessor, and a handful of documentary references spread across the same period, it is instructive to draw an analogy with a later period. Barrie Cook (1999) has made a study of the use of the Byzantine gold bezant in England in the high Middle Ages, when gold coins were not produced in England. Documentation of the royal finances for this period is substantial, and leaves no real doubt that gold bezants were circulating in England in considerable numbers. However, none have yet been found in England dating from this period. This indicates that limited survival is not a reliable guide to the number of coins in circulation, especially since the high value and relative rarity of gold must have meant that it was often melted down and re-used. The possibility of a more substantial gold coinage from the reign of Offa cannot therefore be lightly dismissed. It is true that two of the three coins differ from the regular Mercian coinage, being struck only in the names of their respective moneyers, Pendræd and Ciolheard (Figure 15.1, nos 17–18). This, together with their execution, and especially the unusually high relief of the bust on the Pendræd coin, could be seen as indications that they were presentation issues rather than regular currency, but gold coins would only have been used for high value transactions, and additional care may have been taken with such 'high status' coins.

The third gold coin of Offa has attracted considerable attention, as it is an imitation of a gold dinar of the Abbasid Caliph Al Mansur, dated 157 AH (AD 774), which has 'OFFA REX' placed upside down in relation to a blundered but still discernible Arabic inscription (Figure 15.1, no. 19). This piece has been interpreted as an offering piece to the pope, since its earliest recorded provenance is in

Rome.[5] However, Blunt pointed out that Offa would have been unlikely to commission a coinage containing the Islamic profession of faith as a gift to the pope, and that the condition of the coin suggests that it may have circulated in currency. Furthermore, Islamic gold coins circulated widely in Italy and the whole Mediterranean, and the coin may thus be interpreted as a coin devised for use in international trade (Blunt, 1961: 51; Archibald, 1991: 190), an issue which Offa's letter to Charlemagne indicates was something which concerned him.

The Mercian supremacy established by Offa faltered on his death, but quickly recovered under Coenwulf (796–821). In Mercia, Offa was succeeded by his son Ecgfrith, but he only survived his father by a few months, and no coins survive in his name. This is not especially surprising since, throughout the Middle Ages, a delay of several months before the introduction of a new coinage was not unusual after a peaceful succession (Blunt *et al.*, 1963: 7). Coinage at London was apparently introduced relatively quickly following Coenwulf's accession to the throne, and initially Coenwulf's coinage was restricted to London. This is reflected by the fact that Coenwulf's early coinage has a considerably larger number of London moneyers than later in the reign, when Coenwulf was also able to issue coins in Kent and East Anglia.

In Kent, the local pretender Eadberht Praen is known both from documentary sources and from his coinage, and it was not until 798 that Coenwulf succeeded in establishing his authority both over Kent and the Canterbury moneyers. In East Anglia, the brief reign of Eadwald is known only from his coins, and no precise date is known for Coenwulf's assumption of authority there. However, coins of comparatively early style were struck for Coenwulf by East Anglian moneyers, and it is likely that he re-established Mercian overlordship before the end of the century, probably *c.* 798 (Blunt *et al.*, 1963: 5–7, 26).

Having established his authority in all three kingdoms, Coenwulf seems to have ruled unchallenged, despite wars against the Welsh which eventually led to his death in 821. His coinage likewise continued in all three areas. In Kent, however, Coenwulf installed his brother Cuthred as king rather than ruling directly, and only reverted to direct authority following Cuthred's death in 807. The two brothers seem to have shared authority amicably, and the Canterbury moneyers apparently struck coins of similar types for both brothers throughout the reign of Cuthred, with the introduction of a portrait type for both kings *c.* 805 (Figure 15.1, no. 20 and Figure 15.2, no. 1).[6] Coenwulf also re-established a joint coinage with the archbishop of Canterbury.

---

5. For references to early interpretations of this coin, see Blunt (1961: 50–1 and note 38).
6. The evidence here is ambiguous, and it may be that the Canterbury moneyers only struck coins of 'Cuthred' type for Coenwulf after his brother's death (Hugh Pagan, pers. comm.).

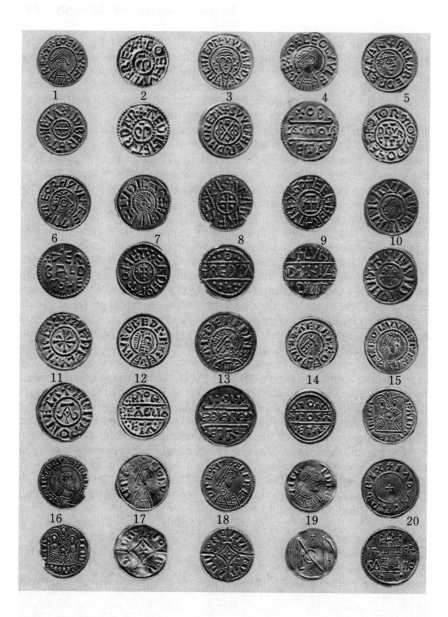

Figure 15.2 Mercian coins © The Trustees of the British Museum. Reproduced by kind permission of the Trustees of the British Museum. 1. Silver penny of Coenwulf, king of Mercia, moneyer Tidbearht; 2. Silver penny of Coenwulf, king of Mercia and Archbishop Æthelheard, probably minted in Canterbury; 3. Silver penny of Wulfred, archbishop of Canterbury, moneyer Swefherd; 4. Silver penny of Ceolwulf I, king of Mercia, moneyer Oba; 5. Silver penny of Baldred, king of Kent, moneyer Diormod; 6. Silver penny of Beornwulf, king of Mercia, moneyer Werbald; 7. Silver penny of Ludica, king of Mercia, moneyer Eadnoth; 8. Silver penny of Wiglaf, king of Mercia,

Archbishop Æthelheard had issued coins jointly with Offa, but was forced to flee Kent during the brief reign of Eadberht Praen, spending part if not all of his exile on the Continent. When Coenwulf seized power in Kent, Æthelheard returned, and the joint coinage resumed until his death in 805 (Figure 15.2, no. 2) (Blunt *et al.*, 1963: 5–12).

While Æthelheard was very clearly pro-Mercian, his successor Wulfred (who came of Mercian noble stock) was more independent, and a coinage was issued in his name alone (Figure 15.2, no. 3), initially with the legend DOROVERNIA CIVITAS on the reverse. This has been taken to indicate that only a single moneyer struck coins for him, and that it was thus superfluous to record the moneyer's name, although in later types Wulfred issued coins with the moneyer's name, and with the mint name DOROVERNIA contracted to a central monogram. Despite this independence, relations between Coenwulf and Wulfred seem to have been untroubled except for a brief period 817–821. It is tempting to link an anonymous archiepiscopal issue with this period, but Blunt *et al.* (1963: 19–22) argued that this belongs with an anonymous secular issue which followed the death of Coenwulf (see below) and that the style of Wulfred's First Monogram type suggests that it coincided with Coenwulf's later issues. This in turn suggests that Wulfred's coinage continued undisturbed throughout his conflict with Coenwulf.

The latter part of Coenwulf's reign also saw the development of a new minting centre in Kent, at Rochester. Minting apparently began there after the death of Cuthred, probably *c.* 810. The attribution of this particular group of coins to Rochester is based on their stylistic similarity with coins of Coenwulf's successor Ceolwulf which carry the mint signature DOROBREVIA, the Latin name of Rochester, and with later coins of Ecgberht of Wessex which carried an abbreviated form of the title *Sanctus Andreus Apostolicus,* after the patron saint of Rochester Cathedral (Blunt *et al.*, 1963: 22). The latter years of Coenwulf thus saw the production of coins in East Anglia, London, Canterbury and Rochester.

cont.
moneyer Redmund; 9. Silver penny of Ecgberht, king of Wessex, Lundonia type; 10. Silver penny of Berhtwulf, king of Mercia, moneyer Brid; 11. Silver penny of Æthelwulf, king of Wessex, Brid; 12. Silver penny of Burgred, king of Mercia, Lunette type, moneyer Beagstan; 13. Silver penny of Æthelred, king of Wessex, Lunette type, moneyer Ethelred; 14. Silver penny of Alfred, king of Wessex, Lunette type, moneyer Bosa; 15. Silver penny of Ceolwulf II, king of Mercia, Two Emperors type, moneyer Ealdulf; 16. Silver penny of Alfred, king of Wessex, Two Emperors type, moneyer Cenred; 17. Silver penny of Ceolwulf, king of Mercia, Cross & Lozenge type, moneyer Liofwald; 18. Silver penny of Alfred, king of Wessex, Cross & Lozenge type, moneyer Liafwald; 19. Silver penny of Alred, king of Wessex, London Monogram type, uncertain moneyer; 20. Silver penny of Edward the Elder, king of Wessex, Fortress type, moneyer Eadmund.

The breadth of authority enjoyed by Offa and Coenwulf did not long survive the latter's death, and the focus of power in southern England shifted dramatically from Mercia to Wessex. As in the reign of Offa, the surviving coinage provides the strongest evidence for shifts in political authority, and the next ten years saw considerable political instability throughout the former Mercian 'empire'. Coenwulf was succeeded by his brother Ceolwulf I, who was accepted as ruler in Mercia and East Anglia, and to a lesser extent in Kent. However, his rule even in Mercia was both uncertain and short-lived, and he was deposed in 823, to be replaced by Beornwulf, whose origins are unknown. Beornwulf was similarly unsuccessful, and apparently exercised no authority in Kent, while his failure to maintain power in East Anglia led to his death there in 825. He was succeeded by one of his ealdormen, Ludica, who also reigned for only two years. His authority was limited to Mercia itself, together with its traditional sub-kingdoms, and his reign saw the final loss to Mercia of East Anglia, with the re-emergence of a local East Anglian dynasty under Athelstan I. He was succeeded in Mercia by Wiglaf, who also ruled for only two years before Mercia itself was conquered by Ecgberht of Wessex in 829. Ecgberht's control of Mercia was even more short-lived, however, and Wiglaf recovered his authority the following year, remaining king of Mercia until his death in 839.

All these changes are reflected in the coinage. Ceolwulf seems to have been able to issue coins in Mercia and East Anglia (Figure 15.2, no. 4), although he apparently had considerably fewer moneyers working for him in London than Coenwulf had in his latter years. The situation in Kent is more complicated. We know that Ecgberht of Wessex conquered Kent in 825, from a local Kentish king called Baldred, who had apparently replaced Ceolwulf as ruler there. The date of Baldred's accession is uncertain, but the evidence of the coinage suggests that he may have been a rival to Ceolwulf from very early in the latter's reign. While at least six moneyers had struck coins in the name of Coenwulf at Canterbury before his death, only two of these struck in Ceolwulf's early portrait type. Even these two, together with three others, seem to have been hedging their bets, as they all issued a coinage with no royal name at all. Instead, the moneyer's name and title surrounded the royal bust on one side, with the mint signature DOROBERNIA CIVITAS on the other. The anonymous coinage can be divided into two groups according to the type of bust shown. The first follows the bust type used on the coins of Coenwulf and Ceolwulf, while the second shows the hair looking like some kind of bonnet. This 'Bonnet' type is also found on coins of Baldred, and on early coins of Ecgberht from Canterbury (Blunt *et al.*, 1963: 14–19). This continuity of type might suggest that the Canterbury moneyers already supported Baldred's claims during Ceolwulf's reign, but that they did not dare to recognize him openly on their coins until after Ceolwulf's death in 823.

By contrast, Ceolwulf maintained his authority more successfully at

Rochester, perhaps because Mercian power remained stronger in West Kent, closer to the Mercian border. Under Ceolwulf there were three or even four moneyers striking in Rochester compared with two under Coenwulf, and there is no equivalent of the anonymous coinage at Canterbury (Blunt *et al.*, 1963: 24–5; Lyon, 1968, 219–23). Nevertheless, as at Canterbury, Ceolwulf's coins were succeeded first by those of Baldred (Figure 15.2, no. 5), then by those of Ecgberht of Wessex, and thereafter the coins of Kent form part of the monetary history of Wessex, rather than of Mercia.

The production of Mercian coins in East Anglia lasted only a few years longer. East Anglian moneyers struck coins in the names of both Beornwulf and Ludica (Figure 15.2, nos 6–7), and it is notable that most, if not all, of the coins of these two kings were struck in East Anglia. Beornwulf may possibly have issued coins from London (this possibility rests on a single damaged coin), but Ludica apparently did not (Blunt *et al.*, 1963: 25–36; Pagan, 1986: 47). This may indicate that, as at Canterbury under Ceolwulf, the moneyers were reluctant to acknowledge the authority of the new kings, but hesitated to proclaim their loyalty to other claimants on their coins. Following Ludica's death in 827, however, coinage in London revived on a small scale under Wiglaf (see Figure 15.2, no. 8) and it may be that Wiglaf's claims had been preferred in London throughout the short-lived reigns of his two predecessors. Wiglaf's authority did not, however, extend to East Anglia, where a local dynasty emerged under Athelstan I. Both the kingdom and the coinage of East Anglia remained independent of Mercia thereafter (Blunt *et al.*, 1963: 25–6; Pagan, 1982).

Despite the comparative overall length of his reign, the coinage of Wiglaf is insubstantial, doubtless due in part to the brief interruption to his rule when Ecgberht of Wessex conquered Mercia in 829. The *Anglo-Saxon Chronicle* tells us that Wiglaf obtained his kingdom again in 830, and the coinage also reflects only a very short period of rule for Ecgberht. Two types are known on which Ecgberht styles himself 'REX M(ERCIORUM)', one of which explicitly celebrates his possession of the Mercian minting centre with the legend 'LVNDONIA CIVITAS' (Figure 15.2, no. 9). This links stylistically with the other coins, struck by the moneyer Redmudh, and it is possible that Redmudh was the only moneyer striking in London at this period. Coins of the two types together are only known in single figures. Redmudh also struck coins for Wiglaf, of which again only small quantities are known. Blunt *et al.* (1963: 34) suggested that stylistic similarities between Redmudh's Ecgberht coins and those struck for Wiglaf indicate that the latter were struck close to 830, although they firmly attribute these coins to Wiglaf's second reign. However, Pagan (1986: 47) has pointed out that these coins might immediately pre-date Ecgberht's reign, and thus be an issue of Wiglaf's first reign. Whichever is the case, if any coins were struck at all in Mercia after Wiglaf 'obtained the kingdom' again, it would appear to have been at most a brief single issue, followed by the greater part of ten years in which no coins were issued in Mercia at all.

In this respect, the 830s are unique. Coinage in southern Mercia can be traced back at least 50 years before into the early coinage of Offa and, including the earlier anonymous small flan pennies, it is likely that the issue of coinage by Mercian kings extended back for over a century. Mercian coinage revived again under Berhtwulf (839–852), while coinage continued in the intervening period in both East Anglia and Kent, the latter now firmly under the control of Wessex (Pagan, 1986: 46–7). It seems most unlikely that Mercia briefly reverted to a non-monetary economy, and the absence of coinage for the greater part of Wiglaf's reign is likely to reflect limitations in his political authority rather than economic problems. Here the phrasing of the *Anglo-Saxon Chronicle* may be significant. In telling us that Wiglaf 'obtained' the kingdom of Mercia from Ecgberht, the *Chronicle* does not actually tell us that he reconquered the kingdom, although Blunt *et al.* (1963, 4) followed Stenton (1971, 229–31) in interpreting it that way. In fact the wording seems more likely to imply that he received the kingdom back as a client king of Ecgberht. If this were so, it would make sense of the apparent cessation of coin striking within Mercia itself. Ecgberht as overlord would have no need to issue coins from London, since he already controlled both Canterbury and Rochester, while Wiglaf might well have been prohibited from issuing coins in his own name as a reminder of his client status.

The political situation changed following the accession of Æthelwulf in Wessex in 839, and Berhtwulf in Mercia in 840. Mercian coinage revived under Berhtwulf, apparently with the active cooperation of Æthelwulf's moneyers (North, 1961). A broad pattern of cooperation and alliance between the kings of Mercia and Wessex is visible thereafter in the coinage until the final collapse of the Mercian kingdom around 880. This pattern of cooperation is probably to be seen as a response to the external threat posed by the increasing scale of Viking attacks, and James Booth (1998) has argued that Berhtwulf's revival of the Mercian coinage was part of a deliberate policy of economic regeneration, together with Æthelwulf, following Viking raids on both London and Rochester in 842. The precise monetary relationship between Berhtwulf's early coinage and the coins of Æthelwulf is not entirely clear. Berhtwulf's first coinage is stylistically very similar to the second phase of Æthelwulf's 'portrait' coinage at Rochester, while one of Berhtwulf's moneyers, Brid, also appears on other coin types of Æthelwulf at Rochester (Figure 15.2, nos 10–11). It thus seems clear that Berhtwulf's first coinage is closely linked with Rochester, even though the town was now firmly part of greater Wessex.

What is less clear is the nature of the link with Rochester. Although it has been suggested that Berhtwulf might actually have had minting rights at Rochester itself, the stylistic link need only suggest that the dies for Berhtwulf's first coinage were cut in Rochester, with the coins themselves more plausibly struck in London, within the kingdom of Mercia (Lyon, 1968: 228–9; Pagan, 1986: 55–6; Booth, 1998). It would certainly make sense, following a decade or more without minting activity in London, that Berhtwulf should turn to the nearest mint outside his own kingdom to find the necessary skills to revive Mercian coinage. Actually striking the coins was not a particularly skilled task, nor can one assume that the procedures surrounding the issue of new coins would have been particularly taxing to inexperienced moneyers, but die-cutting requires more skill. While Æthelwulf's permission may have been required for Berhtwulf to employ the Rochester die-cutters, there is no need to interpret this as a full-blown monetary alliance. In producing designs similar to those of Æthelwulf, the die-cutters would simply have been producing dies of a familiar type. Furthermore, there is a commonly repeated pattern in monetary history for a kingdom introducing coinage to base the design on that of an established and familiar foreign coinage. In the absence of a Mercian coinage in the 830s, it is likely that the coinage of Wessex served in its stead, and would thus be familiar. That Berhtwulf's coinage was a re-introduction, rather than an innovation, is only a minor variation on a broader pattern.

Once re-established by Berhtwulf, the Mercian coinage had less need to lean on that of Wessex, and Berhtwulf's later issues are more independent. Under his successor Burgred (852–874), the revival of the power of Mercian coinage was completed. As Hugh Pagan (1965; 1986: 57–63) has commented, his coinage was apparently commoner and more widely circulated in England than any since the Roman occupation, although recent finds of new types of Offa now suggest that Offa's coinage may have been equally extensive. Although the silver content of the coinage of both Mercia and Wessex declined dramatically in this period, as a consequence of the wars against the Vikings, the power of Burgred's coinage was demonstrated when first Æthelred I of Wessex (865–871) and then his brother Alfred (871–899) chose to harmonize the design of their own coinage with that of Burgred (see Figure 15.2, nos 12–14). This reflects a broader pattern of alliance between Mercia and Wessex, in which Burgred married the sister of Æthelred and Alfred, and called on Wessex for military assistance against both the Welsh and the Vikings (Keynes, 1998).

Burgred's coinage, and that of his Wessex imitators, took the form of the so-called 'lunette' type, with a regal bust on the obverse, and a moneyer's name in three lines on the reverse. Variations in the design allow division into a number of sub-types. Pagan's detailed study of the coinage (Pagan, 1965) revealed that establishing the relative chronology and the attribution to individual mints of the various types is extremely complicated, and Lyon (1968: 232) has also commented that the classification of Burgred's coinage is 'by no means straightforward'. For present purposes, it is sufficient to note that Burgred issued coins of 'lunette' type in large numbers from London while coins of the same type were issued in Canterbury first for Æthelred, then Alfred, with Burgred's coinage accounting for something over half the joint issue. Some of Burgred's moneyers also struck coins for the Wessex kings, and it is possible that both Burgred and Alfred issued coinage from London in 874. The same year, however, Mercia was conquered by the Vikings. Burgred was forced to flee the kingdom, and died in exile in Rome, while Mercia was divided between the Vikings and a native Mercian ruler called Ceolwulf, whom the *Anglo-Saxon Chronicle* (versions A and E, *sub* 874) describes dismissively as 'a foolish king's thegn'.

Following Burgred's exile, the balance of power shifted towards Alfred. It is clear from the coinage that Ceolwulf II was more than the puppet that the *Anglo-Saxon Chronicle*, writing both with hindsight and a pro-Wessex agenda, suggests. It is unclear precisely which parts of Mercia he controlled when he first became king, and it is possible that initially London may have been controlled by Alfred. What is clear is that Alfred and Ceolwulf quickly developed a monetary alliance in which Ceolwulf was an equal partner (Blackburn and Keynes, 1998). The two kings issued a joint coinage, now surviving in a single example of each king, which carried a sub-Roman bust with the name of the respective king on one side, and a sub-Roman design showing two emperors side by side on the other (see Figure 15.2, nos 15–16). The same design had been used on some of the early anonymous small flan pennies, and Blackburn (1998) has recently argued that this should not be interpreted as symbolic of alliance between the two kings. However, he argued in the same paper that Alfred's coin designs demonstrate a careful interest in Roman coin designs. This interest, coupled with the rarity of the coins compared with Alfred's substantive types, suggests that this may indeed have been a symbolic issue to indicate a renewal of the Mercia–Wessex alliance.

While the status of the 'Two Emperors' type may be debatable, there is no doubt that Alfred and Ceolwulf issued a substantive joint currency, together with Archbishop Æthelred of Canterbury, in the form of the 'Cross and Lozenge' type (Figure 15.2, nos 17–18). This type is named from its reverse design, which is derivative of a design found on coins of Offa. The inspiration for the joint type thus came once more from Mercia rather than Wessex. Coins of this type were apparently struck for both rulers in London, while Canterbury and Winchester produced the same type for Alfred (with a single Winchester-style coin in the name of Ceolwulf). An unidentified mint, probably in the west, produced coins of the same type for Alfred, and another unidentified mint, possibly somewhere in West Mercia, produced coins of the same type for Ceolwulf (Blackburn and Keynes, 1998: 134–49).

We do not know what became of Ceolwulf; whether he was killed by the Vikings, or died naturally, or even fled into exile like his predecessor Burgred. Nor do we know at precisely what date independent Mercian rule came to an end. The *Anglo-Saxon Chronicle* (versions A and E, *sub* 886) refers to Alfred 'occupying' London in 886, and granting the city to Ealdorman Æthelred of Mercia, and we are told that in the same year he was accepted as ruler of all the English and the British not under Viking rule (Keynes, 1998: 12–14). A coinage of Alfred with a bust on one side and a monogram of the name 'LVNDONIA' on the other has traditionally been thought to commemorate this event (Figure 15.2, no. 19). This interpretation has now been questioned, partly on the basis of the coinage. The London monogram type appears to follow on directly from Alfred and Ceolwulf's Cross and Lozenge coinage, and it is highly unlikely that this survived as late as 886. A Mercian regnal list indicates that Ceolwulf reigned for five years, which would place the end of his reign some time around 879 (Keynes, 1998: 12), and there is no reason to suppose that Alfred would have waited several years before introducing his own next coinage. Nor does the reference to Alfred 'occupying' London in 886 necessarily imply that the city had only recently come into his hands, since the destruction caused by Viking raids might well have occasioned repairs to the city at that point even if the city had been ruled by Alfred for several years.

Opinions differ as to precisely how early Alfred may have assumed direct authority over London and southern Mercia, and introduced the London monogram coinage. Archibald (1991: 286) has suggested that it may have been as early as 878, when Alfred divided England with the Viking leader Guthrum at the Treaty of Wedmore. More recently, Blackburn (1998: 116–21) has suggested that the coinage was introduced slightly later, around 880, to accommodate the five years given to Ceolwulf in the regnal list, with a short pause before Alfred introduced the new coin type. Either way, Mercia ceased to exist as an independent kingdom after the reign of Ceolwulf II, and Mercian coinage was reduced to the issues of Alfred in the south, and the Vikings in the north. Like the London coins, rare issues from Gloucester and Oxford may indicate that Alfred was establishing the authority of Wessex in towns that had previously belonged to Mercia (Blackburn, 1998: 121–2), but for the latter part of Alfred's reign, a single coin type (with minor variations) was in use throughout his expanded realm. The coinage of the southern Danelaw was probably also issued at least in part in what had earlier been Mercia, but the attributions of the Danelaw coinage are too complex to discuss in detail here.[7]

Although the history of Mercia as a fully independent kingdom effectively ended with Alfred's assumption of authority over the whole of southern England, a sense of separate Mercian identity remained strong throughout much of the tenth century. Nowhere is this more visible than in the coins, although the title 'Rex Merciorum' does not appear on tenth-century coins. Under Alfred's successor Edward the Elder, Mercia remained semi-independent under Edward's sister Æthelflæd, 'Lady of the Mercians', and her husband ealdorman

---

7. For more detailed discussion of coinage in the Danelaw see Lyon and Stewart (1961), and Blunt *et al.* (1989: 97–107).

Æthelred. Although coinage remained a strictly royal prerogative, and all coins of the period were struck in the name of Edward, several of Edward's coin types, including the attractive 'pictorial' types (Figure 15.2, no. 20) are now recognized as Mercian issues (Blunt *et al.*, 1989: 97–107). Following the death of Æthelflæd, Edward brought Mercia more directly under royal control, but even after his son Athelstan was recognized as king of both Mercia and Wessex, the pattern of regional coinage continued, and distinct regional differences can be observed in the coins of his successors, even though these differences are often comparatively subtle (Pagan, 1997). It was not until late in the reign of Edgar, around 20 years after the subjection of the Danelaw, that a unified national coinage was introduced across the whole of England.[8] It is notable that it was Edgar, who ruled briefly as king of a separate Mercia 955–957 before succeeding to Wessex as well, who chose to bring recognizably Mercian coinage to an end, as part of the process of forging a unified kingdom of England.

Acknowledgements

The author is grateful to Marion Archibald, Stewart Lyon and Hugh Pagan, all of whom read earlier drafts of this chapter and provided many helpful comments. Any errors which remain are, of course, the responsibility of the author.

---

8. The nature of Edgar's coinage reform has been hotly debated. The best introduction to the subject is Jonsson (1987).

Part IV

The Visual Culture of Mercia

Figure 16.1 The Sandbach Crosses, Cheshire © English Heritage

16 Constructing Iconographies: Questions of Identity in Mercian Sculpture

Jane Hawkes

It is generally accepted that sculpture produced south of the Humber in the eighth and early ninth centuries can be distinguished, or considered as separate from, its North Humbrian counterparts. It is deemed to have certain characteristics, such as animal and vegetal ornament, that endow it with a specifically Mercian (South-Humbrian) identity. The perceived distinction is explicit in the classic studies of the material, such as those by Brown (1937) and Kendrick (1938), where the carvings merit discussion under separately headed sections that group them as a cohesive whole. The more recent work on establishing schools of sculpture has, to a certain extent, counteracted such 'grand narratives' by pinpointing local similarities and regional differences within the perceived Mercian geo-polity (e.g. Cramp, 1977; Sidebottom, 1994), but the notion of a definable Mercian identity in pre-Viking sculpture remains.

The plantscroll carved on the two crosses at Bakewell in Derbyshire, for instance, distinguished by its tightly scrolled, almost leafless, fleshy branches and the stylized floriate arrangement of its 'berries', is recognized as similar to those at Bradbourne and Eyam (Routh, 1937: pls II, VIII, XIV; Cramp, 1977: 224; Sidebottom, 1994: 72–79), being the products of a school of carvers active in the Peak District of central Mercia in the late eighth and early ninth centuries. At the same time the motif is recognized as differing significantly from contemporary scrolls found in eastern Mercia (e.g. at Breedon-on-the-Hill, Leics.), where the branches, arranged in a regular S-scroll, sprout stylized leaves, flowers and berries (Cramp, 1977: Fig. 50). Despite such distinctions, these plantscrolls are nevertheless deemed to be sufficiently 'similar' in their 'differences' to their North Humbrian counterparts to allow them to be grouped together as the products of a 'Greater Mercia' (Cramp, 1977: 191). The flexibility inherent in such constructs, however, has proved insufficient to accommodate the ninth-century sculpture from western Mercia, at Sandbach in Cheshire (Figure 16.1).[1]

---

1. These include the North and South crosses standing in the marketplace of

Here, the animal-head terminals of the plantscroll carved on the south face of the North cross in the market place are a feature deemed to be characteristic of Mercian art (Brown, M.,1996: 164–172), being found in ninth-century manuscripts such as the Tiberius Bede (London, British Library, Cotton MS Tiberius C.ii), the Barberini Gospels (Rome, Vatican, Biblioteca Apostolica, MS Barberini Lat. 570), the Book of Cerne (Cambridge, University Library, MS Ll.1.10), and the Royal Bible (London, British Library, MS Royal 1.E.vi) (Alexander, 1978: pls 165, 169–72, 310–11; Wilson, 1984: pl. 103; cf. Wheeler, 1977; Brown, M., 1996), but in these instances the motif terminates in letters rather than plantscrolls. A sculptural version of the animal-head terminal from Cropthorne (Worcs.), although found in association with vegetal ornament, evolves from a well-foliated plantscroll: that at Sandbach is a leafless 'treescroll' with a segmented stem, found elsewhere in south-western England, at West Camel (Somerset), where it occurs without the distinctive terminals (Cottrill, 1935: pl. XIV). Such carvings, tenuous in their 'similarity' to Sandbach, are far removed geographically and, in the case of West Camel, a 'Mercian' identity is debatable (although see Cramp, 1977: 192).

The general characteristics of the creatures featured elsewhere at Sandbach (on the north and west faces of the North cross, and the east and south faces of the South cross, in the market place),[2] with their broad muzzles, gaping jaws, prominent eyelids and interlaced tongues (Figure 16.2a), can be identified as broadly 'Mercian' according to parallels identifiable in the Book of Cerne, the Tiberius Bede and the Royal Bible, while the way their hindquarters develop into interlace can also be regarded as characteristic of Mercian art, occurring as it does in the eighth-century St Petersburg Gospels (St Petersburg, State Public Library, cod. F.v.1.8: Alexander, 1978: pl. 190), and in metalwork contexts, such as the decoration of the ninth-century Witham pins, for which a 'Midlands' origin has been considered (Webster and Backhouse, 1991: no. 184; see also Webster, Chapter 18 in this volume). In a sculptural context, however, 'Mercian' attribution is less clear as, although it survives on sculptures of eighth- and ninth-century date from Elstow (Beds.) and Gloucester (Webster and Backhouse, 1991: no. 20, Fig. 25), it also features on pieces from the south-west, at West Camel and Dalton in Devon (Cottrill, 1935: pl. XIV).

Consideration of the figural ornament raises slightly different

---

cont.

    Sandbach, dateable to the first half of the ninth century; the head of a third cross, now set on the South cross; and three diminutive shafts and two pieces of a coped tombstone standing in the churchyard. Four stones now cemented into the wall of the south porch of the parish church at Bakewell, Derbyshire (Routh, 1937: nos 9, 13–15) probably emerged from the same centre of production (Hawkes, 1998).

2. See also the animal head terminating the interlacing hindquarters of the beast on the west face of the northern Sandbach cross (Figure 16.2a).

problems (see, e.g. Sidebottom, 1994: 72–3), as studies establishing
local groups of carvings usually consider such decoration to be of
secondary importance to the non-figural motifs. To a certain extent,
this apparent neglect can be explained by the comparative rarity of
figural sculpture in the pre-Viking period (Bailey, 1980: 24–5; 1996:
11–12; Hawkes, 1999: 204–5). Yet, at Sandbach there is more figural
carving than any other type of decoration: figures occupy all four faces
of the southern cross and three faces of the northern shaft. Academic
disregard of figural decoration can also be explained by the fact that
such ornament is (arguably) more reflective of the models lying behind
the schemes than is the case with the non-figural motifs; this raises
issues not usually relevant to the scholarly concerns surrounding
examination of the animal and vegetal ornament. On the northern
Sandbach cross the figural style reflects the influence of numerous
sources while dependence on these varies considerably.

The nimbed, oval face of Mary and the crucified Christ (Figure
16.5a) betray a late antique western provenance, while the nimbed,
bearded face of the other male figures (e.g. John in the Crucifixion
scene), probably derives, through the portrayal of the bearded figure of
Christ in the Road to Calvary scene (see Figure 16.2b), from a model
not too far removed from an early eastern Mediterranean source
(Hawkes, 1998). The profile heads, with their long foreheads and
pointed chins and beards (e.g. Simon of Cyrene in the Calvary scene
and Mary of the Annunciation: Figure 16.2b), are not common in pre-
Viking sculpture in Mercia (or indeed in Anglo-Saxon England
generally), but they do appear in Pictish material of eighth- and
ninth-century date (RCAHMS, 1982: 192–211 and 1984: 206–11;
Ritchie, 1989: 25–7, 41–5, 57), and in Irish contexts: in the Book of
Kells, *c.* 800 (Meehan, 1994: e.g. pls 7–8, 22, 62, 95), and in later
sculpture, such as the South cross at Castledermot, Co. Kildare
(Harbison, 1992: Fig. 107). It has been argued that the figural style on
this, and other Irish monuments, is the development of a native style
already established in works such as the Book of Kells, but which had
its origins in works produced in southern England in the early eighth
century, whence it spread to Scotland and Iona during the eighth and
early ninth centuries, and through Ireland during the course of the
ninth century (e.g. Calvert, 1979; Henderson, 1978 and 1982). It is
possible, therefore, that the profile faces at Sandbach provide an
instance of this distinctive Insular style after its establishment in
southern England in the eighth century.[3] Alternatively, it may

---

3. The figures' clothing reflects the same diverse influences. The short-skirted tunic
   of the profile figures is comparable with Insular examples of the ninth century
   (Owen-Crocker, 1986: 121–6), while the long, pleated flared robe worn by Christ
   on the North cross (Figure 16.5b) is best paralleled in the eighth-century Turin
   and Lichfield Gospels (Alexander, 1978: pls 209–13), and the long robes worn by
   the other figures suggest dependence on a late antique model type; the drooping
   hemline and scalloped edges indicate an original depiction of clothing clinging to
   the legs.

(a)   (b)

Figure 16.2 (a) Animal ornament, west face of the North cross, Sandbach.
(b) Road to Calvary and Annunciation, west face of the North cross,
Sandbach. Photos: Jane Hawkes

demonstrate a dependence on figural styles already circulating in
Ireland and Scotland during the first half of the ninth century (Hawkes,
1997). Whether this is indeed the case, the figural styles featured on
the North cross reflect the influence of a number of different sources,
ranging from Mediterranean works of the late antique period, to
Insular art of the eighth and ninth centuries, all of which vary in the
extent of their dependence on those models.

Clearly, certain problems are encountered in attempts to situate the
carvings at Sandbach by means of the criteria usually invoked to assess
the local and regional identities of Anglo-Saxon sculpture. While well-
provenanced carvings are employed to define the schools of eastern
and central Mercian sculpture, it is in manuscript decoration that the
best parallels for Sandbach are located – parallels which can provide
only a broadly Mercian setting. The inability to establish a more
localized identity is largely due to the notable lack of pre-Viking
sculpture in the immediate vicinity of Sandbach (Sidebottom, 1994:
106–8). Such absence means there is little with which the monuments

can be compared, and the widely dispersed nature of the sculptural comparanda is thus almost inevitable.[4] Nevertheless, while extending the corpus of potential comparanda to include media other than sculpture does provide a generally 'Mercian' setting, it also highlights discrepancies in the medium-specific nature of much of the decoration. The tendency to associate animal-head terminals with lettering rather than vegetal ornament in manuscripts, for instance, is undoubtedly due to the comparative rarity of plantscrolls in Anglo-Saxon manuscripts of the eighth and ninth centuries,[5] while it is prolific in a carved medium where its use is determined by its iconographic potential and the function of the monument: vinescrolls are ideally suited to the tall narrow dimensions of the cross-shaft, serving to transform the monument into the Tree of Life which is the Cross.

The extent to which the Sandbach monuments can be considered 'Mercian' or identified with a West Mercian regional school of production, is, therefore, at least questionable. If, however, they are considered according to different criteria, such as the intentions lying behind their design and figural iconography, other readings relating to questions of identity are possible.

The manner in which the figural sculpture of 'Mercia' is organized has often been regarded as characterized by the use of arched architectural settings (e.g. Cramp, 1977: 224–5; Sidebottom, 1994: Distribution Map 26; see also Brown, M., 1996: 80–1, 116). In the east this is certainly the case. At Breedon-on-the-Hill (Leics), and Peterborourgh, Castor and Fletton (Cambs) many of the figures are set within their own arched niches, while the arches themselves grow from slender columns with distinctive capitals and bases (Kendrick, 1938: pl. XXXI; Webster and Backhouse, 1991: Figs 22–24). The same tendency is also discernible in the Peak District where the figures are set within arched frames that are of different proportions to those featured on the East Mercian carvings, but which are still arguably architectural in their inspiration (Routh, 1937: pls II, IX, XIV).

At Sandbach, small niches proliferate (Figures 16.2 to 16.5). On both cross-shafts the figures are set within their own compartments. Even the fragments in the churchyard display the same fetish. There is, however, no sense in which these frames can be considered architectural features; indeed, many of the cells are not even arched.

---

4. Although the vagaries of survival and access to stone may also explain the widely dispersed nature of the sculptural parallels, the wealth of material surviving in eastern and central Mercia indicates that such logistical considerations do not provide a complete explanation.

5. Although rare, plantscrolls that could be considered closely analogous to those featured in a sculptural medium are not unknown in Anglo-Saxon manuscript contexts, e.g. Barberini Gospels '*Chi Rho*' page, f.18 (Alexander, 1978: pl. 170). In an Irish context the details of f. 309r in the Book of Kells (Mac Lean, 1999: Fig. 15.2) provide another possible parallel. It is interesting to note that in these instances the branches of the plants do not terminate in the animal heads featured on the sculpture at Sandbach.

Figure 16.3 Lozenge decoration, east face of the South cross, Sandbach. Photo: Jane Hawkes

Here, the act of compartmentalizing the decoration seems to have been the foremost principle of design. To enclose the decoration, regardless of the disposition and shape of the frame, to incorporate all possible varieties of frame, was such a primary consideration that the distinctive layout may not even be a reflex of cultural or regional identity (Cramp, 1989: 225).

The use of lozenge shapes intersected by prominent bosses featured on the South cross (Figure 16.3), for instance, is rare in sculptural contexts, but it is not unusual in metalwork contexts (e.g. the eighth-century Tassilo Chalice and the late ninth-century Fuller Brooch: Wilson, 1984: pls 1, 161). Likewise, the manner in which some of the figures are contiguous with the roll-moulding on the North cross (e.g. Figure 16.5) is remarkably similar to the effect achieved on open-work metal artefacts, such as the Irish Crucifixion plaques, where figures are joined to each other and the frame for functional reasons (Bourke, 1993: Fig. 21.1). The influence of metalwork techniques could also explain the numerous pellets set around the carved figures on both the crosses (Figures 16.2b, 16.5a and b): they are skeuomorph

Figure 16.4 (a) Cross-head, east face of the North cross, Sandbach

(b) Adoration of the Magi, east face of the North cross, Sandbach. Photos: Jane Hawkes

nails, from an object such as an open-work metal artefact, that, having no function in a stone medium, have become a decorative motif. Such features strongly suggest that dependence on metalwork models controlled the form of the settings at Sandbach and made the frames the dominant features they are.

Thus, although Sandbach shares with other 'Mercian' sculpture a tendency to compartmentalize its figural decoration, this is where the 'similarity' ends. The compartments themselves are not comparable, and the organizational principles underlying the arrangement are very different. So different are they, that the degree of influence exerted by the model is probably more relevant than notions of a common Mercian or West Mercian identity. It is not simply one panel, or one element of the decoration that has been influenced by metalwork techniques; these are consistent across both monuments and metal may even have been incorporated into their original design. The large boss at the centre of the North cross-head is surrounded by four small circular holes of equal size and depth, apparently designed to hold a metal appliqué that encircled or covered the boss (Figure 16.4a), and the plain mouldings framing the narrative scenes congruent to an area of apparent damage on the West face of the cross also surround the hole, implying that it does not represent secondary damage (Figure 16.2b). As with other pre-Viking monuments, it probably once contained a large inset (Bailey, 1990; Henderson, 1994).

Such metalwork effects, so strikingly retained in the design of the Sandbach crosses, were probably intentional, integral to what the monuments were intended to signify in the landscape in which they stood. Here, stone was being deliberately employed to recreate the brilliantly glittering and gem-encrusted metal crosses that were a familiar part of ecclesiastical furnishings. At Sandbach, the institution of the Church, by virtue of its sign, the Cross, has been removed from the confines of a building and made monumental in the landscape, permanently visible, for all to see.[6]

The intention of enshrining and proclaiming the presence of the Church and all it represents is not simply discernible in the design of the Sandbach crosses, although this is the most obvious method employed. It is reinforced by the figural iconography, as an examination of the scenes extant on the east face of North cross demonstrates (Figure 16.1). These comprise the Adoration of the Magi (near the top of the shaft), with the Virgin and Child on the left and the three Magi placed, as busts, one above the other on the right (Figure 16.4b). Below is the Crucifixion, with Christ on the cross surmounted by symbols of the sun and moon, surrounded by the four evangelist symbols, and flanked at the foot of the crucifix by Mary and John. In the socle of the crucifix is the Adoration of the Manger with an

---

6. It is also likely that references to the Apocalyptic *'Crux Gemmata'* were also being invoked (Higgitt, forthcoming).

Figure 16.5 (a) Crucifixion and adoration of the manger, east face of the North cross. **(b)** Transfiguration and *Traditio Legis cum Clavis*, east face of the North cross, Sandbach. Photos: Jane Hawkes

angel hovering over the child in a crib flanked by the ox and ass (Figure 16.5a). Below this is the Transfiguration, consisting of Christ standing between Moses with the Law of the Old Testament, and Elijah (on the right) with a scroll depicting the Word of the Prophets; the Voice of God is symbolized by the bird (probably to be identified as the dove of the Holy Spirit) hovering above his head (Hawkes, 1995: 215–17). In the roundel at the base of the shaft is the *Traditio Legis cum Clavis*, where Christ is flanked by Paul with the New Law (on the left) and Peter with the keys of heaven, on the right (Figure 16.5b). The iconography of these scenes is extensive and complex, both in terms of the individual images and in the way they relate to each other. Together they present a consistent message concerning the Church and its sacraments as founded on, and validated through, the incarnation and salvation of Christ, the divine made human.

In biblical exegesis the Adoration of the Magi (Figure 16.4b) was nearly always explained as the first occasion on which God manifested himself to humanity through Christ. It was interpreted as signifying humanity adoring the Godhead, and more specifically, the inclusion of the Gentiles in that act. These ideas were common, not just in the writings of the earliest Church writers, but also in the works of Insular exegetes (e.g. the Hiberno-Latin commentary, *In Matthaei Evangelium Exposito* 1: 2, in *PL* 92: 13).[7] The scene at Sandbach would thus have signified the adoration of three heathen Gentiles from the far reaches of the earth who present their gifts in recognition of Christ's divine and saving nature.

At another level the Magi would also have been seen as prototypes of the Church congregation which, in faithful veneration, approach the altar (*In Matt.* 1: 2, in *PL* 92: 12–13). Although such eucharistic themes are potentially relevant to any image of the Magi, the way the event is juxtaposed with the Crucifixion at Sandbach makes such a reading more than just possible. Iconographically, therefore, the scene articulates the theophany, the adoration and bearing witness necessarily attendant on such events, as well as the sacrament of the Eucharist.

The Crucifixion (Figure 16.5a), like any such image, would have invoked, at the very least, consideration of Christ's sacrifice, the Eucharist and the salvation of humanity. In addition, the way the cross fills and quarters the scene is emblematic of the universal relevance of the event. This was a patristic commonplace, being popularized through the writings of Ambrose, Augustine and Jerome in their identification of the dimensions of the cross as identical with the love of Christ.[8] In the ninth century, Alcuin was to refer to the universal and saving nature of the cross in the same tradition:

> Indeed as it lay, the cross stretched out to all the four quarters of the world, east and west, north and south, because even so by his passion Christ draws all people to him.[9]

It is to this understanding of the cross that the symbols of the sun and moon and evangelists at Sandbach add a certain emphasis. The

---

7. Although this commentary is listed by Lapidge and Sharpe (1985: 336, no. 1269) as of dubious Hiberno-Latin provenance, it is more generally accepted as having been written within the Irish tradition (McNally, 1969, 17–19; 1970: 676–7; Kelly, 1989–90: 412, no. 82; Wright, 1990: 105–6, no. *27). I am grateful to Dr Jennifer O'Reilly for her advice on this issue.

8. For example, Augustine, *Tractate 118: In S. Johannis Evangelium* (Willems, 1954, *CCSL* 36: 657); see Coatsworth (1979: 1, 24–7, 67–82), for further references.

9. *Iacens vero crux quatuor mundi partes appetit, orientem videlicet, et occidentem, aquilonem et meridiem, quia et Christus per passionem suam omnes gentes ad se trahit* (*De Divini Officiis* 18, in *PL* 101: 1208).

evangelists, who recorded the event in their gospels, guaranteed the spread of Christianity to the far ends of the earth. Thus the arrangement of their symbols around the crucifix signifies not only the witnessing of Christ's salvation, but also that that salvation embraces the entire world. Likewise the sun and moon refer, not only to the darkness that fell over the earth at the time of Christ's death (Matthew 27: 45; Mark 25: 33; Luke 23: 44; Gospel of Nicodemus 8: 10, in James, 1924: 94–146), but to the involvement of the natural world in the death of the Creator; they signify the roles of Christ as the Son of God and Lord of the Cosmos. The ideas are found in works as diverse as the Old English poem 'The Dream of the Rood', whose account of the Crucifixion was probably circulating in Anglo-Saxon England from the eighth century onwards,[10] and (at the end of the period) Ælfric's sermon on the Crucifixion, which follows Gregory the Great's homily on the Epiphany (Swanton, 1970; Thorpe, 1844: 108; *Homilia X. ii: In Epiphania Domini*, in *PL* 76: 1110; see O'Reilly, 1998).

These themes of universality and witnessing are further expanded by the presence of Mary and John who act as historical witnesses to the event and as reminders of Christ's words from the cross (John 19: 26–27; see Aldhelm, *De Virginitate (Prosa)*, in Ehwald, 1919: 235, translated in Lapidge and Herren, 1979: 59–132, at 64). More importantly they also connect the Crucifixion to other events in the cycle of Christian history: Mary provides a link between the mysteries of the Passion and those of the Incarnation (see e.g. Bede, *In Lucae Evangelium Exposito* 1: 1, in Hurst, 1960, *CCSL* 120: 36–7), while John associates the Crucifixion with the Final Resurrection. It was his account of the Passion (John 18–19) that was read during the liturgical commemoration of the event (for discussion, see Okasha and O'Reilly, 1984: 45; see also Lenker, 1997: 317) and as presumed author of the Book of Revelation he was regarded as witness to the Second Coming (e.g. Aldhelm, *De Virginitate (Prosa)*, in Ehwald, 1919: 235).

Thus the iconography of the Crucifixion scene, while carrying the usual references associated with such images, highlights the universal application of the sacrifice, and the witnessing of the event by those who were able to affirm and spread the message of its salvation to the far corners of the world. Mary and John further link the event to others central to Christianity, including the Incarnation which is depicted above and below.

The usual significance of the Adoration of the Manger (Figure 16.5a), a specific iconographic version of the Nativity, was to downplay the event as a virgin birth and highlight it as the manifestation of God

---

10. Although the Old English poem known as 'The Dream of the Rood' survives in the early eleventh-century Vercelli Manuscript (Swanton, 1970), phrases from the poem's account of the Crucifixion survive in runic form on the Northumbrian shaft at Ruthwell, Dumfriesshire, in a manner that can be regarded as integral to the design of the monument and so dated to the eighth century.

on earth, recognized and adored by the created world. In such instances the natural world is represented by the two animals thought to symbolize humanity in general, but also the heathen Gentiles in particular. As Ambrose put it in his commentary on Luke's account of the Nativity (*Expositionis in Lucam* 2: 43, in Adriaen, 1957, *CCSL* 14: 50), the beasts in their stalls symbolize the peoples of the pagan world to be nourished by the abundance of 'sacred food' (*alimoniæ sacræ*). The angel, not usually included in pictorial versions of the Adoration, was nevertheless a common feature in ecclesiastical writings on the subject. Ambrose follows his account of the ox and ass with a reference to the angels by invoking Mark 1: 13 ('And he was with the beasts and the angels ministered unto him'), to indicate the humility and divinity found in the Christ child at his birth:

> Fulfilled now is the prophecy. The Lord is praised from the heavens; and he is seen on earth ... As in one is a sign of mercy, in the other you behold a witness of divine power. It was because of men he suffered beasts; it was because of himself he is proclaimed by angels.[11]

Here, the notions of revelation and adoration expressed by the Adoration of the Magi are extended to include Christ revealed and adored at his birth by the beasts of the natural world, the humanity they represent, and the angels of heaven.

Moreover, the Adoration of the Manger had another, eucharistic, significance. Bede's commentary on Luke's account of Christ's birth (*In Luc.* 1: 2, in Hurst, 1960, *CCSL* 120: 49–50) makes the association by referring to the Child in the crib as 'the bread of angels' (*panis angelorum*), and the ox and ass feeding from the manger as those Christians who, as 'sanctified beasts' (*sancta animalia*), feed from 'the corn of his flesh' (*carnis suæ frumento*). Ælfric, in the eleventh century, deriving his ideas from the earlier writings of Gregory the Great and Bede, makes the same link in his sermon on Christ's Nativity (*Sermo de Natale Domini*, in Thorpe, 1844: 34): the birth of Christ was the birth of the Eucharist provided by Christ's death and resurrection; the child in the manger, wrapped in swaddling bands, was the Eucharist that clothes Christians in an 'immortal tunic' (*undeadlican tunecan*).

Thus, as with the Adoration of the Magi and the Crucifixion, the iconography of the Adoration of the Manger at Sandbach has a potentially multivalent significance. The theme of revelation and universal adoration is presented by the beasts and angel attendant on

---

11. *Impleta igitur prophetia est. Laudatur de coelis Dominus, et videtur in terris ... ut in altero misericordiae insigne, in altero divinae indicium potestatis agnoscas. Tuum est quod bestias patitur, suum quod ab angelis praedicatur* (*Expos. Lucam* 2: 52, in Adraien, 1957, *CCSL* 14: 53).

the crib, while the lack of distinction between the Crucifixion and Adoration of the Manger scenes (the latter being actually enclosed within the base of the crucifix), points to a specific association of that event with the Eucharist.

The two lower images, the Transfiguration and the *Traditio Legis cum Clavis*, continue these themes, but also introduce a slightly different iconographic element, one which is concerned with the establishment of the Church on earth. The Transfiguration (Figure 16.5b) represents yet another moment when the divinity of God was manifested on earth in the body of his Son, but as this particular theophany immediately preceded Christ's crucifixion it was generally interpreted as a sign of the resurrection to come. The notion is present in the biblical accounts of the event, where the subject of Christ's conversation with Moses and Elijah is revealed to confirm the link with the forthcoming Passion (Matthew 17: 3–9; Mark 9: 3–9). Thus, the most common interpretation of the event, confirmed at the Council of Nicæa in 325, was that it proved Christ's divine nature which would guarantee the resurrection of his body. The literary tradition makes it clear, however, that it was not only Christ's divine power that was manifested on Mount Tabor. The presence of Moses and Elijah was also deemed significant because between them they symbolized the Old Law and the Words of the Prophets that were transformed and consolidated by Christ and united in the foundation of his Church. Thus Augustine viewed the two patriarchs as witnesses, not only of Christ's divine nature, but also of his Church, while the Voice of God marked the moment when the Church on earth was established in Christ (*Sermo LXXVIII. De Verbis Evangelii Matthaei, xvii.18*, in *PL* 38: 491; see also Leo the Great, *Tractatus LI: Lectio sancti evangelii secundum Mattheum*, in Chavasse, 1973, *CCSL* 138A: 296–303; Hilary of Poitiers, Remigius, Jerome and John Chrysostom, in Toal, 1958: 69–71, 40–43). This evaluation clearly extends the theme of witnessing and veneration found in all the scenes on this face of the cross-shaft, adding the patriarchs to the Gentiles, humanity in general, the creatures of the natural world, and the angels of heaven, while it expands the iconographic reference to include the Church.

The lowermost scene, the *Traditio Legis cum Clavis* (Figure 16.5b) is extremely unusual in the form it takes at Sandbach, including, as it does, both Peter and Paul with the keys and the Law. It is an iconographic arrangement that was not established in Christian art before the ninth century, the earliest surviving instance of the scheme being that at Müstair, Switzerland, dated to *c.* 800. Here, in a foundation that enjoyed the direct patronage of Charlemagne, the frescoes provided an extended commentary on the integral relationship of Church and State in the Carolingian world (e.g. Birchler, 1954). The *Traditio Legis cum Clavis*, set in one of the apses of the church, was pivotal to the programme, illustrating Peter and Paul as the two apostles responsible for spreading the Gospel and founding the Church throughout the world. While the Church was founded on Peter (after

Christ's words to him recorded in Matthew 16: 18), Paul was deemed to have set down the Law (which, in the case of Müstair, was upheld by the State) that the faithful Christian was expected to follow in order to gain entrance to heaven, over which Peter had the power of binding and loosing. The scheme at Sandbach provides the only other extant example of the scene produced at a time contemporary with the Müstair fresco. Compared with the other images on the cross-shaft it represents a remarkably new scene in an early ninth-century Anglo-Saxon context. Moreover, it makes explicit the iconographic references to the establishment and authority of the earthly Church implicit in the preceding scenes.

Early Christian sermons on the Transfiguration, set above the *Traditio Legis cum Clavis*, certainly explore the connections between the two. Augustine, when explaining the significance of the transfigured Christ, uses the analogies of Paul, his preaching to the Gentiles and the establishment of the Church (*Sermo LXXVIII*, in *PL* 38: 490). Leo the Great, discussing the Transfiguration, combines Peter's experience of divine revelation on Mount Tabor with his foundation of the Church of Rome through which, he argues, eternal life is possible for all faithful Christians (*Tractatus* LI.1, in Chavasse, 1973, *CCSL* 138A: 296–97). Such literary links suggest the juxtaposition of Transfiguration and *Traditio Legis cum Clavis* at Sandbach is not accidental. Visually, it seems deliberate: the bar-throne of the transfigured Christ extends up from the frame surrounding the *Traditio Legis*, while the feet of the two Old Testament figures at the Transfiguration develop into tendrils that pass into the roundel framing the lower scene. Christ transfigured is set above Christ donating the Law and keys of Heaven, while Paul holding the New Law is depicted immediately below Moses carrying the Old Law. To this extent the decoration links the two scenes, as the characters in them are linked in the exegetical tradition. As the foremost of the apostles in the spreading of the Gospels, Peter and Paul at Sandbach are further associated with the Transfiguration to the extent that that scene symbolizes the confirmation of the Church in Christ, while the *Traditio Legis cum Clavis* signifies its establishment on earth.

Such correspondences serve to highlight the references to the institution of the Church implicit in the scenes above. The Church is, after all, the institution that facilitates the celebration of the sacraments, such as the Eucharist, and it is the Church that preserves, propagates and continues to bear witness to Christ and his message of universal salvation, even to the far corners of the world: the iconographic themes of the Adoration of the Manger, the Crucifixion and the Adoration of the Magi. If the monument is read from top to bottom, the iconography of the two lowermost scenes is integral to what has preceded them in that the themes of recognition and confirmation of Christ's divinity are continued in the figures of Peter and Paul, and Elijah and Moses. But at the same time a clear statement concerning the establishment of the earthly Church through those chosen and appointed by God is also presented. Once articulated, it is possible to re-read the shaft from bottom to top in such a way that the entire programme presents an unequivocal statement about the power, authority and working of the Church.

Historically this is not an entirely unfeasible reading of the figural iconography. The reign of Coenwulf, and that of Offa before him (that collectively ended in *c.* 821), enjoyed a constant flurry of diplomatic activity with the Carolingian court, particularly between 787 and 803 when papal envoys accompanied those from Gaul during the Mercian royal elevation of Lichfield to the status of an archbishopric (Stenton, 1918; 1933; Levison, 1946: 111–32; Deanesly, 1965; Mayr-Harting, 1972: 182; Heath, 1973; Simms-Williams, 1975; Hart, 1977; Bullough, 1980: 160–72; Hicks, 1993: 134; Keynes, 1995: 35–41), and it is perhaps not irrelevant to note here that Sandbach lies within the Anglo-Saxon diocese of Lichfield (Hill, 1981; Higham, 1994b: 167–8). The contacts established in the course of such activities would certainly provide the opportunity for the transmission of knowledge concerning the production of images in the Carolingian world, especially those being produced in royal foundations. Against this background the sculpture at Sandbach could be regarded as articulating the continuing aspirations of the senior clergy in the region in the decade after Lichfield lost its archdiocesan status, and that Carolingian images of ecclesiastical authority were being invoked as part of that agenda. Such suggestions would certainly be in keeping with what is known of the tendencies of the Mercian royal and ecclesiastical hierarchies of the late eighth and early ninth centuries to imitate things prestigious and Carolingian. Access to the varied and contemporary material evident in the figural decoration of the monuments can be explained within the context of the visits made to, and from, papal legates and Carolingian dignitaries (both regal and ecclesiastical) which marked the events of the period, while the Transfiguration and *Traditio Legis cum Clavis* (expressing, as they do, the investment of divine authority in the Church), would be particularly appropriate in such a cultural climate. Within the overall design of the east face of this cross these scenes, situated as they would have been at the eye-level of the spectator, function as confirmation of an iconographic programme that systematically extols the power and authority vested in the establishment of Christ's Church on earth – or perhaps, in this case, the institution of the Church in western Mercia.

Figure 17.1 Sandstone figure panel. Breedon-on-the-Hill. The Conway Library, Courtauld Institute of Art

17 Classicism of Southumbrian Sculpture

Richard Jewell

In approaching the subject of this chapter, one fundamental question presents itself: what is Classicism? Kendrick saw the early history of English art as being a series of struggles between barbaric and classical aesthetic tendencies, the former being defined by its expression of organic forms in dynamic abstract and linear terms, the latter by its use of naturalism and modelling to achieve its effect (Kendrick, 1938: 1). In Southumbria, by the end of the eighth century and during the earlier ninth, in sculpture, as in manuscripts, many of the more forward-looking works show a noticeable leaning towards this latter aesthetic.

George Henderson (1972, 97–153; 1999, 56–135) has stressed the importance of the Roman Imperial tradition to Early Christian imagery and its proselytizing impact. Before the Carolingian era the Christians of the West still looked to Constantinople and the Byzantine emperors as the direct lineal descendants of Imperial Rome and Augustus Caesar, and many revered contemporary Rome as the source of their own Christianity. Regardless of their subject matter, relics of Classical and Late Antique art were imbued both with Imperial prestige and Roman Christian significance to the newly-Christianized 'barbarians': by the same token, King David and Charlemagne were both endowed with the authority of an Augustus.

Early medieval ecclesiastical metalwork objects, particularly crosses, were repositories of precious Antique portrait gems, perhaps presumed to be Christian rulers or saints, just as Constantine's *Labarum*, the original Christian imperial standard, had featured portraits of the emperor's family as well as Christ's monogram.

On a formal level, Classical naturalism was also important for its rendering of physical presence, bringing figures to life, and thus reinforcing their Christian message. Likewise, Anglo-Saxon animal ornament broke with its abstracted Germanic and Hiberno-Saxon past under the influence of East Christian art.

The pagan English aesthetic did not accord prominence to naturalistic ornament, and it is only in the wake of the introduction of foreign exemplars by the Church that it took its place in English art.

The variety of these sources, as well as receptivity towards them, seem greatly to have increased towards the end of the eighth century and early in the ninth, both in England and Carolingian Europe. Late Antique, Early Christian and earlier Byzantine art all played their part, as well as more nearly contemporary Roman and Italo-Byzantine art. Works from these periods might on occasion be imbued with the spirit and style of 'perennial Hellenism', like Classical Greek, Hellenistic and early Imperial Roman art, and when such models inspired the sculptors of Southumbria, they, like their contemporaries in the Carolingian schools, were capable of producing work to which the term Classicism can be applied in a stricter sense. Nevertheless, in general they seem to have been responding more to decorative elements and non-classicizing figural tendencies in East Christian art (as well as, of course, continuing insular preoccupations), than mainstream Carolingian artists did after the establishment of the Palace School at Aachen in the last few years of the eighth century (Beckwith, 1964: 38).

The largest and most important group of sculpture in the region, comprising friezes and relief-carved panels, is at Breedon-on-the-Hill, Leicestershire, let into various walls of the later church of St Mary and St Hardulph (see Clapham, 1927; Cramp, 1977; on the friezes only, Jewell, 1986). The decorative friezes are of two types, referred to respectively as the narrow and broad friezes: one, about 17 cm high, carved with single and double-stemmed vine scrolls; the other, about 22 cm high, bearing a wide range of ornamental motifs in panels of varying length, separated by thin vertical strips. They are chiefly of a hard, fine-grained Permian calcareous sandstone from Nottinghamshire, although a few blocks are of oolite (Jewell, 1986: note 4).

The friezes possess features which show them both to be the work of one group of craftsmen, and make them unique in Anglo-Saxon sculpture. Despite the small scale of the carvings, they have considerable depth, the strong undercutting of the forms sometimes making them partially free-standing. This deep-shadowed carving technique applies as much to the boldly modelled foliate scrolls of the narrow frieze, with their cupped leaf forms, as to the varied ornament of the broad frieze; and they form a stylistically homogeneous group to which only one of the figure panels is closely related.

Apart from the geometrical ornament, the decorative motifs used on the broad frieze are culled from various early Byzantine sources. The birds, animals and figures of the inhabited scrolls, and of most of the non-geometrical panels, are only mildly subjected to the Anglian mannerisms which affect the style of contemporary animal ornament in the East Midlands – Lindsey and Middle Anglia, as seen for example in the Witham pins, Gandersheim Casket, and Hedda Stone (Webster and Backhouse, 1991: no. 184, Fig. 24; Marth, 2000).

There are few contemporary sculptural parallels in Mercia and the South of England, while the sometimes close affinities between the creatures of the inhabited scroll and early ninth-century Northumbrian sculpture, especially the Easby and Hoddom crosses, are in the nature of period resemblances, reflecting the revived interest in late antique models common to Mercian and Northumbrian sculptors in this period (see Webster and Backhouse, 1991: Fig. 12). With the exception of Easby, Northumbrian sculpture of the late eighth and early ninth centuries is generally more conservative in style, with a tendency towards a provincial heaviness and stiffness in its copying of Roman models for figure subjects (e.g. Otley, Rothbury) and a more barbarizing treatment of its animal ornament (e.g. Croft, Morham) (see Cramp, 1971; Hawkes, 1997; Webster and Backhouse, 1991: No. 115; Kendrick, 1938: pl. 93.3). The same is true of the Peak District crosses, themselves Northumbrian derivatives, and notable in this context only for the late antique-looking horseman on the Bakewell cross-shaft, which has a close parallel in the broad frieze (Cramp, 1977: Fig. 60c).

In Southumbria the closest relatives of the Breedon animals are found in manuscripts, chiefly the Codex Bigotianus (Paris, Bibl. Nat., MSS lat. 281 and 298) where two large initials are divided into regular panels, each enclosing a single bird or animal (see figure on p.12, Alexander, 1978: 60, ills 166, 168); these find parallels in sixth- to seventh-century sculpture in Italy, as does the panelled arrangement, suggesting that they depend on earlier Italo-Byzantine models. Of particular interest is the chancel screen slab (96 × 104 cm), probably from S. Maria *in Aracoeli*, in the Palazzo Senatorio, Rome (Ermini, 1974: no. 32, pl. XI). This is divided into square compartments containing animals and birds which are comparable to Breedon in their liveliness and in the technical level and height of relief of their carving. The animal types and their square-compartmented arrangement are also strongly reminiscent of the Codex Bigotianus initials. Sixth-century Byzantine sculpture in the East can also show remarkable stylistic analogies with the Breedon inhabited scroll, especially a screen slab from Elbistan, now in the Archaeological Museum, Istanbul, with its centaur and spear-wielding huntsman (Jewell, 1986: pl. 46b).

Most of the contemporary parallels for the ornament of the Breedon friezes in Carolingian art on the Continent are found in manuscripts, particularly those of the Court School group, dating from *c*. 781–*c*. 800. In the Godescalc Evangelistary (Paris, Bibliothèque Nationale, Nouv. acq. lat. 1203, folios 21b, 77a) and the Dagulf Psalter (Vienna, Österreichische Nationalbibliothek, Codex 1861, folio 21b), vine scrolls and foliage can be compared with the narrow frieze, and in the Psalter a striking parallel for the deeply faceted pelta panel of the broad frieze is seen (folio 64, Jewell, 1986: pl. 31a). In the more mature Harley and Soissons Gospels the early Christian motifs of groups of birds or inhabited vine columns are based on sixth-century models and panels of the broad frieze, like the cockerels and falcons and the vintage scene, are of similar derivation. The bird group in the Book of Kells (Dublin, Trinity College Library, MS 58) betrays the similar interests of the Hiberno-Saxon world at the turn of the eighth century (Alexander, 1978: ill. 258).

The revivalist spirit, and sometimes the subjects, of the carvings of the Breedon broad frieze parallel the art of Charlemagne's court, but the Court School, with its increasingly self-conscious search for an authentic antique classicism, is more likely to have provided the inspiration or the impetus than the models. From the style of the sculpture, most of the models seem to have been earlier ivories and textiles from the Christian East. This is most obvious in the inhabited scrolls.

The single vine scroll of the narrow frieze, however, is firmly linked with late eighth- and early ninth-century sculpture in northern and central Italy, especially in its use of hollow trefoil leaves, which have few, if any, parallels in earlier sculpture outside Italy. Moreover, the leaf whorls and coiled tendril offshoots, not seen elsewhere in Anglo-Saxon sculpture in this form, are closely paralleled on a marble cross, dated 801–802 by S. Giovanni di Monte, now in Bologna Museum (photograph Conway Library, Courtauld Institute, London) and in Brescian examples of similar date (Jewell, 1986: n. 21). The trefoil with oval leaves appears for the first time in England at Breedon and is later seen on western Mercian sculpture of the ninth century at Wroxeter (Salop), Cropthorne (Worcs.) and Acton Beauchamp (Herefs.) and recurs on a later piece at Breedon (see Wilson, 1984: ill. 126; Kendrick, 1938: pl. 80. 2, 3). It is much more frequent in contemporary north Italian sculpture. Another feature of the Breedon scroll which could be of Italian derivation is the varied sequence and pairing of the volute endings of three principal types: trefoils, grape bunches and single leaves (Jewell, 1986: 98). But it should not be forgotten that the appearance of these leaf forms and scrolls in Italy is itself a reflection of the influence of Syrian ecclesiastics throughout the seventh and eighth centuries (Dalton, 1925: 301). The appearance of related Italo-Syrian foliage in the Godescalc Evangelistary and Dagulf Psalter also reflects their borrowings from contemporary Italian art.

The narrow frieze belongs to a sub-Roman and Byzantine tradition of strip friezes, in stone stucco and terracotta, bearing continuous vine scroll ornament, with seventh-century examples in Gaul, Rome and Visigothic Spain (Jewell, 1986: 99).

A strongly Italianate scroll of similar date to Breedon is also found at Britford in Wiltshire, where the stunted palmette-derived lappets attached to the insides of the volutes are coupled with enclosed heart-shaped berry bunches, both north Italian features. Scrolls with features of palmette-derivation occur elsewhere in earlier ninth-century sculpture in Wessex, at Codford St Peter, in Kent at Reculver, and in Northumbria on the cross-shaft formerly in Lowther Castle, Cumbria (see Tweedle, in Webster and Backhouse, 1991: No. 208; Wilson, 1984: ills 65–8; Bailey and Cramp, 1988: ills 428, 430, 432–5, 436–43). There is also a hint of it on one of the fragments at South Kyme, Lincs; these also include one with quite a classical-looking horizontal key pattern of open design (Cramp, 1977: fig. 54c). Their prominent moulded frames suggest a panel, and Baldwin Brown was reminded of Italian *Cancelli* (Baldwin Brown, 1937: 181, pl. 48). In this respect it is interesting to note that fragments of a stucco relief from the Abbey of S. Caprasio, Aulla (Liguria), founded 884 (Verzone, 1945: nos 34–5, pl. 28), bear foliage, a key pattern border and moulded frames, all of which are similar to the corresponding motifs on the South Kyme fragments which, although earlier, could well reflect a knowledge of Italian church furniture.

At Breedon the sculptors responsible for the friezes also carved a figural panel of the same sandstone (Figure 17.1; Cramp, 1977: 207, 210, fig. 55). It measures only 48 × 25 cm but has a depth of carving as great as 5 cm. The two figures stand side by side in a slightly cramped manner, with shoulders hunched and their heads inclined inwards. Despite the whitish surface encrustation produced by calcification, they still appear to have tender and benign expressions. Both hold plant stems ending in cupped leaves similar to those in the panel with fighting beasts in the broad frieze. Their long flowing garments cling to the arms and legs revealing the forms beneath, and forming V-shaped folds between the legs. The figure on the left has crimped hair and a beard and holds a square book in his draped left hand. The other figure, which may be female, has smooth hair and is unbearded; this figure holds up in both hands a V-shaped swathe of drapery which clings to and spreads out against the right leg, from the knee downwards, with low, widely spaced ridges of drapery following the curve of the leg beneath. The constriction of the wide, horizontally crimped folds between the legs into a thin cluster of finely incised narrow folds, as they approach the left hand, in which they are held, admirably conveys the effect of the clutching and pulling upwards of the robe's diaphanous material.

Both figures appear to be on tiptoe, a formula which avoided foreshortening the feet (cf. the Bewcastle Christ; see Bailey and Cramp, 1988: ill. 94). The fully-modelled feet have their nearest counterpart in Mercian sculpture on the large figure panel at Fletton (Cramp, 1977: 210, fig. 56a). The rounded left arm of this figure also parallels the Breedon panel (Fig. 17.2a).

Like the sculpture of the friezes, the depth of relief, combined with vigorous undercutting, has the effect of casting the background into such deep shadow that the carving appears almost to be detached from it. The treatment of the figures in this panel is humanistic rather than conventional and the modelling soft and rounded, neither of which features is seen to the same extent in any of the other figure sculptures at Breedon or in the Peterborough area. Apart from their gently bowed posture they have little in common with this group, which is of limestone. The essential difference is in their drapery, with its cavernous folds which are so much more voluminous than the flat bands of drapery on the Fletton and Castor figures (Figure 4.1) and the related apostle panel at Breedon. This difference is not surprising, as the entire group of sandstone sculpture stands apart from early ninth-century work elsewhere in the Mercian region.

Figure 17.2 (a) Relief panel, Fletton. **(b)** Frieze section, Fletton. The Conway Library, Courtauld Institute of Art

The style of the two-figure panel is inexplicable in the context of Anglo-Saxon sculpture or of contemporary Carolingian work, being a more faithful imitation of a Hellenistic style than even the ivories of Charlemagne's reign, in which there is a tendency to over-emphasize the linear element in the folds of classical drapery, at the expense of volume, as on the covers of the Lorsch Gospels (Beckwith, 1964: 38).

The scale of the Breedon panel, as well as its deep-shadowed carving technique, does lead one to think of ivories, but of late Antiquity rather than the Carolingian period. Only a relatively small number of these combine modelling nearly in the round with a delicate, pliant drapery style: the pair of fifth-century panels, possibly from Gaul, in the Louvre, with scenes of six classical poets and their muses, is particularly relevant (Natanson, 1953: fig. 27). Here the figures are carved in the highest possible relief, the limbs and heads being partially or completely undercut; the classical garments are of thin, clinging drapery, revealing the form of the legs, modelled in the round beneath U-shaped folds which on certain of the figures are very close in style to the figure on the right in the Breedon panel, which sports a band of drapery folds at the top of the legs very like those of the girdles worn by two of the Muses, and the little cluster of folds on the right upper arm of the other figure is closely paralleled on the top left-hand Muse (Clio). But despite its classicizing drapery style, the crimped hair of this figure probably reflects a contemporary Anglo-Saxon male fashion seen both on the corbel heads of the broad frieze end blocks and a near contemporary coin of Offa (Jewell, 1986: 109).

The other complete sandstone panel at Breedon measures 62 x 50 cm and is carved in a relief of about 6 cm with a lion *passant guardant* pawing a sinuous stemmed plant, within a chamfered frame (Cramp, 1977: fig. 53b). The surface is weathered, but this detracts little from the bold effect of the carving. Similar panels have not survived in pre-Conquest sculpture elsewhere, but the initial 'I' in the Codex Bigotianus includes a lion in the same heraldic posture within a square panel. The orientalizing paired lions in oval foliate compartments on the broad frieze are its closest relatives at Breedon (Cramp, 1977: fig. 52b), but the style of neither the animal nor the plant find precise parallels there. This panel, therefore, could be later in date. It probably occupied an exterior position in the Anglo-Saxon church; examples can be found in later Continental architecture such as Pomposa Abbey (early eleventh century) of external panels bearing a single 'heraldic' lion. A tenth-century panel from Stara Zagora in Bulgaria (Filow, 1919: pl. 2) has the lion in a recessed frame as at Breedon, and the similarity of format and posture suggests that both were following Byzantine prototypes of a similar kind.

Two other well-known figure sculptures at Breedon, together with related pieces at Peterborough, Fletton and Castor, are of oolitic limestone. All would seem to date from the second half of the eighth and earlier ninth century, although they display a bewildering variety of styles, mixing Late Antique, Byzantine, East Christian and Anglian elements more freely than the sandstone sculpture.

One of the best known is the arched panel at Breedon probably depicting the Virgin Mary (Cramp, 1977: 210, fig. 58a). The prominent veil is like that worn by the Mary of the Hedda Stone, and it has been pointed out that English devotion to Mary seems to have been on the increase in the late eighth century; the church's dedication to St Mary and St Hardulph may well go back this far (Cramp, 1977: 210). But the book has more affinity with images of Christ, the Evangelists and the Apostles than that of the Virgin, and may indicate that the sculptor has confused her attributes. The absence of a nimbus harks back to early Christian and Byzantine art, and there can be little doubt that this was an icon, or cult image of the Virgin; its hieratic frontality indicates such a function and the half-length portrayal follows a convention adopted in some Byzantine icons. An early appearance of the icon in the medium of low relief sculpture is seen in the late sixth- or early seventh-century panels from Hagios Polyeuktos in Istanbul (Harrison, 1989: figs 136–142).

The drapery style, with its system of fine median-incised parallel folds grouped together in gently curving bands, has its origin in

Byzantine art of the seventh century, such as the mosaic of the 630s in Hagios Dimitrios, Salonika (Kitzinger, 1976), showing the patron saint between Bishop John and the Prefect Leontius, whose drapery is particularly similar; while the heavy triangular folds over the Virgin's hand are like those at the hem of the Bishop's cope. The rigidly fixed staring gaze of the Virgin could also derive from Byzantine art, and is seen in the Salonika mosaic; the head of Leontius, it will also be observed, is rather small in proportion to his height and set on broad shoulders, both features of the Breedon Virgin. It seems possible that the sculptor had seen a Byzantine or Italo-Byzantine icon of the seventh century.

Drapery conventions similar to those of the Breedon Virgin panel are used in the Corbie Psalter (Amiens, Bibliothèque Municipale, MS 18, folio 46a), of *c.* 800, which combines eastern with Insular features in its historiated initials (see Porcher, 1965). In sculpture, the St Michael panel at Fletton and the Apostle panel at Breedon come closest in style. A more sharply delineated version is used for the Castor Apostle (Cramp, 1977: Fig. 4.1). With its delicate blend of tender humanism and exquisite linear design, the Castor Apostle is one of the masterpieces of Anglo-Saxon art – a sculptural counterpart of the Barberini Gospels Evangelist portraits, themselves perhaps an East Midlands product of the same period (see Webster, 2000: 67, 68, 69; Bailey, 2000, 43–51; Farr, 2000, 59–61).

The thin dainty hands and feet of the St Michael and the two Apostle figures seem to follow an Anglian convention, with the fingers and toes indicated only by closely spaced incisions, and little attempt at modelling or anatomical realism. Stronger Insular tendencies are explicit in the undersized oval face of the Virgin, with holes for eyes, triangular nose and slit mouth. The disproportionately large right hand, with its elongated fingers, is an expressive feature with many Anglo-Saxon parallels, such as the base of the Bishop Auckland cross of the later eighth century (Kendrick, 1938: pl. 52); or in British Library, Royal MS I.E. vi, f. 43, of the earlier ninth (Alexander, 1978: ill. 161). It is also a recurrent element in the Corbie Psalter figures, as well as occurring in certain Late Antique works (including some Coptic textiles) and in the Utrecht Psalter, itself thought to be inspired by a Late Antique model.

The more classicizing head of the Fletton St Michael with its close-cropped curls resembles examples in contemporary Northumbrian sculpture such as the head of the apostle figure, possibly St Peter, at the top left of the middle block of the Easby cross shaft (Longhurst, 1931: pl. 26.1). The nimbed figure on the much larger and more monumental vertical panel at Fletton (Figure 17.2a), who holds a scroll in his right hand, is markedly different from the St Michael, except as regards his stance and the style of the head. The shoulders are broader, the arms more massive and the feet more naturalistically treated; the drapery style is much closer to the antique, with broader folds across the legs, which are quite distinct from the stylized bands of fine parallel folds which form the drapery of St Michael. Its style is not the delicate Hellenistic classicism of the sandstone figure panel, which seems to have more in common with ivories, or the translation of classical drapery into heavy cylindrical folds, seen in the Breedon angel panel (Figure 17.4), but it is closely akin to Byzantine figural sculpture in stone, like the reliefs on the ends of the fifth-century Sarcophagus of the Prophet Elias (so-called) in the Braccioforte Cemetery, Ravenna (Figure 17.3), which represent the Annunciation (a) and the Visitation (b). The drapery folds in the latter relief are particularly similar, as is the treatment of the feet, which are fully modelled but lacking in surface detail.

The Fletton figure most probably represents a prophet. An early prototype for this panel is seen in the stucco figures of prophets, modelled in low relief, set in pairs flanking the windows of the Baptistry of the Orthodox in Ravenna (*c.* 450). These are given more elaborate architectural frames, but the lively gestures of the figures recall the Fletton Prophet and one of them holds a rolled-up scroll in a similar manner.

The Castor and Breedon apostle panels are fragments of slabs bearing a procession of apostolic figures, based on early Christian sarcophagus frontals. In its use of pilasters as dividers, the Breedon piece can be compared to sarcophagi, e.g. at Toulouse and Rodez, where the Apostles are set in consecutive flat architectural frames (Le Blant, 1886: pls 42a and 22a). Castor, with the figures beneath arches, compares with many earlier sarcophagi, for instance one at Narbonne

(a)   (b)

Figure 17.3 End panel of sarcophagus: **(a)** the Annunciation; **(b)** the Visitation. Ravenna, Braccioforte Cemetery. The Conway Library, Courtauld Institute of Art

where a two-pronged foliate sprig is seen in each of the spandrels, a feature of both the Castor and Hedda Stone arcades (Le Blant, 1886: pl. 43b). A fragment of a roofed monument – although with a flat unornamented pilaster strip divider – is also seen at Bakewell (Cramp, 1977: fig. 60a).

The Fletton frieze blocks bear bust-length figures in the same style as the St Michael, with which they may be contemporary. They are very different in format and style from the Breedon friezes; quite apart from the busts of angels and three other nimbed figures under an arcade, the ornament is full of a whimsical Anglian inventiveness, compared with which the Breedon broad frieze is a model of late antique sobriety. In one panel of the Fletton frieze four peacocks are reduced to mere elements in an abstract symmetrical design; in another a dancing man holds the tails of two bipeds; but most extraordinary of all is the pelta ornament accompanying the angels (Figure 17.2b), in which each of the peltas has been hollowed out to enclose an inner pelta, which in turn wraps itself round a well-modelled bird whose head and body protrude from one end and tail-tip from the other; all this being done with extreme geometrical precision and technical skill: not in the least a 'prickled senseless pattern', and certainly nothing to do with bats (Kendrick, 1938: 177; Cramp, 1977: 211).[1]

When we turn to the famous angel panel in the ringing chamber of the tower at Breedon, we see East Christian art writ large (Figure 17.4). Measuring 93 × 53 cm, it is set high up in the middle of the south wall between two Norman windows, and having been there since the tower was built in the twelfth century, is in very good condition. Like the Virgin panel, it has a pseudo-architectural frame; the plain pilasters are set on triple-stepped bases and have rounded capitals with cups out of which the arch springs. The spandrels are not recessed, the outer edge of the arch being defined only by an incision. The figure is impressively massive, virtually filling the arch with its wings, while the right wing-tip just overlaps the left pilaster. The feathers are summarily indicated by incised lines only on the lower half of this wing. The drapery folds are thick, heavy and tube-like. The head faces half right, but the right ear is treated as if in profile; the eyes are moulded and the pupils are not drilled; the hair, of shoulder length, is formed of heavy bulbous curls bound by a fillet.

The right hand is held out frontally, and the angel gives the Greek form of the blessing. In the left he holds a long staff, its cruciform head having lozenge-shaped arms and fitting into a socket on the end of the staff. Its bottom section, which had a spherical terminal like the Fletton St Michael's, has been broken off. The left foot takes the weight

---

1. The square block at Fletton with symmetrically arranged flat acanthus leaves is of a different stone, has no frame, and is not part of the frieze. It probably dates from late in the tenth century.

Figure 17.4 Relief panel (Archangel Gabriel), Breedon-on-the-Hill. The Conway Library, Courtauld Institute of Art

of the body which leans slightly to the right, a classicizing pose suggesting movement.

On either side of the angel is a conventional plant springing from behind the bases; the straight stems each issue a pair of fleshy hollowed leaves and end in a fully modelled pomegranate. On the left, the leaves emerge from sockets on the side of the stem.

An early prototype for the Breedon angel can be seen in the Archangel Michael on the Constantinopolitan ivory diptych-wing in the British Museum, of *c.* 520. Despite the obvious differences between the drapery styles and architectural frames, there seems to be a general typological connection, and the spatial ambiguities between the figure and its setting are inherent in both.

Closer stylistic affinities can be seen in the more expressionistic ivory panel of the annunciation in the back-rest of Maximian's throne in Ravenna, of the mid-sixth century (see Natanson, 1953: pl. 38). The treatment of the face is decidedly similar and the wings are nearly as sparsely feathered as at Breedon. The Ravenna Gabriel has obvious iconographical links with the Breedon angel: both are stepping forwards and raise their right hand to give the Greek blessing. I would suggest that the Breedon sculptor wished to represent the Angel Gabriel of the Annunciation: a fitting subject for a church dedicated to the Virgin.

The Corbie Psalter (Amiens, Bibliothèque Municipale, MS 18) offers near parallels for the facial type and other details of the Angel panel, the bust of an angel on folio 28b showing a similar treatment of the hair and of the plump, heavily modelled face, with a band under the jaw suggesting a double chin (see Porcher, 1965). On folio 108b, the cruciform staff-head and its method of attachment are noteworthy, and on folio 46a a figure holds a foliate wand which is a close relative of the plants on the panel (Kendrick, 1938: 177; Cramp, 1977: 211). These two plants are symbolic of the angel's heavenly origin; in iconographical terms they are related to the Flowers of Paradise which stud the ground in representations of heavenly scenes, such as on mosaics in San Vitale, Ravenna. Similar conventional flowers with pomegranate-like heads, are used on a Coptic stele of the fifth century in Cairo, with the Madonna and Child in an arched frame, where they spring from behind the bases, as at Breedon (Cecchelli, 1946: 211). In Anglo-Saxon sculpture, pairs of plants are placed beside figures on the ninth-century cross-shafts at Edenham, Lincolnshire, and Newent, Gloucestershire (Clapham, 1930: pl. 21; Kendrick, 1938: pl. 77).

An exact parallel for the plant on the left of the angel in the panel at Breedon is found on a carved architrave block of the sixth century, produced under direct Syrian influence, in S. Giuliano, Spoleto (Serra, 1961: no. 122, pl. 48).[2] Despite their probable Constantinopolitan origin, the stylistic affinities of the Ravenna Annunciation and the other Christological panels in the throne of Maximian also lie with Syria, or possibly Egypt, and it appears to me that the Breedon sculptor used as his model an ivory of mid or later sixth-century date, either from Syria, or from Alexandria under Syrian influence. The drawings of the Corbie Psalter also show Syrian influences, and the parallels between them and the Breedon Angel reflect their mutual interest in earlier models from the Eastern Mediterranean region (Cramp, 1977: 210–11). I would suggest that the angel panel is of much the same date as the Psalter, the very end of the eighth century. None of its features point to a later date, and the details of the arch and the heavy tubular drapery folds betray the hand of the Insular sculptor in a way that looks backwards into the eighth century. This is also a feature of the Corbie Psalter's drapery style.

Another example of this rather ponderous Eastern-inspired

---

2. Serra dates the architrave block to the seventh to eighth centuries.

sculpture is the small panel in Peterborough Cathedral bearing two standing figures under a double arch (Cramp, 1977: fig. 58b). They each hold a staff, and their conical hats, frequently seen also in the Corbie Psalter (ff. 87b, 110b and 138b; Henry, 1974: fig. 71), may indicate that they represent Eastern ecclesiastical dignitaries. Their faces are much worn, but the little drill-holes of the eyes, and the slits indicating the mouths – both of which are also features of the Breedon Virgin and Castor Apostle – are just visible.

The shaft between the two figures is square in section, with a triangular capital supporting the solid spandrel between the arched recesses in which the figures stand. From the insides of the arches, where they spring from the capital, emerge two fleshy drooping stems ending in frond leaves; similar drooping stems, also ending in frond leaves, spring from halfway down the shaft on either side, and are gripped by the figures.

The detail of the stems ending in pointed leaves hanging down from a triangular capital is closely paralleled in the Book of Kells (Dublin, Trinity College Library, MS 58, f. 4a; Henry, 1974: pl. 7). The origin of this curious detail lies in Syria, where the triangle, often arranged in tiers (as in the Book of Kells) is a motif encountered in both architecture and sculpture.[3] Françoise Henry (1974: 215–16) has discussed the close points of contact in their ornament between the Corbie Psalter and the Book of Kells which both date from *c.* 800. It is most probable that the Peterborough panel is also of this date.

A small sandstone figure panel fragment at Breedon, not yet mentioned, is of great interest[4] (Figure 17.5a). At its base is a broad roll-moulded frame; on it is set a rectangular plinth the face of which is divided, by double line incisions, into two squares with crossing diagonal single line incisions. Standing on the plinth was a figure, whose right lower leg and left foot alone survive; the carving is cut back to a depth of about 5 cm. The right leg, which is seen sideways on, is finely carved and naturalistically rounded, with a slim ankle; the damaged left foot, perched on the corner of the plinth on the right-hand side, and projecting beyond the top edge, is seen frontally and points downwards. A short section of the hem of the figure's knee-length tunic is seen at the top of the fragment; of its front, a deep-shadowed S-shaped fold survives; the back of the hem with a straight edge, and gently undulating surface, is seen behind and below this.

Resting on the base on the left, beside the plinth, is a pot of spherical shape with a double-ribbed neck; around its waist are three incised lines. The neck overlaps another pot immediately above, of similar type but having only two incised lines at the waist.

---

3. Cf. the low relief carving on a seventh-century window valve in the Damascus Museum, no. 14108.
4. Apparently unpublished, this intriguing little piece is set in a lead-lined recess in the South wall of the South aisle, close to other fragments. Possibly it came to light during restoration work in 1959, like the Apostle panel.

Figure 17.5 (a) Panel fragment: miracle at Cana. Breedon-on-the-Hill. **(b)** Ivory panel: miracle at Cana © Courtesy of the Board of Trustees of the Victoria and Albert Museum

The stance of the feet – one in profile, the other frontal and downward pointing – reminds us of the Breedon angel, and the drapery fold is treated similarly to the edges of the hem in this panel, which likewise appear to hang lower at the back than the front.

The pots, or wine jars, give us a hint that we are dealing with a representation of the Cana Miracle. This subject, of frequent occurrence in early Christian art, appears on one of the ninth-century cross-shaft fragments at Dewsbury in Yorkshire, but this carving is of quite a different order with a strongly provincial style (Baldwin Brown, 1937: 181 f., pl. 48). The composition is crowded to fit into a narrow panel on the shaft and has no basis in early Christian models. In contrast, the carving on the Breedon fragment is classicizing in style and of high quality. The leg and the wine jars show a grasp of volumetric modelling as impressive as the Breedon two-figure panel. There is a strong possibility that this, too, was based on an ivory carving, although perhaps of later date, as the ivory of the Cana Miracle which provides the closest parallel for the carving technique of the leg and drapery in the Breedon fragment is the small panel in the Victoria and Albert Museum (Figure 17.5b). In his study of the group of ivories to which it belongs, Weitzmann (1972) assigned it to about the middle of the eighth century, from Syria, Palestine or Egypt.

From the similarity in the stance of his right leg and left foot (partially hidden by the pots as at Breedon), the water-pourer on the left in the ivory could well suggest a reconstruction of the figure in the Breedon fragment, along similar lines, but facing the other way. The spherical pots, or jars, in the fragment are quite unlike the stemmed vases in this ivory. They are more closely paralleled in the Andrews Diptych, which is sometimes dated to the fifth century, where the jars in the Cana scene have the same rotund bodies with double line incisions as at Breedon (Volbach, 1976: no. 233, pl. 108). If the Breedon panel is of the early ninth century as I would suggest, then it is of great significance as the only example of this subject in Anglo-Saxon sculpture. Moreover, it, along with other examples from Sandbach, Dewsbury, Rothbury, Masham, and Bakewell, provides further evidence of ambitious narrative relief for this period in England (see also Hawkes, Chapter 16 in this volume).

Biblical narrative sculpture is rare in Mercia, one other example, quite different in style, being the Wirksworth slab, with its crowded jumble of New Testament scenes executed in sub-Northumbrian fashion in the late eighth century (Hawkes, 1995a). But no account of Classicism in Southumbria could omit the Reculver cross fragments, and here there is an Ascension with a very close iconographical parallel on an early Christian ivory (Kozodoy, 1986: 67–8, pl. 33a); also the lower portions of apostle figures whose drapery forms a cascade of frilly folds on either side and diagonally across the legs – a feature also convincingly paralleled on another fifth-century ivory of an apostle and in Carolingian copies of early Christian ivories such as the Lorsch Gospels book covers (Victoria and Albert Museum, 1963: pl. 2; Beckwith, 1964: pl. 3). The comparisons suggest that Reculver presents rather small-scale versions in stone of small-scale sculptures in ivory – precisely as in the Cana fragment, broad frieze and related two-figure panel at Breedon (the angel is on a larger scale), and done at much the same date. The carving is good, but no better than much contemporary sculpture in Northumbria and Mercia. It is not alone in imitating Mediterranean models, because examples of eighth- and ninth-century Anglo-Saxon Classicism survive at Easby, Otley, Breedon, Fletton, and elsewhere.

Generally, the Reculver drapery style is not similar to the Mercian/ Anglian group, but the Fletton Prophet, with its fifth-century Ravennate forebears, appears not so far removed in this respect if compared with the angel fragment (Kozodoy, 1986: pl. 34c). However, it is not the figure style that fixes the Reculver fragments in the earlier ninth century, but the foliage of the scroll surrounding the busts on one surviving piece (Kozodoy, 1986: pl. 36d). Despite dating it early, Kendrick (1938) pointed out the similarity of the leaves on the inside of the volutes to Britford, itself based on North Italian sculpted examples of foliage of the late eighth and ninth centuries. Nonetheless, as Tweddle and Budny have realized, the real clincher is the pointed leaf turned under its own stem (Tweddle *et al.*, 1995: 55–6).

Combining classicizing busts with such a scroll at this date must be a manifestation of that Anglo-Saxon inventiveness in its handling of earlier models so often seen in the Breedon frieze, where the birds and animals transcend the merely decorative and become almost living creatures – even the centaur with wings on his shoulders, and at Fletton, where early Christian birds are wrapped in peltas, and the resulting zoo-geometrical ornament used as an accompaniment to the busts of classicizing angels on the same scale, almost blending with their wings.

Dating of the sculpture at Breedon and in the Peterborough area is necessarily conjectural, although accurately dated comparative material in some cases makes it less so. But I believe it is possible to attempt a chronological sequence for the group on the basis of style, assigning the various sculptures to notional decades, thus:

1. Hedda Stone and Gandersheim Casket, *c.* 770–80
2. Breedon, Apostle, and Castor, Apostle, *c.* 780–790
3. Breedon, friezes, two-figure panel and angel, and Peterborough, two-figure panel, *c.* 800–10
4. Fletton, 'Prophet', *c.* 810–20
5. Fletton, St Michael and friezes, and Breedon Virgin, *c.* 820–30

In conclusion, during much of the period under discussion in this chapter, *c.* 770–830 (i.e. from early in Offa's reign till the end of the Mercian Supremacy), the Classicism of Southumbrian sculpture parallels and is coeval with – but is rarely dependent on – the Carolingian Renaissance; often using the same fifth- to sixth-century source material, although evincing a greater interest in East Christian decorative art, and always eschewing acanthus ornament in favour of Syrian-derived plant scrolls.

The real Anglo-Carolingian style is the Winchester style of the tenth and eleventh centuries. Like its Continental model, it excels mainly in miniatures and ivories rather than sculpture. As a fitting postscript to this survey, it is pleasing to note the finest surviving example of Winchester-style decorative sculpture on the Wolverhampton Column, in the Mercian heartland (Cramp, 1975: 187–9, pls 16, 17). In some ways this is a tenth-century successor to the Breedon friezes, and, like them, has no sculptural parallels in the South of England.

18 Metalwork of the Mercian Supremacy

Leslie Webster

In marked contrast to the profuse and independently dated Anglo-Saxon metalwork of the seventh and later ninth centuries, apart from a very few major items, metalwork of the eighth and early ninth centuries has received comparatively little attention in art-historical surveys of the period, despite some honourable exceptions, such as Brøndsted (1924), Smith (1924), Bakka (1963), and Wilson (1964).[1] This was a period of exceptional absorption of, and experimentation in, new-wave Mediterranean and Oriental influences, as the many surveys of the high art of sculpture and manuscript decoration of this period demonstrate.[2] The restlessly inventive and often playful decoration of manuscripts such as the Tiberius group, and the Barberini Gospels, or of the Castor and Breedon sculptures characterize a new excitement in adapting orientalizing styles such as the interlaced plant and animal decoration of Lombard Italy,[3] and a more illusionistic classicizing style of figural representation, to the established traditions of Insular animal and abstract curvilinear art. Though many of the same stylistic traits are equally evident in the minor arts of metalwork and bone and ivory carving, their smaller scale rarely permits great complexity, and perhaps partly for this reason, they have attracted less attention. A further inhibiting factor in discussion of this group has been the significant lack of secure chronological pegs on which to hang theories of development and dissemination – it is a melancholy fact that not a single eighth-century coin hoard contains decorated metalwork, and indeed, that there is no independently datable piece of metalwork between the late seventh-century composite brooch from Boss Hall, Ipswich (from a coin-dated burial with a terminus post quem of 690)

---

1. Wilson (1964: 9–21); and see also Webster and Backhouse (1991: 220–39).
2. For example, Bruce-Mitford (1967: 797–825), Plunkett (1998a).
3. For this kind of exemplar, see *Il Futuro dei Langobardi: l'Italia e la costruzione dell'Europa di Carlo Magno* (2000), especially Chapter 6, 'L'Italie dei ducati Langobardi', pp. 229–99; and J. Mitchell, 'L'Italia e l'Inghilterra anglo-sassone', pp. 402–13.

and the Æthelwulf ring, for which the earliest possible date is 828 (Webster and Backhouse, 1991: 51–3; Wilson, 1964: 5–9).

Equally, the very portability of metalwork and bone carvings makes the identification of politico-regional styles, or attribution to individual monastic houses, a rather more speculative issue than it is with the theoretically less mobile medium of sculpture (though of course sculptors could and did move around as readily as any portable bone carving or metal book-fitting) or even manuscripts; in both these fields, a framework of art-historical attribution has been constructed by major studies on schools and *Schriftprovinzen*, in ways which till recently were hardly possible with metalwork.[4] Moreover, the reconciliation of art-historical evidence with political or religious contexts and events is a delicate issue at the best of times, and it is certainly a wise rule that evidence needs independent evaluation before attempting any integration with historical data.[5] In such constrained conditions, it should perhaps not surprise that few have negotiated a more detailed engagement with this fluid and seemingly intractable body of material.

As a result of all these factors, those who wish to arrive at a definition of Mercian metalwork will have to search in some unexpected places, since some of the most significant discussion of this topic occurs as peripheral comment in studies of sculpture and manuscripts. One searches in vain in Mercian Studies (Dornier, 1977a) for any essay on metalwork alongside those on manuscripts and sculpture; however, several perceptive and significant comments on metalwork are embedded in Rosemary Cramp's chapter on schools of Mercian sculpture in that volume. Equally Richard Jewell (1982 and 1986) and Steven Plunkett (1998a and 1998b) have made valuable observations on other genres including metalwork and bone carvings in their recent contributions to the study of Mercian sculpture. Conversely, Egil Bakka's groundbreaking study (Bakka, 1963) reviews with many important insights a whole range of highly relevant metalwork from the alienated context of Norwegian Viking graves, most of which he barely attributes, since it can only be located in its country of origin with considerable circumspection. Earlier and broader studies such as those of Smith (1924), Kendrick (1938: 164–78) and Bruce-Mitford (1967), display some reluctance to sufficiently distinguish the scope and characteristics of what they categorize as 'Mercian', or the overlapping but not coterminous 'Anglian' and 'Southumbrian' styles from 'Northumbrian' style, or to address the crucial question of how these can be identified in terms of portable decorated items. The kind of outcome which may ensue from lack of precision in defining such terms is to be seen in the attribution of

---

4. See, for example, Kendrick (1938), Cramp (1977), Alexander (1978), Jewell (1982 and 1986), Bailey (1990), Webster and Backhouse (1991: 195–220), Brown, M. (1996: 22–3, 162–78) and elsewhere in this volume.
5. See for example, the observations of Mac Lean (1998: 185) and Wilson (1964: 5–9, 12–14).

the closely related Ormside bowl and Bischofshofen cross to North-umbria, quite possibly because of the bowl's Cumbrian findspot (e.g. Kendrick, 1938: 150–1; Bruce-Mitford, 1967: 782; and see further below); yet, as Bakka observed, the bowl's closest affinities lie much further south, in central Mercia (Bakka, 1963: 58). Craftsmen as well as artefacts travel, and the eighth century was clearly a period of considerable cultural flux (Henderson, 1998; Plunkett, 1998a), further complicating an already complex scenario of stylistic identity and transmission; nevertheless, even the rather ragged impression of the evidence that may be gleaned from the literature suggests the existence of a core of metalwork (and bone carving) which may be related to a regional, and in a few cases, particular ecclesiastical, context.

This situation, in which pointers to localization were noted,[6] but firm characterization of a metalwork style and its ascription to a

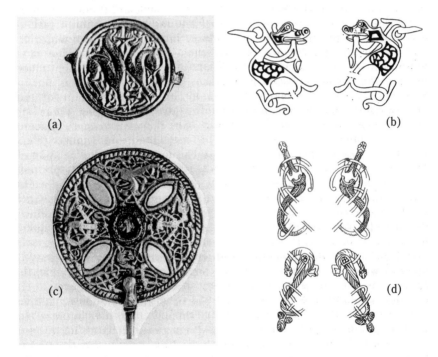

Figure 18.1 Mercian beasts: (a) brooch, Flixborough, Lincs. (a) and (c) © the Trustees of the British Museum; (b) details, brooch from the Pentney, Norfolk, hoard (drawing C. Miller); (c) detail, linked pin-set, R. Witham at Fiskerton, Lincs; (d) details, Gandersheim Casket (drawing, L. Webster). Not to scale

6. As, for example, in Kendrick's typically acute perception of a fen-edge stylistic milieu, even though he rather separated this from his sculpture-centred discussion of Mercian style (Kendrick, 1938: 168–71).

'Mercian' orbit were always difficult, is now changing. The last few years have seen important advances, both in a dramatically increased available volume of data, and in our understanding of its distribution. Some of this is the product of controlled excavation on high-status, sometimes religious, sites such as those at Brandon, Suffolk, and Flixborough, N. Lincs. (see Figures 18.1 and 2); a very few major finds have been discovered by chance, such as the Pentney hoard, which was found by a grave-digger (Webster and Backhouse, 1991: 229–31) (Figure 18.8); but the crucial factor has undoubtedly been the explosion of metal detecting as a hobby. The numismatists were the first to acknowledge the significant benefits to study of plotting the numerous stray finds (mostly detected) of Anglo-Saxon pennies, especially the secondary *sceatta* series, the current coinage for much of the eighth century. We now know that these were struck in over 20 mints, from Southampton to York, in at least seven regions, and using some 5,000 dies (Metcalf, 1994: 315). The radically altered picture of the nature of the economic infrastructure and scale of organization implied by all this activity not only shows how a similarly systematic approach to the finds of non-numismatic metalwork might produce equally interesting results; it also has implications for our under-standing of the mechanisms whereby other kinds of decorated artefacts were produced and distributed – not least because a number of the motifs used on this coinage are very closely related to equivalents in other media, especially to metalwork and manuscript art (Webster, 2001). There is much yet to be understood in this sphere; but despite the fact that not all detected finds can be reliably plotted, and that there is a degree of lowland zone bias inherent in the areas routinely detected,[7] the mapping of these individual metalwork stray finds is beginning to substantiate in a very striking way the existence of what may with increasing confidence be termed a Mercian stylistic province.

At the same time, fresh opportunities have recently arisen to survey and evaluate the field; first of all, the paper from which this review has arisen was given in its original version at the session on Mercian Art organized by Michelle Brown and Carol Farr at the Leeds International Medieval Conference in 1997; and more recently two other forums held in Germany in 1999 have provided further valuable opportunities for revisiting aspects of Mercian art in the light of new material, and for discussion (see Webster, 2001; and Webster, 2000; Bailey, 2000; Farr, 2000). What follows here will therefore summarize my main conclu-sions set out in these two papers, to which the curious are referred for detailed analysis and illustration of style vocabulary, and comparisons with similar elements in sculpture and manuscript art of this period.

The principal elements of this style as seen in metalwork, and variously categorized as Anglian or Mercian, consist of a range of

---

7. That is, south and east of a diagonal line drawn from the Tees to the Exe.

animal, plant and abstract motifs, combined together in a fairly consistent set of variations. Dominant in this vocabulary are spright-ly birds and beasts, often in opposed pairs, which prance, step, perch or writhe, sometimes in interlace, or among the twining stems and berry bunches of vines and other plants. Some beasts are clearly playful quadrupeds or bipeds, with pricked ears, grinning jaws and lolling tongues, as on brooches from Flixborough, N. Lincs., and Pentney, Norfolk, or the high-stepping beasts on some of the west Norfolk-centred series Q *sceattas* (Metcalf, 1994: 483–501, pl. 23); others are lizard-like, with scaly bodies and gripping hands, like creatures on one of the R. Witham, Lincs., pins and on the Gandersheim Casket; all may have pricked or furled wings, or more conventional animal bodies (Figure 18.1). The birds are equally sportive, striding and prancing as vigorously as the beasts; occasionally human and other hybrids also occur, as on the Gandersheim Casket and one of the Brandon, Suffolk, pins (Figure 18.2). The interlace and plants in which these creatures clamber or are entrammelled are composed of slender meshes and tendrils, with elegantly pointed or trefoiled leaves and delicately modelled berry clusters. Even at its least accomplished, as on the Leicester brooch or the Asby Winderwath plaque (Webster and Backhouse, 1991: 228–9; Youngs, 1999), this is a refined, lively, even teasing style, in which a sometimes serious iconographic content (as on the Bischofshofen cross, the Gandersheim Casket and the Asby Winderwath plaque)[8] is still framed with the lightest of touches.

Animal heads as a theme on their own are also very prominent in this style; whether as playful grinning volutes on many kinds of artefact from pin-heads and brooches to the Gandersheim Casket and the Bischofshofen cross (Figure 18.3), or as shovel-snouted or fanged gapers and gnashers which are particularly (though by no means exclusively) seen on weapon fittings such as the Beckley pommel and Fetter Lane, London, hilt, the Thames scabbard mount, and the St Ninians Isle chapes and pommel (Figures 18.6a, 18.4a and b). Hiberno-Saxon elements also play a part in this mélange, as they do in Mercian manuscript art and in sculpture;[9] sometimes in the spiral hip joints of shovel-snouted creatures of the kind just mentioned, as on two dies, one from Canterbury, one from Lincolnshire (Figure 18.4a, c, d); sometimes less obviously, as on the Fetter Lane pommel, on the Asby Winderwath plaque, and in the whirling triskeles seen on some of the secondary *sceattas*, such as the series L23a London mint type (Metcalf, 1994: 451–2). This motif, along with key pattern and other abstract ornament occasionally seen in metalwork, has long since ceased to have an exclusively Hiberno-Saxon or Northumbrian resonance, and has become adopted into the mainstream art of Southumbrian culture.

---

8. See, for a discussion of this, Elbern (1990), Youngs (1999) and Webster (2000).
9. For example, in the Vespasian Psalter, the Stockholm Codex Aureus and the Barberini Gospels, all at the very least with Mercian associations, and the last very probably made at a centre such as Peterborough.

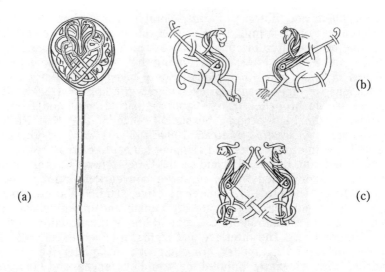

Figure 18.2 Mercian birds and human hybrids: (a) pin, Brandon, Suffolk (drawing, Suffolk Archaeological Unit); (b) bird details, Gandersheim Casket; (c) human hybrids, Gandersheim Casket (drawings, b and c, L. Webster). Not to scale

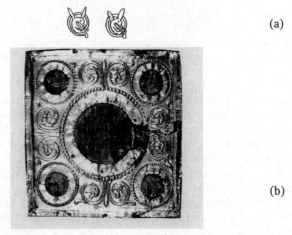

Figure 18.3 Animal-headed volutes: (a) details of metal mounts, Gandersheim Casket (drawing, L. Webster); (b) details from Bischofshofen cross (photograph, O. Anrather). Not to scale

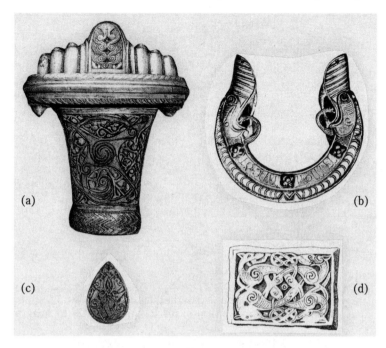

Figure 18.4 Shovel-snouts and swirling joints: (a) sword hilt, Fetter Lane, London; (b) scabbard chape, St Ninians Isle hoard (photographs (a), (b) © the Trustees of the British Museum; (c) die, Canterbury, Courtesy of Dr M. O. Budny; (d) die, Lincolnshire (drawing, Department of Culture, Media and Sport). Not to scale

When the provenanced metalwork (and bone carving) of this kind that we can currently identify is plotted (Map 10), a very striking distribution begins to emerge. It should moreover be borne in mind that what appears on this rather primitive map is not only the tip of a large iceberg of unreported or unprovenanced items, but is already out of date at the time of writing, and will be still more so by the time this is published. From the north side of the Thames at London up to the Humber, a style province of metalwork items begins to take shape, with (as Kendrick long ago observed on the basis of far fewer items) a marked concentration around the Fen edge, and in the east midlands – not only right in the Mercian heartland, but, as Richard Bailey, Steven Plunkett and others have stressed, an area dominated ecclesiastically by Peterborough, its daughter foundations such as Breedon, and other religious centres such as that at Brandon, Suffolk (Plunkett, 1998a: 204–5; Bailey, 2000). Beyond the core area, a few finds extend the range into southern Northumbria, with provenances such as Pontefract, Market Weighton and hardly surprisingly, the major ecclesiastical and political centre and emporium of York. Beyond this, the very

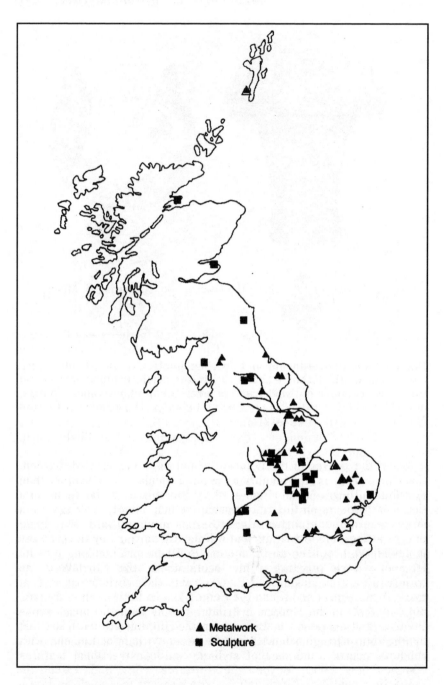

Map 10 Distribution of finds of eighth- to early-ninth-century zoomorphic metalwork and sculpture (map, L. Webster)

Figure 18.5 Extended drawings, the Ormside bowl (drawing C. Miller)

rare outliers become, as things tend to when further away from the point of origin, more extraordinary. The Asby Winderwath plaque, from a high-status settlement way up in the Cumbrian Pennines is possibly a local – but quite faithful – imitation of the style, given that its form recalls Hiberno-Saxon and Irish mounts of similar shape (Youngs, 1999). The lonely disc-headed pin recently excavated within the monastic site at Hartlepool (Daniels *et al.*, 1997) may also represent a simplified local version of a type well represented at Flixborough, Brandon, and elsewhere within the core area. More interesting, however, is the case of the Ormside, Cumbria, bowl, often described, as we have seen, as Northumbrian, on no particular grounds other than tradition and provenance (Figure 18.5). But this item was found in a grave in the churchyard at Ormside, which clearly belongs to a northern group of Viking furnished burials in churchyards;[10] it could therefore have come to this resting place from far afield, and very likely did. While it is certain that some Southern orientalizing stylistic influences were reaching a few sculptors in the North-West, as Rosemary Cramp has shown is the case with the nearby cross-shaft at Dacre, Cumbria (Bailey and Cramp, 1988: 90–1), the stylistic affiliations of the bowl place it firmly not only with the mischievous animal frieze sculptures at Breedon-on the-Hill, but also with the lost eighth-century hanging bowl from the River Witham at Lincoln, with which it shares a number of stylistic and constructional features

---

10. As, for example, similar burials at Wensley, North Yorkshire, and Repton, Derbyshire. See *From Viking to Crusader: Scandinavia and Europe 800–1200* (1992: 318–19).

(Wilson, 1964: pl. 2c; Webster and Backhouse, 1991: 172–3). Bakka's suggestion, mentioned above, that it is a Southumbrian product is surely correct (Bakka, 1963: 57–8); and if this is the case, then with it must also go the great Anglo-Saxon altar cross now at Bischofshofen near Salzburg, which is stylistically extremely close (Webster and Backhouse, 1991: 170–3). That other most famous Anglo-Saxon export to the continent, the Gandersheim Casket, can also now be more precisely located within a Mercian context (Marth, 2000). The much disputed (and secondary) inscription on the base which may or may not refer to Ely led Kendrick and others to assign the Casket confidently to this region (Kendrick, 1938: 169–70); more recently, Richard Jewell, Steven Plunkett and Richard Bailey (Jewell, 1982: Chapter 6, note 7; Plunkett, 1998a: 211; Bailey, 2000) have independently proposed an origin at the Anglo-Saxon monastic foundation at Peterborough, based on a detailed comparison with sculpture from Peterborough itself and from its daughter houses at Breedon, Fletton, and Castor. The identification of this object as a chrismal, and its highly complex exegetic programme may lend further credence to this suggestion (Webster, 2000). It may be added that the elegant and elaborate decoration not only of the whale bone panels from which it is constructed, but also of the metal frame which holds the panels together, is wholly consistent with the vocabulary of other metalwork (and indeed the lone piece of bone carving)[11] found within the Mercian area.

The most extreme and northerly spot on the map represents the two chapes and sword pommel from the St Ninians Isle, Shetland, hoard of Pictish and other silver. These have always been regarded as strongly influenced by Anglo-Saxon metalwork (Wilson, 1973: 58–60, 64–76, 120–1, 137–40; Webster and Backhouse, 1991: 223–4), but the more recent discovery of the elaborately decorated sword pommel found within an Anglo-Saxon royal domain near Beckley, Oxon., and of a pyramidal sword fitting from near Bawtry, Notts., both significantly related in style to the St Ninians hoard sword fittings, casts a new light on these pieces (Figures 18.6a and b). A visible Mercian influence on some major items of eighth-century Pictish sculpture has long been argued by Isabel Henderson and others (Henderson, 1967: 150–7; 1994: 81; Plunkett, 1998a), suggesting direct contact between Mercia and Pictland; high-status trappings such as these sword fittings might have been a very likely diplomatic gift from a Mercian king such as Æthelbald (716–757), who is recorded as having had dealings with his powerful Pictish contemporary, Oengus son of Fergus (d.761). Whatever the mechanisms by which Mercian art styles and – if the new parallels from Mercia's heartland convince – Mercian artefacts came to Pictland, the evidence of both sculpture and metalwork suggests that these contacts were more than casual.

---

11. A whalebone panel fragment from Larling, Norfolk. See Webster and Backhouse (1991: 179).

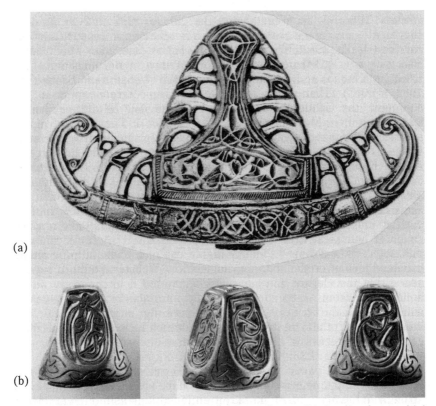

Figure 18.6 (a) Sword pommel, Beckley area, Oxon.; (b) details of pyramidal sword fitting, Bawtry, Notts. Scale 1:1 © the Trustees of the British Museum

In general, and despite some degree of overlap, a picture emerges from this exercise of a significant divide between metalwork south and north of the Humber, and of the Thames. For a start, there is altogether less eighth-century metalwork beyond these limits, a factor which cannot be entirely due to the differential activities of detectorists, since some of these areas are rich in retrieved finds of eighth-century coins, and of ninth- and tenth-century metal artefacts. We may also consider, despite their relative paucity, the much more Hiberno-Saxon style of contemporary decorated metal artefacts retrieved from Northumbrian contexts such as Dundrennan, Dumfries., Hartlepool, Whitby and York (see Webster and Backhouse, 1991: 137, 141–2), compared with the metalwork here identified as Mercian. The York helmet, for instance, has an inscription in Hiberno-Saxon display capitals, recording a name, Oshere, which would not have looked out of place on a contemporary Northumbrian king-list; its fiercely grinning animal heads on the eyebrows and lateral and rear ends of the crest, as Tweddle has shown, are much closer to eighth-century Hiberno-Saxon metalwork and manuscript equivalents than they are to examples from contemporary metalwork and manuscripts ascribed to the Southern or Mercian groups (Tweddle, 1992: 1140: Figs 569–70). The same can be said of the head seen from above at the front end of the crest (Tweddle, 1992: 1154: Fig. 577). The zoomorphic decoration on the nasal has close correspondences with the decoration of the unlocalized, but very possibly Northumbrian, St Petersburg Gospels, and the robust, compact and extremely regular interlace into which the animals dissolve, distinguished by a median line, has more in common with the compact and solid interlace of eighth-century Northumbrian sculpture, such as that on the Abercorn cross-shaft (Cramp, 1984: pl. 266), than with the lighter, less disciplined, interlace associated with entwining animals seen in the art of Southumbria (e.g. Tweddle, 1992: Fig. 429, and Figs 579, 580). A similar emphasis on geometric rigour, and some tendency towards covering surfaces with abstract motifs such as interlace and key pattern also seem more pronounced in these finds than in the southern group, where interlace and animals seem to cohabit on a more regular and equal basis. Only a few outliers decorated in this style occur in southern contexts – the predominantly interlace-decorated tweezers from Reculver, for example, a Northumbrian origin for which is supported by its animal head terminals, which have the characteristic comma-shaped ears of the Northern strap-end group (Webster and Backhouse, 1991: 233; Thomas, 1996: 81–2).

But what is particularly revealing about the mapping of this metalwork is its negative distribution, rather than its presence. For apart from the few outliers already mentioned, this kind of metalwork is virtually unknown, not only in Northumbria, but even more strikingly, in Wessex and in Kent, where penetration is almost non-existent.[12] As noted above, this cannot be to any significant degree the product of differential detecting, as contemporary coins as well as ninth- and tenth-century metalwork have been found in considerable quantity in these areas. Even more revealing, however, is the comparison of this distribution with the area defined by the itineraries of the Mercian kings, as mapped by David Hill (Hill, 1981: map 145); if this is further compared with the equivalent map of the itineraries of the kings of Wessex (Hill, 1981: map 146), the boundary between the two kingdoms is as plain to see, as is the stark divide in the distribution of the contemporary metalwork. All of this, and the striking correlation with the distribution of closely related sculpture (Cramp, 1977: Fig. 49; Plunkett, 1998b), confirm beyond reasonable doubt the origin of this distinctive metalwork within the greater Mercian kingdom.

A related issue deserves consideration in this context of a

---

12. I know of only one piece in this style from south of the Thames – the die from Canterbury (Budny and Graham-Campbell (1981); Webster and Backhouse (1991: 222)).

geographically defined Mercian stylistic zone; namely, the relationship of eighth- and early ninth-century Mercian metalwork to the emergent Trewhiddle style. This distinctive style, named after the hoard of coins and decorated silver artefacts deposited at Trewhiddle, Cornwall, *c.* 868, dominated metalwork from Wessex to Northumbria throughout much of the ninth century, and is clearly related to decoration in manuscripts of the so-called Tiberius Group, notably the Tiberius Bede (B.L. Cotton MS Tiberius C.ii) and the Royal Bible (B.L. Royal MS 1 E.vi),[13] both dated within the second quarter of the ninth century. It is characterized by a use of small discrete fields, usually set in beaded borders, containing combinations of frisky, often speckled, animals, leafy plant scrolls and geometric motifs, all usually reserved against a niello background. It has long been recognized that, in a general sense, these elements can all be traced back to the Mercian stylistic tradition outlined above. Its geographical and chronological ranges, however, are very different; objects decorated in the style abound in areas where Mercian metalwork barely or never penetrated, such as Wessex and Kent; and it appears wholly to supersede the Hiberno-Saxon tradition in Northumbria. The Trewhiddle style's occurrence in a number of hoards and other closely dated contexts between (possibly) 828/839 and 875 also suggests that its heyday was centred on the middle third of the ninth century, when it was certainly favoured by the Wessex royal family, as exemplified by the surviving rings associated with the names of King Æthelwulf (839–858) and his daughter Æthelswith (853–874) (Figures 18.7a, b).[14]

The discovery in 1977 of the hoard of six silver disc brooches at Pentney, Norfolk, has, however, suggested that the origins of this style are more intimately associated than had been suspected with the Mercian animal style seen on some of these brooches (Webster and Backhouse, 1991: 229–31) (see Figure 18.8). This hoard contains two pairs of brooches and two singletons, all but the smallest apparently

 (a)  (b)

Figure 18.7 Rings associated with (a) King Æthelwulf of Wessex and (b) his daughter, Queen Æthelswith of Mercia © the Trustees of the British Museum.

13. See Wilson and Blunt (1961), Wilson (1964: esp. 25–7), Wilson (1984: 94–6) and Budny (1985: 780, 785–7).
14. These rings might indeed have been made to commemorate two royal marriages: that of Æthelwulf to Judith, Charles the Bald's daughter in 856, and Æthelswith's to Burgred of Mercia in 853.

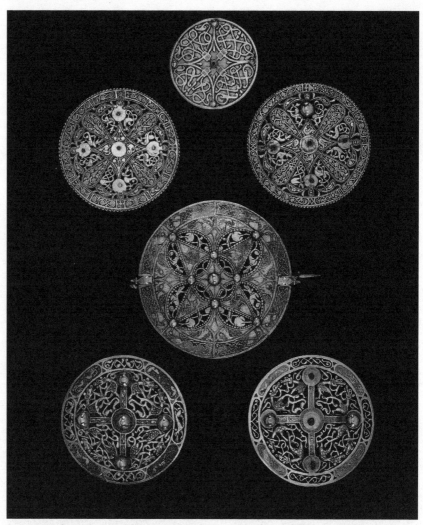

Figure 18.8 Hoard of six disc brooches from Pentney, Norfolk © the Trustees of the British Museum

unworn, suggesting that the others may therefore be contemporary. The smallest brooch belongs to the late eighth century, and has plant ornament in the Mercian tradition, and the largest brooch is in fully-fledged Trewhiddle style; but the two pairs contain elements of both styles, most strikingly on the second pair of openwork brooches, where the larger central beasts are metalwork versions of the rampant beasts familiar from Mercian sculpture, and the smaller animals in the border cartouches are pure Trewhiddle style, some indeed very similar in detail to animals in the Royal Gospels canon tables (Figure 18.9). On

Figure 18.9 Brooch from the Pentney, Norfolk, hoard (drawing, C. Miller).

stylistic grounds, this combination thus seems likely to date to the first third of the ninth century; no coins were associated with the hoard, but one possible context for burial might be the first Viking raids in East Anglia, in the 840s. Shared distinctive traits with other Trewhiddle-style pieces from around the Wash also suggest that these brooches could have been made in that region, where, as we have already noted, there is a concentration of eighth- and early ninth-century metalwork in the Mercian style. This striking assemblage, perhaps significantly buried at the very time that Mercia's power was on the wane (Hart, 1977: 56–7), seems to belong to the cusp of the transition from the earlier Mercian style to its more widespread and dominant successor.

Thus, in a sense, the Pentney brooches both represent the apogee and the aftermath of this distinctive, high-status metalwork style, and its geographical heartland. No doubt future discoveries, large and small, will amplify and sharpen this picture; but I believe that the current evidence allows us at last with some confidence to speak of a Mercian style province for this metalwork, as much as for its parallels in other media.

Acknowledgements

The author would like to thank the following for their help and inspiration during the gestation of this chapter: Richard Bailey, Michelle Brown, Carol Farr, James Graham-Campbell, Richard Jewell, Kevin Leahy, Steven Plunkett, Sue Youngs, Egon Wamers and David Wilson.

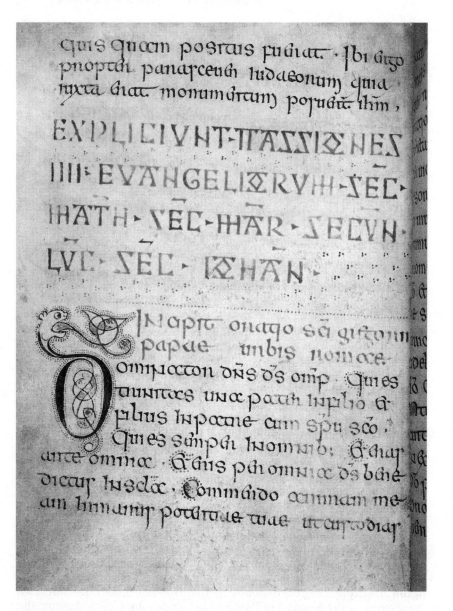

quis quam postuis puduat. Ibi ergo
propter panarceuch ludaeonum quia
iuxta diat monumétum posuert ihm,

EXPLICIVHT·PASSIØHES
IIII·EVAHGELIØRVH·SĒC·
IHĀTH·SĒC·MĀR·SECVH·
LVC·SĒC·IØHĀN·

INapit onatio sā grego̅n̅
papae unbis nomoce
Omnipoten dn̅s d̅s omp. Qui es
trinitas una patth lupho et
plius lupocone cun s̅p̅u s̅c̅o̅;
Qui es sunpdi luomnib; et chay
ante omnaa. et gus pdi omnaa d̅s bne-
dicatur lusdic. Commendo animam me-
am lin amp potestate tuae ut anytodiay

Figure 19.1 Book of Nunnaminster, London, B.L. Harley MS 2965, f. 16v
© The British Library. Courtesy of the British Library Board.

19 Mercian Manuscripts? The 'Tiberius' Group and Its Historical Context

Michelle P. Brown

The elusive nature of a Mercian 'identity' is reflected in the hesitancy and dispute which pervade discussions concerning the attribution of manuscripts to its monastic scriptoria.[1] This circumspection may mirror the fragmented picture of the historical development of this undoubtedly important but equally enigmatic 'kingdom'. Sandwiched between the 'golden ages' of Bede's Northumbria and the Wessex of Alfred and his successors, the intervening period has been comparatively neglected and only recently has it begun to be recognized as an important phase during which the achievements of the Insular world were consolidated and transmitted to the new order of tenth-century England, even in the face of political and military upheaval. It has long been observed by historians that stability is not a prerequisite of cultural achievement. It is, however, likely to impact upon the survival rate of evidence of material culture. The ninth century in particular has tended to be written off as a period of decline and of Viking attack and devastation. The chronological extent of this has been exaggerated, with important books such as the Book of Cerne and the Royal Bible being made during the second quarter of the century and the literary output of Alfred and his circle commencing during the final quarter, but the attendant loss of evidence remains a significant factor. Nonetheless, although eclipsed in popular imagination by their Hiberno-Saxon counterparts, some of the finest examples of Anglo-Saxon art were produced South of the Humber under the Mercian 'hegemony' – the Vespasian Psalter, the Stockholm Codex Aureus, the

---

1. For further details of the manuscripts cited in this chapter, see the appropriate entries in the following: J. J. G. Alexander, *Insular Manuscripts, 6ᵗʰ to the 9ᵗʰ Century* (London, Harvey Miller, 1978); E. A. Lowe, *Codices Latini Antiquiores* (11 vols and suppl., Oxford, Oxford University Press, 1934–72); L. Webster and J. M. Backhouse (eds), *The Making of England. Anglo-Saxon Art and Culture AD 600–900 (BM / BL exhibition catalogue)*, London, British Museum Press, 1991).

Book of Cerne, the Royal Bible, the Pentney brooches, the Gandersheim Casket and the sculptures of Breedon-on-the-Hill.

One of the distinctive features which forms a recurrent theme throughout these southern English works, in whichever medium, is a whimsical brand of animal ornament, whether in the form of 'independent' heraldic beasts and grotesques, or of brontosaurus-like biting beast-heads which form the terminals of sections of ornament or of display letters where they munch voraciously upon letter-strokes to form a distinctive lacertine display script. A typical exponent of these features is a copy of Bede's *Historia Ecclesiastica* (British Library, Cotton MS Tiberius C.ii) which has given its name to the South-umbrian 'Tiberius' group of manuscripts (see figure on p. 88). This has also been known as the 'Canterbury' group, highlighting a basic problem which has dogged discussion: the magnet principle of manuscript attribution in which one known centre attracts otherwise unattributed 'floating' works, by default. In rectifying such tendencies the pendulum often initially swings too far in the other direction. Such considerations pervaded the duel of the pen between Sisam and Kuhn in the 1950s concerning the origins of the Book of Cerne (Kuhn, 1948: 619–27 and 1957: 368–9; Sisam, 1956: 9–10 and 1957: 372–3). Kuhn accepted a direct patronage association with Bishop Aedeluald of Lichfield and therefore attributed the whole group to Mercia, while Sisam reasserted a Canterbury focus for the group although admitting that Cerne might be a provincial outlier. Notwithstanding such polarized debate, how did the concept of the group evolve?

As early as 1868 Westwood attributed the Vespasian Psalter to Canterbury (Westwood, 1868: 43–6) and it was joined by the Tiberius Bede, the Royal Bible and the Book of Cerne in Zimmermann's work (Zimmermann, 1916, III: 25, 108, 135–6, 294–6). Kendrick, however, discerned a marked difference in style in Cerne and declared it to be 'the first undoubtedly Mercian manuscript' (Kendrick, 1938: 165–7). He was followed in this by Wormald, who perceived a connection between the evangelist symbols of Cerne (see figure on p. 146), the Royal Bible, the Stockholm Codex Aureus and the Gospels of St Augustine, on which they might all have depended. While viewing this symbol type as that current in Canterbury in the pre-Carolingian period, he distinguished Cerne as a probable Mercian product of the first half of the ninth century (Wormald, 1954; reptd 1984: 13–35). This was not generally accepted and Henry could still claim that Cerne and the Barberini Gospels were Lindisfarne products of the late eighth century (Henry, 1964, II: 60–4, 71, 73). In 1964 Wright defined what he saw as the sequence of major Canterbury books: Vespasian Psalter (first half of the eighth century); Stockholm Codex Aureus (second half of the eighth century); Royal Bible (late eighth century); Tiberius Bede (eighth to ninth century); Book of Cerne (early ninth century, written at Canterbury, possibly for Bishop Aedeluald of Lichfield) (Wright, 1964: 116–17). He viewed the Vespasian Psalter and the Stockholm Codex Aureus as precursors of the 'Tiberius' group, writing that 'the

Tiberius style is known to have been influential on the Continent in the last decade of the eighth century, and so the first example of the style – Royal 1.E.vi – must be dated *saec.*VIII*ex.* The relative chronology of this sequence of manuscripts thereby places the Vespasian Psalter in the first half of the eighth century' (Wright, 1967: 79). Alexander extended the group somewhat to include the Vespasian Psalter, the Stockholm Codex Aureus, the Blickling Psalter, the Royal Bible, the Tiberius Bede, which he ascribed to eighth- and ninth-century Canterbury while leaving the question of a Mercian origin for Cerne open (Alexander, 1978: 55–60, 84–5). Wheeler and Jewell highlighted Southumbrian sculptural parallels for the group while Wilson, Budny and Webster have explored links with metalwork (Wheeler, 1977: 235–44; Jewell, 1982: 303 and Chapter 17 in the present vol.; Wilson, 1984: 83, 91, 96; Budny, 1985: 686, 697–8; Webster, Chapter 18 in this volume). In the *Making of England* exhibition catalogue (Webster and Backhouse, 1991: 195–220) and *The Book of Cerne* (Brown, M., 1996: 164–77). I argued in favour of completely relinquishing the 'Canterbury' alternative nomenclature for the 'Tiberius' group, to avoid regional specification, and discussed the stylistic features of decoration and script associated with the group, extending their regional diffusion across a broader area of Mercian cultural activity (including Kent) to form what I have termed the 'Mercian *Schriftprovinz*', capable of encompassing the political components of greater Mercia, Kent and Wessex during the eighth and ninth centuries, rather as the '*Irische Schriftprovinz*' has been extended to embrace seventh- to eighth-century Northumbria.

A feature of many of the later representatives of the Tiberius group is that they are written in minuscule script. There is significant evidence of experimentation and innovation in the formation of high-class minuscule scripts for diplomatic use in Southumbrian scriptoria during the late eighth and early ninth centuries, perhaps related to contemporaneous developments on the Continent in the formulation of caroline minuscule. A perception of the authority of writing fostered by its use in a liturgical context had helped to shape its use as had its integration with orality in the administrative and legal spheres from the time of its introduction and use to record the law-code of King Ethelberht I of Kent at the opening of the seventh century (Brown, M. 2000 and forthcoming). In the atmosphere of heightened litigation and of manipulation of corporate assembly in the form of councils and synods which pervaded southern England during the reigns of Offa and Coenwulf, written records played an increasingly important role. The survival rate of original documents of the period is patchy, with most extant examples being attributable to Christ Church Canterbury, to Worcester and possibly to Winchester or Sherborne (S 1438 and S 298, which might also be Christ Church products, however). The material that does survive at least provides a chronological and something of a regional context against which to assess some of the surviving books. I have associated closely one of the Tiberius manuscripts, Paris, B.N., lat.

10861, a collection of saints' lives, with charters written at Christ Church from around 810–825 (Brown, M., 1987). The 'mannered minuscule' which I have associated with Canterbury script of this period is directly related to the programme of litigation pursued by Archbishop Wulfred (805–832), himself a Mercian nobleman and an active scribe, in his attempts to stave off Mercian royal encroachment and to regain Canterbury's property and privileges in the wake of the relegation of Offa's rival archbishopric of Lichfield (Brown, M., 1987 and 1996). The cursive minuscule and decorated lacertine display scripts of the Paris Saints' Lives may be related to those found in other members of the group, allowing it to act as something of a reference point in discussions of their origins. In a monographic study of the Book of Cerne (which I concluded to be a product of Worcester, or perhaps Lichfield, of the 820s–840s) I pursued this line further and, along with a consideration of provenance evidence, suggested the following groupings for Tiberius group members of the late eighth and early ninth centuries (Brown, M., 1996: 162–72).

Mercian School
Barberini Gospels (Vatican, Bibl. Apost., Barb. lat. 570)
B.L., Harl. MS 7653
B.L., Royal MS 2.A.xx
B.L., Harl. MS 2965
Salisbury Cathedral Lib., MS 117 (etc.)
B.L., Cotton MS Vespasian B.vi (ff. 104–9)
Bodleian Lib., Hatton 93
Book of Cerne (Camb. Univ. Lib., MS Ll.1.10)

Canterbury School
Paris, B.N., MS lat. 10861
B.L., Cotton MS Tiberius C.ii
B.L., Royal MS 1.E.vi (etc.)
(Camb., Corpus Christi Coll., MSS 69, 144, 173?)

West Saxon (influenced?) School
(B.L., Eg. MS 1046?)
Wilfred Merton Collection, MS 42
B.L., Royal MS 4.A.xiv
Bodleian Lib., Bodley 426

Having subsequently had the opportunity of viewing the manuscript in the flesh, I would now add the St Petersburg Gospels (St Petersburg, State Lib., Cod. F.v.1.8). Visually, the palette of this work, with its grey-blues and brick reds, is akin to that of the Book of Cerne and Hatton 93. The prancing Bambi-like creature which dominates its 'Liber' page has also long been compared to its gilded cousin on f. 3 of Cerne. The display script of the St Petersburg Gospels lacks the fully lacertine character and the linking beast heads of the later members of the Tiberius group, but in other respects its ribbon-like black letters, although ill-disciplined in their march across the page, could be seen as precursors of those found in Barberini and Cerne (see figures on p. 144 and p. 291). The text script is half-uncial, of the regular, rounded variety associated with the Lindisfarne Gospels and its associates and termed 'reformed Phase II half-uncial' by Julian Brown (Brown, 1982). It carries none of the distinctive minuscule tendencies or calligraphic distortions and whimsical grotesque or zoomorphic decorative features associated with the later Tiberius manuscripts, but this is not, perhaps, surprising if it represents an earlier stage of development in the mid to late eighth century. Given the historical background to the conversion of Mercia and the development of key dioceses, such as Lichfield, a dependence upon Northumbrian traditions and models is to be expected. It may similarly be observed within the Barberini Gospels. Like so many of the great expressions of Insular culture, much of its impact lies in the skilful fashion in which it blends features and influences drawn from many different ethnic and regional sectors of the post-Roman world. In this sense it is encyclopaedic, with the result that, when considering its origins, scholars will often tend to focus upon individual ingredients and emphasize those at the expense of others, to favour a specific area. Thus, Lindisfarne, York, Mercia and Canterbury have all been seriously considered as the source of its genesis. I have stated elsewhere my views concerning the scribal hands at work in Barberini (Webster and Backhouse, 1991: no. 160; Brown, M., 1996: 167–8). Of the four scribes, two practise half-uncial scripts of mainstream, post-Lindisfarne Gospels, Northumbrian character. Another uses an unusual version of the same script, characterized by its competent, neat aspect with small letter-bows and attenuated ascenders and descenders. In a curious way its aspect appears to foreshadow that familiar in caroline minuscule. The remaining scribe employs a script which is similar in overall aspect, but which builds in some distinctive calligraphic variants (ligatures, distorted bows, occasional reversals of ductus) and, most notably, he allows his artistic skills expression by elaborating his minor initials with beast heads and by utilizing extensive line-fillers and runover symbols in his *mise-en-page* (see figure on p. 294). These include a number of amusing human and grotesque components related to those encountered in Cerne, the Paris Saint's Lives and the Tiberius Bede. The Book of Cerne, which can be dated to the 820s–840s (Brown, M., 1996), is the ultimate exponent of this phenomenon, with a whole herd of brontosaurus-like creatures articulating its breviate Psalter. I have also discussed the late Tiberius-group context for such features as a relevant chron-ological context for their other principal source, the Book of Kells (Brown, M., 1994). Perhaps the earliest occurrence of such zoo- or anthropomorphic runover symbols was first noted by me in the form of a single bird on f. 50v of the Codex Bigotianus (Paris, B.N., MSS lat. 281 and 298), an uncial Gospel book which I have suggested may be a Worcester product of the late eighth century, although Kent is also a possible place of origin (Brown, M., 1996: 120, 167) (see figure on p. 12). The Codex Bigotianus is also distinguished by a panelled treatment of its major initials inhabited by independent beast motifs of 'Mercian' character.

There is a demonstrable context for Bigotianus' particular style of uncial scipt in Mercia. The Ismere Diploma (B.L., Cotton Aug. II.3; S 89), a grant by King Æthelbald of land in Worcs., dating to 736, is a probable example of the early uncial of the Worcester scriptorium. Another early instance of Mercian uncial is the section added, perhaps by a female scribe, to a volume containing an inscription that indicates ownership by Abbess Cuthswith of Inkberrow, Worcs. (Sims-Williams, 1976; Brown, 2001a). Later eighth-century examples of Worcester's uncial might include a copy of the *Rule of St Benedict* (Bodl., Hatton 48) and a *Paterius* (Worcester, Cathedral Lib., MS 4). Worcester's interest in the production of uncial manuscripts may have been further stimulated by the receipt of an impressive gift from King Offa. His attested political interests in Northumbria (including the marriage of his daughter to King Æthelred of Northumbria in 792) may have facilitated his acquisition of one of the great Ceolfrith Bibles, written at Wearmouth/Jarrow prior to the abbot's departure for Rome in 716. The copy he took with him to present to the Pope survives as the Codex Amiatinus (Florence, Bibl. Medicea-Laurenziana, MS Amiatino 1); fragments of one or both of the other two volumes, one for Wearmouth, the other for Jarrow, have also come to light (B.L., Add. MSS 37777 and 45025 and Loan MS 81). A copy of an alleged charter of 780 (Wharton, I, 1691: 470) refers to Offa's donation to Worcester of a *'magnam Bibliam cum duabus armillis ex auro'*. Subsequent tradition equates this with a Bible which Offa caused to be copied from an exemplar in S. Paulo *fuori le mure* in Rome. However, the Middleton fragments of one of the Ceolfrith Bibles (B.L., Add. MS 45025), which were used as estate document wrappers by the Willoughby family at Wollaton Hall, Notts. (as, at some point, were the other known fragments) were discovered along with fragments of an early eleventh-century Worcester cartulary of unusually large format, corresponding to the dimensions of the Bible leaves. St Wulfstan is thought to have had charters copied into the Bible in Worcester Cathedral (as recorded in Hemmings Cartulary, B.L., Cotton Tiberius A.xii, see Turner, 1916: xli–xlii; Ker, 1948; Webster and Backhouse, 1991: 123) and there is a distinct possibility, raised by these fragments, that Offa's magnanimous gift was indeed a Ceolfrith Bible (Brown, M., 1996: 166; Wood, 1994). The overtly romanizing appearance of these Wearmouth/Jarrow pandects may have been enough to engender a later association with Italy, as indeed also occurred in the case of the Codex Amiatinus. If Offa did indeed obtain one of these remarkable volumes, we cannot know the manner in which he did so. Whatever the truth of the matter, there is certainly some evidence here of Offa's involvement in book patronage. It may be worth noting that he is, unusually for a southern English ruler prior to Athelstan, commemorated in the Durham Liber

Vitae (B.L., Cotton MS Domitian A.vii) which is thought to be either a Lindisfarne or Wearmouth/Jarrow book begun during the ninth century (Brown, M., 1989: 162). Perhaps, like Athelstan, Offa had direct dealings with the North East as an ecclesiastical patron. Alcuin certainly anticipated his political or military intervention at the time of his son-in-law's murder. Another possible route of acquisition may have been York, where, it seems, Alcuin may have seen one of the Ceofrith Bibles, as indicated by his quotation of one of their headings in his *Carmina 69* (Corsano, 1987: 3–34, 20–2; Brown, M., 2000, 2001b, forthcoming). Perhaps the Viking menace was leading to evacuation of key treasures and personnel.

To return to the Barberini Gospels, in addition to Northumbrian features of its script and text, its ornament has some connections with the North. Its foliate motifs have been compared to those found upon the Bewcastle cross sundial panel and with the Ormside Bowl. However, as Leslie Webster points out in Chapter 18 of this volume, the bowl is equally likely to have been made in Mercia and was simply found in Northumbria. Barberini's minor decoration and display script undoubtedly find their home in the late Tiberius group. Its evangelist miniatures are indebted to Byzantine sources, signalled by their bearded figures, painterly modelling and stylized spatial settings. Their foliate ornament, and some of the volume's grotesques, are exotic and eastern in their resonances, and reliance upon similarly exotic models may be responsible for the echoes of similarity which are found, for example, on the Bewcastle cross. Such cultural influences are also a distinctive feature of the Mercian sculptures such as those at Breedon-on-the-Hill, Castor, Fletton and Peterborough (centres closely linked in their foundation history). These centres also provide sculptural context for the Barberini figure style. The other major context is, of course, the earlier members of the Tiberius group made in Kent: the Vespasian Psalter (see figure on p. xii and cover illustration) and the Stockholm Codex Aureus. These have traditionally been ascribed to Canterbury, where they were in the later Middle Ages, but I have recently reaffirmed another possibility: that they were made at Minster-in-Thanet, a centre known from Boniface's correspondence to have been actively producing high-grade books (including chryso-graphy) in the earlier eighth century (Brown, M., 2001a). The exotica pervade both the Kentish and mainstream Mercian representatives of the Tiberius group and would appear to have been a feature of Southumbrian style in the period of Mercian supremacy. Trade relations under Offa and ecclesiastical and diplomatic contacts with the Carolingian Empire may have helped to foster such trends, perhaps most tangibly demonstrated by Offa's coinage modelled upon that of the caliphate, and events such as Charlemagne's distribution of the Avar treasure (some of which is known to have come to England) may have furnished a direct stimulus. In view of the historical background and of available cultural models, a *de luxe* manuscript made in Offa's Mercia (whether in eastern or western Mercia, in Kent or by a team assembled for this and similar purposes) might be expected to conflate

Northumbrian, Kentish, Continental, Byzantine and Christian Orient ingredients – of the sort encountered in the Barberini Gospels and, at a later period and in a different style, in the Book of Cerne.

There are a number of other issues of particular historical and cultural significance which are raised by the Tiberius group. One of these is the question of evidence of female literacy in Anglo-Saxon England, which I have discussed in a recent paper (Brown, 2000a). It is noteworthy that the depleted body of evidence for book production in Mercia includes the best candidates as books made by and/or owned by women. Abbess Cuthswith of Inkberrow has already been mentioned as the probable owner of a copy of Jerome's Commentary *in Ecclesiastes* (Würzburg, Universitätsbibliothek, M.p.th.q.2, probable ownership inscription of Cuthswith, f. 1) in which a lacuna was filled, around 700, in an uncial script emulating that of this fifth- to sixth-century Italian book itself, perhaps by one of the nuns in her charge. A little later, in the 730s, Abbess Eadburh of Minster-in-Thanet was supplying books to Boniface's mission and may have left her ownership mark on p. 47 of Bodleian, MS Selden Supra 30[3418], an *Acts of the Apostles* in an eighth-century English uncial hand (New Palaeographical Soc., 2nd Ser.: pl. 56). The early addition on p.70 of a prayer in the feminine voice bolsters the suggestion of female use, and of the possibility of origin within the convent. The volume later belonged to St Augustine's, Canterbury, but then Thanet's property had passed to that centre by the eleventh century, and perhaps as early as the ninth in the wake of the Viking invasions (Brooks, 1984: 203–6; Brown, M., 2001a; Emms, forthcoming). Rosamond McKitterick suggested that, if this uncial were to be seen as scriptorium specific, the natural home for palaeographically related works such as the Vespasian Psalter and the Stockholm Codex Aureus (with their characteristic use of gold, a feature particularly requested of Eadburh by Boniface) would also be Minster-in-Thanet (McKitterick, 1989a; Brown, M., 2001a). The later St Augustine's provenance of the former and the seizure and ransom of the latter by Vikings might also accord with a scenario of earlier Thanet ownership. The St Augustine's origins of the Royal Bible, one of the scribes of which has been linked by Mildred Budny to the hand which added the interlinear Old English gloss to the Vespasian Psalter in the mid-ninth century, might also thereby be called into question in favour of Thanet although manufacture at or for Canterbury remains probable. Thus the former alternative sobriquet for the Tiberius group, the 'Canterbury group' is open to attack not only from Mercian members of the group, but also from elsewhere in Kent. The supply of essential liturgical tools to cathedrals and monasteries, as well as the mission fields, by nuns would also find a Continental parallel with evidence for such provision in the Merovingian orbit by the nuns of Rebais, Faremoutiers-en-Brie, Jouarre, Chelles and possibly Kitzingen and Tauberbischofsheim (McKitterick, 1989a: 30–1; Brown, M., 2001a). It is interesting in this context that Goscelin's *life* of St Mildreth/Mildred of Minster-in-Thanet ascribes to her the copying of a

Psalter while she was studying at Chelles (Emms, forthcoming). A later abbess of Thanet was, of course, Cwoenthryth, heir of King Coenwulf and also abbess of Winchcombe, proprietary house of Coenwulf's royal regime. Winchcombe was the royal archival repository (see B.L., Stowe Ch. 15, S 1436), and in a sense Cwoenthryth may therefore be seen as the chief archivist of the Mercian royal house. Like Archbishop Wulfred, Cwoenthryth pursued an energetic programme of litigation and charter production in the defence of her rights (Brown, M., 1987, 1996 and 2001a). It is not unlikely that she would have maintained Thanet's interest in book production. Cwoenthryth and Wulfred should certainly be seen as significant channels of shared interests and models between Kent and Mercia. In this they may well have been joined by other members of the upper echelons of the church hierarchy, such as Bishop Heahberht of Worcester who seems, like Wulfred, to have been concerned with the reform of proprietary houses within his diocese upon Carolingian lines (Brooks, 1984: 133–4, 155–64, 175–80; Cubitt, 1990 and 1995; Brown, M., 1996: 164–5, 183). We know little of Bishop Aedeluald of Lichfield, who may be celebrated in the Book of Cerne, but it has been suggested that he too may have joined Archbishop Wulfred in his reforms, including the introduction of canons in accordance with the influence of the Rule of Chrodegang of Metz, although the evidence for this is preserved only in the later medieval Lichfield Chronicle (Brooks, 1984: 133–4, 153–64; VCH, 1970: 140; Brown, M., 1996: 182–3; Wharton, I, 1691: 431, 444–5, 448, 459, 465). If Wulfred did indeed seek to promote a spirit of collaboration and solidarity amongst the Southumbrian episcopacy, to stave off royal and lay encroachment and under the influence of Carolingian church reformers, this might be reflected in the Carolingian traits of codicology, experimentation with minuscule scripts and iconographic and artistic features which are to be found in the later members of the Tiberius group (Brooks, 1984; Cubitt, 1990 and 1995; Claussen, 1992; Keynes, 1994a; Brown, M., 1996). Such a context would have nurtured the phenomenon of the 'Mercian *Schriftprovinz*' as well as formulating distinctive local expressions within it. The similarities and the differences between the various members of the group are to be expected within such a scenario. Taken as a whole, the extant Tiberius group manuscripts may not amount to anything like the exuberant blossoming of learning and culture which was occurring in a contemporary Carolingian milieu, but they are impressive and influential in their way and are a useful, if cracked, mirror of the period of Mercian hegemony in which they were made. That an elaborate, large-scale *de luxe* Bible (B.L., Royal MS 1.E.vi), which makes conscious reference to Carolingian book production and to the artistic traditions of Charlemagne's court and Ravenna but which nonetheless is a celebration of the English contribution to the transmission and editing of Scripture, should have been produced in Kent while the Vikings were battering at the door is ample warning that this era should not be seen as a feeble 'tailing off' of Insular culture.

Further important textual and provenance evidence pointing to female manufacture and/or use are to be found in the Tiberius group prayerbooks. Of these four volumes, only the Book of Cerne fails to present significant evidence of female association. The Royal Prayerbook, the Book of Nunnaminster and even the fragmentary Harley 7653 all contain material couched in the feminine, or even more indicatively a mixed gender, voice and litanies or readings with a marked female slant. The Royal Prayerbook also appears geared towards medical interest. Both this and Harley 7653 evince a later Worcester provenance. Nunnaminster is closely related to these others in text and style. There is good circumstantial evidence to suggest that by the late ninth century it was in the possession of a Mercian noblewoman, Ealhswith, who was married to King Alfred of Wessex and who may have bequeathed her prayerbook, along with other property, to her foundation of the Nunnaminster in Winchester. If a royal woman of Mercian background had a taste for such a book at this time, it might be considered a possibility that these works had belonged to Mercian royal or aristocratic women at the time of their production during the first quarter of the ninth century. If, as has been suggested, the Book of Cerne was a bishop's book, it may be that powerful church women, such as Cwoenthryth, might also have aspired to such works of private devotion (Kuypers, 1902; Brown, M., 1996, 2001a).

The Tiberius prayerbooks mark a new stage in the development of the devotional tradition of the West. The Psalter, of which an extrapolated version occurs in the Book of Cerne, was the principal focus of private, and public, prayer throughout much of the Middle Ages, challenged only, from its arrival in the mid-thirteenth century onwards, by the Book of Hours (essentially an abbreviated reflection, for lay use, of the monastic round of the Divine Office). Within the Tiberius prayerbooks may be charted the development of a structured, thematic devotional tradition which in some ways prefigures the Book of Hours. The earliest of the group, Harley 7653 which probably dates to the turn of the century, is too fragmentary to indicate if it was themed (Birch, 1889; Kuypers, 1902; Morrish, 1982, 1986 and 1988; Brown, M., 1996 and 2001a). It may even have been a pamphlet of the sort thought to have acted as sources for the other members of the group. The Book of Nunnaminster (see figure on p. 278) centres upon a meditation upon the life of Christ. It is probably not greatly different in date and origin (probably diocese of Worcester, first quarter of the ninth century) from the Royal Prayerbook, which takes as its theme, in its Gospel lections concerning miracles of healing and its prayers and charms, the figure of Christ as the *medicus* or healer and the health, spiritual and physical, of mankind. It has been suggested that it may have served as a quasi-practical tool for a physician – perhaps even a female physician (Kuypers, 1902; Morrish, 1982; Webster and Backhouse, 1991: no. 163; Brown, M., 1996; Brown, M., 2001a). The Book of Cerne is the most sophisticated in its textual structure and compilation of materials, centring upon a protracted meditation on the doctrine of the Communion of Saints. There has been a great deal of debate concerning whether the Bishop Aedeluald named in an acrostic poem and the breviate Psalter in Cerne was the bishop of Lichfield (818 × 830) or his earlier namesake, the bishop of Lindisfarne (721 × 724–740) (Kuypers, 1902; Sisam, 1956–7; Kuhn, 1948, 1957: Dumville; Morrish, 1982, 1986, 1988; Brown, M., 1996). Palaeographical, textual, codicological and art historical evidence would indicate that the volume was actually made in western Mercia sometime during the 820s–840s and I have suggested that, even if the earlier bishop is to be associated with the Psalter, that the orthography of the acrostic itself would suggest that it was either composed with reference to Aedeluald of Lichfield or strategically altered with him in mind (Brown, M., 1996). Individual prayers from the Tiberius group compilations were to influence both the Carolingian and later Anglo-Saxon devotional traditions, but their sophisticated approach towards thematic structure was not perpetuated.

Another feature of these prayerbooks which is noteworthy is that they indicate that, in early ninth-century Mercia, there was some knowledge of Greek and Hebrew, and certainly an appreciation of the value of these languages as cultural indicators of erudition and cosmopolitanism (Lapidge, 1988; Berschin, 1991; Bodden, 1988; Brown, 1996; Howlett, 1998). They also confirm, along with the diplomatic record, that standards of latinity were loose, to say the least (Dumville, 1972). It may be particularly apposite in this respect to note that the earliest extant example of written Old English prose occurs in the Book of Cerne, in the form of an introductory exhortation to prayer which gives the key to the meaning of Cerne and to its practical use as an intercessory link with the eternal communion. I have, I hope, shown this to be an original, integral component of the book, in the hand of its single artist-scribe (Dumville, 1972; Brown, M., 1996; Brown, M., 2001a). Cerne also contains an Old English gloss to one of its most important prayers, the Lorica of Loding which is considered so efficacious that it should be recited thrice daily, which opens the suite of prayers that begins on f. 43 (see figure on p. 144). This gloss is in the hand of the artist-scribe and was probably conceived as part of the primary programme of work. At a similar period a continuous Old English gloss was also added to the Vespasian Psalter in Kent. Prior to the Viking incursions and Alfred's famed revival of learning, the seeds were being sown in Mercia and in areas which had been under its influence, of more extensive written vernacular literacy. This phenomenon may be seen against a broader backdrop of new perceptions of how language and script could be used, which were to develop further from the late ninth century onwards.

That Mercian works such as the Books of Nunnaminster and Cerne were apparently available as models in Winchester from the later ninth century helps to account for the degree of influence of Mercian pointed minuscule script, decoration and, to some extent, of text which can be detected in later West Saxon works (Bestul, 1986; Brown, M., 1996: 142, 160). Such elements of continuity are likewise evinced in later Mercian works such as the copy of Aldhelm's *de Virginitate* (B.L, Royal MS 5.F.iii) owned by Bishop Werferth of Worcester, Alfred's tutor and a key figure in his scholarly team which included churchmen from Francia, Celtic Wales and Mercia. A Mercian role in the Alfredian revival, the continued operation of Worcester in 'free Mercia' and the West Saxon succession to the control of Kent ensured that the legacy of Mercia and its culture continued to inform the emergence of a new England.

The Barberini Gospels, Vatican, Biblioteca Apostolica, Barb Lat. 570, f. 15.
© The Biblioteca Apostolica Vaticana. By kind permission of the Prefect of
the Biblioteca Apostolica Vaticana.

Part V

Mercia in Retreat

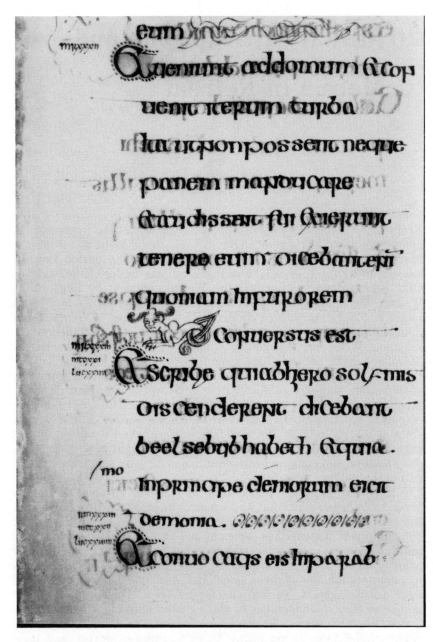

eum

Uenerunt addomum &co
uenit iterum turba
ita utqon possent neque
panem manoucare
&cum dissent sui exierunt
tenere eum oicebanteni
quoniam hifurorem
Conuersus est
&scribe quiabhero solimis
ois oenclerent dicebant
beelsebubhabech &quia.
Inprmcipe demorum eicit
demonia.
Conuocatis eisinparab

The Barberini Gospels, Vatican, Biblioteca Apostolica, Barb Lat. 570, detail, f. 5v. © The Biblioteca Apostolica Vaticana. By kind permission of the Prefect of the Biblioteca Apostolica Vaticana.

20 Military Institutions and Royal Power

Gareth Williams

Reading the *Anglo-Saxon Chronicle*, it is easy to get the impression of almost continual warfare throughout Anglo-Saxon history, not least in Mercia during the eighth and ninth centuries. The period saw the subjection by force of neighbouring kingdoms under Æthelbald and Offa, repeated warfare against the Welsh, conquest by Ecgberht of Wessex, the re-emergence of at least limited independence for Mercia under Wiglaf, and prolonged conflict with a succession of Viking armies culminating in the disappearance of Mercia as an independent kingdom. When not engaged in conflict with external enemies, the Mercian nobility seem to have been quite content to fight each other: the lack of any lasting line of clear dynastic succession points to considerable factional conflict within what was a large and disparate kingdom, made up of many different tribal groups. This brief summary of course overstates the extent of full-blown warfare in the period, since it merely reflects the fact that warfare when it did occur was regarded as sufficiently noteworthy for chroniclers to report. Even so, the evolution and collapse of the Mercian state were shaped, to a great extent, by military activity.

For all the apparent importance of warfare, however, we know remarkably little about what warfare actually involved. How large were the armies of the eighth and ninth centuries? How were they raised and equipped? Was warfare the right and duty of every free man, or a purely aristocratic pastime? Did Mercian warriors fight for king or country, or for both, or for neither? The *Anglo-Saxon Chronicle* rarely has answers for any of these questions, and other sources that shed light on the subject are few and far between. This problem is not unique to Mercia, and applies in varying extents to the whole of Anglo-Saxon England. Between them, Asser and the Chronicle provide slightly fuller information about Alfred's military reforms, and texts such as the Burghal Hidage and the Domesday Book, together with wills and charters, also provide valuable information, but for no area or era is the information very complete.

This paucity of information has often led students of Anglo-Saxon warfare to select details from very different times and places, and to weave them into broad generalizations about 'Anglo-Saxon' warfare which ignore the fact that the evidence spans over five hundred years, and that for much of that time England was far from united. The extent to which texts like the Domesday Book can be used at all as evidence for Offa's Mercia is questionable, to say the least, and any study of military institutions in Mercia needs to focus much more closely on evidence which is directly relevant, although material from other kingdoms both in the British Isles and elsewhere may help to give a broader context for the development of Mercian institutions.

Before proceeding to look at Mercian military institutions in more detail, it is nevertheless useful to summarize the main schools of thought on Anglo-Saxon military organization. The most widespread view from the nineteenth century to the 1960s saw Anglo-Saxon warfare largely in the context of ideas of a Germanic 'folk'-based society. According to this view, it was both the right and the duty of every free-born man to bear arms. The Anglo-Saxon *fyrd* was seen as a mass levy of peasant farmers, to be summoned at the will of the king or his representatives. This reflects a view of society which generaly emphasized the importance of the free peasant farmer rather than the nobility. This view was accepted by the majority of Victorians, modified by Frederic Maitland, and subsequently developed and elaborated by Sir Frank Stenton in *Anglo Saxon England* (1971: 290–91).

An opposed view was presented by H. Munro Chadwick (1907), and developed further by Eric John (1960: 138–9; 1966: 128–53; 1996: 51–3). This saw warfare as primarily an aristocratic occupation, reflecting a greater emphasis on the importance of the nobility in the Anglo-Saxon period. According to this theory, Anglo-Saxon warfare was organized along more or less feudal lines, with an aristocracy which served the king in exchange for grants of land. Armies were seen as smaller, and the free peasant farmer had little role, either in warfare specifically or in the broader context of landholding and society. Under this view, the only contribution the *ceorl* made to warfare was in the supply train.

A third position was developed by Warren Hollister (1962), in his book *Anglo-Saxon Military Institutions on the Eve of the Norman Conquest*. He combined elements of both the previous approaches, to develop a theory of a double system of military organization. He drew a distinction (not found in contemporary accounts) between the 'select fyrd', a comparatively small warrior elite, and the 'great fyrd', a much larger force which also included free peasant farmers around the professional core of the 'select fyrd'. Depending on the nature of the military emergency, the 'select fyrd' or the 'great fyrd' might be called out. It was possible for royal officials to call out the fyrd from individual shires, but only the king himself had the right to call out the 'great fyrd' across the whole kingdom. A similar view was presented by Maurice Powicke (1962), who emphasized the subdivision of the national fyrd into provincial and shire forces. Although both Hollister and Powicke were primarily concerned with the end of Anglo-Saxon

England, and leaned heavily on post-conquest material, they also drew in earlier material to help build their arguments, and the 'select fyrd'/'great fyrd' model has often been cited as if it applied across a much broader period of Anglo-Saxon history than Hollister himself suggested.

All the historians cited above approached the subject by building models based on their broader interpretation of Anglo-Saxon society, and then bringing together pieces of evidence from very different times and places to support the model. More recent works have tended to focus on more specific problems in particular times and places. Two such works have particular relevance to the study of the Mercian military establishment. The first is Nicholas Brooks' (1971) seminal article, 'The development of military obligations in eighth- and ninth-century England.' Brooks made a detailed study of the appearance in charters of the reservation from general immunities, of the three so-called 'common burdens' of service in the army, and the building and manning of bridges and fortresses. While pointing to a number of problems posed by the distribution of surviving charters from the different Anglo-Saxon kingdoms, and also by local scriptorial traditions, he was able to show that the evidence as it stands suggests that the three obligations did not develop simultaneously in all the kingdoms. Furthermore, the evidence suggests that Mercia appears to have had a leading role in developing these obligations, with bridge-work and fortress-work first appearing in Mercia in 749, in the reign of Æthelbald, and apparently spreading into Kent in the 790s under Offa's overlordship.

A second extremely important work is Richard Abels' (1988) book on lordship and military obligation. He traces the development of military obligations throughout Anglo-Saxon history, but unlike the earlier synthetic works he points to changes in the style of warfare and military organization throughout the period. In particular, he follows Brooks in seeing the eighth century as an important period in the development of royal authority over the military establishment, as a consequence of the growing use of bookland tenure, with the next major changes arising as a result of Alfred's reforms in Wessex in the late ninth century. Abels relates military organization to lordship and to royal authority. While accepting the existence of a substantial and well organized levy in the later Anglo-Saxon period, he portrays Anglo-Saxon warfare down to the late ninth century as largely, though not exclusively, restricted to a military elite: kings, those who held land of the kings, and also those to whom they granted land in turn, together with the household followers of all three groups. These obligations became more strictly controlled as a result of bookland tenure, but reflected a formalization of an earlier system based on private warbands and temporary grants of land. Abels' views thus to some extent follow the earlier work of Eric John in regarding warfare as relatively small scale, and largely confined to the aristocracy.

Abels makes two points of particular importance to any study of

Anglo-Saxon military organization in the eighth century. First, he argues that in the seventh and early eighth century, more emphasis should be placed on personal lordship than on royal rights. A king owed his position to being accepted as lord by the nobility, and particularly by his potential rivals. Only those who accepted his lordship had any duty to serve him, and other claimants would continue to exercise lordship over their own followers, and the king's authority thus depended on whether he could command greater resources than his rivals. Bookland tenure, although it created hereditary rights for the landholder, also created hereditary duties, and it was with the spread of bookland tenure in the eighth century that Abels links the development of royal authority over a system of military obligations (Abels, 1988: 43–57). Abels also notes an important problem with using early lawcodes as evidence for any sort of general military obligation. While conceding that even *ceorls* might be liable to pay *fyrdwite,* the fine for failing to perform the military service due from them, he points out that there is nothing within the lawcodes which necessarily implies that all *ceorls* had a duty of military service to the king. He argues that individual *ceorls* might owe military service to their lord (who might then owe service to the king, or might even be the king) and that such men would indeed be liable for penalties if they failed to serve, but that there is no evidence that the majority of the *ceorlisc* class had no such obligations. He further notes that the lawcodes in any case represent an assertion of royal rights to which the kings aspired, rather than necessarily factual accounts of general practice (Abels, 1988: 13–16).

Abels' work coincided with Timothy Reuter's work on Frankish military organization in the late eighth and early ninth centuries (1985; 1992). It has long been noted that the end of Charlemagne's military expansion in the early ninth century coincided with the introduction in Frankish capitularies of military obligations, which spread the burden of military obligations even onto those who held too little land to serve individually. This has traditionally been seen as an indication of the exhaustion of the Frankish military capacity by Charlemagne's almost annual campaigns, and the fact that the Carolingian empire simultaneously switched from aggressive expansion to becoming a target for the attacks of others has been taken as a consequence of this supposed military exhaustion, which left the empire unable to defend itself. Reuter turns this argument on its head. He argues that for logistical reasons, Charlemagne's campaigning armies must always have been relatively small, irrespective of whether there was any technical obligation of military service on all free Frankish men. The campaigns, he argues, were undertaken by groups of professional warriors, well armed and well horsed, and therefore wealthy enough to purchase both arms and horses. Such an army could not have been particularly large, partly because relatively few people could have supported themselves on such campaigns, and partly because of the difficulty of provisioning large armies over any sort of distance.

According to Reuter, the decision of whether or not to participate in Charlemagne's campaigns was based to some extent on a form of cost–benefit analysis. Those who had the wealth to equip themselves, and to be able to to leave their lands in the care of others, and who foresaw sufficient profit, whether through plunder or rewards from the king, to justify the expense and the risk, would join the expeditions. Others would not. Reuter further argues that the wealth and power of Charlemagne made the Frankish kingdom an attractive target for raiding in the late eighth and early ninth centuries, but that plunder-based military service was poorly suited to a system of national defence. Within this system, there were still expenses and risk, but no chance of profit, and thus no direct motivation to defend lands other than those in which the warriors had a vested interest. It was thus to create a more stable defence network that Charlemagne introduced military obligations across a wider section of Frankish society, and the fact that he was in a position to do so indicates the great extent of his authority, rather than the exhaustion of the Frankish state.

Reuter's arguments are persuasive, and have important implications for the development of military institutions in Anglo-Saxon England. If even a ruler like Charlemagne relied heavily on the greed of the warrior aristocracy to undertake aggressive warfare, and campaigned with relatively small armies as a result, it seems unlikely that the rulers of any of the less powerful Anglo-Saxon kingdoms would have exercised much greater authority over their own military establishments. To trace the development of military obligations in Mercia, it is therefore helpful to propose a model based on Reuter's analysis of the Frankish material. First, this means drawing a distinction between offensive and defensive warfare. Second, it is necessary to consider the preconditions for the development of defence systems.

Offensive warfare could be undertaken on much the same cost–benefit terms as Reuter suggests for the Franks. This does not exclude the possibility that those who held land of the king were obliged to provide service in the king's host when required to do so, whether for offensive or defensive purposes, but the number of landholders within the Mercian kingdom was probably not great, and even those obliged to serve may have been reluctant and even recalcitrant if they did not foresee sufficient gain in return for their service. This approach to offensive warfare can be seen to cover Mercian campaigns from the seventh century to the collapse of the Mercian kingdom in the ninth century. Damian Tyler (forthcoming) has recently argued that offensive warfare was a more effective tool for Mercian royal power in the late seventh century than under Æthelbald and Offa, precisely because the Mercian military establishment was well suited to the exaction of plunder/tribute, but lacked the organization and power to sustain lasting conquests. While Coenwulf seems to have been more successful in holding his conquests unchallenged, even he found it necessary to appoint his brother Cuthred, who presumably had his own warband, as sub-king in Kent in the early part of his reign, and the

Mercian hegemony collapsed completely following Coenwulf's death. The infighting between rival claimants to the Mercian kingdom in the 820s, like the earlier seizure of the kingdom by first Æthelbald and then Offa, further suggests that any member of the royal house might have access to a band of followers to support any potential claim to royal authority.

Defensive warfare shows both more systematic organization and more change and development in the course of the eighth and ninth centuries. The imposition of defensive military obligations depends on four factors. First, there would have to be sufficient administrative facility for the system to be organized. Second, there would have to be an established idea of the nation or polity as something worth defending. Third, there would have to be a sufficient external threat to make defence necessary. Finally, there would have to be a sufficiently strong central power to enforce compliance from those not inclined to serve of their own accord. The first of these was provided in Mercia by the literate administration of Christian churchmen from the late seventh century onwards. The dating of the second is less clear. The Tribal Hidage, now mostly accepted as dating from the late seventh century, presents a picture of fragmented groups, each with a separate identity, and the extent to which any members of the smaller groups or kingdoms felt any loyalty towards a broader concept of Mercia is unclear.[1] By the late eighth century, most of those groups had lost their separate identities and had been absorbed into the Mercian kingdom, but this process is poorly documented, and did not necessarily take place simultaneously in all areas. Mercia's central position, completely surrounded by other kingdoms, both Anglo-Saxon and Welsh, made the kingdom particularly liable to external threats, especially once absorption of the smaller kingdoms removed the buffer states between Mercia and the other major kingdoms. It is important to note in this respect that the development of military obligations on bookland apparently took place in Mercia under Æthelbald and Offa, at the height of the Mercian supremacy. This is consistent with the requirement for strong royal authority to enforce compliance with the new system, but the probability that Æthelbald and Offa thought it necessary to introduce new systems of defence does emphasize that Mercia's pre-eminence in the eighth century did not go unchallenged. Thus, all four of the preconditions for national defence systems probably existed by the mid-eighth century, and most, if not all, may even date back to the end of the seventh century (Williams, forthcoming).

The obligation to serve in the royal host probably goes back before the beginning of the eighth century in Mercia, although it is not specifically documented as a royal right, as it is in the laws of Ine of

---

1. A useful overview of interpretations of the Tribal Hidage is provided by Rumble (1996).

Wessex (Brooks, 1971: 69). It is also unclear precisely at what point the short-term granting of land in loan in return for service was replaced by booking land in perpetuity, with precise definitions of the service due included in the charter by which the land was 'booked'. Almost certainly this was a gradual process, beginning with a number of individual grants to the Church, followed by the appropriation by the lay aristocracy of what had originally been a clerical privilege. The potential problems of granting land in perpetuity, with clerical immunities, and without clear reservations of the king's right to military service from his landholders, are clearly stated in Bede's famous letter to Archbishop Ecgberht of York in 734, in which he complains that land given to false monasteries cannot be used to reward the nobility for military service to their kingdom (*EHD*, 735–45; John, 1960: 64–79; Brooks, 1971: 74–5). It is possibly an attempt to curb such abuse of clerical privilege in Mercia that made Æthelbald the target of a series of letters from Bishop Boniface in 747, in which he is accused of unheard-of oppression of churchmen within his lands, and specifically of forcing them to labour on royal building projects. This is consistent with the first specific mention of the obligations of bridgework and fortress work as reserved royal rights within a general grant by Æthelbald of immunities on Church lands at the Synod of Gumley in 749. Following so closely on Boniface's letters, it seems not unreasonable to see the terms of the Synod of Gumley as a negotiated settlement as to precisely which rights the king could demand (*EHD*, 751–6; John, 1996: 52). However, charter survival is so patchy for this period that one cannot exclude the possibility that these rights may go back further (Brooks, 1971).

The matter is further complicated by the fact that, although bridgework and fortress work became standard obligations throughout Mercia in the eighth and ninth centuries, no visible traces remain of any fortified bridges or towns which can be precisely dated. At present, only three Mercian *burhs* show any sign of defences from this period. Excavations at Hereford, Tamworth and Winchcombe have revealed layers of urban defences below those built as part of the burghal programme of Æthelflæd, Lady of the Mercians, in the early tenth century. However, although these have been interpreted as belonging to the period of Mercian supremacy in the mid-eighth century, there is no conclusive evidence to date these early defences to the eighth century rather than the ninth (Bassett, 1996, forthcoming). There is even less evidence to support the suggestion that Mercia in the eighth century possessed a network of burghal reforms which predated Alfred's reforms in Wessex by a century.[2] The evidence of Offa's Dyke is similarly inconclusive. The construction of such a major military structure immediately points both to strong royal power and to a strong sense of threat. However, we have no contemporary

---

2. For this suggestion, see Haslam (1987).

documentation concerning its construction, and while it is possible that some equivalent of bridgework and fortress work was placed as an obligation on the inhabitants of the border areas, as discussed by David Hill elsewhere in this volume, there is no reason to prefer this possibility to any other form of conscripted labour. One should note that the earliest phase of the Danevirke, a comparable (albeit shorter) structure across the Jutland peninsula, defending Denmark's southern border, is now dated to *c.* 700 (Andersen, 1998), although few would accept the existence of anything resembling bookland obligations in Denmark at that period. Danevirke also provides a note of caution concerning the attribution of Offa's Dyke. The earliest attribution of the Dyke to Offa is in Asser's *Life of Alfred*, in which he writes that Offa built an earthwork 'from sea to sea'. A similar claim is made in the Frankish Annals for the Danish king, Godred, in 808, apparently a reference to Danevirke. However, although several phases of construction have now been identified in the Danevirke, no phase corresponding to Godred's period has yet been identified (Scholz, 1972; Andersen, 1998), suggesting that at most he undertook repairs to existing structures, or perhaps redeveloped only a very limited area of the Danevirke which has not yet been excavated.

Recent work on Offa's Dyke raises similar problems. It now seems clear that the Dyke did not stretch 'from sea to sea', and that the 'missing sections' never existed, rather than having disappeared. Nor does there seem to be much evidence of the multiple phases of construction to be associated with continuous usage. Furthermore, there is no firm dating evidence to tie the construction to the reign of Offa (Hill, 2000; Worthington, forthcoming). The combination of strong royal power and external threat is certainly consistent with the reign of Offa, and the conflict between Offa and the kings of Powys is discussed in more detail elsewhere in this volume by David Hill. In particular, Hill points to the evidence presented by the inscription on the so-called Pillar of Eliseg for a forceful assertion of Powysian independence for a period of nine years during the reign of Offa. Since the latest interpretations of the extent of Offa's Dyke suggest that it coincides very closely with the border between Mercia and Powys, the reign of Eliseg provides a very plausible context for the construction of the Dyke, although the evidence for this is far from conclusive (Hill, 2000; Worthington, forthcoming). If this interpretation is correct, however, it provides strong evidence for Offa's power to undertake a very substantial defensive mobilization in the short term, but it neither indicates how this was undertaken, or that Offa had the authority (or perhaps the need) to sustain the long-term garrisoning and upkeep of the Dyke.

The inconclusive evidence of Offa's Dyke and the *burhs* aside, it does seem that Mercian royal authority over military obligations continued to develop under Offa. Service in the host appears together with bridgework and fortress work in a Mercian charter of *c.* 793–6, and it is also in this period that the three obligations appear specifically for the first time in Kent, as reservations in a general grant of immunities to the Kentish Church by Offa at the Synod of Clofesho (Brooks 1971: 78–9). This has traditionally been dated to 792, but Donald Bullough (forthcoming) has recently pointed out that it may have taken place somewhat later than previously thought, although clearly before Offa's death in 796. The terms of the Synod provide interesting evidence of the limitation of Offa's authority in Kent. Sir Frank Stenton (1971) suggested that Offa's authority in Kent early in his reign was far from secure, and that the Battle of Otford in 776 saw the beginning of some years of Kentish independence, and this seems consistent with the numismatic evidence for Kentish kingship in the late eighth century, discussed elsewhere in this volume (Williams, Chapter 15 this volume). That Offa was in control in Kent in the 790s is also clear from the coinage, as well as from the fact that he was in a position to demand military service from the men of Kent at all. However, the limitation of Offa's authority there is also clear from the fact that service was limited to 'Campaigns within Kent against pagan seamen with migrant fleets, and amongst the South Saxons as necessity dictates, and the construction of bridges and fortifications against the pagans, again within the borders of the Kentish people' (Brooks, 1971: 79).

There is no suggestion that the Kentish people regarded themselves as part of a 'Greater Mercia', and there is no mention of any duty to serve Offa within the bounds of his own kingdom. It is also interesting that the terms of the obligations stress the new external threat posed by the Vikings as a condition of service. The obligations are thus quite explicitly consistent with the requirements for a specific regional identity and external threat mentioned above, and the willingness of the Kentish Church to accept them may have as much to do with their own vested interests as with Offa's authority.

The fragile nature of Mercian authority in both East Anglia and Kent is highlighted by the fact that both kingdoms revolted under their own local claimants on the death of Offa.[3] That the Mercian kingdom retained considerable military resources is demonstrated by the fact that Coenwulf was able to reassert Mercian authority in Kent by 798, and in East Anglia possibly even sooner. Coenwulf then maintained his position in both kingdoms, as well as in Mercia itself, without any evidence of even the temporary military reverses which Offa is known to have suffered. Within Kent, he not only regained control of the coinage as a potent symbol of authority, but continued Offa's policy of imposing on the Kentish people military obligations against Viking raiders (Brooks, 1971: 80; Williams, Chapter 15 in this volume). He was also able to campaign repeatedly in Wales, as discussed by Hill in

---

3. The Kentish revolt under Eadberht Praen is well documented, but East Anglian independence at this time is known only from the numismatic evidence. See Williams, Chapter 15 in this volume.

Chapter 12 in this volume. The fact that he was killed on his last campaign, and that the Mercian hegemony was so swiftly overturned by Ecgberht of Wessex following his death, together with the fact that his reign is less well documented than that of Offa, has probably contributed to the reign of Coenwulf being overshadowed by that of his more illustrious predecessor. Nevertheless, in a period in which one of the main foundations of kingship was military power, Coenwulf seems to have exercised a kingship just as firmly based as that of Offa, even if there is no evidence that his ambitions were quite so exalted.

Despite the swift resumption of royal authority under Coenwulf and full command of the military resources of Mercia and her client kingdoms, Mercian royal power was not yet so firmly established that it could survive either a weak king, or a contested kingship. On the death of Offa, and very shortly thereafter his son, Mercian authority collapsed, but Coenwulf was apparently able to restore it very substantially within two years. On the death of Coenwulf, Mercian power similarly collapsed, but this time nobody was able to restore it effectively. This almost certainly reflects the fact that royal control of military institutions was still extremely personal. One of the requirements mentioned earlier for an effective national defence system was royal authority strong enough to enforce military service from those who would not necessarily provide it of their own free will.

The collapse of the Mercian supremacy in the 820s can be explained by a number of factors. First, both East Anglia and Kent had retained the separatist tendency which had caused them to seek independence following the death of Offa, and their task was probably made easier by the death of Coenwulf in North Wales. Although we have few details of the circumstances surrounding his death, he is unlikely to have died alone, and his death would not have passed unnoticed by his Welsh enemies. For the king to be killed, presumably a significant proportion of the Mercian military establishment would have fallen with him, while even the survivors would have been on the wrong side of Mercia to deal with insurrections in East Anglia and Kent. Furthermore, since (to judge from our admittedly limited sources) for over twenty years there had been peace in East Anglia and Kent, but repeated conflict on the Welsh border, and since the Welsh could have been expected to take heart from Coenwulf's death, the Welsh border probably seemed a greater threat to Mercian security in the short term.

Second, neither Coenwulf's brother and successor Ceolwulf nor, after his brief reign and deposition in 823, his successors seem to have been powerful leaders. Although Ceolwulf, Beornwulf, Ludica, and Wiglaf are generally seen as ruling sequentially in swift succession, it is far from clear that the order of succession was quite so neat. The numismatic evidence suggests that while Ceolwulf had some authority in Mercia, East Anglia and West Kent, he was unable to exert his authority throughout the whole of Kent, and failed to control the important mint of Canterbury, while none of his succesors seem to have had any power in Kent at all. While Beornwulf and Ludica are known as kings of Mercia, they apparently issued coins only in East Anglia, while Wiglaf issued coins only in Mercia. It may well be that, rather than a clear sequence of succession, these rulers represent a group of rival claimants of royal blood, each backed by is own personal warband, who were successful in having their kingship recognized in different areas at different times (Williams, Chapter 15 in this volume). Since, with the partial exception of Ceolwulf, they struggled to exercise established royal rights over coinage, it is likely that they faced a similar struggle to control the military establishment. It is perhaps significant that Beornwulf, having gained control of the East Anglian moneyers was nevertheless killed in East Anglia. While bookland may in theory have created a hereditary obligation to serve the king irrespective of personal bonds of lordship, a disputed succession provided a perfect opportunity for those not tied directly to any of the parties by personal bonds to stand aloof until the winner emerged, on the grounds that it was unclear to whom the obligation was owed. If the succession was disputed, it therefore seems likely that the military establishment of the various Mercian kings of the 820s was largely limited to the personal warbands of the individual leaders.

A further point to be noted is that while Mercia apparently lacked a strong leader after the death of Coenwulf, Wessex possessed one in the form of Ecgberht. Ecgberht himself demonstrates that in some ways little had changed since the early eighth century. Like Æthelbald of Mercia before him, he spent much of his youth in exile, but retained a sufficient personal following that he was able to establish himself first as king of his own kingdom, and then as the effective overlord of much of southern England. Although a local Kentish claimant, Baldred, briefly emerged to challenge Ceolwulf's overlordship, and probably ruled independently after Ceolwulf's deposition, Ecgberht conquered Kent in 825 and thereafter it remained under the domination of Wessex. In 829, Ecgberht even succeeded in conquering Mercia, or at least a part of it. The extent of Ecgberht's control of Mercia is uncertain. The *Anglo-Saxon Chronicle*, not noted for its impartial reporting of events, describes him as conquering the kingdom, and there is no doubt that he controlled London, at least briefly, since he issued a small coinage there with the title of king of Mercia. However, the Mercian king Wiglaf had survived, and 'obtained' the kingdom of Mercia from Ecgberht in 830.

This has often been taken to indicate a Mercian reconquest, but may simply represent an accommodation between Ecgberht and Wiglaf, in which Wiglaf 'obtained' the kingdom in return for a recognition of Ecgberht's overlordship. This would be consistent with the fact that Wiglaf issued few, if any, coins during the remaining nine years of his reign, although issuing coins was now well established as a royal prerogative in Mercia, and there seems no obvious economic reason for the cessation of coinage. Nevertheless, whether Wiglaf reconquered Mercia or negotiated an accommodation, it seems clear that he continued to command enough of the Mercian military establishment to represent at least a potential threat to Ecgberht's authority. This may simply mean that, like others before him, he went into exile and took his personal warband with him, but it is also possible that he had retained control of part of Mercia, and was able to mobilize the landholders who owed service to the king. Ecgberht may also have struggled to command sufficient military resources to hold both Kent and Mercia in direct subjection, and have been willing to reach an accommodation over Mercia in order to consolidate his hold on Kent. This is, necessarily, somewhat speculative, since we have so little evidence for this period, but it makes sense in the context of the military establishment that seems to have evolved in Mercia in the eighth century and which, on the basis of the charter evidence, was developing in Wessex in the early to mid-ninth century (Brooks, 1971: 80–2).

Mercian power underwent a limited revival after the death of both Ecgberht and Wiglaf, and under their respective successors Æthelwulf and Berhtwulf the escalation of the external threat posed by the Vikings seems to have encouraged cooperation rather than conflict between Mercia and Wessex. This is reflected in the re-establishment of the Mercian coinage under Berhtwulf (840–852), apparently with at least the sanction of Æthelwulf, if not necessarily a full-blown monetary alliance. Links became even stronger under Berhtwulf's successor Burgred (852–874), who married Æthelwulf's daughter, and in Burgred's reign the forces of Mercia and Wessex campaigned together against both the Vikings and the Welsh. The relationship between Mercia and Wessex in this period is discussed in detail in Chapter 21 in this volume by Simon Keynes, and it would therefore be superfluous to comment in any detail on the political events leading to the final collapse of Mercia as an independent kingdom some time around the year 880. A few points should, perhaps, be made about the military resources and royal power in Mercia in those final years.

The ultimate collapse of the Mercian kingdom, and the survival of Wessex, and the fact that our written sources are primarily products of the Wessex court, have led to the view that Mercia was somehow a weaker kingdom than Wessex, and that Burgred and his successor Ceolwulf were somewhat inadequate compared with their contemporaries in Wessex, especially Alfred the Great. There may be some truth in this, and Alfred's reforms marked a fundamental shift in the development of Anglo-Saxon military organization (Abels, 1988: 58–78; Peddie, 1999). However, Alfred was exceptional by European rather than purely English standards in his success against the Vikings, and it is important to note that, despite its eventual collapse, Mercia proved much more resilient than either East Anglia or Northumbria. It survived the first overwintering of the Vikings in Nottingham, and even after Burgred's exile and the division of the kingdom in 874, a form of the kingdom of Mercia continued until the death of Ceolwulf II, c. 880. Even then, English Mercia remained a distinct area under the overlordship of Alfred, the ally of both Burgred and Ceolwulf. This implies the continued existence of some Mercian military forces throughout this period.

Second, Burgred's calls to Wessex for military assistance, first against the Welsh and again to besiege the Vikings in Nottingham, do not necessarily betoken military weakness. The Welsh posed a potential threat to both Mercia and Wessex, and both had an interest in keeping their Welsh neighbours subdued. The difficulty of raising a large army for campaigns has already been discussed, but combining the resources of two major kingdoms was probably the best way to build up a substantial size, especially since the recurrent threat of the Vikings must have required that both kingdoms keep part of their forces at home for defence. Furthermore, such a military alliance was not unprecedented, and even such a strong ruler as Æthelbald had fought together with the men of Wessex against the Welsh (*ASC, sub.* 743). The siege of Nottingham also represents something of a special case. Siege warfare in this period was very unsophisticated, and the defending side had a huge advantage when facing assault. The only way that this could be countered was by raising a very substantial army. This ploy was unsuccessful at Nottingham, but it should be noted that Alfred himself tended to be unsuccessful at besieging Viking armies within his own kingdom in the earlier part of his reign. It was only from the 880s, once the burghal system was in place and he was in a position to control lines of supply effectively, and feed his own army efficiently while denying any supplies to the Vikings, that he routinely began to force the Vikings out of their defensive positions (Abels, 1997; Peddie, 1999: 148–63). By the standards of the time, Burgred's attempt to gather additional forces makes perfect sense, and should not necessarily be taken as a sign of weakness. His exile is less ambivalent, since being driven out of his own kingdom by invaders can only be interpreted as a military failure. Again, however, it is possible to over-simplify the situation, especially compared with the promotion of Alfred as hero in the surviving sources. As discussed earlier, exile was by no means uncommon in the eighth and ninth centuries, nor was it necessarily permanent. This applied not just to pretenders who returned as kings, like Æthelbald and Ecgberht, but even to kings themselves. One of the reasons why the Northumbrian chronology of the eighth and ninth centuries is confused is that both Æthelred I and Æthelred II were deposed, only to resume their royal power. Burgred's exile abroad is comparable with Alfred's exile from power in the marshes at Athelney. What sets the two apart is Burgred's death shortly afterwards. Had Alfred died at Athelney, there would have been no 'Alfred the Great', and the conquest of Wessex would have become permanent. That is not to say that Burgred intended to return, nor that he would necessarily have been successful if he had, and it may be that his decision to go to Rome may indicate that he was already ill and recognized that he was unable to lead the fight against the Vikings effectively.

Whatever the circumstances of Burgred's departure, the Mercian kingdom survived a little longer under the rule of Ceolwulf II. Although he is dismissed by West Saxon sources writing after the event as a 'foolish king's thegn', and as a puppet of the Vikings, the evidence of both charters and coins makes it clear that he had royal power, and was accepted as an ally (and probably an equal) by Alfred (Keynes, 1998 and Chapter 21 in this volume). The fact that he was able to establish himself as king despite the presence of the Viking army in Mercia must indicate that he had military forces at his disposal. The Vikings were not all-powerful, but there is no reason to believe that they would not have taken the whole of Mercia had there been no continued Mercian resistance, much less promoted a local king as a potential focus of opposition. The precise nature of Ceolwulf's military resources is unclear, but his control of the coinage suggests that he was able to exercise royal rights, and it seems likely that he continued to command the same military obligations as his predecessors, albeit in a diminished kingdom of Mercia.

Even after Mercia ceased to exist as a separate kingdom, it remained a significant military power. Although Ealdorman Æthelræd ruled under the overlordship of Alfred, Asser tells us that it was fear of his 'tyranny' that induced a number of Welsh rulers also to accept Alfred's overlordship as a form of protection, indicating that under Æthelræd Mercia retained the capacity to mount aggressive campaigns (Keynes and Lapidge, 1983: 96). Furthermore, as is well recorded, a large part of the conquest of the southern Danelaw (much of which had formerly been part of Mercia) was undertaken first by Æthelræd, and subsequently by his widow Æthelflæd. Although Æthelflæd was the daughter of Alfred the Great, and followed his military policy in the building of a network of fortified *burhs,* it was as the 'Lady of the Mercians', not as a West Saxon princess, that she made her military achievements. The continued use of distinctively Mercian coinage in the early tenth century as a symbol of quasi-royal authority is discussed elsewhere in this volume. Furthermore, while the use of a network of *burhs* to provide a system of defence in depth reflects the influence of Wessex, the link between fortifications and the Mercian state follows a tradition which can be traced back to Æthelbald in the mid-eighth century.

The development of military obligation and royal authority in Mercia can be summarized briefly thus: A system of personal lordship, rather than state kingship, in early Mercia, probably lasting until some point in the reign of Æthelbald; the introduction of reserved royal rights on bookland under Æthelbald, extended under Offa and continued under Coenwulf, but with the traditional personal bond between lord and follower surviving alongside this extended royal authority; an apparent collapse of royal authority in Mercia in the 820s; a revival of royal authority and the Mercian state under Berhtwulf and Burgred, which to some extent survived both the Viking conquest and the imposition of West Saxon overlordship. The precise scale, and the degree of standardization of the Mercian military establishment simply cannot be calculated on the basis of the limited evidence available, but current thinking tends towards aggressive warfare being limited to a relatively small elite, while defensive warfare probably necessitated calling on a wider section of society, both for defensive armies and garrisons, and for the physical construction of bridges and fortresses.

21 Mercia and Wessex in the Ninth Century

Simon Keynes

Offa, king of the Mercians, died on 29 July 796 and was buried at Bedford. His son Ecgfrith, who had been consecrated king of the Mercians in 787, died on 17 December 796. Offa's son-in-law Æthelred, king of the Northumbrians, had been killed near the River Cover, in North Yorkshire, on 18 April 796. After a short period of political disruption, the kingdom of the Northumbrians had been brought under the control of Eardwulf; and the turmoil occasioned by disruption in Mercia, most notably in Kent and East Anglia, appears to have settled down soon after the accession of Coenwulf, king of the Mercians (796–821). Nonetheless, in the eyes and mind of one contemporary observer, viewing developments in his native land from a vantage point in Charlemagne's kingdom, these were dangerous times in Britain, and the 'death of kings' (*mors regum*) was a sign of misery. Alcuin was moved, of course, by the sense of uncertainty which attended the passing of an old order and its replacement by something new; but there is no mistaking his particular regret, in respect of the Mercians, that the aspirations of many had come to nought. His own analysis was expressed in the terms which came most naturally to him, in words borrowed from the psalmist (Ps. 127): 'Except the Lord build the house, they labour in vain that build it; except the Lord keep the city, the watchmen waketh but in vain.' As he added in his own words: 'Man proposes, God disposes' (*Homo cogitat, Deus iudicat*).[1]

Alcuin was not to know (at this stage) that the 'Mercian Supremacy' would continue for some time after the death of King Offa; for if Offa himself is kept in his proper perspective, Coenwulf emerges as a most respectable fifth in the line of Mercian overlords. The Mercian regime was able to maintain its interests not only throughout midland England, between the Thames and the Humber, but also in Lindsey, East Anglia, Essex, and the South-East. Numismatic evidence demonstrates that the

---

1. Alcuin, *Epist.*, no. 124 (Allott, 1974: no. 160). For exposition of this letter, see Bullough (1993). For further discussion of Alcuin's views, see Keynes, forthcoming a.

regime continued to exercise some form of control over commercial activity in London, and Coenwulf sought to secure his position in the South-East by appointing his brother Cuthred to rule in Kent.[2] It was a period when links were cultivated between political and ecclesiastical establishments in Mercia and equivalent centres of power and influence in Kent. It is, moreover, symbolic of a larger truth that during this period (*c.* 810) an unknown scholar, presumably working in association with ecclesiastical and secular authorities of the day, felt the need and had the resources to assemble material seemingly intended to reduce his world to order, including a collection of episcopal lists for the whole Church of the English (Figure 21.1), and a set of royal genealogies for dynasties ruling in different parts of Britain (though not, it seems, including the Saxon lines of Wessex, Sussex and Essex).[3] Yet it could not last. Tension steadily increased between the representatives of the Mercian regime and Wulfred, archbishop of Canterbury (805–832); and following Wulfred's powerful assertion of episcopal rights, represented by the canons of the council of Chelsea (816), matters deteriorated in ways which in certain quarters must seriously have undermined confidence in the Mercian regime.[4]

The end of the Mercian supremacy in the 820s

A Mercian at the end of the ninth century would not have looked back at the 820s with much sense of nostalgia. According to a contemporary observer, Coenwulf's death in 821 precipitated an outbreak of disputatious behaviour throughout the land:

> After the death of Coenwulf, king of the Mercians, many disagreements and innumerable disputes arose among leading persons of every kind – kings, bishops, and ministers of the churches of God – concerning all manner of secular affairs, so that in various places the churches of Christ were greatly despoiled, in goods, lands, revenue, and all matters.[5]

---

2. For Coenwulf and Cuthred, see Keynes (1993b: 113–18).
3. For this collection of material (now B.L. Cotton Vespasian B. vi, fols 104–9), see Keynes, forthcoming a.
4. The classic exposition of Coenwulf's dispute with Wulfred is Brooks (1984: 133–6, 180–97 and 322–3). See also Wormald (1982: 127–8); Kirby (1991: 186–7); Keynes (1993b: 118); Cubitt (1995: 191–203); and Kelly, 'Wulfred', in Lapidge *et al.* (1999: 491–2).
5. S 1435 (Kelly, 1998: no. 15), recording a settlement at the council of *Clofesho*, 825: 'Post mortem uero Coenwulfi regis Merciorum multe discordie et innumerabiles dissonancie extollebantur contra uniuscuiusque principalium personarum, regum et episcoporum et pastorum ecclesiarum Dei erga plurima secularia negocia, ita ut multum dispoliate fuerant per loca diuersa ӕcclesie Christi in rebus, in terris<?> , in tributo, in omnibus causis [. . .].' See also Keynes (1993b: 119).

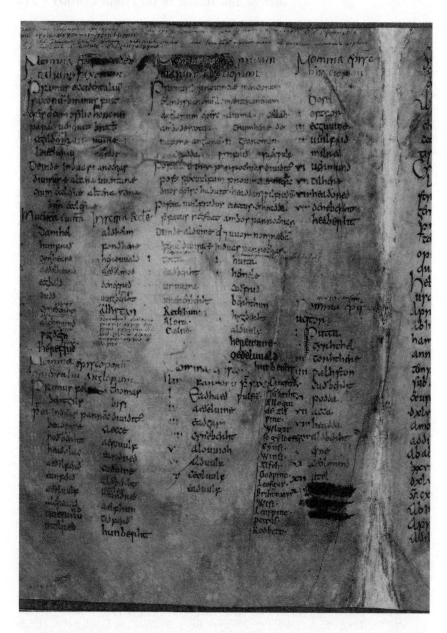

Figure 21.1 Episcopal lists for the sees of Wessex, East Anglia, and Mercia. London, B.L., Cotton MS Vespasian B.vi, f. 108v. © The British Library Board. Courtesy of the British Library Board.

It was perhaps the kind of outbreak which followed the passing of a strong ruler who had kept faction and discord in check, like the pagan reactions in the seventh century or the 'anti-monastic' reaction in the tenth; and it was attended by other indications that the Mercian regime collapsed inwards upon itself in the 820s.[6] It was at about this time that Cynehelm (St Kenelm), son of the late King Coenwulf, was reputedly murdered by his jealous sister, and it is presumably a sign of further internal dissension that Coenwulf's successor Ceolwulf I was 'deprived of his kingdom' in 823. The *Anglo-Saxon Chronicle* reports that in 824 two ealdormen, Burghelm and Muca, 'were killed' (*wurdon ofslægene*). Burghelm is not to be found in any charters of the period, but was probably Mercian, and Muca can be identified as one of the staunch supporters of Ceolwulf's regime.[7] At successive councils of *Clofesho*, in 824 and 825, King Beornwulf was obliged to give way to Archbishop Wulfred in the ongoing dispute about the Kentish minsters, notably involving Coenwulf's daughter Cwoenthryth;[8] and at about this time Beornwulf appears to have appointed a certain Baldred to rule Kent in his interest.[9] It was not a good time for the Mercians to face any opposition. In 825 Ecgberht, king of the West Saxons, defeated Beornwulf at the battle of *Ellendun* (Wroughton, Wilts.), and in the process broke the long-standing Mercian supremacy in the South-East.[10] Soon afterwards the East Angles appealed to Ecgberht for peace and protection, 'because of their fear of the Mercians', and then rose up and killed Beornwulf for themselves. In 827, in what might have been yet another manifestation of internal dissension, King Ludeca was killed, 'and his five ealdormen with him', and Wiglaf succeeded to the kingdom.[11] Ecgberht went on from strength to strength. In 829 he conquered the kingdom of the Mercians, 'and he was the eighth king who was *Bretwalda* [ruler of Britain]'; coins were struck in his name at London as 'king of the Mercians', and a Mercian regnal list accorded him a reign of one year (829–830). Wiglaf seems to have been restored to his former position

---

6. For discussion of the Mercian collapse in the 820s, see Wormald (1982: 128), and Kirby (1991: 188–92).
7. S 186–7.
8. S 1434 and 1436, on which see Brooks (1984: 180–6), and Keynes (1994a: 11–13).
9. Keynes (1993b: 119–20).
10. For a possible fragment (in Latin translation) of a lost vernacular poem on the subject of battles, culminating with the battle of *Ellendun*, see HH, *HA* iv.29 (ed. Greenway, 1996: 262, with comment, p. cii).
11. *ASC*, s.a. 825, 827. In the absence of any charters issued by Ludeca, the five ealdormen in question cannot be securely identified; possibilities include Beornoth, Bofa, Cuthred, Eadberht, Ealhheard, Ecgberht, Uhtred and Wulfred, who appear in the early 820s but not in the 830s (Keynes, 1993a, Table XVII). The statement in JW, *Chron.*, s.a. 825 (ed. Darlington *et al.*, 1995: 244), to the effect that Ludeca was killed when invading East Anglia in order to avenge the death of his kinsman Beornwulf, is perhaps no more than a construction put upon the *ASC* by a Worcester chronicler in the late eleventh or early twelfth century.

in 830; and a charter drawn up in his name, on 1 September 831, tacitly acknowledged the interruption.[12] Clearly, something was rotten in the state of Mercia. The kind of political disruption which followed the death of Æthelbald, in 757, and the deaths of Offa and Ecgfrith, in 796, had been masked on those occasions by the rapid imposition of new regimes; and it is as if, in the 820s, the Mercians were simply unable to get their act together.

The Mercian polity in the ninth century

It is all too easy, therefore, to disregard the last fifty years of Mercia's history as an independent kingdom, from c. 830 to c. 880, as a sad tale of a kingdom withering away on the vine which had sustained it for so long. Perhaps it is more accurately a case of a kingdom reverting to its natural state. The text known to modern scholarship as the Tribal Hidage reminds us of the highly complex composition of the extended Mercian realm in the seventh and eighth centuries.[13] Of course, our understanding of the Mercian polity has many other dimensions (ranging from the exploitation of natural resources, and the development of towns and fortifications, to the role of religious houses in society and politics, the significance of schools of sculpture, and the vitality of other aspects of religious culture), and no-one could doubt that soaring aspirations were entertained on behalf of its rulers. Yet for all the posturing, it is questionable how much progress was made, under Æthelbald and Offa, in the transformation of this vast region into anything approximating to a unified territorial realm.[14] For all that we know, the kingdom of the Mercians remained in the early ninth century much the same as it had been in the middle of the seventh century: a loose confederacy of the Anglian peoples of the Midlands, between the Thames and the Humber, united in their recognition of a single ruler drawn from among their own number, traditionally the ruler of the Mercian peoples of the upper Trent valley, but by no means necessarily conscious of themselves as a single people with a distinctive political tradition. It has been well said and for good reason that 'The Age of Offa was perhaps the end of England's heroic age';[15] yet it is not in ninth-century Mercia that one might expect to find the first signs of whatever age would follow.

What we need is an indication of Mercia's internal political organization, and an explanation of its capacity to survive. It is a

---

12. On the circumstances of Wiglaf's restoration, see Keynes (1993b: 122–4). The charter (S 188) was issued 'in the first year of my second reign' (*anno primo secundi regni mei*).
13. Dumville (1989: 227); Stafford (1985: 94–6); Gelling (1992: 79–85); and Keynes (1995: 21–5 and 27).
14. Cf. Yorke (1990: 114 and 124).
15. Wormald (1982: 128).

significant aspect of Mercian history in the ninth century, as it had been of West Saxon history in the eighth, that successive kings stood in no known relationship to their respective predecessors; and just as a West Saxon chronicler had made up for the difficulty by stating of each king that his ancestry 'goes back to Cerdic',[16] so too are modern historians inclined to resolve Mercian kingship into a protracted rivalry between representatives of at least three different dynasties, each with names alliterating on a particular letter of the alphabet.[17] The principle is sound enough, since practices of name-giving in Anglo-Saxon England sometimes extended to the maintenance of alliteration within a family, or repetition of whole elements. We can but turn to the charters of the ninth-century kings of the Mercians in search of elucidation.[18] The 'C' dynasty centres on King COENWULF, identified in Mercian royal genealogies as son of CUTHBERHT. Coenwulf's brother, CUTHRED, was installed by Coenwulf as king of Kent (798–807). At least three men were styled 'kinsman' (*propinquus*) of either Coenwulf or Cuthred in the early ninth century, namely Coenwald, Cyneberht and Ceolwulf.[19] COENWALD, apparently a son of Cuthred, seems to have maintained a presence with his father in Kent, and recurs among the witnesses to Coenwulf's charters in 811–812.[20] CYNEBERHT, who took precedence over Coenwald in 811–812, may have been a brother of Coenwulf and Cuthred, or a son of Cuthred who had not joined his father.[21] CEOLWULF attested several charters in 814–815, and seems to have held office, or enjoyed status, as a *dux*;[22] he may have been another brother of Coenwulf and Cuthred. Coenwulf is otherwise known to have had a son, CYNEHELM, better known to posterity as St Kenelm of Winchcombe, and a daughter CWOENTHRYTH, abbess of Minster-in-Thanet (Kent), who is alleged to have been involved in

---

16. The basic formula 'þæs cyn geþ to Cerdice' is found in the West Saxon Regnal List, which originated in the late ninth century (and forms a preface to *ASC*, MS. A). Cf. *ASC*, s.a. 757, 786, on Cynewulf and Cyneheard, and Beorhtric: 'and hiera/ his ryhtfederen cyn geþ to Cerdice' ('and their/his true paternal ancestry goes back to Cerdic').
17. For an exposition of this view of ninth-century politics, see Dumville (1977: 98); Wormald (1982: 128 and 138); Stafford (1985: 102–4); Thacker (1985: 9–14); Yorke (1990: 118–20); and Kirby (1991: 194). See also Rollason (1983: 5–9).
18. The charters themselves are registered as S 152–226. The evidence of the witness-lists is set out in Keynes (1993a: Table XVII) ('Attestations of laymen in Mercian charters, 797 – *c.* 920'). The analysis which follows is an expanded form of Keynes (1998: 5, n. 17).
19. The notion that Cunred, abbot of St Augustine's, Canterbury, was a kinsman of Coenwulf and Cuthred depends on S 159, in which the name of Abbot Cunred was substituted in one manuscript for that of the actual beneficiary, Eanberht (who on this reading of the evidence was the kinsman in question): see Kelly (1995: 63–70 (no. 16) and 208–9), and cf. Thacker (1985: 10).
20. Charters of Cuthred (and Coenwulf): S 39 and 41. Charters of Coenwulf: S 168, 165, 169, 170.
21. Charters of Coenwulf: S 168, 165, 169.
22. S 175 ('Signum manus Ceoluulfi ducis'), 176 (ditto), 177 ('Signum manus Ceoluulfi regis propinqui') and 172, dated 814; and S 178, dated 815.

Cynehelm's death.[23] The problem lies in judging how much further to extend the principle in relation to the careers of other C-men in charters. Cuthberht, father of Coenwulf, is conceivably the person of that name who attested charters in the latter part of Offa's reign as a *princeps* (ruler) or *dux* (ealdorman), and who may have had connections in the east midlands.[24] A *princeps* or *dux* called CYNEHELM attested Coenwulf's charters in the first decade of the ninth century, but is not likely to have been the king's son, in which case we have in him another potential royal kinsman on the loose.[25] It would be economical to suppose that the Ceolwulf *dux* who was Coenwulf's brother was the Ceolwulf who succeeded Coenwulf as King Ceolwulf I (821–823). The Cyneberht who was conceivably Cuthred's son, and thus Ceolwulf's nephew, may well be the Cyneberht prominent among the lay witnesses from the early 820s (in the reign of Ceolwulf) to the mid-840s (in the reign of Berhtwulf). It is rather more difficult to judge whether Ceolberht, Ceolheard, Ceolmund and Ceolweard, who appear as *principes* or *duces* in the late eighth and early ninth centuries, were necessarily members of the same family; and perhaps one should hesitate before prolonging the kin-group for another fifty years to include King Ceolwulf II (874–879).[26] The cohesion displayed by this family in the early ninth century is impressive, but the question arises whether the family represents a detachment of the 'Mercian' royal dynasty, in so far as there was such a thing, or a kin-group of separate origin making the best of its own opportunities. It may be significant that the religious house favoured by the family was not in the Mercian heartland, but at Winchcombe, in Gloucestershire. And while the claim entertained on their behalf was that Coenwulf was descended from Coenwealh, a brother of Penda (father of Wulfhere and Æthelred) and of Eowa (progenitor of Æthelbald and Offa), it is not altogether unlikely that Ealdorman Cuthberht and his kin represent the ascendancy of a new group, and that they fabricated a connection with the earlier Mercian overlords when it became politically expedient for them to do so.

Taking their cue from the cohesive identity of the 'C' dynasty, modern historians have created a rival 'B' dynasty, which would appear to have struggled for its existence from the mid-eighth to the early

---

23. Love (1996: lxxxix–cxxxix and 50–89); see also her entry on Kenelm, in Lapidge *et al.* (1999: 269).
24. S 1412 (BCS 271) is a charter by which Beonna, abbot of *Medeshamstede* [Peterborough], sold land at Swineshead, Lincs., to Cuthberht, *princeps*, with reversion to the minster.
25. It was conceivably this Ealdorman Cynehelm who is the subject of S 152 (dated 797), purportedly a charter by which King Coenwulf confirmed a grant of Glastonbury abbey to Cynehelm and his successors. William of Malmesbury was commendably reluctant to identify this Cynehelm as Coenwulf's son of the same name. See WM, *DAntG*, chs. 49–51 (ed. Scott, 1981: 106–10). See also Abrams (1996: 335–7).
26. Thacker (1985: 10); Yorke (1990: 118–19 and 123).

tenth century. The earliest potential members of the kin include Offa's adversary Beornred, in 757, and his son-in-law Beorhtric, king of the West Saxons (786–802), to whom might be added Baldred, king of Kent in the early 820s, and Ealdorman Burghelm, killed in 824.[27] There is, of course, no compelling reason why any of these men should have had anything to do with each other, or indeed with one or more of the three kings of the Mercians in the central decades of the ninth century whose names similarly began with 'B', namely BEORNWULF (823–825), BERHTWULF (840–852) and BURGRED (852–874). Yet we do notice the same proclivity towards alliteration. Beornwulf had a brother BYNNA;[28] and Berhtwulf had at least two sons, BERHTRIC, who attested charters in the mid–840s,[29] and BERHTFERTH, who gained notoriety for his alleged complicity in the murder of Wigstan, son of Wigmund, in 849, and who can perhaps be identified as the Berhtferth 'king's son' who attested a West Saxon charter in 868.[30] Two other putative members of the B-dynasty are the atheling BEORNOTH (presumably a son of Berhtwulf or Burgred), and his son BERHTSIGE (who appears in the late 890s and early 900s).[31] We might ask ourselves where the B-kings came from. Beornwulf was quite possibly the *dux* of that name who attested a charter of Coenwulf in 812 and one of Ceolwulf in 823, although not in a position which suggested much prospect of future advancement; Berhtwulf was conceivably the layman of that name who attested a charter of King Wiglaf in 836; and Burgred may be the *dux* of that name who attested a charter of King Berhtwulf in the mid–840s (Figure 21.2).[32] The names are by no means common in ninth-century charters, and in each case the attestations are chronologically compatible with elevation to kingship; yet to judge from their attestations, these were not men who could have had much expectation of the distinction about to be thrust upon them. The succession of kings of the 'B' dynasty was interrupted by Ludeca (826–827) and Wiglaf (827–829, 830–840), before being restored in the persons of Berhtwulf and Burgred. Ludeca is a largely unknown quantity, but it should be noted that he too had appeared previously as a *dux*, in the

---

27. For Beornred, see Dumville (1977: 98), Wormald (1982: 138) and Yorke (1990: 112). For the suggestion that Beorhtric was a '(?) Mercian nominee to the throne of Wessex', see Collins (1991: 334). For Baldred, see Yorke (1990: 119); a Baldred attests a charter of Berhtwulf in the mid-840s (S 204) and charters of Burgred (S 206, 212). For Burghelm, see *ASC*, s.a. 824.
28. S 1433 and 1436–7.
29. S 198 and 205.
30. For the involvement of Berhtferth, son of King Berhtwulf, in the murder of St Wigstan, see JW, *Chronicon*, *s.a.* 849 (ed. Darlington *et al.*, 1995: 262). The Berhtferth *filius regis* who attested S 539 (868), was conceivably the same son of Berhtwulf, or a son of Burgred; see Keynes (1998: 11, n. 40), and Keynes (1994b: 1130–1).
31. *ASC*, s.a. 903, and Keynes (1998: 39, n. 168). Unfortunately, there is no sign of a family member called Beowulf.
32. Beornwulf: S 170 (812) and 187 (823). Berhtwulf: S 190 (836). Burgred: S 204 (*c.* 845).

Figure 21.2 Charter of Berhtwulf, king of the Mercians, issued *c.* 845, granting land at Wootton Underwood, Bucks., to Forthred his thegn. Canterbury, Dean and Chapter, Chart. Ant. C. 1280. By kind permission of the Dean and Chapter of Canterbury

entourage of King Beornwulf in 824, without any indication of particular distinction.[33] Some of the several *principes* or *duces* called Wigbald, Wigberht, Wigcga, Wigferth and Wigheard, prominent in Mercian charters in the late eighth and early ninth centuries, could be resolved with little further exercise of the imagination into a family of Wigs; and while there happens not to be any sign among them of a Wiglaf, it would be churlish not to include among their number the person of that name who became king of the Mercians in the wake of Ludeca's demise in 827. King Wiglaf is known to have had a son called Wigmund.[34] According to hagiographical tradition, Wigmund married Ælfflæd, daughter of Ceolwulf I, presumably in the hope of gaining something from association with the C-dynasty; but their son Wigstan fell foul of Berhtferth, scion of the B-dynasty, and had to make do with innocent martyrdom, burial at Repton, and sainthood.[35] There is, incidentally, no sign during Burgred's reign of the 'foolish king's thegn' called Ceolwulf, who became King Ceolwulf II; and two possible occurrences in Burgred's reign of the Æthelred who became Æthelred, Lord of the Mercians, constitute all that is known of the origins of their last ruler.[36]

The 'dynastic' construction put on Mercian history in the ninth century has much to recommend it, as long as we do not lose sight of three facts. In the first place, there is no guarantee that the C-, B- and W-dynasties were branches of the ancient 'Mercian' royal house, as opposed to other kin-groups on the make. By the same token, there is no reason to suppose that they necessarily originated in the Mercian heartland of the upper Trent valley. Second, those who rose to become rulers of the Mercians in the ninth century appear in several cases to have attested the charters of their immediate predecessors, though never with any striking degree of prominence or consistency. The implication seems to be that royal succession among the Mercians in the ninth century was far from predictable, and that it depended more on the ability of one among a profusion of *principes* or *duces* to secure support from among their own number, after a king's death, and to gain recognition from them all as the new king, *primus inter pares*. Third, there is more to know about the Mercian polity than the

---

33. S 1433–4.
34. A charter of King Wiglaf for Archbishop Wulfred, issued in 831 at Wychbold (Worcs.) (S 188), is attested by Wigmund *filius regis*.
35. For Wigstan and Berhtferth, see JW, *Chronicon, s.a.* 849 (ed. Darlington *et al.*, 1995: 262). See also Rollason (1983: 5–9); Thacker (1985: 12–13); Rollason (1989: 117–18); Yorke (1990: 119–20); and Kirby (1991: 194). If we may believe the tale, Wiglaf had been succeeded [in the late 830s] by his son Wigmund, who had married Ælfflæd; Wigmund died, and was succeeded by Berhtwulf; Berhtferth, son of Berhtwulf, wished to marry Ælfflæd; Wigstan, son of Wigmund, opposed it; and Berhtferth killed Wigstan [in 849]. On the dynastic role of women, see Stafford, Chapter 3 in this volume.
36. S 212 (866) and 214 (869); the latter is shown in Fig. 21.3 For Æthelred and Alfred, see Keynes (1998: 19–34).

respective fortunes of its competing dynasties, and much to be learnt from surviving charters about other aspects of the Mercian regime during the last fifty years of its existence. For the earlier part of the ninth century we have 'Mercian' charters from Kent (and Sussex), as well as from Mercia itself; but for the reigns of Berhtwulf (840–852), Burgred (852–874) and Ceolwulf II (874–879), and for Ealdorman Æthelred (*c.* 880–911), we are almost entirely dependent on material from Mercia alone. The majority of the charters are from the archives of Worcester cathedral, so special attention should be reserved for two charters, both preserved in their original form (from the archives of Christ Church, Canterbury), both in favour of laymen, and both all the more significant for representing diplomatic practices which obtained elsewhere in the kingdom. One is a remarkable vernacular charter by which King Berhtwulf granted land at Wotton Underwood (Bucks.) to his thegn (*minister*) Forthred, in the mid-840s (Figure 21.2).[37] The other is a charter by which King Burgred and Queen Æthelswith ('coronata stemma regali Anglorum regina') granted land at *Upthrop* (unidentified) to Wulflaf in 869, with restriction thereafter to the male line (Figure 21.3).[38] Both charters show the Mercian king going about his business accompanied by an impressive array of bishops, ealdormen, and others. If only more charters like them had chanced to survive, we would have a better understanding of the Mercian regime in the mid-ninth century, and might even hesitate before regarding the kingdom as one in a state of terminal decline. Even Ceolwulf II issued charters and coins of a kind which is difficult to reconcile with the judgement of those who wrote him off in the early 890s as a 'foolish king's thegn'.[39]

The ninth-century kings of the Mercians take their places, therefore, *among* rather than *above* those who moved in the upper echelons of the social hierarchy in the Mercian regime; and we turn to the charters, again, in the hope of forming a better idea of the identity, unfolding careers, and local or personal associations of all those whom we may judge from attestations to have formed part of this secular elite. There is a basic distinction between those styled 'ealdorman' (*dux*, a term apparently synonymous with *princeps*) and those not accorded a title of any kind, and one can but hope that the names of the ealdormen meant more in the ninth century than they do now: Beornoth (*c.* 798–825), Heardberht (*c.* 798–816), Cynehelm (*c.* 800–811), Ceolweard (*c.* 803–811), Eadberht (*c.* 809–825), Sigered (*c.* 816–848), Cyneberht (*c.* 822–845), Ælfstan (*c.* 830–852), Æthelheard (*c.* 830–855), Humberht (*c.* 835–866), Beornheard (*c.* 852–869), Æthelwulf (*c.* 855–871), Beornoth

---

37. S 204 (Canterbury, Dean and Chapter, Chart. Ant. C. 1280) = *OSFacs.* i. 8. For further discussion of the charter, see Baines (1979) and Kelly (1990: 55–6).
38. S 214 (BL Cotton Augustus ii. 76) = *BMFacs.* ii. 39.
39. For Ceolwulf's charters, see S 215 (*EHD*, no. 95) and 216. For his coins, see Blackburn and Keynes (1998). For his treatment in the *Chronicle*, see Keynes (1998: 18–19).

Figure 21.3 Charter of Burgred, king of the Mercians, dated 869, granting land at Upthrop [unidentified] to Wulflaf. London, B.L., Cotton MS Augustus ii. 76 © The British Library, courtesy of the British Library Board

(*c.* 855–884), and others like them. The careers of these men often span two or more reigns, as if there was at least some continuity irrespective of the changes at the top. But what kind of men were they? One might assume that these *principes* or *duces* were appointed to their high office by the king, and assigned responsibility for one or other of the former satellite provinces, now integrated as ealdormanries into an enlarged kingdom of Mercia.[40] An alternative possibility is that some if not all of the *principes* or *duces* were themselves the hereditary or chosen leaders of different peoples within the extended Mercian world, who owed their status to the position which they held or to the standing which they enjoyed locally, and who acknowledged the overall sovereignty of the Mercian king. Two of their number who can be placed in some other context may be typical of the rest. Humberht was distinctively prominent during the reigns of Wiglaf, Berhtwulf and Burgred, and is known to have been *princeps* of the *Tomsæte*, in the very heartland of Mercia; and Æthelred (Mucel) is described by Asser as ealdorman 'of the *Gaini*'.[41] If only on this basis one might suppose that the ealdormen are more likely to have been rulers of their own peoples, who acknowledged the authority of the Mercian king, than persons appointed by the king to hold a particular office in a particular part of his kingdom. It is also significant that we do not gain much sense, from the charters, of men serving the king at a lower level of the hierarchy, and accompanying him on his peregrinations around his realm. We encounter a *pedisequus* or two;[42] a *thelonius* (toll-gatherer), and a person who might be regarded as a royal priest;[43] but what we seem to miss is a group identifiable as a *body* of thegns (*ministri*), standing out by virtue of the *regularity* of their occurrences in the witness-lists of the king's charters, who might have represented office-holders within the king's household.

The question arises whether the operation of royal government in Mercia necessarily involved an elaborate administrative infrastructure, or whether the kings exercised their powers in ways which left less of a trace. The scarcity of surviving charters for some of the key parts of the kingdom, not to mention the absence of other forms of documentation, impede our understanding of this matter, but it is

---

40. For discussion along these lines, see, e.g., Chadwick (1905a: 168–70, 259–60, 290–2, 317–18); Oman (1949: 366–74); and esp. Stenton (1971: 304–6). For more recent discussion, see, e.g., Hart (1977: 58–9); Thacker (1981: 204–5) (*princeps*); and Yorke (1990: 125–6).
41. For Humberht and the *Tomsæte* (S 197), see Yorke (1990: 124) and Keynes (1994a: 39–40). One might have expected that the leader of the *Tomsæte* would be the king of the Mercians. For Mucel and the *Gaini* (Asser, *Vita Ælfredi regis*, ch. 29), see Keynes and Lapidge (1983: 240–1).
42. E.g. Æthelheah, *pedisequus* (later *dux*) of King Coenwulf (S 168, 169); Cuthred, *pessessor* or *pedisequus* of King Coenwulf (S 170, 1861); Bola, *pedisequus* of King Beornwulf (S 1434, 1436); Alfred, *pedisequus* of King Wiglaf (S 188).
43. For the *thelonius*, and for the royal priest (Piot), see Keynes (1994a: 48, with n. 206).

clear enough that the Mercian regime sustained itself in the time-honoured way. Kings and ealdormen were able to demand services from their people in respect of their land, and were inclined in certain circumstances to grant exemptions from at least some of these services, with reservation of those pertaining to military service;[44] though it has been noted that the tendency of kings to sell extensive privileges to religious houses may reflect a shortage on their part of more tangible resources, like money and land.[45] And lest it be supposed that the Mercians were isolated in their midland strongholds, it should be noted that one charter, issued in 848, seeks to protect the interests of ambassadors and messengers coming to the king's court from overseas, from Wessex, or from Northumbria.[46] The significant question is whether the kingdom was divided, in the ninth century, into territorial divisions approximating to shires, each placed by the king under an ealdorman, and whether there is any sign of formally constituted sub-divisions set up for administrative, judicial, financial, military and social purposes. Absence of evidence is not evidence of absence; but the likelihood is that the process of extending such arrangements from Wessex into Mercia was not begun until the late ninth or early tenth century.[47]

The West Saxon polity in the ninth century

If we turn our attention to the kingdom of the West Saxons in the ninth century, we seem in several respects to be entering a different world. It is the case that the *Anglo-Saxon Chronicle* does good service for the West Saxon regime by providing it with deep roots, a strong sense of purpose and direction, and the kind of credibility which arises from a profusion of circumstantial detail. It is also the case that the law-code of King Ine (688–726) throws light on the organization and structure of the kingdom at a relatively early stage in its development,[48] and, in its association with the law-code of King Alfred (871–899), lends the West Saxon polity of the eighth and ninth centuries the appearance of order

---

44. Several charters which afford an insight into the Mercian regime in the central decades of the ninth century are readily accessible in *EHD*: S 190 (*EHD*, no. 85), 192 (ibid., no. 86), 1271 (ibid., no. 87), 206 (ibid., no. 90), 207 (ibid., no. 91), 208 (ibid., no. 92), and 215 (ibid., no. 95). For the reservation of military service in Mercian charters, from the mid-eighth century onwards, see Brooks (2000a: 39–42 and 46).
45. Wormald (1982: 138–9). One should add, of course, that circumstances were not conducive to the preservation of ninth-century Mercian charters in favour of laymen.
46. S 197 (above, n. 41).
47. On these matters, see Stenton (1971: 336–8); Taylor (1957); Gelling (1992: 125–45); and Stafford (1985: 137–43). Cf. Campbell (1995: 53): 'In the mid-ninth century Wessex certainly and Mercia probably had an ealdorman for each shire.'
48. For Ine's law-code, see *EHD*, no. 32. For important general observations on Ine's law-code, see Wormald (1999: 103–6). Cf. Keynes (1995: 26–7).

and respectability. At the same time, it has become axiomatic in modern scholarship that the Mercians are known to us from the testimony of their victims, rivals, and critics; and that if only we had comparable material we would realize how much like their neighbours they were. The point is well made, but the notion that significant differences existed between the two polities arises of its own accord from analysis of charters, where the evidence is more evenly balanced.

West Saxon charters of the eighth and ninth centuries are preserved in a variety of archives, providing a form of control for documents which would be difficult to assess in isolation from each other.[49] The charters issued in the second half of the eighth century reflect the kingdom's ability to preserve its independence at a time of sustained Mercian supremacy elsewhere in Southumbria, and suggest that King Cynewulf (757–786) and King Beorhtric (786–802) may have been able to consolidate the foundations laid by Ine in the late seventh century.[50] Another factor which contributed to the rise of Wessex was the obvious strength of the royal dynasty established by King Ecgberht (802–839). It has been suggested that the line originated in Kent, since Ecgberht's father Ealhmund had been king of Kent in the mid–780s, but the natural presumption remains that the line was genuinely West Saxon, and that it was not the son who went from Kent into Wessex, but the father who had strayed from Wessex into Kent.[51] The combination of archaeological and numismatic evidence adds a further dimension to our understanding of the dynamics of the kingdom of Wessex in this early period, by reminding us of its economic prosperity, and of its access to foreign markets.[52] One gets the impression that in the first quarter of the ninth century Ecgberht may have focused attention on his position in Wessex, securing his resources in the South-West before turning to contemplate an extension of his interests to the East, and perhaps in particular towards the lucrative markets of London and Kent.[53] The tale of his success, culminating in 829 with his 'conquest' of the kingdom of the Mercians, followed by his expedition to receive

---

49. For a survey of West Saxon charters of the period up to the death of King Ecgberht, see Edwards (1988). For West Saxon charters of the period from 839 to 899, see Keynes (1994b). The evidence of the witness-lists is set out in Keynes (1993a, Table XXI) ('Attestations of laymen in West Saxon charters of the ninth century'). The analysis which follows is an expanded form of Keynes (1998: 5, n. 16).
50. Keynes, forthcoming a.
51. Ibid.
52. For the excavations at Southampton, see Morton (1992: I, 26–30 and 59–77); and Andrews (1997: II, 252–6); see also Morton (1999). For the earliest West Saxon coinage (with the suggestion that it was minted at Southampton), see Dolley (1970) and Blackburn (1986: 294–5).
53. The distribution of single finds of eighth- and ninth-century coinage reflects the inclusion of Southampton in the area of economic activity which also includes London and Kent; see Dolley and Metcalf (1958: 462) and Keynes, forthcoming a, n. 117, with references.

the submission of the Northumbrians, does not need to be retold.[54] It must suffice to stress the long-term significance of his accommodation with Wiglaf in the 830s, and the foresight displayed in his dealings with ecclesiastical and political interests in Kent, symbolized most effectively by the agreement reached at the council of Kingston in 838.[55] Ecgberht's son Æthelwulf (839–858) contributed further to the process, in the 840s, by carefully cultivating his interests in Kent, and, in the 850s, by cultivating other interests not only on the Continent (represented by his dealings with the Carolingians and with the papacy) but also at home and in Heaven (represented by his 'Decimation' of 854–855). He gave Burgred and the Mercians some help against the Welsh, and gave the English a taste of victory over the Vikings. Yet although Æthelwulf did so much to raise the prestige of the monarchy (and to secure the continuation of his line), he resolved nonetheless to divide the kingdom after his death into its two component parts, with Æthelbald (to be followed by Æthelred and Alfred) in the West and Æthelberht in the East. It was Æthelbald's early death, in 860, that prompted the agreement among the surviving brothers whereby Æthelberht succeeded to the kingdom as a whole, with the prospect of Æthelred and Alfred to follow.[56] It is arguably to the credit of the brothers that they ignored their father's intentions, and saw the advantages of building a unified kingdom across southern England from Cornwall to Kent; for while we need not doubt that there was much to be gained from access to the natural resources of the South-West, the brothers cannot have been oblivious to everything that Canterbury, and London, would always have to offer.[57] It is also to their credit that they saw the advantages of maintaining an alliance with Burgred, in the economic interests of both parties and against the forces of the common enemy.

Yet there was more to the strength of Wessex in the ninth century than effective dynastic management. The charters of the late eighth and ninth centuries take us deeper into the political and social fabric of the kingdom, and suggest what appears to be a telling contrast with corresponding structures in the kingdom of Mercia. In the charters of Cynewulf, Beorhtric and Ecgberht, we encounter a profusion of

---

54. Wormald (1982: 139–40); Yorke (1990: 148–9); Kirby (1991: 189–95).
55. Brooks (1984: 197–200); Wormald (1982: 140); Keynes (1993b: 121–4) and (1994: 1112–14). Kirby (1991: 192–3) suggests that Ecgberht's successes in the 820s were owed to Frankish support, and that it was the withdrawal of that support, *c.* 830, that occasioned a reversal of West Saxon fortune and recovery of independence in Mercia and East Anglia.
56. Keynes and Lapidge (1983: 314–16); and for the reunification of the kingdom, as reflected in charters, see Keynes (1993b: 128–30). Cf. Kirby (1991: 200–4).
57. For an important demonstration of the potential significance, to Alfred, of the natural resources in the South-West, see Maddicott (1988); though perhaps there is less to be said for the notion that the exploitation of these resources was necessitated by a collapse in the east (cf. ibid., pp. 7–12, 17, 48). See also Balzaretti, *et al.* (1992: 162–3).

prefecti, a term which denotes men set up in authority over others, presumably appointed to their high office by the king.[58] The term *prefectus* was superseded in the later ninth century by *dux* (*ealdorman* in the vernacular), concealing what may have been a fundamental difference between the men who bore this title in the two kingdoms. If the *duces*, or ealdormen, seem in Mercia to have been the leaders of their respective peoples, who gave their support to the one among their number whom they recognized as king, the *duces* seem in Wessex to have been men placed by kings in control of particular shires, who held their office at the king's pleasure. It is well known that the ancient shires of southern England came into being under different circumstances: Cornwall and Devon took shape from ancient king-doms; Dorset and Somerset were named after those who lived in proximity to (or were governed from) the royal estates at Dorchester and Somerton; Wiltshire and Hampshire denote the territories dependent upon or governed from the royal estates at Wilton and Southampton; while Sussex, Surrey and Kent, like Cornwall and Devon, were old political entities.[59] It is possible to make good sense of the succession to the various ealdormanries in the ninth century,[60] and it is instructive to find the ealdormen themselves leading their shire levies into battle against the Vikings already in the 840s and 850s.[61] The contrast with Mercia could not be more striking. It is otherwise worth noting that *thegns* (*ministri*) are conspicuous by their presence in ninth-century West Saxon charters, as if the kings were encouraging the development of a hierarchy of lesser officials, some of whom may have held office in the royal household.

The emergence of a new political order

A major historical issue in the ninth century is how to account for the decline of Mercia and the ascendancy of Wessex, and how to characterize the political order which had emerged by the end of Alfred's reign. There is no simple answer, such as a decisive battle leading to permanent political change, or the unexpected intervention of a third party affecting one kingdom more than the other. Rather, and unsurprisingly, a complex combination of factors was at work. The implosion of the Mercian regime in the 820s should not distract us from the larger picture. While it is necessary to make due allowance for the inequalities of the source material at our disposal, the overall impression which emerges from analysis of ninth-century charters is that Mercia and Wessex differed from each other in significant

---

58. Thacker (1981: 211–12) (*prefectus*).
59. Brooks (2000c: 121–2); Campbell (1995: 43, n. 9).
60. Keynes (1993a, Table XXII).
61. *ASC, s.a.* 840, 845, 851, 853, 860.

respects, and in ways which might help us to understand what happened in the face of sustained Viking attack.[62] It is not that structures in Wessex were more advanced or more effective than equivalent structures in Mercia; simply that they were different, and perhaps better adapted to survive in the changing circumstances. The point is not to *expect* Mercia to be on a par with Wessex, or to judge one kingdom by standards derived from the other. Dynastic strength in Wessex was matched by continuity of political purpose: the close involvement with the South-East in the 830s, 840s and 850s gave way to the more effective integration of Kent in the 860s; and the relationship cultivated with the rulers of the Mercians found expression not only in a form of monetary union but also in the military alliances and dynastic marriages of 853 and 868. The impact of the Viking raids was clearly an important factor, seeming to threaten the very survival of the Christian faith.[63] The presence of Vikings (perhaps more so than a reading of Bede) made people all the more conscious of their common identity, both as English and as Christians, while the seemingly systematic 'conquest' of the kingdoms of East Anglia (870), Mercia (874) and Northumbria (875) kept the pressure on Wessex to succeed where others had failed. It has been suggested that the Viking raids had a devastating effect on Kent in the mid-ninth century, prompting the West Saxons to exploit their natural resources in the South-West.[64] Yet while one can be sure that the West Saxons did just that, they also understood that it was the importance of London and the River Thames to the economy of the whole of southern England which would determine the shape of any long-term political solution.

Does this bring us any closer to an understanding of Mercia's 'collapse' in the 860s and 870s?[65] On the face of it, the evidence is damning. Burgred's immediate reaction when the Vikings invaded Mercia in the winter of 867–868 had been to appeal to the West Saxons for help. The Mercians 'made peace' with the Vikings at London in 871–872 (in other words bought them off), and again at Torksey in 872–873, before capitulating at Repton in 873–874. Burgred was driven out of the country, and set off for Rome with his wife Æthelswith and their small entourage.[66] The *Anglo-Saxon Chronicle* is contemptuous in its treatment of Ceolwulf II, both in its account of the circumstances of his accession in 874, in the wake of Burgred's departure, and in its account of the division of the kingdom in 877, when the eastern part passed under Viking control. The chronicler

---

62. On the difficulty of making any such comparisons, see Brooks (2000b: 48–9) and Kirby (1991: 192).
63. Brooks (2000b: 59–62).
64. See Maddicott (1988: 7–9) and above, n. 57.
65. Wormald (1982: 138–9); Yorke (1990: 123–4); Kirby (1991: 194–5).
66. *ASC, s.a.* 874. For further evidence of their passage to Rome, see Keynes (1997: 109–10 and 115–16), with Plate 2.

makes no mention, however, of whatever lay behind the apparent demise of Ceolwulf, *c.* 879, or of what happened thereafter, leaving a modern reader wholly in the dark. It may be that Alfred's victory at Edington, in 878, and Ceolwulf's demise, *c.* 879, gave Alfred the stature and the opportunity to fill a political vacuum; and that the kingdom of Mercia, as a political entity, did not collapse, but was taken by Ealdorman Æthelred into a new political order. For the product of all these circumstances was the birth in the early 880s of the Alfredian 'Kingdom of the Anglo-Saxons', conceived as a polity for all the English people who were not under subjection to the Danes (whether in Mercia, Wessex, or the South-East), given more formal expression in 886 in connection with Alfred's restoration of the city of London, and destined to be transformed in the 920s into King Æthelstan's 'Kingdom of the English'.[67] Modern historians determined to stand up for Mercia may be more sensitive to Mercian feelings than the Mercians were themselves; for while some Mercians, in the late ninth century, would naturally have objected to the ending of their separate political identity, others might have been able to accept the development as part of a new way forward.

Historians of Anglo-Saxon England cannot afford to underestimate the Mercian dimension.[68] If we look at the seventh century from Northumbria, the eighth century from the Continent, the ninth century from Wessex, the tenth century from inside a monastery, and the eleventh century from behind a shield-wall, we never get much sense of the contribution from Mercia. Yet all three of the kings who presided over the English at periods of most significant political change in the ninth and tenth centuries could not have done without it: the Mercians had vital parts to play in Alfred's inspirational 'Kingdom of the Anglo-Saxons', in Æthelstan's visionary 'Kingdom of the English', and in Edgar's realization of the same. When a chronicler reported the appointment of Eadric Streona, in 1007, as ealdorman of the Mercians, the phrase used was 'throughout the kingdom of the Mercians' (*geond Myrcnarice*); and it is testimony of a kind to the power of the office that when it came into the wrong hands it proved as threatening to the security of England as it had once been essential to its making.

---

67. For the 'Kingdom of the Anglo-Saxons' (*c.* 880–927), see Keynes (1998: 34–9) and Keynes (2001).
68. For a recent assessment of the Mercian contribution to English history (unpublished at the time of writing), see Walker (2000).

Bibliography

Abels, R. (1988), *Lordship and Military Obligation in Anglo-Saxon England*. London, British Museum Press.

Abels, R. (1997), 'English logistics and military organisation, 871–1066: the impact of the Viking wars', in A. Nørgård Jørgensen and B.L. Clausen (eds), *Military Aspects of Scandinavian Society in a European Perspective, AD 1–1300*. Copenhagen, National Museum, pp. 257–65.

Abrams, L. (1996), *Anglo-Saxon Glastonbury: Church and Endowment*. Studies in Anglo-Saxon History **8**, Woodbridge, Boydell and Brewer.

Adams, B. and Jackson, D. (1992), 'The Anglo-Saxon cemetery at Wakerley, Northamptonshire: excavations by Mr D. Jackson 1968–9', *Northamptonshire Archaeology*, **22**: 69–178.

Adriaen, M. (ed.) (1957), *Sanctus Ambrosius – Expositio Evangelii Secundum Lucam*, in *CCSL* 14, Turnhout, Brepols.

Alexander, J. J. G. (1978), *Insular Manuscripts, 6th to the 9th Century*. London, Harvey Miller.

Allen, J. R. and Anderson, A. O. (1903), *The Early Christian Monuments of Scotland: A Classified, Illustrated, Descriptive List of the Monuments, with Analysis of Their Symbolism and Ornamentation*. London, Society of Antiquaries of Scotland (reprinted 1993, Balgavies, Pinkfoot Press).

Allott, S. (1974), *Alcuin of York: His Life and Letters*. York, William Sessions Ltd.

Andersen, H. H. (1998), *Danevirke og Kovirke: Arkæologiske undersøgelser 1861–1993*. Aarhus, Jysk Arkæologisk Selskab.

Anderson, A. O. and Anderson, M. O. (1991), *Adamnan's Life of Columba*. Oxford, Clarendon Press.

Anderson, B. (1991), *Imagined Communities: Reflections on the Origins and Spread of Nationalism* (2nd edn). London, Verso.

Anderson, M. A. O. (1980), *Kings and Kingship in Early Scotland*. Edinburgh, Scottish Academic Press.

Andrew, W. J. (1911), 'A numismatic history of the reign of Stephen', *British Numismatic Journal*, **8**: 87–136.

Andrews, P. (1995), 'Excavations at Redcastle Furze, Thetford, 1988–9', *East Anglian Archaeology*, **72**: 24–7.

Andrews, P. (ed.) (1997), *Excavations at Hamwic*, II: *Excavations at Six*

Dials. CBA Research Report **109**, York, Council for British Archaeology.

Andrews, P. and Penn, K. (1999), 'Excavations in Thetford, north of the river, 1989–90', *East Anglian Archaeology*, **87**: 88–90.

Angenendt, A. (1984), *Kaiserherrschaft und Königstaufe.* Berlin, W. de Gruyter.

Angenendt, A. (1990), *Das Frühmittelalter: Die abendländische Christenheit von 400 bis 900.* Stuttgart, Kohlhammer.

Anonymous (1999), 'New Saxon horse burial in Suffolk', *British Archaeology*, **50**: 5.

Archibald, M. M. (1985), 'The coinage of Beonna in the light of the Middle Harling hoard', *British Numismatic Journal*, **55**: 10–54.

Archibald, M. M. (1991), contributions in L. Webster and J. Backhouse (eds), *The Making of England: Anglo-Saxon Art and Culture, AD 600–900.* London, British Museum Press.

Archibald, M. M. and Fenwick, V. with Cowell, M. R. (1995), 'A sceat of Ethelberht I of East Anglia and recent finds of coins of Beonna', *British Numismatic Journal* **65**: 1–19.

Atkin, M. (1993), 'The Norwich Survey 1971–1985: a retrospective view', in J. Gardiner (ed.), *Flatlands and Wetlands: Current Themes in East Anglian Archaeology*, East Anglian Archaeology, **50**: 127–43.

Audouy, M. (1984), 'Excavations at the Church of All Saints, Brixworth, Northamptonshire, 1981–2', *Journal of the British Archaeological Association*, **137**: 1–44.

Axboe, M. (1982), 'The Scandinavian gold bracteates', *Acta Archaeologica*, **52**: 1–87.

Ayre, J. and Wroe-Brown, R. with Malt, R. (1996), 'Aethelred's Hythe to Queenhithe: the origin of a London Dock', *Medieval Life*, **5**: 14–25.

Backes, M. and Dölling, R. (1969), *Art of the Dark Ages.* New York, Abrams.

Bailey, K. (1989), 'The Middle Saxons', in S. Basset (ed.), *The Origins of Anglo-Saxon Kingdoms.* London and New York, Leicester University Press, pp. 108–22 and 265–9.

Bailey, R. N. (1980), *Viking Age Sculpture.* London, William Collins Sons and Co. Ltd.

Bailey, R. N. (1990), *The Meaning of Mercian Sculpture.* Sixth Brixworth Lecture (1988), Leicester, University of Leicester, Vaughan Papers in Adult Education, **34**.

Bailey, R. N. (1996), *England's Earliest Sculptors.* Toronto, Pontifical Institute of Medieval Studies.

Bailey, R. N. (2000), 'The Gandersheim Casket and Anglo-Saxon stone sculpture', in R. Marth (ed.), *Das Gandersheimer Runenkästchen, Internationales Kolloquium Braunschweig, 24.–26. März 1999.* Braunschweig, Herzog Anton Ulrich Museum: pp. 43–52.

Bailey, R. N. and Cramp, R. (1988), *Cumberland, Westmoreland and Lancashire North of the Sands, Corpus of Anglo-Saxon Stone Sculpture in England. 2*, Oxford, Oxford University Press for the British Academy.

Baines, A. H. J. (1979), 'The boundaries of Wotton Underwood', *Records of Buckinghamshire*, **21**: 141–53.

Bakka, E. (1963), *Some English Decorated Metal Objects Found in Norwegian Viking Graves. Contributions to the Art History of the Eighth Century A.D. Årbok for Universitetet i Bergen. Humanistik Serie 1963*. **1**, Bergen, University of Bergen.

Baldwin Brown, G. (1937), *Anglo-Saxon Sculpture: The Arts in Early England*. **6.2**, E. Sexton (ed.), London, John Murray.

Balkwill, C. (1993), 'Old English *wic* and the origin of the hundred', *Landscape History*, **15**: 5–12.

Balzaretti, R. *et al.* (1992), 'Debate: trade, industry and the wealth of King Alfred', *Past & Present*, **135**: 142–88.

Bannerman, J. (1999) 'The Scottish takeover of Pictland and the relics of St Columba', in D. Broun and T. O. Clancy (eds), *Spes Scotorum: Hope of the Scots*. Edinburgh, T & T Clark: pp. 71–94.

Barnwell, P. S. (1991), '*Epistula Hieronimi de gradus Romanorum*: an English school book', *Historical Research*, **64**: 77–86.

Barraclough, G. and Parker, G. (eds) (1993), *The Times Atlas of World History* (4th edn). London, Times Books.

Bartrum, C. (ed.) (1966), *Early Welsh Genealogical Tracts*. Cardiff, Wales University Press.

Bassett, S. (1983), *The Wootton Wawen Project. Interim Report No. 1*. Birmingham, University of Birmingham School of History.

Bassett, S. (1986), *The Wootton Wawen Project. Interim Report No. 4*. Birmingham, University of Birmingham School of History.

Bassett, S. (1989a), 'Churches in Worcester before and after the conversion of the Anglo-Saxons', *Antiquaries Journal*, **69**, 225–56.

Bassett, S. (ed.) (1989b), *The Origins of the Anglo-Saxon Kingdoms*. London, Leicester University Press.

Bassett, S. (1992), 'Church and diocese in the West Midlands: the transition from British to Anglo-Saxon control', in J. Blair and R. Sharpe (eds), *Pastoral Care before the Parish*. Leicester, London and New York, Leicester University Press: pp. 13–40.

Bassett, S. (1996), 'The administrative landscape of the diocese of Worcester in the tenth century', in N. Brooks and C. Cubitt (eds), *St Oswald of Worcester: His Life and Influence*. Leicester, Leicester University Press: pp. 147–73.

Bassett, S. (2000), 'How the west was won: the Anglo-Saxon take-over in the West Midlands', *Anglo-Saxon Studies in Archaeology and History*, **11**: 107–18.

Bassett, S. (forthcoming), 'Burhs in the period of Mercian supremacy', in D. Hill and M. Worthington (eds), *Æthelbald and Offa*. Oxford, British Archaeological Reports, Br. Ser.

Bately, J. M. (1988), 'Old English prose before and during the reign of Alfred', *Anglo-Saxon England*, **17**: 93–138.

Bateman, T. (1861), *Ten Years' Digging in Celtic and Saxon Grave-hills*. London and Derby, J. R. Smith and W. Bemrose and Sons.

Beckwith, J. (1964), *Early Medieval Art*. London, Thames and Hudson.

Berglund, B. (1994), 'The Ystad project', in S. Helmfrid (ed.), *Landscape and Settlements*. Stockholm, National Atlas of Sweden: pp. 18–21.

Berschin, W. (1991), *Biographie und Epochenstil im lateinischen Mittelalter*, 3, Karolingische Biographien 750–920, Stuttgart, Hiersemann.

Bestul, T. H. (1986), 'Continental sources of Anglo-Saxon devotional writing', in P. E. Szarmach (ed.), *Sources of Anglo-Saxon Culture*. Kalamazoo, Medieval Institute Publications, Western Michigan University: pp. 103–26.

Biddle, M. (1984), 'London on the Strand', *Popular Archaeology*, July: 23–7.

Biddle, M. (1989), 'A city in transition: 400–800', in M. D. Lobel (ed.), *The City of London from Prehistoric Times to c. 1520: The British Atlas of Historic Towns*. 3, Oxford, Oxford University Press: pp. 20–9.

Biddle, M. and Kjølbye-Biddle, B. (1985), 'The Repton Stone', *Anglo-Saxon England*, 14: 233–92.

Biddle, M. and Kjølbye-Biddle, B. (1992), 'Repton and the Vikings', *Antiquity*, 66: 36–51.

Bieler, L. (1979), *The Patrician Texts in the Book of Armagh*. Scriptores Latini Hiberniae, 10, Dublin, Institute for Advanced Studies.

Binchy, D. A. (1962), 'The passing of the old order', in B. Ó Cuív (ed.), *The Impact of the Scandinavian Invasions on the Celtic-Speaking Peoples c. 800–1100 AD: Introductory Papers Read at Plenary Sessions of the International Congress of Celtic Studies Held in Dublin, 6–10 July, 1959*. Dublin, Institute for Advanced Studies: pp. 119–32.

Binns, A. (1995), 'Pre-Reformation dedications to St Oswald in England and Scotland: a gazetteer', in C. Stancliffe and E. Cambridge (eds), *Oswald: Northumbrian King to European Saint*. Stamford, Paul Watkins: pp. 241–71.

Birch, W. de Gray (1881), *Memorials of Saint Guthlac of Crowland*. Wisbech, Leach and Son.

Birch, W. de Gray (1885–99), *Cartularium Saxonicum*. 3 vols and index. London, Whiting and Co (reprinted 1964, New York, Johnson Reprint Co.).

Birch, W. de Gray (ed.) (1889), *An Ancient Manuscript Belonging to St Mary's Abbey, or Nunnaminster, Winchester*. London, Hampshire Record Society.

Birchler, L. (1954), 'Zur Karolingischen Architektur und Malerei in Munstair-Mustair', in L. Birchler (ed.), *Frühmittelalterliche Kunst in den Alpenländern*. Lausanne, L. Birchler, E. Pelichet and A. Schmid: pp. 167–252.

Bitterauf, T. (ed.) (1905), *Die Traditionen des Hochstifts Freising*. Munich (reprinted 1967, Aalen, Scientia Verlag).

Blackburn, M. (1986), 'The Anglo-Saxons and Vikings: eighth–tenth centuries', in P. Grierson and M. Blackburn, *Medieval European Coinage, with a Catalogue of the Coins in the Fitzwilliam Museum, Cambridge*, I: *The Early Middle Ages (5th–10th Centuries)*. Cambridge, Cambridge University Press, pp. 267–326.

Blackburn, M. (1995), 'Money and coinage', in R. McKitterick (ed.), *The New Cambridge Medieval History c. 700–c. 900*, **2**, Cambridge, Cambridge University Press: pp. 538–59.

Blackburn, M. A. S. (1998), 'The London mint in the reign of Alfred', in M. A. S. Blackburn and D. N. Dumville (eds), *Kings, Currency and Alliances: History and Coinage of Southern England in the Ninth Century.* Woodbridge, Boydell: pp. 105–24.

Blackburn, M. A. S. and Keynes, S. D. (1998), 'A corpus of the *Cross-and-Lozenge* and related coinages of Alfred, Ceolwulf II and Archbishop Æthelred', in M. A. S. Blackburn and D. N. Dumville (eds), *Kings, Currency and Alliances: History and Coinage of Southern England in the Ninth Century.* Woodbridge, Boydell and Brewer: pp. 125–50.

Blackburn, M. A. S. and Pagan, H. (1986), 'A revised check-list of coin hoards from the British Isles, *c.* 500–1100', in M. A. S. Blackburn (ed.), *Anglo-Saxon Monetary History.* Leicester, Leicester University Press: pp. 291–313.

Blackmore, L. (1988a), 'The pottery', in R. Cowie and R. L. Whytehead with L. Blackmore, 'Two Middle Saxon occupation sites: excavations at Jubilee Hall and 21–22 Maiden Lane, WC2', *Transactions of the London and Middlesex Archaeological Society*, **39**: 81–110.

Blackmore, L. (1988b), 'The metalwork', in R. Cowie and R. L. Whytehead with L. Blackmore, 'Two Middle Saxon occupation sites: excavations at Jubilee Hall and 21–22 Maiden Lane, WC2', *Transactions of the London and Middlesex Archaeological Society*, **39**: 127–31.

Blackmore, L. (1989), 'The pottery', in R. L. Whytehead and R. Cowie with L. Blackmore, 'Excavations at the Peabody site, Chandos Place, and the National Gallery', *Transactions of the London and Middlesex Archaeological Society*, **40**: 71–107.

Blackmore, L. (1995), 'The Middle Saxon pottery', in P. Mills, 'Excavations at the dorter undercroft, Westminster Abbey', *Transactions of the London and Middlesex Archaeological Society*, **46**: 69–124.

Blackmore, L. (1997), 'From beach to burh: new clues to entity and identity in 7th- to 9th-century London', in G. De Boe and F. Verhaeghe (eds), *Urbanism in Medieval Europe – Papers of the Medieval Europe Brugge 1997 Conference* 1: 123–32.

Blackmore, L. (1999) 'Aspects of trade and exchange evidenced by recent work on Saxon and medieval pottery from London', *Transactions of the London and Middlesex Archaeological Society*, **50**: 38–54.

Blackmore, L. (forthcoming) 'Pottery: trade and tradition', in D. Hill and R. Cowie (eds), *Wics: The Early Medieval Trading Centres of Northern Europe.* Sheffield, Sheffield Academic Press.

Blackmore, L. and Cowie, R. (forthcoming), 'Saxon and medieval Battersea: excavations at Althorpe Grove, 1975–78', *Surrey Archaeological Collections.*

Blackmore, L. and Redknap, M. (1988), 'Saxon and early medieval

imports to the London area and the Rhenish connection', in
D. Gaimster, M. Redknap and H-H. Wegner (eds), *Zur Keramik des Mittelalters und der beginnenden Neuzeit im Rheinland: Medieval and Later Pottery from the Rhineland and its Markets*. Oxford, British Archaeological Reports, International series **S440**: pp. 223–39.

Blackmore, L., Bowsher, D., Cowie, R. and Malcolm, G. (1998), 'Royal Opera House', *Current Archaeology*, **14**: 60–3.

Blair, J. (1989), 'Frithuwold's kingdom and the origins of Surrey', in S. Basset (ed.), *The Origins of Anglo-Saxon Kingdoms*. London, Leicester University Press: pp. 97–107 and 263–5.

Blair, J. (ed.) (1990), *Saint Frideswide's Monastery at Oxford: Archaeological and Architectural Studies*. Stroud, Alan Sutton Publishing.

Blair, J. (1991), *Early Medieval Surrey: Landholding, Church and Settlement before 1300*. Stroud, Alan Sutton Publishing and Surrey Archaeological Society.

Blair, J. (1992), 'Anglo-Saxon minsters: a topographical review', in J. Blair and R. Sharpe (eds), *Pastoral Care before the Parish*. Leicester, Leicester University Press: pp. 226–66.

Blair, J. (1994), *Anglo-Saxon Oxfordshire*. Stroud, Alan Sutton Publishing.

Blair, J. (1995a), 'Anglo-Saxon pagan shrines and their prototypes', *Anglo-Saxon Studies in Archaeology and History*, **8**: 1–28.

Blair, J. (1995b), 'Debate: ecclesiastical organisation and pastoral care in Anglo-Saxon England', *Early Medieval Europe*, **4**: 193–212.

Blair, J. (1996), 'Palaces or minsters? Northampton and Cheddar reconsidered', *Anglo-Saxon England*, **25**: 97–121.

Blair, J. (1999) 'Bampton, St. Mary's', *Church Archaeology*, **3**: 56.

Blake, E. O. (ed.) (1962), *Liber Eliensis*. London, Royal Historical Society.

Blinkhorn, P. (forthcoming), *The Ipswich Ware Survey*. Medieval Pottery Research Group Monographs, London, Department of the Environment.

Blunt, C. E. (1961), 'The coinage of Offa', in R. H. M. Dolley (ed.), *Anglo-Saxon Coins, Studies Presented to F. M. Stenton*. London, Methuen: pp. 39–62.

Blunt, C. E., Lyon, C. S. S. and Stewart, B. H. I. H. (1963), 'The coinage of Southern England, 796–840', *British Numismatic Journal*, **32**: 1–74.

Blunt, C. E., Stewart, B. H. I. H. and Lyon, C. S. S. (1989), *Coinage in Tenth-Century England*. Oxford, Oxford University Press.

Bodden, M. C. (1988), 'Evidence for knowledge of Greek in Anglo-Saxon England', *Anglo-Saxon England*, **17**: 217–46.

Böhme, H. W. (1986), 'Das Ende der Römerherrschaft in Britannien und die angelsächsische Besiedlung Englands im 5. Jahrhundert', *Jahrbuch des römisch-germanischen, Zentralmuseums*, Mainz, **33**: 469–574.

Bolton, W.F. (1954), 'The Middle English and Latin poems of Saint Guthlac', unpublished PhD thesis, Princeton University.

Bolton, W.F. (1959), 'The Latin revisions of Felix's *Vita Sancti Guthlaci*', *Mediaeval Studies,* **21**: 36–52.

Bond, J. M. (1996), 'Burnt offerings: animal bone in Anglo-Saxon cremations', *World Archaeology,* **28**: 76–88.

Booth, J. (1998), 'Monetary alliance or technical co-operation? The coinage of Berhtwulf of Mercia (840–52)', in M. A. S. Blackburn and D. N. Dumville (eds), *Kings, Currency and Alliances: History and Coinage in Southern England in the Ninth Century,* Woodbridge, Boydell: pp. 63–103.

Boretius, A. (ed.) (1883), *Capitularia regum Francorum,* **1**, MGH, *Legum sectio.* **2**, Hannover, Hahn.

Bougard, F. (1995), *La justice dans le royaume d'Italie de la fin du VIIIe siècle au début du XIe siècle.* Rome, Bibliothèque des écoles françaises d'Athènes et de Rome **291**.

Bourke, C. (1993), 'The chronology of Irish crucifixion plaques', in M. Spearman and J. Higgitt (eds), *The Age of Migrating Ideas,* Edinburgh, National Museums of Scotland and Alan Sutton Publishing: pp. 175–81.

Bowler, D. (1983), 'Rangoon Street', *Popular Archaeology,* **5.6**: 13–18.

Bowman, S., Ambers, J. and Leese, M. (1990), 'Re-evaluation of British Museum radiocarbon dates issued between 1980–84', *Radiocarbon,* **32**: 59–79.

Bowsher, D. and Malcolm, G. with Cowie, R. (forthcoming), *Saxon London: Excavations at the Royal Opera House 1989–1997,* London, Museum of London Archaeology Service.

Bowsher, J. (1999), 'Saxon foreshore at Temple Place', *London Archaeologist,* **9.3**: 82–9.

Brigham, T. (1990), 'The Late Roman waterfront in London', *Britannia,* **21**: 99–183.

Bromwich, R. and Williams, I. (ed. and trans.) (1972), *Armes Prydein, The Prophecy of Britain, From the Book of Taliesin.* Dublin, Dublin Institute for Advanced Studies.

Brøndsted, J. (1924), *Early English Ornament.* Copenhagen and London, Levin and Munksgaard, Hachette.

Brooks, N. P. (1971), 'The development of military obligations in eighth- and ninth-century England', in P. Clemoes and K. Hughes (eds), *England Before the Conquest: Studies in Primary Sources Presented to Dorothy Whitelock.* Cambridge, Cambridge University Press: pp. 69–84.

Brooks, N. P. (1984), *The Early History of the Church of Canterbury: Christ Church from 597 to 1066.* Leicester, Leicester University Press.

Brooks, N. P. (1989a), 'The formation of the Mercian kingdom', in S. Bassett (ed.), *The Origins of the Anglo-Saxon Kingdoms.* London, Leicester University Press: pp. 159–70.

Brooks, N. P. (1989b), 'The creation and early structure of the kingdom of Kent', in S. Bassett (ed.), *The Origins of Anglo-Saxon Kingdoms,* London, Leicester University Press: pp. 55–74.

Brooks, N. P. (2000a), 'The development of military obligations in eighth- and ninth-century England', in *Communities and Warfare 700–1400*. London, Hambledon Press: pp. 32–47.

Brooks, N. P. (2000b), 'England in the ninth century: the crucible of defeat', *Transactions of the Royal Historical Society*, 5th ser., **29** (1979), 1–20, reprinted in *Communities and Warfare 700–1400*. London, Hambledon Press: pp. 48–68.

Brooks, N. P. (2000c), 'The administrative background to the Burghal Hidage', *Burghal Hidage and Anglo-Saxon Fortifications, Communities and Warfare 700–1400*. London, Hambledon Press: pp. 114–37.

Brooks, N. P., Gelling, M. and Johnson, D. (1984), 'A new charter of King Edgar', *Anglo-Saxon England*, **13**: 137–55.

Broun, D. (1994), 'The origin of Scottish identity in its European context', in B. E. Crawford (ed.), *Scotland in Dark Age Europe*. St Andrews, University of St Andrews: pp. 21–31.

Broun, D. (2000), 'The seven kingdoms in *De Situ Albaniae*: a record of Pictish political geography or an imaginary map of Alba', in E. J. Cowan and R. A. McDonald (eds), *Alba: Celtic Scotland in the Medieval Era*. East Linton, Tuckwell: pp. 24–42.

Brown, G. B. (1937), *Anglo-Saxon Sculpture: The Arts in Early England*. **6.2**, E. H. L. Sexton (ed.), London, John Murray.

Brown, M. P. (1987), 'Paris, Bibliothèque Nationale, lat. 10861 and the scriptorium of Christ Church, Canterbury', *Anglo-Saxon England*, **15**: 119–37.

Brown, M. P. (1989), 'The Lindisfarne scriptorium from the late seventh to the early ninth century', in G. Bonner, D. Rollason and C. Stancliffe (eds), *St Cuthbert, His Cult and His Community to AD 1200*. Woodbridge, Boydell and Brewer: pp. 151–63.

Brown, M. P. (1991), 'Continental symptoms in insular codicology: historical perspectives', in P. Rück (ed.), *Pergament*. Sigmaringen, Thorbecke: pp. 57–62.

Brown, M. P. (1994), 'Echoes: the Book of Kells and southern English manuscript production', in F. O'Mahony (ed.), *The Book of Kells. Proceedings of a Conference at Trinity College, Dublin, 6 September 1992–9 September 1992*. Aldershot, Scolar Press: pp. 133–43.

Brown, M. P. (1996), *The Book of Cerne: Prayer, Patronage and Power in Ninth-Century England*. London, The British Library.

Brown, M. P. (2000), '"In the Beginning was the Word": books and faith in the age of Bede', The Jarrow Lecture, 2000, Newcastle-upon-Tyne, St Paul's Church Jarrow.

Brown, M. P. (2001a), 'Female literacy in Anglo-Saxon England: the evidence of the ninth-century prayerbooks', in C. Kay and L. Sylvester (eds), *Lexis and Texts in Early English: Essays Presented to Jane Roberts*. Antwerp, Editions Rodopi.

Brown, M. P. (2001b), 'Anglo-Saxon manuscript production: issues of making and using', in P. Pulsiano and E. Traherne (eds), *Anglo-Saxon Literary Culture*.

Brown, M. P. (forthcoming), 'Building Babel: the architecture of the early western written vernaculars', in L. Brownrigg and M. Smith (eds), *Proceedings of the Oxford Conference in the History of the Book, 2000.*

Brown, P. (1996), *The Rise of Western Christendom: Triumph and Diversity, AD 200–1000.* Oxford, Blackwell.

Brown, P. R. (1996 for 1993), 'Beccel and the theme of death in *Guðlac B*', *Mediaevalia*, **19**: 273–97.

Brown, T. J. (1982), 'The Irish element in the insular system of scripts to c. A.D. 850', in H. Loewe (ed.), *Iren und Europa im früheren Mittelalter*, I, Stuttgart, Klett-Cotta: pp. 101–19 (reprinted in J. Bately, M. P. Brown and J. Roberts (eds), *A Paleographer's View: Selected Writings of Julian Brown.* 1993, London, Harvey Miller: pp. 201–20).

Bruce-Mitford, R. L. S. (1967), 'The reception by the Anglo-Saxons of Mediterranean art following their conversion from Ireland and Rome', *Settimane di Studio del centro Italiano di Studi sull'alto Medioevo*, **14**, Spoleto, Presso la Sede del Centro: pp. 797–825.

Bruce-Mitford, R. L. S. (1974), *Aspects of Anglo-Saxon Archaeology.* London, Victor Gollancz.

Bruce-Mitford, R. L. S. (1978), *The Sutton Hoo Ship-Burial II: Arms and Regalia.* London, British Museum Press.

Budny, M. O. (1985), 'London, British Library MS. Royal 1.E.VI: the anatomy of an Anglo-Saxon Bible fragment', unpublished PhD thesis, University of London.

Budny, M. O. and Graham-Campbell, J. A. (1981), 'An eighth-century bronze ornament from Canterbury and related works', *Archaeologia Cantiana*, **97**: 7–25.

Bullough, D. A. (1980), *The Age of Charlemagne.* London, Ferndale Editions.

Bullough, D. A. (1983), 'Alcuin and the Kingdom of Heaven: liturgy, theology and the Carolingian age', in U.-R. Blumenthal (ed.), *Carolingian Essays.* Washington, DC, Catholic University of America Press (reprinted and revised in Bullough 1991: pp. 161–240).

Bullough, D. A. (1991), *Carolingian Renewal: Sources and Heritage.* Manchester, Manchester University Press.

Bullough, D. A. (1993), 'What has Ingeld to do with Lindisfarne?', *Anglo-Saxon England*, **22**: 93–125.

Bullough, D. A. (forthcoming), 'From traders to raiders? Frisians, Franks and Northmen', in D. Hill and M. Worthington (eds), *Æthelbald and Offa*, Oxford, British Archaeological Reports Series.

Byrne, F. J. (1966), 'Historical note on Cnogba (Knowth)', in appendix to G. Eogan, 'Excavations at Knowth, Co. Meath, 1962–1965', *Proceedings of the Royal Irish Academy*, **66C**: 383–400.

Byrne, P. (2000), 'Ciannachta Breg before Síl nÁeda Sláine', in A. P. Smyth (ed.), *Seanchas: Studies in Early and Medieval Irish Archaeology, History and Literature in Honour of Francis J. Byrne.* Dublin, Four Courts Press: pp. 121–26.

Byrnes, M. (2000), 'The Árd Ciannachta in Adomnán's *Vita Columbae*:

a reflection of Iona's attitude to the Síl nÁeda Sláine in the late seventh century', in A. P. Smyth (ed.), *Seanchas: Studies in Early and Medieval Irish Archaeology, History and Literature in Honour of Francis J. Byrne*. Dublin, Four Courts Press: pp. 127–36.

Calvert, J. A. (1979), *The Early Development of Irish High Crosses and their Relationship to Scottish Sculpture in the Ninth and Tenth Centuries*. Ann Arbor: University of Michigan Press.

Cambridge, E. and Rollason, D. (1995), 'Debate: the pastoral organisation of the Anglo-Saxon church: a review of the "Minster Hypothesis"', *Early Medieval Europe*, 4: 87–104.

Campbell, D. and Lane, A. (1989), 'Llangorse: a tenth-century royal *crannog* in Wales', *Antiquity*, 63: 675–81.

Campbell, J. (1979a), 'Bede's words for places', in P. Sawyer (ed.), *Places, Names and Graves*. Leeds, University of Leeds: 34–54 (reprinted in Campbell 1986b: pp. 99–120).

Campbell, J. (1979b), 'Bede's *reges* and *principes*', Jarrow Lecture, St Paul's Church, Jarrow (reprinted in Campbell 1986b: pp. 85–98).

Campbell, J. (1982), *The Anglo-Saxons*. Oxford, Phaidon Press.

Campbell, J. (1986a), 'Some twelfth-century views of the Anglo-Saxon past', in J. Campbell, *Essays in Anglo-Saxon History*, London, Hambledon: pp. 209–28.

Campbell, J. (1986b), *Essays in Anglo-Saxon History*, London, Hambledon.

Campbell, J. (1995), 'The late Anglo-Saxon state: a maximum view', *Proceedings of the British Academy*, 87: 39–65.

Caruth, J. and Anderson, S. (1999), 'RAF Lakenheath Saxon cemetery', *Current Archaeology*, 163: 244–50.

Carver, M. O. H. (1990), 'Pre-Viking traffic in the North Sea', in S. McGrail (ed.), *Maritime Celts, Frisians and Saxons*. Council for British Archaeology Research Report, 71: pp. 117–125.

Carver, M. O. H. (1998), *Sutton Hoo: Burial Ground of Kings?* London, British Museum Press.

Cavadini, J. (1993), *The Last Christology of the West: Adoptionism in Spain and Gaul, 785–820*. Philadelphia, University of Pennsylvania Press.

Cecchelli, C. (1946), *Mater Christi*. 1, Rome, F. Ferrari.

Chadwick, H. M. (1905a), *Studies on Anglo-Saxon Institutions*. Cambridge, Cambridge University Press.

Chadwick, H. M. (1905b, 1907 and 1924), *The Origin of the English Nation*. Cambridge, Cambridge University Press.

Chambers, R. W. (1967), *Beowulf: An Introduction to the Study of the Poem*. 3rd edn, Cambridge, Cambridge University Press.

Chaplin, R. E. (1971), *The Study of Animal Bones from Archaeological Sites*. London, Seminar Press.

Charles-Edwards, T. M. (1993), *Early Irish and Welsh Kinship*. Oxford, Clarendon Press.

Charles-Edwards, T. M. (1995), 'Language and society among the Insular Celts, AD 400–1000', in M. J. Green (ed.), *The Celtic World*. London, Routledge: pp. 711–13.

Charles-Edwards, T. M. (1999), *The Early Mediaeval Gaelic Lawyer.* Quiggin Pamphlets on the Sources of Mediaeval Gaelic History 4, Department of Anglo-Saxon, Norse and Celtic, Cambridge, University of Cambridge.

Charles-Edwards, T. M. (2000), ' "The Continuation of Bede", *s.a.* 750: high-kings, kings of Tara and "Bretwaldas" ', in A. P. Smyth (ed.), *Seanchas: Studies in Early and Medieval Irish Archaeology, History and Literature in Honour of Francis J. Byrne.* Dublin, Four Courts: pp. 137–45.

Charles-Edwards, T. M. (forthcoming), *The Origins of Wales.*

Chavasse, A. (ed.) (1973), *Sancti Leonis Magni Romani Pontificis Tractatus Septem et Nonaginta,* in *CCSL* **138**, **138A**, Turnhout, Brepols.

Chibnall, M. (ed.) (1969), *The Ecclesiastical History of Orderic Vitalis.* **2**, Oxford, Clarendon Press.

Chick, D. (1997), 'Towards a chronology for Offa's coinage: an interim study', *The Yorkshire Numismatist,* **3**: 47–64.

Clancy, T. O. (1998), *The Triumph Tree: Scotland's Earliest Poetry, AD 550–1350.* Edinburgh, Canongate.

Clapham, A. W. (1913), 'The Benedictine Abbey of Barking: a sketch of its architectural history and an account of recent excavations on its site', *Transactions of the Essex Archaeological Society,* **12**: 69–87.

Clapham, A. W. (1927), 'The carved stones at Breedon-on-the-Hill, Leicestershire, and their position in the history of English art', *Archaeologia,* **77**: 219–40.

Clapham, A. W. (1930), *English Romanesque Architecture.* **1** *Pre-Conquest,* Oxford, Clarendon Press.

Clarke, H. and Ambrosiani, B. (1991), *Towns in the Viking Age.* Leicester, Leicester University Press.

Clarke, H. B., Ní Mhaonaigh, M. and Ó Floinn, R. (1998), *Ireland and Scandinavia in the Early Viking Age,* Dublin, Four Courts Press.

Classen, P. (1965), 'Karl der Grosse, der Papsttum und Byzanz', in W. Braunfels (ed.), *Karl der Grosse, Lebenswerk und Nachleben.* **1**, Düsseldorf, Schwann: pp. 537–608.

Classen, P. (1972), 'Karl der Grosse und der Thronfolge im Frankenreich', in *Festschrift für H. Heimpel,* **3**. Göttingen, Veröffentlichungen der Max-Planck-Instituts für Geschichte, 36: 109–34.

Claussen, M. A. (1992), 'Community, tradition and reform in early Carolingian Francia: Chrodegang and the canons of Metz Cathedral', unpublished PhD dissertation, University of Virginia.

Clayton, M. (1996), 'Hermits and the contemplative life in Anglo-Saxon England', in P. Szarmach (ed.), *Holy Men and Holy Women: Old English Prose Saints' Lives and Their Contexts.* Albany, State University of New York Press: pp. 147–75.

Coates, R. (1990), 'On some controversy surrounding *Gewissae/ Gewissei,* Cerdic and Ceawlin', *Nomina,* **13**: 1–11.

Coatsworth, E. (1979), 'The iconography of the crucifixion in pre-conquest sculpture in England', 2 vols, unpublished PhD thesis, University of Durham.

Colgrave, B. (ed. and trans.) (1927), *The Life of Bishop Wilfrid by Eddius Stephanus*. Cambridge, Cambridge University Press.

Colgrave, B. (ed. and trans.) (1956), *Felix's Life of Saint Guthlac*. Cambridge, Cambridge University Press.

Colgrave, B. and Mynors, R. A. B. (eds and trans.) (1969), *Bede's Ecclesiastical History of the English People*. Oxford, Oxford University Press.

Collingwood, R. G. and Myres, J. N. L. (1936), *Roman Britain and the English Settlements*. Oxford, Clarendon Press.

Collins, R. (1990), 'Pippin I and the Kingdom of Aquitaine', in P. Godman and R. Collins (eds), *Charlemagne's Heir: New Perspectives on the Reign of Louis the Pious (814–840)*. Oxford, Oxford University Press: pp. 362–89.

Collins, R. (1991), *Early Medieval Europe 300–1000*. London, Macmillan

Conner, P. (1993a), *Anglo-Saxon Exeter: A Tenth-Century Cultural History*. Woodbridge, Boydell.

Conner, P. (1993b), 'Source studies, the Old English *Guthlac A* and the English Benedictine reformation', *Revue bénédictine*, **103**: 380–413.

Connolly, S. and Picard, J-M. (trans.) (1987), 'Cogitosus: *Life of St. Brigit*', *Journal of the Royal Society of Antiquaries of Ireland*, **117**, 5–27.

Cook, B. J. (1999), 'The Bezant in Angevin England', *Numismatic Chronicle*, **159**: 255–75.

Coplestone-Crow, B. (1989), *Herefordshire Place-Names*. Oxford, British Archaeological Reports, Br. ser. **214**.

Corsano, K. (1987), 'The first quire of the Codex Amiatinus and the Institutiones of Cassiodorus', *Scriptorium*, **41**: 3–34.

Costambeys, M. (1999), 'Piety, property and power in eighth-century central Italy', unpublished PhD thesis, University of Cambridge.

Cottrill, F. (1935), 'Some pre-conquest stone carvings in Wessex', *Antiquaries Journal*, **15**: 144–51.

Cowie, R. (1988a), 'A gazetteer of Middle Saxon period sites and finds in the Strand/Westminster area', *Transactions of the London and Middlesex Archaeological Society*, **39**: 37–46.

Cowie, R. (1988b), 'The excavation at Maiden Lane', in R. Cowie and R. L. Whytehead with L. Blackmore, 'Two Middle Saxon occupation sites: excavations at Jubilee Hall and 21–22 Maiden Lane, WC2', *Transactions of the London and Middlesex Archaeological Society*, **39**: 67–75.

Cowie, R. (1989), 'Excavations at the National Gallery, 1987', in R. L. Whytehead and R. Cowie with L. Blackmore, 'Excavations at the Peabody site, Chandos Place, and the National Gallery', *Transactions of the London and Middlesex Archaeological Society*, **40**: 58–71.

Cowie, R. (1992), 'Archaeological evidence for the waterfront of Middle Saxon London', *Medieval Archaeology*, **36**: 164–8.

Cowie, R. (forthcoming), 'English *wics*: problems with discovery and interpretation', in D. Hill and R. Cowie (eds), *Wics: The Early*

Medieval Trading Centres of Northern Europe. Sheffield, Sheffield Academic Press.

Cowie, R. and Whytehead, R. (1989), '*Lundenwic*: the archaeological evidence for Middle Saxon London', *Antiquity*, **63**: 706–18.

Cowie, R. and Whytehead, R. L. with Blackmore, L. (1988), 'Two Middle Saxon occupation sites: excavations at Jubilee Hall and 21–22 Maiden Lane, WC2', *Transactions of the London and Middlesex Archaeological Society*, **39**: 47–163.

Cowie, R. with Harding, C. (2000), 'Saxon settlement and economy from the Dark Ages to Domesday', in *The Archaeology of London: An Assessment of the Archaeological Evidence for Human Habitation in the Area now Covered by Modern Greater London.* London, Museum of London Archaeology Service, pp. 171–206.

Cox, D. C. (1975), 'The Vale estates of the Church of Evesham, *c.* 700–1086', *Vale of Evesham Historical Society Research Papers*, **5**: 25–50.

Cramp, R. J. (1971), 'The position of the Otley crosses in English sculpture of the eighth to ninth centuries,' in K. Milajcik (ed.), *Kolloquium über spätantike und frühmittelalterliche Skulptur*, **2**, Mainz am Rhein, Philip von Zabern: pp. 55–63.

Cramp, R. J. (1975), 'Anglo-Saxon sculpture of the reform period', in D. Parsons (ed.), *Tenth-Century Studies.* Chichester, Phillimore: pp. 184–99.

Cramp, R. J. (1977), 'Schools of Mercian sculpture' in A. Dornier (ed.), *Mercian Studies.* Leicester, Leicester University Press: pp. 191–233.

Cramp, R. J. (1984), *County Durham and Northumberland (2 parts), Corpus of Anglo-Saxon Sculpture.* **1**, Oxford, Oxford University Press for The British Academy.

Cramp, R. J. (1989), 'The artistic influence of Lindisfarne within Northumbria', in G. Bonner, D. Rollason and C. Stancliffe (eds), *St Cuthbert, His Cult and His Community to AD 1200.* Woodbridge, Boydell Press: pp. 213–28.

Crawford, J. (1968), 'St Bertellin of Stafford', *The Downside Review*, **86**: 56–67.

Cruickshank, G. (2000), 'The Battle of Dunnichen and the Aberlemno Battle-scene', in E. J. Cowan and R. A. McDonald (eds), *Alba: Celtic Scotland in the Medieval Era.* East Linton, Tuckwell.

Cubbin, G. P. (ed.) (1996), *MS D, The Anglo-Saxon Chronicle, a Collaborative Edition*, **6**, MS D, Cambridge, Brewer.

Cubitt, C. R. E. (1990), 'Anglo-Saxon church councils, c. 650–c. 850', unpublished PhD dissertation, University of Cambridge.

Cubitt, C. R. E. (1995), *Anglo-Saxon Church Councils, c. 650–c. 850.* London, Leicester University Press.

Dalton, O. M. (1925), *East Christian Art.* Oxford, Clarendon Press.

Daniels, R., Brewster, L. and Jones, J. (1997), 'An eighth-century pin from Hartlepool', *Archaeological Journal*, **154**: 214–17.

Darlington, R. R., Bray, J. and McGurk, P. (eds and trans.) (1995), *The Chronicle of John of Worcester.* **2**, Oxford, Oxford University Press.

Davies, W. (1977), 'Annals and the origins of Mercia', in A. Dornier, *Mercian Studies*. Leicester, Leicester University Press: pp. 17–29.

Davies, W. (1978), *An Early Welsh Microcosm: Studies in the Llandaff Charters*. London, Royal Historical Society.

Davies, W. (1979), *The Llandaff Charters*. Aberystwyth, National Library of Wales.

Davies, W. (1982), *Wales in the Early Middle Ages*. Leicester, Leicester University Press.

Davies, W. (1988), *Small Worlds: The Village Community in Early Medieval Brittany*. London, Duckworth.

Davies, W. (1990), *Patterns of Power in Early Wales*. Oxford, Oxford University Press.

Davies, W. (1993), 'Celtic kingships in the early middle ages', in A. J. Duggan (ed.), *Kings and Kingship in Medieval Europe*. London, King's College London Medieval Studies 10: pp. 101–24.

Davies, W. and Vierck, H. (1974), 'The contexts of Tribal Hidage: social aggregates and settlement patterns', *Frühmittelalterliche Studien*, 8: 223–93.

Davis, A. and de Moulins, D. (1988), 'The plant remains', in R. Cowie and R. L. Whytehead with L. Blackmore, 'Two Middle Saxon occupation sites: excavations at Jubilee Hall and 21–22 Maiden Lane, WC2', *Transactions of the London and Middlesex Archaeological Society*, 39: 139–47.

Davis, R. (trans.) (1992), *The Lives of the Eighth-Century Popes (Liber Pontificalis)*. Liverpool, Liverpool University Press.

Davis, R. (trans.) (1995) *The Lives of the Ninth-Century Popes (Liber Pontificalis)*. Liverpool: Liverpool University Press.

Day, W.R. (1997), 'The monetary reform of Charlemagne and the circulation of money in early medieval Campania', *Early Medieval Europe*, 6: 25–46.

de Moulins, D. and Davis, A. (1989), 'The plant remains', in R. L. Whytehead and R. Cowie with L. Blackmore, 'Excavations at the Peabody site, Chandos Place, and the National Gallery', *Transactions of the London and Middlesex Archaeological Society*, 40: 134–48.

Deanesly, M. (1965), 'The Anglo-Saxon Church and the papacy', in C. H. Lawrence (ed.), *The English Church and the Papacy in the Middle Ages*. New York, Fordham University Press: pp. 31–62.

Delogu, P. (1995), 'Lombard and Carolingian Italy', in R. McKitterick (ed.), *The New Cambridge Medieval History c. 700–c. 900*, 2, Cambridge, Cambridge University Press: pp. 290–319.

Depeyrot, G. (1994), *Richesse et société chez les mérovingiens et carolingiens*. Paris, Editions Errances.

Dickins, B. (1936–8), 'Queen Cynethryth of Mercia', *Proceedings of the Leeds Philosophical and Literary Society: Literary and Historical Section*, 4: 54.

Dix, B. (1986–7), 'The Raunds Area Project: second interim report', *Northamptonshire Archaeology*, 21: 3–29.

Dixon, P., Marshall, P., Palmer-Brown, C. and Samuels, J. (1994),

Newark Castle Studies: Excavations 1992–1993. Newark, Newark Castle Trust.

Doherty, C. (1984), 'The use of relics in early Ireland', in P. Ní Chatháin and M. Richter (eds), *Irland und Europa: die Kirche im Frühmittelalter*. Stuttgart, Klett-Cotta: pp. 89–101.

Doherty, C. (1991), 'The cult of St Patrick and the politics of Armagh in the seventh century' in J-M. Picard (ed.), *Ireland and Northern France, AD 600–850*. Dublin, Four Courts Press: pp. 53–94.

Dolley, M. (1970), 'The location of the Pre-Alfredian mint(s) of Wessex', *Proceedings of the Hampshire Field Club*, **27**: 57–61.

Dolley, R. H. M. (1960), 'Coin hoards from the London area as evidence for the pre-eminence of London in the Later Saxon period', *Transactions of the London and Middlesex Archaeological Society*, **20**: 37–50.

Dolley, R. H. M. and Metcalf, D. M. (1958), 'Two stray finds from St. Albans of coins of Offa and of Charlemagne', *British Numismatic Journal*, **28**: 459–66.

Dool, J., Wheeler, H., Birss, R., Annable, R. and Mackreth, D. (1985), 'Roman Derby: excavations 1968–1983', *Derbyshire Archaeological Journal*, **105**: 7–345.

Dornier, A. (ed.) (1977a), *Mercian Studies*. Leicester, Leicester University Press.

Dornier, A. (1977b), 'The Anglo-Saxon monastery at Breedon-on-the-Hill, Leicestershire', in A. Dornier (ed.), *Mercian Studies*. Leicester, Leicester University Press: pp. 155–68.

Drinkall, G. and Foreman, M. (1998), *The Anglo-Saxon Cemetery at Castledyke South, Barton-on-Humber*. Sheffield, Sheffield Academic Press.

Duby, G. (1971), 'Des sociétés médiévales', inaugural lecture, Collège de France, Paris, Gallimard.

Duby, G. (1974), *The Early Growth of the European Economy*. London, Arnold.

Dümmler, E. (ed.) (1895), Alcuin, *Epistolae, Epistolae Karolini Aevi*. MGH, Berlin, Weidmann.

Dumville, D. N. (1972), 'Liturgical drama and panegyric responsory from the 8th century: a re-examination of the origin and contents of the 9th-century section of the Book of Cerne', *Journal of Theological Studies*, n. s. **23**, pt 2: 374–406.

Dumville, D. N. (1976), 'The Anglian collection of royal genealogies and regnal lists', *Anglo-Saxon England*, **5**: 23–50.

Dumville, D. N. (1977), 'Kingship, genealogies, and regnal lists', in P. H. Sawyer and I. N. Wood (eds), *Early Medieval Kingship*. Leeds, University of Leeds Press: pp. 72–104.

Dumville, D. N. (1983), 'Brittany and "Armes Prydein Vawr"', *Études Celtiques*, **20**: 145–59.

Dumville, D. N. (ed.) (1985), *The Historia Brittonum, 3, The 'Vatican Recension'*. Cambridge, Cambridge University Press.

Dumville, D. N. (1989a), 'Essex, Middle Anglia, and the expansion of

Mercia in the South-East Midlands', in S. Bassett (ed.), *The Origins of Anglo-Saxon Kingdoms*. London, Leicester University Press: pp. 123–40.

Dumville, D. N. (1989b), 'The Tribal Hidage: an introduction to its texts and their history', in S. Bassett (ed.), *The Origins of the Anglo-Saxon Kingdoms*. London, University of Leicester Press: pp. 225–30.

Dumville, D. N. (1992), *Wessex and England from Alfred to Edgar*. Woodbridge, Boydell.

Dyer, C. (1980), *Lords and Peasants in a Changing Society*. Cambridge, Cambridge University Press.

Dyer, C. (1991), *Hanbury: Settlement and Society in a Woodland Landscape*. Department of English Local History Occasional Papers, ser. 4, **4**. London, Leicester University Press.

Dyson, T. and Schofield, J. (1984), 'Saxon London', in J. Haslam (ed.), *Anglo-Saxon Towns in Southern England*. Chichester, Phillimore: pp. 285–313.

Earle, J. (1857), 'Offa's Dyke, in the neighbourhood of Knighton', *Archaeologia Cambrensis*, 3rd series, **10**: 201–9.

Earle, J. (1892), *The Deeds of Beowulf: An English Epic of the Eighth Century Done into Prose*. Oxford, Oxford University Press.

Eckenstein, L. (1896), *Women under Monasticism: Chapters on Saint-Lore and Convent Life Between A.D. 500 and A.D. 1500*. Cambridge, Cambridge University Press.

Edwards, H. (1988), *The Charters of the Early West Saxon Kingdom*. British Archaeological Reports, British ser. 198. Oxford, British Archaeological Reports.

Ehwald, R. (ed.) (1919), *Aldhelmi Opera* (Monumenta Germaniae Historica: Auctorum Antiquissimorum, **15**). Berlin, Weidmann.

Ekwall, E. (1954), *The Street Names of the City of London*. Oxford, Clarendon Press.

Ekwall, E. (1960), *The Concise Oxford Dictionary of English Place-Names*. 4th edn, Oxford, Clarendon Press.

Elbern, V. (1990), 'Zwischen England und Oberitalien; die sogenannte insulare Kunstprovinz in Salzburg', in *Jahres- und Tagesbericht des Görres Gesellschaft 1989*: pp. 196–111.

Emms, R. (forthcoming), 'St Augustine's Abbey Canterbury and the "first books of the whole English Church"'.

Erkens, F. R. (1993), '*Sicut Esther Regina*. Die westfrankische Königin als *consors regni*', *Francia*, **20**: 15–38.

Ermini, L. P. (ed.) (1974), *La Diocesi di Roma, Corpus della scultura altomedievale*, **7.1**, Spoleto, Centro italiano di studi sull'alto medioevo.

Etchingham, C. (1996), *Viking Raids on Irish Church Settlements in the Ninth Century*. Maynooth Monographs, Series Minor, **1**. Maynooth, Department of Old and Middle Irish, St. Patrick's College.

Etchingham, C. (1999), *Church Organisation in Ireland AD 650 to 1000*. Maynooth, Laigin Publications.

Everson, P. (1977), 'Excavations in the vicarage garden at Brixworth', *Journal of the British Archaeological Association*, **130**: 55–122.

Everson, P. (1993), 'Pre-Viking settlement in Lindsey', in A. Vince (ed.), *Pre-Viking Lindsey*. Lincoln, City of Lincoln Archaeological Unit: pp. 91–100.

Everson, S. (ed. and trans.) (1988), Aristotle, *The Politics*. Cambridge, Cambridge University Press.

Evison, V. I. and Hill, P. (1996), *Two Anglo-Saxon Cemeteries at Beckford, Hereford and Worcester*. York, CBA Research Report **103**.

Faith, R. (1997), *The English Peasantry and the Growth of Lordship*. London, Leicester University Press.

Faral, E. (1929), *La Légende arthurienne*. 3, Paris, Bibliothèque de l'École des hautes études, Sciences historiques.

Farid, S. (1997), 'An archaeological assessment report and publication proposal for a site at 6–16 Old Church Street, Royal Borough of Kensington and Chelsea', PreConstruct Archaeology unpublished report.

Farid, S. and Brown, G. (1997), 'A butchery site in *Lundenwic*', *London Archaeologist*, **8.6**: 146–52.

Farley, M. (1979), 'Burials in Aylesbury and the early history of the town', *Records of Buckinghamshire*, **21**: 116–21.

Farmer, D. H. (1978), *The Oxford Dictionary of Saints*. Oxford, Clarendon Press.

Farr, C. (2000), 'The Gandersheim casket compared with Anglo-Saxon manuscripts', in R. Marth (ed.), *Das Gandersheimer Runenkästchen, Internationales Kolloquium Braunschweig, 24.–26. März 1999*. Braunschweig, Herzog Anton Ulrich Museum: pp. 53–62.

Filow, B. D. (1919), *Early Bulgarian Art*. Bern, Paul Haupt Academical Bookstore.

Finberg, H. P. R. (1972), *The Early Charters of the West Midlands*. 2nd edn, Leicester, Leicester University Press.

Finsterwalder, P. W. (ed.) (1929), *Die Canones Theodori Cantuariensis und ihre Überlieferungsformen*. Weimar.

Fletcher, E., Biddle, M. and Kjølbye-Biddle, B. (1988), 'The churches of Much Wenlock', *Journal of the British Archaeological Association*, **141**: 178–83.

Foard, G. (1985), 'The administrative organisation of Northampton-shire in the Saxon period', *Anglo-Saxon Studies in Archaeology and History*, **4**: 185–272.

Ford, W. J. (1976), 'Settlement patterns in the central region of the Warwickshire Avon', in P. H. Sawyer (ed.), *Medieval Settlement, Continuity and Change*. London, Edward Arnold: pp. 274–94.

Ford, W. J. (1996), 'Anglo-Saxon cemeteries along the Avon valley', *Transactions of the Birmingham and Warwickshire Archaeological Society*, **100**: 59–98.

Forsberg, R. (1950), *A Contribution to a Dictionary of Old English Place-Names*. Uppsala, Nomina Germanica, **9**.

Forsyth, K. (1997), *Language in Pictland*. Utrecht, de Keltische Draak.

Foster, S. M. (1996), *Picts, Gaels and Scots*. London, Batsford.

Foster, S. M. (ed.) (1998), *The St Andrews Sarcophagus: A Pictish*

Masterpiece and Its International Connections. Dublin, Four Courts Press.

Fouracre, P. (1992), 'Cultural conformity and social conservatism in early medieval Europe', *History Workshop Journal*, **33**: 152–61.

Fouracre, P. (2000), *The Age of Charles Martel*. London, Longman.

Fouracre, P. and Gerberding. R. (1996), *Late Merovingian France: History and Hagiography 640–720*. Manchester, Manchester University Press.

Fox, C. (1955), *Offa's Dyke: A Field Survey of the Western Frontier Works of Mercia in the 7th and 8th Centuries AD*. London, The British Academy and Oxford University Press.

Franklin, M. J. (1984), 'The identification of minsters in the Midlands', *Anglo-Norman Studies*, **7**: 69–88.

Freestone, I. and Gaimster, D. (1997), *Pottery in the Making: World Ceramic Traditions*. London, British Museum Press.

Frere, W. H. and Brown, L. E. G. (eds) (1903–15), *The Hereford Breviary*. London, Henry Bradshaw Society **26**, **40** and **46**.

From Viking to Crusader: Scandinavia and Europe 800–1200 (1992), exhibition catalogue. Paris, Berlin and Copenhagen, Nordic Council of Ministers, Council of Europe.

Fulk, R. D. (1992), *A History of Old English Meter*. Philadelphia, University of Pennsylvania Press.

Gai, S. (1999), 'Die Pfalz Karls des Grossen in Paderborn. Ihre Entwicklung von 777 bis zum Ende der 10. Jahrhunderts', in C. Stiegmann and M. Ivernhoff (eds), *799 – Kunst und Kultur der Karolingerzeit: Karl der Grosse und Papst Leo III. in Paderborn: Beiträge zum Katalog der Ausstellung Paderborn 1999*. Mainz, Verlag Philipp von Zabern, pp. 183–96.

Gaimster, M. (1998), *Vendel Period Bracteates on Gotland: on the Significance of Germanic Art*. Lund, Almquist and Wiksell International.

Gaimster, M., Haith, C. and Bradley, J. (1998), 'Medieval Britain and Ireland in 1997', *Medieval Archaeology*, **42**: 107–90.

Garrison, M. D. (1995), 'Alcuin's world through his letters and verse', unpublished PhD dissertation, University of Cambridge.

Garton, D. (1987), 'Dunston's Clump and the brickwork plan field systems at Babworth, Nottinghamshire: excavations 1981', *Transactions of the Thoroton Society of Nottinghamshire*, **91**: 16–73.

Geake, H. (1997), *The Use of Grave-Goods in Conversion-Period England, c.600–c.850*. Oxford, British Archaeological Reports, Br. ser. **261**.

Gelling, M. (1953), 'The boundaries of the Westminster charters', *Transactions of the London and Middlesex Archaeological Society*, **11**: 101–3.

Gelling, M. (1978), *Signposts to the Past*. London, Dent.

Gelling, M. (1989a), 'The early history of western Mercia,' in S. Bassett (ed.), *The Origins of Anglo-Saxon Kingdoms*. London, University of Leicester Press.

Gelling, M. (1989b), 'The place-names Burton and variants', in S. C. Hawkes (ed.), *Weapons and Warfare in Anglo-Saxon England*. Oxford, Oxford University Committee for Archaeology: pp. 145–53.

Gelling, M. (1992), *The West Midlands in the Early Middle Ages.* Leicester, Leicester University Press.

Gelling, M. (1993), 'Why aren't we speaking Welsh?', *Anglo-Saxon Studies in Archaeology and History,* **6**: 51–6.

Gem, R. (1993a), 'Architecture of the Anglo-Saxon church, 735 to 870: from Archbishop Ecgberht to Archbishop Ceolnoth', *Journal of the British Archaeological Association,* **146**: 29–66.

Gem, R. (1993b), 'The episcopal churches of Lindsey in the early 9th century', in A. Vince (ed.), *Pre-Viking Lindsey.* Lincoln, City of Lincoln Archaeology Unit: pp. 123–7.

Gillingham, J. (1971), *The Kingdom of Germany in the High Middle Ages.* London, Historical Association.

Godman, P. (1982), 'Introduction', in P. Godman (ed.), *The Bishops, Kings and Saints of York.* Oxford, Oxford University Press: pp. xxxiii–xciii.

Goffin, R. (1988), 'The Saxon daub', in R. Cowie and R. L. Whytehead with L. Blackmore, 'Two Middle Saxon occupation sites: excavations at Jubilee Hall and 21–22 Maiden Lane, WC2', *Transactions of the London and Middlesex Archaeological Society,* **39**: 114–19.

Gonser, P. (ed.) (1909), *Das angelsächsische Prosa-Leben des hl. Guthlac.* Heidelberg, Anglistische Forschungen, **27**.

Goody, J. (1968), 'Introduction' in J. Goody (ed.), *Succession to High Office.* Cambridge, Cambridge University Press: pp. 1–56.

Gover, J. E. B., Mawer, A. and Stenton, F. M. (1942), *The Place-Names of Middlesex.* English Place-Name Society, **18** Cambridge, Cambridge University Press.

Gradon, P. O. E. (ed.) (1958), *Cynewulf's 'Elene'.* London, Methuen.

Green, C., Green, I., Dallas, C. and Wild, J. P. (1986–87), 'Excavations at Castor, Cambridgeshire in 1957–58 and 1973', *Northamptonshire Archaeology,* **21**: 109–48.

Green, H. J. M. (1963), 'Secrets of Whitehall: evidence of Roman, Saxon and medieval Westminster revealed during the current rebuilding of the Treasury and Downing Street – Part 1', *Illustrated London News,* **242**: 1004–7.

Greenway, D. (ed.) (1996), *Henry, Archdeacon of Huntingdon, Historia Anglorum.* Oxford, Clarendon Press.

Grierson, P. (1959), 'Commerce in the Dark Ages: a critique of the evidence', *Transactions of the Royal Historical Society,* 5th series, **9**: 123–40.

Grierson, P. (1965), 'Money and coinage under Charlemagne', in W. Braunfels (ed.), *Karl der Grosse. Lebenswerk und Nachleben,* **1**. Düsseldorf, Schwann: pp. 501–36.

Grierson, P. (1979), *Dark Age Numismatics.* London, Variorum.

Grierson, P. and Blackburn, M. A. S. (1986), *The Early Middle Ages (5th–10th centuries), Medieval European Coinage, with a Catalogue of the Coins in the Fitzwilliam Museum, Cambridge.* **1**, Cambridge, Cambridge University Press.

Grimes, W. F. (1968), *The Excavation of Roman and Medieval London.* London, Routledge and Kegan Paul.

Gruffydd, R. G. (1978), 'Canu Cadwallon ap Cadfan', in R. Bromwich and R. Brinley Jones (eds), *Astudiaethau ar yr Hengerdd,* Cardiff, Gwasg Prifysgol Cymru.

Gundlach, W. (ed.) (1892), *Codex Carolinus, MGH Epistolae,* **3**, Berlin, Weidmann.

Gwenogvryn Evans, J. and Rhys, J. (eds) (1893), *The Text of the Book of Llan Dâv.,* Oxford, Pwllheli.

Haddan, A. W. and Stubbs, W. (1871), *Councils and Ecclesiastical Documents Relating to Great Britain and Ireland.* **3**, Oxford, Clarendon Press.

Haefele, H. F. (ed.) (1959), Notker the Stammerer, *Gesta Karoli Magni Imperatoris, MGH Scriptores Rerum Germanicarum in Usum Scholarum.* Berlin, Weidmann.

Hagen, A. (1995), *A Second Handbook of Anglo-Saxon Food and Drink: Production and Distribution.* Hockwold cum Wilton, Anglo-Saxon Books.

Hall, D. (1981), 'The origins of open-field agriculture: the archaeological fieldwork evidence', in T. Rowley (ed.), *The Origins of Open Field Agriculture.* London, Croom Helm: pp. 22–38.

Hamerow, H. (1993), *The Anglo-Saxon Settlement, Excavations at Mucking.* **2**, London, English Heritage and British Museum Press.

Hampe, K. (ed.) (1898), Leo III, *Epistolae, MGH, Epistolae* **4**. Hannover, Hahn.

Harbison, P. (1992), *The High Crosses of Ireland: An Iconographical and Photographic Survey.* 3 vols, Bonn, Dr Rudolf Habelt GMBH.

Hardy, T. D. and Martin, C. T. (eds and trans.) (1888), *Lestorie des Engles Solum la Translacion Maistre Geffrei Gainer.* **1**, Public Record Office, Rerum Britannicarum Medii Aevi Scriptores (Chronicles and Memorials of Great Britain and Ireland during the Middle Ages), London, Her Majesty's Stationery Office.

Harrison, M. (1989), *A Temple for Byzantium.* Austin, University of Texas Press.

Hart, C. R. (1971), 'The Tribal Hidage', *Transactions of the Royal Historical Society,* 5th series, **21**: 133–57.

Hart, C. R. (1977), 'The kingdom of Mercia', in A. Dornier, *Mercian Studies.* Leicester, Leicester University Press: pp. 43–61.

Haslam, J. (1987), 'Market and fortress in England in the reign of Offa', *World Archaeology,* **19**: 76–93.

Hässler, H-J. (1994), 'Neue Ausgrabungen in Issendorf, Niedersachsen', *Studien zur Sachsenforschung.* **9**, Hannover, Selbstverlag Hässler.

Hässler, H-J. (ed.) (1999), *Studien zur Sachsenforschung.* **12**, Oldenburg, Isensee.

Hawkes, J. (1995a), 'The Wirksworth slab: an iconography of *humilitas*', *Peritia,* **9**: 246–89.

Hawkes, J. (1995b), 'A question of judgement: the iconic programme at

Sandbach, Cheshire', in C. Bourke (ed.), *From the Isles of the North.* Belfast, HMSO: pp. 213–20.

Hawkes, J. (1997a), 'Symbols of the Passion or power? The iconography of the Rothbury cross-head', in C. Karkov, R. Farrell, and M. Ryan. (eds), *The Insular Tradition.* Albany, State University of New York Press: pp. 27–44.

Hawkes, J. (1997b), 'Columban Virgins: iconic images of the Virgin and Child in insular sculpture', in C. Bourke (ed.), *Studies in the Cult of Saint Columba.* Dublin, Four Courts Press: pp. 107–35.

Hawkes, J. (1998), 'Breaking the silence: the Road to Calvary at Sandbach, Cheshire', in A. M. Luiselli Fadda and É. Ó Carragáin (eds), *Le Isole Britanniche e Roma in Età Romanobarbarica.* Rome, Herder: pp. 37–48.

Hawkes, J. (1999), 'Northumbrian sculpture: questions of context', in J. Hawkes and S. Mills (eds), *Northumbria's Golden Age.* Stroud, Sutton Publishing: pp. 204–15.

Hawkes, J. and Mills, S. (eds) (1999), *Northumbria's Golden Age.* Stroud, Sutton Publishing.

Hayes, P. and Lane, T. (1992), *The Fenland Project, Number 5: Lincolnshire Survey, the South-West Fens.* East Anglian Archaeology **55**, Ipswich, Suffolk County Planning Department.

Heath, P. (1973), 'The medieval church', in R. B. Pugh (ed.), *Victoria County History: Staffordshire.* **3**, London, Oxford University Press: pp. 1–43.

Heather, P. (1996), *The Goths.* Oxford, Basil Blackwell.

Heighway, C., Garrod, A. and Vince, A. (1979), 'Excavations at 1 Westgate Street, Gloucester, 1975', *Medieval Archaeology*, **23**: 98–158.

Henderson, G. (1972), *Early Medieval.* Harmondsworth, Pelican Books.

Henderson, G. (1985), 'The imagery of St. Guthlac of Crowland', in W. M. Ormrod (ed.), *England in the Thirteenth Century: Proceedings of the 1984 Harlaxton Symposium.* Nottingham: University of Nottingham: 76–94.

Henderson, G. (1999), *Vision and Image in Early Christian England.* Cambridge, Cambridge University Press.

Henderson, I. (1967), *The Picts: Ancient Peoples and Places.* London, Thames and Hudson.

Henderson, I. (1978), 'Sculpture north of the Forth after the take-over by the Scots', in J. Lang (ed.), *Anglo-Saxon and Viking Age Sculpture and its Context.* Oxford, British Archaeological Reports, Br. ser. **49**: pp. 47–73.

Henderson, I. (1982), 'Pictish art and the Book of Kells', in D. Whitelock, R. McKitterick, and D. Dumville (eds), *Ireland in Early Medieval Europe: Studies in Memory of Kathleen Hughes.* Cambridge, Cambridge University Press: pp. 79–105.

Henderson, I. (1994), 'The insular and Continental context of the St Andrews sarcophagus', in B. E. Crawford (ed.), *Scotland in Dark Age Europe.* St Andrews, St John's House Papers, **5**: pp. 71–102.

Henderson, I. (1998), '*Primus inter Pares*: the St Andrews sarcophagus and Pictish sculpture' in S. Foster. (ed.), *The St Andrews Sarcophagus: A Pictish Masterpiece and its International Connections.* Dublin, Four Courts Press: pp. 97–167.

Hennessy, W. M. (ed.) (1866), *Chronicum Scotorum: A Chronicle of Irish Affairs to 1135.* Public Record Office, *Rerum britannicarum medii aevi scriptores.* London, Her Majesty's Stationery Office.

Henry, F. (1964), *L'Art Irlandais.* 2, St Léger-Vauban, Zodiaque.

Henry, F. (1974), *The Book of Kells.* London, Thames and Hudson.

Hicks, C. (1993), *Animals in Early Medieval Art.* Edinburgh, Edinburgh University Press.

Higgitt, J. (forthcoming), 'Theorising Anglo-Saxon stone sculpture: ways of seeing, response', in F. Orton and C. Karkov (eds), *Theorising Anglo-Saxon Stone Sculpture.* Kalamazoo, Western Michigan University Press.

Higham, N. (1992a), 'King Cearl, the battle of Chester and the origins of the Mercian "overkingship"', *Midland History,* **17**: 1–15.

Higham, N. (1992b), *Rome, Britain and the Anglo-Saxons.* London, Seaby.

Higham, N. (1994a), *The English Conquest: Gildas and Britain in the Fifth Century.* Manchester, Manchester University Press.

Higham, N. (1994b), *The Origins of Cheshire.* Manchester, Manchester University Press.

Higham, N. (1995), *An English Empire: Bede and the Early Anglo-Saxon Kings.* Manchester, Manchester University Press.

Hill, D. (1974a), 'Offa's and Wat's Dykes: some exploratory work on the frontier between Celt and Saxon', in T. Rowley (ed.), *Anglo-Saxon Settlement and Landscape, British Archaeological Report,* **6**: 102–7.

Hill, D. (1974b), 'The interrelation of Offa's and Wat's Dyke', *Antiquity,* **48**: 309–12.

Hill, D. (1977), 'Offa's and Wat's Dykes: some aspects of recent work, 1972–1976', *Transactions of the Lancashire and Cheshire Antiquarian Society,* **79**: 21–33.

Hill, D. (1981), *An Atlas of Anglo-Saxon England.* Oxford, Basil Blackwell.

Hill, D. (2000), 'Offa's Dyke: pattern and purpose', *Antiquaries Journal.* **80**: 195–206.

Hill, D. and Cowie, R. (eds) (forthcoming), *Wics: The Early Medieval Trading Centres of Northern Europe.* Sheffield, Sheffield Academic Press.

Hill, D. and Rumble, A. R. (1996), *The Defence of Wessex: The Burghal Hidage and Anglo-Saxon Fortifications.* Manchester, Manchester University Press.

Hill, J. M. (1981), 'The soldier of Christ in Old English prose and poetry', in P. Meredith (ed.), *Essays in Honour of A. C. Cawley,* Leeds Studies in English, NS **12**: 57–80.

Hines, J. (1984), *The Scandinavian Character of Anglian England in the*

Pre-Viking Period. Oxford, British Archaeological Reports, Br. ser. **124**.

Hines, J. (1993), *Clasps, Hektespenner, Agraffen: Anglo-Scandinavian Clasps of Classes A-C of the 3rd Century AD: Typology, Diffusion and Function*. Stockholm, Kungl. Vitterhets Historie och Antikvitets Akademien.

Hines, J. (1994), 'The becoming of the English: identity, material culture and language in early Anglo-Saxon England', *Anglo-Saxon Studies in Archaeology and History*, **7**: 49–59.

Hines, J. (1995), 'Cultural change and social organisation in early Anglo-Saxon England', in G. Ausenda, *After Empire: Towards an Ethnology of Europe's Barbarians*. Woodbridge, Boydell Press: pp. 75–88.

Hines, J. (1997), *A New Corpus of Anglo-Saxon Great Square-Headed Brooches*. Reports of the Research Committee of the Society of Antiquaries of London, **51**, Woodbridge, Boydell and Brewer.

Hines, J. (1999), 'Review of Drinkall and Foreman (1998)', *Medieval Archaeology*. **43**: 308–11.

Hinton, D. A. (1993), 'A smith's hoard from Tattershall Thorpe, Lincolnshire', *Anglo-Saxon England*, **22**: 147–66.

Hinton, D. A. (2000), *A Smith in Lindsay: The Anglo-Saxon Grave at Tattershall Thorpe, Lincolnshire*. Monograph 16, London, Society for Medieval Archaeology.

Hodges, R. (1982), *Dark Age Economics: The Origins of Towns and Trade AD 600–1000*. London, Duckworth.

Hodges, R. (1991), *Wall-to-Wall History: The Story of Roystone Grange*. London, Duckworth.

Hodges, R. and Whitehouse, D. (1983), *Mohammed, Charlemagne and the Origins of Europe*. London, Duckworth.

Holder-Egger, O. (ed.) (1911), Einhard, *Vita Karoli Magni, MGH Scriptores rerum Germanicarum in usum scholarum*. Hannover, Hahn.

Hollister, C.W. (1962), *Anglo-Saxon Military Institutions on the Eve of the Norman Conquest*. Oxford, Clarendon Press.

Holt, J. C. (1965), *Magna Carta*. Cambridge, Cambridge University Press.

Hooke, D. (1978–79), 'Anglo-Saxon landscapes of the West Midlands', *Journal of the English Place-Name Society*, **11**: 3–23.

Hooke, D. (1981a), *The Landscape of Anglo-Saxon England: The Charter Evidence*. Oxford, British Archaeological Reports, Br. ser. **95**.

Hooke, D. (1981b), 'The Droitwich salt industry: an examination of the West Midland charter evidence', in J. Campbell, D. Brown, and S. Hawkes (eds), *Anglo-Saxon Studies in Archaeology and History*. Oxford, British Archaeological Reports, Br. ser. **92**: pp. 123–69.

Hooke, D. (1983), *The Landscape of Anglo-Saxon Staffordshire: The Charter Evidence*. Keele, University of Keele Department of Adult Education.

Hooke, D. (1985a), *The Anglo-Saxon Landscape: The Kingdom of the Hwicce*. Manchester, Manchester University Press.

Hooke, D. (1985b), 'Village development in the West Midlands', in D. Hooke (ed.), *Medieval Villages*. Oxford University Committee for Archaeology, Monograph No **5**: pp. 125–54.

Hooke, D. (1988a), 'Early forms of open-field agriculture in England', *Geografiska Annaler*, **70 B (1)**: 113–31 (reprinted with corrections in U. Sporrong (ed.) (1990) *The Transformation of Rural Society, Economy and Landscape*. Stockholm, University of Stockholm Department of Human Geography: pp. 143–51).

Hooke, D. (1988b), 'Regional variation in southern and central England in the Anglo-Saxon Period and its relationship to land units and settlement', in D. Hooke (ed.), *Anglo-Saxon Settlements*. Oxford, Basil Blackwell: pp. 123–51.

Hooke, D. (1989), 'Pre-Conquest woodland: its distribution and usage', *Agricultural History Review*, **37**: 113–29.

Hooke, D. (1990), *Worcestershire Anglo-Saxon Charter-Bounds*. Woodbridge, Boydell Press.

Hooke, D. (1992), 'The use of early medieval charters as sources for the study of settlement and landscape evolution', in A. Verhoeve and J. A. J. Vervloet (eds), *The Transformation of the European Rural Landscape: Methodological Issues and Agrarian Change 1770–1914*. Brussels, Standing European Conference for the Study of the Rural Landscape: pp. 39–47.

Hooke, D. (1996), 'Reconstructing Anglo-Saxon landscapes in Warwickshire', *Transactions of the Birmingham and Warwickshire Archaeological Society*, **100**: 99–116.

Hooke, D. (1997a), 'The Anglo-Saxons in England in the seventh and eighth centuries: location in space', in J. Hines (ed.), *The Anglo-Saxons from the Migration Period to the Eighth Century: An Ethnographic Perspective*. Woodbridge, Boydell Press: pp. 65–85.

Hooke, D. (1997b), 'Early medieval estates in central England: a case study', in J. Kubková, J. Klápste, M. Jezeká, P. Meduna, *et al.*, *Life in the Archaeology of the Middle Ages*. Prague, Archeologicky ustav AV CR: pp. 234–45.

Hooke, D. (1998a), 'Medieval forests and parks in southern and central England', in C. Watkins (ed.), *European Woods and Forests, Studies in Cultural History*. New York, CAB International: pp. 19–32.

Hooke, D. (1998b), *The Landscape of Anglo-Saxon England*. Leicester, Leicester University Press.

Hooke, D. (forthcoming), 'Names and settlement in the Warwickshire Arden', in D. Hooke and D. Postles (eds), *Names, Time and Place, Festschrift for R. A. McKinley*. Oxford, Leopard's Head Press: pp. 32–45.

Hope-Taylor, B. (1977), *Yeavering: An Anglo-British Centre of Early Northumbria*. London, HMSO.

Horstmann, C. (ed.) (1887), *The Life of Saint Werburge of Chester, by Henry Bradshaw*. Early English Text Society, Original Series **88**, London, N. Trübner and Co.

Horstmann, C. (ed.) (1901), *Nova Legenda Anglie: As Collected by John of Tynemouth, John Capgrave, and Others, and First Printed, with New Lives, by Wynkyn de Worde A.D. MDXUI.* 2 vols, Oxford, Clarendon Press.

Howe, M. D. (1984), 'Three Anglo-Saxon burials from Alwalton, Cambridgeshire', *Northamptonshire Archaeology*, **19**: 53–61.

Howlett, D. (1998), 'Hellenic learning in Insular Latin: an essay on supported claims', *Peritia*, **12**: 54–78.

Howlett, D. (2000), 'The structure of *De Situ Albaniae*', in S. Taylor (ed.), *Kings, Clerics and Chronicles in Scotland, 500–1297*. Dublin, Four Courts: pp. 124–45.

Hughes, K. (1970), 'Some aspects of Irish influence on early English private prayer', *Studia Celtica*, **5**: 48–61.

Hughes, K. (1971), 'Evidence for contacts between the Churches of the Irish and the English from the Synod of Whitby to the Viking Age', in P. Clemoes and K. Hughes (eds), *England Before the Conquest: Studies in Primary Sources Presented to Dorothy Whitelock*. Cambridge, Cambridge University Press: pp. 49–67.

Hughes, K. (1973), 'The Welsh-Latin chronicles: Annales Cambriae and related texts', *Proceedings of the British Academy*, **59**: 233–58.

Hughes, K. (1980), *Celtic Britain in the Early Middle Ages*. Woodbridge, Boydell.

Hurst, D. (ed.) (1960), *Beda Venerabilis In Lucae Evangelium – In Marcae Evangelium*, in *CCSL* **120**, Turnholt, Brepols.

Hurst, J. D. (1997), *A Multi-Period Salt Production Site at Droitwich: Excavations at Upwich*. York, CBA Research Report, **107**.

Hyslop, M. (1963), 'Two Anglo-Saxon cemeteries at Chamberlain's Barn, Leighton Buzzard, Bedfordshire', *Archaeological Journal*, **120**: 161–200.

Iamartino, G. (1992), '"Militia Christi" e crociata nei secoli XI–XIII', *Miscellanea del Centro di studi medioevali*, **13**: 785–822.

Il Futuro dei Langobardi: l'Italia e la costruzione dell'Europa di Carlo Magno (2000), exhibition catalogue, Brescia.

Innes, M. (2000), *State and Society in the Early Middle Ages: The Middle Rhine Valley 400–1000*. Cambridge, Cambridge University Press.

Jackson, K. H. (1959), 'Edinburgh and the Anglian occupation of Lothian', in P. Clemoes (ed.), *The Anglo-Saxons: Studies Presented to Bruce Dickins*. London, Bowes & Bowes: pp. 35–47.

James, M. R. (1909–12), *A Descriptive Catalogue of the Manuscripts in the Library of Corpus Christi College Cambridge*. 2 vols, Cambridge, Cambridge University Press.

James, M. R. (1924), *The Apocryphal New Testament*. Oxford, Clarendon Press.

James, S., Marshall, A. and Millett, M. (1984), 'An early medieval building tradition', *Archaeological Journal*, **141**: 182–215.

Janssen, W. (1972), *Issendorf. Ein Urnenfriedhof der späten Kaiserzeit und der Völkerwanderungszeit. Vol. 1 Die Ergebnisse der Ausgrabung 1967*. Hildesheim, Lax Verlag.

Jenkins, D. and Owen, M. E. (1983), 'The Welsh marginalia in the

Lichfield Gospels. Part I', *Cambridge Medieval Celtic Studies,* **5**: 37–66.

Jenkins, D. and Owen, M. E. (1984), 'The Welsh marginalia in the Lichfield Gospels. Part II: The "Surexit" memorandum', *Cambridge Medieval Celtic Studies,* **7**: 91–120.

Jewell, R. H. I. (1982), 'The pre-Conquest sculpture at Breedon-on-the-Hill, Leicestershire', unpublished PhD dissertation, University of London.

Jewell, R. H. I. (1986), 'The Anglo-Saxon friezes at Breedon-on-the-Hill, Leicestershire', *Archaeologia,* **108**: 95–115.

Johansson, C. (1975), *Old English Place-Names Containing Lēah.* Stockholm, Almqvist and Wiksell International.

John, E. (1960), *Land Tenure in Early England.* Leicester, Leicester University Press.

John, E. (1966), *Orbis Britanniae.* Leicester, Leicester University Press.

John, E. (1992), 'The point of Woden', *Anglo-Saxon Studies in Archaeology and History,* **5**: 127–34.

John, E. (1996), *Reassessing Anglo-Saxon England.* Manchester, Manchester University Press.

Jones, C. A. (1995), 'Envisioning the *cenobium* in the Old English *Guthlac A*', *Mediaeval Studies,* **57**: 259–91.

Jones, C. W. (ed. and trans.) (1947), *Saints' Lives and Chronicles in Early England.* Ithaca, Cornell University Press.

Jones, M. (1994), 'St Paul in the Bail, Lincoln: Britain in Europe?', in K. Painter (ed.), *'Churches Built in Ancient Times': Recent Studies in Early Christian Archaeology.* London, Society of Antiquaries and Accordia Research Centre: pp. 325–47.

Jones, T. (ed.) (1955), *Brut y Tywysogion or the Chronicle of the Princes, Red Book of Hengest Version.* Cardiff, University of Wales Press.

Jonsson, K. (1987), *The New Era: The Reformation of the Late Anglo-Saxon Coinage Commentationes de Nummis Saeculorum IX-XI, In Suecia Repertis.* Nova Series **1**, Stockholm and London, Royal Coin Cabinet and Spink and Son.

Kasten, B. (1997), *Königssöhne und Königsherrschaft. Untersuchungen zur Teilhabe am Reich in der Merowinger- und Karolingerzeit.* Hannover, Hahn.

Keene, D. (1995), 'London in the Early Middle Ages 600–1300', *London Journal,* **20.2**: 9–21.

Kelleher, J. V. (1971), 'Uí Maine in the annals and genealogies to 1225', *Celtica,* **9**: 61–112.

Kelly, J. F. (1989–1990), 'A catalogue of early medieval Hiberno-Latin biblical commentaries II', *Traditio,* **45**: 393–434.

Kelly, S. (1990), 'Anglo-Saxon lay society and the written word', ed. R. McKitterick, *The Uses of Literacy in Early Mediaeval Europe.* Cambridge, Cambridge University Press: pp. 36–62.

Kelly, S. (1992), 'Trading privileges from eighth-century England', *Early Medieval Europe,* **1.1**: 3–28.

Kelly, S. E. (ed.) (1995), *Charters of St Augustine's Abbey, Canterbury, and Minster in Thanet*. Anglo-Saxon Charters, **4**, Oxford, Oxford University Press.

Kelly, S. E. (ed.) (1998), *Charters of Selsey*. Anglo-Saxon Charters, **6**, Oxford, Oxford University Press.

Kemp, R. (1991), 'The archaeology of 45–54 Fishergate', in T. O'Connor (ed), *Bones From 45–54 Fishergate, The Animal Bones* **4**. *The Archaeology of York* **15**, London: Council for British Archaeology for the York Archaeological Trust: pp. 211–20.

Kendrick, T. D. (1938), *Anglo-Saxon Art to A.D. 900*. London, Methuen.

Kendrick, T. D. and Radford, R. C. A. (1943), 'Recent discoveries at All Hallows, Barking', *Antiquaries' Journal*, **23**: 14–18.

Ker, N. R. (1938), 'Membra disiecta', *British Museum Quarterly*, **12**: 130–4.

Ker, N. R. (1948), 'Hemming's Cartulary', in R. W. Hunt (ed.), *Studies in Medieval History Presented to F. M. Powicke*. Oxford, Clarendon Press.

Ker, N. R. (1957) *Catalogue of Manuscripts Containing Anglo-Saxon*. Oxford, Clarendon Press.

Keynes, S. (1990), 'Changing faces: Offa, King of Mercia', *History Today*, **40**: 14–19.

Keynes, S. (1993a), *An Atlas of Attestations in Anglo-Saxon Charters c. 670 – 1066*. Cambridge, University of Cambridge, Department of Anglo-Saxon, Norse, and Celtic (publication forthcoming)

Keynes, S. (1993b), 'The Control of Kent in the Ninth Century', *Early Medieval Europe*, **2.2**: 111–31.

Keynes, S. (1994a), *The Councils of Clofesho* [Brixworth Lecture 1993]. Vaughan Paper 38, Leicester, University of Leicester.

Keynes, S. (1994b), 'The West Saxon charters of King Æthelwulf and his sons', *English Historical Review*, 109: 1109–49.

Keynes, S. (1995), 'England, 700–900', in R. McKitterick (ed.), *The New Cambridge Medieval History c. 700–c. 900*, **2**, Cambridge, Cambridge University Press: pp. 18–42.

Keynes, S. (1997), 'Anglo-Saxon Entries in the *Liber Vitae* of Brescia', J. Roberts and J. L. Nelson with M. Godden (eds), *Alfred the Wise: Studies in Honour of Janet Bately on the Occasion of her Sixty-fifth Birthday*, Cambridge, D. S. Brewer: pp. 99–119.

Keynes, S. (1998), 'King Alfred and the Mercians', M. A. S. Blackburn and D. N. Dumville (eds), *Kings, Currency and Alliances: History and Coinage of Southern England in the Ninth Century*. Woodbridge, Boydell and Brewer: pp. 1–45.

Keynes, S. (2001), 'Edward, King of the Anglo-Saxons', in D. Hill and N. J. Higham (eds), *Edward the Elder*. London: Routledge: pp. 40–66.

Keynes, S. (forthcoming a), 'The Kingdom of the Mercians in the eighth century', in D. Hill and N. J. Higham (eds), *Æthelbald and Offa*. Oxford: British Archaeological Reports.

Keynes, S. (forthcoming b), 'The power of the written word: Alfredian England 871–899', in T. Reuter (ed.), *Alfred the Great*.

Keynes, S. and Lapidge, M. (eds and trans.) (1983), *Alfred the Great:*

Asser's Life of King Alfred and Other Contemporary Sources. Harmondsworth, Penguin Classics.

King, P. D. (ed.) (1987), *Charlemagne. Translated Sources.* Kendal, P. D. King.

Kinsley, A. G. (1989), *The Anglo-Saxon Cemetery at Millgate, Newark-on-Trent, Nottinghamshire.* Nottingham, Department of Classical and Archaeological Studies, University of Nottingham.

Kinsley, A. G. (1993), *Broughton Lodge: Excavations on the Romano-British Settlement and Anglo-Saxon Cemetery at Broughton Lodge, Willoughby-on-the-Wolds, Nottinghamshire 1964-8.* Nottingham, Department of Classical and Archaeological Studies, University of Nottingham.

Kirby, D. P. (1991), *The Earliest English Kings.* London, Unwin Hyman.

Kirby, D. P. (1994), 'The political development of Ceredigion, c. 400-1081', in J. L. Davies and D. P. Kirby (eds), *From the Earliest Times to the Coming of the Normans, Ceredigion County History. 1*, ed. I. G. Jones, Cardiff: pp. 318-42.

Kitzinger, E. (1976), 'Byzantine art in the period between Justinian and Iconoclasm', in E. Kitzinger, *The Art of Byzantium and the Medieval West.* Bloomington, University of Indiana Press.

Klingelhöfer, E. (1992), *Manor, Vill and Hundred: The Development of Rural Institutions in Early Medieval Hampshire.* Studies and Texts **112**. Toronto, Pontifical Institute of Mediaeval Studies.

Knowles, D. and Hadcock, R. N. (1971), *Medieval Religious Houses: England and Wales.* Harlow, Longman.

Koehler, W. (1958), *Die Hofschüle Karl des Grossen, Die karolingische Miniaturen. 2*, Berlin, Deutscher Verein für Kunstwissenschaft.

Kotzor, G. (ed.) (1981), *Das altenglische Martyrologium.* Munich, Bayerische Akademie der Wissenschaften, Phil-Hist. Klasse, Abhandlungen NF **88/1,2**.

Kozodoy, R. (1986), 'The Reculver Cross', *Archaeologia*, **108**: 67-94.

Kraus, O. (ed.) (2001), *Tiere, Menschen, Götter: wikingerzeitliche Kunststile und ihre neuzeitliche Rezeption.* Hamburg, Veröff Joachim Jungius-Ges. Wiss. **90**.

Kuhn, S. M. (1948), 'From Canterbury to Lichfield', *Speculum*, **23**: 619-27.

Kuhn, S. M. (1957), 'Some early Mercian manuscripts', *Speculum*, n. s. **8**: 355-70.

Kurtz, B. P. (1926), 'From St. Antony to St. Guthlac: a study in biography', *University of California Publications in Modern Philology*, **12**: 103-46.

Kurze, F. (ed.) (1895), *Annales Regni Francorum, MGH Scriptores Rerum Germanicarum in Usum Scholarum.* Hannover, Hahn.

Kuypers, A. B. (1902), *The Prayer Book of Aedeluald the Bishop, Commonly Called the Book of Cerne.* Cambridge, Cambridge University Press.

Lapidge, M. (1981), 'Some Latin poems as evidence for the reign of Athelstan', *Anglo-Saxon England*, **9**: 62-71.

Lapidge, M. (1988), 'The study of Greek at the school of Canterbury in the seventh century', in M. Herren (ed.), *The Sacred Nectar of the Greeks: The Study of Greek in the West in the Early Middle Ages.* London, King's College: pp. 169–94.

Lapidge, M. (1996), *Anglo-Latin Literature 600–899.* London, Hambledon.

Lapidge, M., Blair, J., Keynes, S. and Scragg, D. (eds) (1999), *The Blackwell Encyclopaedia of Anglo-Saxon England.* Oxford, Blackwell.

Lapidge, M. and Herren, M. (eds and trans.) (1979), *Aldhelm: The Prose Works.* Cambridge, D. S. Brewer.

Lapidge, M. and Sharpe, R. (1985), *A Bibliography of Celtic-Latin Literature 400–1200.* Dublin, Royal Irish Academy.

Lauer, P. (1900), *Le règne de Louis IV d'Outremer.* Paris, Bibliothèque de l'École des Hautes Études.

Lauer, P. (1910), *Robert I et Raoul de Bourgogne, rois de France, 923–36.* Paris, Bibliothèque de l'École des Hautes Études.

Leahy, K. (1993), 'The Anglo-Saxon settlement of Lindsey', in A. Vince (ed.), *Pre-Viking Lindsey.* Lincoln, City of Lincoln Archaeological Unit: pp. 29–44.

Le Blant, E. (1886), *Les sarcophages chrétiens de la Gaule.* Paris, Ministère de l'instruction publique, Collection de documents inédits sur l'histoire de France.

Leeds, E. T. (1936), *Early Anglo-Saxon Art and Archaeology.* Oxford, Clarendon Press.

Lenker, U. (1997), *Die westsächsische Evangelienversion und die Perikopenordnungen im angelsächsischen England.* Munich, Wilhelm Fink Verlag.

Levison, W. (1946), *England and the Continent in the Eighth Century.* Oxford, The Clarendon Press.

Lewis, A. (1978), 'Anticipatory succession of the heir in early Capetian France', *American Historical Review*, **83**: 906–27.

Leyser, K. J. (1979), *Rule and Conflict in an Early Medieval Society.* London, Edward Arnold (reprinted 1989, Oxford, Basil Blackwell).

Liebermann, F. (1889), *Die Heiligen Englands.* Hannover, Hahn'sche Buchhandlung.

Liebermann, F. (1894), *Über die Leges Anglorum saeculo xiii inuente Londoniis collectae.* Halle, Max Niemeyer.

Liebermann, F. (ed.) (1903–16), *Die Gesetze der Angelsachsen.* Halle, Max Niemeyer.

Lloyd, J. E. (1939), *A History of Wales.* 3rd edn, London, Longmans.

Locker, A. (1988), 'The fish bones', in R. Cowie and R. L. Whytehead with L. Blackmore, 'Two Middle Saxon occupation sites: excavations at Jubilee Hall and 21–22 Maiden Lane, WC2', *Transactions of the London and Middlesex Archaeological Society*, **39**: 149–50.

Locker, A. (1989), 'Fish bones', in R. L. Whytehead and R. Cowie with L. Blackmore, 'Excavations at the Peabody site, Chandos Place, and the National Gallery', *Transactions of the London and Middlesex Archaeological Society*, **40**: 148–50.

Lohier, F. and Laporte, J. (eds) (1936), *Saint Wandrille, Gesta sanctorum patrum Fontanellensis coenobii*. Rouen, Société de l'histoire de Normandie.

Longhurst, M. (1931), 'The Easby cross', *Archaeologia*, **81**: 43–7.

Losco-Bradley, S. and Wheeler, H. M. (1984), 'Anglo-Saxon settlement in the Trent valley: some aspects', in M. L. Faull (ed.), *Studies in Late Anglo-Saxon Settlement*. Oxford, Oxford University Department for External Studies: pp. 101–14.

Lot, F. (1891), *Les Derniers Carolingiens: Lothaire, Louis V, Charles de Lorraine, 954–991*. Paris, Bibliothèque de l'École des Hautes Études.

Loud, G. (1981), 'The *Gens Normannorum* – myth or reality?', *Anglo-Norman Studies*, **4**: 104–16.

Love, R. C. (ed.) (1996), *Three Eleventh-Century Anglo-Latin Saints' Lives*. Oxford, Clarendon Press.

Loveluck, C. P. (1998), 'A high-status Anglo-Saxon settlement at Flixborough, Lincolnshire', *Antiquity*, **72**: 146–61.

Lucy, S. (1999), 'Changing burial rites in Northumbria AD 500–750', in J. Hawkes and S. Mills (eds), *Northumbria's Golden Age*. Stroud, Sutton Publishing: pp. 12–43.

Lyon, C. S. S. (1968), 'Historical problems of Anglo-Saxon coinage – (2) The ninth century – Offa to Alfred', *British Numismatic Journal*, **37**: 216–38.

Lyon, C. S. S. (1969), 'Historical problems of Anglo-Saxon Coinage – (3) Denominations and weights', *British Numismatic Journal*, **38**: 204–25.

Lyon, C. S. S. and Stewart, B. H. I. H. (1961), 'The Northumbrian Viking coins in the Cuerdale hoard', in R. H. M. Dolley (ed.), *Anglo-Saxon Coins*. London, Methuen: pp. 96–121.

Mac Airt, S. and Mac Niocaill, G. (eds) (1983), *The Annals of Ulster (to A.D. 1131)*. Dublin, Institute for Advanced Studies.

MacGowan, K. (1987), 'Saxon timber structures from the Barking Abbey excavations 1985–6', *Essex Journal*, **22.2**: 35–8.

MacGowan, K. (1996) 'Barking Abbey', *Current Archaeology*, **13.5**: 172–5.

MacGregor, A. (2000) 'A seventh-century pectoral cross from Holderness, East Yorkshire', *Medieval Archaeology*, **44**, 217–22.

Mackreth, D. F. (1996), *Orton Hall Farm: A Roman and Early Anglo-Saxon Farmstead*. East Anglian Archaeology **76**, Ipswich, Suffolk County Planning Department.

Mac Lean, D. (1998) 'The Northumbrian perspective' in S. Foster (ed.), *The St Andrews Sarcophagus: A Pictish Masterpiece and its International Connections*. Dublin, Four Courts Press: pp. 179–208.

Mac Lean, D. (1999), 'Northumbrian vine-scroll ornament and the Book of Kells', in J. Hawkes and S. Mills (eds), *Northumbria's Golden Age*. Stroud, Sutton Publishing: pp. 178–90.

MacQuarrie, A. (1993), 'Kings of Strathclyde, c400–1018', in A. Grant and K. Stringer (eds), *Medieval Scotland, Crown, Lordship and Community: Essays Presented to Geoffrey Barrow*. Edinburgh, Edinburgh University Press: pp. 1–19.

Mac Shamhráin, A. S. (1996), *Church and Polity in Pre-Norman Ireland:*

The Case of Glendalough. Maynooth Monographs, **7**, Maynooth, An Sagart.

Maddicott, J. R. (1988), 'Trade, industry and the wealth of King Alfred', *Past and Present*, **123**: 3–51.

Maddicott, J. R. (2000), 'Two frontier states: Northumbria and Wessex, c. 650–750', in J. R. Maddicott and D. M. Palliser (eds), *The Medieval State: Essays Presented to James Campbell*. London, Hambledon: pp. 39–40.

Magnus, B. (1997), 'The Firebed of the Serpent: myth and religion in the Migration period mirrored through some golden objects', in L. Webster and M. Brown, *The Transformation of the Roman World AD 400–900*. London, British Museum: pp. 194–207.

Maloney, C., with de Moulins, D. (1990), *The Upper Walbrook Valley in the Roman Period: The Archaeology of Roman London*. **1**, London, Council for British Archaeology Research Report **69**.

Marth, R. (ed.) (2000), *Das Gandersheimer Runenkästchen, Internationales Kolloquium Braunschweig, 24.–26. März 1999*. Braunschweig, Herzog Anton Ulrich Museum.

Mayr-Harting, H. (1972), *The Coming of Christianity to Anglo-Saxon England*. London, B. T. Batsford.

McClure, J. and Collins, R. (eds and trans.) (1994), *Bede, The Ecclesiastical History of English People*. Oxford, Oxford University Press.

McCone, K. (1982), 'Brigit in the seventh century: a saint with three Lives?', *Peritia*, **1**: 107–45.

McGurk, P. (ed.) (1998) *The Chronicle of John of Worcester*, **3**: *The Annals from 1067 to 1140 with the Gloucester Interpolations and the Continuation to 1141*. Oxford Medieval Texts, Oxford, Oxford University Press.

McKinley, J. (1994), *The Anglo-Saxon Cemetery at Spong Hill, North Elmham: Part VIII The Cremations*. East Anglian Archaeology, **69**, Gressenhall.

McKitterick, R. (1983), *The Frankish Kingdom under the Carolingians 751–987*. Harlow, Longman Higher Education.

McKitterick, R. (1989a), 'Nuns' scriptoria in England and Francia in the eighth century', *Francia*, **19**, 1. Sigmaringen, Thorbecke (reprinted 1994, in R. McKitterick, *Books, Scribes and Learning in the Frankish Kingdoms, 6th–9th Centuries*. Aldershot, Variorum).

McKitterick, R. (1989b), *The Carolingians and the Written Word*. Cambridge, Cambridge University Press.

McKitterick, R. (1990), 'Women in the Ottonian Church: an iconographic perspective', in W. J. Shiels and D. Wood (eds), *Women in the Church: Papers Read at the 1989 Summer Meeting and the 1990 Winter Meeting of the Ecclesiastical History Society*. Oxford, Basil Blackwell: pp. 79–100.

McNally, R. E. (1969), 'The imagination and early Irish biblical exegesis', *Annuale Mediaevale*, **10**: 5–27.

McNally, R. E. (1970), 'The three holy kings in early Irish Latin writing', in P. Granfield and J. Jungman (eds), *Kyriakon: Festschrift Johannes Quasten.* **2**, Münster, Verlag Aschendroff: pp. 667–90.

McNeil, R. (1983), 'Two 12th century *wich* houses in Nantwich, Cheshire', *Medieval Archaeology*, **27**: 40–88.

McNeill, J. T. and Gamer, H. M. (eds and trans.) (1938), *Medieval Handbooks of Penance.* New York, Columbia University Press.

Meadows, I. (1996–7),'The Pioneer Helmet', *Northamptonshire Archaeology*, **27**: 191–3.

Meadows, I. (1997), 'Wollaston: the 'Pioneer' burial', *Current Archaeology*, **154**: 391–5.

Meaney, A. L. (1964), *A Gazetteer of Early Anglo-Saxon Burial Sites.* London, George Allen and Unwin.

Meaney, A. L. and Hawkes, S. C. (1970), *Two Anglo-Saxon Cemeteries at Winnall, Winchester, Hampshire.* Monograph **4**, London, Society for Medieval Archaeology.

Meehan, B. (1994), *The Book of Kells.* London, Thames and Hudson.

Mellows, C., and Mellows, W. T. (trans. and eds) (1980), *The Peterborough Chronicle of Hugh Candidus.* 3rd edition, Peterborough, Peterborough Museum Society.

Mellows, W. T. (ed.) (1949), *The Chronicle of Hugh Candidus, a Monk of Peterborough.* London, Oxford University Press.

Merrifield, R. (1983), *London – City of the Romans.* London, Batsford.

Metcalf, D. M. (1963), 'Offa's pence reconsidered', *Cunobelin*, **9**: 37–52.

Metcalf, D. M. (1966), 'A coinage for Mercia under Æthelbald', *Cunobelin*, **12**: 26–39.

Metcalf, D. M. (1977), 'Monetary affairs in Mercia in the time of Æthelbald', in A. Dornier (ed.), *Mercian Studies.* Leicester, Leicester University Press: pp. 87–106.

Metcalf, D. M. (1993–4), *Thrymsas and Sceattas in the Ashmolean Museum, Oxford.* 3 vols, Oxford, Royal Numismatic Society/ Ashmolean Museum.

Metcalf, D. M. (ed.) (1987), *Coinage in Ninth-Century Northumbria.* Oxford, British Archaeological Reports, Br. ser. **180**.

Meyer, K. (1901), 'The expulsion of the Déssi', *Y Cymmrodor*, **14**: 101–35.

Meyer, K. (1907), 'The Expulsion of the Déssi', *Ériu*, **3**: 135–42.

Meyer, K. (ed. and trans.) (1912), Hail Brigit. *An Old-Irish Poem on the Hill of Alenn.* Halle and Dublin, Max Niemeyer and Hodges, Figgis and Co.

Millett, M. (1980), 'The Thames Street section: 1974', in C. Hill, M. Millett and T. Blagg, *The Roman Riverside Wall and Monumental Arch in London.* Special Paper **3**, London, London and Middlesex Archaeological Society.

Milne, G. (1985), *The Port of Roman London.* London, Batsford.

Milne, G. (1992), *Timber Building Techniques in London c.900–1400.* Special Paper **15**, London, London and Middlesex Archaeological Society.

Milne, G. (forthcoming), *Archaeology After the Blitz: Medieval*

Excavations Near Cripplegate, London 1946–1968. London, English Heritage.

Milne, G. and Goodburn, D. (1990), 'The early medieval port of London AD 700–1200', *Antiquity*, **64**: 629–36.

Moisl, H. (1981), 'Anglo-Saxon royal genealogies and Germanic oral tradition', *Journal of Medieval History*, **7**: 215–48.

Moody, T. W., Martin, F. X. and Byrne, F. J. (eds) (1984), *A New History of Ireland* **9**. *Maps, Genealogies, Lists. A Companion to Irish History* **2**, Oxford, Clarendon Press.

Morris, A. M. (1999), 'The Anglian abbey of *Medeshamstede*: its sphere of influence and its Northumbrian connections', unpublished MA dissertation, University of Leicester.

Morris, J. (ed.) (1975), *Domesday Book, Middlesex*. Chichester, Phillimore.

Morris, J. (ed. and trans.) (1980), *Nennius – British History and The Welsh Annals*. Chichester, Phillimore.

Morris, R. (1989), *Churches in the Landscape*. London, Dent.

Morrish, J. (1982), 'An examination of literature and learning in the 9th century', unpublished PhD dissertation, University of Oxford.

Morrish, J. (1986), 'King Alfred's Letter as a source of learning in England', in P. E. Szarmach (ed.), *Studies in Earlier Old English Prose*. Binghamton, SUNY: pp. 87–107.

Morrish, J. (1988), 'Dated and datable manuscripts copied in England during the ninth century: a preliminary list', *Medieval Studies*, **50**: 512–38.

Morton, A. (1999), 'Hamwic in context', in M. Anderton (ed.) *Anglo-Saxon Trading Empires: Beyond the Emporia*. Glasgow, Cruithne Press: pp. 48–62.

Morton, A. D. (ed.) (1992), *Excavations at Hamwic*, 1: *Excavations 1946–83, Excluding Six Dials and Melbourne Street*. CBA Research Report 84, London, Council for British Archaeology.

Muir, B. J. (ed.) (1994), *The Exeter Anthology of Old English Poetry: An Edition of Exeter Dean and Chapter MS 3501*. 2 vols, Exeter, University of Exeter Press.

Müller-Wille, M., Dorfler W., Meier, D. and Kroll, H. (1988), 'The transformation of rural society, economy and landscape, during the first millennium AD: archaeological and palaeobotanical contributions from Northern Germany and Southern Scandinavia', *Geografiska Annaler*, **70**: 53–68.

Mynors, R. A. B., Thomson, R. M. and Winterbottom, M. (eds and trans.) (1998), *William of Malmesbury, Gesta Regum Anglorum*. Oxford Medieval Texts, Oxford, Oxford University Press.

Myres, J. N. L. (1986), *The English Settlements*. Oxford, Clarendon Press.

Nash-Williams, V. E. (1950), *The Early Christian Monuments of Wales*. Cardiff, University of Wales Press.

Natanson, J. (1953), *Early Christian Ivories*. London, Tiranti.

Nelson, J. L. (1983), 'The Church's military service in the ninth century: a contemporary comparative view?', *Studies in Church History*, **20**: 15–30 (reprinted in Nelson, 1986b: 117–32).

Nelson, J. L. (1986a), 'Brunhild and Balthild in Merovingian history', in J. L. Nelson (ed.), *Politics and Ritual in Early Medieval Europe.* London, Hambledon: pp. 1–48.

Nelson, J. L. (1986b), *Politics and Ritual in Early Medieval Europe.* London, Hambledon.

Nelson, J. L. (1986c), ' "A king across the sea": Alfred in Continental perspective', *Transactions of the Royal Historical Society,* **36**: 45–68 (reprinted in Nelson, 1999: ch. II).

Nelson, J. L. (1987), 'The Lord's anointed and the people's choice: Carolingian royal ritual', in D. Cannadine and S. Price (eds), *Rituals of Royalty: Power and Ceremonial in Traditional Societies.* Cambridge, Cambridge University Press: pp. 137–80 (reprinted in Nelson, 1996: 99–132).

Nelson, J. L. (1989), 'Translating images of authority: the Christian Roman emperors in the Carolingian world', in M. M. Mackenzie and C. Roueché (eds), *Images of Authority. Papers presented to Joyce Reynolds.* Cambridge, Cambridge Philological Society: pp. 195–205 (reprinted in Nelson 1996: 89–98).

Nelson, J. L. (1990), 'Literacy in Carolingian government', in R. McKitterick (ed.), *The Uses of Literacy in Early Medieval Europe.* Cambridge, Cambridge University Press: pp. 258–96 (reprinted in Nelson, 1996: 1–36).

Nelson, J. L. (1992), *Charles the Bald.* London, Longman.

Nelson, J. L. (1995), 'Kingship and royal government', in R. McKitterick (ed.), *The New Cambridge History, c. 700–c. 900.* **2**, Cambridge, Cambridge University Press: pp. 383–430.

Nelson, J. L. (1996), *The Frankish World 750–900.* London, Hambledon.

Nelson, J. L. (1997), 'Early medieval rites of queen-making and the shaping of medieval queenship', in A. Duggan (ed.), *Queens and Queenship in Medieval Europe.* Woodbridge, Boydell: pp. 301–15.

Nelson, J. L. (1998), 'Making a difference in eighth-century politics: the daughters of Desiderius', in A. C. Murray (ed.), *After Rome's Fall: Narrators and Sources of Early Medieval History. Essays Presented to Walter Goffart.* Toronto, University of Toronto Press: pp. 171–90.

Nelson, J. L. (2000), 'Rulers and government', in T. Reuter (ed.), *The New Cambridge Medieval History, c. 900–c. 1024.* **3**, Cambridge, Cambridge University Press: pp. 95–129.

Nenk, B. S., Haith, C. and Bradley, J. (1997), 'Medieval Britain and Ireland in 1996', *Medieval Archaeology,* **41**: 241–328.

Nenk, B. S., Margeson, S. and Hurley, M. (1992), 'Medieval Britain and Ireland in 1991', *Medieval Archaeology,* **36**: 184–308.

Newman, J. (1999), 'Wics, trade, and the hinterlands – the Ipswich region', in M. Anderson (ed.), *Anglo-Saxon Trading Centres: Beyond the Emporia.* Glasgow, Cruithne Press: pp. 32–47.

Ní Dhonnchadha, M. (1993), 'The *Lex innocentium*: Adomnán's law for women, clerics and youths, 697 A.D.', *Historical Studies* (Irish Conference of Historians), **19**: 58–69.

Nielsen, P. O., Randsborg, K. and Thrane, H. (1993), *The Archaeology of Gudme and Lundeborg. Papers Presented at a Conference at Svendborg, October 1991.* Archaeologiske Studier **10**, Copenhagen, Akademisk Forlag.

Nightingale, P. (1983), 'The ora, the mark and the mancus, weight-standards and the coinage in eleventh-century England (part I)', *Numismatic Chronicle*, **143**: 248–57.

Noble, F. (1983), *Offa's Dyke Reviewed*, M. Gelling (ed.), British Archaeological Reports, Br. ser. **114**.

Noble, T. F. X. (1984), *The Republic of St Peter: The Birth of the Papal State, 680–825*, Philadelphia, University of Pennsylvania Press.

North, J. J. (1961), 'The coinage of Berhtwulf of Mercia (840–52)', *Spinks Numismatic Circular*, **69**: 213–15.

Ó Carragáin, É. (1981), 'How did the Vercelli collector interpret *The Dream of the Rood?*', in P. M. Tilling (ed.), *Studies in English Language and Early Literature in Honour of Paul Christophersen*. Coleraine, New University of Ulster: pp. 63–104.

Ó Corráin, D. (1981), 'The early Irish churches: some aspects of organisation', in D. Ó Corráin (ed.), *Irish Antiquity. Essays and Studies Presented to Professor M. J. O'Kelly*. Cork, Tower Books (reprinted 1994, Dublin, Four Courts Press): pp. 327–41.

Ó Corráin, D. (1986), 'Historical need and literary narrative', in D. Ellis Evans, J. G. Griffith and E. M. Jope (eds), *Proceedings of the 7th International Congress of Celtic Studies, Oxford 1983*. Oxford, Cranham Press: pp. 141–58.

Ó Corráin, D. (1995), 'Ireland, Scotland and Wales, *c.*700 to the early eleventh century', in R. McKitterick (ed.), *The New Cambridge Medieval History, c. 700–c. 900*. **2**, Cambridge, Cambridge University Press: pp. 43–63.

Ó Muraíle, N. (2000), 'Some early Connacht population groups', in A. P. Smyth (ed.), *Seanchas: Studies in Early and Medieval Irish Archaeology, History and Literature in Honour of Francis J. Byrne*. Dublin, Four Courts Press: pp. 161–77.

Ó Riain, P. (1995), 'Pagan example and Christian practice; a reconsideration', in D. Edel (ed.), *Cultural Identity and Cultural Integration. Ireland and Europe in the Early Middle Ages*. Dublin, Four Courts Press: pp. 144–56.

O'Brien, M. A. (1962), *Corpus Genealogiarum Hiberniae*. Dublin, Institute for Advanced Studies (reprinted 1976).

O'Connor, T. P. (1991), *Bones From 45–54 Fishergate, The Animal Bones* **4**, *The Archaeology of York*. **15**, London: Council for British Archaeology for the York Archaeological Trust.

O'Connor, T. P. (forthcoming), 'On the interpretation of the animal bone assemblages from wics', in D. Hill and R. Cowie (eds), *Wics: The Early Medieval Trading Centres of Northern Europe*. Sheffield, Sheffield Academic Press.

O'Donovan, J. (ed.) (1848–51), *Annala Ríoghachta Éireann. Annals of the Kingdom of Ireland by the Four Masters from the earliest period to the year 1616*. 7 vols, Dublin (reprinted 1990, Dublin, De Búrca Rare Books).

Okasha, E. and O'Reilly, J. (1984), 'An Anglo-Saxon portable altar: inscription and iconography', *Journal of the Warburg and Courtauld Institutes*, **47**: 1–31.

Oman, C. (1949), *England before the Norman Conquest*. [1910] 9th edn, London, Methuen.

O'Reilly, J. (1998), 'Patristic and insular traditions of the evangelists: exegesis and iconography', in A. M. Luiselli Fadda and É. Ó Carragáin (eds), *Le Isole Britanniche e Roma in Età Romanobarbarica*. Rome, Herder: pp. 49–94.

Oswald, A. (1954), *The Church of St. Bertelin at Stafford*. Birmingham, City of Birmingham Museum and Art Gallery.

Owen-Crocker, G. R. (1986), *Dress in Anglo-Saxon England*. Manchester, Manchester University Press.

Ozanne, A. (1963), 'The Peak dwellers', *Medieval Archaeology*, **7**: 15–52.

Pagan, H. E. (1965), 'A third gold coin of Mercia', *British Numismatic Journal*, **34**: 8–10.

Pagan, H. E. (1968), 'A new type for Beonna', *British Numismatic Journal*, **37**: 10–15.

Pagan, H. E. (1970), 'Northumbrian numismatic chronology in the ninth century', *British Numismatic Journal*, **37**: 1–15.

Pagan, H. E. (1982), 'The coinage of the East Anglian kingdom from 825–870', *British Numismatic Journal*, **52**: 41–83.

Pagan, H. E. (1986), 'Coinage in southern England, 796–874', in M. A. S. Blackburn (ed.), *Anglo-Saxon Monetary History*. Leicester, Leicester University Press: pp. 45–65.

Pagan, H. E. (1997), 'Internal Monetary Frontiers in 10th-century England', unpublished paper given at the 12th International Numismatic Congress, Berlin.

Parsons, D. (1996), 'Before the parish: the church in Anglo-Saxon Leicestershire', in J. Bourne (ed.), *Anglo-Saxon Landscapes in the East Midlands*. Leicester, Leicestershire Museums, Arts and Records Service: pp. 11–35.

Peddie, J. (1999), *Alfred: Warrior King*. Stroud, Sutton.

Pertz, G. H. (ed.) (1826a), *Annales Laureshamenses, MGH Scriptores*. **1**, Hannover [np]: pp. 22–39.

Pertz, G. H. (ed.) (1826b), *Annales Nazariani, MGH Scriptores*. **1**, Hannover [np]: pp. 23–44.

Phillimore, E. (ed.) (1888), 'The Annales Cambriae and the Old Welsh genealogies from Harleian MS. 3859', *Y Cymmrodor*, **9**: 141–83.

Pilch, H. (1990), 'The last Vercelli homily: a sentence-analytical edition', in J. Fisiak (ed.), *Historical Linguistics and Philology*. Berlin and New York, Mouton de Gruyter: pp. 297–336.

Pirie, E. J. E. (1996), *Coins of the Kingdom of Northumbria, c. 700–867*. Llanfyllin, Galata Press.

Pirie, E. J. E. (in progress), 'The purse-hoard of Northumbrian stycas', in D. Bowsher and G. Malcolm with B. Cowie (eds), *Saxon London:*

Excavations at the Royal Opera House 1989–1997. London, Museum of London Archaeology Service.

P.L., Patrologia Latina. 221 vols, ed. J. P. Migne, Paris, J. P. Migne and Garnier Frères: 1841–1880 (with volumes reissued by Garnier to 1905).

Plummer, C. (ed.) (1892–99), *Two of the Saxon Chronicles Parallel.* 2 vols, Oxford, Clarendon Press.

Plummer, C. (ed.) (1896), *Venerabilis Baedae Historiam Ecclesiasticam Gentis Anglorum; Historiam Abbatum, Epistolam ad Echeretum, una cum Historia Abbatum Auctore Anonymo.* Oxford, Clarendon Press.

Plunkett, S. (1998a), 'The Mercian perspective', in S. Foster (ed.), *The St Andrews Sarcophagus: A Pictish Masterpiece and its International Connections.* Dublin, Four Courts Press: pp. 202–26.

Plunkett, S. (1998b), 'Anglo-Saxon stone sculpture and architecture in Suffolk' in S. West (ed.), *A Corpus of Anglo-Saxon Material from Suffolk, East Anglian Archaeology.* **84**, Ipswich, Suffolk County Council Archaeology Service: pp. 323–57.

Poppe, E. (1986), 'A new edition of *Cáin Éimíne Báin*', *Celtica*, **18**: 35–52.

Porcher, J. (1965), 'La peinture provinciale', in W. Braunfels and H. Schnitzler (eds), *Karl der Grosse.* **3**, Düsseldorf, L. Schwann: 54–73, Figs 6–10, pl. XXV.

Porter, G. (1997), 'An early medieval settlement at Guildhall, City of London', in G. De Boe and F. Verhaeghe (eds), *Urbanism in Medieval Europe – Papers of the 'Medieval Europe Brugge 1997 Conference'.* **1** Zellick, Institute for Archaeological Heritage: pp. 147–52.

Powicke, M. (1962), *Military Obligation in Medieval England.* Oxford, Clarendon Press.

Powlesland, D. (1997), 'Early Anglo-Saxon settlements, structures, form and layout', in J. Hines (ed.), *The Anglo-Saxons from the Migration Period to the Eighth Century: An Ethnographic Perspective.* Woodbridge, Boydell Press: pp. 101–17.

Rackham, J. (1994a), 'Economy and environment in Saxon London', in J. Rackham (ed.), *Environment and Economy in Anglo-Saxon England. A Review of Recent Work on the Environmental Archaeology of Rural and Urban Anglo-Saxon Settlements in England.* London: Council for British Archaeology Research Report, **89**: 126–35.

Rackham, J. (ed.) (1994b), *Environment and Economy in Anglo-Saxon England: A Review of Recent Work on the Environmental Archaeology of Rural and Urban Anglo-Saxon Settlements in England.* London, Council for British Archaeology Research Report, **89**.

Rackham, J., Locker, A. and West, B. (1989), 'Animal remains', in R. L. Whytehead and R. Cowie with L. Blackmore, 'Excavations at the Peabody site, Chandos Place, and the National Gallery', *Transactions of the London and Middlesex Archaeological Society*, **40**: 148–70.

Radner, J. N. (1978), *Fragmentary Annals of Ireland.* Dublin, Dublin Institute for Advanced Studies.

Rahtz, P. (1976), *Excavations at St Mary's Church, Deerhurst, 1971–73*. London, CBA, Research Report **15**.

Rahtz, P. and Meeson, R. (1992), *An Anglo-Saxon Watermill at Tamworth: Excavations in the Bolebridge Street area of Tamworth, Staffordshire in 1971 and 1978*. London, CBA, Research Report **83**.

Rahtz, P. and Watts, L. (1997), *St Mary's Church, Deerhurst, Gloucestershire: Fieldwork, Excavations and Structural Analysis, 1971–1984*. Woodbridge, Boydell Press.

RCAHMS (1982), Royal Commission on the Ancient and Historical Monuments of Scotland: *Argyll: An Inventory of the Monuments*. **4** (Iona), Edinburgh, HMSO.

RCAHMS (1984), Royal Commission on the Ancient and Historical Monuments of Scotland: *Argyll: An Inventory of the Monuments*. **5** (Islay, Jura, Colonsay and Oronsay), Edinburgh, HMSO.

Redknap, M. (1991a), 'The Saxon pottery from Barking Abbey: part 1, local wares', *London Archaeologist*, **6.13**: 353–60.

Redknap, M. (1991b), *The Christian Celts: Treasures of Late Celtic Wales*. Cardiff, National Museum of Wales.

Redknap, M. (1992), 'The Saxon pottery from Barking Abbey: part 2, the continental imports', *London Archaeologist*, **6.14**: 378–81.

Reilly, K. (in progress), 'The animal and fish bone', in D. Bowsher and G. Malcolm with R. Cowie (eds), *Saxon London: Excavations at the Royal Opera House 1989–1997*. London, Museum of London Archaeology Service.

Rennel of Rodd, Lord (1963), 'The land of Lene', in I. Ll. Foster and L. Alcock (eds), *Culture and Environment: Essays in Honour of Sir Cyril Fox*. London, Routledge and Kegan Paul: pp. 307–26.

Reuter, T. (1985), 'Plunder and tribute in the Carolingian empire', *Transactions of the Royal Historical Society*, 5th ser. **35**: 75–94.

Reuter, T. (1991), *Germany in the Early Middle Ages, 800–1056*. London, Longman.

Reuter, T. (1992), 'The end of Carolingian military expansion', in P. Godman and R. Collins (eds), *Charlemagne's Heir: New Perspectives on the Reign of Louis the Pious (814–840)*. Oxford, Oxford University Press: pp. 391–405.

Reynolds, A. (1999), *Later Anglo-Saxon England: Life and Landscape*. Stroud, Tempus.

Reynolds, S. (1983), 'Medieval *origines gentium* and the community of the realm', *History*, **68**: 375–90.

Rhodes, M. (1980), 'The Saxon pottery', in C. Hill, M. Millett and T. Blagg (eds), *The Roman Riverside Wall and Monumental Arch in London*. London, London and Middlesex Archaeological Society Special Paper, **3**: 97–98.

Rhys, T. (1908) 'All around the Wrekin', *Y Cymmrodor*, **21**.

Richards, J. D. (1987), *The Significance of Form and Decoration of Anglo-Saxon Cremation Urns*. Oxford, British Archaeological Reports, Br. ser. **166**.

Richards, J. D. (1999), 'Cottam: An Anglian and Anglo-Scandinavian settlement on the Yorkshire Wolds', *Archaeological Journal*, **156**: 1–110.

Riché, P. (1976), *Education and Culture in the Barbarian West*. Columbia, University of South Carolina Press.

Richmond, H. (1986), 'Outlines of church development in Northamptonshire', in L. A. S. Butler and R. K. Morris (eds), *The Anglo-Saxon Church: Papers on History, Architecture and Archaeology in Honour of Dr H. M. Taylor*. London, CBA, Research Report **60**: pp. 176–87.

Rickett, R. (1995), *The Iron Age, Roman and Early Saxon Settlement: The Anglo-Saxon Cemetery at Spong Hill, North Elmham*. **7**, Gressenhall, East Anglian Archaeology **73**.

Riddler, I. (1990), 'Saxon handled combs from London', *Transactions of the London and Middlesex Archaeological Society*, **41**: 9–20.

Rigold, S. E. R. (1961 and 1966), 'The two primary series of sceattas', *British Numismatic Journal*, **30**: 6–53, and *British Numismatic Journal*, **35**: 1–6.

Riley, H. T. (ed.) (1893), *Ingulph's Chronicle of the Abbey of Croyland with the Continuations by Peter of Blois and Anonymous Writers*. London, George Bell and Sons.

Riley, H. T. (trans.) (1854), *Ingulf's Chronicle of the Abbey of Croyland with the Continuations by Peter of Blois and Anonymous Writers*. London [n.p.].

Ritchie, A. (1989), *Picts*. Edinburgh, HMSO.

Roberts, J. (1970), 'An inventory of early Guthlac materials', *Mediaeval Studies*, **32**: 193–233.

Roberts, J. (1977), 'St Bartholomew's Day: a problem resolved?', *Medium Ævum*, **46**: 16–19.

Roberts, J. (1979), *The Guthlac Poems of the Exeter Book*. Oxford, Clarendon Press.

Roberts, J. (1981), 'The Exeter Book: *Swa is lar 7 ar to spowendre spræce gelæded*', *Dutch Quarterly Review of Anglo-American Letters*, **11**: 302–19.

Roberts, J. (1986), 'The Old English prose translation of Felix's *Vita sancti Guthlaci*', in P. Szarmach (ed.), *Studies in Earlier Old English Prose*. Albany, State University of New York Press: pp. 363–79.

Roberts, J. (1988), '*Guthlac A*: sources and source hunting', in E. D. Kennedy, R. Waldron and J. Wittig (eds), *Medieval English Studies Presented to George Kane*. Woodbridge, Suffolk, D. S. Brewer: pp. 1–18.

Roberts, J. (1997), '*Fela martyra* "many martyrs": a different view of Orosius's city', in J. Roberts, J. L. Nelson and M. Godden (eds), *Alfred the Wise*. Cambridge, D. S. Brewer: pp. 155–78.

Roberts, J. (2000), 'The English saints remembered in Old English anonymous homilies', in P. Szarmach (ed.), *Old English Prose: Basic Readings*. London, Garland Publishing: pp. 433–61.

Robertson, A. J. (1986), *Anglo-Saxon Charters*. (reprint) Holmes Beach, FL, W. W. Gaunt.

Robinson, G. W. (1916), *The Life of Saint Boniface by Willibald*. London, Humphrey Milford.

Rodwell, W. (1984), 'Churches in the landscape', in M. L. Faull (ed.), *Studies in Late Anglo-Saxon Settlement*. Oxford, Oxford University Department for External Studies: pp. 1–23.

Rollason, D. W. (1978), 'List of saints' resting-places in Anglo-Saxon England', *Anglo-Saxon England*, **7**: 61–93.

Rollason, D. W. (1981), *The Search for Saint Wigstan*. Vaughan Papers, **27**, Leicester, Leicester University Press.

Rollason, D. W. (1982), *The Mildrith Legend: A Study in Early Medieval Hagiography in England*. Leicester, Leicester University Press.

Rollason, D. W. (1983), 'The cults of murdered royal saints in Anglo-Saxon England', *Anglo-Saxon England*, **11**: 1–22.

Rollason, D. W. (1989), *Saints and Relics in Anglo-Saxon England*. Oxford, Blackwell.

Rosier, J. L. (1970), 'Death and transfiguration: *Guthlac B*', in J. L. Rosier (ed.), *Philological Essays: Studies in Old and Middle English Language and Literature in Honour of Herbert Dean Meritt*. The Hague, Mouton: pp. 82–92.

Rosser, G. (1989), *Medieval Westminster 1200–1540*. Oxford, Clarendon Press.

Routh, R. E. (1937), 'A corpus of the pre-conquest carved stones of Derbyshire', *Archaeological Journal*, **94**: 1–42.

Rowland, J. (ed. and trans.) (1990), *Early Welsh Saga Poetry: a Study and Edition of the Englynion*. Cambridge, D. S. Brewer.

Rowley, T. (1972), *The Shropshire Landscape*. London, Hodder and Stoughton.

Rumble, A. R. (1977), ' "Hrepingas" reconsidered', in A. Dornier (ed.), *Mercian Studies*. Leicester, Leicester University Press: pp. 169–72.

Rumble, A. R. (1996a), 'Appendix III The Tribal Hidage: an annotated bibliography', in D. Hill and A. Rumble, *The Defence of Wessex: The Burghal Hidage and Anglo-Saxon Fortifications*. Manchester, Manchester University Press: pp. 182–8.

Rumble, A. R. (1996b), 'An edition and translation of the Burghal Hidage, together with Recension C of the Tribal Hidage', in D. Hill and A. Rumble (eds), *The Defence of Wessex: The Burghal Hidage and Anglo-Saxon Fortifications*. Manchester, Manchester University Press: pp. 14–35.

Rumble, A. R. (1996c), 'The known manuscripts of the Burghal Hidage', in D. Hill and A. Rumble (eds), *The Defence of Wessex: The Burghal Hidage and Anglo-Saxon Fortifications*. Manchester, Manchester University Press: pp. 36–59.

Salisbury, C. R. (1981), 'An Anglo-Saxon fish-weir at Colwick, Nottinghamshire', *Transactions of the Thoroton Society of Nottinghamshire*, **85**: 26–36.

Salisbury, C. R. (1991), 'Primitive British fishweirs', in G. L. Good, R. H. Jones and M. W. Ponsford (eds), *Waterfront Archaeology*. London, CBA Research Report **74**: 76–87.

Sawyer, P. H. (1968), *Anglo-Saxon Charters: An Annotated List and Bibliography*. London, Royal Historical Society.

Sawyer, P. H. (1977), 'Kings and merchants', in P. H. Sawyer and I. N. Wood (eds), *Early Medieval Kingship*. Leeds, School of History, University of Leeds: pp. 139–58.

Sawyer, P. H. (1998a), *Anglo-Saxon Lincolnshire: A History of Lincolnshire*. 3, Lincoln, Society for Lincolnshire History and Archaeology.

Sawyer, P. H. (1998b), *From Roman Britain to Norman England*. 2nd edn, London, Routledge.

Scharer, A. (1982), *Die angelsächsische Königsurkunde im 7. und 8. Jahrhundert*. Vienna, Böhlau.

Scharer, A. (1988), 'Die Intitulationes der angelsächsischen Könige im 7. und 8. Jahrhundert', in H. Wolfram and A. Scharer (eds), *Intitulatio III. Lateinische Herrschertitel und Herrschertitulaturen vom 7. bis zum 13. Jahrhundert*. Vienna, Böhlau: pp. 9–74.

Schofield, J. (1994), 'Saxon and medieval parish churches in the City of London: a review', *Transactions of the London and Middlesex Archaeological Society*, **45**: 23–145.

Scholz, B. W. with B. Rogers (1972), *Carolingian Chronicles*. Ann Arbor, University of Michigan Press.

Schülke, A. (1999), 'On Christianization and grave-finds', *European Journal of Archaeology*, **2**.1: 77–106.

Schülke, A. (forthcoming), 'Die "Christianisierung" als Forschungsproblem der südwestdeutschen Gräberarchäologie', *Zeitschrift für Archäologie des Mittelalters*.

Scott, J. (ed.) (1981), *The Early History of Glastonbury: An Edition, Translation and Study of William of Malmesbury's 'De Antiquitate Glastonie Ecclesie'*. Woodbridge, Boydell and Brewer.

Scragg, D. G. (ed.) (1992), *The Vercelli Homilies and Related Texts*. Early English Text Society, Original Series **300**, Oxford, Oxford University Press.

Scull, C. (1993), 'Archaeology, early Anglo-Saxon society and the origins of Anglo-Saxon kingdoms', *Anglo-Saxon Studies in Archaeology and History*, **6**: 65–82.

Scull, C. (1999), 'Social archaeology and Anglo-Saxon kingdom origins', *The Making of Kingdoms: Anglo-Saxon Studies in Archaeology and History*, **10**: 17–24.

Serjeantson, R. M. and Longden, H. I. (1913), 'The parish churches and religious houses of Northamptonshire: their dedications, altars, images and lights', *Archaeological Journal*, **70**: 217–452.

Serra, J. (1961), *Diocesi di Spoleto, Corpus della scultura altomedievale*. **2**, Spoleto, Centro italiano di studi sull'alto medioevo.

Sharpe, R. (1982), '*Vitae S. Brigitae*: the oldest texts', *Peritia*, **1**, 81–106.

Shoesmith, R. (1982), *Excavations on or Close to the Defences, Hereford City Excavations*. **2**, London, CBA Research Report **46**.

Sidebottom, P. (1994), 'The schools of Anglo-Saxon stone sculpture in the North Midlands', unpublished PhD thesis, University of Sheffield.

Sidell, J. (in progress), 'The eggshell', in D. Bowsher and G. Malcolm with R. Cowie (eds), *Saxon London: Excavations at the Royal Opera House 1989–1997*. London, Museum of London Archaeology Service.

Sims-Williams, P. (1975), 'Continental influence at Bath monastery in the seventh century', *Anglo-Saxon England*, **4**: 1–10.

Sims-Williams, P. (1976), 'Cuthswith, seventh-century abbess of Inkberrow, near Worcester, and the Würzburg manuscript of Jerome on Ecclesiastes', *Anglo-Saxon England*, **5**: 1–21.

Sims-Williams, P. (1983a), 'Gildas and the Anglo-Saxons', *Cambridge Medieval Celtic Studies*, **6**: 1–30.

Sims-Williams, P. (1983b), 'The settlement of England in Bede and the *Chronicle*', *Anglo-Saxon England*, **12**: 1–41.

Sims-Williams, P. (1990), *Religion and Literature in Western England, 600–800*. Cambridge, Cambridge University Press.

Sims-Williams, P. (1994–5), 'Historical need and literary narrative: a caveat from ninth-century Wales', *Welsh History Review*, **17**: 11–20.

Sims-Williams, P. (1993), 'The provenance of the Llywarch hen poems: a case for Llan-gors, Brycheiniog', *Cambrian Medieval Celtic Studies*, **26**: 27–63.

Sisam, K. (1953a), 'Anglo-Saxon royal genealogies', *Proceedings of the British Academy*, **39**: 287–346.

Sisam, K. (1953b), *Studies in the History of Old English Literature*. Oxford, Clarendon Press.

Sisam, K. (1956–7), 'Canterbury, Lichfield and the Vespasian Psalter', *Review of English Studies*, n. s. **7**: 1–10 and 113–31, and n. s. **8**: 372–3.

Small, A., Thomas, A. C., and Wilson, D. M. (1973), *St Ninians Isle and Its Treasure. Aberdeen University Studies Series*, **152**, Oxford, Oxford University Press for the University of Aberdeen.

Smith, A. H. (1956), *English Place-Name Elements, Part II*. Cambridge, English Place-Name Society, **26**.

Smith, R. A. (1914), 'Irish brooches of five centuries', *Archaeologia*, **65**, 223–50.

Smith, R.A. (1924), 'Examples of Anglian Art', *Archaeologia*, **74**: 233–54.

Stafford, P. (1985), *The East Midlands in the Early Middle Ages*. Leicester, Leicester University Press.

Stafford, P. (1997), *Queen Emma and Queen Edith, Queenship and Women's Power in Eleventh-Century England*. Oxford, Blackwell.

Stafford, P. (1998), *Queens, Concubines and Dowagers: The King's Wife in the Early Middle Ages*. 2nd edn, London, Leicester University Press.

Stafford, P. (forthcoming), 'Gender and inheritance in Alfred's family history' in T. Reuter (ed.), *Alfred the Great*.

Stancliffe, C. (1983), 'Kings who opted out', in P. Wormald, D. Bullough, and R. Collins (eds), *Ideal and Reality in Frankish and Anglo-Saxon Society: Studies Presented to J. M. Wallace-Hadrill*. Oxford, Basil Blackwell: pp. 154–76.

Stancliffe, C. (1995a), 'Oswald, "Most Holy and Most Victorious King of the Northumbrians"', in C. Stancliffe and E. Cambridge (eds), *Oswald: From Northumbrian King to European Saint*. Stamford, Paul Watkins: pp. 33–83.

Stancliffe, C. (1995b), 'Where was Oswald killed?', in C. Stancliffe and E. Cambridge (eds), *Oswald: From Northumbrian King to European Saint*. Stamford, Paul Watkins: pp. 84–96.

Stancliffe, C. (1999), 'The British Church and the mission of Augustine', in R. Gameson (ed.), *Saint Augustine of Canterbury and the Conversion of England*. Stroud, Sutton: pp. 124–30.

Stenton, D. M. (1970), *Preparatory to Anglo-Saxon England, Being the Collected Papers of Frank Merry Stenton*. ed. by D. M. Stenton, Oxford, Clarendon Press.

Stenton, F. M. (1918), 'The supremacy of the Mercian kings', *English Historical Review*, **33**: 433–52 (reprinted, 1970, *Preparatory to Anglo-Saxon England*. D. M. Stenton (ed.), Oxford, Clarendon Press: pp. 48–66).

Stenton, F. M. (1933), 'Medeshamstede and its colonies', in J. G. Edwards, V. H. Galbraith, and E. F. Jacob (eds), *Historical Essays in Honour of James Tait*. Manchester, Manchester University Press: pp. 312–26 (reprinted 1970, *Preparatory to Anglo-Saxon England*. D. M. Stenton (ed.), Oxford, Clarendon Press: pp. 179–92).

Stenton, F. M. (1942), 'The historical bearing of place-name studies: the place of women in Anglo-Saxon society', *Trans. R. Hist. Soc.*, ser. 4, **25**: 1–13 (reprinted 1970, *Preparatory to Anglo-Saxon England*. D. M. Stenton (ed.), Oxford, Clarendon Press, 1970: pp. 314–24).

Stenton, F. M. (1971), *Anglo-Saxon England*. 3rd edn, Oxford, Clarendon Press.

Stevenson, W. H. (ed.) (1904), *Asser, Life of King Alfred*. Oxford, Clarendon Press.

Stevenson, W. H. (ed.) (1959), *Asser's Life of King Alfred*. Oxford, Oxford University Press.

Stewart, B. H. I. H (1978), 'Anglo-Saxon gold coins', in R. A. G. Carson and C. M. Kraay (eds), *Scripta Nummaria Romana*. London, Spink: pp. 143–72.

Stewart, I. (1986), 'The London mint and the coinage of Offa', in M. A. S. Blackburn (ed.), *Anglo-Saxon Monetary History*. Leicester, Leicester University Press: pp. 27–43.

Stocker, D. (1993), 'The early church in Lincolnshire: a study of sites and their significance', in A. Vince (ed.), *Pre-Viking Lindsey*. Lincoln, City of Lincoln Archaeology Unit: pp. 101–22.

Stocker, D. and Went, D. (1995), 'The evidence for a pre-Viking church adjacent to the Anglo-Saxon barrow at Taplow, Buckinghamshire', *Archaeological Journal*, **152**: 441–50.

Stott, P. (1991), 'Saxon and Norman coins from London', in A. Vince (ed.), *Finds and Environmental Evidence, Aspects of Saxo-Norman London*. **2**, London, London and Middlesex Archaeology Society Special Paper, **12**: 279–325.

Stuiver, M. and Pearson, G. W. (1986), 'High-precision calibration of the radiocarbon timescale, AD 1950–500 BC', *Radiocarbon*, **28** (**2B**): 805–38.

Sutherland, D. S. and Parsons, D. (1984), 'The petrological contribution to the survey of All Saints' Church, Brixworth, Northamptonshire: an interim account', *Journal of the British Archaeological Association*, **137**: 45–64.

Swanton, M. J. (ed.) (1970), *The Dream of the Rood*. Manchester, Manchester University Press.

Swanton, M. J. (ed. and trans.) (1996), *The Anglo-Saxon Chronicle*. London, I. M. Dent.

Sweet, H. (ed.) (1871), *King Alfred's West-Saxon Version of Gregory's Pastoral Care*. Early English Text Society, Original Series **45, 50**, London, Oxford University Press.

Tabacco, G. (1989), *The Struggle for Power in Medieval Italy*. Cambridge, Cambridge University Press.

Talbot, C. H. (1954), *The Anglo-Saxon Missionaries in Germany*. London, Sheed and Ward.

Tangl, M. (ed.) (1916), *S. Bonifatii et Lulli Epistolae, Epistolae Selectae*. **1**, Berlin, Monumenta Germaniae Historica, Hannover, Hahn.

Tatton-Brown, T. (1984), 'The towns of Kent', in J. Haslam (ed.), *Anglo-Saxon Towns in Southern England*. Chichester, Phillimore: pp. 1–36.

Taylor, C. S. (1957), 'The origin of the Mercian shires', *Gloucestershire Studies*, ed. H. P. R. Finberg. Leicester, Leicester University Press: pp. 17–45.

Taylor, H. M. (1971), 'Repton reconsidered: a study in structural criticism', in P. Clemoes and K. Hughes (eds), *England Before the Conquest: Studies in Primary Sources Presented to Dorothy Whitelock*. Cambridge, Cambridge University Press: pp. 351–89.

Taylor, H. M. (1977), *Deerhurst Studies*, **1**: *The Anglo-Saxon Fabric 1971–76*. Cambridge, privately published.

Taylor, H. M. (1978), *Anglo-Saxon Architecture*. **3**, Cambridge, Cambridge University Press.

Taylor, H. M. (1987), 'St Wystan's church, Repton, Derbyshire: a reconstruction essay', *Archaeological Journal*, **144**: 205–45.

Taylor, H. M. and Taylor, J. (1965), *Anglo-Saxon Architecture*, 2 vols. Cambridge, Cambridge University Press.

Thacker, A. (1982), 'Chester and Gloucester: early ecclesiastical organization in two Mercian broughs', *Northern History*, **18**: 199–211.

Thacker, A. T. (1981), 'Some terms for noblemen in Anglo-Saxon England, c.650–900', *Anglo-Saxon Studies in Archaeology and History*. **2**, British Archaeological Reports, Br. Ser., **92**: 201–36.

Thacker, A. T. (1985), 'Kings, saints, and monasteries in pre-Viking Mercia', *Midland History*, **10**: 1–25.

Thacker, A. T. (1995), '*Membra disjecta*: the division of the body and the diffusion of the cult', in C. Stancliffe and E. Cambridge (eds), *Oswald: Northumbrian King to European Saint*. Stamford, Paul Watkins: pp. 97–127.

Thomas, G. (1996), 'Silver wire strap-ends from east Anglia', *Anglo-Saxon Studies in Archaeology and History*. **9**, Oxford University Committee for Archaeology: pp. 81–100.

Thorpe, B. (ed.) (1844), *The Homilies of the Anglo-Saxon Church*. **1**, London, The Aelfric Society.

Thorpe, B. (ed.) (1848), *Florentii Wigorniensis monachi Chronicon ex Chronicis*. **1**, London, English Historical Society.

Timby, J. R. (1993), 'Sancton I Anglo-Saxon cemetery: excavations carried out between 1976 and 1980', *Archaeological Journal*, **150**: 243–365.

Timby, J. R. (1996), *The Anglo-Saxon Cemetery at Empingham II, Rutland: Excavations Carried out 1974 and 1975*. Oxford, Oxbow Books.

Toal, M. F. (ed.) (1958), *The Sunday Sermons of the Great Fathers*. **2**, London, Longmans.

Tremp, E. (ed.) (1995), Astronomer, *Vita Hludowici Imperatoris, MGH Scriptores Rerum Germanicarum in Usum Scholarum*. Hannover, Hahn.

Turner, C. H. (1916), *Early Worcester Manuscripts*. Oxford, Clarendon Press.

Tweddle, D. (1991), 'Sculpture', in L. Webster and J. Backhouse (eds), *The Making of England: Anglo-Saxon Art and Culture AD 600–900*. London, British Museum Press, 239–42.

Tweddle, D. (1992), *The Anglian Helmet from 16–22 Coppergate, The Archaeology of York: The Small Finds*. **17/8**, London, Council for British Archaeology, for the York Archaeological Trust.

Tweddle, D., Biddle, M., Kjølbye-Biddle, B. and Barnes, M. (1995), *South-East England, Corpus of Anglo-Saxon Stone Sculpture*. **4**, Oxford, Oxford University Press and British Academy.

Tyers, I., Hillam, J. and Groves, C. (1994), 'Trees and woodland in the Saxon period: the dendrochronological evidence', in J. Rackham (ed.), *Environment and Economy in Anglo-Saxon England: A Review of Recent Work on the Environmental Archaeology of Rural and Urban Anglo-Saxon Settlements in England*. London, Council for British Archaeology Research Report, **89**: pp. 12–22.

Tyler, D. (forthcoming), 'Orchestrated violence and "The Supremacy of the Mercian Kings"', in D. Hill and M. Worthington (eds), *Æthelbald and Offa*. Oxford, British Archaeological Reports.

Vaughan, R. (1958), *Matthew Paris*. Cambridge, Cambridge University Press.

Verzone, P. (1945), *L'Arte preromanica in Liguria*. Turin, A. Viglongo and Co.

Victoria and Albert Museum (1963), *Late Antique and Byzantine Art*. London, HMSO.

Victoria History of the Counties of England (1970), *A History of the County of Stafford*. **3**, London, Constable.

Vierck, H. (1970–71), 'Pferdegräber im angelsächsischen England', in M. Müller-Wille, 'Pferdegrab und Pferdeopfer im frühen Mittelalter',

Berichten van de Rijksdienst voor het Oudheidkundig Bodemonder-zoek. **20–21**: 189–98 and 218–20.

Vince, A. (1983), 'In search of Saxon London: the view from the pot shed', *Popular Archaeology*, **5.4**: 33–7.

Vince, A. (1984), 'The Aldwych: Saxon London discovered?', *Current Archaeology*, **8.4**: 310–12.

Vince, A. (1988), 'The economic basis of Anglo-Saxon London', in R. Hodges and B. Hobley (eds.), *The Rebirth of Towns in the West AD 700–1050*. London, CBA Research Report, **68**: 83–92.

Vince, A. (1990), *Saxon London: An Archaeological Investigation*. London, Seaby.

Vince, A. (1991a), 'The development of Saxon London', in A. Vince (ed.), *Finds and Environmental Evidence, Aspects of Saxo-Norman London*. **2**, London, London and Middlesex Archaeology Society Special Paper, **12**: 409–35.

Vince, A. (ed.) (1991b), *Finds and Environmental Evidence, Aspects of Saxo-Norman London*. **2**, London, London and Middlesex Archaeology Society Special Paper, **12**.

Vleeskruyer, R. (ed.) (1953), *The Life of St. Chad: An Old English Homily*. Amsterdam, North-Holland Publishing Company.

Volbach, W. F. (1976), *Elfenbeinarbeiten der Spätantike und des frühen Mittelalters*. 3rd edn, Mainz, Von Zabern.

Wade, K. (1988), 'Ipswich', in R. Hodges, and B. Hobley (eds), *The Rebirth of Towns in the West AD 700–1050*. London, CBA Research Report **68**: 93–100.

Wade, K. (forthcoming), 'Ipswich', in D. Hill and R. Cowie (eds), *Wics: The Early Medieval Trading Centres of Northern Europe*. Sheffield, Sheffield Academic Press.

Wade-Evans, A. W. (ed.) (1944), *Vitae sanctorum Britanniae et genealogiae*, History and Law Series, **9**. Cardiff: University of Wales Press.

Wager, S. J. (1998), *Woods, Wolds and Groves: The Woodland of Medieval Warwickshire*. Oxford, British Archaeological Reports, Br. ser. **269**.

Wainwright, F. T. (1945), 'The chronology of the Mercian register', *English Historical Review*, **60**: 388–9.

Wainwright, F. T. (1975a), 'Aethelflaed, Lady of the Mercians', in F. Wainwright (ed.), *Scandinavian England*. Chichester, Phillimore: pp. 305–25.

Wainwright, F. T. (1975b), *Scandinavian England: Collected Papers*. H. P. R. Finberg (ed.), Chichester, Phillimore.

Walker, I. W. (2000), *Mercia and the Making of England*. Stroud, Sutton.

Wallace-Hadrill, J. M. (1965), 'Charlemagne and England', in W. Braunfels (ed.), *Karl der Grosse. Lebenswerk und Nachleben*. **1**, Düsseldorf, Schwann: 683–98 (reprinted in Wallace-Hadrill, 1975: 155–80).

Wallace-Hadrill, J. M. (1971), *Early Germanic Kingship in England and on the Continent*. Oxford, Oxford University Press.

Wallace-Hadrill, J. M. (1975), *Early Medieval History*. Oxford, Oxford University Press.

Wallace-Hadrill, J. M. (1988), *Bede's 'Ecclesiastical History of the English People': A Historical Commentary*. Oxford, Clarendon Press.

Warner, G. F. (1928), *The Guthlac Roll*. Oxford, Roxburghe Club.

Watson, W. J. (1993), *The History of the Celtic Placenames of Scotland*. Edinburgh, Birlinn. Reprint of Edinburgh and London: William Blackwood, 1926.

Webster, L. (1997), 'Heirs of Rome: the shaping of Britain AD 400–700', in L. Webster and M. Brown, *The Transformation of the Roman World AD 400–900*. London, British Museum: pp. 208–48.

Webster, L. (2000), 'Style and function of the Gandersheim casket,' in R. Marth (ed.), *Das Gandersheimer Runenkästchen, Internationales Kolloquium Braunschweig, 24.–26. März 1999*. Braunschweig, Herzog Anton Ulrich Museum: pp. 63–72.

Webster, L. (2001), 'The Anglo-Saxon hinterland: animal style in Southumbrian eighth-century England, with particular reference to metalwork' in O. Krause (ed.), *Tiere, Menschen, Götter: wikingerzeit-liche Kunststile und ihre neuzeitliche Rezeption*. Hamburg, Veröff. Joachim Jungius-Ges. Wiss. **90**: pp. 39–62.

Webster, L. and Backhouse, J. (1991), *The Making of England: Anglo-Saxon Art and Culture AD 600–900*. London, British Museum Press.

Weitzmann, K. (1972), 'The ivories of the so-called Grado Chair', *Dumbarton Oaks Papers,* **26**: 43–91.

Welch, M. (1992), *The English Heritage Book of Anglo-Saxon England*. London, Batsford.

Werminghoff, A. (ed.) (1906), *Concilia Aevi Karolini* [742–842] **1**, *MGH Legum sectio* **3**, *Concilia* **2(i)**. Hannover, Hahn.

West, B. (1989), 'Animal remains: material hand-collected', in R. L. Whytehead and R. Cowie with L. Blackmore, 'Excavations at the Peabody site, Chandos Place, and the National Gallery', *Transactions of the London and Middlesex Archaeological Society,* **40**: 150–68.

West, B. with Rackham, J. (1988), 'Birds and mammals', in R. Cowie and R. L. Whytehead with L. Blackmore, 'Two Middle Saxon occupation sites: excavations at Jubilee Hall and 21–22 Maiden Lane, WC2', *Transactions of the London and Middlesex Archaeological Society,* **39**: 150–4.

West, S. E. (1985), *West Stow: The Anglo-Saxon Village*. East Anglian Archaeology **24**, Ipswich, Suffolk County Planning Department.

West, S. E. (1998), *A Corpus of Anglo-Saxon Material from Suffolk, East Anglian Archaeology*. **84**, Ipswich, Suffolk County Council Archaeology Service.

Westwood, J. O. (1868), *Facsimiles of the Miniatures and Ornaments of Anglo-Saxon and Irish Manuscripts*. London, Day and Son.

Wharton, H. (1691), *Anglia Sacra*. **I**, London, R. Chiswel (reprinted 1969, Farnborough, Gregg International Publishers).

Wheeler, H. (1977), 'Aspects of Mercian art: the Book of Cerne', in

A. Dornier (ed.), *Mercian Studies*. Leicester, Leicester University Press: pp. 235–44.

Wheeler, H. (1979), 'Excavation at Willington, Derbyshire, 1970–72', *Derbyshire Archaeological Journal*, **99**: 58–220.

Wheeler, R. E. M. (1934), 'The topography of Saxon London', *Antiquity*, **8**: 290–303.

White, R. and Barker, P. (1998), *Wroxeter: Life and Death of a Roman City*. Stroud, Tempus.

Whitelock, D. (1951), *The Audience of Beowulf*. Oxford, Clarendon Press.

Whitelock, D. (1955), *English Historical Documents*. **1** *c*. 500–1042. London: Eyre and Spottiswoode.

Whitelock, D. (1965), *The Anglo-Saxon Chronicle: A Revised Translation*. 2nd (corrected) impression, London, Eyre and Spottiswoode.

Whitelock, D. (1966), 'The prose of Alfred's reign', in E. G. Stanley (ed.), *Continuations and Beginnings*. London, Nelson: pp. 67–103.

Whitelock, D. (1979), *English Historical Documents*. **1**, *c*. 500–1042, 2nd edn, London, Eyre Methuen.

Whitelock, D., Douglas, D. C. and Tucker, S. I. (1961), *The Anglo-Saxon Chronicle*. London, Eyre and Spottiswoode.

Whitwell, B. (1991), 'Flixborough', *Current Archaeology*, **126**: 244–7.

Whytehead, R. L. (1985), 'The Jubilee Hall site reveals new evidence of Saxon London', *Rescue News*, **37**: 6–7.

Whytehead, R. L. (1988), 'The excavation at Jubilee Hall', in R. Cowie and R. L. Whytehead with L. Blackmore, 'Two Middle Saxon occupation sites: excavations at Jubilee Hall and 21–22 Maiden Lane, WC2', *Transactions of the London and Middlesex Archaeological Society*, **39**: 49–66.

Whytehead, R. L. with Bowsher, D. (1989), 'The Peabody Site', in R. L. Whytehead and R. Cowie with L. Blackmore, 'Excavations at the Peabody site, Chandos Place, and the National Gallery', *Transactions of the London and Middlesex Archaeological Society*, **40**: 38–58.

Whytehead, R. L. and Cowie, R. with Blackmore, L. (1989), 'Excavations at the Peabody site, Chandos Place, and the National Gallery', *Transactions of the London and Middlesex Archaeological Society*, **40**: 35–176.

Wickham, C. (1981), *Early Medieval Italy: Central Power and Local Society, 400- 1000*. London, Macmillan.

Wickham, C. (1995a), 'Rural society in Carolingian Europe', in R. McKitterick (ed.), *The New Cambridge Medieval History, c. 700– c. 900*. **2**, Cambridge, Cambridge University Press: pp. 510–37.

Wickham, C. (1995b), 'Monastic lands and monastic patrons', in R. Hodges (ed.), *The 1980-86 Excavations Part II, San Vincenzo al Volturno*. **2**, Archaeological Monographs of the British School at Rome, **9**, London, British School at Rome: pp. 138–52.

Wilkinson, D. J. and McWhirr, A. D. (1998), *Cirencester: Anglo-Saxon Church and Medieval Abbey*. Cirencester Excavations, **4**, Cirencester, Cotswold Archaeological Trust.

Willems, R. (ed.) (1954), *Sanctus Augustinus – In Iohannis Evangelium Tractatus*, in *CCSL* **36**, Turnhout, Brepols.

Williams ab Ithel, J. (ed.) (1860), *Annales Cambriae*. London, Rolls Series.

Williams, D. and Vince, A. (1997), 'The characterisation and interpretation of Early to Middle Saxon granitic tempered pottery in England', *Medieval Archaeology*, **41**: 214–20.

Williams, G. (forthcoming), 'Military obligations and Mercian supremacy in the eighth century' in D. Hill and M. Worthington (eds), *Æthelbald and Offa*. Oxford, British Archaeological Reports.

Williams, I. (ed.) (1955), *Armes Prydein o lyfr Taliesin*. Cardiff, Gwasg Prifysol Cymru.

Williams, J. H., Shaw, M. and Denham, V. (1985), *Middle Saxon Palaces at Northampton*. Archaeological Monograph **4**, Northampton, Northampton Development Corporation.

Williams, P. W. (1983), *An Anglo-Saxon Cemetery at Thurmaston, Leicestershire*. Leicester, Leicester Museums, Art Galleries and Records Service.

Wilson, D. (1992), *Anglo-Saxon Paganism*. London, Routledge.

Wilson, D. M. (1964), *Anglo-Saxon Ornamental Metalwork 700–1100 in the British Museum. Catalogue of Antiquities of the Later Anglo-Saxon Period*, **1**, London, British Museum.

Wilson, D. M. (1973), 'The treasure' in A. Small, A. C. Thomas and D. M. Wilson, *St Ninians Isle and its Treasure*. Oxford, Oxford University Press: pp. 45–148.

Wilson, D. M. (1984), *Anglo-Saxon Art: From the Seventh Century to the Norman Conquest*. London, Thames and Hudson.

Wilson, D. M. and Blunt C. E. (1961), 'The Trewhiddle hoard', *Archaeologia*, **98**: 75–122.

Winder, J. and Gerber-Parfitt, S. (forthcoming), 'The oyster shells', in D. Bowsher and G. Malcolm with R. Cowie (eds), *Saxon London: Excavations at the Royal Opera House 1989–1997*. London, Museum of London Archaeology Service.

Winterbottom, M. (1978), *Gildas: The Ruin of Britain and Other Documents*. Chichester, Phillimore.

Wood, I. (1991), 'Saint-Wandrille and its hagiography', in I. N. Wood and G. A. Loud (eds), *Church and Chronicle in the Middle Ages: Essays Presented to John Taylor*. London, Hambledon: pp. 1–14.

Wood, I. (1994), 'The most holy Abbot Ceolfrid', Jarrow Lecture, Newcastle-upon-Tyne, St Paul's Church, Jarrow.

Wood, M. (1981), *In Search of the Dark Ages*. London, BBC.

Woods, H. (1987), 'Excavations at Wenlock Priory, 1981–6', *Journal of the British Archaeological Association*, **140**: 36–75.

Woolf, A. (1998), 'Pictish matriliny reconsidered', *Innes Review*, **44**: 147–67.

Woolf, A. (forthcoming), 'Onuist son of Uurguist: *tyrannus carnifex* or a David for the Picts?', in M. Worthington and D. Hill (eds), *Æthelbald, Beornred and Offa: The Eighth-Century Kings of Mercia and Their World*. Oxford, British Archaeological Reports.

Wormald, F. (1954), 'The miniatures in the Gospels of St. Augustine, Corpus Christi College, Cambridge, MS 286', Cambridge, Cambridge University Press (reprinted 1984, in J. J. G. Alexander, T. J. Brown and J. Gibbs (eds), *Francis Wormald: Collected Writings*. London and Oxford, Harvey Miller and Oxford University Press: pp. 13–35).

Wormald, P. (1982), 'The age of Bede and Æthelbald', 'The age of Offa and Alcuin', and 'The ninth century', in J. Campbell (ed.), *The Anglo-Saxons*. London, Phaidon: pp. 70–100, 101–28, 132–59.

Wormald, P. (1991), 'In search of King Offa's "law-code"', in I. Wood and N. Lund (eds), *People and Places in Northern Europe, 500–1600: Studies Presented to Peter Hayes Sawyer*. Woodbridge, Boydell and Brewer: pp. 25–45.

Wormald, P (1996a), 'BL Cotton MS. Otho B. xi: a supplementary note', in D. Hill and A. Rumble, *The Defence of Wessex: The Burghal Hidage and Anglo-Saxon Fortifications*. Manchester, Manchester University Press: pp. 59–68.

Wormald, P. (1996b), 'The emergence of the *regnum Scottorum*: a Carolingian hegemony?', in B. E. Crawford (ed.), *Scotland in Dark Age Britain*. St Andrews, University of St Andrews Press: pp. 131–60.

Wormald, P. (1999), *The Making of English Law: King Alfred to the Twelfth Century, I: Legislation and its Limits*. Oxford, Blackwell.

Worthington, M. (forthcoming), 'Offa's Dyke', in M. Worthington and D. Hill (eds), *Æthelbald, Beornred and Offa: The Eighth-Century Kings of Mercia and Their World*. Oxford, British Archaeological Reports.

Wright, C. D. (1990), 'Hiberno-Latin and Irish influenced biblical commentaries, Florilegia and homily collections', in F. M. Biggs, T. D. Hill and P. E. Szarmach (eds), *Sources of Anglo-Saxon Literary Culture: A Trial Version*. New York, Center for Medieval and Early Renaissance Studies: pp. 87–123.

Wright, C. E. (1939), *Cultivation of Saga in Anglo-Saxon England*. London, Oliver and Boyd.

Wright, D. H. (1964), 'Review of P. Hunter Blair', *The Moore Bede*, in *Anglia*, **82**: 110–17.

Wright, D. H. (1967), 'The Vespasian Psalter (B.M. Cotton Vespasian A.I)', *Early English Manuscripts in Facsimile*, **14**, Copenhagen, Rosenkilde and Bagger.

Wroe-Brown, R. (1998), 'Bull Wharf: Queenhithe', *Current Archaeology*, **14**: 75–7.

Yorke, B. A. E. (1983), 'Joint kingship in Kent c.560 to 785', *Archæologia Cantiana*, **99**: 1–19.

Yorke, B. A. E. (1985), 'The kingdom of the East Saxons', *Anglo-Saxon England*, **14**: 1–36.

Yorke, B. A. E. (1990), *Kings and Kingdoms of Early Anglo-Saxon England*. London, Seaby.

Yorke, B. A. E. (1995), *Wessex in the Early Middle Ages*. Leicester, Leicester University Press.

Yorke, B. A. E. (2000), 'Political and ethnic identity: a case study of Anglo-Saxon practice', in B. Frazer and A. Tyrrell, *Social Identity in Early Medieval Britain*. London, Leicester University Press: pp. 69–89.

Youngs, S. M. (ed.) (1989), *'The Work of Angels'. Masterpieces of Celtic Metalwork, 6th–9th Centuries AD*. London, British Museum Publications.

Youngs, S. M. (1997), 'Recent finds of insular enameled buckles', in C. E. Karkov, R. T. Farrell and M. Ryan (eds), *The Insular Tradition*. New York, State University of New York Press: pp. 189–209.

Youngs, S. M. (1999), 'A Northumbrian plaque from Asby Winderwath, Cumbria', in J. Hawkes and S. Mills (eds), *Northumbria's Golden Age*. Stroud, Sutton: pp. 281–95.

Zimmermann, E. H. (1916), 'Vorkarolingische Miniaturen', *Denkmäler Deutscher Kunst, III: Malerei*. Berlin, Deutscher Verein für Kunstwissenschaft.

Zipperer, S. (1999), 'Coins and currency – Offa of Mercia and his Frankish neighbours', in U. Von Freeden, U. Koch and A. Wieczorek (eds), *Völker an Nord- und Ostsee und die Franken*. Bonn: pp. 121–7.

General Index

Index of Manuscripts Cited